American Voices

American Voices

CULTURE AND COMMUNITY

THIRD EDITION

Dolores laGuardia
University of San Francisco

Hans P. Guth
Santa Clara University

Mayfield Publishing Company
Mountain View, California
London • Toronto

LIBRARY OF CONGRESS CATALOGING–IN–PUBLICATION DATA
laGuardia, Dolores.
    American voices : culture and community /
Dolores laGuardia, Hans P. Guth. — 3rd ed.
      p.   cm.
   ISBN 1-55934-934-4
   1. Readers—United States.   2. Pluralism (Social sciences)—
Problems, exercises, etc.   3. Ethnology—United States—Problems,
exercises, etc.   4. Ethnic groups—Problems, exercises, etc.
5. Culture—Problems, exercises, etc.   6. English language—
Rhetoric.   7. Critical thinking.   8. College readers.   I. Guth,
Hans Paul.   II. Title.
PE1127.H5L25   1997
808'.0427—dc21   97-25112
                                                               CIP

Manufactured in the United States of America
10   9   8   7   6   5   4   3

Mayfield Publishing Company
1280 Villa Street
Mountain View, California 94041

Sponsoring editor, Thomas V. Broadbent; production, Rogue Valley Publications;
manuscript editor, George Dyke; text designer, TS Design Group; cover designer,
Laurie Anderson; manufacturing manager, Randy Hurst. The text was set in
11/12 Bembo by Thompson Type and printed on 45# Penntech Penn Plus by
R. R. Donnelley & Sons Co., Inc.

Cover image: Lawrence Ferlinghetti, *Unfinished Flag of the United States*

Acknowledgments and copyrights continue at the back of the book on
pages 733–738, which constitute an extension of the copyright page.

 Printed on acid-free, recycled paper.

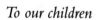

To our children

TO THE INSTRUCTOR

American Voices is a textbook for the courses in writing and critical thinking that are at the core of the student's general education. We aim at helping students become alert readers, more purposeful and effective writers, and thinking members of the larger community. We focus on issues that define our diverse, multicultural society as it charts its future. The book is built around selections by committed writers who demonstrate the power of the written word to record, interpret, and change the social and cultural reality in which we live.

The Goals of *American Voices*

 • REDEFINING AMERICA   This book is part of the search for a new national identity that honors diversity while searching for community. The text explores the promise of a multicultural America, examining the issues that confront us on the way to a richer, pluralistic meeting of majority and minority cultures. The central focus of the book is the challenge of honoring diversity while searching for the common center.

 • EXPLORING TODAY'S ISSUES   The book is organized around major concerns in our changing social and cultural awareness. In each chapter, readings cluster around a central theme:

1 INITIATION: Growing Up American—exploring the diverse experiences of young Americans

2 NEW WORLD: Diversity and Community—honoring the true richness of American culture

3 CONTESTED HISTORY: Rediscovering America—heeding revisionist readings of our shared history

4 OUTSIDERS: Unheard Voices—listening to those marginalized in our affluent society

5 IDENTITY: Rethinking Race—reexamining race as an unresolved challenge to the American dream

6 CULTURE WARS: Constructing Gender—exploring the current redefinition of gender roles

7 MEDIA WATCH: Image and Reality—watching the media mold our perception of reality

8 ROLE MODELS: In Search of Heroes—looking for sources of inspiration for alienated youth

9 LANGUAGE: Bond or Barrier?—probing the power of language to unite or divide us

10 VIOLENCE: Living at Risk—exploring ways of coping with the epidemic of violence

11 ENVIRONMENT: Participating in Nature—renewing our bonds with the world of nature

12 UNCERTAIN FUTURE: Dream or Nightmare—envisioning Utopian and dystopian tomorrows

▪ BALANCED REPRESENTATION   Readers of earlier editions of *American Voices* responded to its selection of authentic American voices representing a "wide and challenging variety of ways to be human and to perceive the world." Half of the writers in this new edition represent minority backgrounds or alternative lifestyles; half of the writers or more are women. In the words of one reviewer, many of "the writings in *American Voices* are by women who happen to be writers as opposed to writers whose profession it is to be 'women' for their readers." At the same time, to help instructors address the concerns of embattled white males, we include writers like Daniel J. Boorstin on the positives in American history, Carl Bernstein on journalistic standards, and Robert Bly on the search for male role models for a new generation.

▪ TEACHING INDEPENDENT THINKING   Instruction in critical thinking aims at validating the students' independent judgment. The goal is to develop our students' ability to reexamine familiar ideas, to take a serious look at issues, and to make up their own minds. Critical thinking requires the willingness to confront opposing views or plays off differing perspectives on major issues. The readings in this text invite students to participate in the dialogue, introducing them to the dialectic of pro and con. On politically sensitive topics, we guard against presenting the textbook authors' views as the approved, correct slant on an issue.

▪ FOSTERING STUDENT PARTICIPATION   The apparatus in *American Voices* promotes students' involvement in their reading and provokes classroom interaction. Headnotes go beyond routine biography to highlight an author's experience and commitment. **Thought Starters** focus students' attention and activate what they bring to a selection. The after-selection apparatus validates the range of reader response by asking questions that do not have a single correct answer. Questions labeled **The Responsive Reader** direct attention to key points. Questions and suggested topics labeled **Talking, Listening, Writing** encourage students to formulate their own personal reactions and to engage in a dialogue with their classmates, often in preparation for both informal and more structured writing assignments. **Collaborative Projects** for group work introduce students to the challenges and rewards of collaborative learning.

▪ INTEGRATING READING AND WRITING   A writing workshop follows each chapter, with guidelines and activities in each workshop focused on a major writing or thinking strategy. We help teachers move from experience to exposition, providing the bridge from personal-experience writing to more academic, more public forms of discourse. A rich sampling of student papers helps instructors bridge the gap between professional and student writing and encourages students to find their own voices, to trust their own authority as witnesses and thoughtful observers.

▪ ASSURING FLEXIBILITY   The organization of *American Voices* suggests a course outline that many teachers have found workable. However, chapters, reading selections, and writing workshops are self-contained and may be rearranged to suit the needs of different classes or programs. An alternative rhetorical table of contents enables instructors to shift from a thematic, issues-oriented emphasis to an emphasis on rhetorical strategies.

Features of the Third Edition

The third edition builds on features that have appealed to teachers and students and that set *American Voices* apart from competitors:

▪ ENGAGING WITH CURRENT ISSUES   We seek out thought-provoking, discussion-generating writing about current issues. The selections in the third edition explore topics including bad parenting; the resurgence of anti-immigrant sentiment; the forgotten people of America's prison gulag archipelago; role models for alienated youth; gender balance in the media; the black middle class; the attack on affirmative action; the O. J. trials and the racial divide; the media furor over Black English; gay-bashing and the growing acceptance of gays; the soulless modern corporation; and the pornographer as free speech hero.

▪ STRENGTHENED THEMATIC FOCUS   We have strengthened the sequence of chapters for clearer focus on key issues. We have moved up the key chapter on diversity and community; now Chapter 2, it integrates Ursula Le Guin on heartland America and Harvey Milk on the city of neighborhoods. Chapter 4 on "Outsiders" includes new materials on those marginalized in our society—students neglected in American schools; Americans buried in our prisons; Americans with disabilities. Separate new chapters on rethinking race (5) and constructing gender (6) deal with major forces affecting the individual's search for identity.

▪ READING-BASED AND RESEARCH-BASED WRITING   We encourage the current trend toward giving students help early with papers drawing on their reading (Writing Workshop 3) and toward having them work with investigative papers that provide shorter alternatives—and also trial runs—for longer library papers (Writing Workshop 11). At the same time, we have greatly expanded the treatment of computer searches and of documentation (MLA and APA) for the full-length documented paper in Writing Workshop 12.

Acknowledgments

It has again been a privilege and a pleasure to work on this book with the dedicated professionals at Mayfield Publishing. We owe a special debt to the many colleagues in the writing movement who have made the core courses in the general education curriculum more responsive to the needs of today's students. We have again taken to heart excellent advice from our reviewers: Dr. Kathleen Bell, University of Central Florida; Marlene S. Bosanko, Tacoma Community College; Susanne Bounds, Morehead State University; Judy Daniel, University of Minnesota–Morris; Bruce R. Henderson, Fullerton College; Kim Martin Long, Shippensburg University of Pennsylvania; Peggy A. Moore, College of the Siskiyous; Ed Moritz, Indiana University–Purdue University; and Roslyn Z. Weedman, Delta College. Above all, we have learned much from our students. Often, struggling against odds, they have maintained their faith in American education. Their candor, intelligence, and idealism have been a marvelous antidote to cynicism, burnout, and apathy.

D. laGuardia
H. Guth

TO THE STUDENT

In reality, society and the individual are not antagonists. Culture provides the raw material of which individuals make their lives. If it is meager, the individual suffers. If it is rich, the individual has a chance to rise to the opportunity.

—*Ruth Benedict*

This book asks you to read, think, and write about who you are as a person. Who are you—as an individual and as part of a nation? What makes each of us the people we are? Where do we come from, and where are we headed? What shapes our thinking, our values, our loyalties?

The readings in this book invite you to think about how your sense of self is shaped by sometimes conflicting influences. How important is family or social status? How much does gender matter, and how rigid are gender roles in our society? How important are ethnic or national origin and racial identity? (Is much of who we are already programmed by class, gender, or race?) How have religious influences, work experiences, or health issues shaped your outlook? Where do you stand on issues that fuel the basic controversies in our society—the racial divide, out-of-control violence, "family values," proliferating prisons, sexual orientation?

Working with this book, you will have a chance to think about what you have in common with others, about shared experiences and commitments. In our diverse, multicultural society, what are the things that provide a common bond? At the same time, you will have a chance to think about what *separates* you from others. How real are the barriers that divide us? What are the forces in our society that make for hostility, suspicion, or even paranoia? What is the outlook for our common future?

Americans have prided themselves on being independent individuals, making their own choices. We each have the right to be our "own person"—not just a cog in the machine or a number in the college computer. As Americans, we have the right to say "No." We have the right to talk back to government officials, elders in the family, peer groups at school or college, preachers, teachers, advocates of causes, or whoever wants to tell us what we should think and do. Nevertheless, the choices we make are shaped by the culture in which we live. We have the option of conforming to the traditional lifestyles of our families—urban or rural, strict or permissive, liberal or conservative. We choose to adapt or reject our heritage, staying close to or distancing ourselves from a Southern or Mexican or Irish or Italian past. We each in our own way come to terms with our inherited faiths—Catholic, Baptist, Mormon, Jewish, Buddhist, Muslim, or other.

A culture is a traditional way of living, of thinking and feeling. A culture, for better or for worse, provides traditional answers to basic questions: How important am I as an individual compared with the survival of society? What are my obligations to family—to parents, to siblings, to relatives in need? What jobs are open to me—to someone of my family background, gender, or social status? How am I expected to love, court, marry, have children? Is it all right to divorce? to have an abortion? What is valued in my culture? Who is judged successful, and why? Who is considered beautiful, and why? What is considered sinful, offensive, or taboo?

In these and similar matters, many people adapt to their own needs the traditions of family, neighborhood, or church. Many swim in a traditional lifestyle the way fish swim in the sea. For many others, however, growing up means deciding to move on, to make their own personal declaration of independence. They find themselves reexamining their roots, their assumptions, their loyalties. They reach a point in their lives where they have to decide. Should they work in the family's hardware store or go to college? Should they convert to Catholicism? Should they marry one of their own kind or someone from a different background or religion? Should they follow in the footsteps of a mother or father—or should they enter a profession where people of their gender, their skin color, or their ethnic background are still a rarity?

American culture is not a single monolithic culture where everybody has to think, talk, and act the same. It is a rich, evolving culture where communities and individuals do not stay the same. America is a multicultural society, with many traditions clashing at times and at other times blending in a rich new synthesis. A commuter might start his day in a mainly Spanish-speaking Texas country town and drive through white suburbs to a predominantly black downtown, interspersed with areas with shop signs in Chinese or Vietnamese. Many Americans have always been bilingual—using another language or a down-home dialect in their families or neighborhoods, in addition to the standard English of school and office.

Americans do not all have names like Harriman or Saltonstall. The *Mayflower,* bringing dissident English Puritans to New England, was a small boat. Many Americans are descended from Irish peasants driven off their land by famine, from orthodox Jews, or from freed slaves. Others are descended from displaced persons—Ukrainians, Poles, Lithuanians—uprooted by Hitler's war machine. Many Americans trace their ancestry to the refugees from failed revolutions or lost wars (Germany in 1848; Hungary in the first stirrings of revolt against Stalinism; Vietnam). Many (perhaps two million or more) trace their ancestry at least in part to Native Americans living on the fringes of the white society that drove them from their land. Many Americans have Mexican ancestors who lived in the Southwest before the Americanos came or who came across the border in search of work. Other Americans are descended from Puerto Ricans, or from Chinese laborers who built the railroads of the West, or from Japanese families who were taken to relocation camps in the desert during World War II.

As our country approaches the twenty-first century, Americans face fateful questions: Are the forces that drive us apart becoming stronger? Will racial strife turn our cities into armed camps? Are class distinctions—layers of wealth and privilege—resurfacing that immigrants from traditional societies thought they had left behind? Will the widening gulf between the rich and the poor make us "two nations"? Or can we achieve a richer new synthesis? What would it take to achieve a true pluralism? Can we envision a pluralistic society that values the contributions of many cultural strands, with people of different ties and backgrounds respecting and learning from one another?

CONTENTS

ALTERNATIVE RHETORICAL TABLE OF CONTENTS

ABOUT THE EDITORS

Dolores laGuardia teaches at the University of San Francisco, where she developed a humanities sequence titled "American Voices: Ourselves and Each Other," with courses focused on African Americans, Asian Americans, Latinos, Native Americans, religious minorities, and alternative lifestyles. She has served as the writing specialist for a large federal grant designed to improve writing instruction at the community college level and has done curriculum work for a number of San Francisco Bay Area institutions. She has conducted workshops on computer education at the prestigious Troitsk Institute outside Moscow. She is coauthor with Hans Guth of *American Visions: Multicultural Literature for Writers* (1995) and of *Issues across the Curriculum* (1997).

Hans P. Guth (Santa Clara University) has worked with writing teachers and spoken at professional meetings in most of the fifty states. He has spoken on redefining the canon and using multicultural materials at national and regional conferences. He is coauthor of *Discovering Literature* (second edition, Prentice Hall, 1997) and of *You the Writer* (Houghton Mifflin, 1997) and is the author of numerous other composition texts. He was codirector and program chair of the annual Young Rhetoricians' Conference in Monterey from 1984 to 1994 and has recently organized workshops at Oxford and at Heidelberg University.

Reading, Writing, Thinking

What is this book supposed to do for you?

- *This book should help you become a better reader.* How much do you get out of your reading? Much of what writers write about comes from what they read. To understand their society and the larger world, they do more than listen to the seven o'clock news. They read about current events, trying to get more than one side of the story. They turn to experts who can explain past history and new trends. They read to find out what is behind the current buzzwords—workfare, self-esteem, a "Eurocentric" curriculum, "the color-blind society."

- *This book should help turn you into a better writer.* How good are you at putting your ideas into words? On subjects like racism among the young or the pros and cons of sex education, you learn to draw on your own personal experience and observation. You listen to the testimony of people who have undergone "downsizing" and "restructuring," and you work out your own conclusions about trends in the job market. When arguments get heated, you learn to listen to the other side and to think about what it would take to influence your intended audience. You learn to hold your own in an ongoing discussion and make your voice heard.

- *This book should help you organize your thinking.* How good are you at sizing up an issue and thinking the matter through? This book should nudge you toward thinking more critically—going beyond hearsay or "what everybody says," checking out relevant facts, weighing the pros and cons. Writing seriously about a subject means exploring it, checking things out, and making up your own mind.

PREVIEW: THE RESPONSIVE READER

An educated person is first of all someone who reads. Readers have a chance to go beyond the headline news to the why, the so what, and the what now. They can go beyond a candidate's endorsement of a strong America to a study of the candidate's funding, voting record, political alliances, and pet causes. When they hear a company spokesperson present the corporate line in a labor dispute, readers can find out how the issue

1

looks from the other side of the negotiating table. On a subject like sexual harassment or abortion, they can find out how the issue looks from the other side of the gender gap or the other side of the aisle.

How do you become a better reader?

■ *First, a good reader is a receptive reader.* Receptive readers read along attentively, taking in what the writer is trying to say. They look early for a hint or a preview of the writer's main points and how the writer supports them or makes them stick. They are not satisfied with the "general idea" but pay attention to the ramifications—the important details, the important ifs and buts. Reading an article on the role of the National Collegiate Athletic Association in deciding who can compete in college sports, an attentive reader may take in information on questions like the following:

> How did the NCAA become the body ruling on eligibility of college athletes? Who are these people—who elects them or gets to vote? What has been their influence on academic standards for high school athletes? What kind of "solid" coursework is required? (Do coaches get to decide what is solid academic work—for instance, ruling out courses with the label *interdisciplinary*?) Do students rejected or vetoed by the NCAA have any recourse? Is the growing influence of the NCAA part of a more general movement to raise academic standards for "jocks"?

■ *A good reader is at the same time a responsive reader.* Responsive readers make what they read their own. They do not accept everything the writer says at face value or as gospel truth. As you read along, there should be a running commentary going on in your mind: What is new here, and what is familiar? What assumptions do I bring to this topic, and which seem to be shared by the writer? Where do *I* stand on this issue? What do I know that perhaps the writer did not know? What would I say if I were asked to testify on this topic?

■ *A good reader is likely to read with the writer's eye.* Start to look at something you read as the work of a fellow writer. How did the author get the audience to pay attention? How did she or he dramatize the issue— bring the topic to life? How carefully or how aggressively does the writer state the main point? What backup is there—personal witnessing, facts or hard data, expert testimony, inside information? How does the piece as a whole take shape?

Remember: Listen first before you start talking back. Before you argue with a writer, before you reject or endorse what a writer says, take in what the writer is trying to say. Track how a piece of writing develops. As an alert reader, you need to keep questions like the following in mind:

■ What is the key issue or key question? How is it introduced?

■ Is there an early statement or an early hint of the author's answer to the central question? Is there a **thesis**? (Where is the author's message stated most directly or most eloquently?)

▪ Does the argument hinge on a key term like *culture, assimilation,* or *affirmative action*? Where and how is it defined? (Are there key examples or test cases that clarify the term?)

▪ Where are we headed? Is there an early hint of an overall plan or organizing strategy? For instance, is an article going to contrast the then and now? Is it going to start with surface first impressions and then take a look behind the scenes? Is the writer going to look first at arguments pro and then at arguments con?

▪ How solid is the array of examples or evidence that the author presents to support a general point? Which are most striking or convincing? (Which are drawn from personal experience or observation?)

▪ Does the author bring in expert testimony, insider's information, or eyewitness reports? Where and how?

▪ Does the author recognize possible objections or counterarguments? Are they brushed off, or are they taken seriously?

▪ Does the conclusion merely summarize, or does it go a step beyond what the author said before? For instance, is there a clinching final example or an effective punchline? Does the author relate his argument to the larger picture?

Assume you are reading a *Time* essay on "The Fear of Losing a Culture." The comments after each of the following excerpts illustrate how an alert reader might interact with the text:

Richard Rodriguez

Children of a Marriage

What is culture?

The immigrant shrugs. Latin American immigrants come to the United States with only the things they need in mind—not abstractions like culture. Money. They need dollars. They need food. Maybe they need to get out of the way of bullets.

Most of us who concern ourselves with Hispanic-American culture, as painters, musicians, writers—or as sons and daughters—are the children of immigrants. We have grown up on this side of the border, in the land of Elvis Presley and Thomas Edison; our lives are prescribed by the mall, by the DMV and the Chinese restaurant. . . .

(It might seem strange that immediately after asking the key question—"What is culture?"—the author would mention immigrants too concerned about the necessities of life to worry about the issue. However, this reference serves to put the question in *perspective*. It is the sons and daughters of immigrants who face the question of what is "Hispanic American culture." So especially do painters, musicians, and writers.)

Hispanics fear losing ground in any negotiation with the American city. We come from an expansive, an intimate culture that has been judged second-rate by the United States of America. For reasons of pride, therefore, as much as of affection, we are reluctant to give up our past. Hispanics often express a fear of "losing" culture. Our fame in the United States has been our resistance to assimilation.

The symbol of Hispanic culture has been the tongue of flame—Spanish. But the remarkable legacy Hispanics carry from Latin America is not language—an inflatable skin—but breath itself, capacity of soul, an inclination to live. The genius of Latin America is the habit of synthesis . . .

(By now the writer, a Mexican American himself, has focused on what he sees as the central difference between Americans of Spanish-speaking descent and other minority groups. Hispanic or Latino Americans want to "belong to America" without *giving up* their distinctive history and their distinctive culture. This passage already introduces the author's answer to this dilemma. The key word is *synthesis*—the gift of creating a richer blend from diverse materials. The reader will now expect some striking or convincing examples of what the author means by synthesis.)

What Latin America knows is that people create one another as they marry. In the music of Latin America you will hear the litany of bloodlines—the African drum, the German accordion, the cry from the minaret.

The United States stands as the opposing New World experiment. In North America the Indian and the European stood apace. Whereas Latin America was formed by a medieval Catholic dream of one world—of meltdown conversion—the United States was built up from Protestant individualism. The American melting pot washes away only embarrassment; it is the necessary initiation into public life. The American faith is that our national strength derives from separateness, from "diversity." The glamour of the United States is a carnival promise: You can lose weight, get rich as Rockefeller, touch up your roots, get a divorce.

(As expected, this passage gives examples of how in Latin America strands from different cultures have combined in a richer new blend, or synthesis. The author reinforces this point by *contrasting* the Catholic Latin American tradition, with its dream of one world, with the Protestant North American tradition of individualism—of striking out on your own, of leaving your past behind.)

Immigrants still come for the promise. But the United States wavers in its faith. As long as there was space enough, sky enough, as long as economic success validated individualism, loneliness was not too high a price to pay. (The cabin on the prairie or the Sony Walkman.)

As we near the end of the American century, two alternative cultures beckon the American imagination—both highly communal cultures—the Asian and the Latin American. The United States is a literal culture. Americans devour what we might otherwise fear to become. Sushi will make us corporate warriors. Combination Plate #3, smothered in mestizo gravy, will burn a hole in our hearts. . . . Latin America offers communal riches: an undistressed leisure, a kitchen table, even a full sorrow.

(As the traditional American ideal of "everyone for himself" no longer works in our crowded interdependent world, Americans have a choice of two possible models for a more "communal" culture—the Asian and the Latin American. The author is now ready for his conclusion, in which he redefines the familiar term *assimilation* so that it will no longer stand for a one-way street. It will no longer mean the assimilation or takeover of one culture by another. It will stand for a mutual influencing and richer new blend. As the author says at the end of his essay: "Expect bastard themes, expect ironies, comic conclusions. For we live on this side of the border, where Kraft manufactures bricks of 'Mexican style' Velveeta, and where Jack in the Box serves 'Fajita Pita.' . . . Expect marriage. We will change America even as we will be changed.")

Where do *you* stand on the issue of a multicultural America that will be a rich blend of different cultural strands? The commitments of Rodriguez' readers are likely to range over a whole spectrum of opinion. At one end of the spectrum might be people with Anglo-Saxon names who carry "English Only" buttons and who wish they could build electrified barbed wire fences along the Mexican border high enough to keep out any further migrants to the north. At the other end of the spectrum might be people who have decided that for minorities to try to join the "mainstream" is a mirage. The only hope is for people to band together with those of their own race or culture to advance their cause.

As a responsive reader, you will be asking yourself questions like the following:

- How does my own experience compare with that of the author?
- How much of this article is fact or hard data, and how much is one person's opinion?
- When the author cites authorities and insiders, do I accept them as authoritative sources? (Do I "take their word for it"?)
- Is the author's argument balanced or one-sided? Is there something to be said on the other side?
- How much of this piece of writing is special pleading? (Is this author beholden to a party line? Does the author sound like a spokesperson for a special interest?)

- How narrow or how broad is this writer's appeal? (Does the writer write off a whole group of people because of ethnicity, race, gender, or lifestyle?)

A good reader is not simply a passive reader, dutifully taking notes. Ideally, your reading will trigger your writing. You will be moved to write in order to talk back. You may want to clarify something that the writer obscured or glossed over. You may feel the need to correct a stereotype or a misrepresentation. You may want to pay tribute to someone the writer ignored. Whether you agree or not, a strong reading selection will make you think. It will stimulate you to think the matter through.

YOUR TURN: How Well Do You Read?

How well do you read? Use the following (slightly shortened) essay by a well-known columnist to test your capacity for close, responsive reading. The questions that precede the text will walk you through the essay. They will ask you to pinpoint the ideas and the features that give the essay shape and direction. How well do you follow the author's trend of thought? How quick are you to take in key points and key examples?

Answer the following questions as you work your way through the essay:

- What does the *title* make you expect?
- What is the common pattern in the examples Goodman uses for her *introduction*? What word provides the common thread? (What meanings or associations does it have for you?)
- How does the introduction lead up to the central idea or *thesis*? How does the thesis serve as a preview of the basic contrast that shapes much of the essay?
- What kind of *support* does Goodman offer to clarify and develop the basic contrast? How does she use material from personal experience or observation? How does she go beyond it?
- Where does Goodman offer a *concession*—anticipating possible objections, admitting that there are exceptions to her claims?
- What does the *conclusion* add to the essay? Does it merely summarize, or does it go beyond what the author has already said? (How does the last sentence circle back to the title of the essay?)
- Can you relate Goodman's points in any way to your personal experience or observation? (Can you make a *personal connection*?)
- Do you agree with the author wholeheartedly, or do you want to take issue with any of her points? What would you say if you were asked to respond to her or talk back?

Ellen Goodman

We Are What We Do

I have a friend who is a member of the medical community. It does not say that, of course, on the stationery that bears her home address. This membership comes from her hospital work.

I have another friend who is a member of the computer community. This is a fairly new subdivision of our economy, and yet he finds his sense of place in it.

Other friends and acquaintances of mine are members of the academic community, or the business community, or the journalistic community. Though you cannot find these on any map, we know where we belong.

None of us, mind you, was born into these communities. Nor did we move into them, U-Hauling our possessions along with us. None has papers to prove we are card-carrying members of one such group or another. *Yet it seems that more and more of us are identified by work these days, rather than by street.*

In the past, most Americans lived in neighborhoods. We were members of precincts or parishes or school districts. My dictionary still defines community first of all in geographic terms, as "a body of people who live in one place."

But today fewer of us do our living in that one place; more of us just use it for sleeping. Now we call our towns "bedroom suburbs," and many of us, without small children as icebreakers, would have trouble naming all the people on our street.

It's not that we are more isolated today. It's that many of us have transferred a chunk of our friendships, a major portion of our everyday social lives, from home to office. As more of our neighbors work away from home, the work place becomes our neighborhood. . . .

We may be strangers at the supermarket that replaced the corner grocer, but we are known at the coffee shop in the lobby. We share with each other a cast of characters from the boss in the corner office to the crazy lady in Shipping, to the lovers in Marketing. It's not surprising that *when researchers ask Americans* what they like best about work, they say it is "the shmooze (chatter) factor." When they ask young mothers at home what they miss most about work, it is the people.

Not all the neighborhoods are empty, nor is every work place a friendly playground. Most of us have had mixed experiences in these environments. *Yet* as one woman told me recently, she knows more about the people she passes on the way to her desk than on her way around the block. . . .

It's not unlike the experience of our immigrant grandparents. Many who came to this country still identified themselves as members of the Italian community, the Irish community, the Polish community.

They sought out and assumed connections with people from the old country. Many of us have updated that experience. We have replaced ethnic identity with professional identity, the way we replaced neighborhoods with the work place. . . .

I don't think that there is anything massively disruptive about this shifting sense of community. The continuing search for connection and shared enterprise is very human. *But I do feel uncomfortable with our shifting identity.* The balance has tipped and we seem increasingly dependent on work for our sense of self.

If our offices are our new neighborhoods, if our professional titles are our new ethnic tags, then how do we separate ourselves from our jobs? Self-worth isn't just something to measure in the marketplace. But in these new communities, it becomes harder and harder to tell who we are without saying what we do.

PREVIEW: THE PROCESS OF WRITING

A well-organized piece of writing does not surface on your computer screen or blank sheet of paper ready-made. The question for you as a writer is: How is a finished piece of writing *produced*? The beautiful Greek vase you see on display in a museum was once a lump of clay. It went through a process of shaping and finishing that took time and care. Writing worth reading similarly goes through a process. It goes through phases of focusing, gathering, shaping, revising, and final editing. Experienced writers make allowance for trial and error, for promising leads that do not work out, for second thoughts, and for last-minute adjustments.

The stages in the writing process intermesh—for instance, you may start revising or working in second thoughts while still hunting for further material. Besides, different writers have their own ways of picking a subject, working up materials, and pulling them into shape. However, the following are dimensions of the writing process to which productive writers do justice in one way or another:

TRIGGERING What makes writers write? What triggers writing— what brings it on? On the most basic level, we may write because of an immediate practical need. We write a résumé because we need a job. We write to a judge or a planning commission to head off a decision that would hurt. But such practical writing easily shades over into other kinds. A woman who writes to complain about job discrimination is likely to find herself talking not just about her own case but other cases as well. She will find herself writing about a topic that matters to more than one person.

Writers write because they have something to say to other people. Here are some of the motives that may trigger your writing:

- *Writers write to explain.* After studying a troubling question, they share their answers with a larger audience. They write about oil spills, youth gangs in Los Angeles, or teenage suicide. They turn to their readers to say: "Listen! It's important! I want to explain it to you."

▪ *Writers write to talk back.* Suppose the governor of the state identifies a major problem of American education: Teachers care only about fat paychecks. A language arts teacher who was hired at a salary lower than the bus driver's may have thoughts on this topic. A writing teacher who spends hours each day commuting between two low-paying jobs may feel moved to talk back.

▪ *Writers write to set the record straight.* You may be reading about how Southern whites supposedly feel about Southern blacks, or about how American males allegedly feel about women, and you find yourself saying: "That's not the way it is! I know something about this from firsthand experience! Let me set you straight."

▪ *Writers write to air grievances.* They appeal to their readers' sense of fairness. They write to register their solidarity with the homeless or the unemployed.

GATHERING To write an authentic, convincing paper, you have to immerse yourself in the subject. You may start by calling up from the memory bank of past experience the images, events, buzzwords, and arguments that cluster around your topic. You may follow up by reading up on it, discussing it with friends and roommates, or interviewing people who might have the inside story. Your finished paper should show that you are an attentive reader, an alert listener, a scribbler of notes, a collector of newspaper clippings, and a patron of the photocopy machine.

Develop the habit of taking notes. Here are some **prewriting** techniques that can help you work up a rich fund of material for a paper:

▪ **Brainstorming** roams freely over a topic. It dredges up any memories, images, events, or associations that might prove useful. Exploring the ideas related to the word *macho,* for instance, you jot down anything that the word brings to mind. You write quickly and freely, allowing one idea to lead to another. There will be time later to sort out these preliminary jottings—to see how they add up, to see what goes with what. Right now, the idea is to mobilize everything you already know, to bring to the surface anything you remember.

The following brainstorming exercise has already brought together much promising material. What major points for a paper are beginning to come into focus?

Macho: Big, muscular, unfeeling, rough—harsh, moves to kill. (Sylvester Stallone: I hate what he promotes.) Negative impression. Hard, craggy faces with mean eyes that bore holes in you.

Men who have to prove themselves through acts of violence. The man who is disconnected from his feelings, insensitive to women's needs—cannot express himself in a feeling manner.

The word seems to have negative connotations for me because I work part-time in a bar. I am forever seeing these perfectly tanned types who come on to a woman. As a child, macho meant a strong male type who would take care of me—paternal, warmth in eyes. John Wayne: gruff, yet you feel secure knowing someone like this was around.

Crude, huge—the body, not the heart—tendency to violence always seems close to the surface. Looks are very important. Craggy face. Bloodshed excites them. Arnold Schwarzenegger muscles, gross.

Tend to dominate in relationships—desire for control. "Me Tarzan—you Jane."

▪ **Clustering** is a different method of letting your mind bring memories and associations to the surface. Instead of letting the items that come to mind march down the page, clustering makes them branch out from a central core. You pursue different chains of association started by a key word or stimulus word. More so than in brainstorming, a pattern takes shape. You begin to see connections; different items begin to fall into place.

Here is a cluster exploring the associations of the word *tradition*. It is followed by a write-up of the material generated by the cluster:

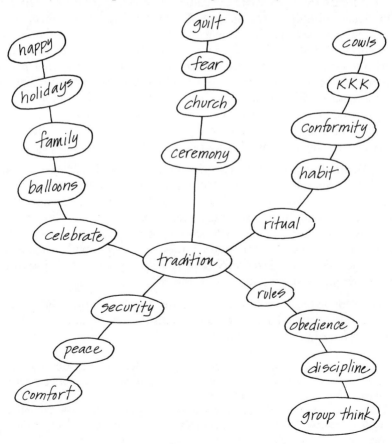

Tradition to many of us means first of all nostalgic memories of Christmas or Easter or Passover, happy hours spent with family and friends, birthday celebrations with balloons and ice cream cake and candles. In the traditional family, there is a sense of security—of knowing what to do, of relying on the tried and true. However, we also feel the weight of tradition—feeling guilty about not going to mass, feeling fear of retribution for our sins and backslidings. The inherent danger in tradition is the reliance on groupthink. Blind obedience to traditional rules and regulations can lead to unquestioned acceptance of cruel or idiotic practices. When we look at the dual nature of tradition, we see interlocking elements that can suddenly cover the face of love with a cowl of enmity and violence.

▪ **Discovery frames** are sets of questions that can guide you in exploring a topic. Suppose you are working on an up-to-date definition of feminism. What does the term mean to someone of your generation? The following discovery frame provides a model that you may want to adapt for other current topics. What materials could you fill in under the tentative headings?

POPULAR STEREOTYPES What popular associations cluster around the term? What stereotypes does it bring to mind? (Are people still talking about "women's libbers"?)

HISTORICAL BACKGROUND What is the history of feminism? What have been outstanding leaders, role models, and key events? (What do you know about Sojourner Truth, Elizabeth Cady Stanton, or Margaret Mead?)

RELATED TERMS How is the word related to similar terms— *emancipation, women's liberation, the suffragist movement, the women's movement?*

MEDIA COVERAGE What is current media coverage of the movement? What images of women are projected in the news, in movies, in advertising?

PERSONAL CONNECTION What role have feminist concerns played in your own experience?

COMMON MEANING What seems to be the core meaning? What is the common thread in your various examples?

LOOKING AHEAD What does the future hold? (Is "equity feminism" replacing "victim feminism"? Are more working-class women joining the movement?)

SHAPING How does a writer turn a rich collection of unsorted material into a coherent paper? Successful writers again and again employ three basic organizing strategies:

▪ *Bring a central issue into focus.* A focused paper does not roam over a variety of topics, giving opinions about this and that. Instead, an effective paper zeroes in on an issue or a limited area and does it justice. Early in a paper, try to give readers an answer to a basic question: What is the issue? What is this all about?

For instance, much acrimonious debate has swirled about recent initiatives to outlaw affirmative action. You may want to focus on one key issue: Is it true that affirmative action is damaging to its beneficiaries' self-esteem? Some African American academics and business people say they hate the idea that people always assume they made their way as "affirmative action hires." On the other hand, one black intellectual said he would rather feel bad in a good job at a prestige university than feel bad walking the streets without a job. Do minority students and minority faculty members at your school have thoughts on the subject?

▪ *Push toward a thesis.* What is your paper as a whole going to say? What is it going to prove? After exploring the topic, looking at the evidence, reading and talking about the issue, you need to move toward a summing up. What conclusion or conclusions do your findings point to? What is going to be your main point? What is going to be your **thesis**— your central idea, your unifying overarching thought?

Try summing up the central message of your paper in a sentence that will serve as your thesis statement early in a paper. You may want to use the next few sentences to spell out the full meaning of what you claim or assert.

> THESIS: *Vocational education, many experts claim, is forever trying to catch up with the real world.* The educational system is preparing people for jobs that have already been taken by robots. . . .
>
> THESIS: *American business is "downsizing," causing a rapid decline in employee loyalty.* Executives improve a company's balance sheet by slashing payrolls, leaving insecure workers alienated from a company and a system that has no regard for their interests. . . .
>
> THESIS: *Faulty communication torpedoes relationships.* The authors of several recent best-sellers claim it's not that people dislike each other or develop diverging interests. It's simpler than that: They misunderstand or misread what the other person is saying. . . .

A traditional model for a short paper is **thesis-and-support**. Early in the paper, you stake out a claim. You make an assertion. Then you go on to support it. You follow it up with convincing backup material: examples, evidence, statistics, expert testimony, insiders' insights, firsthand personal experience.

▪ *Work out a meaningful overall plan.* If you are to take your readers with you, they need to feel that you have a planned itinerary. How are you going to lay out your material? What is your program? In an early stage of a writing project, start jotting down a scratch outline or **working outline**. A working outline helps you visualize your tentative plan. (By definition a working outline is subject to revision.) The following might be a student's working outline for a paper in defense of affirmative action:

traumatic injustices of the past
   (the recent *Rosewood* movie chronicles the massacre and destruction of a black community in postslavery times)
continued de facto segregation
   (inner-city schools are more segregated than ever, and courts are retreating from forced integration)
lack of minority role models
   (lack of black teachers, doctors, and police makes young blacks cynical about education supposedly leading to better jobs)

Your readers need to know where you are headed—and they appreciate early hints of what lies ahead. Often an effective thesis statement already hints at the overall plan:

THESIS: Race relations in this country have moved from legally sanctioned discrimination, through the legal outlawing of discrimination, to the struggle to change deeply ingrained personal attitudes about race.

(The reader will expect that a major section of the paper will be devoted to each of these three stages.)

▪ *Line up your supporting material.* Follow up or follow through: Support any points you make with key examples or relevant evidence. Bring in material from interviews, quotable quotes.

REVISING When you finish the first run-through of a paper, remind yourself: This is a first draft. Whenever possible, allow a day or more before you go back to an early draft for rereading and revision. Genuine revision goes beyond surface corrections—correcting misspelled words or names, putting in missing commas. It involves some real rethinking. When you come back to a paper after a time, you are likely to see missing links, exaggerated claims, or detours and backtrackings.

Each paper is different, and each paper has its own strengths and weaknesses. Even so, teachers, reviewers, and editors often find themselves repeating familiar advice. Consider guidelines like the following:

▪ *Sharpen your focus.* What is the basic problem, and what are the two or three possible answers? What is the striking contrast or contradiction that your paper will try to resolve? Look at the before-and-after versions of the title and introduction of a paper on rape. In revising the beginning of the paper, what did the writer do to sharpen its focus? (What sentence in the revised version can serve as a central thesis? What kind of program or agenda is the revised version setting up for the rest of the paper?)

BLURRED: **Rape: An Examination of Data**

In recent years, the subject of rape has become more and more frequently discussed and analyzed. A growing number of women seem to believe that rape is statistically on the rise. Men often seem to view claims of vastly increased occurrence of rape with skepticism, finding themselves cast in the position of having to defend themselves against often-quoted statistics that tag them as dangerous to women. Conversely, women often seem to view a vast portion of the male population with suspicion and fear.

FOCUSED: **Rape: A Growing Division Between the Sexes?**

Men and women increasingly seem to react differently to the subject of rape. Women seem to view the incidence of rape as growing at a fearful rate. They seem to regard a large portion if not a majority of the male population with fear and suspicion. Men, on the other hand, often seem to view the current spate of statistics and reports with skepticism, suspecting that the media are sensationalizing the topic. They often find themselves in the position of having to defend themselves against the image of the male as predatory and dangerous toward women.

- *Review your organizing strategy.* For example, should you go more consistently from the simple to the difficult? (Lead up better to the parts of your paper that are challenging or controversial? Put your readers in an assenting mood first?) Or, before you start showing what is wrong with a new theory, should you take more time to explain what it is?
- *Build up and develop your examples.* In the first-draft stage, student writing often stays on a very general level. Try to bring a general point to life by presenting a striking, dramatic example. Go from the general to the specific—and back again. How do your reactions differ for the before-and-after versions of the following passage?

GENERAL: In patriarchal societies, men are in a position of power where women are often powerless to confront an accuser. It is ironic that rape, a crime that often enables women to identify their attackers, at the same time often leaves them in a position that forces them to keep silent and not seek remedy. Many women keep their secret to themselves, afraid that they will not be believed.

SPECIFIC: It is ironic that rape, a crime that often enables women to identify the attacker, often leaves them in a position that forces them to keep silent and not seek remedy. About five years ago, one of my best friends and I were pulling into a gas station; standing at another pump was a medium-built, thirtyish middle-class male. "Back up and get out of here. That man raped me," my friend blurted out. I was outraged. I wanted to stop the car, get out, confront him, spit on him, get his name into the paper, let everyone know. But all she wanted to do was hide, leave, deny, fade away, let go. I could feel her fear, her shame at the memory, her desire to put it behind her although it was glaring her in the face.

I was shocked, amazed, and saddened that not even I knew. She said that almost no one else did—a boyfriend at the time, the police. She was raped by an acquaintance; the gas station customer was a classmate. The police had discouraged her from pressing charges. The circumstances made a conviction too precarious to attempt. She asked me not to tell anyone.

• *Add a striking firsthand quote.* Issues come to life when we hear the authentic voices of the people involved.

SECONDHAND: The headline in *USA Today* read, "Rape Victim Speaks Out on 20/20." After emotional weeks in the courtroom, the victim in a celebrity rape trial told her side of the story.

FIRSTHAND QUOTATION: The headline in *USA Today* read, "Rape Victim Speaks Out on 20/20." After emotional weeks in the courtroom, the victim in a celebrity rape trial was ready to be heard—ready to tell the world her story. "People have judged me without knowing all the facts, without knowing me as a person. I want to clear it up," she said in the interview. Why is this woman being judged? Why does she have to "clear" things up?

EDITING   Final editing is your chance to take care of misspellings, awkward or confusing punctuation, garbled sentences, and confused or misused words. Remember that text on a computer screen or printout looks deceptively finished. Proofread carefully, checking your text line by line and word by word. Here are examples of high-priority items to look for in final editing:

• *Look for familiar spelling demons.* Make sure you have not misspelled the "unforgivables": *receive, definite, believe, similar, separate, used to, a lot* (two words). Check common problem words: *accommodate, government, predominant, environment, occurred.* Watch for confusing pairs: *accept* (take in) but *except* (take out); *affect* (change in part) but *effect* (the whole result).

• *Avoid the* it's *trap.* Save yourself grief by changing any *it's* to *it is* (if that is what you mean). Use *its* if that is what it should be (the band and *its* vocalist).

- *Check for apostrophes with possessives.* (What belongs with what?) Distinguish between singular (one *person's* problems) and plural (both my *parents'* attitude).

- *Hook up sentence fragments.* Look for sentence fragments that should be linked to a preceding sentence from which they have been split off *(To fight disease. Living in the city. Which proved untrue.).*

Chimpanzees were bred for experiments *to fight disease.*

- Use the semicolon as your handbook instructs you.

Speed kills; caution saves lives.

YOUR TURN: Responding to Peer Review

How do you react to comments on your writing? Remember that **feedback** is an important stage of the writing process. Much business writing is reworked in response to comments from coworkers, superiors, or consultants. Much professional writing is revised in response to criticism from editors or reviewers. Many writing classes today adopt a workshop format, with students rewriting early drafts in response to comments from instructors and peers.

When you participate in **peer review** (oral or written) in class, try to combine the two basic functions of a good editor: First, recognize and reinforce what a writer does well. Second, offer constructive suggestions for improving what is weak or has gone wrong. Pay attention to larger questions of purpose, audience, and organization as well as to spelling and punctuation. You might use the following questions as a guide for your participation in peer review:

Guidelines for Peer Review

1. What is the writer trying to do?
2. Does the writer bring a limited topic into focus? How well does the writer bring the topic or the issue to life?
3. Is there a central idea, or thesis? Should it be spelled out more clearly or forcefully?
4. Is there a preview or overview of the overall plan? Do readers get a sense of the writer's strategy? Does the plan seem to work?
5. How solid is the writer's follow-up or backup of major points? What is the quality of examples, evidence, or support from authorities? Which examples are strong? Which are weak?
6. Are there effective transitions—does the writer take the reader along from point to point? Are turning points or major stages in the argument signaled clearly enough?

7. What is confusing, and what is especially clear? What sentences seem muddy? What problems are there with spelling or punctuation?
8. Who might be the ideal reader for this paper? Who is ignored or left out?
9. Where do you agree? Where do you disagree, and why?
10. What would you say or write if you had a chance to respond to the writer?

Prepare a peer review of the following paper and compare your responses with those of others.

No Heroes

In todays society young people find few worthy objects for loyalty or outlets for devotion. They join groups ranging from neighborhood gangs to Neo-nazi groups because they need something to be loyal to or to believe in. To better understand this assessment we must look at the past and try to determine what worthy objects used to be available for young people to pledge their support.

The traditional symbols for hero worship fall into three categories: political, military, and sports figures. These seem to reflect well the more popular forms of hero worship in our society—unless we count such idols as rock musicians, movie stars, or outlaws (Jesse James, Bonnie and Clyde).

In the past young adults had political figures to look up to and respect. Respect is the important word here. Today the offices and titles are still there, but much of the dignity attached to them has been lost. Political leaders like Franklin Roosevelt and Harry Truman were admired by millions. John Kennedy still lives on in people's memories as a symbol of idealism and a new Camelot. Nixon ("I am not a crook") did much to cheapen the office of the president with the Watergate scandal. Recently we have had fund-raising scandals with politicians routinely getting tax breaks for rich constituents or accepting donations from foreign sources. *Politician* has become a dirty word for many voters.

The decline in loyalty towards the military is due largely to unpopular wars like those fought in Korea and Vietnam. We were no longer rallying around the flag as we had done for World War I and World War II. People blamed the Cold War for drawing funds away from domestic programs into a huge arms buildup. Many people object to money spent on foreign aid. Why should we help others when our own country has unsolved problems?

It has also become increasingly difficult to hero-worship athletes in todays society. In baseball, we no longer have athletes like Babe Ruth, Lou Gehrig, Willie Mays, Stan Musial, or Mickey Mantle. Players who played the game with respect for the sport and a love of simply playing. Today we have players who hold out for million-dollar salaries with no concern for the fans. We have players who are in trouble with the law and perform below the standards their million-dollar contracts seem to call for.

With all these problems in our society today, one can understand why young people seach for new outlets for their loyalties. Instead of Little League baseball, they get involved in neighborhood gangs. They make heroes of rap singers who glorify violence against women. Young people have lost faith in the values of the establishment and are finding it hard to find worthy alternatives.

PREVIEW: WRITING AND THINKING

What is the relationship between writing and thinking? What kind of thinking gives shape to your writing? The computer has shortened the distance between the way we think and the way we write. Much writing at the computer is the electronic equivalent of "thinking out loud." We may start with still miscellaneous notes. We notice tentative connections, and half-formed ideas begin to take shape. We massage these, rejecting some and following up others. Some tentative overall scheme begins to take shape. We feed in further supporting material.

Much "critical thinking" is designed to clear the ground for the really productive work of weighing evidence and drawing logical conclusions. To make possible fruitful investigation and discovery, we often first have to question stale, familiar ideas and traditional think schemes. To promote thinking that generates new ideas for new situations, we have to be open to new questions and new possibilities.

For instance, what are productive **problem-solving** strategies? The problem might be how to dispose of a city's garbage at a time when people do not want garbage dumps or landfills or incinerators in their neighborhoods. How do we move from problem to solution? One productive procedure is to brainstorm possible solutions, however far-fetched. (Maybe we could load the garbage on a train and take it to the desert.) Then, by ourselves or in a group, we look at the various options. We start to put aside those that for one reason or another seem wrong. Various alternatives might prove too expensive or too unpopular. They might be too experimental, or they may have been tried before and have failed. By a process of elimination, we might arrive at the option that would solve the problem, at least for a time.

How can we study and practice effective thinking strategies? Our thoughts do not stand still so that we could easily chart or schematize them. Nevertheless, we can chart some basic thinking strategies that we see at work again and again when people face a problem or try to think through a subject. Several major think schemes provide models for the kind of reasoning that leads to sound conclusions. Often the writer presents the conclusions first and then shows the reasoning that led up to them.

REACHING GENERAL CONCLUSIONS Much productive thinking goes from the specific to the general. This generalizing, or **inductive**, model is a discovery mode. It starts from careful observation or data gathering and tries to find the common pattern, the connecting thread. The generalizing or inductive model puts input first: We do not launch unsupported opinions but *earn* the right to have an opinion. Before we generalize, we take a close look at our experience, our observation, our data.

Some powerful writing follows the inductive model. James Baldwin, in his classic essay, "Notes of a Native Son," takes us on a journey of discovery to make us see the workings of racial discrimination in World War II New Jersey. Baldwin first re-creates his experiences with hallucinatory intensity:

> he is refused service at a place called "The American Diner"
>
> the waitress in a fancy restaurant tells him, almost apologetically, "We don't serve Negroes here"
>
> in an outburst of uncontrollable rage, he hurls a water pitcher at the waitress
>
> he is chased from the restaurant by a murderous mob
>
> a friend misdirects the pursuers and saves Baldwin's life
>
> he goes over the experience again and again in his mind ("the way one relives and automobile accident after it has happened and one finds oneself alone and safe")

He then, after pondering the experience, draws his conclusion:

> I could not get over two facts, both equally difficult for the imagination to grasp, and one was that I could have been murdered. But the other was that I had been ready to commit murder.

The strength of the generalizing model is that it stays close to firsthand experience or close to the facts. It shows a respect for the readers, who are invited to look for themselves, to reach their own conclusions. A standard application is to lay several related incidents end to end to show the common pattern. A typical paper will present the general conclusion first and then present the detailed examples that led to it:

A Tale of Three Cities

GENERAL POINT: We treat the homeless not as fellow human beings but as an embarrassment; we hide them for appearances' sake.

Incident 1: One of the major parties holds its national convention in a big city. The city authorities busily clean up the litter. They pick up the homeless and put them in shelters.

Incident 2: The other major party holds its convention in a big city. The city authorities spruce up the city. Filth is picked up; beggars and homeless people are made to move on or are moved to temporary shelters.

Incident 3: An important foreign visitor—the Pope, the Queen of England—arrives. The city authorities spruce up the city; they make beggars and the homeless less visible, as above.

In practice, writers do not usually start out toward general conclusions from a totally clean slate. They will often start with tentative ideas. They try out working hypotheses or follow hunches. To do an honest job of thinking the matter through, the important thing is to be willing to revise tentative generalizations as the evidence accumulates.

WEIGHING THE PRO AND CON Much thinking does not proceed in a linear fashion or straight line from evidence to conclusion. We often first lean one way and then another. The play of **pro and con** makes us explore both sides of an issue. We often feel that to arrive at a balanced conclusion we have to line up arguments in favor and arguments against. We can then weigh their respective merits. Often a convincing piece of writing moves from point to counterpoint and from there to a reasonable conclusion. The play of pro and con allows us to weigh the evidence and balance conflicting claims. It is a safeguard against narrow, one-sided views; it keeps us from jumping to conclusions.

The playing off of conflicting ideas, of point and counterpoint, is the method of **dialectic**. The classic scheme for a pro and con argument is *thesis* (first major point)—*antithesis* (counterpoint)—*synthesis* (a richer, balanced view taking both sides into account).

The following might be a student writer's rough notes for a typical pro and con topic: Should motorcycle riders have to wear safety helmets?

CON—arguments against helmets

> freedom of the open road, sense of liberation, free spirits
>
> outdoor types: exhilaration of being exposed to the elements vs. isolation in excessively cushioned metal cage
>
> cost and inconvenience in dragging/storing the clumsy helmets
>
> principle of choice vs. state interference

PRO—arguments in favor of helmets

> severe nature of injuries, often more ghastly than in car accidents
>
> strain on hospitals, rehabilitation services, horrendous cost to community
>
> trauma to the other motorist (who knows he/she is implicated in the death or maiming of another human being)

BALANCED CONCLUSION: need to protect the public and fellow motorists should overrule the individual's desire for freedom

The pro-and-con approach is especially appropriate to hotly debated issues: affirmative action, English Only, bilingual education, censorship. The commitment to listen to the other side counteracts our tendency to raise our voices and shout people down. The willingness to reconsider, to take a second look, is a prerequisite of rational discussion.

ARGUING FROM PRINCIPLE Logic books used to concentrate heavily on a third major thinking strategy. Much argument does not start from a patient gathering of the facts. It starts from what we already know, or think we know. The **deductive** model starts with a general principle and applies it to a specific situation. (This model reverses the itinerary of the inductive model.) You can model such arguments as follows:

> IF: Federal guidelines bar colleges from discriminating against students on the basis of gender.
>
> AND IF: The local women's college still bars male students.
>
> THEN: The college is in violation of federal guidelines.

When we argue from principle, we start from basic assumptions and apply them to specific cases. Writers who argue from principle appeal to shared values. Much depends on the reader's accepting the basic assumptions, or **premises**. On the topic of capital punishment, for instance, accepting premises like the following is likely to make you agree with a writer rejecting the death penalty:

> Premise 1: The poor must have the equal protection of the law (but they cannot afford the best, expensive legal help and therefore are much more likely to receive the death penalty than the rich).
>
> Premise 2: Minorities deserve equal treatment before the law (but the death penalty is applied to them much more often than to whites).
>
> Premise 3: People innocently convicted must have a chance to be rehabilitated (but the mistake cannot be rectified if the people are dead).

You can chart an argument based on these premises according to the "IF- AND IF-THEN" formula:

> IF: Justice requires the justice system to be willing to correct its mistakes—to reverse judicial error.
>
> AND IF: Capital punishment makes the reversal of a wrongful verdict impossible.
>
> THEN: Capital punishment is inherently unjust.

Students of logic have paid much attention to how such arguments work and how they go wrong. They call a formal deductive argument that moves from a first premise through a second premise to a valid conclusion a **syllogism**. The first premise is the more general or more inclusive one (major premise): "All human beings are mortal." The second premise is the more limited or specific one (minor premise): "Socrates is a human being." The justified logical conclusion is: "Socrates is mortal."

You can chart a formal syllogism like this:

FIRST PREMISE: Women are not eligible to join the Troglodyte Club.

SECOND PREMISE: Luisa is a woman.

CONCLUSION: Therefore, Luisa is not eligible to join the Troglodyte Club.

A **faulty syllogism** results when we try to get more out of our premises than they warrant:

FIRST PREMISE: All human beings are mortal.

SECOND PREMISE: My dog is mortal.

CONCLUSION: Therefore, my dog is a human being.

Here, we are misreading the first premise. It is not exclusive; it does not say: "All human beings *and no other kinds of living beings* are mortal." We should really read it to mean: "All human beings (and perhaps also many other beings) are mortal." Here is a common faulty syllogism:

FIRST PREMISE: All Marxists quote Marx.

SECOND PREMISE: Professor Guth quotes Marx.

CONCLUSION: Therefore, Professor Guth is a Marxist.
                        (What is wrong here?)

THINKING AND LOGICAL FALLACIES Advocates of straight thinking warn us of other similar pitfalls. Sometimes we fail to think straight because someone is manipulating our reactions. How are our reactions being steered when the cutting down of trees is described as "harvesting"? The word *harvest* might lead us to believe that in a few years the trees will grow again. They would provide another crop—although, in the case of redwood trees, the last "crop" took between two hundred and eight hundred years to grow.

However, often we manage to reach wrong conclusions on our own. Logicians take inventory of familiar **logical fallacies**—familiar kinds of shortcut thinking or predictable ways of reaching the wrong conclusion. Sometimes these are the product of our natural tendency to go for the simple answer or the quick fix. Problems like the following are likely to hurt your credibility as a writer:

ad hominem *Ad hominem* arguments aim at the person (usually below the belt) instead of addressing the issue. Instead of discussing your ideas about health care, for instance, your opponent might call attention to a messy divorce, an alcoholic relative, your visits to a psychiatrist, or your sexual orientation.

hasty generalization Knowing a few Vietnamese students hardly gives us the right to generalize about "how Asians think." (Filipino, Japanese, Chinese, and Vietnamese students might think alike in some ways, but it would be a formidable task to pinpoint the similarities and test our conclusions.) Similarly, we should not make sweeping generalizations about "what the American people want." Elections provide a rough measure of what people want, and often it is different from what we had hoped for. (And often these elections are decided by a few percentage points.)

unrepresentative sample We cannot determine student sentiment on current issues by talking only to members of fraternities and sororities. We need to listen as well to co-op dwellers, people living on their own close to the campus, and commuters. We should probably talk to reentry students, minority students, and part-time students.

post hoc fallacy *Post hoc* is short for the Latin for "after this, therefore because of this." "First this and then that" does not always mean cause and effect. If it rained after the rainmaker performed a ceremony, it might have rained anyway without his help. If a hurricane strikes after a nuclear test, there might or might not be a causal connection.

false analogy Is our nation like a lifeboat—with only so many spaces? Would it be swamped if we allowed an unlimited number of the people floundering in the water to climb aboard? It is true that no nation has unlimited resources, and absorbing too many immigrants might "swamp" cities and institutions. However, sooner or later the analogy breaks down. Immigrants have often developed new resources and taken new initiatives (which newcomers to a lifeboat could not do). And as a nation, we depend on people *outside* the lifeboat for resources and for trade that brings employment.

rationalization When we rationalize, we go for creditable explanations. When something goes wrong, we look for explanations that sound reasonable and at the same time clear us of blame. When you do poorly in a class with a teacher of a different gender or ethnicity, the reason may well be that the teacher is prejudiced against your kind. But the reason may also be that the subject is difficult or that you did not have enough time to study. When you become wary of rationalization, you try to distinguish between a legitimate grievance and an excuse.

slanting Court procedures require prosecutors and defense attorneys to share evidence favoring the other side. The wary reader knows that interested parties tend to slant the data or suppress damaging evidence. They exaggerate everything that favors their cause and simply leave out complicating or contrary testimony. Skeptical readers ask: On this issue, who has an axe to grind? Who has an interest in tampering with the evidence or cooking the books?

bandwagon Advertisers and public relations experts try to sway us by letting us know that "everybody does it" or "everyone thinks so." What is fashionable or trendy carries people along when it comes to selling ideas as well as shoes.

smokescreen Propagandists know how to hide damaging or disturbing information behind a verbal smokescreen. "Collateral damage" stands for civilians killed, maimed, and bombed out in attacks officially aimed at military targets. "Ethnic cleansing" stands for the practice of loading women, old men, and children into cattle cars after burning down their homes.

YOUR TURN: Assessing Arguments

How do you react to the following arguments? Which do you think are sound? Where would you take issue with the speaker or writer—and on what grounds?

1. Professor Minkin is from a middle-class background. She can't be expected to sympathize with the poor.

2. Where there is smoke, there is fire. There would not be charges of corruption against the mayor if he were totally innocent.

3. Only people born in the U.S. can be elected president. Henry Kissinger was born in Germany. He cannot become president of the United States.

4. In some state universities, tuition fees have gone up by as much as forty percent in the last few years. What we witness here is a concerted attempt to deprive minority students of an education.

5. Just about everyone agrees that the current welfare system perpetuates the cycle of dependency. We need to get able-bodied adults off the welfare rolls and stop rewarding welfare mothers for having additional children.

6. Students work best in a relaxed, supportive atmosphere. Tests generate anxiety and lead to cramming and abuse of coffee, pills, and other stimulants. Therefore, tests work against true learning.

7. Newspapers have been piling up on the driveway across the street. It looks as if the people went away on vacation. Or perhaps someone is sick and does not come out to pick up the papers.

8. The police found empty beer cans in the back of the overturned car. The driver must have been drinking.

9. In the local high schools, the dropout rates for minority students are at an all-time high. A recent study showed that fewer black or Hispanic candidates are about to receive advanced degrees than two or three years ago. At prestige institutions like the Harvard Law School, minority representation has hardly budged in recent years. America's minorities are not winning the race for equal educational opportunity.

10. Two of my coworkers at the chemical factory died of lung cancer. The safety precautions at the plant are totally inadequate.

Starting a Journal

How do you make writing a habit? To help make writing a natural, familiar activity, start a journal or writer's log. Write in your journal maybe twice a week, writing entries ranging maybe from half a single-spaced page to a page or more. Your first entries might be about yourself. You might talk about your roots, your family background, your memories (happy or unhappy) of school, or your major interests.

Gradually, you will be branching out: Use your journal to record a running commentary on what you observe, view, and read. Write about incidents that make you think—what happened? Why did it shake you up or change your mind about something? Write about people that matter to you. You might want to react to news stories that make you angry or glad. Record conversations that touched a nerve. Write about visits to the theater or to a museum.

In your journal, you will be writing spontaneously and informally. Your instructor may ask to read all or a sampling of it—but mainly as an interested reader, without a red pencil in hand. You may share entries with your classmates. You will be able to be more candid or unguarded than in formal papers. You will be able to put down first impressions as well as second thoughts, puzzling questions as well as tentative answers.

In addition to giving you practice in verbalizing your thoughts and feelings, your journal will serve you as a source of material for more struc-tured papers. Often an entry will already contain the germ of an idea for a paper. For instance, in developing the paper, you might use what you already have but look for related similar incidents, fill in background for something that happened, tell your reader more about the people involved, or bring the story up to date.

Use the first few entries of your journal for a **personal résumé**. Write entries under headings like the following:

- Roots—family background, ethnic or racial identity, the meeting of cultures

- Schooling—teachers and classmates, goals and obstacles, successes and failures

- Flashlight memories—vividly remembered incidents that have a special meaning for you
- Jobs—part-time jobs, experiences as counselor or mentor, initiation to the workplace
- Personal issues—personal goals and commitments, causes you support, unresolved problems in your life

Study the following sample journal entries. What might each writer do to expand the entry into a fully developed paper?

Roots

I lived with my family in Saigon, South Vietnam, until the age of six, when the communist government took over. The situation at that time was very tense; some people lost their lives, families, or property. My family lost everything but our lives, and we moved to a small town, where I went to school and spent the rest of the day helping my parents at home. Unfortunately, our lives got worse and worse and my parents decided to sell their last valuables and try to escape to seek a better life. My parents had hoped to be able to afford for all of us to escape, but unfortunately my father and brother had to be left behind at the last. This was against my hope and that of my parents. During our escape, I had to hide from the police beneath the deck of a small boat. We spent nine days on the ocean and were robbed by Thai pirates. They raped most of the women. One girl was killed, but four of us were safe, including my mother and me. We were hiding under the men's bodies, and luckily the pirates did not see us. After reaching Malaysia, I spent four months in a small refugee camp, where I suffered from loneliness, hunger, and lack of water. We were finally transferred to the Philippines for another six months. Finally, we were accepted as residents in America. Now I realized that I, as well as my parents, had paid so much for a word—freedom.

Schooling

I am a Hispanic woman and proud of who I am. But there was a time of my life when I was ashamed of myself. I went to a primarily white elementary school, but there were a few blacks, Hispanics, and Asians. The white kids would call the Hispanics beaners and greasers. I didn't understand the words exactly, but I knew they were aimed at my kind. Once at lunch time, I opened my lunch box, which contained two pieces of white bread with smashed beans in between them. One blond, blue-eyed boy with red pants and striped shirt said to me: "Yuck! What is that brown junk in your sandwich?" Thereafter I would eat by myself or open my lunch box slowly to see what was in it first. I wanted to be just like the rest of the kids and not be called names or have different food and a different skin color. When the class put on a play called Sleeping Beauty, I was the witch's crow, with my face

painted green and my nose with a black beak. I always wondered why I
didn't get better parts, like the princess or even the witch. After I
graduated from high school and was on my own, I realized I didn't
have time to feel sorry for myself. I started to research my background
as a Hispanic woman and found my culture to be interesting and inspiring.
I know only that parents should raise their children with love and free
of racism, realizing that we are all the same. Now I am proud and not afraid
of names.

Personal Issues

There are ways of talking about a group with which I identify that
offend me. As a woman, terms that offend me include *babe* and *baby*. Women
are not infants, and when they are called these names, the implication is
that women are childish, immature, and unable to take care of themselves.
Chick and *fox*: Women are not feathered or furry animals. If these terms
are used to "compliment a female's appearance," why not compliment her
intelligence? her sense of humor? her ability in sports? Even the word *lady*
can connote a submissive, subservient, "polite" woman. Granted, words are
"just words." However, they are often a fairly accurate indicator of how a
person might act. Unfortunately, I was able to see the connection between
words and feelings at first hand. I had grown close to my cousin Ben, who
was funny and pleasant to be around. My first warning flag went up when
he referred to a movie as a "chick flick." I was working in his father's store,
and one day when I asked a customer if I could help him, he said: "I don't
want no goddamn woman waiting on me!" As I stood there agape, my uncle
helped him and laughed at the "joke." Needless to say I was upset and later
voiced my concern. That night I received a phone call from Ben. He told me
that I really ought to toughen up if I wanted to make it in the business
world. He proceeded to say that women should "know their place." I lost
all respect for him that night.

1

Initiation: Growing Up American

I never write about anything I have not experienced myself.
— *Shelby Steele*

One writes out of one thing only—one's own experience. Everything depends on how relentlessly one forces from this experience the last drop, sweet or bitter, it can possibly give.
— *James Baldwin*

There are so many young brothers and sisters coming to the forefront, writers who have decided that we can tell our stories any way we damn well please.
— *Terry McMillan*

Gabriele Rico, author of *Writing the Natural Way,* says that everyone has a story. We all have a story to tell that reveals who we are and how we became who we are. When we trust the listener or reader enough, we may tell that story. Many such stories are stories of growing up, of initiation. We move from an earlier stage to a new stage that requires us to learn. We face a challenge that may seem new and overwhelming to us but that (we discover later) many others before us had to face in their own way. We find ourselves reliving an archetypal experience—reliving a pattern that has been played out by many earlier generations.

One such archetypal experience is the move from a protected childhood environment to a world of adult problems. We may slowly discover that a person we trusted has serious flaws. (The idol has feet of clay.) We may discover that we are outgrowing an institution or a set of ideas that at one time seemed to serve all our intellectual or spiritual needs.

For many young Americans, that archetypal experience of growing up has been a move from one world to another—from country to city, or from the old-country ways of immigrant parents to the American world of school and profession. Often that move is a time of confusion, of divided loyalties. It is a time of breaking away and searching for a new identity. People find themselves torn between conflicting loyalties—to different cultures, different ways of life, and often different languages. Sometimes the initiation or awakening centers on the rediscovery of a culture or a language that was part of the family's past but that had been buried in the attempt to assimilate, to become part of the mainstream of American life. Many of the following selections tell the story of such a journey in quest of the writer's identity.

A DAUGHTER'S STORY

Nguyen Louie

Is there a typical American student? Or is it typically American for every-one to have the right to be his or her own person? What is familiar or predictable about the following life story of a fellow student? Is there anything representative about waystations in her life, about her relationship with her parents, or about her thoughts and feelings while growing up? What if any-thing is different or unexpected about Nguyen's story? In what ways is her story different from yours? Can you relate to some of the things that make it different? Nguyen Louie wrote this autobiographical essay when she was a student at Brown University. It was first published in Ms. *magazine as part of a series of testimonies exploring mother-daughter relationships.*

Thought Starters: Has the "generation gap" become a cliché? Or is it still a live issue for many young Americans during their growing up?

I was born two days before International Women's Day (IWD). As I   *1* was growing up, this was always a hectic time of year because my mother was busy going to meetings and organizing programs for the IWD event. I resented the fact that it seemed to take precedence over my birthday. I always wanted a full-fledged birthday party with a dozen friends, junk food, and presents. Instead, I stayed in day care with other children whose mothers were members of the the Third World Women's Alliance. On my eleventh birthday I was allowed to be part of the IWD event; I gave a speech in front of 300 people to raise money for a child care center in Angola. My mother coached me and bought me a purple jumpsuit for the occasion. For the first time, I was doing something that might make a difference on the other side of the world. I think I grew more during that five-minute speech than I had during the previous year. That's when I realized why my mother did what she did and why it was important.

My parents were at Berkeley during the sixties. They agitated for the development of ethnic studies, dropped out of school, and protested against the Vietnam war. They were very liberal. They also gave me a lot of freedom to grow on my own. With that flexibility, I didn't feel the need to rebel. I don't really understand the kinds of relationships my girlfriends have with their mothers. Usually their mothers were overprotective, mak-ing my friends want to defy them even more. Although my mom and I are not equals, we are best friends. I can talk to her, confide in her, laugh with her, and cry with her.

We weren't always so close. As a young child, I was resentful that she didn't have much time to spend with me. I felt closer to my father; he did things with me. We watched videos, ate potato chips, played board games, and went for walks together. When my dad brought his paperwork home, I would poke around and ask him what he was doing. My parents were probably gone from home the same amount of time, but I blamed my mother more. I guess it was because I thought my mother was supposed to be around.

When I was six, my mother became pregnant with my brother, Lung San. I was lonely and looked forward to having a sibling to play with, but I didn't expect my parents to spend so much time with him and not with me. Again, I blamed my mother. I tried to run away, but made it only to the corner because I wasn't supposed to cross the street. Consequently I was forced to compromise with my parents and accept my new role as a responsible big sister, one who was too mature to have tantrums and run away. By age 12, I preferred to stay home from the conventions my parents went to and take care of my brother.

Looking back, I realize that my mother always made sure we had quality time together. My father and I were content to bum around the house, but my mother insisted that we go out and do things. We went on excursions to the Berkeley marina, Golden Gate Park, and Chinatown, and we took family vacations in Santa Cruz and Hawaii. Although it may sound cheesy, my family is very trusting, loving and closely knit. 5

I used to feel pressure to be active in my mother's causes. I felt that I was letting her down if I didn't go to meetings. Being active was the right thing to do, but it wasn't always what I wanted to do. I wanted to be a "normal" teenager, to go to the movies or bowling with my friends. Often it seemed like my parents did not have any fun; they were always gone, and they came home exhausted. I wasn't able to see that their work was interesting or worthwhile. To me, it seemed oppressive. In a lot of ways I am more conservative than my mom. I often fight change. My mom wants me to get out there and be more active, and sometimes I just don't think I have the time or energy for it. I just want to be myself.

When I was 13, my parents sent me to Cuba for a month with an international youth organization. My mother said, "It willl open your eyes, and you'll learn so much." I adamantly did not want to go. My body was changing and I had started to menstruate, and I was insecure and anxious about having to deal with guys or compete with girls on this trip. The mere thought of it terrified me. But my parents were firm; they put me on the plane, and I went.

My parents were right. It was an eye-opening experience. Delegations of young people had come to Cuba from all over the world. I learned how impoverished some other kids were and about the struggles they were going through. When I went home I felt I had a responsibility to do something, to use the information I had gained and become more active. I started out with good intentions, but my resolve dwindled when I went to junior high school. There were cliques that required being popular and looking cute, and I wanted to be myself. I didn't want to change myself to fit into any clique. I was often lonely and miserable. I hated junior high.

In high school I discovered it was O.K. to be myself. In fact, it was cool to be an individual. I became secure and comfortable with myself and made a lot of good friends who accepted me for who I was. When I was a sophomore I was a founding member of the Asian Awareness Club. When complaints arose about Asian students getting beaten up and kicked in the hallways, we organized workshops on interracial relationships and Asian stereotypes. Part of what I liked about the club was organizing with my friends and deciding to do it on my own. My parents weren't telling me, "You are going to this meeting and will learn something from it." I planned the meetings and the different issues we discussed.

I decided to go to Brown because of its academic diversity and the   *10* fact that it offered the flexibility of creating your own major. Also, being at home with my parents was too comfortable; I needed to get out on my own and be more independent. Breaking away from my parents was the hardest thing for me to do. But my parents made the transition easier by flying out with me to the East Coast and giving me lots of support.

When I got to Brown, I went through a difficult time. I had never been so aware of my socioeconomic background, but at Brown it seems that the majority of the students have been through private East Coast preparatory schools, and I felt they had the upper hand. I also found it strange to meet so many students whose primary goal is to make money. Many students aspire to be doctors not because they want to help people, but in order to have extravagant lifestyles. I was disheartened by this attitude. The first semester was a struggle for me. My parents stressed that although grades are important, they are not matters of life and death. They just said, "Do the best you can." I still feel the need to work, but the pressure is coming from within myself.

I am a feminist by my own interpretation: I believe that men and women are equal physically and intellectually; therefore, they are entitled to equal rights, treatment, and respect. I take this for granted, and I immediately assume people are wrong for thinking otherwise. It's almost instinctive. Yet I would never introduce myself as a feminist; I am a Chinese-Korean-American young woman. Being a feminist is an integral part of who I am, but it is not all that I am.

I can't see myself being as much of an activist as my mother, but activism is definitely a part of me. It's in my blood. I'm not sure whether that's a blessing or a curse. I plan to tap into the activism on campus, but I don't want to devote my life to it. I prefer to deal with things on a personal level. What I want from life is to achieve my maximum potential, to be happy, and to be comfortable. I want to find a balance.

The Responsive Reader

1. What do you learn about the mother's involvement as an organizer or activist? What is the author's attitude toward her mother? How did it develop or change during her growing up? (Does the author consider herself an "activist"?)

2. Has the term *liberal* become a dirty word in our society? In what sense were Louie's parents "liberals"? What do you learn here about traditional liberal causes? Why would ethnic studies be one of them?

3. Terms like *sibling rivalry, quality time,* and the desire to be *normal* are familiar to students of pop psychology and of talk shows focusing on personal concerns. Are these terms just buzzwords? What role did they play in Louie's growing up?

4. "Educational experiences" that people might mention in a vita might include travel and contrasting experiences at different stages of their schooling. What was eye-opening about the author's trip to Cuba? What made the difference between her junior high and her high school experience?

5. How did the author become aware of the role of race and ethnicity? What shaped her attitude toward or interest in "diversity"? How did she become aware of the role of class in American society?

6. Louie says, "I am a feminist by my own interpretation." What *is* her own version of feminism? How does it compare with yours or with your definition of the term?

Talking, Listening, Writing

7. Do you think Nguyen Louie could be called a typical or representative young American? Why or why not? Do you think she has had a privileged or sheltered experience while growing up? Do you think she has allowed herself to be steered too much by her parents?

8. Was there a waystation or a turning point in your growing up when you discovered the role of poverty, of race, of class, or of gender in our society?

9. Is there activism on your campus? What form does it take? Who gets involved? Do you?

LAKOTA WOMAN

Mary Crow Dog

Lakota Woman *(written with Richard Erdoes) is the story of Mary Crow Dog, who grew up on a reservation in South Dakota in a one-room cabin, without a father in the house and without running water or electricity. Her publisher said about her, "Rebelling against the aimless drinking, punishing missionary school, narrow strictures for women, and violence and hopelessness of reservation life, she joined the new movement of tribal pride sweeping Native American communities in the sixties and seventies and eventually married Leonard Crow Dog, the movement's chief medicine man, who revived the outlawed Ghost Dance." William Kunstler has called the book the "moving story of a Native American woman who fought her way out of bitterness and despair to find the righteous ways of her ancestors." When she was a child on the reservation, Mary Crow Dog says, "Indian religion was forbidden. Children were punished for praying Indian, men were jailed for taking a sweat bath. Our sacred pipes were broken, our medicine bundles burned or given to museums." For a time, before she set out in search of the native traditions of her people, she conformed to the image of the Christian convert. She remembers being confirmed in a white dress, with veil and candle—"white outside and red inside, the opposite of an apple." What in her story fits in with what you know about the indigenous peoples of North America? What changes your mind about the experience of Native Americans?*

Thought Starters: What shaped your early impressions of Native Americans? Have recent readings, movies, or television shows changed the way you think about them?

It is not the big, dramatic things so much that get us down, but just being Indian, trying to hang on to our way of life, language, and values while being surrounded by an alien, more powerful culture. It is being an iyeska, a half-blood, being looked down upon by whites and full-bloods alike. It is being a backwoods girl living in a city, having to rip off stores in order to survive. Most of all it is being a woman. Among Plains tribes, some men think that all a woman is good for is to crawl into the sack with them and mind the children. It compensates for what white society has done to them. They were famous warriors and hunters once, but the buffalo is gone and there is not much rep in putting a can of spam or an occasional rabbit on the table.

As for being warriors, the only way some men can count coup now-adays is knocking out another skin's teeth during a barroom fight. In the old days a man made a name for himself by being generous and wise, but now he has nothing to be generous with, no jobs, no money; and as far as our traditional wisdom is concerned, our men are being told by the white missionaries, teachers, and employers that it is merely savage superstition they should get rid of if they want to make it in this world. Men are forced to live away from their children, so that the family can get ADC—Aid to Dependent Children. So some warriors come home drunk and beat up their old ladies in order to work off their frustration. I know where they are coming from. I feel sorry for them, but I feel even sorrier for their women.

To start from the beginning, I am a Sioux from the Rosebud Reservation in South Dakota. I belong to the "Burned Thigh," the Brule Tribe, the Sicangu in our language. Long ago, so the legend goes, a small band of Sioux was surrounded by enemies who set fire to their tipis and the grass around them. They fought their way out of the trap but got their legs burned and in this way acquired their name. The Brules are part of the Seven Sacred Campfires, the seven tribes of the Western Sioux known collectively as Lakota. The Eastern Sioux are called Dakota. The difference between them is their language. It is the same except that where we Lakota pronounce an *L,* the Dakota pronounce a *D.* They cannot pronounce an *L* at all. In our tribe we have this joke: "What is a flat tire in Dakota?" Answer: "A b*d*owout."

The Brule, like all Sioux, were a horse people, fierce riders and raiders, great warriors. Between 1870 and 1880 all Sioux were driven into reservations, fenced in and forced to give up everything that had given meaning to their life—their horses, their hunting, their arms, everything. But under the long snows of despair the little spark of our ancient beliefs and pride kept glowing, just barely sometimes, waiting for a warm wind to blow that spark into a flame again.

My family was settled on the reservation in a small place called He-Dog, after a famous chief. There are still some He-Dogs living. One, an old lady I knew, lived to be over a hundred years old. Nobody knew when she had been born. She herself had no idea, except that when she came into the world there was no census yet, and Indians had not yet been given Christian first names. Her name was just He-Dog, nothing else. She always told me, "You should have seen me eighty years ago when I was pretty." I have never forgotten her face—nothing but deep cracks and gullies, but beautiful in its own way. At any rate very impressive.

On the Indian side my family was related to the Brave Birds and Fool Bulls. Old Grandpa Fool Bull was the last man to make flutes and play them, the old-style flutes in the shape of a bird's head which had the elk power, the power to lure a young girl into a man's blanket. Fool Bull lived a whole long century, dying in 1976, whittling his flutes almost until his last day. He took me to my first peyote meeting while I was still a kid.

He still remembered the first Wounded Knee, the massacre. He was a young boy at that time, traveling with his father, a well-known medicine man. They had gone to a place near Wounded Knee to take part in a Ghost Dance. They had on their painted ghost shirts which were supposed to make them bulletproof. When they got near Pine Ridge they were stopped by white soldiers, some of them from the Seventh Cavalry, George Custer's old regiment, who were hoping to kill themselves some Indians. The Fool Bull band had to give up their few old muzzle-loaders, bows, arrows, and even knives. They had to put up their tipis in a tight circle, all bunched up, with the wagons on the outside and the soldiers surrounding their camp, watching them closely. It was cold, so cold that the trees were crackling with a loud noise as the frost was splitting their trunks. The people made a fire the following morning to warm themselves and make some coffee and then they noticed a sound beyond the crackling of the trees: rifle fire, salvos making a noise like the ripping apart of a giant blanket; the boom of cannon and the rattling of quick-firing Hotchkiss guns. Fool Bull remembered the grown-ups bursting into tears, the women keening: "They are killing our people, they are butchering them!" It was only two miles or so from where Grandfather Fool Bull stood that almost three hundred Sioux men, women, and children were slaughtered. Later grandpa saw the bodies of the slain, all frozen in ghostly attitudes, thrown into a ditch like dogs. And he saw a tiny baby sucking at his dead mother's breast.

I wish I could tell about the big deeds of some ancestors of mine who fought at the Little Big Horn, or the Rosebud, counting coup during the Grattan or Fetterman battle, but little is known of my family's history before 1880. I hope some of my great-grandfathers counted coup on Custer's men, I like to imagine it, but I just do not know. Our Rosebud people did not play a big part in the battles against generals Crook or Custer. This was due to the policy of Spotted Tail, the all-powerful chief at the time. Spotted Tail had earned his eagle feathers as a warrior, but had been taken East as a prisoner and put in jail. Coming back years later, he said that he had seen the cities of the whites and that a single one of them contained more people than could be found in all the Plains tribes put together, and that every one of the wasičuns' factories could turn out more rifles and bullets in one day than were owned by all the Indians in the country. It was useless, he said, to try to resist the wasičuns. During the critical year of 1876 he had his Indian police keep most of the young men on the reservation, preventing them from joining Sitting Bull, Gall, and Crazy Horse. Some of the young bucks, a few Brave Birds among them, managed to sneak out trying to get to Montana, but nothing much is known. After having been forced into reservations, it was not thought wise to recall such things. It might mean no rations, or worse. For the same reason many in my family turned Christian, letting themselves be "white-manized." It took many years to reverse this process.

My sister Barbara, who is four years older than me, says she remembers the day when I was born. It was late at night and raining hard amid thunder and lightning. We had no electricity then, just the old-style kerosene lamps with the big reflectors. No bathroom, no tap water, no car. Only a few white teachers had cars. There was one phone in He-Dog, at the trading post. This was not so very long ago, come to think of it. Like most Sioux at that time my mother was supposed to give birth at home, I think, but something went wrong, I was pointing the wrong way, feet first or stuck sideways. My mother was in great pain, laboring for hours, until finally somebody ran to the trading post and called the ambulance. They took her—us—to Rosebud, but the hospital there was not yet equipped to handle a complicated birth, I don't think they had surgery then, so they had to drive mother all the way to Pine Ridge, some ninety miles distant, because there the tribal hospital was bigger. So it happened that I was born among Crazy Horse's people. After my sister Sandra was born the doctors there performed a hysterectomy on my mother, in fact sterilizing her without her permission, which was common at the time, and up to just a few years ago, so that it is hardly worth mentioning. In the opinion of some people, the fewer Indians there are, the better. As Colonel Chivington said to his soldiers: "Kill 'em all, big and small, nits make lice!"

I don't know whether I am a louse under the white man's skin. I   *10* hope I am. At any rate I survived the long hours of my mother's labor, the stormy drive to Pine Ridge, and the neglect of the doctors. I am an iyeska, a breed, that's what the white kids used to call me. When I grew bigger they stopped calling me that, because it would get them a bloody nose. I am a small woman, not much over five feet tall, but I can hold my own in a fight, and in a free-for-all with honkies I can become rather ornery and do real damage. I have white blood in me. Often I have wished to be able to purge it out of me. As a young girl I used to look at myself in the mirror, trying to find a clue as to who and what I was. My face is very Indian, and so are my eyes and my hair, but my skin is very light. Always I waited for the summer, for the prairie sun, the Badlands sun, to tan me and make me into a real skin.

The Crow Dogs, the members of my husband's family, have no such problems of identity. They don't need the sun to tan them, they are full-bloods—the Sioux of the Sioux. Some Crow Dog men have faces which make the portrait on the buffalo Indian nickel look like a washed-out white man. They have no shortage of legends. Every Crow Dog seems to be a legend in himself, including the women. They became outcasts in their stronghold at Grass Mountain rather than being whitemanized. They could not be tamed, made to wear a necktie or go to a Christian church. All during the long years when practicing Indian beliefs was forbidden and could be punished with jail, they went right on having their ceremonies, their sweat baths and sacred dances. Whenever a Crow Dog got together with some relatives, such as those equally untamed, unregenerated Iron Shells, Good Lances, Two Strikes, Picket Pins, or Hollow Horn Bears, then you could hear the sound of the can gleska, the drum, telling all the world that a Sioux ceremony was in the making. It took courage and suffering to keep the flame alive, the little spark under the snow.

The first Crow Dog was a well-known chief. On his shield was the design of two circles and two arrowheads for wounds received in battle— two white man's bullets and two Pawnee arrow points. When this first Crow Dog was lying wounded in the snow, a coyote came to warm him and a crow flew ahead of him to show him the way home. His name should be Crow Coyote, but the white interpreter misunderstood it and so they became Crow Dogs. This Crow Dog of old became famous for killing a rival chief, the result of a feud over tribal politics, then driving voluntarily over a hundred miles to get himself hanged at Deadwood, his wife sitting beside him in his buggy; famous also for finding on his arrival that the Supreme Court had ordered him to be freed because the federal government had no jurisdiction over Indian reservations and also because it was no crime for one Indian to kill another. Later, Crow Dog became a leader of the Ghost Dancers, holding out for months in the frozen caves and ravines of the Badlands. So, if my own family lacks history, that of my husband more than makes up for it.

Our land itself is a legend, especially the area around Grass Mountain where I am living now. The fight for our land is at the core of our existence, as it has been for the last two hundred years. Once the land is gone, then we are gone too. The Sioux used to keep winter counts, picture writings on buffalo skin, which told our people's story from year to year. Well, the whole country is one vast winter count. You can't walk a mile without coming to some family's sacred vision hill, to an ancient Sun Dance circle, an old battleground, a place where something worth remembering happened. Mostly a death, a proud death or a drunken death. We are a great people for dying. "It's a good day to die!" that's our old battle cry. But the land with its tar paper shacks and outdoor privies, not one of them straight, but all leaning this way or that way, is also a land to live on, a land for good times and telling jokes and talking of great deeds done in the past. But you can't live forever off the deeds of Sitting Bull or Crazy Horse. You can't wear their eagle feathers, freeload off their legends. You have to make your own legends now. It isn't easy.

The Responsive Reader

1. Mary Crow Dog says, "As a young girl I used to look at myself in the mirror, trying to find a clue as to who and what I was." Who is she? What are key elements in her sense of self?

2. What is her attitude toward Native American men? How does she describe and explain their behavior? How does she contrast their past and their present?

3. What do you learn here about the buried or half-forgotten past that, the author says, was for many years "not thought wise to recall"? What is the author's relation to "our people's story"? What do you learn about customs, traditions, beliefs?

Talking, Listening, Writing

4. Some writers speak for themselves as individuals; others give voice to the experience of many. They speak for a group, for a region, or for a generation. Would you consider Mary Crow Dog an effective and representative spokesperson for Native Americans? Why or why not?

5. A later essay in this book examines the issue of "White Guilt" (Shelby Steele, p. 274). Do you think white Americans today should feel guilty about the treatment of Native Americans now and in the past? Why or why not?

6. Are you in favor of people like Mary Crow Dog restoring the forgotten or formerly banned culture and religion of their group?

7. Mary Crow Dog says, "You have to make your own legends now. It isn't easy." What does she mean?

Collaborative Projects

8. How much do you know about the American Indian Movement or other organizations dedicated to recovering the cultural heritage of a group in American society? Are there comparable organizations for Spanish-speaking Americans (Chicanos, Latinos), for blacks or African Americans, or for Asian Americans? Pool your knowledge or relevant background with that of other students in your class.

STEP FORWARD IN THE CAR, PLEASE

Maya Angelou

> *Maya Angelou has had a spectacular career as writer, poet, singer, dancer, actor (she acted in* Roots*), and writer-producer of a ten-part television series. She was part of the civil rights movement, working as the Northern coordinator for the Southern Leadership Conference. She lived for several years in Ghana editing the* African Review. *Angelou has told her story in a series of autobiographical volumes, including* I Know Why the Caged Bird Sings *(which first introduced her to a large audience);* Gather Together in My Name; Singin', Swingin' and Gettin' Merry like Christmas; *and* The Heart of a Woman. *She was born in St. Louis, Missouri; after the breakup of her parents' marriage, she went to live with her grandmother in Arkansas among Southern rural blacks who, she says, valued age more than wealth and religious piety more than beauty. She early came to know poverty, the neglected segregated schools, and the fear of violence at the hands of white people and of abuse by her own people as well. She became an unmarried teenage mother at age sixteen. Her grandmother ran a country store in Sparks, Arkansas, a small Southern town where many of her contemporaries knew only to "chop cotton, pick cotton, and hoe potatoes," all the while dreaming of being "free, free from this town, and crackers, and farming, and yes-sirring and no-sirring." They all "needed to believe that a land existed somewhere, even beyond the Northern star, where Negroes were treated as people." The following excerpt focuses on a crucial stage of Angelou's journey toward making this dream come true. A much sought-after speaker-performer, Angelou published a collection of poetry,* I Shall Not Be Moved, *in 1990 and read her poem "On the Pulse of the Morning" at President Clinton's inauguration in 1993.*

Thought Starters: What does the term *racism* mean to you? Where do you hear it used, and by whom? To judge from your own observation, how does racism work? What are its roots? How can it be overcome?

My room had all the cheeriness of a dungeon and the appeal of a   *1* tomb. It was going to be impossible to stay there, but leaving held no attraction for me, either. The answer came to me with the suddenness of a collision. I would go to work. Mother wouldn't be difficult to convince; after all, in school I was a year ahead of my grade and Mother was a firm believer in self-sufficiency. In fact, she'd be pleased to think that I had that much gumption, that much of her in my character. (She liked to speak of herself as the original "do-it-yourself girl.")

Once I had settled on getting a job, all that remained was to decide which kind of job I was most fitted for. My intellectual pride had kept me from selecting typing, shorthand, or filing as subjects in school, so office work was ruled out. War plants and shipyards demanded birth certificates, and mine would reveal me to be fifteen, and ineligible for work. So the well-paying defense jobs were also out. Women had replaced men on the streetcars as conductors and motormen, and the thought of sailing up and down the hills of San Francisco in a dark-blue uniform, with a money changer at my belt, caught my fancy.

Mother was as easy as I had anticipated. The world was moving so fast, so much money was being made, so many people were dying in Guam, and Germany, that hordes of strangers became good friends overnight. Life was cheap and death entirely free. How could she have the time to think about my academic career?

To her question of what I planned to do, I replied that I would get a job on the streetcars. She rejected the proposal with: "They don't accept colored people on the streetcars."

I would like to claim an immediate fury which was followed by the *5* noble determination to break the restricting tradition. But the truth is, my first reaction was one of disappointment. I'd pictured myself, dressed in a neat blue serge suit, my money changer swinging jauntily at my waist, and a cheery smile for the passengers which would make their own work day brighter.

From disappointment, I gradually ascended the emotional ladder to haughty indignation, and finally to that state of stubbornness where the mind is locked like the jaws of an enraged bulldog.

I would go to work on the streetcars and wear a blue serge suit. Mother gave me her support with one of her usual terse asides, "That's what you want to do? Then nothing beats a trial but a failure. Give it everything you've got. I've told you many times, 'Can't Do is like Don't Care.' Neither of them has a home."

Translated, that meant there was nothing a person can't do, and there should be nothing a human being didn't care about. It was the most positive encouragement I could have hoped for.

In the offices of the Market Street Railway Company, the receptionist seemed as surprised to see me there as I was surprised to find the interior dingy and drab. Somehow I had expected waxed surfaces and carpeted floors. If I had met no resistance, I might have decided against working for such a poor-mouth-looking concern. As it was, I explained that I had come to see about a job. She asked, was I sent by an agency, and when I replied that I was not, she told me they were only accepting applicants from agencies.

The classified pages of the morning papers had listed advertisements *10* for motorettes and conductorettes and I reminded her of that. She gave me a face full of astonishment that my suspicious nature would not accept.

"I am applying for the job listed in this morning's *Chronicle* and I'd like to be presented to your personnel manager." While I spoke in supercilious accents, and looked at the room as if I had an oil well in my own backyard, my armpits were being pricked by millions of hot pointed needles. She saw her escape and dived into it.

"He's out. He's out for the day. You might call him tomorrow and if he's in, I'm sure you can see him." Then she swiveled her chair around on its rusty screws and with that I was supposed to be dismissed.

"May I ask his name?"

She half turned, acting surprised to find me still there.

"His name? Whose name?"   15

"Your personnel manager."

We were firmly joined in the hypocrisy to play out the scene.

"The personnel manager? Oh, he's Mr. Cooper, but I'm not sure you'll find him here tomorrow. He's . . . Oh, but you can try."

"Thank you."

"You're welcome."   20

And I was out of the musty room and into the even mustier lobby. In the street I saw the receptionist and myself going faithfully through paces that were stale with familiarity, although I had never encountered that kind of situation before and, probably, neither had she. We were like actors who, knowing the play by heart, were still able to cry afresh over the old tragedies and laugh spontaneously at the comic situations.

The miserable little encounter had nothing to do with me, the me of me, any more than it had to do with that silly clerk. The incident was a recurring dream concocted years before by whites, and it eternally came back to haunt us all. The secretary and I were like people in a scene where, because of harm done by one ancestor to another, we were bound to duel to the death. (Also because the play must end somewhere.)

I went further than forgiving the clerk; I accepted her as a fellow victim of the same puppeteer.

On the streetcar, I put my fare into the box and the conductorette looked at me with the usual hard eyes of white contempt. "Move into the car, please move on in the car." She patted her money changer.

Her Southern nasal accent sliced my meditation and I looked deep   25
into my thoughts. All lies, all comfortable lies. The receptionist was not innocent and neither was I. The whole charade we had played out in that waiting room had to do with me, black, and her, white.

I wouldn't move into the streetcar but stood on the ledge over the conductor, glaring. My mind shouted so energetically that the announcement made my veins stand out, and my mouth tighten into a prune.

I WOULD HAVE THE JOB. I WOULD BE A CONDUCTORETTE AND SLING A FULL MONEY CHANGER FROM MY BELT. I WOULD.

The next three weeks were a honeycomb of determination with apertures for the days to go in and out. The Negro organizations to whom I appealed for support bounced me back and forth like a shuttlecock on a badminton court. Why did I insist on that particular job? Openings were going begging that paid nearly twice the money. The minor officials with whom I was able to win an audience thought me mad. Possibly I was.

Downtown San Francisco became alien and cold, and the streets I had loved in a personal familiarity were unknown lanes that twisted with malicious intent. My trips to the streetcar office were of the frequency of a person on salary. The struggle expanded. I was no longer in conflict only with the Market Street Railway but with the marble lobby of the building which housed its offices, and elevators and their operators.

During this period of strain Mother and I began our first steps on the long path toward mutual adult admiration. She never asked for reports and I didn't offer any details. But every morning she made breakfast, gave me carfare and lunch money, as if I were going to work. She comprehended that in the struggle lies the joy. That I was no glory seeker was obvious to her, and that I had to exhaust every possibility before giving in was also clear.   *30*

On my way out of the house one morning she said, "Life is going to give you just what you put in it. Put your whole heart in everything you do, and pray, then you can wait." Another time she reminded me that "God helps those who help themselves." She had a store of aphorisms which she dished out as the occasion demanded. Strangely, as bored as I was with clichés, her inflection gave them something new, and set me thinking for a little while at least. Later when asked how I got my job, I was never able to say exactly. I only knew that one day, which was tiresomely like all the others before it, I sat in the Railway office, waiting to be interviewed. The receptionist called me to her desk and shuffled a bundle of paper to me. They were job application forms. She said they had to be filled out in triplicate. I had little time to wonder if I had won or not, for the standard questions reminded me of the necessity for lying. How old was I? List my previous jobs, starting from the last held and go backward to the first. How much money did I earn, and why did I leave the position? Give two references (not relatives). I kept my face blank (an old art) and wrote quickly the fable of Marguerite Johnson, aged nineteen, former companion and driver for Mrs. Annie Henderson (a White Lady) in Stamps, Arkansas.

I was given blood tests, aptitude tests, and physical coordination tests, then on a blissful day I was hired as the first Negro on the San Francisco streetcars.

Mother gave me the money to have my blue serge suit tailored, and I learned to fill out work cards, operate the money changer and punch transfers. The time crowded together and at an End of Days I was swinging on the back of the rackety trolley, smiling sweetly and persuading my charges to "step forward in the car, please."

For one whole semester the streetcars and I shimmied up and scooted down the sheer hills of San Francisco. I lost some of my need for the black ghetto's shielding-sponge quality, as I clanged and cleared my way down Market Street, with its honky-tonk homes for homeless sailors, past the quiet retreat of Golden Gate Park and along closed undwelled-in-looking dwellings of the Sunset District.

My work shifts were split so haphazardly that it was easy to believe 35 that my superiors had chosen them maliciously. Upon mentioning my suspicions to Mother, she said, "Don't you worry about it. You ask for what you want, and you pay for what you get. And I'm going to show you that it ain't no trouble when you pack double."

She stayed awake to drive me out to the car barn at four-thirty in the mornings, or to pick me up when I was relieved just before dawn. Her awareness of life's perils convinced her that while I would be safe on the public conveyances, she "wasn't about to trust a taxi driver with her baby."

When the spring classes began, I resumed my commitment with formal education. I was so much wiser and older, so much more independent, with a bank account and clothes that I had bought for myself, that I was sure I had learned and earned the magic formula which would make me a part of the life my contemporaries led.

Not a bit of it. Within weeks, I realized that my schoolmates and I were on paths moving away from each other. They were concerned and excited over the approaching football games. They concentrated great interest on who was worthy of being student body president, and when the metal bands would be removed from their teeth, while I remembered conducting a streetcar in the uneven hours of the morning.

The Responsive Reader

1. Angelou once described herself as a young Southern woman who grew up determined to "defy the odds." What kind of person is speaking to you in this selection? What are key traits? What kind of voice do you hear?
2. What does the writer want you to learn from this account about the workings of racism—its motives, its ploys, its repercussions?
3. If you were a sociologist, what in this account would you accept as an objective reporting of the facts? How much is the writer's interpretation—her personal slant on what happened to her? (Do you agree or disagree with the way she interprets the facts?)

Talking, Listening, Writing

4. How much of what you read here has to be understood in the context of a black woman's experience? How much of it has parallels in the experience of other groups?
5. "Self-esteem" has become a buzzword in recent years, with some school districts instituting programs to help poorly achieving students

or students alienated from school develop self-esteem. To judge from Angelou's account, what does it take to develop self-esteem? Do you think schools should have programs aimed at fostering it?

6. What has been your own experience with prejudice—as a target or as a perpetrator? Describe a key incident or several learning experiences in vivid detail. What did you learn from your experience?

7. What's in a name? One teacher reported that students in his classes were uncomfortable with being called "white people." Why do you think they were? What are the pros and cons of other possible labels— *Caucasian, Anglo, European, European American*? (What are the pros and cons of *black, Afro-American, African, African American, people of color*?)

8. Tell the story of a challenge or an obstacle that you have faced and overcome or by which you were defeated.

Collaborative Projects

9. Is the job discrimination that Angelou faced a thing of the past? As one of several possible projects suggested in this chapter, you may want to work with a group to quiz students from diverse cultural or ethnic backgrounds concerning this question. What are their perceptions of the obstacles and opportunities they encounter in looking for jobs?

BORN AMONG THE BORN-AGAIN

Garrison Keillor

Garrison Keillor became legendary in the Midwest as the host of A Prairie
Home Companion, *a live radio show originating in St. Paul, Minnesota,
and giving audiences a nostalgic mix of old-style storytelling, savvy appeals to
local pride, the sentimental songs of barbershop quintets and crooners, and
homespun humor delighting in the quirks and foibles of family and neighbors.
Keillor is a master at creating a nostalgic vision of a small-town American
past removed from the upheavals and paranoias of the twentieth century.
He collected many of the stories he told on his show in* Lake Wobegon
Days *(1985), explaining that many were "true stories from my childhood,
dressed . . . up as fiction." He said in an interview in* Time *that he looked
to the stories he heard in his family as a child "as giving a person some sense
of place," reassuring us "that we were not just chips floating on the waves,
that in some way we were meant to be here, and had a history. That we had
standing." In recent years, Keillor has taken his show on the road, showing
an uncanny knack for relating to the local subculture—its history, its folk
music, its in-jokes—in places as far apart as San Jose, California, and
Fairbanks, Alaska, or New York City, New York. In the selection that
follows, Keillor replays a classic story of growing up: A youngster growing up
in a family with strong religious views (or other strong beliefs) starts to rebel
against having to be "different" from his peers. How much in this story shows
Keillor's homespun sense of humor? How much is serious or thought-
provoking?*

Thought Starters: What has shaped your impressions of small-town or
back-country American life? Do you share the nostalgia for a simpler
small-town life?

. . . In a town where everyone was either Lutheran or Catholic, we   *1*
were neither one. We were Sanctified Brethren, a sect so tiny that nobody
but us and God knew about it, so when kids asked what I was, I just said
Protestant. It was too much to explain, like having six toes. You would
rather keep your shoes on.

Grandpa Cotten was once tempted toward Lutheranism by a preacher
who gave a rousing sermon on grace that Grandpa heard as a young man
while taking Aunt Esther's dog home who had chased a Model T across
town. He sat down on the church steps and listened to the voice boom
out the open windows until he made up his mind to go in and unite with

the truth, but he took one look from the vestibule and left. "He was dressed up like the Pope of Rome," said Grandpa, "and the altar and paintings and the gold candlesticks—my gosh, it was just a big show. And he was reading the whole darn thing off a page, like an actor."

Jesus said, "Where two or three are gathered together in my name, there am I in the midst of them," and the Brethren believed that was enough. We met in Uncle Al and Aunt Flo's bare living room, with plain folding chairs arranged facing in toward the middle. No clergyman in a black smock. No organ or piano, for that would make one person too prominent. No upholstery—it would lead to complacence. No picture of Jesus—He was in our Hearts. The faithful sat down at the appointed hour and waited for the Spirit to move one of them to speak or to pray or to give out a hymn from our Little Flock hymnal. No musical notation, for music must come from the heart and not off a page. We sang the texts to a tune that fit the meter, of the many tunes we all knew. The idea of reading a prayer was sacrilege to us—"If a man can't remember what he wants to say to God, let him sit down and think a little harder," Grandpa said.

"There's the Lord's Prayer," said Aunt Esther meekly. We were sitting on the porch after Sunday dinner. Esther and Harvey were visiting from Minneapolis and had attended Lake Wobegon Lutheran, she having turned Lutheran when she married him, a subject that was never brought up in our family.

"You call that prayer? Sitting and reciting like a bunch of school-children?" 5

Harvey cleared his throat and turned to me and smiled, "Speaking of school, how are you doing?" he asked.

There was a lovely silence in the Brethren assembled on Sunday morning as we waited for the Spirit. Either the Spirit was moving someone to speak who was taking his sweet time or else the Spirit was playing a wonderful joke on us and letting us sit, or perhaps silence was the point of it. We sat listening to rain on the roof, distant traffic, a radio playing from across the street, kids whizzing by on bikes, dogs barking, as we waited for the Spirit to inspire us. It was like sitting on the porch with your family, when nobody feels that they have to make talk. So quiet in church. Minutes drifted by in silence that was sweet to us. The old Regulator clock ticked, the rain stopped, and the room changed light as the sun broke through—shafts of brilliant sun through the windows and motes of dust falling through it—the smell of clean clothes and floor wax and wine and the fresh bread of Aunt Flo, which was Christ's body given for us. Jesus in our midst, who loved us. So peaceful; and we loved each other, too. I thought perhaps the Spirit was leading me to say that, but I was just a boy, and children were supposed to keep still.

And my affections were not pure. They were tainted with a sneaking admiration of Catholics—Catholic Christmas, Easter, the Living Rosary, and the Blessing of the Animals, all magnificent. Everything we did was plain, but they were regal—especially the Feast Day of Saint Francis, which they did right out in the open, a feast for the eyes. Cows, horses, some pets, right on the church lawn. The turmoil, animals bellowing and barking and clucking and a cat scheming how to escape and suddenly leaping out of the girl's arms who was holding on tight, the cat dashing through the crowd, dogs straining at the leash, and the ocarina band of third graders playing a song, and the great calm of the sisters, and the flags, and the Knights of Columbus decked out in their handsome black suits—the whole thing was gorgeous. I stared at it until my eyes almost fell out, and then I wished it would go on much longer.

"Christians," my Uncle Al used to say, "do not go in for show," referring to the Catholics. We were sanctified by the blood of the Lord; therefore we were saints, like Saint Francis, but we didn't go in for feasts or ceremonies, involving animals or not. We went in for sitting, all nineteen of us, in Uncle Al and Aunt Flo's living room on Sunday morning and having a plain meeting and singing hymns in our poor thin voices, while not far away the Catholics were whooping it up. I wasn't allowed inside Our Lady, of course, but if the Blessing of the Animals on the Feast Day of Saint Francis was any indication, Lord, I didn't know but what they had elephants in there and acrobats. I sat in our little group and envied them for the splendor and gorgeousness, as we tried to sing without even so much as a harmonica to give us the pitch. Hymns, Uncle Al said, didn't have to be sung perfect, because God looks on the heart, and if you are In The Spirit, then all praise is good.

The Brethren, also known as The Saints Gathered in the Name of *10* Christ Jesus, who met in the living room were all related to each other and raised in the Faith from infancy except Brother Mel, who was rescued from a life of drunkenness, saved as a brand from the burning, a drowning sailor, a sheep on the hillside, whose immense red nose testified to his previous condition. I envied his amazing story of how he came to be with us. Born to godly parents, Mel left home at fifteen and joined the Navy. He sailed to distant lands in a submarine and had exciting experiences while traveling the downward path, which led him finally to the Union Gospel Mission in Minneapolis, where he heard God's voice "as clear as my voice speaking to you." He was twenty-six, he slept under bridges and in abandoned buildings, he drank two quarts of white muscatel every day, and then God told him that he must be born again, and so he was, and became the new Mel, except for his nose.

Except for his nose, Mel Burgess looked like any forty-year-old Brethren man: sober, preferring dark suits, soft-spoken, tending toward girth. His nose was what made you look twice: battered, swollen, very red with tiny purplish lines, it looked ancient and dead on his otherwise fairly handsome face, the souvenir of what he had been saved from, the "Before" of his "Before . . . and After" advertisement for being born again.

For me, there was nothing before. I was born among the born-again. This living room so hushed, the Brethren in their customary places on folding chairs (the comfortable ones were put away on Sunday morning) around the end table draped with a white cloth and the glass of wine and loaf of bread (unsliced), was as familiar to me as my mother and father, before whom there was nobody. I had always been here.

. . . So one Sunday our family traipsed over to a restaurant . . . that a friend of Dad's had recommended, Phil's House of Good Food. The waitress pushed two tables together and we sat down and studied the menu. My mother blanched at the prices. A chicken dinner went for $2.50, the roast beef for $3.75. "It's a nice place," Dad said, multiplying the five of us times $2.50. "I'm not so hungry, I guess," he said. "Maybe I'll just have soup." We weren't restaurantgoers—"Why pay good money for food you could make better at home?" was Mother's philosophy—so we weren't at all sure about restaurant customs. For example, could a person who had been seated in a restaurant simply get up and walk out? Would it be proper? Would it be *legal*?

The waitress came and stood by Dad. "Can I get you something from the bar?" she said. Dad blushed a deep red. The question seemed to imply that he looked like a drinker.

"No," he whispered, as if she had offered to take off her clothes and   *15*
dance on the table.

Then another waitress brought a tray of glasses to a table of four couples next to us. "Martini," she said, setting the drink down, "whiskey sour, whiskey sour, Manhattan, whiskey sour, gin and tonic, martini, whiskey sour."

"Ma'am? Something from the bar?" Mother looked at her in disbelief.

Suddenly the room changed for us. Our waitress looked hardened, rough, cheap; across the room a woman laughed obscenely, "Haw, haw, haw"; the man with her lit a cigarette and blew a cloud of smoke; a swearword drifted out from the kitchen like a whiff of urine; even the soft lighting seemed suggestive, diabolical. To be seen in such a place on the Lord's Day—*what had we done?*

My mother rose from her chair.

"We can't stay. I'm sorry," Dad told the waitress. We all got up and   *20*
put on our coats. Everyone in the restaurant had a good long look at us. A bald little man in a filthy white shirt emerged from the kitchen, wiping his hands. "Folks? Something wrong?" he said.

"We're in the wrong place," Mother told him. Mother always told the truth, or something close to it.

"This is *humiliating*," I said out on the sidewalk. "I feel like a *leper* or something. Why do we always have to make such a big production out of everything? Why can't we be like regular people?"

She put her hand on my shoulder. "Be not conformed to this world," she said. I knew the rest by heart ". . . but be ye transformed by the renewing of your mind, that ye may prove what is that good and acceptable and perfect will of God."

"Where we gonna eat?" Phyllis asked.

"We'll find someplace reasonable," said Mother, and we walked six   25
blocks across the river and found a lunch counter and ate sloppy joes
(called Maid-Rites) for fifteen cents apiece. They did not agree with us,
and we were aware of them all afternoon through prayer meeting and
Young People's.

The Responsive Reader

1. How does Keillor take you into the Brethren's world of attitudes and
   beliefs? What would you stress in trying to initiate an unsympathetic
   listener into their lifestyle, their way of thinking and feeling? (What
   role does Brother Mel play in this story? What does he contribute to
   your understanding of the family's religion?)
2. For the author, what was the appeal of the strange and different
   Catholic tradition?
3. The story leads up to a high point—to a climactic incident that
   dramatizes the boy's feelings about his background, about his family.
   What *are* the boy's feelings? Where do you first become aware of
   them? Do you sympathize with him?

Talking, Listening, Writing

4. Religion often seems a taboo subject in our society. Why? Courts
   ban displays of the Christmas scene on public property as well as
   prayers in public schools or at commencement ceremonies. Why?
   Where do you stand?
5. Have you ever felt the urge to speak up on behalf of a group considered different or alien or undesirable in our society? Speak or write
   in defense of the group.
6. Has the awareness of being "different" played a role in your life or
   in the life of someone you know well? (Or have you ever worried
   about being too much the *same* as everyone else?)

Collaborative Projects

7. Is there a "religious revival" among the young? What kind of religious ideas or religious affiliations appeal to young people today? Help
   organize an informal poll of your classmates that would shed light on
   these questions.

MY FATHER'S OTHER LIFE

Susan J. Miller

> *In the following piece, Susan J. Miller takes up one of the oldest themes of autobiographical writing: conflict between parent and child. In personal memoirs and in fictionalized form in play and story, writers have played out the tension between parent and child, the struggle of the younger generation against the stifling influence of parents, the rebellion of the defiant son against the authoritarian father, the daughter's rejection of the role model provided by the mother. In our society today, bad parenting has become a buzzword heard in articles and books and therapy sessions where people trace their psychological difficulties to childhood traumas. The dysfunctional family has for many become the focus for their explanations of personal and social ills. Miller here tells an archetypal story of disillusionment with the father who was at one time at the center of happier childhood days. She grew up in an impoverished, dysfunctional household in the New York City area. Her grandmother still spoke Yiddish. New York City was then a mecca of jazz aficionados; her father was on the fringe of a jazz scene that featured greats like Charlie Parker, known to his admirers as Bird, and Dizzy Gillespie, the father of bebop.*

Thought Starters: What stories or images do terms like *bad parenting* and *dysfunctional families* bring to mind? What chains of association do they start?

One night, at an hour that was normally my bedtime, I got all dressed   *1*
up, and my mother and father and I drove into New York, down to the
Half Note, the jazz club on Hudson Street. I was thirteen, maybe fourteen,
just beginning teenagehood, and had never gone anywhere that was
"nightlife." I had heard jazz all my life, on records or the radio, my father
beating out time on the kitchen table, the steering wheel, letting out a
breathy "Yeah" when the music soared and flew. When they were cooking,
when they really swung, it transported him; he was gone, inside the music.
I couldn't go on this trip with him, but I thought I could understand it. It
seemed to me that anyone could, hearing that music. Bird, Diz, Pres,
Sweets, Al, Zoot. It was my father's music, though he himself never played
a note.

I knew the players, for about the only friends my parents had were
musicians and their wives. They fascinated me: their pants with black satin
stripes, their battered horn cases. When I was a little kid, I'd lie in bed
listening to them talk their hip talk in the next room. I knew I was the

only kid in our white neighborhood to be overhearing words like "man" and "cat" and "groove," and jokes that were this irreverent and black. I knew they were cool and I loved it.

At the Half Note that night, the three of us walked through the door, and the owner appeared, all excited to see my father, and in the middle of this smoky nightlife room, he kissed my hand. This was real life, the center of something. We sat down. In front of us, on a little stage, were Jimmy Rushing, a powerful singer, and two sax players, Al Cohn and Zoot Sims, whom I'd known all my life. And there was a whole roomful of people slapping the tables, beating out time, breathing "Yeah" at the great moments, shaking their heads, sometimes snapping their fingers, now and then bursting out with "Play it, man," or "Sing it." When the break came, Zoot sat down with us and ate a plate of lasagna or something and didn't say much except for these dry asides that were so funny I couldn't bear it. And there was my dad: these men were his friends, his buddies. They liked the things about my father that I could like—how funny he was, uncorny, how unsentimental, how unafraid to be different from everyone else in the world.

As a child, I didn't know that my father and many of the musicians who sat with their wives in our living room, eating nuts and raisins out of cut-glass candy dishes, were junkies. It wasn't until I was twenty-one, a college senior, that my father told me he had been a heroin addict, casually slipping it into some otherwise unremarkable conversation. The next day, my mother filled in the story. My father had begun shooting up in 1946, when my mother was pregnant with my brother, who is nineteen months older than me. He stopped when I was around thirteen and my brother was fifteen.

I never suspected a thing. Neither did my brother. We never saw any   5 drug paraphernalia. There was a mysterious purplish spot in the crook of my father's elbow, which he said had something to do with the army. His vague explanation was unsatisfactory, but even in my wildest imaginings I never came near the truth. In the Fifties, in the white, middle- and working-class communities where we lived, no one discussed drugs, which were synonymous with the utmost degradation and depravity. My parents succeeded in hiding my father's addiction from us, but as a result, we could never make sense of the strained atmosphere, our lack of money, our many moves. The addiction was the thread that tied everything together, but we didn't know that such a thread existed, and so decisions seemed insanely arbitrary, my mother's emotions frighteningly hysterical. She was terribly depressed, sometimes desperate. I regularly found her sitting, eyes unfocused, collapsed amid the disorder of a household she was too overwhelmed to manage.

My father was from Brighton Beach, Brooklyn, and earned his living dressing windows in women's clothing stores in and around New York

City. Being a window dresser was a touch creative, but most importantly it meant he didn't have to fit in; all he had to do was get the job done. He was a man of socially unacceptable habits. He was fat, he picked his teeth, he burped, he farted, he bit his nails until he had no nails and then he chewed his fingers, eating himself up. He was a high-octane monologuer, a self-taught high-school dropout who constantly read, thought, and talked politics and culture, gobbling up ideas, stuffing himself as fast as he could—with everything.

By the time I was in college my father was taking amphetamines, LSD, mescaline, peyote, whatever he could get. I would receive long letters from him, written when he was coming down from an acid or mescaline trip. Often he tripped alone in the living room of our New Jersey apartment, awake all night, listening to records, writing and thinking while my mother slept. I read pages of his blocky, slanted printing, about how the world is a boat and we are all sinking. Usually I threw them away without finishing them, scanning his stoned raps in front of the big, green metal trash can in the college mail room, picturing him in the living room with the sun rising, wired up, hunched over the paper, filling up the page, wanting me to know all the exciting things he had discovered. Part of me wanted to hear them and love him—and indeed did love him for taking the acid, for taking the chance. But another part shut down, unable to care.

He would not have been a good father even if he hadn't been an addict. By his own admission, he came to parenthood ignorant of love and acquainted only with hate.

My mother told me about my grandmother Esther, the wicked witch of Brighton Beach. According to my mother, my grandmother despised men. She lavished attention on her daughter, my father's only sibling. She dealt in machinations, lies, and deceptions, feeding the fires of hate between father and son, sister and brother. When my father did well in school, his mother scorned him. She tore up a citation he'd won—and then spat on it. She never kissed him, except on the day he went off to boot camp. His mother and my mother, then his young wife, were standing on the platform, saying good-bye. Seeing the other mothers tearfully embracing their sons, his mother was shamed into touching hers: she pecked his cheek.

My father only once told me a story about himself and his mother. I *10* was in college at the time. The two of us were driving on the highway on a beautiful, clear, cold winter day. My father was behind the wheel. Fourteen years earlier, in 1956, his father had died in the hospital while my father and his mother, Esther, were visiting him. My father took Esther home to Brooklyn, where she asked him for a favor. There were some terms in her will she wanted to review. Would he read it out loud to her? (Even in Yiddish my grandmother was illiterate.) My father was tired and upset and somewhat puzzled that his mother wished to go over her will on the night of her husband's death, but he agreed. The will turned out to be simple: Esther's house and savings were to go to Sarah, her daughter. Then he heard himself, the fly in the web, reading: And to my son, Sidney, I leave nothing, because he is no good.

My father stared at the road ahead.

Why, I cried, would she have you read that to her? What did you do?

My father's voice was tired and bitter. She wanted to see what I would do, he said; she wanted to watch my reaction. Ma, I said, I gotta go home now. I'm tired and it's late. I didn't want to show her how bad I felt, I didn't want to give her the satisfaction. I didn't care about the money. Let my fucking sister have the money. But why did she have to write that sentence? Why did she have me read it?

My father started to cry. He had never cried in front of me. His hands loosened their grip on the wheel. The car began to drift into the opposite lane, across the white unbroken line.

Look out, I yelled. He grabbed the wheel and turned us toward   *15* safety. Look out, I yelled, and he did. Look out, I yelled, for what else could I have said?

In August 1988, my father was diagnosed with liver cancer, the result of chronic hepatitis, a disease associated with heroin addiction. The doctors predicted he would live for five months. He tried chemotherapy, ate a macrobiotic diet, enrolled in an experimental holistic treatment program. When I visited him in November, it was clear that things would not turn around.

My mother, who had stuck by him through everything, was still by his side. He was eager to share his latest revelation. A social worker in the treatment program had asked him what he would miss most when he died. He said: I told her that, yeah, sure, I'll miss my wife and my kids, but what I'll miss most is the music. The music is the only thing that's never let me down.

That the revelation would hurt us—my mother especially—never occurred to him. He never kept his thoughts to himself, even if it was cruel to express them. Neither my mother nor I said a word. The statement was the truth of him—not only what he said but also the fact that he would say it to us, and say it without guilt, without apology, without regret.

The Responsive Reader

1. What images or associations do you connect with the jazz scene to which Miller's account takes you? How are your expectations confirmed or disappointed in the opening paragraphs of the essay? What details bring the scene to life for you?
2. Where is the turning point in this essay that introduces you to the other side of the father's life and personality? What is your initial reaction?

3. What was the impact of addiction on the everyday life of the family? What was the impact on the daughter's outlook or personality?
4. What do you learn about the father's childhood or his relationship to his mother as a possible key to the father's personality? Does what you learn change your feelings about the father? Does it excuse him in his daughter's eye—or in yours?
5. At the end, the author circles back to the father's love of music. How and with what effect?

Talking, Listening, Writing

6. In your judgment, is the author too hard on her father?
7. Have you ever experienced disillusionment with someone you admired? Have you ever had mixed feelings or been torn between contradictory emotions about someone important to you?
8. Where in this essay does Miller give a one-paragraph capsule portrait of her father? What is the keynote? Write a similar capsule portrait of someone who has been important in your life.

Collaborative Projects

9. Working with a group, you may want to explore bad parenting, parental abuse, or the dysfunctional family as a recurrent theme in newspaper or magazine articles on family life.

CHILDREN OF THE HARVEST

Lois Phillips Hudson

Many modern societies have or have had migrant populations. In this country, seasonal workers from the rural South came to work in the factories of the North. In the thirties, rural Midwesterners driven from their farms by the dust storms and the Great Depression came to the migrant camps of the West and Northwest. Called "Okies" even when they were not from Oklahoma, they were always on the move—looking for a job to do, a crop to pick, a place to stay, a place to send children to school. They were watched suspiciously by the locals and nudged by the local police to move on. In the West today, Mexican agricultural workers, often officially classified as illegal aliens, live in camps that show on no county map and would pass no health inspection if any official were to seek them out. Born in North Dakota, Lois Phillips Hudson published a novel about the Midwest of the thirties, The Bones of Plenty, *in 1962; she published* Reapers of the Dust: A Prairie Chronicle *in 1965. In the following autobiographical essay, she tells her story of growing up as a child of migrant workers on the wrong side of the tracks, finding herself among the uprooted, the displaced, the dispossessed. What are the things that the young girl telling the following story wonders at? What are basic contrasts between her Midwestern origins and the new world in which she finds herself?*

Thought Starters: Critics of capitalism believe that gross inequalities of wealth are the inevitable result of an unrestricted free-market economy. Observers of America today fear that our country is again, as in the Great Depression, becoming "two nations"—the rich and the poor. Are their fears justified?

On a suffocating summer day in 1937, the thirteenth year of drought   *1*
and the seventh year of depression, with our mouths, nostrils, and eyes full of the dust blowing from our bare fields, my family sold to our neighbors at auction most of the accoutrements of our existence. Then we loaded what was left into a trailer my father had made and drove West to find water and survival on the Washington coast.

During the auction the two classmates with whom I had just finished the fourth grade hung about the desultory bidders giving me looks of respect and undisguised envy. They envied me not so much for the things they could imagine as for the things they couldn't—the unimaginable distance I was going and the unimaginable things along it and at the end of it.

How could any of us have imagined an end to the prairie's limitless sky and the giddy encroachments rising higher and higher against that sky that were the Rocky Mountains? How could we have imagined how in burning summer the forested profiles of the Cascades could echo everywhere the shouts of white falls above us and green rivers below? Who could have imagined, once confronted with their gray expanse, that the waters of Puget Sound were not actually the Pacific, but only a minute stray squiggle of it? Who, finally, could have imagined that there were so many people in the world or that the world could offer them so hospitable a habitation?

There were so many things I could scarcely believe even when I was doing them or looking at them or eating them. We lived in a cabin on an island for a few weeks after we arrived, and it always seemed impossible to me that we could be surrounded by so much water. I spent every moment of the hour-long ferry trip from the mainland hanging over the rail gazing down at the exhilarating wake of my first boat ride. The island was exactly what any island should be—lavish green acres covered with woods and orchards and fields of berries, ringed by glistening sandy beaches richly stocked with driftwood. Once in North Dakota my aunt had brought a very small basket of black cherries to my grandfather's house, and I had made the four or five that were my share last all afternoon. I would take tiny bites of each cherry, then suck the pit and roll it around with my tongue to get the faint remaining taste, till it came out as clean and smooth as a brook-bottom pebble. But on the island I would climb into the trees with my five-year-old sister and have contests with her, seeing which of us could get the most cherries in our mouths at once. Then we would shoot the wet pits, no longer hungrily scoured of their slipperiness, at each other and at the robins who perched above us. Sometimes I would go into the fields with my mother and father and spend an hour helping pick raspberries or blackberries or loganberries or any of the other things they worked in, but there were really only two important things to do—play on the beaches and eat fruit.

It didn't occur to me that things would ever be different again, but one day early in August the last berry was picked and we took the ferry into Seattle, where we bought a big brown tent and a gas stove. We added them to our trailer load and drove back over the green-and-white Cascades, beneath the glacial sunrise face of Mount Rainier, and down into the sweaty outdoor factory that is the Yakima Valley. There the Yakima River is bled for transfusions to the millions of rows of roots, its depleted currents finally dragging themselves muddily to their relieved merger with the undiminishable Columbia. One can follow the Yakima for miles and miles and see nothing but irrigated fields and orchards—and the gaunt camps of transient laborers.

The workers come like a horde of salvaging locusts, stripping a field, moving to the next, filling their boxes or crates or sacks, weighing in,

5

collecting the bonuses offered to entice them to stay till the end of the season, and disappearing again. They spend their repetitive days in rows of things to be picked and their sweltering nights in rows of tents and trailers. We pitched our tent beside the others, far from our pleasant island where the owners of the fields were neighbors who invited my sister and me among their cherry trees. Here the sauntering owners and their bristling foremen never smiled at those children who ran through the fields playing games and only occasionally at those who worked beside their parents.

In North Dakota I had worked on our farm—trampling hay, driving a team of horses, fetching cows, feeding calves and chickens—but of course that had all been only my duty as a member of the family, not a way to earn money. Now I was surrounded by grown-ups who wanted to pay me for working, and by children my own age who were stepping up to the pay window every night with weighing tags in their hands and collecting money. I saw that the time had come for me to assume a place of adult independence in the world.

I made up my mind I was going to earn a dollar all in one day. We were picking hops then, and of all the rows I have toiled my way up and down, I remember hop rows the most vividly. Trained up on their wires fifteen feet overhead, the giant vines resemble monster grape arbors hung with bunches of weird unripe fruit. A man who does not pick things for a living comes and cuts them down with a knife tied to a ten-foot pole so the people below can strip them off into sacks. Hops don't really look like any other growing thing but instead like something artificially constructed— pine cones, perhaps, with segments cleverly cut from the soft, limp, cling- ing leaves that lie next to the kernels of an ear of corn. A hop in your hand is like a feather, and it will almost float on a puff of air. Hops are good only for making yeast, so you can't even get healthily sick of them by eating them all day long, the way you can berries or peas.

Pickers are paid by the pound, and picking is a messy business. Some- times you run into a whole cluster that is gummy with the honeydew of hop aphids, and gray and musty with the mildew growing on the sticky stuff. Tiny red spiders rush from the green petals and flow up your arms, like more of the spots the heat makes you see.

The professionals could earn up to six dollars a day. One toothless 10 grandmother discouraged us all by making as much as anybody in the row and at the same time never getting out of her rocking chair except to drag it behind her from vine to vine. My father and mother each made over three dollars a day, but though I tried to work almost as long hours as they did, my pay at the end of the day would usually be somewhere between eighty and ninety cents.

Then one day in the second week of picking, when the hops were good and I stayed grimly sweating over my long gray sack hung on a child-sized frame, I knew that this was going to be the day. As the after- noon waned and I added the figures on my weight tags over and over again in my head, I could feel the excitement begin making spasms in my stomach. That night the man at the pay window handed me a silver dollar and three pennies. He must have seen that this was a day not for paper but for silver. The big coin, so neatly and brightly stamped, was coolly distant from the blurred mélange of piled vines and melting heat that had put it into my hand. Only its solid heaviness connected it in a businesslike way with the work it represented. For the first time in my life I truly comprehended the relationship between toil and media of exchange, and I saw how exacting and yet how satisfying were the terms of the world. Perhaps because of this insight, I did not want the significance of my dollar dimmed by the common touch of copper pettiness. I gave the vulgar pennies to my little sister, who was amazed but grateful. Then I felt even more grown-up than before, because not everybody my age was in a position to give pennies to kids.

That night I hardly slept, lying uncovered beside my sister on our mattress on the ground, sticking my hand out under the bottom of the tent to lay it on the cooling earth between the clumps of dry grass. Tired as I was, I had written post cards to three people in North Dakota before going to bed. I had told my grandmother, my aunt, and my friend Doris that I had earned a dollar in one day. Then, because I did not want to sound impolitely proud of myself, and to fill up the card, I added on each one, "I'm fine and I plan to pick again tomorrow. How are you?"

I couldn't wait to get to the field the next day and earn another dollar. Back home none of my friends would have dreamed of being able to earn so much in one day. The only thing to do back there for money was to trap gophers for the bounty; and even the big kids, who ran a fairly long trap line and had the nerve to cut the longest tails in half, couldn't make more than twenty cents on a good day, with tails at two cents apiece. I earned a dollar and forty cents the next day and the day after that, and at least a dollar every day for another week until we moved to another place of picking—a pear orchard.

By that time it was September, and most of us children from the rows of tents stood out at the gateway of the camp and waited each day for the long yellow school bus. I had never seen a school bus before, and my sister and I were shy about how to act in such a grand vehicle. We sat together, holding our lunch buckets on our knees, looking out at the trees beside the roads, trying to catch a glimpse of our mother and father on the ladders.

The school had about three times as many pupils in it as there were *15* people in the town back in North Dakota where we used to buy coal and groceries. The pupils who were planning to attend this school all year were separated from those who, like me, did not know how many days or weeks we would be in that one spot. In our special classes we did a great deal of drawing and saw a number of movies. School was so luxurious in comparison with the hard work I had done in North Dakota the previous year that I wrote another post card to Doris, telling her that we never had to do fractions and that we got colored construction paper to play with almost every day. I copied a picture of a donkey with such accuracy that my teacher thought I had traced it until she held the two to the window and saw that the lines were indisputably my own. After that I got extra drawing periods and became very good at copying, which always elicited more praise than my few original compositions.

I was understandably sad when we left that school after two weeks and went to Wenatchee. For the first time, we were not in a regular camp. The previous year my father, recognizing that the crops had not brought in enough to get us through the winter, had taken the train to Wenatchee after the sparse harvest was in and picked apples for a man named Jim Baumann. Baumann wanted him back, so he let us pitch our tent on his land not far from his house. We made camp, and after supper Baumann came down to talk about the next day's arrangements. The school was not so large as the other one, and there was no school bus for us because we were only a half mile away from it. Baumann was shorthanded in the packing shed and needed my mother early in the morning. Besides, there was no reason why she should have to take us to school, because he had a daughter who was in my grade who could walk with us and take us to our respective rooms.

"Why, isn't that lovely!" my mother exclaimed with unwonted enthusiasm. "Now you'll have a nice little girl to play with right here and to be your friend at school."

Her excitement was rather remarkable, considering the dubious reaction she had to everybody else I had played with since we started camping. It hadn't seemed to me that she had liked even the boy who made me a pair of stilts and taught me to walk them. Now here she was favorably predisposed toward somebody I didn't even know. I agreed that it would be nice to have a nice little girl to play with.

The next morning my sister and I sat on the steps of the Baumanns' front porch, where Barbara's mother had told us to make ourselves at home, waiting for her to finish her breakfast. We had already been up so long that it seemed to me we must surely be late for school; I began picturing the humiliating tardy entrance into a roomful of strange faces.

Two of Barbara's friends came down the driveway to wait for her. 20 They both wore the kind of plaid skirts I had been wondering if I could ask my mother about buying—after all, she *had* said all my dresses were too short this fall because of all the inches I'd grown in the summer. The two girls looked at us for a moment, then uncoiled shiny-handled jump ropes and commenced loudly shouting two different rhymes to accompany their jumping.

Barbara came out on the porch, greeted her friends with a disconcerting assurance, jumped down the steps past us, insinuated herself between them, and clasped their hands. "I have to show these kids where the school is," she told them. Turning her head slightly she called, "Well, come if you're coming. We're going to be late." Swinging their arms together, they began to skip down the driveway.

A couple of times on the way to school they stopped and waited until we got near them; I yanked irritably on my little sister's arm and thought about how her shorter legs had been holding me back ever since she was born. I always seemed to be the one who had to drag a little kid along.

The teacher kept me standing at her desk while she called the roll and started the class on a reading assignment. When she looked up at me, I got the irrational impression that I had already managed to do something wrong. She asked where I had come from and I said "North Dakota," thinking it would be simpler than trying to tell all the places I had been in the last three months. She gave me the last seat in a row behind a boy in dirty clothes. As she passed by him she made the faintest sound of exhalation, as though she was ridding her nostrils of a disagreeable smell.

At recess a boy in a bright shirt and new cream-colored corduroy pants yelled "North Dakota, North Dakota!" in a funny way as he ran past me to the ball field. The boy who sat ahead of me came up and said confidentially, "We been out all around here for two years. We come from Oklahoma. We're Okies. That's what you are too, even if you didn't come from Oklahoma." I knew I could never be anything that sounded so crummy as "Okie," and I said so. "Oh, yeah!" he rejoined stiffly. I walked away before he could argue any more and went to find my sister, but the primary grades had recess at a different time, so I went and stood by the door until the period was over. That afternoon I stayed in my seat reading a history book, but the teacher, who seemed to want to go outdoors herself, said "It's better for the room if everybody goes outside for recess." So I went out and stood around the fringes of two or three games and wondered what was funny about North Dakota. Somehow I had the feeling that it would hurt my mother if I asked her.

The last part of the day was given to a discussion period, when each 25 of us who wanted to was given a chance to tell about an important day in his life. The important days of my classmates, all about having a part in a play or learning to ride a bike, seemed so pathetically juvenile that I was impelled to speak. I stood at my seat and told about how I had earned a dollar all in one day in the hop fields.

From two sides of the room Barbara's friends turned to send her looks which I intercepted but found inscrutable. I had been looking at her too, watching for her reaction. A boy near me poked another and whispered in mocking awe, "A whole dollar!"

The boy ahead of me jumped suddenly to his feet, banging his leg against the desk so hard that the entire row shook. "Heck," he cried, "we just come from there, too, and I made more'n a buck and a half *every* day." He gave me a triumphant smile and sat down. Then I knew I hated that boy. That night I told my mother about how there was a mean boy just like those other mean boys at the camps and how the teacher *would* have to put me right behind him. "Well," she sighed, "just try not to pay any attention to him."

By the time I had found my sister after school, Barbara and her friends had gone. The next morning when we went up to the big house she was gone, too.

After that, my sister and I walked together. Sometimes we would be close enough to hear Barbara's friends who were always with her laugh and call her "Bobby." I had never known any Barbaras before, and the name seemed full of unapproachable prestige and sophistication—the name that only a girl with as many dresses as Barbara Baumann would have. "Bobby" was yet more awesome, as if she were as consequential as a boy. At school, if I recited in class, she acted queerly self-conscious, as though she were responsible for me—the way I often felt around my sister when she said something stupid to kids my age.

For various reasons I had that same embarrassed feeling of an en-   *30* forced distasteful relationship with the boy who sat ahead of me. Once in a while somebody in the class would tease me about him or would say something about "the hop pickers." I was bitterly determined to dissociate myself from the boy, and whenever he turned around to talk to me I would pretend he was trying to copy my paper. I would put my hand over it while I kept my eyes glued to the desk and felt my face grow hot.

There were some things about the school I liked very much. We were allowed to use the library a great deal, and for the first time in my life I had access to numbers of books I hadn't already read. By reading at noon and recess I could finish a book at school every two days. I would also have a book at home that I would read in a couple of nights. One of the nice things about living in a tent was that there were hardly any household chores to do and I could read as much as I wanted.

Frosty mornings came with October, and my sister and I would try to dress under the quilts before we got up to eat our oatmeal. Leaves began to blow across the road, apples grew redder with each cold night, pickers hurried from tree to tree, filling the orchards with the soft thunder of hard round fruit rolling out of picking sacks into boxes, and packers worked faster and faster, trying to get the apples twisted up in fancy tissue and into boxes before they jammed up too thickly on the perpetually moving belts. After school my sister and I would go to the box shed behind the big house where Harry, Barbara's big brother, would be nailing boxes together for a nickel apiece. He was always glad to have company, and would let us stand at a respectful distance and watch him pound in nail after nail with two strokes, a tap to set it, then a mighty clout to send it in, three to an end, six to a side.

One afternoon, with the chill blue sky brilliant behind the orange and black Halloween cutouts on the windows, I was sitting at my desk dreamily drawing a witch in a moon when the teacher called my name.

She told me that she wanted me to take all my books out of my desk and take them to the front of the room. Then she told everybody in my row to pack up his books and move one seat back. My heart banged alarmingly up in my throat and I nearly gagged from the sudden acute sensations in my viscera. In North Dakota such drastic action was taken only when an offender, after repeated warnings, had proved too incorrigible to sit anywhere except right in front of the teacher's desk. The fact that I had no idea of why I was now classified as such an incorrigible only augmented my anguish. While books banged and papers and pencils fell to the floor and boys jostled each other in the aisle, I managed to sidle numbly up to the front. I sat down in my new seat, trying not to notice how shamefully close it was to the big desk facing it, and I was careful not to raise my eyes higher than the vase of zinnias standing on the corner nearest me.

When school was out I hurried to find my sister and get out of the schoolyard before seeing anybody in my class. But Barbara and her friends had beaten us to the playground entrance and they seemed to be waiting for us. We started to walk around them but they fell into step with us. Barbara said, "So now you're in the 'A' class. You went straight from the 'C' class to the 'A' class." She sounded impressed.

"What's the 'A' class?" I asked.   35

Everybody made superior yet faintly envious giggling sounds. "Well, why did you think the teacher moved you to the front of the room, dopey? Didn't you know you were in the 'C' class before, 'way in the back of the room?"

Of course I hadn't known. The Wenatchee fifth grade was bigger than my whole school had been in North Dakota, and the idea of subdivisions within a grade had never occurred to me. The subdividing for the first marking period had been done before I came to the school, and I had never, in the six weeks I'd been there, talked to anyone long enough to find out about the "A," "B," and "C" classes.

I still could not understand why that had made such a difference to Barbara and her friends. I didn't yet know that it was disgraceful and dirty to be a transient laborer and ridiculous to be from North Dakota. I thought living in a tent was more fun than living in a house. I didn't know that we were gypsies, really (how that thought would have thrilled me then!), and that we were regarded with the suspicion felt by those who plant toward those who do not plant. It didn't occur to me that we were all looked upon as one more of the untrustworthy natural phenomena, drifting here and there like mists or winds, that farmers of certain crops are resentfully forced to rely on. I didn't know that I was the only child who had camped on the Baumanns' land ever to get out of the "C" class. I did not know that school administrators and civic leaders held conferences to talk about how to handle the problem of transient laborers.

I only knew that for two happy days I walked to school with Barbara and her friends, played hopscotch and jump rope with them at recess, and was even invited into the house for some ginger ale—an exotic drink I had never tasted before.

Then we took down our tent and packed it in the trailer with our *40* mattresses and stove and drove on, because the last apples were picked and sorted and boxed and shipped to the people all over the world, whoever they were, who could afford to buy them in 1937. My teacher wrote a letter for me to take to my next school. In it, she told me, she had informed my next teacher that I should be put in the "A" class immediately. But there wasn't any "A" class in my room, the new teacher explained.

By then I was traveled enough to realize that it was another special class for transients. The teacher showed us movies almost every day.

The Responsive Reader

1. What details, what sights or events, help you relive the experience of the girl telling her story? Which of her experiences or observations in the fields are especially striking or memorable for you?
2. The girl telling her story sees herself as moving toward self-reliance and maturity. In what ways?
3. What is the author's attitude toward or understanding of the larger economic or social system?
4. Does this essay make you think about the schooling of the children of migrant workers? How or why?

Talking, Listening, Writing

5. Is the significance of Hudson's story limited by time and place? Do you think young people have comparable experiences today?
6. In your experience, do teachers and schools treat well-to-do and poor children differently?
7. What can you find out about the role and lives of migrant workers or illegal aliens in your community, county, or state? What do you know from personal experience or observation? Working with a group, try to bring together information from official agencies, news reports, or studies.

Thinking about Connections

Politicians have often talked as if the traditional work ethic were an outstanding quality of the white middle class. What role does the "work ethic" play in the essays by Angelou and Hudson? Is it obsolete today?

DONALD DUK AND THE WHITE MONSTERS

Frank Chin

Frank Chin was one of the first Asian American writers to become known to a wide audience. He attended the University of California at Berkeley in the sixties; in the seventies, he was the first Chinese American to have a play produced on the New York stage. His plays Chickencoop Chinaman *and* Year of the Dragon *attacked the familiar stereotype of Asian males as sinister villains in the Fu Manchu mode. Maxine Hong Kingston, probably the best known Chinese writer in America, has said of him that "the main energy that goes through his work is anger." He has been angry at publishers for publishing four female Asian writers for every Asian male; he has criticized other Chinese American writers for mispresenting and putting down the traditional culture. His spiritual roots are in Chinese myth and in the martial ideal of strong masculine archetypes—independent of state and bureaucracy and trusting "no one." His novel* Donald Duk *(1991) shows another side of his gift for inspiring controversy and mixed reviews. It has been called a "devilishly wild and wacky tale by a word-and-sword slinger of wit, audacity, and intelligence" (Michi Weglyn). The following excerpt—the opening pages of the novel—shows his talent for seeing the humor in issues of ethnic identity that are usually treated in more solemn fashion. As you read the following pages, what kind of humor do you encounter? Do you consider it demeaning or offensive? Why or why not?*

Thought Starters: Writers acknowledging the humorous side of minority experience may be secure enough in their pride to acknowledge the sad and funny side of the rich collective experience of their group. But they may also be accused of perpetuating the self-contempt that makes members of minorities play the clown for a white audience. Is there such a thing as nonoffensive ethnic humor? Where have you encountered it?

Who would believe anyone named Donald Duk dances like Fred 1
Astaire? Donald Duk does not like his name. Donald Duk never liked his name. He hates his name. He is not a duck. He is not a cartoon character. He does not go home to sleep in Disneyland every night. The kids that laugh at him are very smart. Everyone at his private school is smart. Donald Duk is smart. He is a gifted one, they say.

No one in school knows he takes tap dance lessons from a man who calls himself "The Chinese Fred Astaire." Mom talks Dad into paying for the lessons and tap shoes.

Fred Astaire. Everybody everywhere likes Fred Astaire in the old black-and-white movies. Late at night on TV, even Dad smiles when Fred Astaire dances. Mom hums along. Donald Duk wants to live the late night life in old black-and-white movies and talk with his feet like Fred Astaire, and smile Fred Astaire's sweet lemonade smile.

The music teacher and English teacher in school go dreamy eyed when they talk about seeing Fred Astaire and Ginger Rogers on the late-night TV. "Remember when he danced with Barbara Stanwyck? What was the name of that movie . . . ?"

"Barbara Stanwyck?"   5

"Did you see the one where he dances with Rita Hayworth?"

"Oooh, Rita Hayworth!"

Donald Duk enjoys the books he reads in school. The math is a curious game. He is not the only Chinese in the private school. But he is the only Donald Duk. He avoids the other Chinese here. And the Chinese seem to avoid him. This school is a place where the Chinese are comfortable hating Chinese. "Only the Chinese are stupid enough to give a kid a stupid name like Donald Duk," Donald Duk says to himself. "And if the Chinese were that smart, why didn't they invent tap dancing?"

Donald Duk's father's name is King. King Duk. Donald hates his father's name. He hates being introduced with his father. "This is King Duk, and his son Donald Duk." Mom's name is Daisy. "That's Daisy Duk, and her son Donald." Venus Duk and Penny Duk are Donald's sisters. The girls are twins and a couple of years older than Donald.

His own name is driving him crazy! Looking Chinese is driving him   10
crazy! All his teachers are making a big deal about Chinese stuff in their classes because of Chinese New Year coming on soon. The teacher of California History is so happy to be reading about the Chinese. "The man I studied history under at Berkeley authored this book. He was a spellbinding lecturer," the teacher throbs. Then he reads, "The Chinese in America were made passive and nonassertive by centuries of Confucian thought and Zen mysticism. They were totally unprepared for the violently individualistic and democratic Americans. From their first step on American soil to the middle of the twentieth century, the timid, introverted Chinese have been helpless against the relentless victimization by aggressive, highly competitive Americans.

"One of the Confucian concepts that makes the Chinese vulnerable to the assertive ways of the West is 'the mandate of heaven.' As the European kings of old ruled by divine right, so the emperors of China ruled by the mandate of heaven." The teacher takes a breath and looks over his spellbound class. Donald wants to barf pink and green stuff all over the teacher's book.

"What's he saying?" Donald Duk's pal Arnold Azalea asks in a whisper.

"Same thing as everybody—Chinese are artsy, cutesy and chicken-dick." Donald whispers back.

Oh, no! Here comes Chinese New Year again! It is Donald Duk's worst time of year. Here come the stupid questions about the funny things Chinese believe in. The funny things Chinese do. The funny things Chinese eat. And, "Where can I buy some Chinese firecrackers?"

And in Chinatown it's *Goong hay fot choy* everywhere. And some gang   15
kids do sell firecrackers. And some gang kids rob other kids looking for firecrackers. He doesn't like the gang kids. He doesn't like speaking their Chinese. He doesn't have to—this is America. He doesn't like Chinatown. But he lives here.

The gang kids know him. They call him by name. One day the Frog Twins wobble onto the scene with their load of full shopping bags. There is Donald Duk. And there are five gang boys and two girlfriends chewing gum, swearing and smirking. The gang kids wear black tanker jackets, white tee shirts and baggy black denim jeans. It is the alley in front of the Chinese Historical Society Museum. There are fish markets on each side of the Chinatown end of the alley. Lawrence Ferlinghetti's famous City Lights Bookstore is at the end that opens on Columbus Street. Suddenly there are the Frog Twins in their heavy black overcoats. They seem to be wearing all the clothes they own under their coats. Their coats bulge. Under their skirts they wear several pairs of trousers and slacks. They wear one knit cap over the other. They wear scarves tied over their heads and shawls over their shoulders.

That night, after he is asleep, Dad comes home from the restaurant and wakes him up. "You walk like a sad softie," Dad says. "You look like you want everyone to beat you up."

"I do not!" Donald Duk says.

"You look at yourself in the mirror," Dad says, and Donald Duk looks at himself in his full-length dressing mirror. "Look at those slouching shoulders, that pouty face. Look at those hands holding onto each other. You look scared!" Dad's voice booms and Donald hears everyone's feet hit the floor. Mom and the twins are out in the hall looking into his open door.

"I am scared!" Donald Duk says.   20

"I don't care if you are scared," Dad says. His eyes sizzle into Donald Duk's frightened pie-eyed stare. "Be as scared as you want to be, but don't look scared. Especially when you walk through Chinatown."

"How do I look like I'm not scared if I *am* scared?" Donald Duk asks.

"You walk with your back straight. You keep your hands out of your pockets. Don't hunch your shoulders. Think of them as being down. Keep your head up. Look like you know where you're going. Walk like you know where you're going. And you say, 'Don't mess with me, horsepuckie! Don't mess with me!' But you don't say it with your mouth. You say it with your eyes. You say it with your hands where everybody can see them. Anybody get two steps in front of you, you zap them with your eyes, and they had better nod at you or look away. When they nod, you nod. When you walk like nobody better mess with you, nobody will mess with you. When you walk around like you're walking now, all rolled up in a little ball and hiding out from everything, they'll get you for sure."

Donald does not like his dad waking him up like that and yelling at him. But what the old man says works. Outside among the cold San Francisco shadows and the early morning shoppers, Donald Duk hears his father's voice and straightens his back, takes his hands out of his pockets, says "Don't mess with me!" with his eyes and every move of his body. And, yes, he's talking with his body the way Fred Astaire talks, and shoots every gang kid who walks toward him in the eye with a look that says, "Don't mess with me." And no one messes with him. Dad never talks about it again.

Later, gang kids laugh at his name and try to pick fights with him   25
during the afternoon rush hour, Dad's busy time in the kitchen. Donald is smarter than these lowbrow beady-eyed goons. He has to beat them without fighting them because he doesn't know how to fight. Donald Duk gets the twins to talk about it with Dad while they are all at the dining room table working on their model airplanes.

Dad laughs. "So he has a choice. He does not like people laughing at his name. He does not want the gangsters laughing at his name to beat him up. He mostly does not want to look like a sissy in front of them, so what can he do?"

"He can pay them to leave him alone," Venus says.

"He can not! That is so chicken it's disgusting!" Penelope says.

"So, our little brother is doomed."

"He can agree with them and laugh at his name," Dad says. "He can   30
tell them lots of Donald Duk jokes. Maybe he can learn to talk that quack-quack Donald Duck talk."

"Whaaat?" the twins ask in one voice.

"If he keeps them laughing," Dad says, "even if he can just keep them listening, they are not beating him up, right? And they are not calling him a sissy. He does not want to fight? He does not have to fight. He has to use his smarts, okay? If he's smart enough, he makes up some Donald Duck jokes to surprise them and make them laugh. They laugh three times, he can walk away. Leave them there laughing, thinking Donald Duk is one terrific fella."

"So says King Duk," Venus Duk flips. The twins often talk as if everything they hear everybody say and see everybody do is dialog in a memoir they're writing or action in a play they're directing. This makes Mom feel like she's on stage and drives Donald Duk crazy.

"Is that Chinese psychology, dear?" Daisy Duk asks.

"Daisy Duk inquires," says Penelope Duk.   35

"And little Donnie Duk says, *Oh, Mom!* and sighs."

"I do not!" Donald Duk yelps at the twins.

"Well, then, say it," Penelope Duk says. "It's a good line. So *you*, you know."

"Thank you," Venus says.

"Oh goshes, you all, your sympathy is so . . . so . . . so literary. So   *40* dramatic," Donald Duk says. "It is truly depressing."

"I thought it was narrative," Venus says.

"Listen up for some Chinese psychology, girls and boys," Daisy Duk says.

"No, that's not psychology, that's Bugs Bunny," Dad says.

"You don't mean, Bugs Bunny, dear. You always make that mistake."

"Br'er Rabbit!" Dad says.   *45*

"What does that mean?" Donald Duk asks the twins. They shrug their shoulders. Nobody knows what Br'er Rabbit has to do with Dad's way of avoiding a fight and not being a fool, but it works.

One bright and sunny afternoon, a gang boy stops Donald and talks to him in the quacking voice of Walt Disney's Donald Duck. The voice breaks Donald Duk's mind for a flash, and he is afraid to turn on his own Donald Duck voice. He tries telling a joke about Donald Duck not wearing trousers or shoes, when the gangster—in black jeans, black tee shirt, black jacket, black shades—says in a perfect Donald Duck voice, "Let's take the pants off Donald Duk!"

"Oh oh! I stepped in it now!" Donald Duk says in his Donald Duck voice and stuns the gangster and his two gangster friends and their three girlfriends. Everything is seen and understood very fast. Without missing a beat, his own perfect Donald Duck voice cries for help in perfect Cantonese *Gow meng ahhhh!* and they all laugh. Old women pulling little wire shopping carts full of fresh vegetables stop and stare at him. Passing children recognize the voice and say Donald Duck talks Chinese.

"Don't let these monsters take off my pants. I may be Donald Duk, but I am as human as you," he says in Chinese, in his Donald Duck voice, "I know how to use chopsticks. I use flush toilets. Why shouldn't I wear pants on Grant Street in Chinatown?" They all laugh more than three times. Their laughter roars three times on the corner of Grant and Jackson, and Donald Duk walks away, leaving them laughing, just the way Dad says he can. He feels great. Just great!

Donald Duk does not want to laugh about his name forever. There   *50* has to be an end to this. There is an end to all kidstuff for a kid. An end to diapers. An end to nursery rhymes and fairy tales. There has to be an end to laughing about his name to get out of a fight. Chinese New Year. Everyone will be laughing. He is twelve years old. Twelve years old is special to the Chinese. There are twelve years in the Asian lunar zodiac. For each year there is an animal. This year Donald will complete his first twelve-year cycle of his life. To celebrate, Donald Duk's father's old opera mentor, Uncle Donald Duk, is coming to San Francisco to perform a

Cantonese opera. Donald Duk does not want Chinese New Year. He does not want his uncle Donald Duk to tell him again how Daddy was a terrible man to name his little boy Donald Duk, because all the *bok gwai,* the white monsters, will think he is named after that barebutt cartoon duck in the top half of a sailor suit and no shoes.

The Responsive Reader

1. What is a stereotype, and what is the role or power of ethnic stereotypes in our society? Donald is critical of stereotypes and official textbook descriptions of his group—why and where? Does this account modify or confirm stereotypes in your own mind?
2. What is Donald's relation to his Chinese background and to other Chinese?
3. How much in Donald's story stems from his being Chinese American? How much could be part of the story of many other adolescents?

Talking, Listening, Writing

4. Humor is very personal; much of what is funny to one person or group is not a laughing matter to others. How do you relate to the author's sense of humor?
5. A dual or divided cultural heritage may be considered a liability—a source of self-doubt, divided loyalties, or a lacking sense of belonging. It may be considered an asset—a chance for a richer, fuller identity drawing on two different ways of realizing one's human potential. Have you encountered the clash or the merging of two different traditions, two different lifestyles, two different cultures? Do you think of a dual heritage as a liability or an asset?

Collaborative Projects

6. What recognition do some of today's most successful Asian American writers enjoy? Working alone or as a member of a group, look for sources that shed light on the reputation of one of the following: Frank Chin; Amy Tan, author of *The Joy Luck Club* and *The Kitchen God's Wife;* David Henry Hwang, whose *M. Butterfly* won him a Tony Award in 1989; Hawaiian poet Garrett Hongo; Bharati Mukherjee, from India, author of *The Middleman and Other Stories* and the novel *Jasmine.*

Thinking about Connections

Li-Young Lee's poem "Persimmons" (p. 122) also deals with the growing pains of a young Chinese American male. Is the mixture of humor and seriousness similar or different in the two accounts?

FOR MY FATHER

Janice Mirikitani

> And they commanded we dwell in the desert
> Our children be spawn of barbed wire and barracks
> > Janice Mirikitani

Janice Mirikitani is a West Coast poet who coedited Third World Women *(1973), looking for what was "universal, freeing, connective" in Third World literature. She also edited* Ayumi *(1980), an anthology of Japanese American writing. Her poems have ranged from the terrors of Vietnam to the internment of Japanese Americans during World War II. She pays tribute to anonymous poor immigrants from Asia who filled "the sweatsops/the laundries." She writes about Japanese Americans who, like her father, were taken from their homes and businesses to relocation camps like Tule Lake. She expresses her solidarity with Asian women pursued as a mysterious and exotic novelty by blue-eyed men whispering "doubtful words of love."*

Thought Starters: What do you know about the relocation camps of World War II? What do you know about current attempts at reparation or restitution?

He came over the ocean   1
carrying Mt. Fuji on
his back/Tule Lake on his chest
hacked through the brush
of deserts   5
and made them grow
strawberries

> we stole berries
> from the stem
> we could not afford them   10
> for breakfast

his eyes held
nothing
as he whipped us
for stealing.   15

the desert had dried
his soul.

wordless
he sold
the rich,   20
full berries
to hakujin
whose children
pointed at our eyes

            they ate fresh   25
            strawberries
            on corn flakes.

Father,
i wanted to scream
at your silence.   30
Your strength
was a stranger
i could never touch.

iron
in your eyes   35
to shield
the pain
to shield desert-like wind
from patches
of strawberries   40
grown
from
tears.

The Responsive Reader

1. How did the father's experience affect his personality? What kind of
   person had he become? (Is there a key line or passage in the poem
   that for you sums up what the poet says about him?)
2. What is the daughter's attitude toward the father? Is she judging him?
3. Would it have made a difference to the poem if the father had grown
   some crop other than strawberries? Are the strawberries a symbol in
   the poem? Of what? Does the desert become a symbol?
4. What glimpses do you get in this poem of the "hakujin" (or white
   people's) society surrounding this Japanese family?

Talking, Listening, Writing

5. Have you had an opportunity to observe the effect poverty or persecution had on someone's character?
6. Do you think there are some character traits that poor people tend to share? Are there some that rich people share? Are there some that middle-class people share?
7. Do you know any people (or do you know of any people) who spent time in the camps—internment camps, prison camps, concentration camps—that were a major feature of twentieth-century history? What did you learn about their story? Have you heard anyone talk about the camp experience?

Thinking about Connections

Crow Dog, Angelou, Chin, and Mirikitani offer different perspectives on the experience of young Americans from minority backgrounds. Do you see a common theme or common themes? Do you see significant differences?

Writing from Experience

Much powerful writing is rooted in firsthand experience. The life story of Maya Angelou—born in the segregated Old South, overcoming the obstacles in her path, becoming a widely admired performer and poet— has made her a role model for a younger generation. The story of Richard Rodriguez—finding himself the only Mexican kid in an all-white class-room, with only a few words of English—has had a special meaning for readers navigating their own passage from an immigrant past to an American future.

However, even when a writer does not focus exclusively on his or her own story, drawing on personal experience gives a special, authentic touch to the discussion of larger issues. When we read about gender roles or the immigrant experience, we assume that the writer knows the subject at first hand. Reading about affirmative action, we want to know if the author can say: "I was there"—as a target, a beneficiary, a witness, or a close, caring observer. We want to see what theories or statistics mean to the lives of people the author has known or observed. Words are just words until we can relate them to the experience of someone who is involved or who cares.

Writing that draws on personal experience has special strengths:

- When you take stock of your own personal experience, you write about what you know best. No one is more of an expert than you are on what matters to you as a person. Nobody knows more about where and how you grew up. Nobody knows better what home or family meant to you or what helped and hindered you in school or on the job.

- Writing from experience sets up a special confidential relationship between writer and reader. As the writer, you show that you trust your readers enough to share with them your personal thoughts and feelings. The basic assumption in writing that takes stock honestly of the author's own experience is that readers will be able to relate—to see the connection with what matters in their own lives.

TRIGGERING Papers based on personal experience often seem better motivated than other kinds. Here are some reasons to do this kind of writing:

- *People want to share what they have experienced.* When they have faced a serious challenge, they need to tell somebody—if only a diary or journal. Have you ever felt uprooted from friends or from familiar surroundings? Have you ever felt like an outsider in your school or your neighborhood? Have you ever had to live with the aftermath of divorce? These are experiences that may make you want to tell your story. Many people find that writing about a family problem, serious illness, or living with disability helps them cope.

- *People need to sort things out in their own minds.* Have you ever felt torn between feuding parents? Have you ever been divided between what your friends expected and what was expected of you in school? Writing gives you a chance to go back over what happened and try to understand. When you have had difficult relationships with family, or when you had to leave behind a tradition or earlier belief, writing gives you a chance to come to terms with the experience.

- *People feel the need to state a grievance.* When people have been wronged, they may feel the need to go on record. Have you ever witnessed a wrongful arrest? Have you ever seen people denied benefits that you felt were rightfully theirs? When people see injustice, they may want to bear witness (rather than "not get involved"). When you have witnessed an incident of police brutality (or citizen brutality) or bureaucratic bungling, you may feel the need to make your voice heard. When you hear well-financed politicians criticize welfare mothers, you may want to testify in their behalf.

- *People feel the need to pay tribute.* They experience pleasure in sharing what is good—discovering the rewards of tutoring or being a mentor, for instance. They pay tribute to someone who served as a role model or helped them in time of need.

GATHERING What will make a paper about your personal experience become real for your reader? The answer is: Work up a rich fund of material. What sights, sounds, or emotions do you remember? What really happened? What do you remember about the people? What were your honest feelings? Preliminary notes like the following, for a paper about the writer's first experiences in the world of work, have the ring of authentic personal testimony:

The summer before the sixth grade, my mother decided it was time to send me out into the berry fields. I hated it. I made barely any money for the time I was out there. My back ached from bending and picking strawberries, and my hands were forever purple. All my friends were frolicking in the sun while I was stuck in the fields. However, after a few summers of picking, the owners moved me up to the supervising/truck working position. I now got paid by the hour and achieved a status my older brothers had never achieved. This past summer was probably the last summer I will ever work in the fields. I came to love associating with the pickers. The migrant workers are some of the best people I know. Because of working outside, I got a great tan. I know how to drive tractors or tie down trucks, and I was the only girl at my position. However, the time had come to move on. Berry picking was a great experience, but there are other places out there for me too.

Honest writing about personal experience faces up to the good and the bad. Check out the real-life material in the following notes for a student's paper on her and her friends' "health-threatening" struggle to live up to the stereotype of the "ideal woman." She says, "No matter how skinny we became, we never thought we were thin or perfect enough." This is the kind of material that "speaks for itself" even before you start spelling out for your readers what you learned from the experience:

> When I was fifteen, two of my girlfriends taught me to throw up. We thought we were terribly clever; we could gorge with impunity and not gain weight. It was a lark and a clever act of rebellion against the constant punitive dieting we subjected outselves to and that our girlfriends, mothers, and older sisters continued to endure. Within three years, bingeing and purging had become an essential rhythm of my life. For my friend, throwing up was her solution to being thin and not having to diet. To her, it was her rebellion against a system that required women to look skinny and starved. She and her friends would eat vast quantities of food: an entire roast chicken; leftover pasta with salmon in heavy cream sauce; salad with walnuts, Roquefort cheese, and homemade croutons; key lime and apple pies; and peach cobbler with ice cream. By the time she graduated from high school, she was bingeing and purging almost every day. This way she was able to appear "fragile, helpless, and weak—all the qualities so admired in females." Trying to stop, my friend went to therapists, doctors, meetings, and Overeaters Anonymous. A woman running one meeting asked, "Would you be willing to stop if it meant gaining ten pounds?" No one in the group could say yes.

Remember that *telling* your readers about your experiences and feelings is not enough. You need to make them real for your reader. Anchor them to concrete incidents and situations. Re-create the people and situations that inspired your feelings and shaped your thoughts. Re-create the people, the places, the events, so that words will not just remain words. Bring to life real-life incidents that served as an eye-opener for you or for your family or friends.

SHAPING To turn your memories into a structured paper, you focus on what matters. You lay out the material in an order that makes sense. Unsorted experience tends to be miscellaneous. One thing happens after another. Avoid papers that fall into the "and–then" pattern: This happened, and then this happened, and then this happened. An effective paper brings a key issue or concern into focus. It focuses on something that really mattered to you. It may highlight a major strand in your life, leaving much else aside.

In a successful paper about personal experience, different incidents have added up. They have become part of a pattern. The author has pushed toward a **thesis**, or unifying central idea. The following passage by a student of Japanese descent sums up his strong personal feelings. This paragraph could be the key passage of a paper about the experiences that helped make the question of identity a major issue in the student writer's mind:

> "What are you?" I have often been at a loss for words as to how to answer this question. Should I answer, Japanese? American? Japanese American? I do not consider myself fully Japanese, since I have not been brought up with the language and the strict traditional culture. I am not an ordinary American because of obvious visible differences. Trying to answer this question has often left me in an awkward position and has sometimes led me to regret my existence.

Often you can organize a personal experience paper by focusing on the key issue in a series of events. Maybe you will be telling the story of your attempt—successful or not—to make peace with a stepmother who you felt was always watching you "with evil eyes." However, here are some other ways to organize your paper:

- You may write a paper with a major *turning point*—a crucial turn in the road toward becoming your own person.

- You may want to use a strong *then-and-now* pattern to organize your paper. What were assumptions about gender roles when you grew up, and what are they now? How did your own thinking change?

- You might trace the conflict of two strong conflicting influences in your growing up. Perhaps your allegiance was divided between two parents very different in their personalities and commitments; or perhaps you experienced a strong pull between the traditional culture of the home and the peer culture of the neighborhood or school.

A PAPER FOR PEER REVIEW What makes the following personal experience paper a strong paper? What is the connecting thread or unifying idea? What are striking details that a reader might remember? What suggestions would you make for revision? Where do you think the writer might need to work in real-life examples or striking details?

Life on the East Side

I grew up on the east side of my town. Until I moved into the college dorms, the east side was the only environment I really knew. It is not a "Leave it to Beaver" neighborhood. There are no white picket fences, nor do children roam the neighborhood freely. In my neighborhood and in my old high school, drugs and gangs are serious problems. There are few traditional families left. Most kids do not come home from school to parents waiting with milk and cookies but to babysitters or empty houses. While students in other parts of town go to band practice or hang out at the mall with their friends, kids on the east side hang out with their fellow gang members spraypainting the local park.

Living in an environment such as this limits a person's freedom. Growing up, I was denied the luxuries that people from "better" neighborhoods take for granted. In my neighborhood, my friends could not go to the local bowling alley, mall, or miniature golf course without running into gang members. There aren't many places to go for someone without a driver's license because the local hangouts just aren't safe. Driving was especially important to my friends and me because it meant we were not limited to places near our homes and could go to places where we felt more secure. It is sad that fear of violence prevents parents from letting their children go to the local rollerskating rink, but on the east side this is just a reality one accepts.

My family is typical of the east side in that we never had much money. It hasn't been easy coming from a family that lives from paycheck to paycheck. There is always a sense of tension in the house that comes from the uncertainty of not knowing if there is going to be enough money to pay the bills or where the money for unexpected expenses like car repairs will come from. It is hard to watch my parents struggle. Neither of my parents attended college, and they thus had limited options for work. My dad works long hours at a job he doesn't like and consequently usually comes home overtired and in a bad mood. My sister and I have had all our physical and emotional needs met, however. My parents always found the money for things like braces for our teeth, prom dresses, and class trips. Obviously, I have never had a brand new car or taken a trip to Europe, but I have never felt deprived either.

Life on the east side gives one a different perspective. It has taught me realities that I might not otherwise have learned. I do not live in the worst part of town. In high school, I had friends who hated walking down the street to their own houses because they were afraid. At least I can walk through my own neighborhood during the day and feel fairly secure. That I consider a luxury. I have learned not to take anything for granted. I believe people spend too much time obsessed with what they don't have. My house is tiny, and all four of us have to share one bathroom. This used to be a problem for me, and I was jealous of friends who lived in large houses with their own bathrooms. Then I volunteered for work in homeless shelters. Now I am thankful that I have a house.

I learned much during my four years at my east side high school, and much of this learning occurred outside the classroom. With more than four thousand students, the school is a model of cultural and economic diversity. I was lucky to have friends from many different backgrounds. I am comfortable with all races and religions. The school has its problems, but it also has many strengths that outsiders overlook.

Being in college I get to live out a dream. However, the new environment also presents me with new obstacles. While I am not ashamed of my past, I still feel as though I have to prove that I belong here. I have made friends and am treated no differently than anyone else. Yet coming from a school with a bad reputation I feel I have to do everything twice as well as other people. I know that no person is inferior to another person, but there is still a small part of me that can't help feeling tainted by negative images of the east side. However, there are few things I would change about my past. My environment has had much to do with who I am today.

REVISING Always make time for revision. Revising gives you a chance to look at your own writing with the reader's eye. Check a first draft to see what needs work:

▪ *Move in for the closer look.* Build up concrete detail. Add lifelike detail to make your readers visualize the setting. Add physical details, revealing gestures, or favorite sayings to make us see and hear a favorite uncle or cranky neighbor. Act out key events in more striking detail.

▪ *Look for places where you have fallen back on clichés.* Ready-made phrases are handy: "finding oneself," "breakdown in communication," "the fear of commitment." However, make sure such phrases do not sound secondhand. Try your own way of saying what you feel—which may be partly similar to but also in part different from what others have felt before you.

▪ *Check for overgeneralizing.* It is easy to read too much into a single incident. A key incident may dramatize a pattern—but it may also have resulted from an unusual combination of circumstances. (A teacher or a police officer may have had a bad day—just as a heart-warming, generous gesture may have been a once-in-a-lifetime event.)

▪ *Try not to sound too one-sided or self-righteous.* Readers get wary when everything that went wrong in your life was someone else's fault.

▪ *Try not to make everything sound zany, hectic, or funny.* Readers tire of a strained facetious tone. A good tone to aim at may be to be basically serious with an occasional lighter touch.

Topics for Experience Papers (A Sampling)

1. Have you ever rebelled against tradition? Or have you ever returned to a tradition that you had left behind? What led to your change of heart? Was there a turning point? What was the outcome?
2. Have you ever been torn between competing influences on your life or your thinking? Have you ever experienced divided loyalties? How did you sort them out?

3. Have you experienced a change in your religious outlook? For instance, have you or people close to you become or considered becoming "reborn Christians"? Or have you had the experience of leaving a childhood faith behind?

4. Have you encountered special obstacles—or special opportunities—because of who or what you are? What has been your personal experience with discrimination or prejudice? (Or, what is your experience with favoritism or having the "inside track"?)

5. Have you felt defensive about your identity? Have you ever felt ashamed or embarassed about your background? Do you feel resentful or uncomfortable when people pry into where you came from or what you are? How do you cope?

6. In your growing up, have you encountered a challenge to your sense of self-worth? Has a problem in your family or personal life affected your outlook or helped shape your personality?

7. Where and how did you become aware of race? Where did you become aware of the role of ethnicity or varying national origins? What difference has race or ethnicity made in your life?

8. Have you ever discovered a new lifestyle or rediscovered a cultural identity? What difference has it made in your life?

9. Have you ever changed your mind on a major issue? Have you ever had a change of heart on a subject like marriage, having children, abortion, or divorce?

10. What shaped your views on what it means to be a man or a woman? Did you have any role models that influenced or changed your views of gender roles? Have you had occasion to reexamine or revise your views?

11. What has been your initiation into the world of work? What jobs—good or bad—made an impression on you? Do you believe in the "work ethic"?

2

New World: Diversity and Community

We are a people in search of a national community.
—*Barbara Jordan*

It's that same old, same old story. We all have an immigrant ancestor, one who believed in America; one who, daring or duped, took sail.
—*Fae Myenne Ng*

I am giving you a version of America, your America, that you may not have chosen to see or may have missed. I used to travel on the train going out to my job in Queens from the Upper West Side. After a certain subway stop, the entire train is filled with nonwhites. And those people are the people I am writing about, saying they have huge interesting lives.
—*Bharati Mukherjee*

For many years, the unofficial ideology of the United States was that of the melting pot. People would come to this country from across the seas to make a new start—in the words of one refugee from the persecutions and massacres of the Old World, to "start all over again." The promise of America was the promise of equal opportunity—regardless of class, religion, or ethnic origin. Arriving on these shores, the immigrants would leave old allegiances and old hatreds behind to form a new nation.

The American historian Arthur Schlesinger stated a widely held belief when he said,

America has been in the best sense of the term a melting pot, every element adding its particular element of strength. The constant infusion of new blood has enriched our cultural life, speeded our material growth, and produced some of our ablest statesmen. Over

83

17 million immigrants arrived in the single period from the Civil War to World War I . . . the very nationalities which had habitually warred with one another in the Old World have lived together in harmony in the New. America has demonstrated for everyone with eyes to see that those things which unite peoples are greater than those which divide them, that war is not the inevitable fate of mankind.

The policy implementing this belief was assimilation. The goal was to "Americanize" new immigrants as quickly as possible, making them share in a common language and a common culture. Their children would already be new Americans, growing up in a world of baseball, hot dogs, chewing gum, and Coca-Cola.

In the years since Schlesinger wrote, the melting-pot metaphor and the policy of assimilation have come in for much reexamination and revision. The melting-pot theory had not worked, or not worked well, for large segments of American society. Native Americans had been shunted off to reservations in areas where no white people could make a living. African Americans leaving the segregated South found themselves living in segregated inner cities in the North. Many Mexicans, Puerto Ricans, and Cubans were living in Spanish-speaking neighborhoods with strong ties to their own culture. A large new Asian immigration transformed parts of the cities into new Chinatowns or Little Saigons.

Confronted with the limits of assimilation, minority leaders and teachers started to teach a return to the roots. They promoted black pride, pride in the Chicano heritage or *la raza,* or the preservation of Native American traditions. Sociologists and political leaders called for a new recognition of diversity, of pluralism. They asked for recognition of the side-by-side of different languages and cultural strands in a new American "mosaic"—with many different particles fitted together in a rich larger pattern, a larger whole.

Conservative columnists like George Will talk about the "cult of diversity" as a threat to mainstream American culture. Multiculturalism—the recognition of a rich web of cultural influences in American life—has become a fighting word. How will tomorrow's Americans think of diversity and community? How much diversity will our society welcome or accommodate? Will a multicultural society have a common center?

THE MOSAIC VS. THE MYTH

Anna Quindlen

Anna Quindlen became known as a widely syndicated columnist for the New York Times, winning a Pulitzer Prize for commentary in 1992. Like other columnists, she writes about the issues of the day not as an expert—a political scientist, sociologist, or psychologist. She writes as a shrewd, informed observer who helps her readers make sense of the news. Like other columnists, Quindlen is a trend watcher who sizes up and explains the changes in awareness and public consciousness that slowly become part of the way we think about the world in which we live. Like other journalists with liberal or feminist leanings, she has come in for her share of hate mail from angry letter writers. Recently, she has decided to devote more of her time to fiction, her first love. She published her second novel, One True Thing, *in 1994. In the following column, she comments on the gradual change from the melting-pot ideal of American society to a new outlook more tolerant or accepting of diversity.*

Thought Starters: How is American society like a melting pot? How is it like a mosaic? How is it like a "tossed salad"?

There is some disagreement over which wordsmith first substituted 1 "mosaic" for "melting pot" as a way of describing America, but it is undoubtedly a more apt description. And it undoubtedly applies in Ms. Miller's third-grade class and elsewhere in the Lower East Side's Public School 20.

The neighborhood where the school is located is to the immigrant experience what Broadway is to actors. Past Blevitzky Bros. Monuments ("at this place since 1914"), past Katz's Delicatessen with its fan mail hung in the window, past the tenement buildings where fire escapes climb graceful as cat burglars, P.S. 20 holds the corner of Essex and Houston.

Its current student body comes from the Dominican Republic, Cambodia, Bangladesh, Puerto Rico, Colombia, mainland China, Vietnam and El Salvador. In Ms. Miller's third-grade class these various faces somehow look the same, upturned and open, as though they were cups waiting for the water to be poured.

There's a spirit in the nation now that's in opposition to these children. It is not interested in your tired, your poor, your huddled masses. In recent days it has been best personified by a candidate for governor and the suggestion in his campaign that there is a kind of authentic American. That authentic American is white and Christian (but not Catholic), ethnic origins lost in the mists of an amorphous past, not visible in accent, appearance or allegiance.

This is not a new idea, this resilient form of xenophobia. "It is but 5 too common a remark of late, that the American character has within a short time been sadly degraded by numerous instances of riot and lawless violence," Samuel F. B. Morse wrote in an 1835 treatise called "Imminent Dangers to the Free Institutions of the United States through Foreign Immigration," decrying such riffraff as Jesuits.

Times are bad, and we blame the newcomers, whether it's 1835 or 1991. Had Morse had his way, half of me would still be in Italy; if some conservatives had their way today, most of the children at P.S. 20 would be, in that ugly phrase, back where they came from. So much for lifting a lamp beside the golden door.

They don't want to learn the language, we complain, as though the old neighborhoods were not full of Poles and Italians who kept to their mother tongue. They don't want to become American, we say, as though there are not plenty of us who believe we lost something when we renounced ethnicity. "Dagos," my mother said the American kids called them, American being those not Italian. "Wops." How quickly we forget as we use pejoratives for the newest newcomers.

Our greatest monument to immigration, the restored Ellis Island, seems to suggest by its display cases that coming to America is a thing nostalgic, something grandparents did. On the Lower East Side it has never been past tense, struggling with English and poverty, sharing apartments with the bathroom in the hall and the bathtub in the kitchen.

They send their children to school with hopes for a miracle, or a job, which is almost the same thing. This past week the School Volunteer Program, which fields almost 6,000 volunteer tutors, sponsored the first citywide Read Aloud: 400 grown-ups reading to thousands of kids in 90 schools. In P.S. 20, as so many have done before, the kids clutched their books like visas.

It is foolish to forget where you come from, which, in the case of 10 the United States, is almost always somewhere else. The true authentic American is a pilgrim with a small "p," armed with little more than the phrase "I wish. . . ." New ones are being minted in Ms. Miller's class, bits of a mosaic far from complete.

The Responsive Reader

1. Why is the term *mosaic* "a more apt description" for what Quindlen saw on the Lower East Side than *melting pot*? (Or is it?)
2. What does Quindlen say about the nature and history of "xenophobia"—the fear of foreigners—in this country? (Is it alive in your own community or in society at large?)

3. How does Quindlen forge links between the present wave of immigration and America's past? What is her idea of the "true authentic American"?

Talking, Listening, Writing

4. Do you consider yourself a "true authentic American" in Quindlen's terms? Or are you one of those whose ethnic origins are "lost in the mists of an amorphous"—shapeless, indistinct—past?

Collaborative Projects

5. Quindlen says, "It is foolish to forget where you come from." You may want to work on a family history, with special attention to ethnic or regional origins. (Your class may decide to bring these family histories together as a class publication.)

LEGION BARS IMMIGRANT FROM SCHOLARS' CAMP

Dirk Johnson

> *The official oratory of the country long paid homage to America as "a nation of immigrants." St. Patrick's Day for the Irish, Columbus Day for Italians, Hannukah for Jews, Chinese New Year for the Chinese—these and similar ethnic holidays kept alive sentimental attachments to Old Country memories and Old Country ways. Recently, however, immigrant-bashing initiatives have reminded many immigrants and children of immigrants of a traditional undercurrent of anti-immigrant sentiment in American history. Talk show hosts and politicians stirring up the angry white male seemed again to be stoking prejudice against immigrants and minorities. Welfare reform cut off food stamps and disability payments for legal immigrants. The following news story from the* New York Times *focuses on an incident that can serve as a test case for current ambivalent feelings about immigration.*

Thought Starters: Do you agree with the author of the following article that today anger toward immigrants and their children is "a growing sentiment by almost any measure"?

EDGAR, Wis.—Vying to attend a prestigious camp for patriotic   1
young Wisconsin scholars, one student's resume sparkled above the rest: a 16-year-old who earned straight A's, played violin, spoke French and displayed an interest in government.

But Pang Thao, a junior at rural Edgar High School, has been rejected by the camp's sponsor, the American Legion Auxiliary, because she is not a U.S. citizen, even though she will become one in a matter of months.

"Rules are rules, and unfortunately she's not a citizen," said Eileen Knox, a spokeswoman for the Auxiliary. "There are lots of American-born girls who are still waiting in the wings, hoping they can be chosen."

The rejection of Pang, who immigrated with her parents when she was 2 months old, follows a similar incident in Texas earlier this spring. The Houston Stock Show and Rodeo awarded a $10,000 scholarship to a Texas honors student, only to withdraw the prize after learning the winner was not a U.S. citizen.

When it comes to anger toward immigrants and their children—a   5
growing sentiment by almost any measure—Americans usually complain about unskilled and illiterate newcomers draining budgets and services.

But the rejection of the two young scholars, immigration advocates say, illustrates a wellspring of resentment against those who can compete, perhaps too well.

"On the one hand, we encourage assimilation and achievement," said Lucas Guttentag, a lawyer who specializes in immigration for the American Civil Liberties Union, "and we say we want immigrants to learn the values of American society. But then we turn around and exclude these people from the very institutions that imbue those values."

'They don't like me'

The tough immigration bill passed overwhelmingly by the Senate, for example, would deny college financial aid to legal immigrants who are not citizens.

For Pang, the talk of policy and politics can be reduced to something basic. "There are a lot of people out there who don't like me," she said the other night, while on break from her job at her parents' restaurant. "They don't know me. But they don't like me."

Pang hears plenty of the stereotypes about minorities: "They get   *10* more welfare. They don't pay taxes. They're not loyal to America."

She has found herself saying in a flash of defensive anger, "Man, don't you understand? I'm here because my relatives and my ancestors helped the Americans in the war."

The Thaos were among the thousands of Hmongs driven by Communist forces from Laos for helping the United States in the Vietnam War.

Her parents, Long, 38, and Chong Thao, 38, delayed starting the citizenship process until last year. "It is hard to let go when you come from another country," Long Thao said. "It's a part of you. But over time, we understood. This is our home country now. We are Americans."

The family, with six children, struggles financially. The parents run the Thai Cafe in a strip mall in Wausau, a city of 37,000 with a sizable Hmong population. Pang works nights and Saturdays.

Government shutdown

Pang and her parents have been careful not to criticize the American   *15* Legion. They have expressed gratitude to the University of Wisconsin at Whitewater, which recently invited Pang to participate in an international conference there in June, as a consolation for her rejection at the Legion camp, Badger Girls State.

At the time Pang applied to attend the camp, it appeared the citizenship approval might be granted in time. But the shutdown of some government offices in the Washington budget dispute last winter delayed citizenship applications and doomed those hopes.

Those who defend the citizenship rule noted that favoritism for citizens goes back to the nation's founders. They point to the constitutional requirement that the president be born in the United States.

"Citizenship means something," said Knox, of the Legion Auxiliary.

The disappointment in the Thao family has been keen, although Pang, the oldest child, bristles at the notion of people feeling sorry for her. "I'm not complaining," she said. "I'm not whining, and I don't need anyone's pity."

More than anything else, she said, she is bothered by the views of   20
those who believe being born in the United States is a virtue. "I really dislike this idea of some people being superior over others," she said. "Most of the people here are just a mix of nationalities from somewhere else. The difference between me and you is the color of our skin and our background. And that's it."

The Responsive Reader

1. What do you learn in this news story about the young woman and her family and about their history? For you, are they typical American immigrants? Or are they different?
2. In reporting the controversy, is the *New York Times* reporter taking sides? What does he highlight or stress in describing the situation? What are the arguments on both sides?
3. The reporter gives the student the last word. What do you think of her reaction or her attitude?

Talking, Listening, Writing

4. For you, is the difference between being "American-born" or not important or significant? Do you know about any prominent Americans who were foreign-born? What difference does it make?
5. Are your own sympathies with the Legion or with the university that tried to make amends?

Collaborative Projects

6. Working with a group, you may want to investigate the history of "nativist" or anti-immigration sentiment. You may decide to focus on such topics as prejudice against the Irish or against Eastern European immigrants, immigration policies aimed at excluding Asians, or American anti-Semitism.

DIVERSITY AND ITS DISCONTENTS
Arturo Madrid

Arturo Madrid is a native of New Mexico who studied at the University of New Mexico and at UCLA. His first teaching assignment was at Dartmouth; he later became president of the Thomas Rivera Center at the Claremont Graduate School in California. He represents Spanish-speaking Americans of the Southwest who live in lands that were once part of Mexico and for whom the Anglos, or americanos, *were the "immigrants" or new arrivals. The following article is excerpted from a speech he gave at the National Conference of the American Association of Higher Education. He urged his audience of educators to recognize excellence in workers as well as managers, in people who are not glib or superficially sophisticated, and in people regardless of class, gender, race, or national origin. What do you learn from this article about the feeling of being the "other"? At the time Madrid gave his speech, E. D. Hirsch and Alan Bloom were widely quoted pundits writing in defense of traditional academic practices.*

Thought Starters: What does it mean to be "different"? How does it shape a person's outlook and personality?

My name is Arturo Madrid. I am a citizen of the United States, as are my parents and as were my grandparents and my great-grandparents. My ancestors' presence in what is now the United States antedates Plymouth Rock, even without taking into account any American Indian heritage I might have.

I do not, however, fit those mental sets that define America and Americans. My physical appearance, my speech patterns, my name, my profession (a professor of Spanish) create a text that confuses the reader. My normal experience is to be asked, "And where are *you* from?" My response depends on my mood. Passive-aggressive, I answer, "From here." Aggressive-passive, I ask, "Do you mean where I am originally from?" But ultimately my answer to those follow-up questions that will ask about origins will be that we have always been from here.

Overcoming my resentment I try to educate, knowing that nine times out of ten my words fall on inattentive ears. I have spent most of my adult life explaining who I am not. I am exotic, but—as Richard Rodriguez of *Hunger of Memory* fame so painfully found out—not exotic enough . . . not Peruvian, or Pakistani, or whatever. I am, however, very clearly the *other*, if only your everyday, garden-variety, domestic *other*. I will share with you another phenomenon that I have been a part of, that of being a missing person, and how I came late to that awareness. But I've always known that I was the *other,* even before I knew the vocabulary or understood the significance of otherness.

I grew up in an isolated and historically marginal part of the United States, a small mountain village in the state of New Mexico, the eldest child of parents native to that region, whose ancestors had always lived there. In those vast and empty spaces people who look like me, speak as I do, and have names like mine predominate. But the *americanos* lived among us: the descendants of those nineteenth-century immigrants who dispossessed us of our lands; missionaries who came to convert us and stayed to live among us; artists who became enchanted with our land and humanscape and went native; refugees from unhealthy climes, crowded spaces, unpleasant circumstances; and, of course, the inhabitants of Los Alamos, whose sociocultural distance from us was accentuated by the fact that they occupied a space removed from and proscribed to us. More importantly, however, they—*los americanos*—were omnipresent (and almost exclusively so) in newspapers, newsmagazines, books, on radio, in movies, and, ultimately, on television.

Despite the operating myth of the day, school did not erase my otherness. It did try to deny it, and in doing so only accentuated it. To this day what takes place in schools is more socialization than education, but when I was in elementary school—and given where I was—socialization was everything. School was where one became an American, because there was a pervasive and systematic denial by the society that surrounded us that we were Americans. That denial was both explicit and implicit.

Quite beyond saluting the flag and pledging allegiance to it (a very intense and meaningful action, given that the United States was involved in a war and our brothers, cousins, uncles, and fathers were on the frontlines), becoming American was learning English, and its corollary: not speaking Spanish. Until very recently ours was a proscribed language, either *de jure*—by rule, by policy, by law—or *de facto*—by practice, implicitly if not explicitly, through social and political and economic pressure. I do not argue that learning English was not appropriate. On the contrary. Like it or not, and we had no basis to make any judgments on that matter, we were Americans by virtue of having been born Americans and English was the common language of Americans. And there was a myth, a pervasive myth, to the effect that if only we learned to speak English well—and particularly without an accent—we would be welcomed into the American fellowship.

Sam Hayakawa and the official English movement folks notwithstanding, the true text was not our speech, but rather our names and our appearance, for we would always have an accent, however perfect our pronunciation, however excellent our enunciation, however divine our

5

diction. That accent would be heard in our pigmentation, our physiognomy, our names. We were, in short, the *other*.

Being the *other* involves contradictory phenomena. On the one hand being the *other* frequently means being invisible. Ralph Ellison wrote eloquently about that experience in his magisterial novel, *Invisible Man*. On the other hand, being the *other* sometimes involves sticking out like a sore thumb. What is she/he doing here?

For some of us being the *other* is only annoying; for others it is debilitating; for still others it is damning. Many try to flee otherness by taking on protective colorations that provide invisibility, whether of dress or speech or manner or name. Only a fortunate few succeed. For the majority of us otherness is permanently sealed by physical appearance. For the rest, otherness is betrayed by ways of being, speaking, or doing.

The first half of my life I spent downplaying the significance and consequences of otherness. The second half has seen me wrestling to understand its complex and deeply ingrained realities; striving to fathom why otherness denies us a voice or visibility or validity in American society and its institutions; struggling to make otherness familiar, reasonable, even normal to my fellow Americans.
10

I spoke earlier of another phenomenon that I am a part of: that of being a missing person. Growing up in northern New Mexico I had only a slight sense of us being missing persons. *Hispanos,* as we called (and call) ourselves in New Mexico, were very much a part of the fabric of the society, and there were *hispano* professionals everywhere about me: doctors, lawyers, schoolteachers, and administrators. My people owned businesses, ran organizations, and were both appointed and elected public officials.

My awareness of our absence from the larger institutional life of the society became sharper when I went off to college, but even then it was attenuated by the circumstances of history and geography. The demography of Albuquerque still strongly reflected its historical and cultural origins, despite the influx of Midwesterners and Easterners. Moreover, many of my classmates at the University of New Mexico were *hispanos,* and even some of my professors. I thought that would obtain at UCLA, where I began graduate studies in 1960. Los Angeles had a very large Mexican population and that population was visible even in and around Westwood and on the campus. Many of the groundskeepers and food-service personnel at UCLA were Mexican. But Mexican-American students were few and mostly invisible, and I do not recall seeing or knowing a single Mexican-American (or, for that matter, African-American, Asian, or American Indian) professional on the staff or faculty of that institution during the five years I was there. Needless to say, people like me were not present in any capacity at Dartmouth College, the site of my first teaching appointment, and of course were not even part of the institutional or individual mind-set. I knew then that we—a we that had come to encompass American Indians, Asian-Americans, African-Americans, Puerto Ricans, and women—were truly missing persons in American institutional life.

Over the past three decades the *de jure* and *de facto* types of segregation that have historically characterized American institutions have been under assault. As a consequence, minorities and women have become part of American institutional life. Although there are still many areas where we are not to be found, the missing persons phenomenon is not as pervasive as it once was. However, the presence of the *other,* particularly minorities, in institutions and in institutional life resembles what we call in Spanish a *flor de tierra* (a surface phenomenon): we are spare plants whose roots do not go deep, vulnerable to inclemencies of an economic, or political, or social, nature.

Our entrance into and our status in institutional life are not unlike a scenario set forth by my grandmother's pastor when she informed him that she and her family were leaving their mountain village to relocate to the Rio Grande Valley. When he asked her to promise that she would remain true to the faith and continue to involve herself in it, she asked why he thought she would do otherwise. "Doña Trinidad," he told her, "in the Valley there is no Spanish church. There is only an American church." "But," she protested, "I read and speak English and would be able to worship there." The pastor responded, "It is possible that they will not admit you, and even if they do, they might not accept you. And that is why I want you to promise me that you are going to go to church. Because if they don't let you in through the front door, I want you to go in through the back door. And if you can't get in through the back door, go in the side door. And if you are unable to enter through the side door I want you to go in through the window. What is important is that you enter and stay."

Some of us entered institutional life through the front door; others through the back door; and still others through side doors. Many, if not most of us, came in through windows, and continue to come in through windows. Of those who entered through the front door, some never made it past the lobby; others were ushered into corners and niches. Those who entered through back and side doors inevitably have remained in back and side rooms. And those who entered through windows found enclosures built around them. For, despite the lip service given to the goal of the integration of minorities into institutional life, what has frequently occurred instead is ghettoization, marginalization, isolation.

Not only have the entry points been limited, but in addition the dynamics have been singularly conflictive. Gaining entry and its corollary, gaining space, have frequently come as a consequence of demands made on institutions and institutional officers. Rather than entering institutions more or less passively, minorities have of necessity entered them actively, even aggressively. Rather than waiting to receive, they have demanded.

Institutional relations have thus been adversarial, infused with specific and generalized tensions.

The nature of the entrance and the nature of the space occupied have greatly influenced the view and attitude of the majority population within those institutions. All of us are put into the same box; that is, no matter what the individual reality, the assessment of the individual is inevitably conditioned by a perception that is held of the class. Whatever our history, whatever our record, whatever our validations, whatever our accomplishments, by and large we are perceived unidimensionally and dealt with accordingly. I remember an experience I had in this regard, atypical only in its explicitness. A few years ago I allowed myself to be persuaded to seek the presidency of a well-known state university. I was invited for an interview and presented myself before the selection committee, which included members of the board of trustees. The opening question of that brief but memorable interview was directed at me by a member of that august body. "Dr. Madrid," he asked, "why does a one-dimensional person like you think he can be the president of a multidimensional institution like ours?"

Over the past four decades America's demography has undergone significant changes. Since 1965 the principal demographic growth we have experienced in the United States has been of peoples whose national origins are non-European. This population growth has occurred both through birth and through immigration. A few years ago discussion of the national birthrate had a scare dimension: the high—"inordinately high"—birthrate of the Hispanic population. The popular discourse was informed by words such as "breeding." Several years later, as a consequence of careful tracking by government agencies, we now know that what has happened is that the birthrate of the majority population has decreased. When viewed historically and comparatively, the minority populations (for the most part) have also had a decline in birthrate, but not one as great as that of the majority.

There are additional demographic changes that should give us something to think about. African-Americans are now to be found in significant numbers in every major urban center in the nation. Hispanic-Americans now number over 15 million people, and although they are a regionally concentrated (and highly urbanized) population, there is a Hispanic community in almost every major urban center of the United States. American Indians, heretofore a small and rural population, are increasingly more numerous and urban. The Asian-American population, which has historically consisted of small and concentrated communities of Chinese-, Filipino-, and Japanese-Americans, has doubled over the past decade, its complexion changed by the addition of Cambodians, Koreans, Hmongs, Vietnamese, et al.

Prior to the Immigration Act of 1965, 69 percent of immigration 20 was from Europe. By far the largest number of immigrants to the United

States since 1965 have been from the Americas and from Asia: 34 percent are from Asia; another 34 percent are from Central and South America; 16 percent are from Europe; 10 percent are from the Caribbean; the remaining 6 percent are from other continents and Canada. As was the case with previous immigration waves, the current one consists principally of young people: 60 percent are between the ages of 16 and 44. Thus, for the next few decades, we will continue to see a growth in the percentage of non-European-origin Americans as compared to European-Americans.

To sum up, we now live in one of the most demographically diverse nations in the world, and one that is increasingly more so.

During the same period social and economic change seems to have accelerated. Who would have imagined at mid-century that the prototypical middle-class family (working husband, wife as homemaker, two children) would for all intents and purposes disappear? Who could have anticipated the rise in teenage pregnancies, children in poverty, drug use? Who among us understood the implications of an aging population?

We live in an age of continuous and intense change, a world in which what held true yesterday does not today, and certainly will not tomorrow. What change does, moreover, is bring about even more change. The only constant we have at this point in our national development is change. And change is threatening. The older we get the more likely we are to be anxious about change, and the greater our desire to maintain the status quo.

Evident in our public life is a fear of change, whether economic or moral. Some who fear change are responsive to the call of economic protectionism, others to the message of moral protectionism. Parenthetically, I have referred to the movement to require more of students without in turn giving them more as academic protectionism. And the pronouncements of E. D. Hirsch and Allan Bloom are, I believe, informed by intellectual protectionism. Much more serious, however, is the dark side of the populism which underlies this evergoing protectionism—the resentment of the *other*. An excellent and fascinating example of that aspect of populism is the cry for linguistic protectionism—for making English the official language of the United States. And who among us is unaware of the tensions that underlie immigration reform, of the underside of demographic protectionism?

A matter of increasing concern is whether this new protectionism, 25 and the mistrust of the *other* which accompanies it, is not making more significant inroads than we have supposed in higher education. Specifically, I wish to discuss the question of whether a goal (quality) and a reality (demographic diversity) have been erroneously placed in conflict, and, if so, what problems this perception of conflict might present.

As part of my scholarship I turn to dictionaries for both origins and meanings of words. Quality, according to the *Oxford English Dictionary,* has multiple meanings. One set defines quality as being an essential character, a distinctive and inherent feature. A second describes it as a degree of excellence, of conformity to standards, as superiority in kind. A third makes reference to social status, particularly to persons of high social status. A fourth talks about quality as being a special or distinguishing attribute, as being a desirable trait. Quality is highly desirable in both principle and practice. We all aspire to it in our own person, in our experiences, in our acquisitions and products, and of course we all want to be associated with people and operations of quality.

But let us move away from the various dictionary meanings of the word and to our own sense of what it represents and of how we feel about it. First of all we consider quality to be finite; that is, it is limited with respect to quantity; it has very few manifestations; it is not widely distributed. I have it and you have it, but they don't. We associate quality with homogeneity, with uniformity, with standardization, with order, regularity, neatness. All too often we equate it with smoothness, glibness, slickness, elegance. Certainly it is always expensive. We tend to identify it with those who lead, with the rich and famous. And, when you come right down to it, it's inherent. Either you've got it or you ain't.

Diversity, from the Latin *divertere,* meaning to turn aside, to go different ways, to differ, is the condition of being different or having differences, is an instance of being different. Its companion word, diverse, means differing, unlike, distinct; having or capable of having various forms; composed of unlike or distinct elements. Diversity is lack of standardization, of regularity, of orderliness, homogeneity, conformity, uniformity. Diversity introduces complications, is difficult to organize, is troublesome to manage, is problematical. Diversity is irregular, disorderly, uneven, rough. The way we use the word diversity gives us away. Something is too diverse, is extremely diverse. We want a little diversity.

When we talk about diversity, we are talking about the *other,* whatever that other might be: someone of a different gender, race, class, national origin; somebody at a greater or lesser distance from the norm; someone outside the set; someone who possesses a different set of characteristics, features, or attributes; someone who does not fall within the taxonomies we use daily and with which we are comfortable; someone who does not fit into the mental configurations that give our lives order and meaning.

In short, diversity is desirable only in principle, not in practice. Long 30 live diversity . . . as long as it conforms to my standards, my mind set, my view of life, my sense of order. We desire, we like, we admire diversity, not unlike the way the French (and others) appreciate women; that is, *Vive la différence!*—as long as it stays in its place.

What I find paradoxical about and lacking in this debate is that diversity is the natural order of things. Evolution produces diversity. Margaret Visser, writing about food in her latest book, *Much Depends on Dinner,* makes an eloquent statement in this regard:

Machines like, demand, and produce uniformity. But nature loathes it: her strength lies in multiplicity and in differences. Sameness in biology means fewer possibilities and therefore weakness.

The United States, by its very nature, by its very development, is the essence of diversity. It is diverse in its geography, population, institutions, technology; its social, cultural, and intellectual modes. It is a society that at its best does not consider quality to be monolithic in form or finite in quantity, or to be inherent in class. Quality in our society proceeds in large measure out of the stimulus of diverse modes of thinking and acting; out of the creativity made possible by the different ways in which we approach things; out of diversion from paths or modes hallowed by tradition.

One of the principal strengths of our society is its ability to address, on a continuing and substantive basis, the real economic, political, and social problems that have faced and continue to face us. What makes the United States so attractive to immigrants is the protections and opportunities it offers; what keeps our society together is tolerance for cultural, religious, social, political, and even linguistic difference; what makes us a unique, dynamic, and extraordinary nation is the power and creativity of our diversity.

The true history of the United States is one of struggle against intolerance, against oppression, against xenophobia, against those forces that have prohibited persons from participating in the larger life of the society on the basis of their race, their gender, their religion, their national origin, their linguistic and cultural background. These phenomena are not consigned to the past. They remain with us and frequently take on virulent dimensions.

If you believe, as I do, that the well-being of a society is directly related to the degree and extent to which all of its citizens participate in its institutions, then you will have to agree that we have a challenge before us. In view of the extraordinary changes that are taking place in our society we need to take up the struggle again, irritating, grating, troublesome, unfashionable, unpleasant as it is. As educated and educator members of this society we have a special responsibility for ensuring that all American institutions, not just our elementary and secondary schools, our juvenile halls, or our jails, reflect the diversity of our society. Not to do so is to risk greater alienation on the part of a growing segment of our society; is to risk increased social tension in an already conflictive world; and, ultimately, is to risk the survival of a range of institutions that, for all their defects and deficiencies, provide us the opportunity and the freedom to improve our individual and collective lot.

Let me urge you to reflect on these two words—quality and diversity—and on the mental sets and behaviors that flow out of them.

And let me urge you further to struggle against the notion that quality is finite in quantity, limited in its manifestations, or is restricted by considerations of class, gender, race, or national origin; or that quality manifests itself only in leaders and not in followers, in managers and not in workers, in breeders and not in drones; or that it has to be associated with verbal agility or elegance of personal style; or that it cannot be seeded, nurtured, or developed.

Because diversity—the *other*—is among us, will define and determine our lives in ways that we still do not fully appreciate, whether that other is women (no longer bound by tradition, house, and family); or Asians, African-Americans, Indians, and Hispanics (no longer invisible, regional, or marginal); or our newest immigrants (no longer distant, exotic, alien). Given the changing profile of America, will we come to terms with diversity in our personal and professional lives? Will we begin to recognize the diverse forms that quality can take? If so, we will thus initiate the process of making quality limitless in its manifestations, infinite in quantity, unrestricted with respect to its origins, and more importantly, virulently contagious.

I hope we will. And that we will further join together to expand— not to close—the circle.

The Responsive Reader

1. What does it mean to Madrid to be the "other"? What is or was the role of such factors as history, genealogy, appearance (or "physiognomy"), and language in his sense of being different?
2. What was Madrid's experience with or perception of the *americanos*?
3. What was Madrid's experience with the school as the institution most directly representing American society? What was its goal? What was its governing myth? Did it fail or succeed?
4. What are different ways of dealing with minority identity or minority status? How did (and does) Madrid react or cope? Did his attitude or awareness change at different stages in his life?
5. What is Madrid's account of the changes as American colleges and universities try to deal with the issue of diversity? Have the changes been for the better?
6. What is Madrid's last word on the role of diversity in American society?

Talking, Listening, Writing

7. On balance, what do you think predominates in this essay—the "discontents" of the past or the challenges of the future?
8. Have you ever tried to put yourself in the shoes of someone with a history or with grievances and aspirations very different from your own? Tell the story of an experience that opened up for you a new perspective or opened a new window on the world. What did you learn from the experience?

9. Have you ever had difficulty answering the question "Who are you?" or "What are you?"

Collaborative Projects

10. Have the hiring and retention of minority faculty been an issue at your own institution? You and classmates may want to arrange interviews with people who are in a position to know.

MULTICULTURALISM AND THE COMMON CENTER

Diane Ravitch

Diane Ravitch is an influential voice in the debate about the history and future of American education. She is a graduate of the Houston public schools who now teaches history and education at Teachers College, Columbia University. She became known for her book The Troubled Crusade: American Education, 1945–1980 *and for other books about the dilemmas and needs of the American educational system. In 1990 she published* The American Reader: Words That Moved a Nation, *a book collecting classic speeches, poems, songs, arguments, and landmark court decisions that mirror Americans' understanding of themselves as a nation. Representing eloquent voices from Thomas Jefferson, Tom Paine, and Frederick Douglass to Alice Walker, Harvey Milk, and Lorna Dee Cervantes, the book has been called "a journey through the American democratic experience" (Albert Shanker). How far has our society moved toward "cultural pluralism"? What kind of stock-taking takes place in the following article? What second thoughts about multiculturalism does it present?*

Thought Starters: What do current buzzwords like *diversity, pluralism,* and *multiculturalism* mean to you? Have you encountered terms like *Eurocentric* and *ethnocentric*?

As a result of the political and social changes of recent decades, cultural pluralism is now generally recognized as an organizing principle of this society. In contrast to the idea of the melting pot, which promised to erase ethnic and group differences, children now learn that variety is the spice of life. They learn that America has provided a haven for many different groups and has allowed them to maintain their cultural heritage or to assimilate, or—as is often the case—to do both; the choice is theirs, not the state's. They learn that cultural pluralism is one of the norms of a free society; that differences among groups are a national resource rather than a problem to be solved. Indeed, the unique feature of the United States is that its common culture has been formed by the interaction of its subsidiary cultures. It is a culture that has been influenced over time by immigrants, American Indians, Africans (slave and free) and by their descendants. American music, art, literature, language, food, clothing, sports, holidays, and customs all show the effects of the commingling of diverse

1

cultures in one nation. Paradoxical though it may seem, the United States has a common culture that is multicultural.

Our schools and our institutions of higher learning have in recent years begun to embrace what Catherine R. Stimpson of Rutgers University has called "cultural democracy," a recognition that we must listen to a "diversity of voices" in order to understand our culture, past and present. This understanding of the pluralistic nature of American culture has taken a long time to forge. It is based on sound scholarship and has led to major revisions in what children are taught and what they read in school. The new history is—indeed, must be—a warts-and-all history; it demands an unflinching examination of racism and discrimination in our history. Making these changes is difficult, raises tempers, and ignites controversies, but gives a more interesting and accurate account of American history. Accomplishing these changes is valuable, because there is also a useful lesson for the rest of the world in America's relatively successful experience as a pluralistic society. Throughout human history, the clash of different cultures, races, ethnic groups, and religions has often been the cause of bitter hatred, civil conflict, and international war. The ethnic tensions that now are tearing apart Lebanon, Sri Lanka, Kashmir, and various republics of the Soviet Union remind us of the costs of unfettered group rivalry. Thus, it is a matter of more than domestic importance that we closely examine and try to understand that part of our national history in which different groups competed, fought, suffered, but ultimately learned to live together in relative peace and even achieved a sense of common nationhood.

Alas, these painstaking efforts to expand the understanding of American culture into a richer and more varied tapestry have taken a new turn, and not for the better. Almost any idea, carried to its extreme, can be made pernicious, and this is what is happening now to multiculturalism. Today, pluralistic multiculturalism must contend with a new, particularistic multiculturalism. The pluralists seek a richer common culture; the particularists insist that no common culture is possible or desirable. The new particularism is entering the curriculum in a number of school systems across the country. Advocates of particularism propose an ethnocentric curriculum to raise the self-esteem and academic achievement of children from racial and ethnic minority backgrounds. Without any evidence, they claim that children from minority backgrounds will do well in school *only* if they are immersed in a positive, prideful version of their ancestral culture. If children are of, for example, Fredonian ancestry, they must hear that Fredonians were important in mathematics, science, history, and literature. If they learn about great Fredonians and if their studies use Fredonian examples and Fredonian concepts, they will do well in school. If they do not, they will have low self-esteem and will do badly.

At first glance, this appears akin to the celebratory activities associated with Black History Month or Women's History Month, when schoolchildren learn about the achievements of blacks and women. But the point of those celebrations is to demonstrate that neither race nor gender is an obstacle to high achievement. They teach all children that everyone, regardless of their race, religion, gender, ethnicity, or family origin, can achieve self-fulfillment, honor, and dignity in society if they aim high and work hard.

By contrast, the particularistic version of multiculturalism teaches   5
children that their identity is determined by their "cultural genes." That something in their blood or their race memory or their cultural DNA defines who they are and what they may achieve. That the culture in which they live is not their own culture, even though they were born here. That American culture is "Eurocentric," and therefore hostile to anyone whose ancestors are not European. Perhaps the most invidious implication of particularism is that racial and ethnic minorities are not and should not try to be part of American culture; it implies that American culture belongs only to those who are white and European; it implies that those who are neither white nor European are alienated from American culture by virtue of their race or ethnicity; it implies that the only culture they do belong to or can ever belong to is the culture of their ancestors, even if their families have lived in this country for generations.

The war on so-called Eurocentrism is intended to foster self-esteem among those who are not of European descent. But how, in fact, is self-esteem developed? How is the sense of one's own possibilities, one's potential choices, developed? Certainly, the school curriculum plays a relatively small role as compared to the influence of family, community, mass media, and society. But to the extent that curriculum influences what children think of themselves, it should encourage children of all racial and ethnic groups to believe that they are part of this society and that they should develop their talents and minds to the fullest. It is enormously inspiring, for example, to learn about men and women from diverse backgrounds who overcame poverty, discrimination, physical handicaps, and other obstacles to achieve success in a variety of fields. Behind every such biography of accomplishment is a story of heroism, perseverance, and self-discipline. Learning these stories will encourage a healthy spirit of pluralism, of mutual respect, and of self-respect among children of different backgrounds. The children of American society today will live their lives in a racially and culturally diverse nation, and their education should prepare them to do so.

The pluralist approach to multiculturalism promotes a broader interpretation of the common American culture and seeks due recognition for the ways that the nation's many racial, ethnic, and cultural groups have transformed the national culture. The pluralists say, in effect, "American culture belongs to us, all of us; the U.S. is us, and we remake it in every generation." But particularists have no interest in extending or revising American culture; indeed, they deny that a common culture exists. Particularists reject any accommodation among groups, any interactions that blur the distinct lines between them. The brand of history that they espouse is one in which everyone is either a descendant of victims or oppressors. By doing so, ancient hatreds are fanned and recreated in each new generation. Particularism has its intellectual roots in the ideology of ethnic separatism and in the black nationalist movement. In the particularist analysis, the nation has five cultures: African American, Asian American, European American, Latino/Hispanic, and Native American. The huge cultural, historical, religious, and linguistic differences within these categories are ignored, as is the considerable intermarriage among these groups, as are the linkages (like gender, class, sexual orientation, and religion) that cut across these five groups. No serious scholar would claim that all Europeans and white Americans are part of the same culture, or that all Asians are part of the same culture, or that all people of Latin-American descent are of the same culture, or that all people of African descent are of the same culture. Any categorization this broad is essentially meaningless and useless.

Several districts—including Detroit, Atlanta, and Washington, D.C.— have been developing an Afrocentric curriculum. *Afrocentricity* has been described in a book of the same name by Molefi Kete Asante of Temple University. The Afrocentric curriculum puts Africa at the center of the student's universe. African Americans must "move away from a Eurocentric framework" because "it is difficult to create freely when you use someone else's motifs, styles, images, and perspectives." Because they are not Africans, "white teachers cannot inspire in our children the visions necessary for them to overcome limitations." Asante recommends that African Americans choose an African name (as he did), reject European dress, embrace African religion (not Islam or Christianity) and love "their own" culture. He scorns the idea of universality as a form of Eurocentric arrogance. The Eurocentrist, he says, thinks of Beethoven or Bach as classical, but the Afrocentrist thinks of Ellington or Coltrane as classical; the Eurocentrist lauds Shakespeare or Twain, while the Afrocentrist prefers Baraka, Shange, or Abiola. Asante is critical of black artists like Arthur Mitchell and Alvin Ailey who ignore Afrocentricity. Likewise, he speaks contemptuously of a group of black university students who spurned the Afrocentrism of the local Black Student Union and formed an organization called Inter-race: "Such madness is the direct consequence of self-hatred, obligatory attitudes, false assumptions about society, and stupidity."

The conflict between pluralism and particularism turns on the issue of universalism. Professor Asante warns his readers against the lure of universalism: "Do not be captured by a sense of universality given to you by the Eurocentric viewpoint; such a viewpoint is contradictory to your own ultimate reality." He insists that there is no alternative to Eurocentrism, Afrocentrism, and other ethnocentrisms. In contrast, the pluralist says, with the Roman playwright Terence, "I am a man: nothing human is alien to me." A contemporary Terence would say "I am a person" or might be a woman, but the point remains the same: You don't have to be black to love Zora Neale Hurston's fiction or Langston Hughes's poetry or Duke Ellington's music. In a pluralist curriculum, we expect children to learn a broad and humane culture, to learn about the ideas and art and animating spirit of many cultures. We expect that children, whatever their color, will be inspired by the courage of people like Helen Keller, Vaclav Havel, Harriet Tubman, and Feng Lizhe. We expect that their response to literature will be determined by the ideas and images it evokes, not by the skin color of the writer. But particularists insist that children can learn only from the experiences of people from the same race.

Particularism is a bad idea whose time has come. It is also a fashion 10 spreading like wildfire through the education system, actively promoted by organizations and individuals with a political and professional interest in strengthening ethnic power bases in the university, in the education profession, and in society itself. One can scarcely pick up an educational journal without learning about a school district that is converting to an ethnocentric curriculum in an attempt to give "self-esteem" to children from racial minorities. A state-funded project in a Sacramento high school is teaching young black males to think like Africans and to develop the "African Mind Model Technique," in order to free themselves of the racism of American culture. A popular black rap singer, KRS-One, complained in an op-ed article in the *New York Times* that the schools should be teaching blacks about their cultural heritage, instead of trying to make everyone Americans. "It's like trying to teach a dog to be a cat," he wrote. KRS-One railed about having to learn about Thomas Jefferson and the Civil War, which had nothing to do (he said) with black history.

Pluralism can easily be transformed into particularism, as may be seen in the potential uses in the classroom of the Mayan contribution to mathematics. The Mayan example was popularized in a movie called *Stand and Deliver,* about a charismatic Bolivian-born mathematics teacher in Los Angeles who inspired his students (who are Hispanic) to learn calculus. He told them that their ancestors invented the concept of zero; but that wasn't all he did. He used imagination to put across mathematical concepts. He required them to do homework and to go to school on Saturdays and during the Christmas holidays, so that they might pass the Advanced Placement mathematics examination for college entry. The teacher's reference to the Mayans' mathematical genius was a valid instructional device: It was an attention-getter and would have interested even students who were not Hispanic. But the Mayan example would have had little effect without the teacher's insistence that the class study hard for a difficult examination.

Ethnic educators have seized upon the Mayan contribution to mathematics as the key to simultaneously boosting the ethnic pride of Hispanic children and attacking Eurocentrism. One proposal claims that Mexican-American children will be attracted to science and mathematics if they study Mayan mathematics, the Mayan calendar, and Mayan astronomy.

Children in primary grades are to be taught that the Mayans were first to discover the zero and that Europeans learned it long afterwards from the Arabs, who had learned it in India. This will help them see that Europeans were latecomers in the discovery of great ideas. Botany is to be learned by study of the agricultural techniques of the Aztecs, a subject of somewhat limited relevance to children in urban areas. Furthermore, "ethnobotanical" classifications of plants are to be substituted for the Eurocentric Linnaean system. At first glance, it may seem curious that Hispanic children are deemed to have no cultural affinity with Spain; but to acknowledge the cultural tie would confuse the ideological assault on Eurocentrism.

This proposal suggests some questions: Is there any evidence that the teaching of "culturally relevant" science and mathematics will draw Mexican-American children to the study of these subjects? Will Mexican-American children lose interest or self-esteem if they discover that their ancestors were Aztecs or Spaniards, rather than Mayans? Are children who learn in this way prepared to study the science and mathematics that are taught in American colleges and universities and that are needed for advanced study in these fields? Are they even prepared to study the science and mathematics taught in *Mexican* universities? If the class is half Mexican-American and half something else, will only the Mexican-American children study in a Mayan and Aztec mode or will all the children? But shouldn't all children study what is culturally relevant for them? How will we train teachers who have command of so many different systems of mathematics and science?

The efficacy of particularist proposals seems to be less important to their sponsors than their value as ideological weapons with which to criticize existing disciplines for their alleged Eurocentric bias. In a recent article titled "The Ethnocentric Basis of Social Science Knowledge Production" in the *Review of Research in Education,* John Stanfield of Yale University argues that neither social science nor science are objective studies, that both instead are "Euro-American" knowledge systems which reproduce "hegemonic racial domination." The claim that science and reason are somehow superior to magic and witchcraft, he writes, is the product of Euro-American ethnocentrism. According to Stanfield, current fears about the misuse of science (for instance, "the nuclear arms race, global pollution") and "the power-plays of Third World nations (the Arab oil boycott and the American-Iranian hostage crisis) have made Western people more aware of nonscientific cognitive styles. These last events are beginning to demonstrate politically that which has begun to be understood in intellectual circles: namely, that modes of social knowledge such as theology, science, and magic are different, not inferior or superior. They represent different ways of perceiving, defining, and organizing knowledge of life experiences." One wonders: If Professor Stanfield broke his leg, would he go to a theologian, a doctor, or a magician?

The Responsive Reader

1. What is Ravitch's opening account of the general movement toward recognizing diversity in our society? How convincing is it? Is there anything new or debatable?
2. The turning point of the essay comes when Ravitch talks about the downside of the "clash of cultures." What is the basis of her warnings?
3. The heart of this essay is in the distinctions between *pluralism, particularism,* and *universalism* that the author works out. How does she define these terms? What is the gist of her argument concerning them? What are her objections to "particularism"?
4. Does Ravitch seem to do justice to the current objections to a "Eurocentric" tradition in education or American culture?
5. Extended debate about an issue like multiculturalism is often precipitated by a test case —a much-debated, much-analyzed case in point. Is there such a test case in this essay? What role does it play?

Talking, Listening, Writing

6. How "Eurocentric" or how open to diversity has your own schooling been? How much ethnic or cultural diversity have you seen in the teaching in school or college? (How did you react to this aspect of your educational experience?)
7. What has been your observation of the self-image or self-identity of white ethnics—descendants of European immigrants other than English? (For instance, how Polish and how American are Polish Americans?)

Collaborative Projects

8. Recent years have seen a backlash against the movement toward multiculturalism in American education and society. You may want to work with other students to investigate the phenomenon. If you can, interview faculty or officials with reservations or objections on the subject.

Thinking about Connections

Working with other students, you may want to script and stage an imaginary dialogue between Arturo Madrid and Diane Ravitch on the subject of diversity.

ALONG THE PLATTE

Ursula K. Le Guin

Visitors from abroad are often warned not to confuse frantic New York City or laid-back California with the "real America." Between the two coasts lies the American heartland—with its great working-class cities like Detroit, Chicago, or Milwaukee and with vast stretches of rural America where people still drive their pickup trucks down dirt roads listening to country music. Ursula Le Guin is an intensely curious, observant, and politically active observer of the American scene. A native of Berkeley, California, who studied at Radcliffe and Columbia, she has done battle against machos, pro-lifers, enemies of the environment, censors of books for high school students, world hunger, and obliterators of the Native American past. Le Guin is best-known as a writer of science fiction dealing not in futuristic technology and little green men but using the imaginary future to make us ponder the human condition. However, she often writes about her travels through the American countryside and loves the endangered, semiextinct trains whose lonesome whistles tell about far places. What does she like about what she sees on the trip she describes in the following essay? What does she criticize?

Thought Starters: Are there places that you love? Are there places that you hate? What makes the difference?

Some people fly to Tierra del Fuego and Katmandu; some people   1
drive across Nebraska in a VW bus.

Living in Oregon, with family in Georgia, we drive the United States corner to corner every now and then. It takes a while. On the fifth day out of Macon, just crossing the Missouri, we look up to see a jet trail in the big sky. That plane going west will do two thousand miles while we do two hundred. A strange thought. But the strangeness works both ways. We'll drive about four hundred miles today. On foot with an ox-drawn wagon, that distance would take up to a month.

These are some notes from a day and a half on the Oregon Trail.

About ten in the morning we cross the wide Missouri into the West. Nebraska City looks comfortable and self-reliant, with its railyards and grain elevators over the big brown river. From it we drive out into rolling, spacious farmlands, dark green corn, pale yellow hay stubble, darkening gold wheat. The farmhouses, with big barns and a lot of outbuildings, come pretty close together: prosperous land. The signs say: Polled

Shorthorns . . . Hampshire Swine . . . Charolais . . . Yorkshire and Spotted Swine.

We cross the North Fork of the Little Nemaha. The rivers of America have beautiful names. What was the language this river was named in? Nemaha—Omaha—Nebraska . . . Eastern Siouan, I guess. But it's a guess. We don't speak the language of this country.

Down in the deep shade of trees in high thick grass stand three horses, heads together, tails swishing, two black and one white with black tail and mane. Summertime . . .

Around eleven we're freewaying through Lincoln, a handsome city, the gold dome on its skyscraper capitol shining way up in the pale blue sky, and on our left the biggest grain elevator I ever saw, blocks long, a cathedral of high and mighty cylinders of white. On KECK, Shelley and Dave are singing, "Santa Monica freeway, sometimes makes a country girl blue . . ." After a while the DJ does the announcements. There will be a State Guernsey Picnic on Saturday, if I heard right.

Now we're humming along beside the Platte—there's a language I know. Platte means Flat. It's pretty flat along the Platte, all right, but there are long swells in this prairie, like on the quietest sea, and the horizon isn't forever: it's a blue line of trees way off there, under the farthest line of puffball fair-weather clouds.

We cross some channels of the braided Platte at Grand Island and stop for lunch at a State Wayside Park called Mormon Island, where it costs two bucks to eat your picnic. A bit steep. But it's a pretty place, sloughs or channels of the river on all sides, and huge black dragonflies with silver wingtips darting over the shallows, and blue darning-needles in the grass. The biggest mosquito I ever saw came to eat my husband's shoulder. I got it with my bare hand, but a wrecking ball would have been more appropriate. There used to be buffalo here. They were replaced by the mosquitoes.

On along the Platte, which we're going to cross and recross eleven times in Nebraska and one last time in Wyoming. The river is in flood, running hard between its grey willows and green willows, aspens and big cottonwoods. Some places the trees are up to their necks in water, and west of Cozad the hayfields are flooded, hayrolls rotting in the water, grey-white water pouring through fields where it doesn't belong.

The cattle are in pure herds of Black Angus, Aberdeen, Santa Gertrudis, and some beautiful mixed herds, all shades of cream, dun, brown, roan. There's a Hereford bull in with his harem and descendants, big, frowning, curly-headed, like an angry Irishman.

In 1976 Nebraska commissioned ten sculptures for the roadside rest areas along Interstate 80, and going west you see five of them; we stop at each one to see and photograph it, as does the grey-haired man with two daughters who pose with the sculpture for his photograph. The pieces are all big, imaginative, bold. The one we like best resides in a pond a couple miles west of Kearny. It's aluminum in planes and curves and discs; parts of it are balanced to move softly, without sound; all of it floats on the flickering, reflecting water. It's called *The Nebraska Wind Sculpture.* "What is it?" says a grinning man. I say, "Well, the AAA tourbook says it looks like H. G. Wells's Time Machine." He says, "O.K., but what *is* it?"—and I realize he thinks it may be "something," not "just" a work of art; and so he's looking at it and grinning, enjoying the damfool thing. If he knew it was Art, especially Modern Art, would he be afraid of it and refuse to see it at all? A fearless little boy, meanwhile, haunts the pool and shouts, "Look! A lobster!" pointing at a crayfish, and nearly falls into the scummy shallows reflecting the silver Nebraska Wind.

Down the road a town called Lexington advertises itself:

ALL-AMERICAN CITY
ALL-NEBRASKA COMMUNITY

Those are some kind of national and state awards for something, I suppose, but how disagreeable, how unfriendly and exclusive they sound. But then, what other state of the union thought of celebrating the Bicentennial with big crazy sculptures right out for every stranger driving I-80 to see? Right on, Nebraska!

We pull in for the night at a motel in North Platte, a town that has a rodeo every night of every summer every year, and we sure aren't going to miss that. After dinner we drive out Rodeo Road to Buffalo Bill Avenue to the Cody Arena (by now we have the idea that that old fraud came from around here), and the nice cowgirl selling tickets says, trying to give us a senior citizen savings, "Would you be over sixty at all?" No, we can't manage that yet, so she gives us full-price tickets and a beautiful smile. All the seats are good. It's a warm dry prairie evening, the light getting dusty and long. Young riders on young horses mill around the arena enjoying the attention till the announcer starts the show the way all rodeos start, asking us to salute "the most beautiful flag in the world," a pleasure, while the horses fidget and the flag bearer sits stern, but the announcer goes on about how this flag has been "spat and trampled and mocked and burned on campuses," boy, does he have it in for campuses, what decade is he living in? The poison in his voice is pure Agent Orange. More of this "patriotism" that really means hating somebody. Shut up, please, and let's get on with what all us Americans are here to see—and here to do, for ten bucks prize money.

The first cowboy out of the chute, bareback bronc-riding, gets thrown against the fence, and another gets his leg broken right under the stands. Rodeos are hard on horses, hard on cattle, hard on men. A lousy way to earn ten bucks. Ladies, don't let your sons grow up to be cowboys, as the song says. But the calf-roping is done for the joy of skill, of teamwork, horse and man, and the barrel-riding girls are terrific, whipping around those barrels like the spinning cars on a fairground octopus, and

15

then the quirt flicks and the snorting pony lays out blurry-legged and belly to the ground on the home stretch with the audience yipping and yahooing all the way. By now the lady from Longview, Washington, with the six-pack on the next bench is feeling no pain. A bull is trying to destroy the chutes before the rider even gets onto him. The rodeo is one of the few places where people and animals still fully interact. How vain and gallant horses are, not intelligent, but in their own way wise; how fine the scared, wily vigor of the calves and the power of the big Brahma bulls— the terrific vitality of cattle, which we raise to kill. People who want matadors mincing around can have them, there's enough moments of truth for me in a two-bit rodeo.

Driving back after the show over the viaduct across Bayley Yard, a huge Union Pacific switching center, we see high floodlights far down the line make gold rivers of a hundred intertwining tracks curving off into the glare and dazzling dark. Trains are one of the really good things the Industrial Revolution did—totally practical and totally romantic. But on all those tracks, one train.

Next morning we stop at Ogallala for breakfast at the Pioneer Trails Mall. I like that name. Two eggs up, hashbrowns, and biscuits. The restaurant radio loudspeaker plays full blast over the South Platte River roaring past full of logs and junk and way over the speed limit for rivers.

We leave that river at last near where the Denver road splits off, and come into the low, bare hills across it. As the water dries out of the ground and air, going west, the blur of humidity is gone; colors become clear and pale, distance vivid. Long, light-gold curves of wheat and brown plowed land stripe the hills. At a field's edge the stiff wheat sticks up like a horse's mane cropped short. The wind blows in the tall yellow clover on the roadsides. Sweet air, bright wind. Radio Ogallala says that now is the time to be concerned about the European corn borer.

Between the wheat and corn fields scarped table-lands begin to rise, and dry washes score the pastures. The bones of the land show through, yellowish-white rocks. There's a big stockyard away off the road, the cattle, dark red-brown, crowded together, looking like stacked wood in a lumberyard. Yucca grows wild on the hills here; this is range land. Horses roam and graze far off in the soft-colored distances. We're coming to the Wyoming border, leaving this big, long, wide, bright Nebraska; a day and a half, or forty minutes, or a month in the crossing. From a plane I would remember nothing of Nebraska. From driving I will remember the willows by the river, the sweet wind. Maybe that's what they remembered when they came across afoot and on horseback, and camped each night a few miles farther west, by the willows and the cottonwoods down by the Platte.

The Responsive Reader

1. What are striking sights and sounds that an attentive reader might remember after reading this essay? Of which does the author seem

particularly fond? Which, in the words of one student reader, have a special "Midwest flavor"?

2. Where does Le Guin show her fascination with the names of trees, animals, and rivers? Where does her description show a lively imagination? (For instance, the barrel riders whip around the barrel like spinning cars on a fairground octopus.) What other examples of vivid imaginative comparisons can you find? (What do grain elevators have to do with cathedrals? What do Hereford bulls have to do with Irishmen?)

3. Writers of chamber-of-commerce brochures often seem to love everything about the places they tout. Le Guin is often critical in her essay—where and why? What are her standards? (How does her account of the rodeo show both her love of American popular culture and her criticism of it?)

4. What does Le Guin mean when she calls trains "totally practical and totally romantic"?

5. One student reader said, "Le Guin likes the country, and it is not just a long drive to her." What is the secret of Le Guin's positive relationship to the heartland setting she describes? Is there a common denominator?

Talking, Listening, Writing

6. Would you call the sights and sounds Le Guin describes typically American?

7. Have you had any experience with patriotism that "really means hating somebody"?

8. What kind of traveler are you? Do you have a love-hate relationship with the places and people you visit?

9. Write a guide to a part of the country that you but perhaps not many other people know well. Bring the sights and sounds to life for your reader.

Collaborative Projects

10. Many observers are more critical of the lifestyle of ordinary Americans than Le Guin is. Are you? You may want to scout an example of Americana—American popular culture in its natural habitat. Visit a rodeo, county fair, parade, firefighters' picnic, rock concert, blues festival, or the like. Take notes; bring back a detailed report. Can you draw any general conclusions about heartland America or ordinary Americans? (Your class may want to stage a panel discussion of students pooling their observations of the different events they have scouted.)

A CITY OF NEIGHBORHOODS
Harvey Milk

Harvey Milk was an articulate and influential gay member of the Board of Supervisors in San Francisco, a city of great ethnic and cultural diversity. He represented for many the hope for a tolerant and livable city at a time when the values he stood for were threatened by high-rise development destroying the texture of traditional neighborhoods, by urban decay in areas like the Tenderloin, or by poverty and violence in the projects of Hunters Point. (Milk mentions both these areas of the city in the following speech.) Milk and the popular mayor, George Moscone, were gunned down in City Hall by Dan White, a fellow member of the Board of Supervisors who was engaged in a bitter feud with them. As word of the assassination spread, Milk's admirers and supporters came out into the streets in an outpouring of rage and mourning. The following excerpts from a speech given by Harvey Milk were chosen by Diane Ravitch for her American Reader *(1990).*

Thought Starters: Are your local political leaders representative of their community? Why or why not?

Let's make no mistake about this: The American Dream starts with   1
the neighborhoods. If we wish to rebuild our cities, we must first rebuild our neighborhoods. And to do that, we must understand that the quality of life is more important than the standard of living. To sit on the front steps—whether it's a veranda in a small town or a concrete stoop in a big city—and talk to our neighborhoods is infinitely more important than to huddle on the living-room lounger and watch a make-believe world in not-quite living color.

Progress is not America's only business—and certainly not its most important. Isn't it strange that as technology advances, the quality of life so frequently declines? Oh, washing the dishes is easier. Dinner itself is easier—just heat and serve, though it might be more nourishing if we ate the ads and threw the food away. And we no longer fear spots on our glassware when guests come over. But then, of course, the guests don't come, because our friends are too afraid to come to our house and it's not safe to go to theirs.

And I hardly need to tell you that in that 19- or 24-inch view of the world, cleanliness has long since eclipsed godliness. So we'll all smell, look, and actually be laboratory clean, as sterile on the inside as on the out. The perfect consumer, surrounded by the latest appliances. The perfect audience, with a ringside seat to almost any event in the world, without smell, without taste, without feel—alone and unhappy in the vast wasteland of our living rooms. I think that what we actually need, of course, is a little more dirt on the seat of our pants as we sit on the front stoop and talk to our neighbors once again, enjoying the type of summer day where the smell of garlic travels slightly faster than the speed of sound.

There's something missing in the sanitized life we lead. Something that our leaders in Washington can never supply by simple edict, something that the commercials on television never advertise because nobody's yet found a way to bottle it or box it or can it. What's missing is the touch, the warmth, the meaning of life. A four-color spread in *Time* is no substitute for it. Neither is a 30-second commercial or a reassuring Washington press conference.

I spent many years on both Wall Street and Montgomery Street and I fully understand the debt and responsibility that major corporations owe their shareholders. I also fully understand the urban battlefields of New York and Cleveland and Detroit. I see the faces of the unemployed—and the unemployable—of the city. I've seen the faces in Chinatown, Hunters Point, the Mission, and the Tenderloin . . . and I don't like what I see. 5

Oddly, I'm also reminded of the most successful slogan a business ever coined: The customer is always right.

What's been forgotten is that those people of the Tenderloin and Hunters Point, those people in the streets, are the customers, certainly potential ones, and they must be treated as such. Government cannot ignore them and neither can business ignore them. What sense is there in making products if the would-be customer can't afford them? It's not alone a question of price, it's a question of ability to pay. For a man with no money, 99¢ reduced from $1.29 is still a fortune.

American business must realize that while the shareholders always come first, the care and feeding of their customer is a close second. They have a debt and a responsibility to that customer and the city in which he or she lives, the cities in which the business itself lives or in which it grew up. To throw away a senior citizen after they've nursed you through childhood is wrong. To treat a city as disposable once your business has prospered is equally wrong and even more short-sighted.

Unfortunately for those who would like to flee them, the problems of the cities don't stop at the city limits. There are no moats around our cities that keep the problems in. What happens in New York or San Francisco will eventually happen in San Jose. It's just a matter of time. And like the flu, it usually gets worse the further it travels. Our cities must not be abandoned. They're worth fighting for, not just by those who live in them, but by industry, commerce, unions, everyone. Not alone because they represent the past, but because they also represent the future. Your children will live there and hopefully, so will your grandchildren. For all practical purposes, the eastern corridor from Boston to Newark will be one vast strip city. So will the area from Milwaukee to Gary, Indiana. In California, it will be that fertile crescent of asphalt and neon that stretches from Santa Barbara to San Diego. Will urban blight travel the arteries of the freeways? Of course it will—unless we stop it.

So the challenge . . . will be to awaken the consciousness of industry and commerce to the part they must play in saving the cities which nourished them. Every company realizes it must constantly invest in its own physical plant to remain healthy and grow. Well, the cities are a part of that plant and the people who live in them are part of the cities. They're all connected; what affects one affects the others.

In short, the cheapest place to manufacture a product may not be the cheapest at all if it results in throwing your customers out of work. There's no sense in making television sets in Japan if the customers in the United States haven't the money to buy them. Industry must actively seek to employ those without work, to train those who have no skills. "Labor intensive" is not a dirty word, not every job is done better by machine. It has become the job of industry not only to create the product, but also to create the customer.

Costly? I don't think so. It's far less expensive than the problem of fully loaded docks and no customers. And there are additional returns: lower rates of crime, smaller welfare loads. And having your friends and neighbors sitting on that well-polished front stoop. . . .

Many companies feel that helping the city is a form of charity. I think it is more accurate to consider it a part of the cost of doing business, that it should be entered on the books as amortizing the future. I would like to see business and industry consider it as such, because I think there's more creativity, more competence perhaps, in business than there is in government. I think that business could turn the south of Market Area not only into an industrial park but a neighborhood as well. To coin a pun, too many of our cities have a complex, in fact, too many complexes. We don't need another concrete jungle that dies the moment you turn off the lights in the evening. What we need is a neighborhood where people can walk to work, raise their kids, enjoy life. . . .

The cities will be saved. The cities will be governed. But they won't be run from three thousand miles away in Washington, they won't be run from the statehouse, and most of all, they won't be run by the carpetbaggers who have fled to the suburbs. You can't run a city by people who don't live there, any more than you can have an effective police force made up of people who don't live there. In either case, what you've got is an occupying army. . . .

The cities will not be saved by the people who feel condemned to live in them, who can hardly wait to move to Marin or San Jose—or Evanston or Westchester. The cities will be saved by the people who like it here. The people who prefer the neighborhood stores to the shopping mall, who go to the plays and eat in the restaurants and go to the discos and worry about the education the kids are getting even if they have no kids of their own.

That's not just the city of the future; it's the city of today. It means new directions, new alliances, new solutions for ancient problems. The typical American family with two cars and 2.2 kids doesn't live here anymore. It hasn't for years. The demographics are different now and we all know it. The city is a city of singles and young marrieds, the city of the retired and the poor, a city of many colors who speak in many tongues.

The city will run itself, it will create its own solutions. District elections was not the end. It was just the beginning. We'll solve our problems—with your help, if we can, without it if we must. We need your help. I don't deny that. But you also need us. We're your customers. We're your future.

I'm riding into that future and frankly I don't know if I'm wearing the fabled helm of Mambrino on my head or if I'm wearing a barber's basin. I guess we wear what we want to wear and we fight what we want to fight. Maybe I see dragons where there are only windmills. But something tells me the dragons are for real and if I shatter a lance or two on a whirling blade, maybe I'll catch a dragon in the bargain. . . .

Yesterday, my esteemed colleague on the Board said we cannot live on hope alone. I know that, but I strongly feel the important thing is not that we cannot live on hope alone, but that life is not worth living without it. If the story of Don Quixote means anything, it means that the spirit of life is just as important as its substance. What others may see as a barber's basin, you and I know is that glittering, legendary helmet.

The Responsive Reader

1. Why does Milk ask his listeners to reexamine their ideas about progress? How does he ask business to look at their customers and at the "cost of doing business" in a different new light?
2. Where and how does Milk describe his city in the present? What are essential ingredients in his vision of the future? What is his attitude toward people living in the suburbs?
3. What does Milk mean when he says, "The quality of life is more important than the standard of living"?
4. Does the speaker sound sincere to you? (How can you judge?)

Talking, Listening, Writing

5. Are you inclined to agree that there is "more creativity, more competence perhaps, in business than in government"?
6. Would you call Milk a realist or an idealist? Is he a dreamer? (Who was Don Quixote, and what is the story of the helmet to which Milk alludes?)

7. Where have you encountered some of the warmth and human quality that Milk seeks? Try to bring the settings, the events, or the occasions to life for your listeners or readers.
8. Give some serious thought to one major change or development that would make a difference—that would help your community move into a better future. Do everything you can to convince a skeptical audience of the merit of your choice.

Collaborative Projects

9. Are our cities (or is your city) doomed? Working with a group, look for recent and current statistics that might help provide a partial answer to this question. Interpret your findings for your listeners or readers.

MERICANS

Sandra Cisneros

Millions of Americans come from a Spanish-speaking background. Their families may have had ties with the culture of Mexico or Puerto Rico or Cuba. They may have grown up speaking or hearing Spanish and learned English as a second language. Sandra Cisneros was born of a Mexican father and a Mexican American mother in Chicago. She became one of the country's best-known Chicana—short for Mexicana—authors. For her many readers, the stories in her collection The House on Mango Street *brought to life the Spanish-speaking neighborhoods that are enclaves in many American cities. The following story is from a later collection,* Woman Hollering Creek *(1991). The story focuses on Mexican American children visiting their grandmother in Mexico. How American are they? How Mexican are they?* La Virgen de Guadalupe *is the Virgin Mary of Guadalupe, at whose church the grandmother prays. The PRI is the traditional Mexican ruling party, often criticized by progressives for having abandoned the original ideals of the Mexican revolution.*

Thought Starters: What do you know about Hispanic or Latino Americans from sources other than TV or movies? Does your community have a barrio? Does it have Spanish-language stations or publications?

We're waiting for the awful grandmother who is inside dropping   *1*
pesos into *la ofrenda* box before the altar to La Divina Providencia. Lighting votive candles and genuflecting. Blessing herself and kissing her thumb. Running a crystal rosary between her fingers. Mumbling, mumbling, mumbling.

There are so many prayers and promises and thanks-be-to-God to be given in the name of the husband and the sons and the only daughter who never attend mass. It doesn't matter. Like La Virgen de Guadalupe, the awful grandmother intercedes on their behalf. For the grandfather who hasn't believed in anything since the first PRI elections. For my father, El Periquín, so skinny he needs his sleep. For Auntie Light-skin, who only a few hours before was breakfasting on brain and goat tacos after dancing all night in the pink zone. For Uncle Fat-face, the blackest of the black sheep—*Always remember your Uncle Fat-face in your prayers.* And Uncle Baby—*You go for me, Mamá—God listens to you.*

The awful grandmother has been gone a long time. She disappeared behind the heavy leather outer curtain and the dusty velvet inner. We must stay near the church entrance. We must not wander over to the balloon and punch-ball vendors. We cannot spend our allowance on fried cookies or Familia Burrón comic books or those clear cone-shaped suckers that make everything look like a rainbow when you look through them. We cannot run off and have our picture taken on the wooden ponies. We must not climb the steps up the hill behind the church and chase each other through the cemetery. We have promised to stay right where the awful grandmother left us until she returns.

There are those walking to church on their knees. Some with fat rags tied around their legs and others with pillows, one to kneel on, and one to flop ahead. There are women with black shawls crossing and uncrossing themselves. There are armies of penitents carrying banners and flowered arches while musicians play tinny trumpets and tinny drums.

La Virgen de Guadalupe is waiting inside behind a plate of thick   5 glass. There's also a gold crucifix bent crooked as a mesquite tree when someone once threw a bomb. La Virgen de Guadalupe on the main altar because she's a big miracle, the crooked crucifix on a side altar because that's a little miracle.

But we're outside in the sun. My big brother Junior hunkered against the wall with his eyes shut. My little brother Keeks running around in circles.

Maybe and most probably my little brother is imagining he's a flying feather dancer, like the ones we saw swinging high up from a pole on the Virgin's birthday. I want to be a flying feather dancer too, but when he circles past me he shouts, "I'm a B-Fifty-two bomber, you're a German," and shoots me with an invisible machine gun. I'd rather play flying feather dancers, but if I tell my brother this, he might not play with me at all.

"*Girl*. We can't play with a *girl*." Girl. It's my brothers' favorite insult now instead of "sissy." "You *girl*," they yell at each other. "You throw that ball like a *girl*."

I've already made up my mind to be a German when Keeks swoops past again, this time yelling "I'm Flash Gordon. You're Ming the Merciless and the Mud People." I don't mind being Ming the Merciless, but I don't like being the Mud People. Something wants to come out of the corners of my eyes, but I don't let it. Crying is what *girls* do.

I leave Keeks running around in circles—"I'm the Lone Ranger,   10 you're Tonto." I leave Junior squatting on his ankles and go look for the awful grandmother.

Why do churches smell like the inside of an ear? Like incense and the dark and candles in blue glass? And why does holy water smell of tears? The awful grandmother makes me kneel and fold my hands. The ceiling high and everyone's prayers bumping up there like balloons.

If I stare at the eyes of the saints long enough, they move and wink at me, which makes me a sort of saint too. When I get tired of winking saints, I count the awful grandmother's mustache hairs while she prays for Uncle Old, sick from the worm, and Auntie Cuca, suffering from a life of troubles that left half her face crooked and the other half sad.

There must be a long, long list of relatives who haven't gone to church. The awful grandmother knits the names of the dead and the living into one long prayer fringed with the grandchildren born in that barbaric country with its barbarian ways.

I put my weight on one knee, then the other, and when they both grow fat as a mattress of pins, I slap them each awake. *Micaela, you may wait outside with Alfredito and Enrique.* The awful grandmother says it all in Spanish, which I understand when I'm paying attention. "What?" I say, though it's neither proper nor polite. "What?" which the awful grand-mother hears as "¿Guat?" But she only gives me a look and shoves me toward the door.

After all that dust and dark, the light from the plaza makes me *15* squinch my eyes like if I just came out of the movies. My brother Keeks is drawing squiggly lines on the concrete with a wedge of glass and the heel of his shoe. My brother Junior squatting against the entrance, talking to a lady and man.

They're not from here. Ladies don't come to church dressed in pants. And everybody knows men aren't supposed to wear shorts.

"¿*Quieres chicle?*" the lady asks in a Spanish too big for her mouth.

"*Gracias.*" The lady gives him a whole handful of gum for free, little cellophane cubes of Chiclets, cinnamon and aqua and the white ones that don't taste like anything but are good for pretend buck teeth.

"*Por favor,*" says the lady. ¿*Un foto?*" pointing to her camera.

"*Sí.*" *20*

She's so busy taking Junior's picture, she doesn't notice me and Keeks.

"Hey Michele, Keeks. You guys want gum?"

"But you speak English!"

"Yeah," my brother says, "we're Mericans."

We're Mericans, we're Mericans, and inside the awful grand- *25* mother prays.

The Responsive Reader

1. What makes the "awful grandmother" in the story the representative of the Old Country culture and Old Country ways? What do you learn about her religion—about the church where she worships, about saints and miracles, and about her prayers? Why are there so many "don'ts" in what she tells her grandchildren? Why does she think of Americans as barbarians?
2. Does Cisneros intend the American tourists at the end of the story to be stereotypically American? How does Micaela see them? Is she

making fun of them—if so, why? (Does the tourist lady get any credit for having studied Spanish?)

3. Like many young Americans, Micaela and her brothers are somewhere on the spectrum that runs from the Old Country culture to stereotypically all-American ways. Where on the spectrum would you place them? How "Merican" are they? What is revealing about the names they call each other, their play, their fantasy world, their manners?

Talking, Listening, Writing

4. Students with a Hispanic or Latino background point out that part of the traditional culture is the requirement to be respectful toward your elders. Do you think Micaela, the girl telling the story, is too disrespectful or negative about the grandmother? How far has Micaela gone toward being alienated from the traditional culture?

5. Have you ever felt like one of the "in-between" people—unable to identify fully with what was expected of you as a member of a family or group?

PERSIMMONS

Li-Young Lee

> Li-Young Lee, born to Chinese parents in Indonesia, at an early age fled
> with his family from persecution, moving from country to country in search of
> a place to live and be safe. His family finally came to the United States,
> where his father became a Presbyterian minister in Pennsylvania. Lee pub-
> lished Rose, a book of poems, in 1986. He is one of the best known of a
> new generation of bilingual American poets whose poems often explore the
> meeting of two cultures, two worlds. In the meeting of two worlds in this
> poem, what is the symbolic role of the persimmon (the fruit after which the
> poem is named), the father's scroll paintings in a centuries-old Chinese tradi-
> tion, and the monolingual American teacher?

Thought Starters: What has been your exposure to art or literature from
other cultures?

In sixth grade Mrs. Walker   1
slapped the back of my head
and made me stand in the corner
for not knowing the difference
between *persimmon* and *precision*.   5
How to choose

persimmons. This is precision.
Ripe ones are soft and brown-spotted.
Sniff the bottoms. The sweet one
will be fragrant. How to eat: 10
put the knife away, lay down newspaper.
Peel the skin tenderly, not to tear the meat.
Chew the skin, suck it,
and swallow. Now, eat
the meat of the fruit,   15
so sweet,
all of it, to the heart.

Donna undresses, her stomach is white.
In the yard, dewy and shivering
with crickets, we lie naked,   20
face-up, face-down.

I teach her Chinese.
Crickets: *chiu chiu.* Dew: I've forgotten.
Naked: I've forgotten.
Ni, wo: you and me.   25
I part her legs,
remember to tell her
she is beautiful as the moon.

Other words
that got me into trouble were   30
fight and *fright, wren* and *yarn.*
Fight was what I did when I was frightened,
fright was what I felt when I was fighting.
Wrens are small, plain birds,
yarn is what one knits with.   35
Wrens are soft as yarn.
My mother made birds out of yarn.
I loved to watch her tie the stuff;
a bird, a rabbit, a wee man.

Mrs. Walker brought a persimmon to class   40
and cut it up
so everyone could taste
a *Chinese apple.* Knowing
it wasn't ripe or sweet, I didn't eat
but watched the other faces.   45

My mother said every persimmon has a sun
inside, something golden, glowing,
warm as my face.

Once, in the cellar, I found two wrapped in newspaper,
forgotten and not yet ripe.   50
I took them and set both on my bedroom windowsill,
where each morning a cardinal
sang, *The sun, the sun.*

Finally understanding
he was going blind,   55
my father sat up all one night
waiting for a song, a ghost.
I gave him the persimmons,
swelled, heavy as sadness,
and sweet as love.   60

This year, in the muddy lighting
of my parents' cellar, I rummage, looking
for something I lost.
My father sits on the tired, wooden stairs,
black cane between his knees,   65
hand over hand, gripping the handle.

He's so happy that I've come home.
I ask how his eyes are, a stupid question.
All gone, he answers.

Under some blankets, I find a box.   70
Inside the box I find three scrolls.
I sit beside him and untie
three paintings by my father:
Hibiscus leaf and a white flower.
Two cats preening.   75
Two persimmons, so full they want to drop from the cloth.

He raises both hands to touch the cloth,
asks, *Which is this?*

This is persimmons, Father.

Oh, the feel of the wolftail on the silk,   80
the strength, the tense
precision in the wrist.
I painted them hundreds of times
eyes closed. These I painted blind.
Some things never leave a person: 85
scent of the hair of one you love,
the texture of persimmons,
in your palm, the ripe weight.

The Responsive Reader

1. Like other central symbols in poetry, the persimmon in this poem is
   rich in associations and symbolic significance. How often does the
   fruit come up in the poem? What does the fruit mean to the person
   speaking in the poem? What memories and associations does it bring
   to the speaker's mind?
2. What is the role of the teacher in this poem?
3. What is the poet's relation to the scroll paintings and to his father?
4. How does the poem touch on the difficulties and challenges faced
   by the bilingual student?

Talking, Listening, Writing

5. Can you understand and sympathize with the poet's thoughts and feelings in this poem? Or does the speaker seem a stranger to you?

6. As you look back over your own memories, is there an object, a place, or an event that is rich in symbolic meaning for you? Write about it, bringing memories and associations to life for your reader.

Collaborative Projects

7. Do a Quaker reading of this poem with your classmates. (Someone starts reading a stanza, or group of lines, and then stops, with the neighbor picking up the thread.)

WRITING
WORKSHOP 2

Writing from Interviews

Good writers are often good listeners. Before they speak up themselves, they take in what other people have to say. When official pronouncements or statistics leave key questions unanswered, they talk to people who have relevant information. Before they jump into the fray, they listen and get their bearings. They may listen during the course of informal conversations. Or they may set up formal interviews, leading the interviewee through a series of pointed questions (sometimes submitted in advance). When we read the writing of good listeners, we can see that they know what is involved, what they are up against in promoting a new or different point of view. A writer who knows how to listen can make readers feel that they are not simply being preached at from on high but are being addressed by someone who understands what they think and feel.

TRIGGERING You will often want to talk to someone in the know when you wonder: What's the human meaning of these statistics? What's behind this bland public relations announcement? What's behind official denials or alibis? When someone has been accused of wrongdoing, what is that person's side of the story? Here are some sample questions on which a productive interview (or interviews) might shed light:

- What's behind the faceless current immigration statistics? What brought recent immigrants here from a country like Cambodia, Somalia, or the former Soviet Union?
- Do students from diverse ethnic, racial, or cultural backgrounds feel accepted on your campus?
- What happened when separate men's and women's physical education departments were abolished in colleges? What happened to the women who headed the separate women's departments? What happened to the women's teams?
- How do charges of police brutality look from the other side of the desk—from the point of view of police officers or their superiors?

GATHERING When you write a paper on a subject of public interest, you may get helpful ideas from talking with a roommate, a family member, a teacher, a coworker, or a friend. At times your paper may profit from informal conversations with strangers or an exchange overheard on a bus. However, often the most productive source of information and opinion for a paper may be a formal interview or a series of interviews.

When you first approach people to set up an interview, you may find a natural reluctance to set aside time to talk to a stranger. However, once you explain why you value their input, you may find that people love to be consulted as an authority. Many will go on at length on a subject dear to them. Some of the most informative books about what America is and where it is going are published by writers who get Americans to talk— freely, candidly, from the heart. Classics of this genre include such books as Jonathan Kozol's *Rachel and Her Children,* Robert Coles' *Children of Crisis,* Al Santoli's *The New Immigrants,* and Studs Terkel's *Race.*

You will typically prepare a *set of questions* designed to give focus and direction to an interview. (You should, however, be flexible enough to adapt your prepared questions as promising areas of talk open up.) If you are investigating life after retirement, you might come to an interview with a tentative set of questions like the following:

- Is it true that the elderly are a privileged group in our society?
- What did you do before you retired?
- Were you ready for retirement?
- How or why did you retire?
- What do you think about mandatory retirement?
- What about retirement was least like what you expected or the hardest to handle?
- What was best about retirement?
- What advice would you give people starting to plan for retirement?
- If you could turn the clock back thirty years, what would you do differently?

The following is part of a fact-finding interview. The interviewer asked businesslike, open questions. The student interviewer had heard about the superior academic performance of Asian students, and he went to a math teacher to get an insider's point of view. What kind of questions did the interviewer ask? What is the flow of the questions—does one naturally lead to another? How informative and how straightforward are the answers?

QUESTION: On the average, what percentage of your classes is made up of Asian students?

ANSWER: Well, the lower-level courses have very few, but the higher-level courses have many. Of all the students I've taught during the last five years, maybe forty percent have been Asian.

QUESTION: When you say higher-level courses, what classes are you referring to?
ANSWER: Calculus, trigonometry, differential equations.

QUESTION: As for the students in these higher-level math classes, are most of them American-born Asian students, or were they born in other countries?
ANSWER: Many of my students are immigrants, born in Asia. Many of them have come to this country within the last two to ten years.

QUESTION: Do your Asian students tend to score higher on tests and get better grades than other groups of students?
ANSWER: All of us teachers say the same thing to ourselves and to each other. There are more good grades going to Asians than to any other ethnic, racial, or cultural group.

QUESTION: Do you discuss this trend with your peers on an informal or formal basis, say, in staff or departmental meetings?
ANSWER: We discuss it informally. It's hard to discuss it formally with a chairperson sitting in because it seems almost racist to discuss the subject in those terms. We talk informally about what we have noticed and how we feel.

QUESTION: Have you talked to the students about why they do well?
ANSWER: I get various answers, but it boils down to that they learn to use their minds earlier. I don't think that they are necessarily born with higher intelligence, but they are pushed hard from the earliest years. In their home countries, they had to cram and memorize their books. Their curriculum moved faster, so that by the seventh grade they were doing algebra and by the ninth grade they were doing calculus.

QUESTION: What is the driving force or incentive for their success?
ANSWER: They work a lot harder, although we have to remember that others have dropped out along the way, and we see only the hardest workers or better students. The ones that do reach us do better than their American counterparts. Why? I think culturally they have a great respect for learning and for teachers. At home their parents would never think of saying something critical about a teacher.

Many interviewers today cultivate a more aggressive, participatory interviewing style. They may ask provocative questions designed to draw a cautious interviewee out. They may challenge the answers they receive in order to trigger a vigorous exchange of ideas. In the following excerpt from an interview, Frances Lear, publisher of *Lear's* magazine, prods Kate Michelman, president of the National Abortion Rights League, to take a more aggressive stand.

Question: I think a lot of people are pro-choice intellectually but not emotionally. Is that right?
Answer: That's right. Most people agree that women have the right to choose. But some think that means they have to be in favor of

abortion. There's a lot of ambivalence about abortion. There's a big difference between being pro-abortion and pro-choice.

Question: Well, why don't you clarify it? Why aren't you as articulate as the other side?

Answer: I think we are. But for the past eighteen years our efforts were focused mostly in the courts, while our opposition concentrated on political organizing and on communicating to the public, defining the images and the symbols. We haven't been as graphic as they are.

Question: Why not? The pro-choice movement is loaded with journalists.

Answer: But the other side captured the attention of the media because they were on the offensive and we were on the defensive.

Question: You have been at this for a long, long time. Why haven't you come up with a message just as strong and emotional as the right-to-lifers have? Why are you so pure?

Answer: We're not so pure. But we tried to argue in a rational, legal way, and it made the issue abstract for people. . . . Listen, if I wanted to get really emotional and sensationalistic I could show you pictures of women bleeding to death from illegal abortions.

Question: Why don't you?

Answer: I could show pictures of children with cigarette burns all over their bodies—born unwanted, unloved, which is the critical issue here.

From Lear's, August 1992

SHAPING Most published interviews have been more or less extensively edited. The interviewer may have taken a rambling conversation and concentrated on hot current topics and on statements that seem revealing, provocative, or new. (Sometimes the material has been edited to the point where the interviewee says: "I never said that!")

When you write a paper *integrating* the results of an interview, you have a chance to sort out and rearrange the material. You can use revealing comments by your subject to set the scene or to provide biographical background. You can bring out strongly a connecting thread or recurrent theme. How does the writer of the following student paper use revealing details about the person interviewed? What is the connecting strand or the keynote that the writer used to unify the paper?

Picking Up Garbage

Gabriel was born the youngest of thirteen children. He grew up in the old country and has been in the United States for three years. Every morning he goes to his job in the waste land-fill area. When I ask him about his work, he says: "I used to pick up papers in the area. Everybody starts out with that job. Some people are able to save some money that way. Then they go back to the old country, drink and relax for a few months, and then, when they run out of money, come back here. They will always be picking up papers. I don't want to go back. I drive a truck now, and I crush the garbage. I save money."

I ask him about the place where he lives. He is not living with family. "It is a small place with fifteen people living there. I feel bad because we all sleep together in two rooms. I am the first one to go to work in the morning. So when my alarm goes off at 5:30 A.M., everybody is disturbed. I feel bad that everybody wakes up because of the noise from my alarm. But what can I do? I have to work."

Gabriel spends little time at the place where he "lives." He usually works more than five days and goes to school four evenings a week. What does he like least about his job? He says that he does a lot of thinking while he drives the truck. "You know that the American people throw out many things. Much of it is good stuff. I see toys that are brand new. I see radios that are not broken. I see many things that I would like to send to people in my own country. But I cannot pick up any of the things. There is a rule. The driver is not allowed to get out of the truck."

I assume that the company is trying to protect the drivers' health by not letting them handle items from the garbage cans. But Gabriel says that the rule is intended for the driver's safety: Once a driver who climbed out of the truck to pick up something was run over by another driver who did not see him.

"A few times," Gabriel says, "I have taken the chance of losing my job. I got out and picked up a tape recorder once. I brought it home, and it worked perfectly. The Americans throw away so many things like that. It's like throwing away money. Americans are very rich. The people in my country are very poor. Every day I see good things thrown away, and it breaks my heart to crush them. I am destroying what my people could use."

I am looking at the job of the garbage collector from a different perspective since I talked to Gabriel. I used to think that the filth and the smell would bother me most about the job. I found that what bothers Gabriel most is the idea of looking at "waste" all day.

REVISING AND EDITING A paper drawing on one or more oral or printed sources presents special problems of format and mechanics. In editing your paper, check whether you have made it clear who says what. You will often use **direct quotation**—material quoted verbatim, word for word. Make sure you are copying each quotation exactly. Put all material quoted verbatim in quotation marks. (Remember to close the quotation marks at the point where direct quotation, or verbatim quotation, ends.) You will often use a short credit tag to give the credentials of the person quoted:

DIRECT: Julio Sanchez, legal scholar specializing in immigration law, says, "Any coyote in Tijuana can tell you that illegal immigration is inevitable as long as the gap between rich and poor countries continues to grow."

(A colon may take the place of the comma at the beginning of a formal or especially important quotation.)

When you **paraphrase** what someone said, you put someone else's ideas into your own words. Such **indirect quotation** appears in your paper *without* quotation marks:

> INDIRECT: According to Julio Sanchez, legal scholar specializing in immigration law, any guide helping Mexicans cross the border would tell us that illegal immigrants will keep coming as long as the gap between poverty at home and wealth beyond the border continues to grow.

At times you will use a **block quotation** (or chunk quotation) to present a substantial portion of material (four lines or more). Indent a block quotation *ten* spaces, with no additional indent for an initial paragraph break. (Don't use quotation marks—extra indenting signals direct quotation.)

As one vocal critic of the jargon of Washington insiders has said,

> In the language of today's spin doctors and practitioners of doublespeak, the bottom line is that the window of opportunity that enabled us to push the envelope has developed a downside that will negatively impact the parameters of future growth.

In an effective paper, such block quotations are often used sparingly—at strategic places. For the smooth flow of a paper, make sure that much of your quoted material takes the form of **partial quotation** worked organically into your own text. In revising a paper, look for lumpy passages that might need rewriting to integrate quotations better into your own sentences.

> PARTIAL QUOTATION: "Equestrian sports are ideally suited to become a leading women's sport," Coach Hiernan claims. Women have an "intuitive understanding" with the animals they train, and they have the patience often lacking in male riders, who "tend to force the issue."

Topics for Interview Papers (A Sampling)

1. What is it like to be a refugee? an illegal alien? a recent immigrant?
2. What is it like to be a foreign student on your campus?
3. What is it like to grow up in an orthodox Jewish family? in the Mormon church? in a devout Catholic family? in an atheist family?

4. What is it like to be of African American, Asian American, Latino, or other non-Anglo descent in a predominantly Anglo society?
5. What is it like to be a single parent?
6. What is the self-image of police officers today?
7. How do women athletes feel about the role of women's sports at your school?
8. What is it like to live at the minimum-wage level of income? What is it like to live on welfare? What is it like to be unemployed?
9. What is it like to marry someone from a different cultural, ethnic, or racial background?
10. What is it like to live as an American in a foreign country?

3

Contested History: Rediscovering America

Come, my tan-faced children,
Follow well in order, get your weapons ready;
Have you your pistols? have you your sharp-edged axes?
Pioneers! O Pioneers!

—*Walt Whitman*

Nations look in the mirror of their history to understand who they are. They look for inspiration for what lies ahead. However, what they see in the mirror of history is shaped by the agendas of those who do the writing. American history as told in school books was long the story of explorers discovering a new continent. It was the story of pioneers settling the great empty spaces. It told of great white men with Anglo-Saxon names like Lincoln and Grant and Lee making the speeches and riding great horses to glorious victories or defeats. American history was the story of a new nation civilizing the wilderness, throwing off the chains of the feudal European past.

From the point of view of many immigrants, the story of America has always been the story of the distant golden shore. In America, things would be different. People living in wretched conditions, exploited by greedy landlords or brutalized by repressive governments, dreamed of a country at the end of the rainbow where people could be free and equal. People persecuted because they dissented on minor points of doctrine dreamed of a New Jerusalem where they could worship according to the dictates of their conscience.

Much current rewriting of American history has moved both beyond the gung-ho patriotism of "America-first" historians and the traditional myth of America as the land of promise. Much current writing takes into account the point of view of the conquered, the dispossessed, the enslaved. The tide of white invaders that swept over the Americas did not fill an empty space—"virgin land." In the Caribbean islands, the native population, doomed to extinction by the arrival of Columbus and the Spaniards, is variously estimated to have numbered as much as ten million people. Millions of people were brought to the land of the free in chains to work as slaves. California and the Southwest were Mexican before they were annexed to the United States.

How much of what is in traditional history books is fact? How much is legend or myth? What new countermyths are taking hold? How much of a new revised or "revisionist" history are Americans ready to accept?

I WON'T BE CELEBRATING
COLUMBUS DAY

Suzan Shown Harjo

> *Suzan Shown Harjo is of Cheyenne and Muskogee ancestry. She wrote the following guest column for* Newsweek *as the coordinator of the 1992 Alliance, a coalition of Native American groups. In 1991 plans for celebrating the approaching 500th anniversary, or quincentenary, of Columbus' first voyage to America brought into collision radically different visions of America's past. To those organizing the celebrations, Columbus Day meant an occasion to commemorate the discovery of a new continent, leading eventually to the birth of a new nation. Harjo writes from a very different point of view. She sets out to commemorate the native inhabitants of the "New World," who were subjugated, driven from their lands, stripped of their culture and religion, and decimated by wholesale extermination and the white man's diseases. As you read the following article, do you find yourself taking sides between the "Columbus bashers" and the organizers of "Columbus hoopla"?*

Thought Starters: Are you aware of controversies surrounding Columbus Day, Martin Luther King Day, Presidents' Day, or similar commemorative occasions? What is at issue?

Columbus Day, never on Native America's list of favorite holidays,   *1*
became somewhat tolerable as its significance diminished to little more than a good shopping day. But this long year of Columbus hoopla will be tough to take amid the spending sprees and horn blowing to tout a five-century feeding frenzy that has left Native people and this red quarter of Mother Earth in a state of emergency. For Native people, this half millennium of land grabs and one-cent treaty sales has been no bargain.

An obscene amount of money will be lavished on parades, statues and festivals. The Christopher Columbus Quincentenary Jubilee Commission will spend megabucks to stage what it delicately calls "maritime activities" in Boston, San Francisco and other cities with no connection to the original rub-a-dub-dub lurch across the sea in search of India and gold. Funny hats will be worn and new myths born. Little kids will be told big lies in the name of education.

The pressure is on for Native people to be window dressing for Quincentennial events, to celebrate the evangelization of the Americas and to denounce the "Columbus-bashers." We will be asked to buy into the thinking that we cannot change history, and that genocide and ecocide are offset by the benefits of horses, cut-glass beads, pickup trucks and microwave ovens.

The participation of some Native people will be its own best evidence of the effectiveness of 500 years of colonization, and should surprise no one. But at the same time, neither should anyone be surprised by Native people who mark the occasion by splashing blood-red paint on a Columbus statue here or there. Columbus will be hanged in effigy as a symbol of the European invasion, and tried in planned tribunals.

The United Nations has declared 1993 the "Year of the Indigenous 5 People." Perhaps then we can begin to tell our own stories outside the context of confrontation—begin to celebrate the miracle of survival of those remaining Native people, religions, cultures, languages, legal systems, medicine and values. In the meantime, it should be understood that, even in polite society, voices will be raised just to be heard at all over the din of the celebrators.

Native people will continue marking the 500th anniversary of 1491, the good old days in our old countries. There was life here before 1492— although that period of our history is called "pre-history" in the European and American educational systems.

We would like to turn our attention to making the next 500 years different from the past ones; to enter into a time of grace and healing. In order to do so, we must first involve ourselves in educating the colonizing nations, which are investing a lot not only in silly plans but in serious efforts to further revise history, to justify the bloodshed and destruction, to deny that genocide was committed here and to revive failed policies of assimilation as the answer to progress.

These societies must come to grips with the past, acknowledge responsibility for the present and do something about the future. It does no good to gloss over the history of the excesses of Western civilization, especially when those excesses are the root cause of deplorable conditions today. Both church and state would do well to commit some small pots of gold, gained in ways the world knows, to bringing some relief to the suffering and some measure of justice to all.

The United States could start by upholding its treaty promises—as it is bound to do by the Constitution that calls treaties the "Supreme law of the Land." Churches could start by dedicating money to the eradication of those diseases that Native people still die from in such disproportionately high numbers—hepatitis, influenza, pneumonia, tuberculosis.

Church and state could start defending our religious freedom and 10 stop further destruction of our holy places. The general society could help more of our children grow into healthy adults just by eliminating dehumanizing images of Native people in popular culture. Stereotypes of us as sports mascots or names on leisure vans cannot be worth the low self-esteem they cause.

Native people are few in number—under 2 million in the United States, where there are, even with recent law changes, more dead Indians in museums and educational institutions than there are live ones today. Most of us are in economic survival mode on a daily basis, and many of us are bobbing about in the middle of the mainstream just treading water. This leaves precious few against great odds to do our part to change the world.

It is necessary and well past time for others to amplify our voices and find their own to tell their neighbors and institutions that 500 years of this history is more than enough and must come to an end.

Native people will memorialize those who did not survive the invasion of 1492. It is fitting for others to join us to begin an era of respect and rediscovery.

The Responsive Reader

1. How does Harjo employ the rhetoric of protest, the language of dissent? How are the terms she uses to describe this nation's early history different from what you remember from your schooling or early reading? What grievances does she stress? What are major points in her indictment?
2. For you, is there any part of the article that is particularly telling or thought-provoking? Is there any part that you think is particularly unfair?
3. Which of Harjo's charges and arguments are familiar, and which are new to you?

Talking, Listening, Writing

4. What has been your experience with the current rewriting of American history? Have you encountered examples of history revised to reflect the point of view of the exploited, the dispossessed? Explore the contrast between what you might have been taught earlier and the changes now seen in many courses and textbooks.
5. Would you vote to rename "Columbus Day" and call it "Indigenous People's Day"?

Collaborative Projects

6. The current rethinking of the nation's early history has produced reevaluations of figures like Christopher Columbus, Thomas Jefferson, and Father Junipero Serra. For use in a future research project, you may want to look for a recent book or article on one of these or a similar figure. How do current attitudes compare with earlier, more worshipful ones? (Your class may want to organize a panel discussion to pool findings on one or several of these figures.)

WERE THE SPANIARDS *THAT* CRUEL?

Gregorio Cerio

> *In the following article, a contributor to a special issue of* Newsweek *comes to the defense of his Spanish ancestors, trying to clear them of charges of genocide in the conquered lands of the Americas. He tries to show that history is more complex than acknowledged by those who look for clear-cut confrontations of good and evil. The story of colonization is more involved than current attacks on the European invaders lead us to believe: The Spanish conquistadors conquered in alliance with native tribes rebelling against their Aztec or Inca overlords. The European invaders of the Americas were not united in a common quest; Catholic Spaniards were locked in a murderous struggle with the Protestant English. In Spain the treatment of the natives was a matter of disagreement and debate. (Queen Isabella of Spain liberated and sent back to the West Indies a group of Taino natives that Spaniards had brought back to Spain with them as their property.) How convincing or effective is Cerio's effort to exonerate his forebears? What is his line of defense?*

Thought Starters: What were you taught about the Spanish conquest of the New World?

For the Spanish, the Columbus Quincentennial stirred an ambivalent nostalgia, blending pride and pain. Spain's shining memories of its Golden Age, when the nation stood at the summit of world power, have been tarnished by critics who call the 1492 arrival of the Spanish in the New World "an invasion" fueled by greed and leading to "genocide." In their words, Spaniards hear echoes of age-old malevolence: a body of anti-Spanish prejudices they know as *la leyenda negra,* the Black Legend, that tarred the Spanish as incomparably savage and avaricious. It created a national image that Spain is still trying to dispel.

The Black Legend was born in the 16th century, when Spain controlled the greatest empire the West had ever known, stretching from Holland to Austria to Italy, and westward across the Atlantic to the Americas. The Spanish were prosperous, powerful and smug. And almost everyone else in Europe hated them.

Fearful and envious of Spain but poorer and militarily inferior, rival European nations resorted to a paper war, the first modern propaganda campaign. Throughout the century and beyond it, pamphleteers from London to Frankfurt made malice toward the Spanish a byword of patriotism. Their tracts depicted the Spanish as a people inherently barbaric,

1

corrupt and intolerant; lovers of cruelty and bloodshed. "Tyranny," one 1597 French screed began, "is as proper and natural to a Spaniard as laughter is to a man." Others warned that if Europeans had been outraged by the Inquisition, or by Spain's expulsion of the Jews in 1492 (two centuries, it should be noted, after they were expelled from England), these were kindnesses compared to what Spain did in the Americas. William of Orange, the Dutch nobleman who led the Protestants of Holland in revolt against Spanish authority, railed in 1580 that Spain "committed such horrible excesses that all the barbarities, cruelties and tyrannies ever perpetrated before are only games in comparison to what happened to the poor Indians."

Were the Spanish that bad? Well, there's no reason to print up I LOVE THE CONQUEST bumper stickers. As with most legends, la leyenda negra has some basis in fact. Like many invaders, the Spanish committed horrifying atrocities. But savagery was not the norm for the Spanish, or even commonplace. To understand their conduct in the Americas, one must look at the world as the Spanish did in the 15th century. By their standards, they acted with moderation. When the English and French arrived in the Americas, they systematically drove the natives from their land. The Spanish accepted the Indians into their society—however rudely—and sought to provide a philosophical and moral foundation for their actions in the New World.

If that isn't the history presented in many American schoolbooks,   5
novels and films, it is perhaps because the attitudes of most North Americans are a cultural legacy from the same people—English, German, Dutch, French—who fought Spain for 300 years. Varnished and repeated through those centuries, the Black Legend continues to distort our vision of the past, as well as the present, in repugnant stereotypes of Hispanics in both hemispheres, from the vicious *cholo* to the "lazy wetback."

Politics and religion, those two tinderbox subjects, gave the Black Legend its momentum and its staying power. Rivals like France—where even today Spain is sometimes dismissed with the jeer "Africa begins at the Pyrenees"—resented Spanish domination and coveted its empire. Religion added a more visceral animus. Charles V began his reign as King of Spain in 1517, the same year that Martin Luther launched the Protestant Reformation. He was also Holy Roman Emperor, the anointed protector of Christianity, and saw it as his duty to purge the heresy from the Continent. Leading the bloody Counter-Reformation, Spain fought in Germany in the 1540s, began an 80-year war with Holland in 1568 and sent the disastrous Armada against England in 1588. Protestants saw Spain as the agent of the Devil; its extermination was an article of faith. Opening Parliament in 1656, Oliver Cromwell called Spain the "enemy abroad, who is head of the Papal interest, the head of that anti-Christian interest, that is so described in Scripture . . . and upon this account you have a quarrel with the Spaniard. And truly he hath an interest in your bowels."

Ironically, it was Spain's sense of religious mission, and the broad freedom of speech it permitted in its colonies, that helped foster the Black Legend. From Ferdinand onward, Spanish monarchs encouraged candid reports, favorable or unfavorable, on conditions in the Americas. One of the most tireless critics of Spanish rule was a Dominican bishop, Bartolomé de Las Casas, who worked for 50 years to improve the treatment of the Indians. A skilled politician, in 1552 he published a passionate tract called "A Brief Account of the Destruction of the Indies." In graphic and sometimes exaggerated detail, he recounted Spanish cruelties to the Indians, describing, in one instance, how Spaniards hanged natives in groups of 13, "thus honoring our Redeemer and the twelve apostles," then lit fires beneath them.

Spain's enemies ate it up. In the next 100 years, 42 editions of Las Casas's "Brief Account" appeared in Germany, France, Holland and England, some illustrated with lurid engravings by the Dutch artist Theodore DeBry, who had never crossed the Atlantic. One English edition was subtitled "A Faithful Narrative of the Horrid and Unexampled Massacres, Butcheries, and all Manner of Cruelties that Hell and Malice could invent, committed by the Popish Spanish." A U.S. edition of Las Casas was even published in 1898, to bolster support for the Spanish–American War.

Yet, as historian William Maltby points out, "the most powerful indictment of Spain's cruelty and avarice is at the same time a monument to its humanitarianism and sense of justice." Las Casas, other Spanish clergy and their sympathizers were not lonely do-gooders. They embodied a Spanish moral impulse that led the royal court to conduct a soul-searching ethical inquiry into the Spanish Conquest throughout the 16th century. "Spain was constantly debating with itself: 'Am I right, am I wrong? What is it I'm doing with these peoples?'" notes Mexican writer Carlos Fuentes in his television documentary "The Buried Mirror: Reflections on Spain and the New World."

From the beginning of their conquest, the Spanish recognized the   10 need to mediate between the conflicting demands of Christianity and profit. Bernal Díaz, a soldier in the army of Cortés who later wrote a history of the conquest of Mexico, explained the motives of the conquistadors: "We came here to serve God, and also to get rich." It is easy to view the former as a rationale for the latter. But the 16th-century Spanish lived in an age of devotion, when every aspect of life was examined through the lens of religious faith. Spaniards believed they offered the Indians a gift worth any earthly pain: eternal life in heaven.

God had ordained a social hierarchy, most Renaissance Spaniards thought. They accepted Aristotle's concept of "natural slavery"—that large masses of humanity are simply born to serve. The papacy sanctioned slavery and was a large slaveholder. But where the Indians fit in the ranks of mankind baffled the Spanish.

Early on, Isabella of Castile established the policy that Indians who accepted Christianity were free crown subjects. (Those who didn't could be sold into slavery.) But like other subjects, they were expected to pay royal tribute, which could be extracted in the form of labor. With so few colonists, Indian labor was a necessity, but one which, Isabella's counselors reasoned, could teach the natives useful habits of industry. The Spanish devised the *encomienda,* a labor system intended as a sort of trusteeship. A deserving Spaniard was given Indians to use for mining gold or silver or growing cash crops. In return, he would feed the Indians, provide for their instruction in the faith and defend them.

That was the theory. In practice the encomienda varied with the agenda of each Spaniard. Most conquistadors were ex-soldiers, merchants, craftsmen, ex-convicts—"nobodies who wanted to become somebodies," as historian L. B. Simpson put it. Those who wanted to get rich quick and return to Spain drove the Indians hard. Others saw the New World as a permanent home and the Indians as future clients who should be treated well. The encomienda was always, if sometimes only marginally, better than outright slavery. "The people remained in a community even if they were exploited," explains Yale historian David Brion Davis. "They had a certain cultural integrity; their family structure and customs weren't, for the most part, interfered with."

Out of Christian duty, and to keep a close rein on its New World colonies, the Spanish throne consistently ordained that the natives be treated with humane respect. In 1512, Ferdinand's Laws of Burgos provided, among other things, that "no Indian shall be whipped or beaten or called 'dog' or any other name, unless it is his proper name." These and later laws were often ignored or watered down, but under them many Spaniards were punished for mistreating Indians.

Spanish monarchs were also willing to experiment with new systems of government and labor. Las Casas was given a chance to convert an area of Guatemala without the interference of soldiers and met with mixed success. There were four separate, failed experiments on Caribbean islands to see if, given the tools, Indians could live alone like civilized people— that is, like Spaniards. In 1530, Vasco de Quiroga, a Mexican bishop, established a cooperative society in Michoacán, with communal property and what we would call social-welfare benefits.

If these experiments treated the natives as naive children, that is perhaps no more offensive than today's tendency to believe the Indians were helpless before the Spanish. In fact, they were quite resourceful, argues historian Steve Stern: "Indigenous peoples shaped everyday life and social structures much more than our stereotyped imagery would have it." Cortés could not have conquered Mexico without the aid of tribes dominated by the Aztecs. For their help, these natives happily accepted titles, coats of arms and encomiendas from the Spanish crown. The encomienda itself was molded by tributary labor practices long established among the Indians. In many regions, Indians dictated to Spaniards the form and amount of payment to be given. A group of Peruvian Indian chiefs hired a lawyer and sailed to Spain in the 1560s to make a case before Philip II for curtailing

15

the encomienda. In the best political tradition, they even offered him a bribe. "Indians entered into the Spanish legal system to use it for their own purposes," says Stern. "And to some effect."

Always a legalistic people, the Spanish created General Indian Courts where the natives aired their grievances. As historian Philip Wayne Powell wrote, "Spaniards did not try to impose upon America something hypo-critically foreign or inferior to what they lived with at home." Spain's rulers taxed the New World colonists less heavily than their European subjects. In America, the Spanish built schools—23 universities in the New World—that graduated white, mestizo and Indian alike, along with some blacks. They established hospitals to provide the Indians with medical care, such as it was in the era of barber-surgeons and leeches.

If only for economic reasons, the Spanish cared deeply for the welfare of the natives. "Genocide," in fact, may be the unfairest of all the accusa-tions leveled at Spain—if the term is used in its proper sense, to describe the intentional, systematic eradication of a race. Millions of Indians died after the arrival of the Spanish. But a host of pestilences brought from Europe wiped out the vast majority, not war or abuse. The whole of Spain's treatment of the Indians seems almost beneficent compared with the way other colonial powers dealt with natives. "The Spanish made a place for the Indians—as part of the lowest order, but at least they had a place," says Woodrow Borah of the University of California, Berkeley. "North Americans in many cases simply exterminated the Indians." The Spanish mingled with the Indians, at times with the encouragement of the crown. "The Spanish were conquered in turn by those they conquered," says Mexican poet Homero Aridjis. The marriage of blood and cultures created *la raza*—the new mestizo people who compose most of today's Latin Americans. North America, where the natives were excluded, driven off their land and eventually hunted down, remained white. The United States elected several presidents—Andrew Jackson, William Henry Harri-son, Zachary Taylor—who first made a name for themselves as Indian fighters. It is a piece of our heritage that may help explain the potency of U.S. racism.

Spain invested millions worldwide in Columbus Quincentennial pro-jects, still hoping to escape the distortions of the Black Legend. But if the 16th-century Spanish can be granted motives beyond profit, they appear no worse—and often far better—than the nations who castigated them for their sins. Spain committed terrible deeds while bringing "the light of Christianity" to the New World. But history offers no shortage of acts of cruelty performed in the service of religious, social, political and economic ideals. Susan Milbrath, a Florida museum curator whose recent Quincentennial exhibit was greeted with pickets, asks why people concentrate on the morality of Columbus and the Spanish: "The big question to me is, are *human beings* good?" The Black Legend casts a shadow on us all.

The Responsive Reader

1. How real do the ancient religious quarrels between Catholic Spain and Protestant European countries become in this account? What are key historical facts? What are interesting sidelights?
2. How convincing is Cerio's defense or rehabilitation of Spain's role in the New World? What, according to him, were the contemporary justifications or rationalizations for Spain's behavior in the new territories? What is the evidence he presents for soul-searching and humane objectives on the part of the Spaniards?
3. How much of a case does Cerio build for his claim that other colonial powers treated Native Americans worse than the Spaniards did?

Talking, Listening, Writing

4. Does the Cerio article change your mind? In what ways does it make you revise your own thinking?
5. Do you think there is a possible middle ground between the anti-Columbus and the pro-Columbus factions?
6. What have been your opportunities to study and understand the "marriage of blood and cultures" that Cerio calls *la raza*? (How do Spanish-speaking Americans feel about the labels *Hispanic* and *Latino*?)

Collaborative Projects

7. Writers including Octavio Paz, Pablo Neruda, Carlos Fuentes, and Richard Rodriguez have written about the joint Spanish and Indian heritage of Latin America. You may want to look for commentary on the mestizo heritage in the writings of one such writer and report your findings to your classmates.

Thinking about Connections

For you, does Cerio provide a satisfactory answer to the charges brought by Harjo in "I Won't Be Celebrating Columbus Day"? How strong or convincing is his defense?

THE EARTH IS ALL THAT LASTS

Black Elk

> *The following selection tells the story of General Custer's Last Stand from the point of view of a young Lakota fighting on the other side. Custer had served on the Union side in the American Civil War and assumed command of the U.S. Seventh Cavalry in 1866. A few years later, he destroyed an Indian camp after the people there had been promised safety by a military agent. He had a son by a girl who was taken captive there, along with other Cheyenne women and children. Black Elk, who is speaking in this selection, was a teenage boy when Custer, or "Long Hair," with his soldiers (the Wasichus of the story) attacked a large Sioux encampment on the Little Big Horn in 1876. In the ensuing fight, Custer and many of his soldiers lost their lives. Black Elk, a Lakota holy man, told his story many years later when living as a lonely old man in a one-room log cabin among barren hills. John G. Neihardt, who recorded Black Elk's story, was the author of books and poems about Native Americans and the American West.*

Thought Starters: What shaped your ideas about the role of the U.S. military in the conquest of the West? Have you recently seen movies or read books that made you reexamine your ideas about Native Americans and the U.S. Cavalry?

It was the next summer, when I was eleven years old (1874), that the first sign of a new trouble came to us. Our band had been camping on Split-Toe Creek in the Black Hills; and from there we moved to Spring Creek, then to Rapid Creek where it comes out into the prairie. That evening just before sunset, a big thundercloud came up from the west, and just before the wind struck, there were clouds of splittail swallows flying all around above us. . . . The boys tried to hit the swallows with stones and it hurt me to see them doing this, but I could not tell them. I got a stone and acted as though I were going to throw, but I did not. The swallows seemed holy. Nobody hit one, and when I thought about this I knew that of course they could not.

The next day some of the people were building a sweat tepee for a medicine man by the name of Chips, who was going to perform a ceremony and had to be purified first. They say he was the first man who made a sacred ornament for our great chief, Crazy Horse. While they were heating the stones for the sweat tepee, some boys asked me to go with them to shoot squirrels. We went out, and when I was about to shoot at one, I felt very uneasy all at once. So I sat down, feeling queer, and wondered about it. While I sat there I heard a voice that said: "Go at once! Go home!" I told the boys we must go home at once, and we all hurried. When we got back, everybody was excited, breaking camp, catching the ponies, and loading the drags; and I heard that while Chips was in the sweat tepee a voice had told him that the band must flee at once because something was going to happen there.

It was nearly sundown when we started, and we fled all that night on the back trail toward Spring Creek, then down that creek to the south fork of the Good River. I rode most of the night in a pony drag because I got too sleepy to stay on a horse. We camped at Good River in the morning, but we stayed only long enough to eat. Then we fled again, upstream, all day long until we reached the mouth of Horse Creek. We were going to stay there, but scouts came to us and said that many soldiers had come into the Black Hills; and that was what Chips saw while he was in the sweat tepee. So we hurried on in the night towards Smoky Earth River (the White), and when we got there, I woke up and it was daybreak. We camped a while to eat, and then went up the Smoky Earth, two camps, to Robinson, for we were afraid of the soldiers up there.

Afterward I learned that it was Pahuska (Long Hair, General Custer) who had led his soldiers into the Black Hills that summer to see what he could find. He had no right to go in there, because all that country was ours. Also the Wasichus had made a treaty with Red Cloud (1868) that said it would be ours as long as grass should grow and water flow. Later I learned too that Pahuska had found there much of the yellow metal that makes the Wasichus crazy; and that is what made the bad trouble, just as it did before, when the hundred were rubbed out.

Our people knew there was yellow metal in little chunks up there; but they did not bother with it, because it was not good for anything.   5

We stayed all winter at the Soldiers' Town,[1] and all the while the bad trouble was coming fast; for in the fall we heard that some Wasichus had come from the Missouri River to dig in the Black Hills for the yellow metal, because Pahuska had told about it with a voice that went everywhere. Later he got rubbed out for doing that.

The people talked about this all winter. Crazy Horse was in the Powder River country and Sitting Bull was somewhere north of the Hills. Our people at the Soldiers' Town thought we ought to get together and do something. Red Cloud's people said that the soldiers had gone in there to keep the diggers out, but we, who were only visiting, did not believe it. We called Red Cloud's people "Hangs-Around-the-Fort," and our people said they were standing up for the Wasichus, and if we did not do something we should lose the Black Hills.

---

[1][Soldiers' Town: Fort Robinson, in western South Dakota.]

In the spring when I was twelve years old (1875), more soldiers with many wagons came up from the Soldiers' Town at the mouth of the Laramie River and went into the Hills.

There was much talk all summer, and in the Moon of Making Fat (June) there was a sun dance there at the Soldiers' Town to give the people strength, but not many took part; maybe because everybody was so excited talking about the Black Hills. I remember two men who danced together. One had lost a leg in the Battle of the Hundred Slain and one had lost an eye in the Attacking of the Wagons, so they had only three eyes and three legs between them to dance with. We boys went down to the creek while they were sun dancing and got some elm leaves that we chewed up and threw on the dancers while they were all dressed up and trying to look their best. We even did this to some of the older people, and nobody got angry, because everybody was supposed to be in a good humor and to show their endurance in every kind of way; so they had to stand teasing too.

In the Moon When the Calves Grow Hair (September) there was a   *10* big council with the Wasichus on the Smoky Earth River at the mouth of White Clay Creek. I can remember the council, but I did not understand much of it then. Many of the Lakotas were there, also Shyelas and Blue Clouds (Cheyennes and Arapahoes); but Crazy Horse and Sitting Bull stayed away. In the middle of the circle there was a shade made of canvas. Under this the councilors sat and talked, and all around them there was a crowd of people on foot and horseback. They talked and talked for days, but it was just like wind blowing in the end. I asked my father what they were talking about in there, and he told me that the Grandfather at Washington wanted to lease the Black Hills so that the Wasichus could dig yellow metal, and that the chief of the soldiers had said if we did not do this, the Black Hills would be just like melting snow held in our hands, because the Wasichus would take that country anyway.

It made me sad to hear this. It was such a good place to play and the people were always happy in that country. . . .

After the council we heard that creeks of Wasichus were flowing into the Hills and becoming rivers, and that they were already making towns up there. It looked like bad trouble coming, so our band broke camp and started out to join Crazy Horse on Powder River. We camped on Horse-head Creek, then on the War Bonnet after we crossed the old Wasichu's road[2] that made the trouble that time when the hundred were rubbed out. Grass was growing on it. Then we camped at Sage Creek, then on the Beaver, then on Driftwood Creek, and came again to the Plain of Pine Trees at the edge of the Hills.

The nights were sharp now, but the days were clear and still; and while we were camping there I went up into the Hills alone and sat a long

---

[2][Wasichu's road: the Bozeman Trail, which began in Colorado and went to the mining town of Virginia, in Montana.]

while under a tree. I tried to think how I could save that country for my people, but I could not see anything clear.

This made me sad, but something happened a few days later that made me feel good. We had gone over to Taking-the-Crow-Horses Creek, where we found many bison and made plenty of meat and tanned many hides for winter. In our band there was a man by the name of Fat, who was always talking about how fast his horse could run. One day while we were camping there I told Fat my pony could run faster than his could, and he laughed at me and said that only crows and coyotes would think my pony was any good. I asked him what he would give me if my pony could beat his, and he said he would give me some black medicine (coffee). So we ran, and I got the black medicine.

On Kills-Himself Creek we made more meat and hides and were ready to join Crazy Horse's camp on the Powder. There were some Hang-Around-the-Fort people with us, and when they saw that we were going to join Crazy Horse, they left us and started back to the Soldiers' Town. They were afraid there might be trouble, and they knew Crazy Horse would fight, so they wanted to be safe with the Wasichus. We did not like them very much.

After a while we came to the village on Powder River and went into camp at the downstream end. I was anxious to see my cousin, Crazy Horse, again, for now that it began to look like bad trouble coming, everybody talked about him more than ever and he seemed greater than before. . . .

Now and then he would notice me and speak to me; and sometimes he would have the crier call me into his tepee to eat with him. Then he would say things to tease me, but I would not say anything back, because I think I was a little afraid of him. I was not afraid that he would hurt me; I was just afraid. Everybody felt that way about him, for he was a queer man and would go about the village without noticing people or saying anything. In his own tepee he would joke, and when he was on the warpath with a small party, he would joke to make his warriors feel good. But around the village he hardly ever noticed anybody, except little children. All the Lakotas like to dance and sing; but he never joined a dance, and they say nobody ever heard him sing. But everybody liked him, and they would do anything he wanted or go anywhere he said. He was a small man among the Lakotas, and he was slender and had a thin face and his eyes looked through things, and he always seemed to be thinking hard about something. He never wanted to have many things for himself, and did not have many ponies like a chief. They say that when game was scarce and the people were hungry, he would not eat at all. . . .

Crazy Horse kept his village on Powder River with about a hundred tepees, and our band made camp on the Tongue. We built a corral of poles for the horses at night and herded them all day, because the Crows were great horsethieves and we had to be careful. The women chopped and

15

stripped cottonwood trees during the day and gave the bark to the horses at night. The horses liked it and it made them sleek and fat.

When we camped again, one of Red Cloud's loafers who had started back for the Soldiers' Town because they were afraid there might be trouble, came in and said the Crows had killed all his party except himself, while they were sleeping, and he had escaped because he was out scouting.

During the winter, runners came from the Wasichus and told us we   20 must come into the Soldiers' Town right away or there would be bad trouble. But it was foolish to say that, because it was very cold and many of our people and ponies would have died in the snow. Also, we were in our own country and were doing no harm.

Late in the Moon of the Dark Red Calves (February) there was a big thaw, and our little band started for the Soldiers' Town, but it was very cold again before we got there. Crazy Horse stayed with about a hundred tepees on Powder, and in the middle of the Moon of the Snowblind (March) something bad happened there. It was just daybreak. There was a blizzard and it was very cold. The people were sleeping. Suddenly there were many shots and horses galloping through the village. It was the cavalry of the Wasichus, and they were yelling and shooting and riding their horses against the tepees. All the people rushed out and ran, because they were not awake yet and they were frightened. The soldiers killed as many women and children and men as they could while the people were running toward a bluff. Then they set fire to some of the tepees and knocked the others down. But when the people were on the side of the bluff, Crazy Horse said something, and all the warriors began singing the death song and charged back upon the soldiers; and the soldiers ran, driving many of the people's ponies ahead of them. Crazy Horse followed them all that day with a band of warriors, and that night he took all the stolen ponies away from them, and some of their own horses, and brought them all back to the village.

These people were in their own country and were doing no harm. They only wanted to be let alone. We did not hear of this until quite a while afterward; but at the Soldiers' Town we heard enough to make us paint our faces black.

We stayed at the Soldiers' Town this time until the grass was good in the Moon When the Ponies Shed (May). Then my father told me we were going back to Crazy Horse and that we were going to have to fight from then on, because there was no other way to keep our country. He said that Red Cloud was a cheap man and wanted to sell the Black Hills to the Wasichus; that Spotted Tail and other chiefs were cheap men too, and that the Hang-Around-the-Fort people were all cheap and would stand up for the Wasichus. My aunt, who was living at the Soldiers' Town, must have felt the way we did, because when we were breaking camp she gave me a six-shooter like the soldiers had, and told me I was a man now. I was thirteen years old and not very big for my age, but I thought I should have to be a man anyway. We boys had practiced endurance, and we were all good riders, and I could shoot straight with either a bow or a gun.

We were a small band, and we started in the night and traveled fast. Before we got to War Bonnet Creek, some Shyelas joined us, because their hearts were bad like ours and they were going to the same place. Later I learned that many small bands were doing the same thing and coming together from everywhere.

Just after we camped on the War Bonnet, our scouts saw a wagon train of the Wasichus coming up the old road that caused the trouble before.[3] They had oxen hitched to their wagons and they were part of the river of Wasichus that was running into the Black Hills. They shot at our scouts, and we decided we would attack them. When the war party was getting ready, I made up my mind that, small as I was, I might as well die there, and if I did, maybe I'd be known. I told Jumping Horse, a boy about my age, that I was going along to die, and he said he would too. So we went, and so did Crab and some other boys.

When the Wasichus saw us coming, they put their wagons in a circle and got inside with their oxen. We rode around and around them in a wide circle that kept getting narrower. That is the best way to fight, because it is hard to hit ponies running fast in a circle. And sometimes there would be two circles, one inside the other, going fast in opposite directions, which made us still harder to hit. The cavalry of the Wasichus did not know how to fight. They kept together, and when they came on, you could hardly miss them. We kept apart in the circle. While we were riding around the wagons, we were hanging low on the outside of the ponies and shooting under their necks. This was not easy to do, even when your legs were long, and mine were not yet very long. But I stuck tight and shot with the six-shooter my aunt gave me. Before we started the attack I was afraid, but Big Man told us we were brave boys, and I soon got over being frightened. The Wasichus shot fast at us from behind the wagons, and I could hear bullets whizzing, but they did not hit any of us. I do not know whether we killed any Wasichus or not. We rode around several times, and once we got close, but there were not many of us and we could not get at the Wasichus behind their wagons; so we went away. This was my first fight. When we were going back to camp, some Shyela warriors told us we were very brave boys, and that we were going to have plenty of fighting.

We were traveling very fast now, for we were in danger and wanted to get back to Crazy Horse. He had moved over west to the Rosebud River, and the people were gathering there. As we traveled, we met other little bands all going to the same place, until there were a good many of us all mixed up before we got there. Red Cloud's son was with us, but Red Cloud stayed at the Soldiers' Town.

[3][the old road: the Bozeman Trial. The Indians opposed the use of it by gold seekers.]

When we came to the ridge on this side of the Rosebud River, we could see the valley full of tepees, and the ponies could not be counted. Many, many people were there—Oglalas, Hunkpapas, Minneconjous, Sans Arcs, Blackfeet, Brules, Santees, and Yanktonais; also many Shyelas and Blue Clouds had come to fight with us. The village was long, and you could not see all the camps with one look. The scouts came out to meet us and bring us in, and everybody rejoiced that we had come. Great men were there: Crazy Horse and Big Road of the Oglalas; Sitting Bull and Gall and Black Moon and Crow King of the Hunkpapas; Spotted Eagle of the Sans Arcs; the younger Hump and Fast Bull of the Minneconjous; Dull Knife and Ice Bear of the Shyelas; Inkpaduta with the Santees and Yanktonais. Great men were there with all those people and horses. Hetchetu aloh! [It is so indeed!]

About the middle of the Moon of Making Fat (June) the whole village moved a little way up the River to a good place for a sun dance. The valley was wide and flat there, and we camped in a great oval with the river flowing through it, and in the center they built the bower of branches in a circle for the dancers, with the opening of it to the east whence comes the light. Scouts were sent out in all directions to guard the sacred place. Sitting Bull, who was the greatest medicine man of the nation at that time, had charge of this dance to purify the people and to give them power and endurance. It was held in the Moon of Fatness because that is the time when the sun is highest and the growing power of the world is strongest. I will tell you how it was done.

First a holy man was sent out all alone to find the *waga chun,* the holy tree that should stand in the middle of the dancing circle. Nobody dared follow to see what he did or hear the sacred words he would say there. And when he had found the right tree, he would tell the people, and they would come there singing, with flowers all over them. Then when they had gathered about the holy tree, some women who were bearing children would dance around it, because the Spirit of the Sun loves all fruitfulness. After that a warrior, who had done some very brave deed that summer, struck the tree, counting coup upon it; and when he had done this, he had to give gifts to those who had least of everything, and the braver he was, the more he gave away. *30*

After this, a band of young maidens came singing, with sharp axes in their hands; and they had to be so good that nobody there could say anything against them, or that any man had ever known them; and it was the duty of anyone who knew anything bad about any of them to tell it right before all the people there and prove it. But if anybody lied, it was very bad for him.

The maidens chopped the tree down and trimmed its branches off. Then chiefs, who were the sons of chiefs, carried the sacred tree home, stopping four times on the way, once for each season, giving thanks for each.

Now when the holy tree had been brought home but was not yet set up in the center of the dancing place, mounted warriors gathered around the circle of the village, and at a signal they all charged inward upon the center where the tree would stand, each trying to be the first to touch the sacred place; and whoever was the first could not be killed in war that year. When they all came together in the middle, it was like a battle, with the ponies rearing and screaming in a big cloud of dust and the men shouting and wrestling and trying to throw each other off the horses.

After that there was a big feast and plenty for everybody to eat, and a big dance just as though we had won a victory.

The next day the tree was planted in the center by holy men who sang sacred songs and made sacred vows to the Spirit. And the next morning nursing mothers brought their holy little ones to lay them at the bottom of the tree, so that the sons would be brave men and the daughters the mothers of brave men. The holy men pierced the ears of the little ones, and for each piercing the parents gave away a pony to someone who was in need.   35

The next day the dancing began, and those who were going to take part were ready, for they had been fasting and purifying themselves in the sweat lodges, and praying. First, their bodies were painted by the holy men. Then each would lie down beneath the tree as though he were dead, and the holy men would cut a place in his back or chest, so that a strip of rawhide, fastened to the top of the tree, could be pushed through the flesh and tied. Then the man would get up and dance to the drums, leaning on the rawhide strip as long as he could stand the pain or until the flesh tore loose.

We smaller boys had a good time during the two days of dancing, for we were allowed to do almost anything to tease the people, and they had to stand it. We would gather sharp spear grass, and when a man came along without a shirt, we would stick him to see if we could make him cry out, for everybody was supposed to endure everything. Also we made popguns out of young ash boughs and shot at the men and women to see if we could make them jump; and if they did, everybody laughed at them. The mothers carried water to their holy little ones in bladder bags, and we made little bows and arrows that we could hide under our robes so that we could steal up to the women and shoot holes in the bags. They were supposed to stand anything and not scold us when the water spurted out. We had a good time there.

Right after the sun dance was over, some of our scouts came in from the south, and the crier went around the circle and said: "The scouts have returned and they have reported that soldiers are camping up the river. So, young warriors, take courage and get ready to meet them."

While they were all getting ready, I was getting ready too, because Crazy Horse was going to lead the warriors and I wanted to go with him; but my uncle, who thought a great deal of me, said: "Young nephew, you must not go. Look at the helpless ones. Stay home, and maybe there will be plenty of fighting right here." So the war parties went on without me. Maybe my uncle thought I was too little to do much and might get killed.

Then the crier told us to break camp, and we moved over west   40 towards the Greasy Grass (Little Big Horn) and camped at the head of Spring Creek while the war parties were gone. We learned later that it was Three Stars (General Crook) who fought with our people on the Rosebud that time. He had many walking soldiers and some cavalry, and there were many Crows and Shoshones with him. They were all coming to attack us where we had the sun dance, but Crazy Horse whipped them and they went back to Goose Creek where they had all their wagons.

Crazy Horse whipped Three Stars on the Rosebud that day, and I think he could have rubbed the soldiers out there. He could have called many more warriors from the villages and he could have rubbed the soldiers out at daybreak, for they camped there in the dark after the fight.

He whipped the cavalry of Three Stars when they attacked his village on the Powder that cold morning in the Moon of the Snowblind (March). Then he moved farther west to the Rosebud; and when the soldiers came to kill us there, he whipped them and made them go back. Then he moved farther west to the valley of the Greasy Grass. We were in our own country all the time and we only wanted to be let alone. The soldiers came there to kill us, and many got rubbed out. It was our country and we did not want to have any trouble.

We camped there in the valley along the south side of the Greasy Grass before the sun was straight above; and this was, I think, two days before the battle. It was a very big village and you could hardly count the tepees. Farthest up the stream toward the south were the Hunkpapas, and the Oglalas were next. Then came the Minneconjous, the Sans Arcs, the Blackfeet, the Shyelas; and last, the farthest toward the north, were the Santees and Yanktonais. Along the side towards the east was the Greasy Grass, with some timber along it, and it was running full from the melting of the snow in the Big Horn Mountains. If you stood on a hill you could see the mountains off to the south and west. On the other side of the river, there were bluffs and hills beyond. Some gullies came down through the bluffs. On the westward side of us were lower hills, and there we grazed our ponies and guarded them. There were so many they could not be counted.

There was a man by the name of Rattling Hawk who was shot through the hip in the fight on the Rosebud, and people thought he could not get well. But there was a medicine man by the name of Hairy Chin who cured him.

The day before the battle I had greased myself and was going to swim   45 with some boys, when Hairy Chin called me over to Rattling Hawk's tepee, and told me he wanted me to help him. There were five other boys there, and he needed us for the bears in the curing ceremony, because he had his power from a dream of the bear. He painted my body yellow, and my face too, and put a black stripe on either side of my nose from the eyes down. Then he tied my hair up to look like bear's ears, and put some eagle feathers on my head.

Hairy Chin, who wore a real bear skin with the head on it, began to sing a song that went like this:

At the doorway, sacred herbs are rejoicing.

While he sang, two girls came in and stood one on either side of the wounded man; one had a cup of water and one some kind of an herb. They gave the cup and the herb to Rattling Hawk while Hairy Chin was singing. Then they gave him a red cane, and right away he stood up with it. The girls then started out of the tepee, and the wounded man followed, leaning on the sacred red stick; and we boys, who were the little bears, had to jump around him and make growling noises toward the man. When we did this, you could see something like feathers of all colors coming out of our mouths. Then Hairy Chin came out on all fours, and he looked just like a bear to me. Then Rattling Hawk began to walk better. He was not able to fight next day, but he got well in a little while.

After the ceremony, we boys went swimming to wash the paint off, and when we got back many of the people were dancing and having kill talks all over the village, remembering brave deeds done in the fight with Three Stars on the Rosebud.

When it was about sundown we boys had to bring the ponies in *50* close, and when this was done it was dark and the people were still dancing around fires all over the village. We boys went around from one dance to another, until we got too sleepy to stay up any more.

My father woke me at daybreak and told me to go with him to take our horses out to graze, and when we were out there he said: "We must have a long rope on one of them, so that it will be easy to catch; then we can get the others. If anything happens, you must bring the horses back as fast as you can, and keep your eyes on the camp."

Several of us boys watched our horses together until the sun was straight above and it was getting very hot. Then we thought we would go swimming, and my cousin said he would stay with our horses till we got back. When I was greasing myself, I did not feel well; I felt queer. It seemed that something terrible was going to happen. But I went with the boys anyway. Many people were in the water now and many of the women were out west of the village digging turnips. We had been in the water quite a while when my cousin came down there with the horses to give them a drink, for it was very hot now.

Just then we heard the crier shouting in the Hunkpapa camp, which was not very far from us: "The Chargers are coming! They are charging!

The chargers are coming!" Then the crier of the Oglalas shouted the same words; and we could hear the cry going from camp to camp northward clear to the Santees and the Yanktonais.

Everybody was running now to catch the horses. We were lucky to have ours right there just at that time. My older brother had a sorrel, and he rode away fast toward the Hunkpapas. I had a buckskin. My father came running and said: "Your brother has gone to the Hunkpapas without his gun. Catch him and give it to him. Then come right back to me." He had my six-shooter too—the one my aunt gave me. I took the guns, jumped on my pony and caught my brother. I could see a big dust rising just beyond the Hunkpapa camp and all the Hunkpapas were running around and yelling, and many were running wet from the river. Then out of the dust came the soldiers on their big horses. They looked big and strong and tall and they were all shooting. My brother took his gun and yelled for me to go back. There was a brushy timber just on the other side of the Hunkpapas, and some warriors were gathering there. He made for that place, and I followed him. By now women and children were running in a crowd downstream. I looked back and saw them all running and scattering up a hillside down yonder.

When we got into the timber, a good many Hunkpapas were there   55 already and the soldiers were shooting above us so that leaves were falling from the trees where the bullets struck. By now I could not see what was happening in the village below. It was all dust and cries and thunder; for the women and children were running there, and the warriors were coming on their ponies.

Among us there in the brush and out in the Hunkpapa camp a cry went up: "Take courage! Don't be a coward! The helpless are out of breath!" I think this was when Gall stopped the Hunkpapas, who had been running away, and turned them back.

Then another great cry went up out in the dust: "Crazy Horse is coming! Crazy Horse is coming!" Off toward the west and north they were yelling "Hoka hey!" like a big wind roaring, and making the tremolo; and you could hear eagle bone whistles screaming.

The valley went darker with dust and smoke, and there were only shadows and a big noise of many cries and hoofs and guns. On the left of where I was I could hear the shod hoofs of the soldiers' horses going back into the brush and there was shooting everywhere. Then the hoofs came out of the brush, and I came out and was in among men and horses weaving in and out and going upstream, and everybody was yelling, "Hurry! Hurry!" The soldiers were running upstream and we were all mixed there in the twilight and the great noise. I did not see much; but once I saw a Lakota charge at a soldier who stayed behind and fought and was a very brave man. The Lakota took the soldier's horse by the bridle, but the soldier killed him with a six-shooter. I was small and could not crowd in to where the soldiers were, so I did not kill anybody. There were so many ahead of me, and it was all dark and mixed up.

Soon the soldiers were all crowded into the river and many Lakotas too; and I was in the water awhile. Men and horses were all mixed up and fighting in the water, and it was like hail falling in the river. Then we were out of the river, and people were stripping dead soldiers and putting the clothes on themselves. There was a soldier on the ground and he was still kicking. A Lakota rode up and said to me, "Boy, get off and scalp him." I got off and started to do it. He had short hair and my knife was not very sharp. He ground his teeth. Then I shot him in the forehead and got his scalp.

Many of our warriors were following the soldiers up a hill on the   *60* other side of the river. Everybody else was turning back down stream, and on a hill away down yonder above the Santee camp there was a big dust, and our warriors whirling around in and out of it just like swallows, and many guns were going off.

I thought I would show my mother my scalp, so I rode over toward the hill where there was a crowd of women and children. On the way down there I saw a very pretty young woman among a band of warriors about to go up to the battle on the hill, and she was singing like this:

Brothers, now your friends have come!
Be brave! Be brave!
Would you see me taken captive?

When I rode through the Oglala camp I saw Rattling Hawk sitting up in his tepee with a gun in his hands, and he was all alone there singing a song of regret that went like this:

Brothers, what are you doing that I can not do?

When I got to the women on the hill they were all singing and   *65* making the tremolo to cheer the men fighting across the river in the dust on the hill. My mother gave a big tremolo just for me when she saw my first scalp.

I stayed there awhile with my mother and watched the big dust whirling on the hill across the river, and horses were coming out of it with empty saddles. . . .

By then our scouts had reported that more soldiers were coming upstream; so we all broke camp. Before dark we were ready and we started up the Greasy Grass, heading for Wood Louse Creek in the Big Horn Mountains. We fled all night, following the Greasy Grass. My two younger brothers and I rode in a pony drag, and my mother put some young pups in with us. They were always trying to crawl out and I was always putting them back in, so I didn't sleep much.

By morning we reached a little dry creek and made camp and had a big feast. The meat had spots of fat in it, and I wish I had some of it right now.

When it was full day, we started again and came to Wood Louse Creek at the foot of the mountains, and camped there. A badly wounded man by the name of Three Bears had fits there, and he would keep saying: "Jeneny, jeneny." I do not know what he meant. He died, and we used to call that place the camp where Jeneny died.

That evening everybody got excited and began shouting: "The sol- 70
diers are coming!" I looked, and there they were, riding abreast right toward us. But it was some of our own men dressed in the soldiers' clothes. They were doing this for fun.

The scouts reported that the soldiers had not followed us and that everything was safe now. All over the camp there were big fires and dances all night long.

I will sing you some of the songs that our people made up and sang that night. Some of them went like this:

> Long Hair has never returned,
> So this woman is crying, crying.
> Looking over here, she cries.
> · · · · · · · · · ·
> Long Hair, guns I had none.
> You brought me many. I thank you!
> You make me laugh!
> · · · · · · · · · ·
> Long Hair, horses I have none,   75
> You brought me many. I thank you!
> You make me laugh!
> · · · · · · · · · ·
> Long Hair, where he lies nobody knows.
> Crying, they seek him.
> He lies over here.
> · · · · · · · · · ·
> Let go your holy irons (guns).
> You are not men enough to do any harm.
> Let go your holy irons!

After awhile I got so tired dancing that I went to sleep on the ground right where I was.

My cousin, Black Wasichu, died that night.

The Responsive Reader

1. What do you learn from this account about the lifestyle of Black Elk's people? What do you learn about customs, beliefs, legends, ceremonies, treatment of women?

2. The Sioux were legendary as a warrior nation. To judge from this account, how did they think of war? Were their ideas, ceremonies, and customs connected with war similar to or different from ours?

3. What role does Crazy Horse play in this story? What kind of leader is he? What leadership qualities does he have that would be understood or go unrecognized in our society today?

Talking, Listening, Writing

4. *Empathy* is a currently fashionable word for the ability to enter imaginatively into the thoughts and feelings of people from backgrounds different from our own. Can you identify with the world view of the young Lakota whose experience is being remembered in this selection? Why or why not?

5. Throughout history, people have painted their enemies as savage and inhuman (or, to use the word first employed by the ancient Greeks, "barbarian"). In rare instances, cultures have developed traditions allowing them to honor the "noble foe." What is the record of American culture on this score? Do we tend to recognize our enemies as human beings?

Collaborative Projects

6. How have the movies shaped your view of Native Americans' first encounters and last battles with the whites? How did Westerns stereotype Native Americans? What image or images of them emerge from more modern treatments like *Dances with Wolves* or the Canadian *Black Robe*? Your class might want to stage a panel discussion on Native Americans as seen in the mirror of the movies.

DEATH VALLEY EARNS ITS NAME

Irving Stone

> Soon, notice was formally circulated among the emigrants that a certain man, whose name I forget, professing to be an experienced traveler, and explorer of the Great Basin, would lead a company to California by a route far south of the one followed by emigrants thus far.

Immigrants are people who come into *a place (where they are often not wanted). Emigrants are people who are coming* out of *a place, often embarking on an uncertain journey. The quote above is from the diary of Sarah Royce, who survived the journey across the mountains and the "Great American Desert" during the great westward trek of 1849. Many perished from accidents, thirst, or exhaustion; many lost their cattle and wagons to escape with their bare lives. Some, like the ill-fated Donner Party, were surprised by winter and trapped by the deep snow blocking the mountain passes. The author telling the story of one party of emigrants in the following selection is Irving Stone, best-selling author of* Lust for Life *(a biography of the Dutch painter Vincent van Gogh) and* The Agony and the Ecstasy *(a biography of the Italian Renaissance painter and sculptor Michelangelo).*

Thought Starters: What motivated the pioneers who went west, facing legendary hardships? What went on in their minds?

In October of 1849 there assembled at Provo on Utah Lake, some 1 sixty miles south of Salt Lake, a number of traveling groups, families and young men on horseback, unknown to each other prior to this meeting, which would make up the Death Valley Party. The majority of the party had come south to Provo instead of north around Salt Lake to join the California Trail because they had heard the grisly details of the Donner Party. Judging that it was too late to risk the winter snows of the Sierra Nevada, they decided to take the longer but safer route into southern California, then north to the mines. Word had been spread that there would be a rendezvous at Provo for all wishing to travel the Old Spanish Trail.

In the party when it started for Los Angeles on October 9 there were eighty wagons, two hundred fifty people, and one thousand head of horses and cattle. For their guide they hired Captain Jefferson Hunt, a member of the Mormon Battalion who was being sent to California to buy cattle and seed for the community in Salt Lake. Hunt imposed Mormon military discipline on the train: it moved like an army, divided into seven divisions, each under its captain. The train named itself the Sand Walking Company.

No crueler nor more accurate title could be divined.

Captain Hunt made an early error: he took a wrong turning. Though he was soon back on the main trail this undermined confidence in him, and when a Captain Smith with a party of nine Mormons heading for the California mines rode up with a map or waybill which claimed that there was a cutoff, what James Reed of the Donner Party had called "a nigher way," over Walker's Pass from which they could descend into the Tulare Valley close to the mines, and save themselves four hundred wearisome miles, the Sand Walking Company went into a Committee of the Whole around a campfire to debate the desirability of taking Smith's cutoff. When Captain Hunt was asked his opinion, he said he doubted if any white man had ever traveled it; that young men alone might make it but families with wagons would have serious trouble:

"If you all wish to go and follow Smith I will go also. But if even   5 one wagon decides to go the original route, I shall feel bound by my promise to go with that lone wagon."

The Reverend John W. Brier, described in the journal of one of the listeners as a "man who always liked to give his opinion on every subject," declared forcibly for the cutoff, despite the fact he was traveling with a wife and three young sons. So did a number of others.

The next morning, as the wagons and men came to the fork in the road, Smith and the Reverend Mr. Brier prevailed, even as Lansford Hastings and James Reed had helped make the decision for the Donners over the advice of experienced mountain men. Only seven wagons continued on the known trail with Captain Hunt. A hundred wagons seceded, including the Briers, Bennetts, and Arcanes, the Wade and Dale families, all of whom had children, and the entire Jayhawker[1] party of single men.

For two days Smith's party crossed green valleys with plenty of water. But that was as far as the anonymous mapmaker had traveled. Caught in an impassable canyon, with evidence of worse terrain ahead, seventy-two wagons turned back to the Old Spanish Trail. Though they never caught up with Hunt, they followed him into southern California, and arrived in Los Angeles before the seceders had even reached the heart of their inferno.

Smith had also thought better of his decision; he cut back with his mounted Mormons to the Old Spanish Trail and safety without informing the remaining eighty-five emigrants that he had changed his mind. Meeting about their campfire at Misery Mountain, guideless, they too seemed to have little choice but to turn back, when scouts rode into the camp

---

[1][Jayhawker: antislavery guerrillas in Kansas and Missouri before and during the Civil War.]

with the message that they had seen a good pass which would carry them into California.

They decided to plunge ahead, but not as a unified train with a 10 leader; instead they split into three separate groups. The Jayhawkers, young, unencumbered, started out first and fast; the Reverend Mr. Brier's party came next with his three children and two young men who were part of their mess; third, and bringing up the rear, the Bennett, Arcane, and Wade families, the two Earhart brothers with two sons, several unattached men, and twenty-one-year-old William Manly, who was to be their guide. It was Manly's first trip west.

Juliet Brier was born in Bennington, Vermont, September 26, 1813, and educated at a seminary. She was a wisp of a woman, nervous by nature, the mother of three sons, aged eight, seven, and four. The first white woman to enter Death Valley, the sight that greeted her eyes from the ridge of the eastern range was one to strike terror into the stoutest heart: utter, hopeless, unalleviated desolation: eight to fourteen miles wide, one hundred thirty miles long, with the lower-lying, aptly named Funeral Range in the center. There was nothing living as far as the eye could sweep, only windblown and rippled Sahara wastes of sunbaked sand and crusted salt-mud flats, with mountains surrounding on all sides and bearing not a tree, bush, or blade of grass; what H. H. Bancroft, historian of the West, calls:

"The region of mirage, accursed to all living things, its atmosphere destructive even to the passing bird."

When the Reverend Mr. Brier went ahead looking for water, says Mrs. Brier, "I was left with our three little boys to help bring up the cattle. Poor little Kirke gave out and I carried him on my back, barely seeing where I was going."

She stumbled on, hour after hour, in the hot choking dust, the cattle bellowing for water. When darkness fell she lost the two men of the group and had to get on her knees to search out the ox tracks in the starlight. Not until three in the morning did she reach camp, where the men had found hot and cold springs.

It was Christmas morning. At the springs, which they named Fur- 15 nace Creek, one of the men asked, "Don't you think you and the children better remain here?"

"I have never kept the company waiting," replied Mrs. Brier. "Neither have my children. *Every step I take will be towards California.*"

The next morning when they reached the Jayhawker camp the Briers found the young men burning their wagons in order to travel faster: for it needed only one surveying look about them to know that they all faced imminent death.

The Briers also abandoned their wagons, packing their rapidly vanishing foodstuffs on the failing oxen. The Reverend Mr. Brier asked the Jayhawkers for permission to travel with them; the Jayhawkers did not want to be encumbered by a woman and small children, and objected. Then they looked at Mrs. Brier, all skin and bones, and relented. William Manly, leading the Bennett Party, also arrived at the springs. He reports:

"She was the one who put the packs on the oxen in the morning. She it was who took them off at night, built the fires, cooked the food, helped the children, and did all sorts of work when the father of the family was too tired, which was almost all of the time."

The combined train struggled through mile after mile of salt marsh,   20
sinking in sand to their shoe tops. One of the Brier boys remembers:

"Twenty miles across naked dunes, the wind driving the sand like shot into the face and eyes."

Their tongues grew swollen, their lips cracked, the oxen lay down in the sand never to rise again. That night the men climbed up the rock-strewn mountain to the snow line, bringing back snow in their shirts, some eating it hard, others melting it for the cattle.

They went for the next forty-eight hours without water, unable to eat the meat of their slaughtered oxen because they could get nothing down their parched throats. A Dr. Carr suggested that they return to Furnace Creek where there was water; he broke down and cried when Mrs. Brier repeated, "Every step we take will be towards California."

By New Year's Day they camped at the head of the Panamint Valley, totally lost. The stronger of the Jayhawkers pushed ahead, leaving in Mrs. Brier's care the older and weaker men.

The first to die of thirst was the fifty-year-old Reverend Mr. Fish,   25
who was traveling to California in hopes of finding the money to pay off his church's debt in Indiana.

On January 6 the two single men who had been in the Brier mess, and who had the only flour in the party, decided they would strike out alone in the hopes of saving themselves. They baked up all their dough except for a small piece they gave to Mrs. Brier, then shook hands good-bye. Mrs. Brier baked her dough into twenty-two crackers, all they would have for twenty-two days of nightmare and terror.

Next to die was middle-aged William Isham, who crawled four miles on his hands and knees searching for water, then dropped on his face.

"Give up?" cried Juliet Brier. "Oh! I knew what that meant—a shallow grave in the sand."

Their tongues became black and hung out of their mouths. Ahead there was the cruel mirage of the desert: water, an oasis, trees, greenery. When water came it was a muddy pool at what is now Borax Lake; the few remaining cattle stamped into it first, then the humans scooped up the mud-laden water, forcing it down their parched throats.

The next waterless stretch lasted nearly five days. In camp the men,   30
with burnt faces and skeletal frames, lay down and waited for death. Mrs. Brier went behind a rock, prayed to God for strength, then gave them a combined sermon and tongue-lashing that shocked them back onto their

feet. At that moment the Reverend Mr. Richards came running into camp, crying:

"Water! Water! I have found water!"

Four miles away he had come upon a group of Indians, had made friendly signs, then gestures of thirst. The Indians guided him to a brook at the base of the mountains, hidden by shrubs, which ran clear and cold before disappearing into the sands of the desert.

When the party finally struggled to the top of the range and looked back at the valley behind them, they named it Death Valley. But the Mojave Desert into which they descended in the middle of January 1850 was little better: a desert of alkali, with no known trails or springs. Emaciated from dysentery and exhaustion, they faced days of heat, dust, thirst, rocks that cut their feet. One man said, "I will just take a little nap," and never woke up. Another said, "I have a presentiment I shall never reach California," fell off his pony and died. At a spring, one drank too copiously; he was the seventh to perish.

The Reverend Mr. Brier, who had been hobbling along with the aid of crutches, lay down in camp, bade his wife farewell, and closed his eyes. Juliet Brier pleaded with her husband to hold on, gathered some acorns, ground and cooked them and fed them to him from a spoon. He survived.

The Bennett-Manly Party had equally bad luck in trying a southerly   35
trail: they got trapped in the hopeless waste bordered by a black range of mountains through which there could be no conceivable pass. Finding a spring at Tule, near the southern end of the valley, they decided not to dissipate their failing strength, but to remain encamped. Bennett asked young Manly and Rogers, a burly butcher, if they would push on alone, find civilization, and bring back relief. There was neither map nor food the men could take with them, nor knowledge of what lay ahead except days of purgatory.

But they went . . . passing the dead bodies of Jayhawkers who had given out. Their trek, as told by Manly in *Death Valley in '49,* is one of the West's great sagas of man's will against the implacable elements:

"Black and desolate ranges and buttes to the south, great dry plains, salt lakes and slippery alkali water to which we walked, only to turn away again in bitter disappointment, little sheets of ice that saved our lives, hawk and crow diet, lameness . . ."

They got out in fourteen days, sustaining life by sucking on rocks or single blades of grass, breaking trail over trailless mountains, deserts, and valleys until, more dead than alive, they cleared one more range and saw below them the green cattle ranch of San Francisquito.

Settling in for a long wait, the Bennetts took off their wagon covers to make protecting tents for themselves and for the cattle against the heat and sandstorms, rationed their food, watched it vanish. Mrs. Arcane, knowing she must abandon her clothing but not wanting it to be too good for the Indians who would inherit it, dressed herself in her finest garments every day. Captain Richard Culverwell, who had gone exploring, died trying to get back to camp. After three weeks the men agreed:

"If those boys ever get out of this hole they are fools if they ever 40 come back to help anybody."

Manly and Rogers waited only four days to regain their strength, then borrowed horses to load with oranges and other foodstuffs, and spent the next week retracing their steps, exploring for better passes and water holes. When they got their first view of the camp not a soul was in sight; they concluded they had made the journey for nothing.

Manly fired a shot. From under a wagon a man emerged. He threw his arms high over his head and shouted:

"The boys have come! The boys have come!"

They were saved.

The Brier party also emerged, as images of death, onto the opulent 45 hospitality of the Californios who owned San Francisquito ranch. Mrs. Brier came down out of the San Gabriel Mountains, leading her three sons, in rags, the last of the moccasins she had made of the hides of dead oxen worn through; seventy pounds of bone, grit, and indestructibility.

Thirteen men had lost their lives in the Sand Walking Company. The women were tougher; they endured. Juliet Brier's inner strength saved not only her own family but several of the Jayhawkers as well.

The Responsive Reader

1. Stone's account is in part a story of weak and strong leaders. (What is wrong with the guides that fail the emigrants?) What leadership qualities did Stone see in Juliet Brier?
2. Hardship puts people to the test. How do the people in the Sand Walking Party pass the test?

Talking, Listening, Writing

3. Is the pioneering spirit dead in American society today?
4. Try to put yourself in the shoes of one of the anonymous travelers in the story. Write a diary entry sharing your thoughts and feelings.
5. What attracts readers to stories of hardship and disaster? Is the kind of documentary literature represented by this article flourishing or languishing in America today?

Collaborative Projects

6. Does your community keep alive the memory of pioneers or founders? Can you find brochures or other sources commemorating early settlers, early builders? Your class may decide to collaborate on a project devoted to the people involved in the early history of your community.

THE DAY THE SLAVES GOT THEIR WAY

Matthew Kauffman

> *Newspapers, Sunday supplements, and large-circulation magazines have in recent years often turned to a forgotten page from American history. An article might discuss ancient treaty rights that a tribe is trying to recover; another article might focus on the role of black soldiers during the Civil War, or War Between the States. The following selection focuses on the legal after-math of a slave rebellion that is also treated in Robert Hayden's poem "Middle Passage" and in a book that Howard Jones wrote in 1987. The article was first published in Hartford, Connecticut, in the* Hartford Courant. *It appeared on the occasion of the 150th anniversary of the court case that lined up American abolitionists in support of Africans who had staged a successful mutiny on a slave ship bound for Cuba. How does the article change or add to your understanding of the history of slavery in the Americas?*

Thought Starters: What expectations or assumptions do you bring to an article about a mutiny aboard a slave ship? Would you be inclined to consider the story unlikely? Are you predisposed to take sides?

For weeks in the summer of 1839, seafarers along the East Coast had spotted a sleek, black schooner with no national flag waving above its tattered sails. The ship moved slowly, seemingly with no destination, and those who approached the mysterious vessel reported that the crew was composed almost entirely of half-naked black men.

When the crew of a Coast Guard cutter boarded the vessel near Montauk Point, N.Y., on Long Island, they found that the men were slaves who had overpowered their captors at sea, killed four white men and commandeered the schooner. The captain ordered the ship towed to New London, Conn., where, he expected, the slaves would be tried as murderers and mutineers.

But the seizure of the Amistad, as the schooner was called, touched off a two-year legal battle that pitted the governments of two nations against a small group of feisty abolitionists determined to prove that the Africans were enslaved illegally and should be freed.

A celebration of the 150th anniversary of that legal struggle has been planned in New Haven, where the Africans were jailed for much of the time their fate was argued in the courts. The city has scheduled lectures, exhibits, school essay contests, artistic performances, outdoor events and a community dinner.

The case will be celebrated as the first major court victory for the   *5*
anti-slavery forces and as an early example of the involvement of blacks on the frontline of the battle against slavery.

Americans were riveted by the case, but the fate of the Africans is less well-known today. In the early 1970s, Amistad House opened in Hart-ford as a group home for troubled teenage girls, but the house closed in 1983. One of the men who kidnapped Patricia Hearst 15 years ago called himself Cinque after Joseph Cinque, the leader of the rebellion.

Organizers hope the celebration will revive interest in the saga.

"What I would love to see is that it become an integral part of Connecticut history," said Alfred Marder, a New Haven peace worker and a member of the 100-member committee planning the celebration.

The 52 slaves aboard the schooner undoubtedly had little concern for their place in history when they rose up against their Cuban captors. They wanted to go home, so they spared the lives of two men and ordered them to sail east toward Africa. But during the night, the Cubans secretly turned the ship around, and spent nearly two months zig-zagging north along the East Coast, hoping to be rescued.

The Cubans had documents indicating that the Africans were ladinos,   *10*
Africans taken to Cuba before the importation of slaves to the island was outlawed in 1817, but abolitionists suspected that the papers were fraudu-lent. If the blacks had been illegally imported from Africa, the abolitionists argued in court, then they were not slaves guilty of murder, but kidnap victims who acted reasonably to regain their liberty.

The case became a lightning rod for those who opposed slavery, including Roger Sherman Baldwin, who later became governor of Con-necticut and a U.S. senator, and former President John Quincy Adams, who argued the case before the U.S. Supreme Court. A leading abolitionist declared the Amistad case a "providential occurrence" delivered to force a nationwide hearing on the evils of slavery.

Abolitionists, who were determined to keep the Africans, and the issue of slavery, on the minds of Americans, embarked on a tremendous public relations drive, inviting people to visit the Africans in jail, delivering lectures across the country and arranging to have life-size wax dummies made of Cinque and others.

Hundreds and sometimes thousands of people visited the Africans in jail each day. In Hartford, an especially entrepreneurial jailer charged visi-tors 12½ cents each for a peek at the captives.

Despite the excitement, lawyers for the Africans knew they had an uphill battle. The administration of President Martin Van Buren, bowing to pressure from the Spanish government and pro-slavery forces in Amer-ica, worked against the Africans.

Despite Van Buren's inclinations, the Africans won in the lower   *15* court. But the case was appealed to the Supreme Court, and lawyers for the Africans knew that only two of the nine men on the court opposed slavery. Nevertheless, in March 1841, the court granted the Africans the wish expressed by Cinque, who knew only enough English to utter in court the simple plea, "Give me free."

The Africans, the court ruled, were not slaves and were not criminals.

The Africans from the Amistad returned to their homeland 10 months later, but before leaving, the prominent New Haven lawyers who had arranged their defense sought to turn the Africans into Christian missionaries. Cinque and the others took up residence in Farmington, Conn., and spent six hours a day in a classroom. They also cultivated a 15-acre farm and participated in a nationwide tour to help raise money for their voyage home.

The Amistad rebellion rates only a few paragraphs in most encyclopedias and is rarely taught in schools or included in textbooks, said Howard Jones, a University of Alabama history professor who wrote a 1987 book on the case.

New Haven schools, however, are ordering 2,000 booklets on the Amistad affair, and an effort is under way to have the Amistad rebellion featured on a U.S. postage stamp during the sesquicentennial of the Supreme Court decision.

New Haven also hopes to raise $100,000 for a statue of Cinque, *20* which would be erected on the street where the town jail stood.

The Responsive Reader

1. How much do you learn from this article about the Amistad rebellion and its legal aftermath? (What are some of the "hard facts"?)
2. How much knowledge of slavery and the abolitionist movement does the writer assume? How much does he add to your understanding of slavery and of the antislavery forces? (One hundred fifty years later, can you get into the spirit of the abolitionist movement?)

Talking, Listening, Writing

3. What shaped your own views of slavery and abolition? What was the role of teachers, books, the media?
4. Prepare a defense (or an indictment) of the accused "murderers and mutineers."
5. As a member of a school board or similar body, would you vote in favor of commemorating the Amistad affair or a similar historical episode? Why or why not?

Collaborative Projects

6. Your class may want to stage a mock trial of the Amistad group. (You may want to turn to the Hayden poem and the Jones book or to other sources—history books, encyclopedias—for additional information.)

WHY I AM OPTIMISTIC ABOUT AMERICA

Daniel J. Boorstin

Daniel J. Boorstin is one of this country's best-known historians, who served as Librarian of Congress, a position that one editor has called "the highest intellectual honor the U.S. government can bestow." Boorstin grew up in the 1920s in Tulsa, Oklahoma, which he says called itself "The Oil Capital of the World." He became the Pulitzer Prize–winning author of books including The Americans, The Discoverers, *and* The Creators. *At a time when many American historians have focused on the darker side of American history, he has looked in our common past for "lessons in national idealism and political realism." For instance, he has celebrated the Lewis and Clark expedition of 1804–06 into the uncharted territories beyond the Mississippi as an example of the spirit of discovery "that has built our nation"— a "triumph for science and natural history" at the same time that it served the cause of trade and of territorial expansion. In this century, he sees the spirit of exploration and bold leadership exemplified in the 1969 Apollo mission to the moon, but he also sees it threatened by the obsession with "cost-effectiveness," a term that he says "did not enter our language until about 1964." In the article that follows, Boorstin tries to explain the roots of his American brand of optimism at a time when he sees pessimism and negativism prevailing in much of American life.*

Thought Starters: Is America different from other countries? Is it unique among nations? How or why?

You ask what is the basis for my optimism. With a Europe in disarray   *1*
in a century plagued by two murderous World Wars, by genocides without precedent—the German-Nazi massacre of six million and the Stalin-Soviet massacre of 30 million—how can I speak so hopefully about the American future?

One answer is very personal. I was raised and went to public school in the 1920s in Tulsa, Okla., which then called itself "The Oil Capital of the World," but could perhaps have been called "The Optimism Capital of the World." Only 10 years before my family came to Oklahoma, the Indian Territory had been admitted to the Union as the 46th state.

The city thrived on "booster" pride, and before I graduated from Central High School, it boasted two daily newspapers, three skyscrapers, houses designed by Frank Lloyd Wright and a public-school system superintended by the former U.S. Commissioner of Education. The Kiwanis,

Rotary, and Chamber of Commerce competed furiously in projects of civic improvement. For our high school English classes, we memorized and declaimed patriotic orations—from Patrick Henry's "Give Me Liberty or Give Me Death" and Lincoln's "Gettysburg Address" to Henry Grady's "The New South" and Emile Zola's "Plea for Dreyfus." We wrote speeches on the virtues of the federal Constitution for a national contest, which held its finals before the Supreme Court in Washington.

Of course there were dark shadows—like the relentless racial segregation, the brutal race riots of the 1920s, and the Ku Klux Klan. But these were not visible or prominent in my life. The city burgeoned, proudly built a grand new railroad depot, a university, an elegant public library and a city hall—and soon it was embellished by art museums of national rank.

My father was one of the most enthusiastic "boosters," and the growing city seemed to justify his extravagant optimism. I came to sympathize with that American frontier newspaperman who was attacked for reporting as facts the mythic marvels of his upstart pioneer village—including its impressive hotel and prosperous Main Street. In America, he said, it was not fair to object to the rosy reports of community boosters simply because they had "not yet gone through the formality of taking place." I suppose I have never been cured of my distinctively American Oklahoma optimism, bred in the bone and confirmed by the real history of Tulsa.

Another reason for my optimism is in American history. The exhilarating features of our history and culture have in the past been captured in the idea of "American Exceptionalism." This is a long word for a simple idea: the traditional belief that the United States is a very special place, unique in crucial ways. American Exceptionalism is a name too for a cosmopolitan, optimistic and humanistic view of history—that the modern world, while profiting from the European inheritance, need not be imprisoned in Old World molds. And, therefore, that the future of the United States and of its people need not be governed by the same expectations or plagued by the same problems that had afflicted people elsewhere.

How have we lost sight of this beacon?

We have been seduced by the rise of our country as a "superpower." For while power is quantitative, the uniqueness of the United States is not merely quantitative. We have suffered, too, from the consequences of our freedom. Totalitarian societies exaggerate their virtues. But free societies like ours somehow seize the temptation to exaggerate their vices. The negativism of our press and television reporting are, of course, the best evidence of our freedom to scrutinize ourselves. Far better this than the chauvinism of self-righteousness which has been the death of totalitarian empires in our time.

Yet we must never forget that, while to the Old World we were the Unexpected Land, we have ever since been the Land of the Unexpected. The main features of the culture of our United States are just what the wise men of Europe, looking at their own past, could not have conjured up. A short list of the American surprises includes what we have done here with four basic elements of culture—religion, language, law, and wealth.

Religion. By the time of the European settlement of North Amer-   10
ica, the history of the rising nations of Western Europe had been punctuated by torture and massacre in the name of religion. There was the notorious Spanish Inquisition of the 15th century (1478), the bloody Massacre of St. Bartholomew (1572) in France and, in Germany during the very years of the Puritan settlements in New England, the Thirty Years War (1618–1648), which spread into a general conflict between Protestant and Catholic Europe. In that war alone, some 10 percent of the German population was slaughtered in the name of religious orthodoxy.

This seemed not to augur well for a nation like ours, whose Pilgrims were obsessed with religion and had fled England to fulfill their passionate dream. Their religious faith gave them courage to brave the ocean-crossing, the hardships of an unknown land and the risks of hostile natives, despite their lonely remoteness from ancestral homes.

Who could have predicted that the United States, unlike the nations from which our people came, would never suffer a religious war? That the Protestants and Catholics who had tortured and massacred each other in Europe would establish peaceful neighboring communities from New England to Maryland and Virginia? That Jews would here find asylum from ghettos and pogroms? That—though the U.S. would remain conspicuously a nation of churchgoers—the separation of Church and State would become a cornerstone of civic life? Or that public-school principals in the 20th century would be challenged by how to promote a holiday spirit without seeming to favor or neglect Christmas, Hanukkah or Kwanzaa?

Language. In Europe, languages had made nations. Spanish, Portuguese, English, French, German and Italian had produced their own literatures—even before there was a Spain, a Portugal, an England, a France, a Germany or an Italy. But the United States was the first great modern nation without its own language. Our country has been uniquely created by people willing and able to borrow a language.

Oddly enough, the English language has helped make us a congenitally multicultural nation, since most Americans have not come from the land of Shakespeare. So we have learned here that people do not lose their civic dignity by speaking the language of a new community. The English language has been invigorated and Americanized by countless importations of words from German, Italian, French, Spanish, Yiddish and American Indian tongues, among others.

The surprising result is that, without a unique national language, our   15
community has developed a language wonderfully expressive of the vitality and variety of our people. Perhaps we should really call Broken English our distinctive American language, for it bears the mark of our immigrant history.

Law. Nowadays, we can be puzzled at the spectacle of peoples from Russia to South Africa contending over how, whether, and when to adopt a "constitution." They seem to have the odd notion that a "constitution" can be created instantly by vote of a legislature or by a popular election. All this offers a sharp contrast to our Anglo-American experience.

The tradition of a fundamental law—a "constitution"—that we inherited from England reached back to at least the 13th century. The byproduct of a nation's whole history, the unwritten English constitution was a pillar of government and of the people's rights. No one could have foreseen that such a tradition would find a transatlantic written reincarnation in the deliberations of 55 colonials meeting in Independence Hall in Philadelphia in 1787. So our United States was created by a constitution. With another surprising result—that our parvenu nation at the end of the 20th century now lives by the most venerable (and probably most venerated) written constitution in the world. And that the constitution would survive by its very power to be amended (with difficulty).

Yet who could have predicted that a nation whose birth certificate bore the declaration that "all men are created equal" should have been one of the last to abolish slavery? Slavery was abolished in the British Empire in 1833. Still, three decades passed before Lincoln's Emancipation Proclamation of 1863 freed slaves in the Southern secessionist states, followed by the Thirteenth Amendment to the Constitution outlawing slavery in all the United States (1865). The slave trade survived only in certain Muslim states and in parts of Africa.

On the other side, we must note that our only Civil War was fought in a struggle to free a subject people. For this, too, it is hard to find a precedent. And a legacy of the history of slavery in the United States has been the equally unprecedented phenomenon of a conscience-wracked nation. This has led us to create a host of novel institutions—"equal opportunity" laws, "affirmative action," among others—in our strenuous effort to compensate for past injustices.

We should not be surprised that Russians are obsessively suspicious *20* of foreigners coming to their country—after their long domination by the Mongols, their invasion by Napoleon and his forces of "liberation" who burned Moscow, and by the Germans in World War II who left 20 million casualties. No wonder the Russians see the foreigner as the invader or the agent of invaders.

In the United States, we have been luckily free of this stereotype. Instead, our vision of the newcomer has been refracted in the experience of our own recent immigrant ancestors. "Strangers are welcome," Benjamin Franklin explained in his *Information to those Who Would Remove to America* (1782), "because there is room enough for them all, and therefore the old inhabitants are not jealous of them." This has been the mainstream of our history: welcoming the newcomer as worker, customer, community-builder, fellow-citizen-in-the-making. The uniquely American notion of a Nation of Nations was never more vivid than today.

Wealth. We are told that the United States is a *rich* nation. But what really distinguishes us is less our wealth than our radically novel way of measuring a society's material well-being.

Wealth—which was at the center of English mercantilist thinking before the American Revolution—was a static notion. The wealth of the world, measured primarily in gold and silver treasure, was supposed to be a fixed quantity, a pie that could be sliced one way or another. But the size of the pie could not be substantially increased. A bigger slice for Great Britain meant a smaller slice for France or Spain or somebody else, and one nation's gain was another's loss.

Our New World changed that way of thinking. People have come here not for wealth but for a better "way of life." America blurred the boundary between the material and the spiritual. All this was reinforced by the spectacular progress of our technology, exploiting the resources of a rich, little-known and sparsely populated continent.

The American Revolution then was, among other things, a struggle   25
between the time-honored idea of "wealth" and a New World idea of "standard of living." This characteristically American idea appears to have entered our language only at the beginning of this century. It could hardly have been conceived in an Old World burdened with the legacy of feudal "rights," landed aristocracies, royal courts, sacrosanct guild monopolies and ancestral cemeteries. Wealth is what someone possesses, but a standard of living is what people *share*. Wealth can be secretly hoarded, but a standard of living can only be publicly enjoyed. For it is the level of goods, housing, services, health, comfort and education agreed to be appropriate.

All these remarkable transformations of the culture of the Older World add up to American Exceptionalism.

Recently, we have heard apologies for expressions of belief in American uniqueness—as if it were somehow provincial or chauvinist. But our ex-Colonial nation in this post-Colonial age would do well to see what the prescient French man of letters André Malraux observed on his visit to President Kennedy in the White House in 1962: "The United States is today the country that assumes the destiny of man . . . For the first time, a country has become the world's leader without achieving this through conquest, and it is strange to think that for thousands of years one single country has found power while seeking only justice."

And, he might have added, while seeking community. We must see the unique power of the United States, then, not as the power of power, but as the power of example. Another name for history.

The depressing spectacle today of a Europe at war with itself has offered us a melodrama of those same ghosts of ethnic, racial, and religious hate that generations of immigrants have come to America to escape. Now, more than ever, we must inoculate ourselves against these latent perils. Luckily, the states of our federal union are not ethnic, racial, or religious enclaves. Luckily, we have remained a wonderfully mobile people. There is no better antidote to these perils abroad than a frank and vivid recognition of the uniqueness of our history—of the special opportunities offered us. Nor could there be greater folly than refusing to enjoy the happy accidents of our history.

The uniqueness that Jefferson and Lincoln claimed for us, we must   *30* remember, was for the sake of *all* mankind. Our Declaration of Independence takes its cue from "the course of human events." The Great Seal of the United States on our dollar bill still proclaims "Novus Ordo Seclorum"—a new order of the centuries. When before had people put so much faith in the unexpected?

The Responsive Reader

1. What do you learn in Boorstin's opening paragraphs about the American tradition of boosterism? How did it influence his upbringing and education? How is it reflected in his current outlook?
2. Nations have often considered themselves special in the sight of God or favored by destiny. What, according to Boorstin, is the essence of "American Exceptionalism"? In what sense is it a "cosmopolitan, optimistic, and humanistic view of history"?
3. What do you know about the history of religious strife and persecution in the Old World? Which of Boorstin's historical references or allusions do you recognize? How and why was the American experience different?
4. What does Boorstin mean when he says that the United States "was the first great modern nation without its own language"? What evidence can you cite that the English language has been "invigorated and Americanized" by borrowings from many sources? Why should we perhaps call Broken English "our distinctive American language"?
5. How, according to Boorstin, did our "parvenu," or Johnny-come-lately, nation come to live by "the most venerable (and probably most venerated) written constitution in the world"? What is unique about the American attitude toward foreigners or other nations? What other features of the American tradition are "unprecedented" in the legal and political sphere?
6. Americans are often criticized for their materialism. How, according to Boorstin, was the American attitude toward wealth different from that of Old World countries?
7. How, according to this author, is America's power in the world different from that exercised by earlier superpowers?

Talking, Listening, Writing

8. *Pollyanna*—describing a bubbly optimist always ignoring the grim facts—is one of the most American words in the English language. Would you call Boorstin a Pollyanna? Does he recognize the role

of evil in the world and in American history? What role does evil play in his essay?

9. What "latent perils" does Boorstin see that may endanger America's future?

10. Is the American tradition of welcoming the newcomer dead?

Collaborative Projects

11. Are religious divisions and animosities a thing of the past? Working with a group, you may want to interview students and others, trying to determine whether or not they see strong religious feelings as a danger to national harmony.

IN THE AMERICAN SOCIETY
Gish Jen

> *History in school books used to focus heavily on kings and generals and battles and only slowly shifted emphasis toward the lives of ordinary people. A major chapter in American history is the history of the immigrants' America. The family history of many Americans starts with the struggle of first-generation immigrants to integrate into American society—their struggle to make a living in alien surroundings, to overcome hostility or prejudice, to deal with the maze of immigration laws. Gish Jen (she borrowed her first name from the name of a famous actress of the silent-screen era) grew up in the suburbs of New York City as the daughter of Chinese immigrants. She studied at Harvard, Stanford, and the University of Iowa before she went to China, the country of her ancestors, to teach English. She has taught creative writing at Tufts University and the University of Massachusetts. The following short story led to her novel* Typical American, *published in 1991. Some of the people Jen knew as a child were not originally mainland Chinese but came from Taiwan—ruled by the KMT or Kuomintang, the noncommunist Chinese who formed a government-in-exile.*

Thought Starters: How do you feel about immigrants? How do you feel about illegal aliens?

When my father took over the pancake house, it was to send my little sister Mona and me to college. We were only in junior high at the time, but my father believed in getting a jump on things. "Those Americans always saying it," he told us. "Smart guys thinking in advance." My mother elaborated, explaining that businesses took bringing up, like children. They could take years to get going, she said, years.

In this case, though, we got rich right away. At two months we were breaking even, and at four, those same hotcakes that could barely withstand the weight of butter and syrup were supporting our family with ease. My mother bought a station wagon with air conditioning, my father an oversized, red vinyl recliner for the back room; and as time went on and the business continued to thrive, my father started to talk about his grandfather and the village he had reigned over in China—things my father had never talked about when he worked for other people. He told us about the bags of rice his family would give out to the poor at New Year's, and about the people who came to beg, on their hands and knees, for his grandfather to intercede for the more wayward of their relatives. "Like that Godfather in the movie," he would tell us as, his feet up, he distributed paychecks.

1

Sometimes an employee would get two green envelopes instead of one, which meant that Jimmy needed a tooth pulled, say, or that Tiffany's husband was in the clinker again.

"It's nothing, nothing," he would insist, sinking back into his chair. "Who else is going to take care of you people."

My mother would mostly just sigh about it. "Your father thinks this is China," she would say, and then she would go back to her mending. Once in a while, though, when my father had given away a particularly large sum, she would exclaim, outraged, "But this here is the U—S—of—A!"—this apparently having been what she used to tell immigrant stock boys when they came in late.

She didn't work at the supermarket anymore; but she had made it to   5
the rank of manager before she left, and this had given her not only new words and phrases, but new ideas about herself, and about America, and about what was what in general. She had opinions, now, on how downtown should be zoned; she could pump her own gas and check her own oil; and for all she used to chide Mona and me for being "copycats," she herself was now interested in espadrilles, and wallpaper, and most recently, the town country club.

"So join already," said Mona, flicking a fly off her knee.

My mother enumerated the problems as she sliced up a quarter round of watermelon: There was the cost. There was the waiting list. There was the fact that no one in our family played either tennis or golf.

"So what?" said Mona.

"It would be a waste," said my mother.

"Me and Callie can swim in the pool."   10

"Plus you need that recommendation letter from a member."

"Come *on,*" said Mona. "Annie's mom'd write you a letter in a *sec.*"

My mother's knife glinted in the early summer sun. I spread some more newspaper on the picnic table.

"*Plus* you have to eat there twice a month. You know what that means." My mother cut another, enormous slice of fruit.

"No, I *don't* know what that means," said Mona.   15

"It means Dad would have to wear a jacket, dummy," I said.

"Oh! Oh! Oh!," said Mona, clasping her hand to her breast. "Oh! Oh! Oh! Oh! Oh!"

We all laughed: my father had no use for nice clothes, and would wear only ten-year-old shirts, with grease-spotted pants, to show how little he cared what anyone thought.

"Your father doesn't believe in joining the American society," said my mother. "He wants to have his own society."

"So go to dinner without him," Mona shot her seeds out in long arcs   20
over the lawn. "Who cares what he thinks?"

But of course we all did care, and knew my mother could not simply up and do as she pleased. For in my father's mind, a family owed its head a degree of loyalty that left no room for dissent. To embrace what he embraced was to love; and to embrace something else was to betray him.

He demanded a similar sort of loyalty of his workers, whom he treated more like servants than employees. Not in the beginning, of course. In the beginning all he wanted was for them to keep on doing what they used to do, and to that end he concentrated mostly on leaving them alone. As the months passed, though, he expected more and more of them, with the result that for all his largesse, he began to have trouble keeping help. The cooks and busboys complained that he asked them to fix radiators and trim hedges, not only at the restaurant, but at our house; the waitresses that he sent them on errands and made them chauffeur him around. Our head waitress, Gertrude, claimed that he once even asked her to scratch his back.

"It's not just the blacks don't believe in slavery," she said when she quit.

My father never quite registered her complaint, though, nor those of the others who left. Even after Eleanor quit, then Tiffany, then Gerald, and Jimmy, and even his best cook, Eureka Andy, for whom he had bought new glasses, he remained mostly convinced that the fault lay with them.

"All they understand is that assembly line," he lamented. "Robots, they are. They want to be robots." 25

There *were* occasions when the clear running truth seemed to eddy, when he would pinch the vinyl of his chair up into little peaks and wonder if he were doing things right. But with time he would always smooth the peaks back down; and when business started to slide in the spring, he kept on like a horse in his ways.

By the summer our dishboy was overwhelmed with scraping. It was no longer just the hashbrowns that people were leaving for trash, and the service was as bad as the food. The waitresses served up French pancakes instead of German, apple juice instead of orange, spilt things on laps, on coats. On the Fourth of July some greenhorn sent an entire side of fries slaloming down a lady's *massif centrale*. Meanwhile in the back room, my father labored through articles on the economy.

"What is housing starts?" he puzzled. "What is GNP?"

Mona and I did what we could, filling in as busgirls and bookkeepers and, one afternoon, stuffing the comments box that hung by the cashier's desk. That was Mona's idea. We rustled up a variety of pens and pencils, checked boxes for an hour, smeared the cards up with coffee and grease, and waited. It took a few days for my father to notice that the box was full, and he didn't say anything about it for a few days more. Finally, though, he started to complain of fatigue; and then he began to complain that the staff was not what it could be. We encouraged him in this— pointing out, for instance, how many dishes got chipped—but in the end all that happened was that, for the first time since we took over the restaurant, my father got it into his head to fire someone. Skip, a skinny busboy who was saving up for a sportscar, said nothing as my father mumbled on about the price of dishes. My father's hand shook as he wrote out the severance check; and he spent the rest of the day napping in his chair once it was over.

As it was going on midsummer, Skip wasn't easy to replace. We hung   30
a sign in the window and advertised in the paper, but no one called the first week, and the person who called the second didn't show up for his interview. The third week, my father phoned Skip to see if he would come back, but a friend of his had already sold him a Corvette for cheap.

Finally a Chinese guy named Booker turned up. He couldn't have been more than thirty, and was wearing a lighthearted seersucker suit, but he looked as though life had him pinned: his eyes were bloodshot and his chest sunken, and the muscles of his neck seemed to strain with the effort of holding his head up. In a single dry breath he told us that he had never bussed tables but was willing to learn, and that he was on the lam from the deportation authorities.

"I do not want to lie to you," he kept saying. He had come to the United States on a student visa, had run out of money, and was now in a bind. He was loath to go back to Taiwan, as it happened—he looked up at this point, to be sure my father wasn't pro-KMT—but all he had was a phony social security card and a willingness to absorb all blame, should anything untoward come to pass.

"I do not think, anyway, that it is against the law to hire me, only to be me," he said, smiling faintly.

Anyone else would have examined him on this, but my father conceived of laws as speed bumps rather than curbs. He wiped the counter with his sleeve, and told Booker to report the next morning.

"I will be good worker," said Booker.   35

"Good," said my father.

"Anything you want me to do, I will do."

My father nodded.

Booker seemed to sink into himself for a moment. "Thank you," he said finally. "I am appreciate your help. I am very, very appreciate for everything." He reached out to shake my father's hand.

My father looked at him. "Did you eat today?" he asked in   40
Mandarin.

Booker pulled at the hem of his jacket.

"Sit down," said my father. "Please, have a seat."

My father didn't tell my mother about Booker, and my mother didn't tell my father about the country club. She would never have applied, except that Mona, while over at Annie's, had let it drop that our mother wanted to join. Mrs. Lardner came by the very next day.

"Why, I'd be honored and delighted to write you people a letter," she said. Her skirt billowed around her.

"Thank you so much," said my mother. "But it's too much trouble   45
for you, and also my husband is . . ."

"Oh, it's no trouble at all, no trouble at all. I tell you." She leaned forward so that her chest freckles showed. "I know just how it is. It's a secret of course, but you know, my natural father was Jewish. Can you see it? Just look at my skin."

"My husband," said my mother.

"I'd be honored and delighted." said Mrs. Lardner with a little wave of her hands. "Just honored and delighted."

Mona was triumphant. "See, Mom," she said, waltzing around the kitchen when Mrs. Lardner left. "What did I tell you? 'I'm just honored and delighted, just honored and delighted.'" She waved her hands in the air.

"You know, the Chinese have a saying," said my mother. "To do 50
nothing is better than to overdo. You mean well, but you tell me now what will happen."

"I'll talk Dad into it," said Mona, still waltzing. "Or I bet Callie can. He'll do anything Callie says."

"I can try, anyway," I said.

"Did you hear what I said?" said my mother. Mona bumped into the broom closet door. "You're not going to talk anything; you've already made enough trouble." She started on the dishes with a clatter.

Mona poked diffidently at a mop.

I sponged off the counter. "Anyway," I ventured. "I bet our name'll 55
never even come up."

"That's if we're lucky," said my mother.

"There's all these people waiting," I said.

"Good," she said. She started on a pot.

I looked over at Mona, who was still cowering in the broom closet. "In fact, there's some black family's been waiting so long, they're going to sue," I said.

My mother turned off the water. "Where'd you hear that?" 60

"Patty told me."

She turned the water back on, started to wash a dish, then put it back down and shut the faucet.

"I'm sorry," said Mona.

"Forget it," said my mother. "Just forget it."

Booker turned out to be a model worker, whose boundless gratitude 65
translated into a willingness to do anything. As he also learned quickly, he soon knew not only how to bus, but how to cook, and how to wait table, and how to keep the books. He fixed the walk-in door so that it stayed shut, reupholstered the torn seats in the dining room, and devised a system for tracking inventory. The only stone in the rice was that he tended to be sickly; but, reliable even in illness, he would always send a friend to take his place. In this way we got to know Ronald, Lynn, Dirk, and Cedric, all of whom, like Booker, had problems with their legal status and were

anxious to please. They weren't all as capable as Booker, though, with the exception of Cedric, whom my father often hired even when Booker was well. A round wag of a man who called Mona and me *shou hou*—skinny monkeys—he was a professed nonsmoker who was nevertheless always begging drags off of other people's cigarettes. This last habit drove our head cook, Fernando, crazy, especially since, when refused a hit, Cedric would occasionally snitch one. Winking impishly at Mona and me, he would steal up to an ashtray, take a quick puff, and then break out laughing so that the smoke came rolling out of his mouth in a great incriminatory cloud. Fernando accused him of stealing fresh cigarettes too, even whole packs.

"Why else do you think he's weaseling around in the back of the store all the time," he said. His face was blotchy with anger. "The man is a frigging thief."

Other members of the staff supported him in this contention and joined in on an "Operation Identification," which involved numbering and initialing their cigarettes—even though what they seemed to fear for wasn't so much their cigarettes as their jobs. Then one of the cooks quit; and rather than promote someone, my father hired Cedric for the position. Rumors flew that he was taking only half the normal salary, that Alex had been pressured to resign, and that my father was looking for a position with which to placate Booker, who had been bypassed because of his health.

The result was that Fernando categorically refused to work with Cedric.

"The only way I'll cook with that piece of slime," he said, shaking his huge tatooed fist, "is if it's his ass frying on the grill."

My father cajoled and cajoled, to no avail, and in the end was simply forced to put them on different schedules.   *70*

The next week Fernando got caught stealing a carton of minute steaks. My father would not tell even Mona and me how he knew to be standing by the back door when Fernando was on his way out, but everyone suspected Booker. Everyone but Fernando, that is, who was sure Cedric had been the tip-off. My father hald a staff meeting in which he tried to reassure everyone that Alex had left on his own, and that he had no intention of firing anyone. But though he was careful not to mention Fernando, everyone was so amazed that he was being allowed to stay that Fernando was incensed nonetheless.

"Don't you all be putting your bug eyes on me," he said. "*He's* the frigging crook." He grabbed Cedric by the collar.

Cedric raised an eyebrow. "Cook, you mean," he said.

At this Fernando punched Cedric in the mouth; and the words he had just uttered notwithstanding, my father fired him on the spot.

With everything that was happening, Mona and I were ready to be   *75* getting out of the restaurant. It was almost time: the days were still stuffy with summer, but our window shade had started flapping in the evening as if gearing up to go out. That year the breezes were full of salt, as they sometime were when they came in from the East, and they blew anchors and docks through my mind like so many tumbleweeds, filling my dreams with wherries and lobsters and grainy-faced men who squinted, day in and day out, at the sky.

It was time for a change, you could feel it; and yet the pancake house was the same as ever. The day before school started my father came home with bad news.

"Fernando called the police," he said, wiping his hand on his pant leg.

My mother naturally wanted to know what police; and so with much coughing and hawing, the long story began, the latest installment of which had the police calling immigration, and immigration sending an investigator. My mother sat stiff as whalebone as my father described how the man summarily refused lunch on the house and how my father had admitted, under pressure, that he knew there were "things" about his workers.

"So now what happens?"

My father didn't know. "Booker and Cedric went with him to the jail," he said. "But me, here I am." He laughed uncomfortably.

The next day my father posted bail for "his boys" and waited apprehensively for something to happen. The day after that he waited again, and the day after that he called our neighbor's law student son, who suggested my father call the immigration department under an alias. My father took his advice; and it was thus that he discovered that Booker was right: it was illegal for aliens to work, but it wasn't to hire them.

In the happy interval that ensued, my father apologized to my mother, who in turn confessed about the country club, for which my father had no choice but to forgive her. Then he turned his attention back to "his boys."

My mother didn't see that there was anything to do.

"I like to talking to the judge," said my father.

"This is not China," said my mother.

"I'm only talking to him. I'm not give him money unless he wants it."

"You're going to land up in jail."

"So what else I should do?" My father threw up his hands. "Those are my boys."

"Your boys!" exploded my mother. "What about your family? What about your wife?"

My father took a long sip of tea. "You know," he said finally. "In the war my father sent our cook to the soldiers to use. He always said it—the province comes before the town, the town comes before the family."

"A restaurant is not a town," said my mother.

My father sipped at his tea again. "You know, when I first come to the United States, I also had to hide-and-seek with those deportation guys. If people did not helping me, I'm not here today."

My mother scrutinized her hem.

After a minute I volunteered that before seeing a judge, he might try a lawyer.

He turned. "Since when did you become so afraid like your mother?" 95

I started to say it wasn't a matter of fear, but he cut me off.

"What I need today," he said, "is a son."

My father and I spent the better part of the next day standing in lines at the immigration office. He did not get to speak to a judge, but with much persistence he managed to speak to a judge's clerk, who tried to persuade him that it was not her place to extend him advice. My father, though, shamelessly plied her with compliments and offers of free pancakes until she finally conceded that she personally doubted anything would happen to either Cedric or Booker.

"Especially if they're 'needed workers,'" she said, rubbing at the red marks her glasses left on her nose. She yawned. "Have you thought about sponsoring them to become permanent residents?"

Could he do that? My father was overjoyed. And what if he saw to 100 it right away? Would she perhaps put in a good word with the judge?

She yawned again, her nostrils flaring. "Don't worry," she said. "They'll get a fair hearing."

My father returned jubilant. Booker and Cedric hailed him as their savior, their Buddha incarnate. He was like a father to them, they said; and laughing and clapping, they made him tell the story over and over, sorting over the details like jewels. And how old was the assistant judge? And what did she say?

That evening my father tipped the paperboy a dollar and bought a pot of mums for my mother, who suffered them to be placed on the dining room table. The next night he took us all out to dinner. Then on Saturday, Mona found a letter on my father's chair at the restaurant.

> Dear Mr. Chang,
>
> You are the grat boss. But, we do not like to trial, so will runing away now. Plese to excus us. People saying the law in America is fears like dragon. Here is only $140. We hope some day we can pay back the rest bale. You will getting intrest, as you diserving, so grat a boss you are. Thank you for every thing. In next life you will be burn in rich family, with no more pancaks.
>
> Yours truley,
> Booker + Cedric

In the weeks that followed my father went to the pancake house for 105 crises, but otherwise hung around our house, fiddling idly with the sump pump and boiler in an effort, he said, to get ready for winter. It was as though he had gone into retirement, except that instead of moving South, he had moved to the basement. He even took to showering my mother with little attentions, and to calling her "old girl," and when we finally heard that the club had entertained all the applications it could for the year, he was so sympathetic that he seemed more disappointed than my mother.

The Responsive Reader

1. Is there anything "typical" about the success story of this immigrant family? In what ways is the father an American-type "entrepreneur"? In what ways is he a throwback to an earlier patriarchal or paternalistic culture?
2. For many Americans from diverse cultural backgrounds (such as Jews, blacks, or Asians) acceptance into social clubs, fraternal organizations, or fraternities and sororities has been a touchstone of their acceptance into American society. What is the sad and comic story of the mother's ambition to join the country club? What was the upshot?
3. How does this story introduce you to the alternative universe of the illegal alien? What is the illegals' situation and mind-set in this story? What picture do you get of the personnel and the workings of the immigration authorities? (What are finer legal points that play a role in the story?) Why did the father in this story feel a special affinity for the illegals in their struggles with the "deportation authorities"?

Talking, Listening, Writing

4. Did you or any of your friends grow up in a family with Old Country ties? What difference did it make in your or their growing up? (Did you ever hear phrases like "This is not China" or "This is the USA"?)
5. When and where do you encounter references to or arguments against "illegal aliens"? Do you tend to take sides one way or the other?
6. Would you prefer a paternalistic to a hard-nosed "bottom-line" employer?

Thinking about Connections

The selections by Nguyen, Chin, Mirikitani, Johnson, Lee, and Jen all deal with the experiences of Asian Americans. Do you see any common trends or recurrent themes? Or is each person's story different?

INDIAN BOARDING SCHOOL: THE RUNAWAYS

Louise Erdrich

> *Louise Erdrich, of Chippewa and German-American descent, grew up in North Dakota and later went to live in New Hampshire. Her best-selling novel,* Love Medicine *(1984), won the National Book Critics Circle Award; among her other books are* The Beet Queen *(1986),* Tracks *(1988), and* The Bingo Palace *(1994). Her poem is a vivid expression of rebellion against schooling that becomes forced conversion to a different way of life.*

Thought Starters: What are your thoughts about "Americanizing" cultural minorities?

Home's the place we head for in our sleep.   1
Boxcars stumbling north in dreams
don't wait for us. We catch them on the run.
The rails, old lacerations that we love,
shoot parallel across the face and break   5
just under Turtle Mountains. Riding scars
you can't get lost. Home is the place they cross.

The lame guard strikes a match and makes the dark
less tolerant. We watch through cracks in boards
as the land starts rolling, rolling till it hurts   10
to be here, cold in regulation clothes.
We know the sheriff's waiting at midrun
to take us back. His car is dumb and warm.
The highway doesn't rock, it only hums
like a wing of long insults. The worn-down welts   15
of ancient punishments lead back and forth.

All runaways wear dresses, long green ones,
the color you would think shame was. We scrub
the sidewalks down because it's shameful work.
Our brushes cut the stone in watered arcs   20
and in the soak frail outlines shiver clear
a moment, things us kids pressed on the dark

face before it hardened, pale, remembering
delicate old injuries, the spines of names and leaves.

The Responsive Reader

1. What were the runaways running away from? What do you learn about their past history? What do you learn about the system against which they are rebelling? What is in store for them?
2. Much of what we observe in this poem has symbolic meanings and overtones. What vivid details in the runaways' surroundings mirror for them their thoughts and feelings?
3. One editor said that "the language of hurt and injury pervades this poem." What examples can you find? What role does each play in the poem?

Talking, Listening, Writing

4. Does the intense sense of grievance in this poem take you by surprise?
5. In your own experience, has schooling been a means of liberation, widening perspectives and extending opportunities? Or has it been an instrument of oppression—aiming at forced changes in attitudes, narrowing your outlook, or trying to make you over into something you did not want to be?
6. Is there something to be said in defense of policies of enforced Americanization?

Collaborative Projects

7. In the school district(s) in the area where you live, what is the policy regarding cultural diversity? If you can, talk to teachers or administrators in a position to know.

Thinking about Connections

What do the selections by Mary Crow Dog, Suzan Shown Harjo, Black Elk, and Louise Erdrich contribute to your rediscovery of the Native American past?

WRITING
WORKSHOP 3

Writing about Your Reading

Good writers tend to be good readers. When they take a break from working at the keyboard, they pick up a magazine or a book. They browse, or they look something up. They take notes. They are compulsive underliners and collectors of clippings from newspapers.

Effective writers know how to draw on their reading. At the right point in a paper, they refer to an event currently in the news. To clinch an argument, they cite authoritative statistics. For a punchline, they bring in a quotable quote from a media guru like Ellen Goodman or George Will.

TRIGGERING Writers interact with their reading in a number of ways.

- *Reading helps us firm up tentative ideas.* We write to show that something that for us was at first only a hunch was confirmed by our reading. A tentative theory was validated by the testimony of experts or insiders. When we quote, interpret, and integrate what we have read, we show that our ideas are more than superficial impressions. They have the backing of qualified observers.

- *Reading motivates us to talk back.* Much writing is triggered when we say: "Just a minute! That is simply not so," or "That is badly oversimplified!" We then write to set the record straight. We write to show where we agree with other writers and where we think they go wrong. We might be reading a reassuring discussion of slaves' living conditions in the Old South (since slaves were valuable property, owners were not likely to jeopardize their health). We might agree up to a point but soon say: "Yes—but! Look at what has been left out here!"

- *Reading raises questions in our minds.* An author writing about the need to save the spotted owl or to protect the whales can bring an important question into focus while leaving us dissatisfied with the answer he or she provides. We can then set out in search of a better answer.

GATHERING Good writers are not passive readers who read quickly to get "the general idea." Early in an article or in a book, they get the drift of the argument. They size up the writer's agenda. They follow an argument point by point, noting the supporting evidence (or lack of it). They underline or highlight key points; they put question marks or exclamation marks in the margin. They take notes, making sure not to pounce on some minor point or to mispresent the author's intention.

The following might be a student reader's annotated text of a key passage about the traditional struggle between "evolutionists" and "creationists" over what to tell students about the origin of life. Why do many parents object to having students in biology classes study Darwin's account of evolution but not the biblical account of creation?

And what if the creationists win? They might, you know, for there are millions who, faced with the choice between science and their interpretation of the Bible, will choose the Bible and reject science, regardless of the evidence.

This is not entirely because of a traditional and unthinking reverence for the literal words of the Bible; there is also a pervasive uneasiness—even an <u>actual fear—of science</u> that will drive even those who care little for Fundamentalism into the arms of the creationists. For <u>one thing, science is uncertain. Theories are subject to revision;</u> observations are open to a variety of interpretations, and <u>scientists quarrel among themselves.</u> This is disillusioning for those untrained in the scientific method, who thus turn to the rigid certainty of the Bible instead. . . .

<u>Second, science is complex and chilling.</u> The mathematical language of science is understood by very few. The <u>vistas it presents are scary—an enormous universe ruled by chance and impersonal rules, empty and uncaring,</u> ungraspable and vertiginous. How comfortable to turn instead to a small world, only a few thousand years old, and under God's personal and immediate care. . . .

<u>Third, science is dangerous.</u> There is no question but that <u>poison gas, genetic engineering and nuclear weapons and power stations are terrifying.</u> It may be that civilization is falling apart and the world we know is coming to an end. In that case, why not turn to religion and look forward to the Day of Judgment, in which you and your fellow believers will be uplifted into eternal bliss.

Isaac Asimov, "The 'Threat' of Creationism," *New York Times*

Margin annotations:

Keynote: The "Fear" of Science

① Changing Scientific Theories

② "Cold" Scientific Universe

③ Destructive Potential of Science

SHAPING In papers interpreting or arguing with a single source, the basic "Yes, but" pattern often provides the key to the writer's overall plan. For perhaps two-thirds of the paper, you might present, explain, and illustrate the author's position. However, your paper then might reach a turning point where you start saying, "Yes—but." After being a receptive reader for most of the paper, you may feel entitled to voice doubts and reservations about what you have read.

In papers using material from several sources, you need to guard against presenting undigested chunks of material. In an effective paper, the materials you have brought in mesh—without the seams showing. Make sure you integrate—correlate—material from your different sources. Here is an example of how a student reader pulled relevant material from several different sources and then worked them into a smoothly flowing paragraph:

("Man-Made Hearts: A Grim Prognosis," *U.S. News & World Report*)
    "Two winters ago, as William Schroeder sat in his hospital bed sipping a beer and declaring it 'the Coors cure,' the future looked good for permanent artificial hearts. Supporters said the devices might someday become as much of a long-term lifesaver as plastic valves and pacemakers. But by the time Schroeder died on August 6, that talk had all but vanished."

(Robert Bazell, "Hearts of Gold," *The New Republic*)
    "Exotic medical procedures certainly make compelling news stories, and for a time they can elevate relatively unknown medical institutions such as Loma Linda and Humana from obscurity. The trouble is that they are indeed experimental, and often they do not work. In the end they run the risk of attracting considerably more bad publicity than good. Despite hopes to the contrary, it takes more than one operation to make any medical establishment 'number one.' "

(Kathleen Deremy and Alan Hall, "Should Profit Drive Artificial Hearts?" *Business Week*)
    "Experts on medical ethics and health care costs are also questioning the wisdom of the current tests. If the use of artificial hearts becomes widespread, it could add up to $3 billion a year to U.S. health care costs. And that will raise some onerous questions, says Henry Aaron, an economist at Brookings Institution. 'The funding mechanisms are open-ended. The dilemma is: Does everybody get it? If not, who does?' "

(Beth Vaughan-Cole and Helen Lee, "A Heart Decision," *American Journal of Nursing*)
    "Finally, life-extending technology raises the 'right to die' issue. The committee drew the Clarks' attention to the clause in the consent form that stated that the subject could withdraw from the experiment at any time. If the recipient should be crippled physically or psychologically, the extension of life might be more of a curse than a blessing. Who could predict what the patient might want to do if he found himself in an inescapable position in which the activities that make life worthwhile might be impossible? The Clarks understood the alternative and could face that choice if necessary.
    The moral issue of suicide arises, too: The artificial heart recipient has the key that turns off the machinery."

In the finished paragraph, the student writer has used input from these notes to support the central point about the second thoughts that replaced the initial euphoria about the artificial heart:

People have long had false teeth, artificial limbs, and pacemakers—why not an artificial heart? For a while, the future looked bright for another "breakthrough" or a "medical miracle." However, after the death of artificial-heart recipient William Schroeder, many observers had second thoughts about the outlook for the permanent artificial heart as "a long-term lifesaver." Doubts and reservations multiplied. As Robert Bazell said in *The New Republic*, "Exotic medical procedures make compelling news stories" but the "trouble is that they are indeed experimental, and often they do not work." The costs are horrendous: In an article in *Business Week*, Kathleen Deremy and Alan Hall estimated that the widespread use of artificial hearts could add up to $3 billion to the nation's health costs. And the procedure raises thorny questions of medical ethics: Who decides who gets the artificial heart and who is left out? What stand do we take on the "right-to-die" issue—does the patient have the right to suicide? (As Beth Vaughan-Cole and Helen Lee pointed out in *The American Journal of Nursing*, "The artificial heart recipient has the key that turns off the machinery.")

REVISING   Reworking a first draft of a paper drawing on your reading, pay special attention to how you have introduced and identified quoted material. You may want to provide answers to questions like the following: Who said this, and where? What makes this author an authority or a reliable source—what are the quoted author's credentials? What is the point of the quotation—why are you using it here?

Here is a sampling of informative **credit tags** (brief lead-ins to a quotation):

SOURCE: In his article on "Race and Personal Identity in America," Glenn C. Loury talks about the "process of becoming free of the need to have my choices validated by 'the brothers.'"

CREDENTIALS: Ellen Berkowitz, a psychiatrist with the Florida State University program in medical sciences, summed up the current view when she said, "Mental illnesses are just like any other illness, and for the most part they are treatable."

POINT: Lester C. Thurow, in a review of Greider's *One World, Ready or Not*, belittles the fears of those who predict that the speculative excesses of today's financial markets will lead to another great collapse and another Great Depression: "Not even spectacular crashes change the economic system appreciably—much less bring it down."

Read the following sample paper. What use does it make of the student's reading?

Pink Collar Workers

Many women, like myself, when hearing the word "feminist" try to stay as far away as possible. Images of protests, marching libbers on the war path, and loud radical women come to mind. I held many misconceptions about the Women's Movement. (I thought that as many as 80% of these women hated men.) However, after having a Women's Studies class, I feel I understand much more about what the movement is trying to accomplish. After reading about the injustices that women are faced with, I can say without a doubt that I, too, am a feminist.

A conference at Seneca Falls in 1848 represented the first wave of feminism in the U.S. A small assembly affirmed their belief in equality of men and women and wanted to pursue the struggle for sex equality. The first wave of feminism was led by women activists of the antislavery movement. Some extremely outspoken feminists were Susan B. Anthony, Elizabeth Cady Stanton, Lucretia Mott, and Matilda Joslyn Gage. They all agreed that the women's right to vote was the first priority. This was not achieved until 1920, after some seventy-two years of struggle. There was only one single woman of those who had attended the Seneca Falls Convention who was still alive to cast her first vote. The following quote is from Elizabeth Cady Stanton, writing to Lucretia Mott:

> The more I think on the present condition of woman, the more I am oppressed with the reality of her degradation. The laws of our country, how unjust they are! Our customs, how vicious! What God has made sinful, both in man and woman, custom has made sinful in woman alone.

The next quote is from Susan B. Anthony from a letter she wrote to her sister, urging her to join the movement:

> We need not wait for one more generation to pass away in order to find a race of women worthy to assert the humanity of women; and that is all we claim to do.

I grew up with a best friend whose parents, especially her mother, would tell her that as long as she found a "good" man, she wouldn't have to worry about college or a good job. At school, my friend took classes like sewing and cooking. I always felt really bad for her because my parents were exactly the opposite. They always encouraged me to take pre-college classes and to first finish college before settling down. Their philosophy was that I should first be strong in myself and have a good job, then think about marriage. That way, if something was to end the marriage (divorce, death), I could take care of myself. While we were growing up, I was in after-school sports, but my friend wasn't allowed to so she'd go home and wait for me.

Everywhere we look, magazines and movies convey a message of how a woman should look and should be. I once saw an ad selling perfume where there was a beautiful woman's head attached to a snake's body with hands open toward a man. The caption read, "Dare to be tempted." This ad implied that women are like the snake in the garden trying to tempt and deceive men. If people keep seeing ads and movies like that, they will eventually begin to believe them.

Today's women of the second wave of feminism are asking how long before the struggle for equal rights—which has been pursued by feminists every year since 1920—is won. While women have won important rights during the past, some of these rights are still under challenge (e.g., abortion). Statistics show that men's incomes have increased by about 5% over women's during the same period in which women supposedly have been making more marked advances toward equality than before. So, are women more liberated now than before? Until men and women promote support toward women's issues, there will not be any advances. Even if an issue doesn't affect you directly, feminists need to be supportive of each other if any advancements are to be made.

Topics for Papers Based on Reading (A Sampling)

1. How do you react to current rewriting or revision of American history? Choose Harjo's "I Won't Be Celebrating Columbus Day" or Cerio's "Were the Spaniards *That* Cruel?" Write a "Yes, but" paper in which you first sketch any common ground you share with the author. Then go on to present and defend your disagreements.

2. In recent years, there has been much reexamination and imaginative re-creation of the Native American past. Compare the perspective on the Native American past in Black Elk's "The Earth Is All That Lasts" and in one or more recent pieces like Mary Crow Dog's "Lakota Woman" or John Lame Deer's "Listening to the Air" (Chapter 11). Focus on major similarities or differences (or both).

3. Pundits and politicians often complain about fashionable negative attitudes toward America. Trace more positive or affirmative attitudes in one or more of the following: Daniel J. Boorstin's "Why I Am Optimistic about America" (Chapter 3), Jenny Lynn Bader's "Larger Than Life" (Chapter 8), and Harvey Milk's "A City of Neighborhoods" (Chapter 2). (Do these writers share common attitudes or perspectives?)

4. Multiculturalism and diversity have become fighting words in recent years. Write a "Yes, but" paper in which you show where you agree or disagree with Arturo Madrid on diversity or with Diane Ravitch on multiculturalism.

5. Do you see common themes or recurrent topics in readings by or about young Asian Americans? You may want to read or reread selections by Frank Chin, Fox Butterfield (Chapter 5), Janice Mirikitani, and Li-Young Lee.

6. People who distrust abstract theories are fascinated with oral history—the direct and often unedited testimony of ordinary people. Look at such examples as the testimonies of José Luis and Rosa María Urbina (Chapter 4), Black Elk, or Joe Gutierrez (Chapter 4). In what they have to say, what might go beyond or counter to familiar assumptions or often cited theories?

7. Feminists represented in this volume include Maya Angelou, Patty Fisher, Alice Walker, Gloria Steinem, Judi Bari, and Laura Shapiro. Reading the essays by several of these, can you arrive at a composite portrait of a contemporary feminist?

8. History has often been the record of wars, revolutions, invasions, and great ideological confrontations. What dimension of history is represented by the writing of Lois Phillips Hudson, Garrison Keillor, and Irving Stone in this volume? What do they remind us of that in conventional political and military history is left out?

9. Have you read about controversies regarding the preservation of Native American remains in museums and the preservation of Native American burial grounds or religious sites? Find several articles, and write a paper that brings the issues into focus for your readers.

10. Fathers have come in for much criticism in an era concerned about bad parenting. The selections by Miller, Chin, Mirikitani, and Jen talk about a father's role in the family or the relationship between father and child. Write about the father's role in one or more of these selections.

4

Outsiders: Unheard Voices

I feel I am of them—
I feel I belong to those convicts and prostitutes myself,
And henceforth I will not deny them—
For how can I deny myself?

—*Walt Whitman*

The promise of America to successive waves of immigrants was that it had created a new classless society. No longer would society be run for the benefit of a small privileged elite. The blessings of liberty would be available to all. No longer would the many toil so that the few could squander the fruits of honest labor. In some of the great movements of our history, the unfree and disenfranchised reminded American society of its unkept promise. Abolition, the civil rights movement, and the women's movement aimed to make the promise of equal rights come true.

Today, however, observers see everywhere growing evidence of inequality and the failure of human hopes. The gap between the rich and the poor is widening, with millions of American children growing up in poverty and squalor. The United States, holding a sorry record, has a larger percentage of its population in jail than any other country. The gulf that separates a homeless encampment from the high-tech digs of a billionaire like Ross Perot seems as wide as the one that separated the hovel of the French peasant from the Sun King's palace at Versailles. The horrendous dropout rates for minority students in high school and college are an unanswered challenge to the Jeffersonian ideal of an educated citizenry, of free universal education. Poor sections of many American cities have turned into war zones, with guns and drugs out of control.

At the same time, affluent American society seems to be largely turning its back on its poor and sick. The social safety net, the war on poverty, and food stamps for the needy have all been made to seem part of a discredited vocabulary of "tax-and-spend" liberalism. While billionaires

193

flaunt their wealth, Americans with untreated illnesses sleep under highway overpasses and eat out of garbage cans.

Is our society going to heed those who ask us to listen to the unheard voices of the disenfranchised and the dispossessed? Or are the affluent going to insulate themselves from the marginalized, the outsiders? Are we again, like Victorian England, going to be one state but "two nations"—the privileged and those society has written off?

HOMELESS WOMAN LIVING IN A CAR

Anonymous

> *The Diane who speaks to you in the following article is the pseudonym (an assumed name) of a woman from Orange County in California, who wrote her story for the* Los Angeles Times. *Although she joined the ranks of the homeless, she is not mentally ill. She is not an addict. She is holding on to a job, but like many jobs in today's America, it doesn't pay enough for a deposit on a place to live. As she says, "I was one of you." She gave up good earnings and a middle-class lifestyle when catastrophic illness struck her family. She is not without relatives—she lived with a son in Tennessee for a time.*

Thought Starters: What is it like to be homeless? What are the causes of homelessness? Are you one of the "prosperous-looking people" who watch the homeless with suspicion?

I need anonymity, so call me Diane.   1

I try not to be seen as I watch you prosperous-looking people walking from your cars to your offices. If you saw me, your faces would mirror your suspicion and disapproval.

Yet I was one of you. And at least some of you are dancing on the same tightrope over the same abyss into which I have fallen.

None of you know I am here in the car just a few feet away from you—or what it is like once you get here. I can tell you, courtesy of a typewriter for which no one would pay me five desperately needed dollars.

Last night my money added up to $38.67, so I found a cheaper   5
motel. But tonight I will start sleeping in my car. I must eat on $6.23 for the next 10 days. Then there will be a paycheck—enough to keep me in a motel again for about a week. After that, it will be back to the car until the next payday.

Yes, I work for a living, but this job may end soon. And since the pay isn't enough for a deposit on an apartment or even a room, it would be hard to mourn its loss. Except that I have no money, no home, no evident prospects.

My downward spiral from a middle-class Orange County lifestyle began a few years ago. I was divorced and in my 50s, earning $40,000 a year as an editor, when my mother died of cancer. As the only child, I was left to care for an aged father advancing steadily into the dementia of Alzheimer's.

I quit my job, moved to his apartment in Florida and cared for him for two years. We survived on my savings and his annuity. And in 1989 he died, leaving me broke and drained of self-confidence and the ability to concentrate.

News reports told of high unemployment among "older workers," meaning anyone over 40. I was 57. Where did I fit in?

I didn't. 10

Now I drive through the streets of Newport Beach looking for a place to spend the night.

There seems something wrong with each street-side parking space. Here is a house whose windows look directly into my car. Here a space is too near an intersection with heavy traffic. To remain anywhere, I must remain invisible. Yet the one quiet area is also isolated. There is danger in isolation.

Finally, I drive slowly past the Sheraton hotel, with its many parked cars and empty parking spaces. It seems so civilized. I used to come here for business lunches when I worked across the street. Aware of the irony, I check into a space facing the street.

The back seat of my 5-year-old Oldsmobile is too short for sleeping, but the front seats recline. My legs dangle toward the brake and accelerator, yet it seems comfortable enough to think of getting some sleep.

I drop my seat back, but tense whenever footsteps approach. I dread 15 waking to find someone staring at me, so a large, black, cotton knit jacket I place over my head makes me feel nicely invisible. If I were dressed entirely in black, I'd be even less visible. From now on I shall prepare for the night like a cat burglar.

I sleep soundly for two hours, then fitfully for the next hour and a half. To avoid discovery, I must leave before daylight.

This is the first night of what will become four months of living out of my car—long hours of solitude, physical discomfort, boredom and sometimes hunger.

But it will teach me much about myself—and that line beyond which lies permanent hopelessness.

When I awaken, the night sky is beginning to pale. I drive toward McDonald's and sit impatiently in a parking lot for its 6 o'clock opening. I can wait for coffee, but I need the restroom. I take my dish-washing detergent along and manage a passable sponge bath.

After one of the most boring days and nights of my life, I wake up 20 the next morning and drive to Ralph's and spend 69 cents of my remaining $2.56 for a can of tuna. Carrying my tuna back to the car, I find a wallet full of cash and credit cards in the parking lot. I take it to the market manager. As I walk back to my car, I wonder: How hungry or desperate would I have to be to have kept that wallet? I don't know, but I'm not there now and I'm thankful.

I awaken the next morning at 4:30 after sleeping almost five hours.

This is a go-to-work day for me. I work a 40-hour week in four days. But while most people yearn for quitting time, I now look forward to the hours in the office, that place of blissful luxury.

It has hot water, coffee, tea, drinking water, a newspaper, a restroom, my own chair and a place to leave the car. I hope I will be alert enough to do a good day's work.

I manage to perform well. Only in the warm, airless afternoon do I suddenly drop off over my papers and yank instantly awake. I pull through the fog, pour more coffee and focus on my work. The irony is I work for a firm that publishes books advertising apartment rentals and their vast array of comforts and amenities.

Back in my car, one night late, I awaken abruptly. I hear the sound   *25* of a key being slowly worked into my door lock and turned, just inches from my ear. My scalp tingles. The key does not work and is slowly withdrawn. I listen warily. I can lunge for the horn if need be. That could bring someone out of the hotel—and probably end my tenancy at the Sheraton. I wait, unmoving and unseeing under my nighttime shroud.

In a few minutes, I hear a key working the lock of a nearby car door or trunk. It opens and soon closes softly. Then it is quiet. I lie awake, adrenaline rushing, and finally sleep fitfully. This is a cold wash of reality: I am no more immune from danger than anyone else.

This payday has loomed larger in my mind with each passing day. I feel increasing urgency to buy some fresh food, to have a bed to sleep in for a few nights, to soak in a tub. Such expectation allowed me very little sleep last night.

But the paychecks from out of state are delayed; they won't be here until tomorrow.

Tonight I eat my last saved slice of bread and margarine. And, with a wary eye on the gas tank, which reads empty, I drive to the Sheraton yet again.

The paychecks arrive. I check into a motel and almost instantly fall   *30* asleep, unable to enjoy the luxury of tub and television until tomorrow.

I wish I had discovered earlier how much money can be saved by sleeping in the car. It's the only way I know now to save enough to rent a room near my office. Allowing for a night at a motel once a week to catch up on sleep, for laundry and for general self-repair, it will probably take two months or so to save up.

But will I be able to keep up the rent?

When I returned to California from Florida, I finally landed a low-paying but full-time job and was promised rapid advancement. Now I find that the promises are not going to be kept by the corporation that bought this company.

I decide to take a stand: Live up to the promises the company made me or I quit. They praise me but won't budge. I quit, and they look surprised. It was hardly noble or heroic. When you are already living out of your car, it is easier to give up a job. If you have a home, you can imagine losing it.

The downward spiral continues in earnest. The auto life had a   35
rhythm based on paydays. But now there are no more paychecks to come.

My son, who lives in Tennessee, is suspicious. He's been aware that I'm having money problems, but my lack of a permanent phone number and address prompts him to ask me outright if I'm sleeping in my car. I've tried carefully to keep this from him. I don't want to burden him and his family with my financial problems. So when he asks, I laugh it off.

The gas tank is precariously low. I start walking almost everywhere.

It's harder to look for a new job. Without motel room telephones and the workplace, there is no way to leave call-back numbers when responding to ads. I can walk major distances, but it means arriving hot, sweaty and too tired to impress anybody.

I walk as much as 25 miles a day. Now, after seven days of exceptional walking, my left knee is stunningly painful, and the right knee echoes the pain. There are other unfamiliar pains running down the front of my legs. But if I don't start walking, I won't get a gallon of gas into the car and I won't get any food.

So I grit my teeth and walk, overriding the pain with necessity. For   40
the next three days, I continue to walk many miles. The pain fills every part of my brain.

Now I am hobbling, so crippled that I can hardly get in and out of the car. One day of rest makes no improvement, nor do two, nor three. Movement is excruciating.

I have come to a critical time. My days have become a self-defeating spiral of non-accomplishment. Everything I do now is devoted to simple survival. If I don't do something to halt it, I could be on my way into a rougher homelessness. But what can I do?

The Responsive Reader

1. Are you one of those who, in the words of Diane, "are dancing on the same tightrope over the same abyss into which I have fallen"?
2. Does this article change your thinking about the causes of homelessness?
3. Many people block out unpleasant realities. How real does Diane make the problems, deprivations, and dangers of homelessness to you? Can you imagine yourself in her place?

Talking, Listening, Writing

4. How would you answer Diane's final question: "What can I do?"
5. Do you know anyone who is homeless, has no "permanent address," or lives out of a truck or car?

Collaborative Projects

6. How do people in our society come to terms with the growing number of homeless in our midst? How do they explain, deplore, or rationalize what is happening? Have you and fellow students seen the issue taken up in editorials, newspaper columns, letters to the editor, call-ins to talk shows, speeches by politicians, sermons? Can you and your classmates reach any general conclusions about the state of public opinion on this subject?

OUR SCHOOLS AND OUR CHILDREN

Mike Rose

Prestige universities like Harvard, Stanford, Berkeley, UCLA, Columbia, and Chicago are only a few miles down the road from slums. Mike Rose, a university teacher who himself came from the wrong side of the tracks, has been fascinated by the way the American system of education, and especially higher education, helps define and perpetuate the class structure of this country. The son of desperately poor Italian immigrants, Rose has devoted his career to helping students from minority or nonaffluent backgrounds survive in the arena of academic discourse, where many of them enter, in the words of one of Rose's colleagues, "with only an honest face for protection." Like fellow humanists, Rose believes in the untapped potential—the native intelligence and ability to learn of students shortchanged by traditional educational assumptions and procedures. The following selection is the opening essay in Mike Rose's widely read Lives on the Boundary *(1989). He wrote this book to explore how his own early experiences were "reflected in other working-class lives I've encountered: the isolation of neighborhoods, information poverty, the limited means of protecting children from family disaster, the predominance of such disaster, the resilience of imagination, the intellectual curiosity and literate enticements that remain hidden from the schools, the feeling of scholastic inadequacy, the dislocations that come from crossing educational boundaries." Recently Rose published* Possible Lives *as a sequel or companion book to* Lives on the Boundary.

Thought Starters: What do you know about the class structure of traditional societies? Is America still a classless society?

Her name is Laura, and she was born in the poor section of Tijuana, the Mexican border city directly south of San Diego. Her father was a food vendor, and her memories of him and his chipped white cart come back to her in easy recollection: the odor of frying meat, the feel of tortillas damp with grease, and the serpentine path across the city; rolling the cart through dust, watching her father smile and haggle and curse—hawking burritos and sugar water to old women with armloads of blouses and figurines, to blond American teenagers, wild with freedom, drunk and loud and brawny. She came to the United States when she was six, and by dint of remarkable effort—on her parents' part and hers—she now sits in classes at UCLA among those blond apparitions. 1

She has signed up for and dropped the course I'm teaching, remedial English, *four* times during this, her freshman year: twice in the summer before she officially started, once in each of the quarters preceding this one. This is her fifth try. She is with me in my office, and she is scared to death: "I get in there, and everything seems okay. But as soon as we start writing, I freeze up. I'm a crummy writer, I know it. I know I'm gonna make lots of mistakes and look stupid. I panic. And I stop coming."

The Middle Ages envisioned the goddess of grammar, Grammatica, as an old woman. In one later incarnation, she is depicted as severe, with a scalpel and a large pair of pincers. Her right hand, which is by her side, grasps a bird by its neck, its mouth open as if in a gasp or a squawk. All this was emblematic, meant as a memory aid for the budding grammarian. But, Lord, how fitting the choices of emblem were—the living thing being strangled, beak open but silent, muted by the goddess Grammatica. And the scalpel, the pincers, are reminders to the teacher to be vigilant for error, to cut it out with the coldest tool. Laura has never seen the obscure book that holds my illustration of Grammatica, but she knows the goddess intimately, the squinting figure who breathes up to her side whenever she sits down to write.

It is the first week of fall quarter, and I am observing a section of English A, UCLA's most basic writing course, the course that students and many professors have come to call "bonehead." English A students vex universities like UCLA. By the various criteria the institutions use, the students deserve admission—have earned their way—but they are considered marginal, "high risk" or "at risk" in current administrative parlance. "The truly illiterate among us," was how one dean described them.

Dr. Gunner is a particularly gifted teacher of English A. She refuses   5 to see her students as marginal and has, with a colleague, developed a writing course on topics in Western intellectual history. As I watch her, she is introducing her class to the first item on her syllabus, classical mythology. She has situated the Golden Age of Athens on a time line on the blackboard, and she is encouraging her students to tell her what they already know about Greek culture. Someone mentions Aristotle; someone else says "Oedipus Rex . . . and the Oedipus complex." "Who wrote about the Oedipus complex?" asks Dr. Gunner. "Freud," offers a soft voice from the end of the table.

One boy is slouched down in his chair, wearing a baseball cap, the bill turned backward. Two or three others are leaning forward: One is resting his head on his folded arms and looking sideways at Dr. Gunner. A girl by me has set out neatly in front of her two pencils, an eraser, a tiny stapler, and a pencil sharpener encased in a little plastic egg. Talismans, I think. Magical objects. The girl sitting next to her is somber and watches the teacher suspiciously. At the end of the table two other girls sit up straight and watch Dr. Gunner walk back and forth in front of the board. One plays with her bracelet. "Narcissus," says Dr. Gunner. "Narcissus. Who was Narcissus?" "A guy who fell in love with himself," says the boy with his head on his arms.

The hour goes on, the class warms up, students let down their defenses, discussion drifts back and forth along the time line. Someone asks about a book he read in high school called *The Stranger.* Another knows that *renaissance* "means rebirth in the French language." Socrates and Plato get mentioned, as do Mars and Apollo. Dr. Gunner's first name is Eugenia; she writes it on the board and asks the class what Greek word it looks like: "Gene," says the girl with the sharpener and stapler. A halting "genetics" comes from the wary girl. "Eugenia, eugen . . . ," says the boy with the baseball cap, shifting in his chair. "Hey, that means something like race or good race." "Race control," says the boy with his head on his arms.

These are the truly illiterate among us.

It hits you most forcefully at lunchtime: the affluence of the place, the attention to dress and carriage, but the size, too—vast and impersonal, a labyrinth of corridors and classrooms and libraries; you're also struck by the wild intersection of cultures, spectacular diversity, compressed by a thousand social forces. I'm sitting under a canopy of purple jacarandas with Bobby, for Bobby is in a jam. Students are rushing to food lines or dormitories or sororities, running for elevators or taking stairs two at a time. Others "blow it off" and relax, mingling in twos and threes. Fifties fashion is everywhere: baggy pants, thin ties, crew cuts, retro ponytails—but so are incipient Yuppiedom and cautious punk, and this month's incarnation of the nuevo wavo. Palm trees sway on the backs of countless cotton shirts. A fellow who looks Pakistani zooms by on a skateboard. A Korean boy whose accent is still very strong introduces himself as Skip. Two Middle Eastern girls walk by in miniskirts and heels. Sometimes I think I'm teaching in a film by Ridley Scott.

I first met Bobby when he enrolled in a summer program I had   *10* developed for underprepared students. I was visiting the American social history course we offered, listening to the lecturer discuss the role of working women in the late-nineteenth-century mercantile economy. It was an organized, nicely paced presentation. The professor provided a broad overview of the issues and paused to dwell on particularly revealing cases, reading from editorials of the time and from a rich collection of letters written by those women. I was sitting in the back, watching the eighty or so students, trying to get a sense of their involvement, when I noticed this young man down the aisle to my left. He was watching the professor intently. His notebook was open in front of him. His pen was poised. But he wasn't writing. Nothing. I'd look back during the hour: still attentive but still no notes. I caught up with him after class—he knew me from our orientation—and asked how he liked the lecture. "Interesting," he said. So I asked him why he wasn't taking any notes. "Oh, well, 'cause the teacher was just talking about people and reading letters and such. She didn't cover anything important."

For Bobby, and for lots of other freshmen in lots of other colleges, history is a chronicle. History is dates and facts: Who invaded whom?

When? With how many men? And Bobby could memorize this sort of thing like a demon. But *social* history, the history of moods and movements and ordinary people's lives, left Bobby without a clue. He was a star in his inner-city school, and he developed a set of expectations about subjects like history (history is lists of facts) and had appropriated a powerful strategy that fit his expectations (he memorized the lists). Social history was as unfamiliar to him as a Bahamian folktale.

So I sit under the jacarandas with Bobby. His girlfriend joins us. She is having a rough time, too. Both have been at UCLA for about three months now. They completed the summer program, and they are now in the fourth week of fall term. Bobby is talking animatedly about his linguistics course. It is all diagrams and mathematics and glottal stops. It was not what he expected from a course about the study of language. "They're asking me to do things I don't know how to do. All the time. Sometimes I sit in the library and wonder if I'm gonna make it. I mean I don't know, I really don't know." He pauses, looks out across the food lines, looks back at me. He gestures to himself and his girlfriend: "We don't belong at UCLA, do we?"

Students are everywhere. A girl squeals "Vanessa!" and runs over to hug a friend. A big guy with a packpack cuts into the food line. I shift down the bench to make room for a girl with a knee brace. Palm trees swaying on cotton shirts, Pakistanis on skateboards. History woven from letters, language converted to mathematics. A young man who never failed, failing. It's easy to forget what a strange place this is.

The back-to-basics movement got a lot of press, fueled as it was by fears of growing illiteracy and cultural demise. The movement raked in all sorts of evidence of decline: test scores, snippets of misspelled prose, enrollments in remedial courses in our finest schools. Guardians of culture were called on to pronounce and diagnose, and they did. Poets, historians, philologists, and literary scholars were ominously cited in *Newsweek*'s highly influential article, *Why Johnny Can't Write*. Among the many, many children, adolescents, and young adults who became the focus of this national panic were college freshmen like Laura, Bobby, and the members of Eugenia Gunner's English A. People with low SATs; people who wrote poorly. The back-to-basics advocates suggested—and many university faculty members solemnly agreed—that what was needed here was a return to the fundamentals: drills on parts of speech, grammar, rules of punctuation, spelling, usage. All of that. Diagraming sentences too. We've gotten soft. Images of the stern grammarian were resurrected from a misty past: gray, pointer in hand, rows of boys and girls, orderly as syntax, reflected in the flat lenses of his spectacles.

The more things change, the more they remain the same. In 1841   *15* the president of Brown complained that "students frequently enter college almost wholly unacquainted with English grammar." In the mid-1870s, Harvard professor Adams Sherman Hill assessed the writing of students after four years at America's oldest college: "Every year Harvard graduates a certain number of men—some of them high scholars—whose manuscripts would disgrace a boy of twelve." In 1896, *The Nation* ran an article entitled "The Growing Illiteracy of American Boys," which reported on another Harvard study. The authors of this one lamented the spending of "much time, energy, and money" teaching students "what they ought to have learnt already." There was "no conceivable justification," noted a rankled professor named Goodwin, to use precious revenues "in an attempt to enlighten the Egyptian darkness in which no small portion of Harvard's undergraduates were sitting." In 1898 the University of California instituted the Subject A Examination (the forerunner of the writing test that landed Laura, Bobby, and Dr. Gunner's crew in English A) and was soon designating about 30 to 40 percent of those who took it as not proficient in English, a percentage that has remained fairly stable to this day. Another development was this: In 1906 an educational researcher named Franklyn Hoyt conducted the first empirical study to determine if traditional instruction in grammar would improve the quality of writing. His results were not encouraging. Neither were the majority of the results of such studies carried out over the next eighty years. Whatever that stern grammarian was doing to his charges, it didn't seem to affect large numbers of them, historically or experimentally. There is one thing, though, we can say with certainty: He wasn't teaching the earlier incarnations of Laura, Bobby, and most of those in English A. Women, immigrants, children of the working class, blacks, and Latinos occupied but a few of the desks at Brown, Harvard, and the other elite colleges. Those disgraceful students were males from the upper crust.

Statistics are often used to demonstrate educational decay, but let's consider our literacy crisis through the perspective provided by another set of numbers. In 1890, 6.7 percent of America's fourteen- to seventeen-year-olds were attending high school; by 1978 that number had risen to 94.1 percent. In 1890, 3.5 percent of all seventeen-year-olds graduated from high school; by 1970 the number was 75.6 percent. In the 1930s "functional literacy" was defined by the Civilian Conservation Corps as a state of having three or more years of schooling; during World War II the army set the fourth grade as a standard; in 1947 the Census Bureau defined functional illiterates as those having fewer than five years of schooling; in 1952 the bureau raised the criterion to the sixth grade; by 1960 the Office of Education was setting the eighth grade as a benchmark; and by the late 1970s some authorities were suggesting that completion of high school should be the defining criterion of functional literacy. In the United States just over 75 percent of our young people complete high school; in Sweden 45 to 50 percent complete the gymnasium (grades 11 to 12); in the Federal Republic of Germany about 15 percent are enrolled in the *Oberprima* (grade 13). In 1900 about 4 percent of American eighteen- to twenty-two-year-olds attended college; by the late 1960s, 50 percent of eighteen- to nineteen-year-olds were entering some form of postsecondary education. Is this an educational system on the decline, or is it a system attempting to honor—through wrenching change—the many demands of a pluralistic democracy?

It would be an act of hollow and evil optimism to downplay the problems of American schools—the way they're structured and financed, the unevenness of their curricula, the low status of their teachers, their dreary record with the poor and disenfranchised. But what a curious thing it is that when we do criticize our schools, we tend to frame our indictments in terms of decline, a harsh, laced-with-doom assault stripped of the historical and social realities of American education—of its struggle to broaden rather than narrow access, of the increasing social as well as cognitive demands made on it, of our complex, ever-changing definitions of what it means to be literate and what a citizenry should know. How worthy of reflection it is that our policy is driven so often by a yearning for a mythic past or by apples-and-oranges comparisons to countries, past or present, less diverse and less educationally accessible than ours.

"The schools," write social historians David Cohen and Barbara Neufeld, "are a great theater in which we play out [the] conflicts in the culture." And it's our cultural fears—of internal decay, of loss of order, of diminishment—that weave into our assessments of literacy and scholastic achievement. The fact is that the literacy crisis has been with us for some time, that our schools have always been populated with students who don't meet some academic standard. It seems that whenever we let ourselves realize that, we do so with a hard or fearful heart. We figure that things were once different, that we've lost something, that somehow a virulent intellectual blight has spread among us. So we look to a past—one that never existed—for the effective, no-nonsense pedagogy we assume that past must have had. We half find and half create a curriculum and deploy it in a way that blinds us to the true difficulties and inequities in the ways we educate our children. Our purpose, finally, is to root out disease—and, too often, to punish. We write reductive prescriptions for excellence— that seductive, sentimental buzzword—and we are doing it . . . with a flourish. What gets lost in all this are the real needs of children and adults working to make written language their own.

Every day in our schools and colleges, young people confront reading and writing tasks that seem hard or unusual, that confuse them, that they fail. But if you can get close enough to their failure, you'll find knowledge that the assignment didn't tap, ineffective rules and strategies that have a logic of their own; you'll find clues, as well, to the complex ties between literacy and culture, to the tremendous difficulties our children face as they attempt to find their places in the American educational system. Some, like Laura, are struck dumb by the fear of making a mistake; others, like Bobby, feel estranged because familiar cognitive landscapes have shifted, because once-effective strategies have been rendered obsolete; and still others are like the young men and women in Dr. Gunner's classroom: They know more than their tests reveal but haven't been taught how to weave that knowledge into coherent patterns. For Laura, Bobby, and the others the pronouncement of deficiency came late, but for many it comes as early as the first grade. Kids find themselves sitting on the threatening boundaries of the classroom. Marginal. Designated as "slow learners" or "remedial" or, eventually, "vocational."

The Responsive Reader

1. What to you is most striking in the case histories of students that Rose gives here? Why did he select these particular students? What in their stories is most relevant to his argument?
2. Grammar has been a hurdle and an affliction to successive generations of students. Do you recognize any of the methods and assumptions Rose mentions or describes? What does Rose think is wrong with the traditional teaching of grammar? Does his discussion point to more productive methods and approaches?
3. For Mike Rose, the dean talking about "illiterates" and Dr. Gunner teaching mythology seem to represent not only two different personalities but two different philosophies of education. What to you is the key difference? How would you explain it in your own words? What difference does it make?
4. "Standards" and "excellence" are words often found in discussions of American education published by think tanks or printed in the columns of establishment pundits. Why does Rose call excellence "that seductive, sentimental buzzword"? What is wrong with "excellence"? What is wrong with "standards"?
5. Rose fights the fashionable talk about "decline" or "decay" in American education. How? How does he make use of historical background and statistics? What makes his argument persuasive or unconvincing for you?

Talking, Listening, Writing

6. What evidence have you seen that the makeup of the student body in the typical American school or college is determined largely by the social class of the students' parents? What evidence have you seen to the contrary? Do you think it is true that American educational institutions define and perpetuate the class structure of this country?
7. Would you describe your own experiences in the American educational system as mainly positive or mainly negative? Have you encountered teachers like the kind of teacher Mike Rose seems to be? Have you had experiences with teachers, administrators, or "the system" similar to the ones Rose criticizes?

Collaborative Projects

8. In his book, Rose repeatedly refers to the national "panic" about deficiencies of American public schools. Has the panic mode or the volume of complaints about the schools lessened since he wrote the book? Working with a group, you may want to check out current criticism of the schools in the media. Is there anything like a consensus? Are any hopeful directions or initiatives emerging?

TIME

Nathan McCall

During the decade spanning the Reagan and Bush presidencies, the population of America's prison Gulag archipelago tripled from half a million to an estimated million and a half human beings. In some communities, prison construction was one of the few growth industries left. Today, three-strike laws are projected to swell prisons to the point where money spent on jails will outstrip the money the nation spends on schools. Nathan McCall is an African American journalist who went to hell and back in the American prison system and told his story in Makes Me Wanna Holler *(1994). Growing up in a black working-class neighborhood in Portsmouth, Virginia, he had a stepfather who brooked "no hustling, gambling in the streets, or carrying on" and who believed in "work, work, work." (McCall says he and his brothers "saw my old man working hard, and he had nothing.") Like many young black males, McCall was carrying a gun by the time he was fifteen and was in jail by the time he was twenty. After serving three years for armed robbery, he studied journalism at Norfolk State University. He became a reporter for the* Virginia Pilot-Ledger Star *and the* Atlanta Journal and Constitution *and joined the prestigious* Washington Post *in 1989.*

Thought Starters: Is America's large prison population invisible in the American media?

I was standing in my cell doorway, checking out the scene on the floor below, when a white convict appeared in the doorway across from mine. He stood stark still and looked straight ahead. Without saying a word, he lifted a razor blade in one hand and began slashing the wrist of the other, squirting blood everywhere. He kept slashing, rapid-fire, until finally he dropped the razor and slumped to the floor, knocking his head against the bars as he went down.

Other inmates standing in their doorways spotted him and yelled, "Guard! Guard! Guard!" Guards came running, rushed the unconscious inmate to the dispensary, and ordered a hallboy to clean up the pool of blood oozing down the walkway. Later, when I asked the hallboy why the dude had tried to take himself out, he said, "That *time* came down on him and he couldn't take the pressure. You know them white boys can't handle time like us brothers. They weak."

It was a macho thing for a guy to be able to handle his time. Still, every once in a while, time got to everybody, no matter how tough they were. Hard time came in seasonal waves that wiped out whole groups of cats, like a monsoon. Winter was easiest on everybody. There was the sense that you really weren't missing anything on the streets because everyone was indoors. Spring and summer were hell. The Dear John letters started flowing in, sending heartbroken dudes to the fence for a clean, fast break over and into the countryside. Fall was a wash. The weather was nice enough to make you think of home, but winter was just ahead, giving you something to look forward to. Time.

I saw the lifers go through some serious changes about time. Some days, those cats carried theirs as good as anybody else, but other days, they didn't. You could look in their eyes sometimes and tell they had run across a calendar, one of those calendars that let you know what day of the week your birthday will fall on ten years from now. Or you could see in the wild way they started acting and talking that they were on the edge. Then it was time to get away from them, go to the other side of the prison yard, and watch the fireworks. They went *off*. Especially the brothers. They were determined not to go down kicking and screaming and slashing their wrists like the white boys. The brothers considered themselves too hard for that. When the time got to be too much for them, they'd go fuck with somebody and get themselves in a situation where there was no win. It was their way of saying, "Go on, kill me. Gimme a glorious way to get outta this shit."

My time started coming down on me when I realized I'd reached the 5
one-year mark and had at least two to go. I tried to cling tighter to Liz, but that didn't work. After I was transferred from the jail to Southampton, it seemed we both backed out on the marriage plans. She didn't bring it up, and neither did I. Liz's visits and letters slacked off, and I felt myself slipping out of touch with the outside world. When Liz did visit, she seemed distant and nervous, like there was something she wanted to tell me but couldn't get out. That drove me crazy, along with about a hundred thousand other irritations that constantly fucked with my head.

I thought a lot about the irony of the year 1976: It was the year Alex Haley published the slave epic *Roots* and the country was celebrating the two hundredth year of its freedom from tyranny. It seemed that every time I opened a magazine or walked past a TV set, there was talk about the yearlong bicentennial celebration. I'd heard white people brag about being free, white, and twenty-one. There I was, black, twenty-one, and in the penitentiary. It seemed I'd gotten it all wrong.

It's a weird feeling being on the edge and knowing that there's not much you can do about it but hang on. You can't get help for prison depression. You can't go to a counselor and say, "Look, I need a weekend pass. This punishment thing is taking more out of me than I think it was intended to take."

I didn't want to admit to myself that the time was getting to me that much, let alone admit it to anybody else. So I determined to do the macho thing: suffer quietly. Sometimes it got so bad I had to whisper to myself, "Hold on, Nate. Hold on."

Frustrated and depressed, I went to the prison and bought a green spiral-bound tablet and started a journal, partly out of a need to capture my fears and feelings, and partly to practice using the new words I learned. I adopted a journal theme—a quote I ran across by the writer Oliver Wendell Holmes—as encouragement to keep me pushing ahead and holding on:

> I find the great thing in this world is not so much where we stand as in what direction we are moving. To reach the port of heaven, we must sail, sometimes with the wind and sometimes against it— but we must sail, and not drift, nor lie at anchor.

It made me feel better sometimes to get something down on paper 10 just like I felt it. It brought a kind of relief to be able to describe my pain. It was like, if I could describe it, it lost some of its power over me. I jotted down innermost thoughts I couldn't verbalize to anyone else, recorded what I saw around me, and expressed feelings inspired by things I read. Often, the thoughts I wrote down reflected my struggle with time.

> *Each day I inspire myself with the hope that by some miracle of God or act of legislature I will soon regain my freedom. However, from occasional conversations, I find that many other inmates have entertained the same hope— for years.*
> *May 21, 1976*

Even the guys doing less than life had a hard time. Anything in the double digits—ten years to serve, twenty, forty, sixty—could be a backbreaker. I had a buddy, Cincinnati. Real outgoing cat. Every time you saw him, he was talking beaucoup trash. But Cincinnati was doing a hard forty, and it drove him up a wall at least twice a week. He fought it by trying to keep super-busy. With a white towel hung loosely over his shoulder and several cartons of cigarettes tucked under his arm, Cincinnati (we called him that because that's where he was from) would bop briskly across the yard, intent on his missions. He'd stop and jawbone with a group of guys hanging out near the canteen, then hand a carton of cigarettes to one of them and hurry off to the next meeting.

Cincinnati was one of several major dealers at Southampton who used the drug-peddling skills they'd learned on the streets to exploit the crude prison economy. In that economy, cigarettes replaced money as the medium of exchange. Favors and merchandise were negotiated in terms of their worth in packs of cigarettes. For twelve cartons of cigarettes, a guy could take out a contract to have somebody set up on a drug bust, or get them double-banked or shanked. Eight packs could get you a snappy pair of prison brogans from one of the brothers on the shoe-shop crew. For three packs each week, laundry workers would see to it your shirts and pants were crisply starched. Cincinnati liked to get his gray prison shirts starched so that he could turn up the collar and look real cool.

The really swift dealers found ways to convert a portion of their goods to forbidden cash, which they used to bribe guards to get them reefer and liquor, or saved for their eventual return to the streets.

Cincinnati, who was about two years older than me and had logged a lot more street time, was penitentiary-rich. He decorated his cell with plush blue towels and stockpiled so much stuff that the rear wall of his cell looked like a convenience store. It was stacked from floor to ceiling with boxes of cookies, cigarettes, and other stuff he sold, "two for one," to inmates seeking credit until payday.

Watching cats like him, I often thought about Mo Battle and his 15 theory about pawns. Cincinnati handled time and played chess like he lived: He failed to think far ahead and he chased pawns all over the board. In his free time off from the kitchen, where he worked, he busied himself zigzagging across the prison yard, collecting outstanding debts and treating his petty "bidness" matters like they were major business deals.

Cincinnati was playful and cheery most of the time. He was as dark as night and had a shiny gold tooth that gleamed like a coin when he smiled. Short and squat, he had a massive upper body and a low center of gravity, like Mike Tyson. In fact, his voice, high-pitched and squeaky, sounded a lot like Tyson's, too. It was the kind of voice that sounded like it belonged to a child. But nobody mistook Cincinnati for a child. He was a tank, and could turn from nice guy to cold killer in a split second.

He addressed everybody as "bro'." I'd see him on the yard and say, "Yo, Cincinnati, what's happ'nin'?" And if he was in a good mood, he'd say, "Bro' Nate, life ain't nothin' but a meatball."

But time came down on Cincinnati, like it did on everybody else. He had to do at least ten of his forty years before going up for parole. I could tell when he was thinking about it. I'd run into him on the yard and say, "What's happ'nin', Cincinnati?" He'd shake his head sadly and say, "Bro' Nate, I'm busted, disgusted, and *can't* be trusted."

Cincinnati was so far away from home that he never got visits. On visiting days, he usually went out to the main sidewalk on the yard and looked through the fence as people visiting other inmates pulled into the parking lot.

Other times, I could tell how depressed he was by the way he 20 handled defeat on the chessboard. I beat him all the time and taunted him, but sometimes he didn't take it well. Just before I put him in checkmate, he'd get frustrated and knock one of his big arms against the board, sending the pieces crashing to the floor. Then he'd look up with a straight face and say, "Oh, I'm sorry, Bro' Nate. I didn't mean to do that."

We were playing chess one day when Cincinnati stared at the board a long time without making a move. I got impatient. "Go on and move, man! You gonna lose anyway!"

Ignoring me, Cincinnati kept his eyes glued to the board and didn't speak for a long time. After a while, he said, "Bro' Nate, I'm gonna make a break for the fence. I been thinking about it a long time. I got a lotta money saved up. I can get outta state. You wanna come?"

Any inmate who says he's never thought about escaping is either lying or telling the sad truth. The sad truth is, the only dudes who don't think about making a break are those who are either so institutionalized that their thoughts seldom go beyond the prison gates, or who were so poor in the streets that they had been rescued and are glad to be someplace where they are guaranteed three hots and a cot.

There were a few desperate, fleeting moments when I thought half-seriously about making a run. Southampton is ringed by a tall barbed-wire fence with electrical current running through it, but everybody knew the heat was turned off much of the time. Sometimes, I'd stare at that fence and think about how to scale it. I pictured myself tossing my thick winter coat on top of the barbed wire to test the heat and protect my hands, climbing quickly to the top, and leaping to the other side to make my dash before tower guards could get off a good shot. I'd mapped an escape route based on what I'd seen of the area while traveling with the gun gang. I'd thought it through like a chess match, move for move. That's why I didn't try. When I thought it through, I always saw a great chance of getting busted or leading such a miserable life on the run that it would be another form of imprisonment.

Looking at Cincinnati, I jokingly turned down his offer to run. 25
"Naw, brother-man. I'm gonna squat here. I'm expecting a visit from my lady this weekend. I'd hate for her to come and find me gone. Besides, I can handle my bid. You do the crime, you gotta do the time, Jack!"

I forgot about our conversation until a week or two later, when the big whistle at the guard tower sounded, signaling all inmates to go to their cells to be counted. The whistle blew at certain times every day, but on this day, it sounded at an odd hour, meaning there was something wrong. After we went to our cells, the word spread that Cincinnati had made a break. He'd hidden in the attic of the school building, then scrambled over the fence after a posse left the compound to hunt for him.

Following the count, guys in my building (I was in C-3 by then) grew real quiet. Every time someone escaped, I got quiet and privately rooted for him to get away. I sat on my bunk thinking about Cincinnati, trying to picture him out in the pitch dark, his black face sweating, ducking through bushes, hotly pursued by white men with guns and barking dogs. I imagined him low-running across some broad field, dodging lights and listening for suspicious sounds. I imagined the white country folks, alerted to the escape, grabbing their shotguns and joining the hunt.

Some weeks after Cincinnati made his break, he got caught some-where in the state. It saddened me. He was shipped to a maximum-security prison more confining than Southampton, and he got more time tacked on to the forty years that was already giving him hell.

Prison paranoia is a dangerous thing. It can affect a person to the extent that he becomes distrustful of anyone and everyone. Even though my woman has displayed no signs of infidelity, I find myself scrutinizing her behavior each week (in the visiting room), searching her eyes for the slightest faltering trait. I search in hope that I discover none, but hope even more that if there is, I will detect it before it discovers me and slithers back into some obscure hiding place.
June 4, 1976

I walked into the crowded visiting room and took a seat at the table with Liz. My intuition told me that something was up. She'd come alone, without my parents or my son, and her brown eyes, usually bright and cheery, were sad and evasive. In a letter she'd sent to me earlier in the week, she had said there was something she wanted to discuss. I sensed what it was, and I'd come prepared.

We exchanged small talk, then there was this awkward silence. 30 Finally, I spoke, relieving her of a burden I sensed was killing her. "You're seeing someone else, aren't you?"

She nodded. "Yes."

There was a long pause as she waited for my reaction. I looked down at the floor and thought about what I'd just heard. My worst fear had come true. Liz couldn't hang. I'd have to do the time alone. I under-stood. She'd done the best she could. She'd been a helluva lot more sup-portive and reliable than I would have been under the circumstances. The best I could do was be grateful for what she'd done. Take it and grow, as she used to say. I tried to put on a brave face, and I said, "I understand, really. . . . Well, nothing I can do about that but wish you the best. I would like you to hang in there with me, but really, I don't know when I'm gettin' outta here."

She listened quietly and nodded as I talked. When I finished, she didn't say much. We sat there, bummed out, looking at each other. Mr. and Miss Manor. Liz wished me well. Her eyes watered. Then she said good-bye, and left.

I practically ran back to my cell that Saturday morning. I wanted to get back there before the tear ducts burst. It was like trying to get to the bathroom before the bladder gives out. I made it, went inside, and flopped down on a stool. I turned on the stereo, slid in one of my favorite gospel tapes, *Amazing Grace,* by Aretha Franklin, and closed my eyes. The tape opened with a song called "Mary, Don't You Weep." The deep strains of a full gospel choir, comforting the sister of Lazarus after his death, sang in a rich harmony that sent shivers through me:

Hush, Mary, don't you weep.
Hush, Mary, don't you weep.

When I heard those words, the floodgate burst and the tears started   35
streaming down my face. Streaming. The pain ran so deep it felt physical,
like somebody was pounding on my chest. I'd never been hurt by a woman
before. I had never cared enough to be hurt by one. I sat there, leaning on
the cell door, listening to Aretha and crying. Inmates walked past and I
didn't even lift my head. I didn't care who saw me or what they thought.
I was crushed. Wasted. I cried until tears blurred my vision. Then I got
up, picked up my washcloth, rinsed it in the sink, held it to my face, and
cried some more. Liz was gone. I remembered that she had once told me,
"I'll follow you into a ditch if you lead me there." Well, I had led her
there, but she'd never promised to stay.

Sometimes I'd get grinding migraines that lasted for hours on end. I
figured it was caused by the pain of losing Liz, and the stress and tension
hounding me. When the frequency of the headaches increased, I came up
with ways to relieve the stress. I'd leave the place. I'd stretch out on my
bunk, block out all light by putting a cloth over my eyes, and go into deep
meditation or prayer. Starting with my toes, I'd concentrate hard and command every one of my body parts to chill. Often, by the time I reached
my head the tension was gone.

Then I'd take my imagination and soar away from the prison yard.
I'd travel to Portsmouth or some faraway, fictional place. Or I'd venture
beyond the earth and wander through the galaxy, pondering the vastness
of what God has done. I developed a hell of an imagination by doing those
mental workouts, and it put me in touch with my spirit in wondrous ways.
When the concentration was really good, I'd lose all feeling in my body,
and my spirit would come through, making me feel at one with the universe. It was like being high: It felt so good, but I couldn't figure out a
way to make it last.

> *I just witnessed a brutal fight in the cafeteria. The atmosphere was certainly*
> *conducive to violence: hot, odorous air filled with noise and flies. The two*
> *combatants went at each other's throats as if their lives meant nothing to*
> *them. After being confined for an extended period of time, life does tend to*
> *lose its value. I pray that I can remember my self-worth and remain cool.*
> *July 27, 1976*

A group of us from Tidewater were sitting around, sharing funny
tales from the streets and telling war stories about crazy things we'd done.
When my turn came, I told a story about a near stickup on Church Street
in Norfolk. "Yeah, man, we ran across a dude who had nothing but chump
change on him. We got mad 'cause the dude was broke, so we took his
change and started to take his pants. He had on some yellow, flimsy-

looking pants, so we made him walk with us under a streetlamp so we could get a better look at them. When we got under the streetlamp, we could see the pants were cheap. And they were dirty. So we let the dude slide, and keep his pants . . ."

Everybody was laughing. Everybody but a guy from Norfolk named Tony. Squinting his eyes, he leaned over and interrupted, "Did you say the guy had on yellow pants?"

"Yeah."   40

"Goddammit, that was *me* y'all stuck up that night!" he said, pointing a finger at me.

Everything got quiet. The guys looked at me, then at Tony, then back at me. Somebody snickered, and everybody else joined in. I laughed, too, until I looked at Tony and realized he still wasn't laughing. He was hot. He looked embarrassed and mad as hell.

To lighten the mood, I extended my hand playfully and said, "Wow, man, I'm sorry 'bout that. You know I didn't know you then."

Tony looked at my hand like he wanted to spit on it. "Naw, man. That shit ain't funny." The way he said it, I knew he wasn't going to let the thing drop. I knew that stupid macho pride had him by the throat and was choking the shit out of him.

A week or two after the exchange, he came into the library, where I   45
was working, sat in a corner, and started tearing pages out of magazines. The library was filled with inmates. I walked over to the table and said, "Yo, Tony, you can't tear the pages outta the magazines, man. Other people have to read 'em."

He looked up, smiled an evil smile, then ripped out another page and said. "What you gonna do 'bout it? You ain't no killer." The room grew quiet. I felt like all eyes were on me, waiting to see what I would do. I started thinking fast. Tony was stout and muscular and I figured he'd probably do the moonwalk on me if he got his hands on me. He was sitting down and I was standing. I glanced at an empty chair near him. I thought, *I could sneak him right off the bat, grab that chair, and wrap it around his head.* Then I thought about the potential consequences of fighting at work. I could lose my job, get kicked out of the library. I thought, *I gotta let it slide. I have to.* I looked at Tony, shrugged my shoulders, and said, "I ain't gonna do nothin', man. The magazines don't belong to *me*."

Tony sat there, staring at me, and tore more pages out of magazines. I walked away.

Later that night, I thought about it some more. I thought about how he'd come off. I thought, *He disrespected me.* I was too scared to let that man get away with disrespecting me. I felt I had faith that God would take care of me, but whenever I got that scared about something, I relied on what I knew best—faith in self. So I prayed, then set God aside for the time being and put together a shank like I'd learned to make while in the Norfolk jail. I melded a razor blade into a toothbrush handle, leaving the sharp edges sticking out, like a miniature tomahawk. I told one of my buddies what I intended to do. "I gotta get that niggah, man. He disrespected me and tried to chump me down."

The next day, we went looking for Tony on the yard. We spotted him leaving the dispensary with a partner. While my friend kept a lookout for guards, I approached Tony. Without saying anything, I pulled the razor blade and swung it at his throat. He jumped back. I lunged at him again and he flung his arms in front of his face, blocking the blow. The razor slashed his coat. He held up his hands and said, "Hold it, hold it, hold it, man! Be cool. Everything's cool. We all right, man. I ain't got no beef with you."

I pointed the razor at him. "Niggah, don't you *never* take me to be   50
no chump!"

"All right, bro', I was just playing with you yesterday."

I turned and walked away, relieved that he'd backed down and grateful that none of the guards standing on the yard had seen what went down.

My parents came to see me that afternoon. I went into the visiting room still hyper from the scene with Tony. As we talked, I looked at them and wondered what they'd say if they knew I had just risked everything I'd worked for to prove a manhood point. I wondered if Tony was going to try to get some get-back or pay somebody to try to shank me when my back was turned. I wondered if the time was coming down on me so badly that I was losing my grip.

At chow time that evening, my homie Pearly Blue came to the table and sat next to me. There was a slight smirk on his face. I sensed he was feeling a certain delight in knowing he'd warned me to hang tight with my homies to keep hassles away. "Yo, man, I heard you had a run-in with Tony."

"Yeah, a small beef."   55

"I told you these old rooty-poot niggahs will try you if they think you walk alone. . . . You know if you need to make another move on him, the homies can take care of it."

I kept looking straight ahead as I ate. "Naw, man. I got it under control."

I had no problems from Tony the remainder of the time I was at Southampton.

The one thing that seemed to soothe everybody in the joint was music. The loudest, most fucked-up brothers in the place chilled out when they had on a set of headphones. Some white inmates had musical instruments—guitars, saxophones, flutes—and they practiced in their cells at night. Most of the brothers didn't like hearing white music. The brothers would holler through the cell bars, "Cut that hillbilly shit out!"

But one white guy, from some rural Virginia town, was exempt from   60
the hassles. He was a fairly good guitar player, and an even better singer. Every night, before the lights went out, he calmed the building with

music. He sang the same song, and it reverberated throughout the place. He strummed his guitar and sang the John Denver tune "Take Me Home, Country Roads." He sang it in a voice so clean it sounded like he was standing on a mountain crooning down into one of those luscious green valleys he was singing about:

> Country rooaads,
> Take me hoomme,
> To the plaaace
> Where I beloooonng . . .

When those lyrics floated into my cell, I'd sit quietly, lean my head against the concrete wall, and listen. That song reminded me of how lonely I was and made me think of home. It made me think of Liz. It made me think of my son, my family, my neighborhood, my life. Sometimes, when he sang that song, tears welled in my eyes and I'd wipe them away, get into bed, and think some more.

That song seemed to calm everybody in the building, even the baad-asses who were prone to yell through their cells. It had the soothing effect of a lullaby sung by a parent to a bunch of children.

The Responsive Reader

1. Can you empathize with the author of this account of prison life? Why or why not? What kind of person is he? How did the prison experience affect him? How did it shape his attitude toward life?
2. How do the different inmates McCall remembers deal with "doing time"? How do they cope? What strategies do they develop, and how successful are these?
3. Many stories of prison life focus on trying to survive in a brutally violent environment. For the author, what is the point of the story he tells about his confrontation with Tony? What is the point or the lesson of the story for you?
4. How do white people look as seen through the eyes of black inmates? Does McCall think whites and blacks deal differently with the prison experience? Is race a major segregating factor or dividing line in McCall's prison?
5. What is the role of music in McCall's story?

Talking, Listening, Writing

6. Do you tend to think people in jail are a different breed from ordinary law-abiding citizens? Do you know anyone who is doing or has done time? What is the person's story?
7. Critics of the American justice system claim that in our society poor people go to jail. People of color go to jail. Poor people of color go to jail. To judge from McCall's account, are the critics right?

8. What is the racial or ethnic mix and social status of defendants in your local courts?

Collaborative Projects

9. The cost of prison construction and of housing ever-growing numbers of inmates has soared in recent years. What is the bottom line? What statistics are available on the actual and projected costs of the prison industry? (How does the cost of confining a young person for most of his or her life compare, say, with the cost of supporting a welfare family or with the average funds spent in poor neighborhoods on educating a child?)

COMING BACK ACROSS THE RIVER

José Luís and Rosa María Urbina

> *In a country invented as a classless society, many observers see the growth of an underclass performing menial labor and permanently trapped in a black market economy. Agribusiness in California and Texas and garment industry sweatshops in New York City employ immigrants—many without papers— in dismal working conditions. Wealthy Americans hire illegals without paying social security. In his* New Americans: An Oral History *(1988), Al Santoli recorded the results of a nine-month journey across the United States, during which he talked to recent immigrants from sixteen countries. He listened to refugees from Afghanistan and Ethiopia, to a Cuban immigrant who became the mayor of West Miami, and to Guatemalan Indians living in a migrant labor camp. The following testimony tells the story of a couple who came across the river from Juárez in Mexico to El Paso in Texas. Like many other "new Americans" before them, they came as illegal immigrants, outwitting border patrols or immigration authorities—the* migra—*in the search for a place to live and work.*

Thought Starters: Who performs menial tasks in our society? (Who does the dirty work in your community?)

JOSÉ: The majority of the people in our apartment building have the same   *1*
problem as my family. All of us are in El Paso without legal papers. I have
been living here since 1981.

ROSA: I came in 1984, to find work. After José and I were married and
we found a place to live, I brought my children from a previous marriage.
We lived across the river, in Juárez. But I was born further south, in
Zacatecas.

JOSÉ: My hometown is Juárez. Since I was nine years old, I've been coming to El Paso to work. At first I did gardening in people's yards, but I have
stayed in El Paso constantly since 1981, going out to the fields to do farm
work. I used to go to Juárez to visit my relatives at least one day each
month. But in the last year, I haven't gone, because of the new immigration law. To visit Juárez I have to swim across the river. I can't cross the
bridge or the "*migra*" can catch me right there.

   During the past few months, the river has been very high and fast.
That's one reason why not so many people have been crossing lately. I am
not working now, because it isn't the growing or harvesting season on the

big farms. On February 15, we usually begin to plant onions. That is when the main agricultural season begins. But during a three-month period between planting and harvesting, there is no work.

We haven't paid our rent since December. If we're lucky, I can find some part-time work to pay for food. Our baby, José Luís, is two months old. Because he was born in El Paso, he is an American citizen. We can only get food assistance for him. Once in a while, I find a job as a construction laborer, house painter, whatever is available. We use the money to buy food for the baby and the other three children first.

ROSA: I haven't been able to work lately, because the baby is so small. My other children are all in school. Lorenzo is twelve years old, José Rubén is ten, and Miriam is seven. From the time I came to El Paso, I have worked as a housekeeper and minding homes for people. I am not used to staying in the apartment every day, but I have no other choice, because of my small baby.

JOSÉ: Were we ever caught by the *migra* when we crossed the river together? Oh, yes. [Laughs] Lots of times. But the patrolmen are really okay people. They arrest you, ask the usual questions. If you get rough, they will get rough, too. Otherwise they are fine. It all depends on the person who arrests you. If he has a mean personality, he will treat you rudely, whether you are impolite or not. But most of the time, it is a routine procedure.

When the *migra* catch us, they just put us in their truck and take us to their station. They ask our name, address, where we were born. They keep us in a cell maybe three or four hours. Then they put us in a bus and drive us back to Juárez. They drop the women off very near the main bridge. The men are taken a little further away from town.

Our favorite place to cross the river is close to the Black Bridge, which is not far from downtown El Paso. Many of us would stand on the Juárez riverbank and wait for the change of Border Patrol shifts. Each morning, the shift changes between seven-thirty and eight-thirty, sometimes nine-thirty. We learn by observing over long periods of time. And all of our friends have been held in the immigration station. We observed certain patrolmen coming in to work and others checking out after their shifts.

Experienced river crossers pass this information to new people who are just learning the daily routines. Over a period of time, we learn the shift changes by recognizing different officers' faces. Some Mexican people even know the *migra* by name.

ROSA: Suppose I am caught by the patrolmen at seven-thirty in the morning. They will take me to the station and hold me for a few hours, then bus me back to Juárez. I would walk back to a crossing point and try once again. It is like a game. I think the most times I was ever caught by the *migra* was six times in one day. No matter how many times they catch me, I keep coming back.

The majority of the people in the *colonia* where I lived in Juárez worked in El Paso, mostly as housekeepers, construction workers, or helpers in the fields. In the United States there is a lot of work, but in Mexico we have nothing.

JOSÉ: The men, like myself, who work in the fields come across the river at around 2:30 A.M. to meet the buses that take us to the fields from El Paso. The transportation is owned by the *padrone* of the farms, or by the labor-crew chiefs who hire and pay the workers. In the evenings, we ride the buses back to the river. Sometimes I work twelve hours in a day and earn $20. I've learned to check around to see which farms pay the best. Some pay up to $35 a day.

Farm-labor jobs are not very steady. We just grab whatever is open at the moment. I accept anything, any time, as long as it is work. But suppose I take a job that only pays me $12 a day. It would only be enough to cover my transportation and meals in the field. I must find jobs that pay enough to feed my family.

In order to make $25, I must pick seventy-two buckets of chili peppers. That could take me four or five hours; it depends on how fast my hands are. The total amount of buckets we pick depends upon the amount contracted by the big companies in California. For a big contract, we work as long as necessary to complete the order. But the most I can earn in a day is $35.

During the summer, it gets very hot in the fields, up to 110 degrees. We work for eight hours with a half-hour break for lunch. To save money, I bring my lunch from home. The companies usually provide us with a thermos bottle of cold water. The farthest we travel from El Paso is to Lordsburg, New Mexico. That is around three and a half hours by bus. We leave El Paso at 3:00 A.M. For Las Cruces we leave at 5:00 or 5:30 A.M.

ROSA: To my housekeeping jobs I can take a regular El Paso city bus at 7:00 or 8:00 A.M. I usually come home around 3:30 or 4:00 P.M. each day. For a long while, I worked at one house—a Mexican-American family. They started me at $20 a day. Eventually they increased my wages to $25. They live near a large shopping center in the eastern part of town. The job was a little bit easier than working in the factory in Juárez, and paid much better.

In the factory, a whistle blows to let us know when to start, when to stop, when to eat dinner, and when to resume work. Doing housecleaning, I can rest a little when I need to take a short break.

To compare our apartment in El Paso with where I lived in Juárez, I prefer it a little better over there, because in the *colonia* I had a place to hang my clothes after I washed them. The bathroom was outside of the house. But we don't have a bathroom in our apartment here, either. All of the apartments in this part of the building share a toilet on the back stairwell. But in this apartment we have electric appliances, which makes life better than my previous home.

JOSÉ: The landlord who owns this building is very generous. He lets us owe him rent for the months that I am not working. He understands how tough our life is. We pay whatever we can, even if it's only $50. And he knows that, if the day comes where we are raided by immigration officers, we will run.

The rent for this apartment is $125 a month plus electricity. We all live and sleep in this one room. The two boys sleep on the couch. Our daughter, Miriam, sleeps with us on the bed. And the baby sleeps in a crib next to our bed. Fortunately, we have a kitchen, and a closet in this room. Living conditions in Juárez were better, but there was no work at all.

If it is possible, Rosa and I would like to become American citizens. I would have my documents, and the government wouldn't be after us. All we want is to be able to work in peace.

Our dream is to be able to give the children the best of everything. We know that, for them to have a better future and purpose in life, they need a good education. Of the three children in school now, Miriam is the fastest learner. She received an award for being an honor student, the best in her classroom.

We hope the children can finish high school and have the career of their choice. We are going to sacrifice for them, so that they can have the profession that they desire.

I was only allowed to finish grammar school. I am the oldest in my family, of five sisters and two boys. I had to stop going to school when I was twelve, to work with my father to support the family. I would have liked to finish school, but my parents needed me to work. They chose my sisters to study. So I gave up my studies to support my sisters.

At first, I liked working better than going to school. But after a while, I wanted to attend junior high school. But my mother told me that the family couldn't afford for me to go, and she said my sisters seemed to like the books better than I did. So I continued working. My father had a fruit-and-vegetable business. We sold from a pushcart in downtown Juárez, and I came across the river to do some gardening.

Even though I've come to work in Texas and New Mexico for many years, I've never learned to speak much English. I would like to learn, but I've never had the chance to study. I have a lot of responsibility now to provide for the children. It is more important that they have school, so I must work.

The dreams that Rosa María and I had of living in the U.S. and reality are not the same. We hoped to find a job and live comfortably. Now that we are here, our main purpose is to survive.

I worry about our status under the new immigration law. In the previous place where I lived, I paid the rent all the time, but the landlord threw away all of the receipts. So we have no proof that we have been living here enough years to qualify for amnesty.

On the farms where I worked, my employers or crew bosses didn't   *30* keep pay records, because I only worked temporarily at each place. And, besides, I was illegal. So what was the use? If the police showed up, we would be in trouble whether or not the employer had a record. And the employers wanted to protect themselves. They didn't pay us with checks; it was always cash.

Fortunately, the last farmer I worked for took taxes and Social Security out of our wages. He is sending me a W-2 form as proof. I am waiting for it now. But things are getting worse, because the immigration police are putting pressure on people who hire undocumented workers. If the police catch illegals on a job site, the boss can be arrested under the new law. So most places have stopped hiring illegals. For example, my last job in El Paso, I was fired because the *migra* would raid the construction site every day. We would have to stop working and run.

When the planting season begins on the farms, I hope the immigration police don't show up. They raid a farm with a truck and four or five police cars. They position themselves outside the entrance to the farm and wait for us to walk by. They ask us for identification. If we cannot show proof that we are legal, we've had it. They'll take us away.

On the farms where I work, some people are legal and others aren't. If you drive your own car, the police usually won't question you. But if you come to work in the employer's bus, they'll take you away.

ROSA: In town, we don't feel comfortable walking on the street. If the immigration officers see us, they will grab us. We are not afraid for ourselves, because we are accustomed to it. But I worry about the children. They have just begun studying in school here in El Paso. They like it very much. My sons are in the sixth and fifth grades, and Miriam is in second grade. They are learning English very quickly. My oldest boy, Lorenzo, likes social studies and mathematics; he would like to be a doctor. My other son likes the army a lot. He could probably be a good soldier.

JOSÉ: If we become citizens and the United States government asks them   *35* to spend time in the army, we would be honored if they are chosen to serve. We would be very proud of our children for doing their duty for their country.

ROSA: My daughter, Miriam, received a certificate from her teacher. You can ask her what she would like to do when she finishes school.

MIRIAM: [Big grin] I like to study English and mathematics. Some day I would like to be a teacher.

ROSA: In the buildings on this block, the majority of the people are families. In each apartment there are three or four children. This is the only area we found where the landlords don't mind renting to families with kids. The kids play outside, in the alley behind our building. Not many cars pass on this street at night, so it is pretty quiet. But other neighborhoods are more active and there is more crime on the streets.

We would like to have an ordinary life, but our problems with the *migra* are nothing new. If they catch me again and send me back to Juárez, I will just come back across the river.

The Responsive Reader

1. For you, what in this account is a familiar story? What is different from what you might have expected? What is hard to believe or explain?
2. What do you learn here about the workings of the black market economy? What are the methods, procedures, precautions?
3. How traditional are the gender roles in this account?

Talking, Listening, Writing

4. As a citizen and taxpayer, do you feel responsible for this couple and their children? As an employer, would you use their services?
5. The *Chicago Tribune* reviewer of Santoli's book said that "new immigrants are as American as apple pie." Do you think the couple speaking in this account will become "Americanized"? Will their children?

Collaborative Projects

6. You may want to work with a group to investigate estimates of illegal labor practices and the black market economy.

MEMORIES OF FRANK

Mary Kay Blakely

> *Mary Kay Blakely is a free-lance writer whose work has appeared in many magazines and in the "Hers" column in the* New York Times. *The following article from* Psychology Today *was adapted from her book* Wake Me When It's Over *(1989). Blakely here tells the story of her brother's descent into the hell of mental illness, a topic that in our society remains shrouded in superstition and prejudice. Patients and their families carry on a desperate struggle against ignorance, the threat of indeterminate confinement or disabling "cures," legal obstacles to promising drugs or treatments, brutal side effects of medications, cutbacks in public health care, and the constant psychological and financial drain of catastrophic illness. Relatives of people with apparently unsurmountable problems are sometimes told to "let go" and go on with their own lives. Would you have given this advice to the woman writing about her brother in this article?*

Thought Starters: What has been your exposure to or observation of the world of mental illness?

Francis Jude, my eldest brother, was brilliant and witty, the leading *1* madman of my four eccentric siblings, and I miss him enormously. During his brief adult life, he suffered altogether eight nervous breakdowns, serving as many sentences—voluntary and not—in Chicago institutions. Whether his wild imagination caused the stunning chemical changes in his body or the other way around, he surged with inhuman energy during his manic periods, then was flattened for months with tremendous exhaustion. He committed suicide on Nov. 12, 1981.

His doctors diagnosed him as manic depressive, but Frank thought of his illness as a spiritual fever. After his boyhood years as a Catholic seminarian, followed by an earnest search for God in the writings of Buddhist monks, Jewish rabbis, Protestant pastors and, finally, Unitarian ministers, he'd formed a nonsectarian but wholly religious view of events. "We are all like bacteria in a banana," he once wrote after a manic episode, "each doing our own little thing, while the fruit is ripened for God's digestion." It was not unusual for Frank to see signs of God in a bunch of bananas— he saw God everywhere. At times he thought he was God himself, infused with a euphoric rhythm inside his head he called "the beat, the beat, the beat."

Normally reserved and shy, he was charismatic and demonstrative when he was high. Frank ran for governor of Illinois once, on orders from above. He broke through security at *The Chicago Sun Times*, where he brought columnist Mike Royko the good news that he was destined to become Frank's campaign manager. Royko called my parents, and Frank spent the rest of his campaign at the Reed Mental Health Center. The incident did prompt Royko to write a column about Frank, not endorsing his gubernatorial race, but pointing out the faulty security systems at hospitals and newspapers that allowed lunatics to roam freely about the city of Chicago.

Although I am an avowed agnostic myself, I thought Frank's spiritual diagnosis was as credible as anything else. Nevertheless, I felt obliged to argue with him. During his first breakdown in 1967, when he was wired with electrodes and given shock treatments at Loretto Hospital in Chicago, he reported that he'd received messages directly from God himself. The truth arrived in tremendous jolts, he said, just as he expected it would some day. I tried to help him unscramble his brain, pointing out the difference between electricity and divinity. It was machinery, not God, that sent the sizzling jolts through his mind, I explained.

"Truth doesn't fry your brain," I tried pointing out.   5

"Sometimes it *does*," he replied, wide-eyed, as surprised to report this revelation as I was to hear it. A look of sheer lucidity crossed his face, followed by sudden surprise and then vast confusion. It was a silent movie of the chaos inside his head—I could actually *watch* Frank losing his innocence. He shed a great quantity of that innocence in the shock-treatment room at Loretto Hospital, being electrified by truth.

The treatments halted his illness only temporarily. During subsequent breakdowns, he was studied and probed, tested and drugged, interviewed and examined by some of the most famous psychiatrists in Chicago, but no one could cure him. Attempts to stabilize his moods with lithium carbonate failed repeatedly, puzzling his physicians. Frank himself was amazed by the constant motion inside his mind. He said it felt like his head had been clapped between two powerful hands and was orbiting around a spinning discus thrower warming up for a mighty heave. He was anxious for the final thrust, releasing him from the dizzying spins into free flight.

I was one of Frank's main companions throughout his bouts of madness, when his mind rolled out to the ends of human passion. He would hear and see things I couldn't understand, and I spent countless hours arguing with him inside the wards of insane asylums. In polite company, they're referred to as mental health centers, but in the ravaged minds of the inmates, politeness was the first thing to go.

Spending time with Frank and his mad peers was disturbing, because they made the line between sanity and insanity become so murky. After an afternoon arguing with lunatics who spoke truth bluntly, I would go home and watch the evening news, where the president of the most powerful country in the world was declaring war on the tiny island of Grenada. Nobody suggested locking him up. It worried me that mental patients made perfect sense and the president of the United States seemed like a candidate for the Reed Mental Health Center.

Frank would come back from his journeys into madness radically   *10* altered by what he had seen, and I understand now how much I relied on his expeditions. I was too much of a coward to let my own mind roll out full length, having witnessed the devastating price he paid.

His manic bouts were followed by long depressions, as he struggled to apply his dreams to ordinary life. The messages he believed so ardently during his seizures would melt into doubt, and he felt his otherness with an excruciating loneliness. Paralyzed with indecision and fear, he would sleep through those months, sometimes for 20 hours at a time. The fantastic energy abandoned him, and he lifted his thin body out of bed as if it weighed 500 pounds. He described these terrible confrontations with his conscience as "*grand mal* seizures of despair." They were a regular stop on the circular course of his spiritual fevers.

In the spring of 1970, Frank was interned at the Illinois State Psychiatric Institute (ISPI)—it was his fourth breakdown, the most reckless one so far. It was our mother, Kay, who arranged to get him into ISPI after reading a newspaper report about two psychiatrists from the University of Chicago who ran the experimental program. While it was still widely believed among psychiatrists then that bad mothering caused most mental problems, Dr. Herbert Y. Meltzer and Dr. Ronald Moline were among the pioneers who explored manic depression as a result of a chemical imbalance.

Their early experiments turned up evidence of faulty genetic wiring, suggesting that biology, not socialization, triggered the disease. They'd identified a muscle enzyme that seemed to play a role in manic depression, and had been given the 9th floor of ISPI to test their hypothesis. When Kay recognized her son's symptoms in the report—the stunning physical changes Frank underwent during his breakdowns—she scheduled an appointment.

To be admitted to the program, Frank had to submit to a muscle biopsy on his left calf. Kay and I, as part of the "control group," reported to the 9th floor one afternoon to surrender blood and urine samples, ride exercise bikes for five miles, then surrender more samples.

"I'm not sure I belong in anyone's control group," I said to Kay   *15* somewhere during our third stationary mile. I felt so closely related to Frank, I suspected I bordered on manic depression myself. Every one of my siblings lived with this fear. It seemed crazy, trying to retrieve him from the seduction of his madness by pedaling hard for five nonlocomotive miles. Maybe we were the lunatics—I mentioned this possibility to Kay.

She smiled, but didn't encourage a further critique of our going-nowhere ride that afternoon.

Whenever my mother's pale-blue Irish eyes would darken, reflecting her ardor for some imagined improvement in her children—whether it was a cleaner room or better grades or another home permanent despite former disasters—none of us was fool enough to try to dissuade her. She was not a woman who gave up easily, and when madness claimed her eldest, most intelligent, most sensitive son, her eyes took on the deepest blue I'd seen so far. Her smile ruefully acknowledged the absurdity of our circumstances, but her eyes, those two Celtic oracles of unswerving faith, directed me to keep pedaling even harder.

Because the doctors were committed to a theory involving enzymes and brain cells, they couldn't have been counting heavily on answers from psychoanalysis. But because a cure was still unavailable through medicine, the ISPI program included weekly doses of psychotherapy.

I hated the Thursday night sessions, when the patients and their families were collectively grilled under the harsh fluorescent lights of the locked ward. Maybe somewhere in the pasts of these humbled people there were cases of bad mothering or absent fathering or emotional neglect—what family surviving the '50s was exempt?—but I couldn't believe these human errors brought the physical changes in Frank. I knew an unhappy childhood was not the problem. If anything, my parents' unstoppable affection had postponed Frank's crisis. He didn't have his first breakdown under their roof—it happened 240 miles away, at Southern Illinois University the year he left home.

Each week Kay, my father Jerry, my brother Paul and I joined the other families with members impounded on ISPI's 9th floor for a rigorous interrogation of our pasts. My parents exempted Kevin and Gina, the two youngest siblings, in an effort to spare them a direct confrontation with the terrifying look of mental illness, even though they had witnessed Frank's bizarre behavior. Whether obligation or tradition or just plain helplessness prompted this futile treatment, the sessions were unproductive if not outright harmful. One week, Jerry was questioned about his habit of shaking hands with his adult sons, replacing the childhood hugs. The therapist on duty that night suggested our father's formal handshakes had deprived Frank of his affectionate due. This was ridiculous, Paul and I knew.

While my father tried to practice the emotional reserve required of his generation of men, the disguise never completely covered him. I remembered a Saturday morning in June when Jerry paced back and forth across the living-room carpet in his tuxedo, anxiously rehearsing his immediate duties concerning the bride. The task of giving me away clashed with 22 years of loving me, and he was unable to form a single word when I emerged in my wedding dress. Instead, his eyes filled up and his face became bright red, then his smile finally appeared like a period at the end of a long, emotional speech.

I'd seen that expression repeatedly at baptisms and confirmations, basketball games and high-school plays. It was embarrassing to sit next to Jerry when one of his children was on stage because invariably, unable to hold out for the cover of final applause, he would pull out his handkerchief and alert the audience to his severely clogged-up condition. There were plenty of crosses the children of this complicated, emotional man had to bear during the John Wayne-worshipping '50s, but being insufficiently loved was never one of them. Yet in the spring of 1970, a therapist unfamiliar with this history sent Jerry home in despair. He spent the following months doubting himself, believing a dozen more hugs might have saved his son from madness.

Few participants emerged from those evenings without confessing to some charge, but the heaviest guilt was generally accepted by the mothers. During a luckless search for signs of "over-mothering" or "dominance" or "aggression" in Kay one evening, the therapist appeared ready to move on to more promising candidates when he raised a question about "rejection." My mother remembered a night in 1949, when Frank was 3, that still caused her some regrets.

A pediatrician had applied bindings around Frank's head during a visit that afternoon, to flatten the ears a bit. His tiny ears stuck out at what my mother thought was an adorable angle, but the doctor soon convinced her they wouldn't be so adorable when he was a young man. He suggested they would mar his attractiveness, possibly threaten his sex life. As the bindings were applied I imagine the pediatrician caught my mother wincing. That wince appeared hundreds of times as her five offspring somersaulted through childhood—when I got my hand caught in the wringer of the washing machine or one of my brothers had his head stitched in the emergency room. She usually followed the wince with a pat of sympathy, a gesture of comfort.

The doctor, an authoritative man, disapproved of her soft-touch approach. He warned her of the dangers of coddling, especially coddling boys. There were lots of stories then about men whose lives were wrecked by homosexuality because their mothers over-kissed them. Between his ears and his mother, the doctor believed my brother had a very narrow chance for a normal life.

Kay remembered being awake that whole night, listening to cries   25 from the baby's room and wrestling with her urge to scoop him up and comfort him. It took tremendous discipline, but she accepted the punishment of the pediatrician's advice and resisted. She could still hear those cries, she told the therapist at ISPI 21 years later. She winced.

Perhaps that's when my brother may have felt rejected, she volunteered. How could he have known her longing to pick him up, to comfort him? How could he have known she was struggling to follow orders?

Perceiving the fresh scent of guilt, the therapist probed deeper: Maybe she really did think he was homely—maybe she really was unconsciously rejecting him. My mother considered this suggestion for a moment. She looked across the room at my brother, then shook her head slowly. No, she said simply, without further explanation. Even ravaged by illness, even with something untameable coursing through him, Frank was clearly, electrically, a beautiful young man. My mother thought anybody looking at him could see that.

The weekend before Frank's suicide, he visited me in Fort Wayne, coming from Chicago by Greyhound. Over and over that weekend he told me how much he loved me. It was only later, when I went back over our long conversations, that I understood he was also saying goodbye. Ostensibly, he came to deliver a suitcase full of journal notes—jottings made at fever pitch—asking me to be his "translator." The structural ideas for his grand vision were all there, he thought, but lacked fluency. I accepted the sheaf of papers, fully aware that God might appear as an electric chair in the gospel according to Frank.

He, too, was a writer, but had abandoned very nearly all conventional forms in his rush to record gigantic thoughts. Some pages contained only a single sentence, no thoughts leading up to or away from it, like the solitary message of an obsessed placard carrier on the street. ("In the whitest light, the dancer becomes the dance," one page announced.) Frank's journal read like a series of baffling Zen koans, evidence of lunacy or brilliance.

Although it was painful to remember, I cherished that last visit together—it relieved any guilt I might have had about preventing his death. The flimsy gravity of human love cannot stop a man when he's in orbit with divine inspiration. He wasn't depressed that weekend—quite the opposite, in fact. He was riding the crest of a manic high, pacing about my quiet Fort Wayne neighborhood with frenetic energy. He frightened the elderly widow who lived down the street when he serenaded her one midnight on her front lawn. She was lonely, his voices told him, and he thought he had the power to spread around unlimited quantities of love.

I remember watching him through the kitchen window Saturday *30* afternoon as he raked a month's accumulation of leaves with my sons. They filled a large tarp with leaves, then one or both of the kids would jump in and Frank would drag them to the curb. With a mighty heave, unexpectedly strong for his skinny, drug-shaken frame, he'd hoist the kids and leaves into the air.

The sound he emitted with each launch was a peculiar blend of karate yell and manic laugh, his voice undecided whether to expect pain or joy with the final thrust. Then he'd race the kids to the back of the yard and start all over, as if his life depended on filling the street with children and leaves. Long after the kids left the game, he was still filling the tarp.

Like the animated sorcerer's apprentice, he raked feverishly, piercing the night with howls of aching happiness. I stood at the window wondering what he thought he was hauling, to where. He was exceptionally tight-lipped about his plans that weekend. "It's one of those times when the irrational will become rational," he offered cryptically. "I'm in 'that magical moment when *is* becomes *if*...'" He caught himself and stopped quoting e.e. cummings, replacing the rest of the poem with his quiet, lunatic grin. That smile was my personal legacy from Frank.

Sunday I drove Frank to the Greyhound station. Two nights later, Kay called from Chicago. "Hello, darling," she said softly, and I instantly raised both hands to the receiver. Kay saved "darling" for emergencies—her love was made of stronger stuff, herding five children through infancy and adolescence with exacting discipline.

"Are the children in bed?" she asked quietly. I sank into the chair next to the phone, a great ache swelling my throat, cutting off my air. I knew what she had to report. A letter from Frank had arrived that morning: "It was a beautiful letter," she said calmly, huskily, in a voice that had not yet fully recovered from an afternoon of tears. "It made us cry." She paused then, taking in an extra breath of air to hold her brief but heavy summary. "He thanked us for being his parents."

I knew his suicide was not an act of despair; in his own mind, he was committing an act of ultimate faith. It was a death from exhaustion, from the efforts of thinking and striving, and I was grateful he finally reached the end of his pain. 35

His seemingly irrational decision did eventually become rational to me. When I re-read Frank's letters now, freed from the arrogant assumption that I could somehow save him, his brilliance and faith is more accessible to me. Frank thought of his life as "a divine, inscrutable prayer" and believed "my existence does not end with death." Though I'm still an agnostic, I'm inclined to accept his theory of immortality.

Since his permanent departure eight years ago, certain memories—a pile of autumn leaves, a line of familiar poetry—will trigger a rush of recognition, and I feel the beat, the beat, the beat, pumping through me. My own mind, stamped by his, reverberates with an eternal echo of love.

The Responsive Reader

1. What was Frank's history and the nature of his illness? How did it affect his family? How did his family cope?
2. This article alludes to a major shift in modern psychiatry. In recent years, mental-health professionals have increasingly moved away from looking for the roots of mental illness in the patient's traumatic personal experience ("bad mothering," for instance). What do you learn from this article about the shift toward tracing mental illness to physical, biochemical causes? (What did you already know?)

3. Many patients or their families have been in an adversarial relationship with the psychiatric establishment. Is this author hostile toward
the institutions or professionals that serve the mentally ill? What is
her criticism of assumptions or procedures?
4. What glimpses do you get of the attitudes toward mental illness in
the society at large?

Talking, Listening, Writing

5. Do you know of any success stories in the battle against mental
illness? Do you know of any good news on this subject?

Collaborative Projects

6. Patients' families and mental-health professionals have at times been
at odds with organizations like the ACLU (American Civil Liberties
Union) that purport to protect the legal rights of the mentally ill.
What are the issues? What is at stake? Your class may want to commission a group of students with a special interest in this subject to
investigate.

THE OTHER BODY: DISABILITY AND IDENTITY POLITICS

Ynestra King

> *Ynestra King is an outspoken political activist whose books include* Ecofeminism and the Reenchantment of Nature *(1993). In the follow-ing article, first published in* Ms. *magazine, she reminds us that "of all the ways of becoming 'other' in our society, disability is the only one that can happen to anyone, in an instant, transforming that person's life and identity forever." In the dark ages of attitudes toward people with disabilities, physi-cally impaired students like King were shunted off to special classes and special buildings, segregated from "normal" children. In the meantime, society has come a long way. New laws require schools to "mainstream" children with disabilities; ramps and elevators provide improved access to public buildings and transportation. Revolutionary new technologies promise breakthroughs for the blind and the deaf. Why then does King feel an "underlying rage at the system"?*

Thought Starters: Do you know people with disabilities? Are you close to someone with a severe impairment? How do you act around the disabled?

Disabled people rarely appear in popular culture. When they do, their   *1* disability must be a continuous preoccupation overshadowing all other areas of their character. Disabled people are disabled. That is what they "do." That is what they "are."

My own experience with a mobility impairment that is only minorly disfiguring is that one must either be a creature of the disability, or have transcended it entirely. For me, like most disabled people (and this of course depends on relative severity), neither extreme is true. It is an or-ganic, literally embodied fact that will not change—like being a woman. While it may be possible to "do gender," one does not "do disability." But there is an organic base to both conditions that extends far into culture, and the meaning that "nature" has. Unlike being a woman, being disabled is not a socially constructed condition. It is a tragedy of nature, of a kind that will always exist. The very condition of disability provides a vantage point of a certain lived experience in the body, a lifetime of opportunity for the observation of reaction to bodily deviance, a testing ground for reactions to persons who are readily perceived as having something wrong or being different. It is fascinating, maddening, and disorienting. It defies categories of "sickness" and "health," "broken" and "whole." It is in between.

Meeting people has an overlay: I know what they notice first is that I am different. And there is the experience of the difference in another person's reaction who meets me sitting down (when the disability is not apparent), and standing up and walking (when the infirmity is obvious). It is especially noticeable when another individual is flirting and flattering, and has an abrupt change in affect when I stand up. I always make sure that I walk around in front of someone before I accept a date, just to save face for both of us. Once the other person perceives the disability, the switch on the sexual circuit breaker often pops off—the connection is broken. "Chemistry" is over. I have a lifetime of such experiences, and so does every other disabled woman I know.

White middle-class people—especially white men—in the so-called First World have the most negative reactions. And I always recognize studied politeness, the attempt to pretend that there's nothing to notice (this is the liberal response—Oh, you're black? I hadn't noticed). Then there's the do-gooder response, where the person falls all over her/himself, insisting on doing everything for you; later they hate you; it's a form of objectification. It conveys to you that that is all they see, rather like a man who can't quit talking with a woman about sex.

In the era of identity politics in feminism, disability has not only been an added cross to bear, but an added "identity" to take on—with politically correct positions, presumed instant alliances, caucuses to join, and closets to come out of. For example, I was once dragged across a room to meet someone. My friend, a very politically correct lesbian feminist, said, "She's disabled, too. I thought you'd like to meet her." Rather than argue—what would I say? "I'm not interested in other disabled people," or "This is my night off"? (The truth in that moment was like the truth of this experience in every other moment, complicated and difficult to explain)—I went along to find myself standing before someone strapped in a wheelchair she propels by blowing into a tube with a respirator permanently fastened to the back of the chair. To suggest that our relative experience of disability is something we could casually compare (as other people stand by!) demonstrates the crudity of perception about the complex nature of bodily experience.

My infirmity is partial leg paralysis. I can walk anywhere, climb stairs, drive a car, ride a horse, swim, hang-glide, fly a plane, hike in the wilderness, go to jail for my political convictions, travel alone, and operate heavy equipment. I can earn a living, shop, cook, eat as I please, dress myself, wash and iron my own clothes, clean my house. The woman in that wheelchair can do none of these fundamental things, much less the more exotic ones. On a more basic human level I can spontaneously get my clothes off if I decide to make love. Once in bed my lover and I can forget my disability. None of this is true of the woman in the wheelchair. There is no bodily human activity that does not have to be specially negotiated, none in which she is not absolutely "different." It would take a very long time, and a highly nuanced conversation, for us to be able to share experiences as if they were common. The experience of disability for the two of us was more different than my experience is from the daily experience of people who are not considered disabled. So much for disability solidarity.

With disability, one is somewhere on a continuum between total bodily dysfunction—or death—and complete physical wholeness. In some way, this probably applies to every living person. So when is it that we call a person "disabled"? When do they become "other"? There are "minor" disabilities that are nonetheless significant for a person's life. Color blindness is one example. But in our culture, color blindness is considered an inconvenience rather than a disability.

The ostracization, marginalization, and distortion response to disability are not simply issues of prejudice and denial of civil rights. They reflect attitudes toward bodily life, an unease in the human skin, and an inability to cope with contingency, ambiguity, flux, finitude, and death.

Visibly disabled people (like women) in this culture are the scapegoats for resentments of the limitations of organic life. I had polio when I was seven, finishing second grade. I had excelled in everything, and rarely missed school. I had one bad conduct notation—for stomping on the boys' blocks when they wouldn't let me play with them. Although I had leg braces and crutches when I was ready to start school the next year, I wanted desperately to go back and resume as much of the same life as I could. What I was not prepared for was the response of the school system. They insisted that I was now "handicapped" and should go into what they called "special education." This was a program aimed primarily at multiply disabled children, virtually all of whom were mentally retarded as well as physically disabled. It was in a separate wing of another school, and the children were completely segregated from the "normal" children in every aspect of the school day, including lunch and recreational activities. I was fortunate enough to have educated, articulate parents and an especially aggressive mother; she went to the school board and waged a tireless campaign to allow me to come back to my old school on a trial basis—the understanding being that the school could send me to special education if things "didn't work out" in the regular classroom.

And so began my career as an "exceptional" disabled person, not like   10
the *other* "others." And I was glad. I didn't want to be associated with those others either. Apart from the objective limitations caused by the polio, the transformation in identity—the difference in worldly reception—was terrifying and embarrassing, and it went far beyond the necessary considerations my limitations required.

My experience as "other" is much greater and more painful as a disabled person than as a woman. Maybe the most telling dimension of this knowledge is my observation of the reactions of others over the years, of how deeply afraid people are of being outside the normative appearance (which is getting narrower as capitalism exaggerates patriarchy). It is no longer enough to be thin; one must have ubiquitous muscle definition, nothing loose, flabby, or ill defined, no fuzzy boundaries. And of course, there's the importance of control. Control over aging, bodily processes, weight, fertility, muscle tone, skin quality, and movement. Disabled women, regardless of how thin, are without full bodily control.

I see disabled women fight these normative standards in different ways, but never get free of negotiating and renegotiating them. I did it by constructing my life around other values and, to the extent possible, developing erotic attachments to people who had similar values, and for whom my compensations were more than adequate. But at one point, after two disastrous but steamy liaisons with a champion athlete and a dancer (during which my friends pointed out the obvious unkind truth and predicted painful endings), I discovered the worlds I had tried to protect myself from: the disastrous attraction to "others" to complete oneself. I have seen disabled women endure unspeakably horrible relationships because they were so flattered to have such a conventionally attractive individual in tow.

And then there's the weight issue. I got fat by refusing to pay attention to my body. Now that I'm slimming down again, my old vanities and insecurities are surfacing. The battle of dieting can be especially fraught for disabled women. It is more difficult because exercising is more difficult, as is traveling around to get the proper foods, and then preparing them. But the underlying rage at the system that makes you feel as if you *are* your body (female, infirm) and that everything else is window dressing—this also undermines the requisite discipline. A tempting response is to resort to an ideal of self as bodiless essence in which the body is completely incidental, and irrelevant.

The wish that the body should be irrelevant has been one of my most fervent lifelong wishes. The knowledge that it isn't is my most intense lifelong experience.

I have seen other disabled women wear intentionally provocative clothes, like the woman in a wheelchair on my bus route to work. She can barely move. She has a pretty face, and tiny legs she could not possibly walk on. Yet she wears black lace stockings and spike high heels. The other bus occupants smile condescendingly, or pretend not to notice, or whisper in appalled disbelief that this woman could represent herself as having a sexual self. That she could "flaunt" her sexual being violates the code of acceptable appearance for a disabled woman. This woman's apparel is no more far out than that of many other women on our bus—but she refuses to fold up and be a good little asexual handicapped person.

The well-intentioned liberal new campaigns around "hire the handicapped" are oppressive in related ways. The Other does not only have to demonstrate her competence on insider terms; she must be better, by way of apologizing for being different and rewarding the insiders for letting her in. And the happy handicapped person, who has had faith placed in her/

him, must vindicate "the race" because the politics of tokenism assumes that there are in fact other qualifications than doing the job.

This is especially prejudicial in a recession, where there are few social services, where it is "every man for himself." Disabled people inevitably have greater expenses, since assistance must often be paid for privately. In the U.S., public construction of the disabled body is that one either is fully disabled and dysfunctional/unemployable (and therefore eligible for public welfare) or totally on one's own. There is no in-between—the possibility of a little assistance, or exceptions in certain areas. Disabled people on public assistance cannot work or they will lose their benefits. (In the U.S. ideology that shapes public attitudes and public policy, one is either fully dependent or fully autonomous.) But the reality of human and organic life is that everyone is different in some way; there is no such thing as a totally autonomous individual. Yet the mythology of autonomy perpetuates in terrible ways the oppression of the disabled. It also perpetuates misogyny— and the destruction of the planet.

It may be that this clear lack of autonomy—this reminder of mortal finitude and contingency and embeddedness of nature and the body—is at the root of the hatred of the disabled. On the continuum of autonomy and dependence, disabled people need help. To need help is to feel humiliated, to have failed. I think this "help" issue must be even harder for men than women. But any disabled person is always negotiating both the provision-ality of autonomy and the rigidity of physical norms.

From the vantage point of disability, there are some objective and desirable aspects of autonomy. But they have to do with independence. The preferred protocol is that the attendant or friend perform the task that the disabled person needs done in the way the disabled person *asks it to be done.* Assistance from friends and family is a negotiated process, and often maddening. For that reason most disabled people prefer to live in situations where they can do all the basic functions themselves, with whatever special equipment or built-ins are required.

It's a dreadful business, this needing help. And it's more dreadful in   20 the U.S. than in any place in the world, because our heroes are dynamic overcomers of adversity, and there is an inevitable cultural contempt for weakness.

Autonomy is on a continuum toward dependency and death. And the idea that dependency could come at any time, that one could die at any time, or be dismembered or disfigured, and still have to live (maybe even *want to live*) is unbearable in a context that understands and values autonomy in the way we moderns do.

I don't want to depict this experience of unbearabilty as strictly cul-tural. The compromising of the human body before its natural time is tragic. It forces terrible hardship on the individual to whom it occurs. But the added overlay of oppression on the disabled is intimately related to the fear of death, and the acknowledgement of our embeddedness in organic nature. We are finite, contingent, dependent creatures by our very nature; we will all eventually die. We will all experience compromises to our physical integrity. The aspiration to human wholeness is an oppressive idealism. Socially, it is deeply infantilizing.

It promotes a simplistic view of the human person, a static notion of human life that prevents the maturity and social wisdom that might allow human beings to more fully apprehend the human condition. It marginalizes the "different," those perceived as hopelessly wedded to organic existence—women and the disabled. The New Age "human potential movement"—in the name of maximizing human growth—is one of the worst offenders in obscuring the kind of human growth I am suggesting.

I too believe that the potential for human growth and creativity is infinite—but it is not groundless. The common ground for the person— the human body—is a place of shifting sand that can fail us at any time. It can change shape and properties without warning; this is an essential truth of embodied existence.

Of all the ways of becoming "other" in our society, disability is the 25 only one that can happen to anyone, in an instant, transforming that person's life and identity forever.

The Responsive Reader

1. Why does King find the way we respond to people with disabilities "fascinating, maddening, and disorienting"? Why does she object to society expecting that for people like her disability "must be a continuous preoccupation"? Why are first meetings a special problem? Why are encounters with the other sex a special problem? What is wrong with the way "liberals" or "do-gooders" respond to the disabled?
2. Like other spokespersons for the disabled, King is severely critical of "special education" for the students with disabilities. What is the central objection to it?
3. What is wrong with public policies for assisting the disabled? What is wrong with "hire the handicapped" campaigns?
4. King says, "It's dreadful business, this needing help." What makes it so dreadful? Why would it be more dreadful in the U.S. than in any other place? Does King make you understand why disabled people prefer assistance from equipment to assistance from people?

Talking, Listening, Writing

5. What is the exact nature of King's disability? What is her history? Where or how in this article do you find out? Why doesn't she tell you "up front"?

6. Many observers of our culture have criticized the American beauty myth, youth worship, and fitness cult. Why does King see our norms and ideals as imposing a special burden on people like her?

7. What evidence have you seen of increased attention to the needs of people with disabilities? Do you think our society gives too little thought to the needs of the disabled? too much? just about the right amount?

8. In 1997, *Time* reported that "disabled protesters" were denouncing a projected monument commemorating President Franklin Delano Roosevelt—because it showed him, as newsreels had during his presidency, without the wheelchair he was using as the result of being disabled by polio. What principle do you think is at stake here? Would you take sides in the controversy one way or the other?

Collaborative Projects

9. Does your college have policies or programs addressing the needs of students with disabilities? How are they implemented? How meaningful or successful are they?

I STAND HERE IRONING

Tillie Olsen

Tillie Olsen is a working-class woman who without benefit of a Radcliffe education, Guggenheim fellowships, or similar perks bestowed by an elitist establishment became a powerful writer and a force in the women's movement. She came to be widely admired for giving voice to the story of the unheard in American society. She has said, "The power and the need to create, over and beyond reproduction, is native in both women and men. Where the gifted among women (and men) have remained mute, or have never attained full capacity, it is because of circumstances, inner or outer, which oppose the needs of creation." Chronicling the Great Depression of the thirties, Olsen has written with bitter eloquence about poverty, illness, hunger, unemployment, and soul-deadening jobs. Her novel Yonnondio: From the Thirties *(1974) paid tribute to people deprived of their chance to develop into full human beings "so that a few may languidly lie on couches and trill 'how exquisite' to paid dreamers." A native of Omaha, Nebraska, with only a high school education, she lived through grinding poverty to write powerful stories shaking up the complacency of the well-to-do. Her "Tell Me a Riddle" won the O. Henry Award as best short story of the year in 1961. She has since been much honored and has lectured at universities including Amherst and Stanford. In the following story, we look through the eyes of a mother at a daughter who was "the child of anxious, not proud, love." What world do we see through the mother's eyes? (The WPA referred to in the story is the Works Progress Administration, begun in 1935 to provide federally funded jobs for the unemployed during the Great Depression.)*

Thought Starters: Did older members of your family keep alive memories of the Great Depression or of hard times? How did their memories affect their outlook?

I stand here ironing, and what you asked me moves tormented back   *1*
and forth with the iron.

"I wish you would manage the time to come in and talk with me
about your daughter. I'm sure you can help me understand her. She's a
youngster who needs help and whom I'm deeply interested in helping."

"Who needs help." Even if I came, what good would it do? You
think because I am her mother I have a key, or that in some way you could
use me as a key? She has lived for nineteen years. There is all that life that
has happened outside of me, beyond me.

And when is there time to remember, to sift, to weigh, to estimate, to total? I will start and there will be an interruption and I will have to gather it all together again. Or I will become engulfed with all I did or did not do, with what should have been and what cannot be helped.

She was a beautiful baby. The first and only one of our five that was *5* beautiful at birth. You do not guess how new and uneasy her tenancy in her now-loveliness. You did not know her all those years she was thought homely, or see her poring over her baby pictures, making me tell her over and over how beautiful she had been—and would be, I would tell her—and was now, to the seeing eye. But the seeing eyes were few or nonexistent. Including mine.

I nursed her. They feel that's important nowadays. I nursed all the children, but with her, with all the fierce rigidity of first motherhood, I did like the books then said. Though her cries battered me to trembling, I waited until the clock decreed.

Why do I put that first? I do not even know if it matters at all, or if it explains anything.

She was a beautiful baby. She blew shining bubbles of sound. She loved motion, loved light, loved color and music and textures. She would lie on the floor in her blue overalls patting the surface so hard in ecstasy her hands and feet would blur. She was a miracle to me, but when she was eight months old I had to leave her daytimes with the woman downstairs to whom she was no miracle at all, for I worked or looked for work and for Emily's father, who "could no longer endure" (he wrote in his goodbye note) "sharing want with us."

I was nineteen. It was the pre-relief, pre-WPA world of the depression. I would start running as soon as I got off the streetcar, running up the stairs, the place smelling sour, and awake or asleep to startle awake, when she saw me she would break into a clogged weeping that could not be comforted, a weeping I can hear yet.

After a while I found a job hashing at night so I could be with her *10* days, and it was better. But it came to where I had to bring her to his family and leave her.

It took a long time to raise the money for her fare back. Then she got chicken pox and I had to wait longer. When she finally came, I hardly knew her, walking quick and nervous like her father, looking like her father, thin, and dressed in a shoddy red that yellowed her skin and glared at the pockmarks. All the baby loveliness gone.

She was two. Old enough for nursery school they said, and I did not know then what I know now—the fatigue of the long day, and the lacerations of group life in the kinds of nurseries that are only parking places for children.

Except that it would have made no difference if I had known. It was the only place there was. It was the only way we could be together, the only way I could hold a job.

And even without knowing, I knew. I knew the teacher that was evil because all these years it has curdled into my memory, the little boy hunched in the corner, her rasp, "why aren't you outside, because Alvin hits you? that's no reason, go, scaredy." I knew Emily hated it even if she did not clutch and implore "don't go Mommy" like the other children, mornings.

She always had a reason why we should stay home. Momma, you look sick, Momma. I feel sick. Momma, the teachers aren't there today, they're sick. Momma, we can't go, there was a fire there last night. Momma, it's a holiday today, no school, they told me. ₁₅

But never a direct protest, never rebellion. I think of our others in their three-, four-year-oldness—the explosions, the tempers, the denunciations, the demands—and I feel suddenly ill. I put the iron down. What in me demanded that goodness in her? And what was the cost, the cost to her of such goodness?

The old man living in the back once said in his gentle way: "You should smile at Emily more when you look at her." What *was* in my face when I looked at her? I loved her. There were all the acts of love.

It was only with the others I remembered what he said, and it was the face of joy, and not of care or tightness or worry I turned to them— too late for Emily. She does not smile easily, let alone almost always as her brothers and sisters do. Her face is closed and somber, but when she wants, how fluid. You must have seen it in her pantomimes, you spoke of her rare gift for comedy on the stage that rouses a laughter out of the audience so dear they applaud and applaud and do not want to let her go.

Where does it come from, that comedy? There was none of it in her when she came back to me that second time, after I had had to send her away again. She had a new daddy now to learn to love, and I think perhaps it was a better time.

Except when we left her alone nights, telling ourselves she was old enough. ₂₀

"Can't you go some other time, Mommy, like tomorrow?" she would ask. "Will it be just a little while you'll be gone? Do you promise?"

The time we came back, the front door open, the clock on the floor in the hall. She rigid awake. "It wasn't just a little while. I didn't cry. Three times I called you, just three times, and then I ran downstairs to open the door so you could come faster. The clock talked loud. I threw it away, it scared me what it talked."

She said the clock talked loud again that night I went to the hospital to have Susan. She was delirious with the fever that comes before red measles, but she was fully conscious all the week I was gone and the week after we were home when she could not come near the new baby or me.

She did not get well. She stayed skeleton thin, not wanting to eat, and night after night she had nightmares. She would call for me, and I would rouse from exhaustion to sleepily call back: "You're all right, darling, go to sleep, it's just a dream," and if she still called, in a sterner voice, "now go to sleep, Emily, there's nothing to hurt you." Twice, only twice, when I had to get up for Susan anyhow, I went in to sit with her.

Now when it is too late (as if she would let me hold and comfort   25
her like I do the others) I get up and go to her at once at her moan or restless stirring. "Are you awake, Emily? Can I get you something?" And the answer is always the same: "No, I'm all right, go back to sleep, Mother."

They persuaded me at the clinic to send her away to a convalescent home in the country where "she can have the kind of food and care you can't manage for her, and you'll be free to concentrate on the new baby." They still send children to that place. I see pictures on the society page of sleek young women planning affairs to raise money for it, or dancing at the affairs, or decorating Easter eggs or filling Christmas stockings for the children.

They never have a picture of the children so I do not know if the girls still wear those gigantic red bows and the ravaged looks on the every other Sunday when parents can come to visit "unless otherwise notified"— as we were notified the first six weeks.

Oh it is a handsome place, green lawns and tall trees and fluted flower beds. High up on the balconies of each cottage the children stand, the girls in their red bows and white dresses, the boys in white suits and giant red ties. The parents stand below shrieking up to be heard and the children shriek down to be heard, and between them the invisible wall "Not To Be Contaminated by Parental Germs or Physical Affection."

There was a tiny girl who always stood hand in hand with Emily. Her parents never came. One visit she was gone. "They moved her to Rose Cottage," Emily shouted in explanation. "They don't like you to love anybody here."

She wrote once a week, the labored writing of a seven-year-old. "I   30
am fine. How is the baby. If I write my letter nicely I will have a star. Love." There never was a star. We wrote every other day, letters she could never hold or keep but only hear read—once. "We simply do not have room for children to keep any personal possessions," they patiently explained when we pieced one Sunday's shrieking together to plead how much it would mean to Emily, who loved so to keep things, to be allowed to keep her letters and cards.

Each visit she looked frailer. "She isn't eating," they told us.

(They had runny eggs for breakfast or mush with lumps, Emily said later, I'd hold it in my mouth and not swallow. Nothing ever tasted good, just when they had chicken.)

It took us eight months to get her released home, and only the fact that she gained back so little of her seven lost pounds convinced the social worker.

I used to try to hold and love her after she came back, but her body would stay stiff, and after a while she'd push away. She ate little. Food sickened her, and I think much of life too. Oh she had physical lightness and brightness, twinkling by on skates, bouncing like a ball up and down up and down over the jump rope, skimming over the hill; but these were momentary.

She fretted about her appearance, thin and dark and foreign-looking   *35* at a time when every little girl was supposed to look or thought she should look a chubby blonde replica of Shirley Temple. The doorbell sometimes rang for her, but no one seemed to come and play in the house or be a best friend. Maybe because we moved so much.

There was a boy she loved painfully through two school semesters. Months later she told me how she had taken pennies from my purse to buy him candy. "Licorice was his favorite and I brought him some every day, but he still liked Jennifer better'n me. Why, Mommy?" The kind of question for which there is no answer.

School was a worry to her. She was not glib or quick in a world where glibness and quickness were easily confused with ability to learn. To her overworked and exasperated teachers she was an overconscientious "slow learner" who kept trying to catch up and was absent entirely too often.

I let her be absent, though sometimes the illness was imaginary. How different from my now-strictness about attendance with the others. I wasn't working. We had a new baby, I was home anyhow. Sometimes, after Susan grew old enough, I would keep her home from school, too, to have them all together.

Mostly Emily had asthma, and her breathing, harsh and labored, would fill the house with a curiously tranquil sound. I would bring the two old dresser mirrors and her boxes of collections to her bed. She would select beads and single earrings, bottle tops and shells, dried flowers and pebbles, old postcards and scraps, all sorts of oddments; then she and Susan would play Kingdom, setting up landscapes and furniture, peopling them with action.

Those were the only times of peaceful companionship between her   *40* and Susan. I have edged away from it, that poisonous feeling between them, that terrible balancing of hurts and needs I had to do between the two, and did so badly, those earlier years.

Oh there are conflicts between the others too, each one human, needing, demanding, hurting, taking—but only between Emily and Susan, no, Emily toward Susan that corroding resentment. It seems so obvious on the surface, yet it is not obvious. Susan, the second child, Susan, golden- and curly-haired and chubby, quick and articulate and assured, everything in appearance and manner Emily was not; Susan, not able to resist Emily's precious things, losing or sometimes clumsily breaking them; Susan telling jokes and riddles to company for applause while Emily sat silent (to say to me later: that was *my* riddle, Mother, I told it to Susan); Susan, who for all the five years' difference in age was just a year behind Emily in developing physically.

I am glad for that slow physical development that widened the difference between her and her contemporaries, though she suffered over it. She
was too vulnerable for that terrible world of youthful competition, of
preening and parading, of constant measuring of yourself against every
other, of envy, "If I had that copper hair," "If I had that skin. . . ." She
tormented herself enough about not looking like the others, there was
enough of the unsureness, the having to be conscious of words before you
speak, the constant caring—what are they thinking of me? without having
it all magnified by the merciless physical drives.

Ronnie is calling. He is wet and I change him. It is rare there is such
a cry now. That time of motherhood is almost behind me when the ear is
not one's own but must always be racked and listening for the child cry,
the child call. We sit for a while and I hold him, looking out over the city
spread in charcoal with its soft aisles of light. "*Shoogily*," he breathes and
curls closer. I carry him back to bed, asleep. *Shoogily*. A funny word, a
family word, inherited from Emily, invented by her to say: *comfort*.

In this and other ways she leaves her seal, I say aloud. And startle at
my saying it. What do I mean? What did I start to gather together, to try
and make coherent? I was at the terrible, growing years. War years. I do
not remember them well. I was working, there were four smaller ones
now, there was not time for her. She had to help be a mother, and housekeeper, and shopper. She had to set her seal. Mornings of crisis and near
hysteria trying to get lunches packed, hair combed, coats and shoes found,
everyone to school or Child Care on time, the baby ready for transportation. And always the paper scribbled on by a smaller one, the book looked
at by Susan then mislaid, the homework not done. Running out to that
huge school where she was one, she was lost, she was a drop; suffering
over the unpreparedness, stammering and unsure in her classes.

There was so little time left at night after the kids were bedded down. *45*
She would struggle over books, always eating (it was in those years she
developed her enormous appetite that is legendary in our family) and I
would be ironing, or preparing food for the next day, or writing V-mail to
Bill, or tending the baby. Sometimes, to make me laugh, or out of her
despair, she would imitate happenings or types at school.

I think I said once: "Why don't you do something like this in the
school amateur show?" One morning she phoned me at work, hardly
understandable through the weeping: "Mother, I did it. I won, I won; they
gave me first prize; they clapped and clapped and wouldn't let me go."

Now suddenly she was Somebody, and as imprisoned in her difference as she had been in anonymity.

She began to be asked to perform at other high schools, even in
colleges, then at city and statewide affairs. The first one we went to, I only
recognized her that first moment when thin, shy, she almost drowned
herself into the curtains. Then: Was this Emily? The control, the command, the convulsing and deadly clowning, the spell, then the roaring,

stamping audience, unwilling to let this rare and precious laughter out of their lives.

Afterwards: You ought to do something about her with a gift like that—but without money or knowing how, what does one do? We have left it all to her, and the gift has as often eddied inside, clogged and clotted, as been used and growing.

She is coming. She runs up the stairs two at a time with her light   50 graceful step, and I know she is happy tonight. Whatever it was that occasioned your call did not happen today.

"Aren't you ever going to finish the ironing, Mother? Whistler painted his mother in a rocker. I'd have to paint mine standing over an ironing board." This is one of her communicative nights and she tells me everything and nothing as she fixes herself a plate of food out of the icebox.

She is so lovely. Why did you want me to come in at all? Why were you concerned? She will find her way.

She starts up the stairs to bed. "Don't get me up with the rest in the morning." "But I thought you were having midterms." "Oh, those," she comes back in, kisses me, and says quite lightly, "in a couple of years when we'll all be atom-dead they won't matter a bit."

She has said it before. She *believes* it. But because I have been dredging the past, and all that compounds a human being is so heavy and meaningful in me, I cannot endure it tonight.

I will never total it all. I will never come in to say: She was a child   55 seldom smiled at. Her father left me before she was a year old. I had to work her first six years when there was work, or I sent her home and to his relatives. There were years she had care she hated. She was dark and thin and foreign-looking in a world where the prestige went to blondness and curly hair and dimples, she was slow where glibness was prized. She was a child of anxious, not proud, love. We were poor and could not afford for her the soil of easy growth. I was a young mother, I was a distracted mother. There were the other children pushing up, demanding. Her younger sister seemed all that she was not. There were years she did not let me touch her. She kept too much in herself, her life was such she had to keep too much in herself. My wisdom came too late. She has much to her and probably little will come of it. She is a child of her age, of depression, of war, of fear.

Let her be. So all that is in her will not bloom—but in how many does it? There is still enough left to live by. Only help her to know—help make it so there is cause for her to know—that she is more than this dress on the ironing board, helpless before the iron.

The Responsive Reader

1. Why do you think Olsen wrote this story? (Who is the *you* addressed in the story?) What do you think writing this story did for the writer?

2. How do the physical conditions, the circumstances of her life, shape the outlook of the woman telling the story? How does poverty shape her attitude and expectations?

3. What is the role of institutions in this story? (Why do they loom so large?) What is the role of individuals—for instance, the teacher, Emily's father, the old man who lives in the back?

4. What picture of Emily emerges from this story? Can you relate to her as a person? Do you think the picture her mother gives us of her is incomplete or one-sided?

5. What is the narrator's last word on her story and the story of Emily? How do you react to the way the story ends?

Talking, Listening, Writing

6. Some readers of this story empathize with the mother; others criticize her for failing her child. How would you defend the mother? Or how would you justify the charges some readers bring against her?

7. How do you think the situation or the child might have looked when seen from a different point of view? For instance, what might have been the perspective of a teacher or social worker?

8. Tell the story of Emily as she might have told it herself.

Collaborative Projects

9. What are the current statistics about poverty in this country? Who compiles them, and what do they mean? Where do we draw the "poverty line," and how meaningful is the term? Collaborate with other students to explore the answers to these questions.

A GLIMPSE

Walt Whitman

> *Through most of the history of our culture, gay men and lesbian women had to keep their sexual orientation secret. When it became a matter of public record, as in the case of the nineteenth-century poet and playwright Oscar Wilde, it wrecked careers and lives. (When Wilde came back from the prison where he had been sent by British magistrates sputtering with self-righteous indignation, one of his first acts was to write to the press pleading the cause of three children kept in the same brutal dehumanizing jail where he had been confined.) In recent decades, gay and lesbian artists and writers have slowly emerged from the twilight in which they were kept by societal repression. Many of them admired the American poet Walt Whitman (1819–1892), author of* Leaves of Grass *and the "poet of democracy," as a precursor and pioneer. Although he did not openly acknowledge his homosexuality, his celebration of the male human form and the love of comrades made him a prophet of gay liberation.*

Thought Starters: When did you first become aware of the gay lifestyle? How were your early impressions shaped?

A glimpse through an interstice caught,   *1*
Of a crowd of workmen and drivers in a bar-room around the stove
    late of a winter night, and I unremark'd seated in a corner,
Of a youth who loves me and whom I love, silently approaching and
    seating himself near, that he may hold me by the hand,   *5*
A long while amid the noises of coming and going, of drinking and
    oath and smutty jest,
There we two, content, happy in being together, speaking little,
    perhaps not a word.

The Responsive Reader

1. How does this poem go counter to stereotypes about gays?
2. Whitman uses the word *love* twice in this poem. Can you define love in such a way that it includes both heterosexual and homosexual love?
3. How do you think this poem should be read? How should it sound? (What should be the volume, speed, tone of voice?)

Talking, Listening, Writing

4. What prominent gays or lesbians are you aware of in contemporary American life? What do you know about them? How are they treated by the media?

5. What have you read or heard about gay-bashing or homophobia? What have you observed of it at first hand? What psychological or cultural mechanisms are at work?

WRITING
WORKSHOP 4

Drawing Conclusions

What kind of thinking shapes an effective paper? Tracking the thought processes that produce a well-thought-out paper is difficult. The brain moves at computer speed, and ideas surface in our consciousness without our knowing exactly how they took shape. Nevertheless, we can reconstruct common thought patterns that help us make sense of the data we take in. We can chart—at least in simplified fashion—ways our minds process information.

A familiar and productive think scheme finds the common thread in a number of related events. It finds a pattern where at first there was a confusing collection of data. If you get violently ill every time you eat shrimp, you will sooner or later tag shellfish and your allergy to it as the likely culprit. If Asian American students consistently do better than Anglos on a math teacher's tests, she will start looking for some common element in the Asian Americans' backgrounds as the clue to their superior performance.

This kind of thinking is one basic way of moving from fact to **inference**—moving from raw data to what we think they mean. The technical term for thinking that looks for the common element in a set of observations is **induction**, or inductive thinking. If it weren't for inductive thinking, a person allergic to shellfish would keep eating it, and getting sick as a result, forever. Many solidly argued papers line up the examples, the evidence, that all point in the same direction. If it is an effective paper, the reader is likely to say: "Yes, I agree. Looking at the facts or the data, I would have drawn the same conclusion." Typically, the paper presents the general point *early* as the writer's thesis—and then goes on to provide the examples, data, or evidence that led to the general conclusion.

Suppose you ask yourself: "We frequently hear charges of racism—against employers, against the police, against educational institutions. Is racism on the rise?" You look at potentially relevant evidence: the videotape, played over and over on national TV, of a brutal beating of a black motorist by Los Angeles police. You study reports of a multimillion-dollar verdict against a restaurant chain for discriminating against African American customers. If you proceed inductively, you may learn something here that you did not realize before. One student exploring this topic found testimony—by an emergency room physician, by the daughter of an old-style police officer—to the effect that beatings of members of minority groups by police are more common than we like to think. He concluded that what is on the rise is not so much racism as such. A big factor is our heightened *awareness* of it. Alleged racist behavior and racist incidents, he decided, were "under more intense scrutiny" in our society today than they have been in the past. This conclusion became the thesis of his paper.

Obviously, we never approach an issue with a completely open mind. We have preconceptions—opinions to which we are already more or less firmly committed. We may have jumped to conclusions on the basis of limited firsthand experience. We may have accepted without question what we heard in the family or were taught in school. We may be going along with what is widely believed in a group with which we identify. Inductive thinking kicks in when you are ready to say: "What I think about this issue may be based on hearsay, limited evidence, or groupthink. Let me check this out." The conclusion you reach will still be your opinion—but it will be an *informed* opinion. Your readers may find it worthwhile to think about it, argue with it, or make it their own.

TRIGGERING The need to make sense of a rich array of data is one of the most basic human needs. Here are some situations that may trigger a search for general conclusions:

▪ *Much writing charts current trends.* When people find that many available jobs are for temporaries or part-timers, without a pension plan or health benefits, they start checking around to see if this is a widespread pattern. Is it true that many steady and well-paid middle-management positions are gone for good? Is it true that many high-wage manufacturing jobs have been replaced by low-wage jobs in Korea or Taiwan?

▪ *Much writing tests stereotypes or clichés.* For instance, is it true that Americans are incorrigible optimists? (What makes American Peace Corps volunteers go into distant villages thinking they will be able to change age-old patterns of behavior? Was it the experience of getting out from under the stifling tutelage of kings and aristocrats? Was it the experience of being able to start all over somewhere in the wide open spaces of the West? Is the tradition of American optimism wearing thin?)

▪ *Much writing searches for answers to nagging questions.* For instance, who are the homeless? Assuming that the homeless come from many different backgrounds, what are common factors in their histories? (If we could agree on some conclusions about how they got there, we might be able to agree on ways to keep others from traveling the same route.)

GATHERING When we first explore a topic, we may stumble onto related facts that all seem to point roughly in the same direction. Testing or following up our first hunches, we may soon be able to gather relevant information in a more systematic fashion. If you ask, "What is different about the Japanese?" data like the following may soon begin to tell their own story:

Students graduating from twelfth grade:	Japan	90%
	United States	77%
Average daily hours of homework during high school:	Japan	2.0
	United States	.5
Daily absentee rate:	Japan	very low
	United States	9%
Years required of high school mathematics:	Japan	3
	United States (typical)	1
Years required of foreign language (grades 7–12):	Japan	6
	United States	0–2
Engineering majors in undergraduate population:	Japan	20%
	United States	5%

SHAPING A focused paper or a coherent paragraph often results when the writer has funneled related observations into a general conclusion. In a paragraph like the following, the writer has laid related observations end to end. Her general point provides the **topic sentence** that starts the paragraph:

> *I am often treated as a stereotypical blonde.* I have a soft musical voice. I have always had high grades, and I have worked as a tutor to help other students improve theirs. Still, some people do not take me seriously because of the way I look and sound. I have been told to put up my hair in a bun, wear glasses, quit wearing make-up, and work to lower the pitch of my voice. Men are not the only ones doing the stereotyping. I had a female instructor criticize my voice as unprofessional after an oral report. I had a female student tell me during a group project that my "Barbie Doll" voice would make the wrong impression on the audience.

The difference between the thinking that produced this passage and the actual paragraph printed here is a question of what comes first. During the thinking process, we start with the data and then draw a conclusion. However, in most of the writing that presents our findings, we state the general point first and then marshal the evidence that led up to it. When we put the general point first in a paragraph, we call it the topic sentence. When we put the more inclusive or overarching generalization early in a paper, we call it the **thesis**. (Sometimes, you may want to lead your readers up to the general point, simulating the actual process of sorting the data and discovering the common thread.)

Often an effective paper is modeled on the inverted upside-down funnel. What came *out of* the funnel comes first; what went *into* the funnel comes later. The thesis comes first, and then the writer lays out the observations that were funneled into the general conclusion that the thesis sums up. The claim the writer makes comes first; the evidence comes second. The following might be the thesis of a paper about the lack of political involvement among students:

THESIS: A pervasive apathy about political issues marks today's generation of students.

The rest of the paper would then present the evidence that led to this conclusion. Successive paragraphs might focus on points like the following:

- Turnouts for controversial speakers invited to your campus have been small.
- Turnout for elections for student government has been dismal.
- Debates scheduled on topics like AIDS and safe sex have fizzled.
- Few students turned out for special events scheduled to honor minority authors or to recognize outstanding women on campus.

REVISING Whenever you claim to have found a general pattern, you have to guard against jumping to conclusions. Revision is a chance to rethink what your evidence really shows. It is a chance to reword sweeping generalizations. Keep in mind advice like the following:

- *Spell out your thesis.* What exactly are you claiming? It is a lame beginning to start a paper by saying that "certain factors" play a role in prejudice or homelessness. What are they? Which are the most important?
- *Limit your generalizations.* Obviously, readers will not sit still for claims that people of one nationality or religion are marvelously more gifted and generous than another. Neither will educated readers listen patiently to claims that members of any one group are inherently lazy or violence-prone. But less provocative generalizations—about voter apathy, about immigrants on welfare—may also have to be worded more cautiously, with due consideration for exceptions and countertrends. Above all, they will have to be checked against the evidence you are actually able to present.
- *Build your case on representative examples.* Try to present a cross-section of relevant instances. Try to listen to a cross-section of witnesses, pro and con. Do not build your case on one outstanding case that might turn out to be a freak example.

What general conclusions does the author of the following sample paper present to her readers? What data did she funnel into her paper? How real or convincing are the observations on which she based her findings?

Bodies Betrayed by the Mind

> I would do anything to look like a skinny model or a Barbie doll. I used to starve myself for days at a time. I lost a lot of weight, but when I started getting sick and my hair fell out, I started eating and gained it all back. Honestly, if I could, I would stop eating again to be thin, but I physically can't—I get sick instantly. I also have a friend who has severe kidney and mental problems because of anorexia.

The anonymous seventeen-year-old who made this comment represents a feeling and experience common to many young women in the United States.

There are two predominant causes of anorexia and bulimia in young women in particular. Both are a form of social pressure that gives young ladies a standard of beauty to which they feel they need to aspire. "Specialists in eating disorders have concluded that social factors are largely responsible for the rising incidence of eating disorders suffered almost exclusively by young women," claims Larry Percy, a media consultant. The feeling of being pressured is best represented in a health pamphlet on eating disorders that says "guilt about gaining too much weight may develop into fear." At this point the problem has become severe. The causes are not related to food; they are related to how a child has learned to perceive herself and the incessant advertisement of images portraying unnaturally thin women. Thus, many women grow up with a fear of gaining weight and being criticized or belittled by society.

As kids mature they experience waves of competition that either are forgotten or ingrained in them. Parents might be surprised to know that some simple gifts are psychologically harmful to children, like Barbie dolls. Little girls may compare their own bodies with those of the dolls and even begin to compete. Studies have been performed to translate the size of a Barbie doll into a real woman. While the doll's figure varies slightly in size, her waist measurement would not exceed twenty-three inches if human, and would, on average, be closer to seventeen. Her long legs would give her a height ranging from six feet, two inches to seven feet, five inches. A seven foot, five inch Barbie woman would have a bust measurement of thirty-six inches.

When a twelve-year-old compares her body to this popular standard, she is going to be very disappointed and may feel inadequate at a very young age. According to observers of the Barbie phenomenon, not only does Barbie influence women's perceptions of the ideal figure but there are living Barbie fashion models and performers. Laurie Lang of my university's Health Center says, "minority women feel better because they are less visible—I mean, how many black Barbie dolls do you see?"

As young women mature, they are affected more by the media and by images that "define what forms of femininity are acceptable and desirable," according to Larry Percy. Women are faced with models that symbolize how women should look, how they should behave, and how women can expect to be seen by others. Perfection is the ultimate goal. In a Chanel No. 5 perfume ad, there is a picture of French movie idol Catherine Deneuve beside an enlarged bottle of the perfume. She is an ageless, skinny woman with high cheek bones, beautiful eyes, a sexy smile, and gold colored hair. She also looks very elegant. "What Catherine Deneuve's face means to us in the world of magazines and films, Chanel No. 5 seeks to mean and comes to mean in the world of consumer goods. It signifies flawless French beauty, which makes it useful as a piece of linguistic currency to sell Chanel," notes Judith Williamson in her piece on decoding advertisements.

As we delve further into the media's images of perfect beauty, we realize that the images are hardly perfect at all. Various studies (including my own) have concluded that the ideal figure of a woman is slimmer than her own; this is also the figure that is most appealing to men. The models in the media often have a hard time portraying the supreme female image because there has been an "image-slimming effect" of over fifty percent since the turn of the century. Freedman quotes one fashion model as saying it took a crew of people to get her into a pair of size three designer jeans and to carry her into position to be photographed: "To look as I did in that ad, you would have to fast for two months and hold your breath for twenty minutes." Using an illustration of ten different female body types numbered from one to ten in size (excluding height), I asked ten women between the ages of sixteen and twenty to show me how they perceive their own body and how they would like to look. Eight out of ten said they would like to have the second to skinniest figure on the chart and the other two, already that skinny, said they would like to remain the same. The eight identified themselves as being three or more body sizes bigger when often that was not the case. Although the interviewees recognized the fact that the "Twiggy" look is an unhealthy look, the common attitude as captured by one woman seems to be, "They aren't healthy yet they're the ideal. I would love to be the ideal, who wouldn't?"

The university has had trouble getting pamphlets on anorexia and bulimia because of the widespread demand from campuses that have a real problem with eating disorders among their students. A little over ten percent of college women have "a pattern of bingeing and purging," while only two percent of men experience this problem. Many young women are known to take unsafe diuretics and "fat burning" pills. Anorexia and bulimia are associated with numerous health problems that can be life-threatening. It is recognized that certain personality types make certain people more susceptible to eating disorders; however, every person is a candidate. As long as women continue to be bombarded with unhealthy standards of nearly unattainable slimness, the number of victims of eating disorders will steadily increase. Sadly, the media seem to persist in imposing these standards of beauty on an impressionable young society.

"When I watch a commercial or a news broadcast and I see a normal looking spokeswoman, it's shocking!" said a student. The point is valid. Not only have the media caused major health problems and sentiments of insufficiency on the part of women, but they have also begun to measure success, in part, in terms of beauty. Women have to learn to resist this media lure. Women are naturally fatter than men so that they can have babies. Female hormones naturally bind fat cells, giving women breasts and other associated female "swells." If a woman does not interfere with her body's true chemistry is she neither successful nor beautiful? No. She is an individual who recognizes that beauty comes in all forms, shapes, and sizes, and she was probably raised by conscientious parents.

Topics for Papers Drawing Conclusions (A Sampling)

1. In an age of backlash politics, we hear much about the political weight carried by "angry white males." What are white males angry about? Which are the most important or most widely aired grievances?
2. To judge from your own observation, is there such a thing as "recreational drug use"—by people who can take it or leave it?
3. Have you observed common traits or a recurrent pattern in young people who get into trouble with the law?
4. Did your high school or does your college have cliques? Is there a common pattern in the behavior of cliques or of the people who belong to them?
5. We hear much talk about dysfunctional families. To judge from your own observation, how widespread is the phenomenon? What are key elements such families seem to share?
6. To judge from your own observation of our society, how large is the gap between the rich and the poor?
7. On your campus, do people of the same racial or ethnic background tend to flock together? How much mingling is there of people from diverse backgrounds?
8. How serious or how widespread is anti-immigration sentiment in our society? Is "immigrant-bashing" a sign of the times?
9. To judge from your own observation, which immigrant groups have the least (or the most) difficulty in adjusting to their new environment?
10. Is courtesy dead? Are good manners a thing of the past?

5

Identity:
Rethinking Race

It took me a long time and much painful boomeranging of expectations to achieve a realization everyone else seems to have been born with: That I am nobody but myself.

—*Ralph Ellison*

We are so many selves.

—*Gloria Steinem*

"Who am I?" The search for identity has for centuries been a major theme in the imaginative literature of the West. How can we discover our true selves? How can we realize our full human potential? Many discover that a crucial preliminary question is not "Who am I?" but "*What* am I?" We find that our group identity—ethnic origin, race, or social class—limits what we can be. Being a dentist's son or daughter at Stanford University is a different identity from being a student looking for student loans at a community college. Going to a mainly black school in a country town in the South is a different matter from attending a prep school in the East. Who we can be is shaped and often limited by what we are.

For anthropologists, the concept of race has no scientific standing. All human beings are members of the same species, capable of intermarrying. In that basic sense, all human beings are "created equal." Skin color varies from very dark in some tropical climates to very pale in some countries of the frozen North. Members of some ethnic groups in Africa tend to be very short; members of other ethnic groups tend to be very tall (and may be sought after by basketball teams).

Nevertheless, the *perception* of race has often played a crucial and at times murderous role in human history. It has been a powerful divisive influence in the history of this country. Slavery was built on the assumption that some races were created inferior. In the minds of many, the bloodiest war in American history was fought to abolish the institution. Whether and how racism survives in contemporary American society is the subject of much debate and of charges and countercharges. A Jewish student reports that in high school she was called "every name that anti-Semites have created: cheap, smart, rich, stuck up, big-nosed, and JAP."

Race is one, and in recent history perhaps the most deadly one, of the factors that keeps us from being judged by the "content of our character." Being identified as a member of a group, we encounter expectations, pressures, or barriers visible and invisible. Sometimes, these barriers are crudely obvious, as when a country club does not accept Jews. Sometimes, they are more subtle, as when a prominent journal of opinion consistently devalues or undercuts the black leadership. Many feel that race continues to be the great unresolved challenge to traditional American values.

HOW IT FEELS TO BE COLORED ME

Zora Neale Hurston

Zora Neale Hurston once said about the idea of democracy that she was all for trying it out. In fact, she couldn't wait to do so as soon as the Jim Crow laws that legalized discrimination against African Americans were a thing of the past. Hurston was born in Eatonville, an all-black town in Florida, and was working as a domestic when she managed to attend college. She finally went on to Howard University, which has been called "a center of black scholarship and intellectual ferment." As a scholarship student at Barnard College in New York City, she became an associate of the anthropologist Franz Boas, who asked her to return to the South to collect black folk tales. She had earlier published earthy slice-of-life sketches of black life; her classic collection of African American folklore, Mules and Men, *appeared in 1935. Like other students of black dialect and folk tradition, she was accused by militants of perpetuating damaging stereotypes of African Americans as uneducated and unsophisticated. Like other minority artists and writers dependent on white patronage, she was accused of selling out to the white establishment. Although for a time one of the best-known voices of the Harlem Renaissance of the twenties and thirties, she died in a county welfare home and was buried in an unmarked grave. In recent years, feminists have rediscovered her fiction; her masterpiece, the novel* Their Eyes Were Watching God *(1937), is now widely read in college classes. A recent biographer has called her "the most significant unread author in America."*

Thought Starters: How aware are people you know of their separate racial or ethnic identity? Is it constantly on their minds?

I am colored but I offer nothing in the way of extenuating circum-   *1*
stances except the fact that I am the only Negro in the United States whose grandfather on the mother's side was *not* an Indian chief.

I remember the very day that I became colored. Up to my thirteenth year I lived in the little Negro town of Eatonville, Florida. It is exclusively a colored town. The only white people I knew passed through the town going to or coming from Orlando. The native whites rode dusty horses, the Northern tourists chugged down the sandy village road in automobiles. The town knew the Southerners and never stopped cane chewing when they passed. But the Northerners were something else again. They were peered at cautiously from behind curtains by the timid. The more venturesome would come out on the porch to watch them go past and got just as much pleasure out of the tourists as the tourists got out of the village.

The front porch might seem a daring place for the rest of the town, but it was a gallery seat to me. My favorite place was atop the gate-post. Proscenium box for a born first-nighter. Not only did I enjoy the show, but I didn't mind the actors knowing that I liked it. I usually spoke to them in passing. I'd wave at them and when they returned my salute, I would say something like this: "Howdy-do-well-I-thank-you-where-you-goin'?" Usually the automobile or the horse paused at this, and after a queer exchange of compliments, I would probably "go a piece of the way" with them, as we say in farthest Florida. If one of my family happened to come to the front in time to see me, of course negotiations would be rudely broken off. But even so, it is clear that I was the first "welcome-to-our-state" Floridian, and I hope the Miami Chamber of Commerce will please take notice.

During this period, white people differed from colored to me only in that they rode through town and never lived there. They liked to hear me "speak pieces" and sing and wanted to see me dance the parse-me-la, and gave me generously of their small silver for doing these things, which seemed strange to me for I wanted to do them so much that I needed bribing to stop. Only they didn't know it. The colored people gave no dimes. They deplored any joyful tendencies in me, but I was their Zora nevertheless. I belonged to them, to the nearby hotels, to the county— everybody's Zora.

But changes came in the family when I was thirteen, and I was sent   5
to school in Jacksonville. I left Eatonville, the town of the oleanders, as Zora. When I disembarked from the river-boat at Jacksonville, she was no more. It seemed that I had suffered a sea change. I was not Zora of Orange County any more, I was now a little colored girl. I found it out in certain ways. In my heart as well as in the mirror, I became a fast brown— warranted not to rub nor run.

But I am not tragically colored. There is no great sorrow dammed up in my soul, nor lurking behind my eyes. I do not mind at all. I do not belong to the sobbing school of Negrohood who hold that nature somehow has given them a lowdown dirty deal and whose feelings are all hurt about it. Even in the helter-skelter skirmish that is my life, I have seen that the world is to the strong regardless of a little pigmentation more or less. No, I do not weep at the world—I am too busy sharpening my oyster knife.

Someone is always at my elbow reminding me that I am the grand-daughter of slaves. It fails to register depression with me. Slavery is sixty years in the past. The operation was successful and the patient is doing well, thank you. The terrible struggle that made me an American out of a potential slave said "On the line!" The Reconstruction said "Get set!"; and the generation before said "Go!" I am off to a flying start and I must not halt in the stretch to look behind and weep. Slavery is the price I paid for civilization, and the choice was not with me. It is a bully adventure and worth all that I have paid through my ancestors for it. No one on earth ever had a greater chance for glory. The world to be won and nothing to be lost. It is thrilling to think—to know that for any act of mine, I shall get twice as much praise or twice as much blame. It is quite exciting to hold the center of the national stage, with the spectators not knowing whether to laugh or to weep.

The position of my white neighbor is much more difficult. No brown specter pulls up a chair beside me when I sit down to eat. No dark ghost thrusts its leg against mine in bed. The game of keeping what one has is never so exciting as the game of getting.

I do not always feel colored. Even now I often achieve the unconscious Zora of Eatonville before the Hegira. I feel most colored when I am thrown against a sharp white background.

For instance at Barnard. "Beside the waters of the Hudson" I feel my   10
race. Among the thousand white persons, I am a dark rock surged upon, overswept by a creamy sea. I am surged upon and overswept, but through it all, I remain myself. When covered by the waters, I am; and the ebb but reveals me again.

Sometimes it is the other way around. A white person is set down in our midst, but the contrast is just as sharp for me. For instance, when I sit in the drafty basement that is The New World Cabaret with a white person, my color comes. We enter chatting about any little nothing that we have in common and are seated by the jazz waiters. In the abrupt way that jazz orchestras have, this one plunges into a number. It loses no time in circumlocutions, but gets right down to business. It constricts the thorax and splits the heart with its tempo and narcotic harmonies. This orchestra grows rambunctious, rears on its hind legs and attacks the tonal veil with primitive fury, rending it, clawing it until it breaks through to the jungle beyond. I follow those heathen—follow them exultingly. I dance wildly inside myself; I yell within, I whoop; I shake my assegai above my head, I hurl it true to the mark *yeeeeooww*! I am in the jungle and living in the jungle way. My face is painted red and yellow and my body is painted blue. My pulse is throbbing like a war drum. I want to slaughter something—give pain, give death to what, I do not know. But the piece ends. The men of the orchestra wipe their lips and rest their fingers. I creep back slowly to the veneer we call civilization with the last tone and find the white friend sitting motionless in his seat, smoking calmly.

"Good music they have here," he remarks, drumming the table with his fingertips.

Music! The great blobs of purple and red emotion have not touched him. He has only heard what I felt. He is far away and I see him but dimly across the ocean and the continent that have fallen between us. He is so pale with his whiteness then and I am *so* colored.

At certain times I have no race, I am *me*. When I set my hat at a certain angle and saunter down Seventh Avenue, Harlem City, feeling as snooty as the lions in front of the Forty-Second Street Library, for instance. So far as my feelings are concerned, Peggy Hopkins Joyce on the Boule Mich with her gorgeous raiment, stately carriage, knees knocking together in a most aristocratic manner, has nothing on me. The cosmic Zora emerges. I belong to no race nor time. I am the eternal feminine with its string of beads.

I have no separate feeling about being an American citizen and col- 15 ored. I am merely a fragment of the Great Soul that surges within the boundaries. My country, right or wrong.

Sometimes, I feel discriminated against, but it does not make me angry. It merely astonishes me. How *can* any deny themselves the pleasure of my company! It's beyond me.

But in the main, I feel like a brown bag of miscellany propped against a wall. Against a wall in company with other bags, white, red and yellow. Pour out the contents, and there is discovered a jumble of small things priceless and worthless. A first-water diamond, an empty spool, bits of broken glass, lengths of string, a key to a door long since crumbled away, a rusty knifeblade, old shoes saved for a road that never was and never will be, a nail bent under the weight of things too heavy for any nail, a dried flower or two, still a little fragrant. In your hand is the brown bag. On the ground before you is the jumble it held—so much like the jumble in the bags, could they be emptied, that all might be dumped in a single heap and the bags refilled without altering the content of any greatly. A bit of colored glass more or less would not matter. Perhaps that is how the Great Stuffer of Bags filled them in the first place—who knows?

The Responsive Reader

1. There has been much talk about the need for self-esteem—the need for women and minorities to overcome culturally conditioned feelings of inferiority and inadequacy. What is the secret of Hurston's self-esteem?
2. What were major stages in Hurston's awareness of race? (For instance, when was it that she "became" colored? How does she distance herself from other definitions of "Negrohood"? When is she least aware of racial difference?)
3. What is Hurston's last word on the role of race in her life and in the larger society? Do her words seem dated or still valid today?

Talking, Listening, Writing

4. How does Hurston's attitude toward race compare with what you think is predominant in today's generation?
5. What efforts have you observed to restore people's pride in their own racial or ethnic identity? Have you personally participated in such efforts? How successful are they?
6. Have you experienced self-doubt, feelings of inadequacy, or feelings of inferiority? What causes them? How do you cope with them?

Collaborative Projects

7. How much do you know about the art and literature of diverse ethnic or cultural traditions? Your class may want to organize a presentation of poems, tales, songs, or music. (Will you encounter any questions about what is authentic, what is exploitative, or what is offensive or demeaning?)

Thinking about Connections

How does the self-image of a black woman in Hurston's essay compare with the self-image of the young black woman in Maya Angelou's "Step Forward in the Car, Please"?

ON THE JOB

Joe Gutierrez

> *Studs Terkel is known for several best-selling collections of interviews with ordinary Americans. He was born in Chicago in 1912 and grew up there, attending the University of Chicago and the Chicago Law School. He has been a disk jockey, sports commentator, and television emcee; he has hosted a popular talk show for thirty-five years. In books like* Working, Hard Times, *and* American Dreams: Lost and Found, *he proved a good listener, getting the people he interviewed to cut through media hype and political slogans and to talk with amazing honesty about their lives, thoughts, and feelings. The following interview with a fifty-year-old steel worker is from Terkel's latest book,* Race: How Blacks and Whites Feel about the American Obsession *(1992). A reviewer said about this book, "Studs Terkel has got people to say things in such a way that you know at once they have finally said their truth and said it better than they ever believed they could say it."*
>
> *Joe Gutierrez, the person interviewed in the following selection from* Race, *spent four years in a seminary preparing to be a priest but then quit to work in the steel mills like his father. Gutierrez said about his family:*

> My father worked at the Ford plant in Detroit when he first came from Mexico. Then he came to Chicago and the steel mill and worked there as far back as I can remember. . . . My mother was a hillbilly from Georgia. She married at fourteen. We're fifteen children. She didn't speak Spanish and he didn't speak English. I didn't know two words of Spanish until I got out into the steel mill.

> *Gutierrez is of Mexican American descent, with a Mexican father and a North American mother. He says of Spanish Americans, or Latinos, "Latins are right in the middle." In how many ways does the person speaking to you in this interview find himself "right in the middle"?*

Thought Starters: Do you listen to what the person speaking in the following interview calls "working people"? What do you learn?

I didn't identify with Mexicans until people started throwing racism   *1*
around. My name is José but I've always been called Little Joe. The whites
didn't know my last name and thought I was Italian or Greek. So they let
out their true feelings.

I was not accepted by the Mexicans because I couldn't speak the language: "You look white, so you don't want to be a Mexican." I forced myself to learn the language so at least I could get by.

We were the only Mexican family in the neighborhood. The Mexicans, Puerto Ricans, and blacks lived on the East Chicago side by the mills. Now it's all changed. You've got a neighbor that's black, another Puerto Rican, another something else. All on our street.

We were about eight years old, my brother, Vince, and I when we went to a public swimming pool in a park in East Chicago. We took a black kid with us. This was 1948. As soon as we dove in the pool, everybody got out. The lifeguard got out, too, a female. They shut down the pool. I was never raised to be a racist, so I didn't know what it was all about.

There's a certain amount of racism among Mexicans against blacks, and   5
Mexicans against Puerto Ricans. But I see more racism with the blacks than with the white or Latin.

We went through a union election. We're about thirty percent black. Every time I ran for office, there was a solid black vote for the black, regardless of the person. It made no difference. Over the years, I felt it would change because people would look at the person's qualifications. For the most part, it hasn't changed. That's true among Latins also. They'll vote Latin just because he's Latin. Whites? Yeah, pretty much the same.

A good friend of mine, a white from Kentucky, just got elected griever in the metal-plate department. I said, "The black griever we have is simply unqualified; he's done a terrible job. I don't expect the blacks to vote for him. He won't get over twenty votes." He said, "The guy's gonna get a hundred votes." He was right. For three years, the guy did an awful job. They still came out and backed him. I understand the past injustices, but . . .

The guys who are honest say, "Look, we've been down so long, the first time we get somebody to represent the black community, he projects an image of leadership and we overlook the bad. We just want a black there."

It baffles my mind because I've had an ongoing fight in the mills: I don't care if you're black, brown, or white, we're all workers. I sometimes get chastised by the so-called leaders of the Latin community because I don't stand up and say we should all go for *la raza*. There are some Latins who always vote that way. I voted that way before I got involved with the union. I didn't know people. If I saw a Sánchez or Gonzalez or Rodríguez, I voted for him. I met a Cisneros who couldn't write his own name and didn't give a damn about the union, was a company guy. I said nah, nah, nah. He may be Latin but he doesn't represent the interests of working people. I don't care about image.

With whites, what comes first is my pocketbook. I can work with a   10
black, with a Latin, but as soon as I leave that steel mill, I get on South 41 and go back to my world. Here it's a temporary world for eight hours a day, five days a week. When you park your car and walk into that plant,

you walk into another world. All your prejudices, all your hates, you leave in the parking lot.

At the workplace, there's not much tension. You still have people who feel they're treated unfairly because they're black or Latin. When some whites get disciplined, they say, "I'm white, you didn't discipline the black guy." It's a crutch. But in general, it's not there. You're working around heavy equipment and you've got to look out for your buddy. It's very easy to get hurt in a steel mill.

As for whites, there's still a lot of prejudice out there. I know how to erase it. If you give other people a chance—if you give me the opportunity to present my views, maybe you'll get to know me and like me. Look, there's some people you just don't like. It's got nothing to do with color; it's got a lot to do with personality.

Latins are right in the middle. For the longest time, they were classified as blacks. You go to Texas, and Latinos are treated like blacks.

With people losing jobs, there's always got to be somebody to blame. We had nineteen thousand people at Inland Steel. Now we're below ten thousand. For years, whites had all the better jobs. In 1977, the government came in and said you've got to do something about discrimination in the workplace or we'll do it for you. They signed a Memorandum of Understanding that implemented plantwide seniority. It was good for everybody. Now a black or Latino as well as a white could transfer in any department and utilize seniority.

At the time, whites ran the trains, Latins worked on the tracks, and   15
blacks worked in the coke plants. When the changes took place, there was a lot of hatred among whites against minorities in general. "I've worked in this mill for twenty-five years, and here's one of them coming over and bumping me out of a job." It didn't happen that way for the most part, because you still had contract language to go by. You couldn't leapfrog over somebody.

We had an election the other day and won by a landslide. I acted as a watcher. Some voted only for Latins, others only for blacks, and some whites only for whites. Our slate had a president who's white, a Latin who's vicepresident, and two black trustees. It was a mix all around. We voted for the person. We represented the rank-and-file against the old guys. For the most part, we're forty, forty-one years old. You don't have a younger crop because there are no jobs for them.

What's ahead doesn't look good. With a new power plant, a lot of departments will shut down. The coke plants will go. You'll see some of the old hatred coming back. Blacks will say, "You gave us the rotten jobs whites wouldn't take, working on batteries, causing cancer and so forth, and when things get bad, we're the first to go." We're hearing it now. With fewer and fewer jobs, it'll get worse.

I don't like racists—white, black, Latin, anybody. Life's too short for meanness. There was a lot in the army when I was in it. Sometimes it comes out of people you don't expect it from. There's a guy who's decent, a hard worker, a good family man, and he'll say, "That fuckin' nigger." It's like getting hit in the gut. I stop him: "Why do you say that?" He just shrugs. He's Mexican, a deacon in the church. I'm a lector there. I tell this guy, "If a white guy says nigger, the word you use, I bet he calls you spic, taco-bender. Cut out this bullshit."

What's happened is that people were getting tired of the sixties. There was a legitimate grievance among the blacks in this country and a lot of us took part in the marches. But about twelve, fifteen years ago, younger blacks started coming into the steel mills. The older guys found allies among the Latins on the shop floor. But the younger guys came in with one thought in mind: We've been screwed and if we don't keep on their backs, they're gonna screw us again. To them, we're no different than the whites. It started backfiring.

Those of us who were sympathetic are less that way today. I had won   20
over a lot of blacks because I did a good job. But there are some blacks, I swear to God, I don't care what you did, it made no difference. All they saw was black. It's damaging to themselves. What more can a boss wish for?—divide and conquer!

When the government came down with a consent decree, Inland Steel ignored it. Every other company—LTV, Bethlehem, USX—paid minorities monies—two, three thousand dollars apiece—on the basis of years of discrimination at work. Inland Steel paid not a penny. They had a sharp lawyer who said, "Look, people are tired of civil rights, of marches, of busing, of affirmative action. The mood of the country is changing. Let's fight it." The government didn't follow through, and they didn't pay a penny. It's the Reagan years, and Bush is going even further.

I don't think the company is racist. That's too simple. It's the bottom line, the dollar. They don't care about you, no matter what your color is. You're nothing to them. If you're black or Latin or white, if they can set you up against the other workers, they're going to use you. They don't give a damn what color you are. It's the profit.

We have to keep working together, and when we hear the word nigger or spic—or cracker—stand up and say, "I don't appreciate that. Enough of this bullshit!"

The Responsive Reader

1. Like many Americans, Gutierrez does not have a clear-cut racial or ethnic identity. What experiences shaped his sense of who he is or where he belongs?
2. What has shaped his perceptions of the role of race in American life —in the communities in which we live?
3. What are Gutierrez' observations of the role of race on the job? For instance, what does he say about the hierarchy, or pecking order, in

the distribution of jobs? What does he say about company policy on the subject of race? (Does he think it is racist?)

4. Readers of Studs Terkel's books marvel at the candor with which the people he interviews seem to talk about subjects on which many people hide their feelings or lie to both themselves and others. Does anything in this interview seem especially honest or candid? Is there anything that might make you question the speaker's sincerity?

Talking, Listening, Writing

5. What in this interview seems familiar; what seems different or new? Have you had experiences similar to those of Gutierrez—or other experiences that contrast with his?

6. Does this interview make you rethink some of your assumptions about ethnicity and race? How?

7. Would you call Gutierrez a typical American? Why or why not?

8. One reviewer said that Terkel's research "runs directly counter to the meanness of spirit so often expressed and exploited by today's politicians." She said that if Terkel's interviewees are representative, there is a far greater degree of "public consensus" and of "yearning for resolution" than one might imagine. What did she mean? Does this sample interview bear out her observations?

AFFIRMATIVE ACTION
OR NEGATIVE ACTION

Miriam Schulman

> For several decades, affirmative action to correct injustices suffered by minor-
> ities and by women was official government policy. In government employ-
> ment, government contracts, and college admissions especially, programs were
> instituted to step up the representation of underrepresented groups. In recent
> political campaigns, however, affirmative action programs have come under
> attack for giving "special preferences" on the basis of race and gender. A widely
> publicized initiative campaign in California, inspiring similar efforts else-
> where, aimed at making it illegal for any state institution to take race
> or gender into account in dealing with its citizens. According to Nicholas
> Lemann writing in Time magazine, the initiative was predicted to "wipe out
> a host of programs . . . from magnet schools to science tutoring for girls" and
> to "decrease the minority presence at the University of California's two flag-
> ship schools, Berkeley and UCLA." According to some estimates the already
> minimal admission rate of African American students to be trained as mem-
> bers of the country's educational and professional elite would be cut in half.
> (Approved by the voters, the initiative was challenged as unconstitutional and
> got bogged down in the courts.) The following article is from a newsletter
> published by a center for applied ethics at a Catholic university. The author
> is trying to go beyond election-year politics and the anxieties of the proverbial
> angry white male to the ethical and political issues at the heart of the
> controversy.

Thought Starters: Have you or people you know been the beneficiary
or the victim of affirmative action?

It was 1986, and I was having a discussion with my freshman compo-   *1*
sition class at Santa Clara University about racial preference. Several white
students were telling me about friends who should have gotten into SCU
but didn't because the University was accepting so many "affirmative
action students." Others were assuring me that they would have been
accepted at Stanford if some minority student had not gotten their slot.

There were no African American students in the class; at that time,
the freshman African American population at Santa Clara stood at 24 out
of the total 886 freshmen. When I tried to get my students to look at the
numbers and explain why they felt so threatened, they regarded me with
the half-indulgent look college students used to reserve for '60s children
such as myself and shrugged. They knew what they knew.

And me? As much as I liked my students, I found it easy to write off their opinions as racist, or at the least, paranoid.

Ten years later, as the issue of affirmative action threatens to fracture the state of California, I think back on that conversation. It has come to represent for me what is wrong with the public dialogue on this subject: We throw out anecdotal evidence, mixed with a few facts and figures, and then we all retreat into our preconceived ideas without any empathetic consideration of the other side. At least I know I was not really listening to what my students had to say.

I do not mean to suggest that I have changed my mind about affir- 5
mative action. I still support it, which may seem a strange admission in the introduction to an article that I hope will be seen as an evenhanded exploration of the ethical issues involved. But I have come to believe that—in the affirmative action debate, at least—we cannot move forward unless we understand the justice of the other side's position.

At its heart, the controversy over affirmative action is a controversy about justice. When we try to judge the justice of a social policy, we start with the basic premise that everyone should be treated similarly unless there is a morally relevant reason why they should be treated differently. Whatever benefits and burdens the society has to distribute, justice requires them to be allocated on this basis.

For simplicity, I'll confine myself to exploring how this premise applies to race (which, by the way, is how the debate over affirmative action is usually couched, despite the fact that such programs include women and other minorities). Most people agree that the history of slavery and Jim Crow in this country violated the first premise of justice. The color of someone's skin is not a morally justifiable reason for treating people differently.

Ah, but if that's so, say opponents of affirmative action, why is it acceptable to *favor* people because of their skin color? If everyone were treated similarly, wouldn't we have a colorblind society? Indeed, the California Civil Rights Initiative, the ballot proposition that sought to overturn affirmative action, reads like this:

> The state shall not discriminate against, or grant preferential treatment to, any individual or group on the basis of race, sex, color, ethnicity, or national origin in the operation of public employment, public education, or public contracting.

To clarify the values that make us come down on one or the other 10
side in this debate, we must address the justice of preference. In the case of affirmative action, we must decide if there are ever circumstances that make it fair to favor one race over another when it comes to jobs or university admissions.

One answer to that question might be found in the principle of compensatory justice, which states that people who have been treated unjustly ought to be compensated. No reasonable person would argue with the fact that African Americans have suffered more than their share of injustice over the course of U.S. history. Many proponents of affirmative action defend the programs as a kind of reparation for the terrible wrongs of slavery and segregation. The white majority, in this view, must compensate African Americans for unjustly injuring them in the past.

A related concept brings this argument into the present: Affirmative action, proponents hold, neutralizes the competitive disadvantages that African Americans continue to experience because of past discrimination; segregated neighborhoods served by poor schools would be an example.

President Johnson had this justification for preferential treatment in mind when he signed the 1964 Voting Rights Act and said: "You do not take a person who, for years, has been hobbled by chains and liberate him, bring him up to the starting line of a race, and then say, 'You are free to compete . . .' and still justly believe that you have been completely fair."

While the argument for compensatory justice seems persuasive to me, I find that it often plays differently with the folks who are called upon to do the compensating. First of all, many people are not ready to concede their complicity in the wrongs of the past. It's very hard to persuade a young Asian college applicant, whose parents did not arrive in this country for a century after abolition, that she must take responsibility for slavery. Others cannot see how their race puts them at a competitive advantage. Most Appalachian out-of-work coal miners don't see themselves as the beneficiaries of past favoritism.

Even the average white male—who has weaker grounds for rejecting   15
the compensatory argument—is beginning to rebel against racial preference. While it may fall outside the realm of morality to consider whether an argument is popular or not, those of us who want affirmative action to continue must confront the fact that many Americans believe these programs are asking them to take their punishment like . . . well, like a man. A lot of them are refusing to bend over.

I believe there's an equally valid moral argument for affirmative action that avoids the punitive overtones of the justice approach, focusing instead on why these programs are in everyone's best interest. In resolving the affirmative action question for myself, I find the best guidance in a common-good approach to ethics: The common good consists primarily in "ensuring that the social policies, social systems, institutions, and environments on which we depend are beneficial to all. Appeals to the common good urge us to view ourselves as members of the same community, reflecting on broad questions concerning the kind of society we want to become and how we are to achieve that society."

I look around me—at the poverty, crime, and alienation that so disproportionately afflict our minority communities—and I ask myself, Is this the kind of society I want to live in or the world I want my children to grow up in? The answer to that question is much clearer to me than deciding where justice resides in the affirmative action debate.

This is not simply a matter of feeling compassion or guilt, though neither of those responses strikes me as inappropriate. But beyond how I feel, I have a stake in addressing these problems. I know that social blights cannot be confined to a particular neighborhood or community; eventually, I will pay for every angry, jobless, poorly educated person—through the welfare system and through the prison system (the cost of which is fast surpassing schools in California).

However imperfect, affirmative action has made a small dent in the inequities that have characterized the distribution of jobs and educational opportunities in the United States. According to *The New York Times*, "The percentage of blacks in managerial and technical jobs doubled during the affirmative action years. During the same period, as Andrew Hacker pointed out in his book *Two Nations* [Ballantine Books, 1992], the number of black police officers rose from 24,000 to 64,000 and the number of black electricians, from 14,000 to 43,000."

Abolition of affirmative action would clearly reverse these gains. 20 Cities that have dropped minority set-aside programs, for example, have experienced a sharp drop in the percentage of government contracts going to minorities. To say that these programs should be retained is not, however, to ignore the claims of fairness and justice raised by opponents of affirmative action. But I wonder if we need to define these in the competitive manner that has characterized so much of the debate—"You got my spot," as my students might have put it. Wouldn't it be better to create a vision of a society in which my good fortune did not mean your suffering?

Much of the threat my students felt, I now believe, came from the realistic assessment that they faced a dearth of employment and educational prospects. The best way to foster their support for affirmative action would be to address the underlying scarcity.

That was the experience in Atlanta, which, in preparation for the Olympic Games, awarded almost a third of $387 million in construction and vending contracts to women- and minority-owned businesses. "Grumbling has been minimal during Olympic preparations, largely because Atlanta's economy is so strong that work has been plentiful," writes Kevin Sack in *The New York Times*.

A common-good argument for affirmative action is part of a broader approach that envisions a society with plentiful work and good education for everyone. I can imagine the eyeballs rolling as I write these lines. Naive. Utopian. But, really, every ethical system is utopian in that it suggests an ideal. Why is my concept any more idealistic than the California Civil Rights Initiative, which is premised on a colorblind society where no one is ever discriminated against on the basis of race?

The Responsive Reader

1. In the introduction to her article, how does Schulman show that she will try to listen to the other side?
2. What is her basic definition of *justice*? (Is it the same as yours?) How does she apply it to the history of the race issue in this country?
3. What is "compensatory justice"? According to Schulman, what are its limitations as an argument for affirmative action? What is "punitive" about it?
4. What is the essence of the author's "common good" approach to ethics? How does it apply to the current situation in our society and the prospects for its future?
5. What is the author's estimate of the past record or accomplishments of affirmative action? On balance, does she seem to think of it as a success or as a failure?
6. What do you think of Schulman's "Utopian" vision of a future when affirmative action would work without anyone getting hurt?

Talking, Listening, Writing

7. Do you think ethics means a concern with what is good for other people, or can it mean an enlightened concern with what is good for oneself, one's family, or one's group?
8. According to a *Time* article on the history of affirmative action, the idea behind it was that "custom, ethnocentrism, poverty, bad schools, old-boy networking, and a host of other factors would conspire against the new civil rights of African Americans and any real socioeconomic advancement." What is "ethnocentrism"? What is "old-boy networking"? Which of the "factors" listed here are still playing a major role, and which may have become less relevant? How much closer are we to the ideal of a "color-blind" society?

Collaborative Projects

9. Working with a group, you may want to check the current status of anti-affirmative action initiatives or legislation.

WHITE GUILT

Shelby Steele

> *Shelby Steele, now a research fellow at the Hoover Institute, has made many Americans rethink their assumptions about race and racism. He is the son of a black father and a white mother and experienced racism when attending a segregated school in South Chicago. He became an instant celebrity in 1990 when he published* The Content of Our Character: A New Vision of Race in America, *a collection of the essays that he first published in* Harper's *and* The American Scholar. *He has appeared on talk shows and wrote and narrated a television special on the murder of a black teenager by a white mob in Bensonhurst. Steele sees race relations in this country as setting up a scenario in which both blacks and whites play familiar and predictable parts. Blacks play the part of the victim, pressing for redress of their grievances. Whites, suffering from white guilt, salve their consciences by setting up affirmative action programs that are largely ineffectual and counterproductive. Black students agitate against campus racism and are placated by "cheap buyoffs" like separate black dorms. When Steele was active in the civil rights movement in the sixties, all of the eighteen black students at his school, Coe College in Iowa, graduated. Today, at the university where he taught, the dropout rate for African American students is seventy percent. To Steele, these figures mean that blacks must leave behind the politics of victimization and concentrate on maximizing the opportunities that exist. According to Steele, when blacks continue to ask for compensation for past injustices, they perpetuate the wrong "paradigm"—the wrong established pattern to which everything is made to conform. What, according to him, is wrong with the paradigm?*

Thought Starters: Do you listen to or participate in arguments about race? What are the topics or issues?

I don't remember hearing the phrase "white guilt" very much before   *1*
the mid-1960s. Growing up black in the 1950s, I never had the impression that whites were much disturbed by guilt when it came to blacks. When I would stray into the wrong restaurant in pursuit of a hamburger, it didn't occur to me that the waitress was unduly troubled by guilt when she asked me to leave. I can see now that possibly she was, but then all I saw was her irritability at having to carry out so unpleasant a task. If there was guilt, it was mine for having made an imposition of myself. I can remember feeling a certain sympathy for such people, as if I was victimizing them by drawing

them out of an innocent anonymity into the unasked for role of racial policemen. Occasionally they came right out and asked me to feel sorry for them. A caddymaster at a country club told my brother and me that he was doing us a favor by not letting us caddy at this white club and that we should try to understand his position, "put yourselves in my shoes." Our color had brought this man anguish and, if a part of that anguish was guilt, it was not as immediate to me as my own guilt. I smiled at the man to let him know he shouldn't feel bad and then began my long walk home. Certainly I also judge him a coward, but in that era his cowardice was something I had to absorb.

In the 1960s, particularly the black–is–beautiful late 1960s, this absorption of another's cowardice was no longer necessary. The lines of moral power, like plates in the earth, had shifted. White guilt became so palpable you could see it on people. At the time what it looked like to my eyes was a remarkable loss of authority. And what whites lost in authority, blacks gained. You cannot feel guilty about anyone without giving away power to them. Suddenly, this huge vulnerability had opened up in whites and, as a black, you had the power to step right into it. In fact, black power all but demanded that you do so. What shocked me in the late 1960s, after the helplessness I had felt in the fifties, was that guilt had changed the nature of the white man's burden from the administration of inferiors to the uplift of equals—from the obligations of dominance to the urgencies of repentance.

I think what made the difference between the fifties and sixties, at least as far as white guilt was concerned, was that whites underwent an archetypal Fall. Because of the immense turmoil of the civil rights movement, and later the black-power movement, whites were confronted for more than a decade with their willingness to participate in, or comply with, the oppression of blacks, their indifference to human suffering and denigration, their capacity to abide evil for their own benefit and in the defiance of their own sacred principles. The 1964 Civil Rights Bill that bestowed equality under the law on blacks was also, in a certain sense, an admission of white guilt. Had white society not been wrong, there would have been no need for such a bill. In this bill the nation acknowledged its fallenness, its lack of racial innocence, and confronted the incriminating self-knowledge that it had rationalized for many years a flagrant injustice. Denial is a common way of handling guilt, but in the 1960s there was little will left for denial except in the most recalcitrant whites. With this defense lost there was really only one road back to innocence—through actions and policies that would bring redemption.

In the 1960s the need for white redemption from racial guilt became the most powerful, yet unspoken, element in America's social-policy-making process, first giving rise to the Great Society and then to a series of programs, policies, and laws that sought to make black equality and restitution a national mission. Once America could no longer deny its guilt, it went after redemption, or at least the look of redemption, and did so with a vengeance. Yet today, some twenty years later, study after study tells us that by many measures the gap between blacks and whites is widening rather than narrowing. A University of Chicago study indicates that segregation is more entrenched in American cities today than ever imagined. A National Research Council study notes the "status of blacks relative to whites (in housing and education) has stagnated or regressed since the early seventies." A follow-up to the famous Kerner Commission Report warns that blacks are as much at risk today of becoming a "nation within a nation" as we were twenty years ago, when the original report was made.

I think the white need for redemption has contributed to this tragic   5
situation by shaping our policies regarding blacks in ways that may deliver the look of innocence to society and its institutions but that do very little actually to uplift blacks. The specific effect of this hidden need has been to bend social policy more toward reparation for black oppression than toward the much harder and more mundane work of black uplift and development. Rather than facilitate the development of blacks to achieve parity with whites, these programs and policies—affirmative action is a good example—have tended to give blacks special entitlements that in many cases are of no use because blacks lack the development that would put us in a position to take advantage of them. I think the reason there has been more entitlement than development is (along with black power) the unacknowledged white need for redemption—not true redemption, which would have concentrated policy on black development, but the appearance of redemption, which requires only that society, in the name of development, seem to be paying back its former victims with preferences. One of the effects of entitlements, I believe, has been to encourage in blacks a dependency both on entitlements and on the white guilt that generates them. Even when it serves ideal justice, bounty from another man's guilt weakens. While this is not the only factor in black "stagnation" and "regression," I believe it is one very potent factor.

It is easy enough to say that white guilt too often has the effect of bending social policies in the wrong direction. But what exactly is this guilt, and how does it work in American life?

I think white guilt, in its broad sense, springs from a knowledge of ill-gotten advantage. More precisely, it comes from the juxtaposition of this knowledge with the inevitable gratitude one feels for being white rather than black in America. Given the moral instincts of human beings, it is all but impossible to enjoy an ill-gotten advantage, much less to feel at least secretly grateful for it, without consciously or unconsciously experiencing guilt. If, as Kierkegaard writes, "innocence is ignorance," then guilt must always involve knowledge. White Americans *know* that their historical advantage comes from the subjugation of an entire people. So, even for whites today for whom racism is anathema, there is no escape from the knowledge that makes for guilt. Racial guilt simply accompanies the condition of being white in America.

I do not believe that this guilt is a crushing anguish for most whites, but I do believe it constitutes a continuing racial vulnerability—an openness to racial culpability—that is a thread in white life, sometimes felt, sometimes not, but ever present as a potential feeling. In the late 1960s almost any black could charge this vulnerability with enough current for a white person to feel it. I had a friend who had developed this activity into a sort of specialty. I don't think he meant to be mean, though certainly he was mean. I think he was, in that hyperbolic era, exhilarated by the discovery that his race, which had long been a liability, now gave him a certain edge—that white guilt was the true force behind black power. To feel this power he would sometimes set up what he called "race experiments." Once I watched him stop a white businessman in the men's room of a large hotel and convince him to increase his tip to the black attendant from one to twenty dollars.

My friend's tactic was very simple, even corny. Out of the attendant's earshot he asked the man simply to look at the attendant, a frail, elderly, and very dark man in a starched white smock that made the skin on his neck and face look as leathery as a turtle's. He sat listlessly, pathetically, on a straight-backed chair next to a small table on which sat a stack of hand towels and a silver plate for tips. Since the attendant offered no service whatever beyond the handing out of towels, one could only conclude the hotel management offered his lowly presence as flattery to their patrons, as an opportunity for that easy noblesse oblige that could reassure even the harried and weary traveling salesman of his superior station. My friend was quick to make this point to the businessman and to say that no white man would do in this job. But when the businessman put the single back in his wallet and took out a five, my friend only sneered. Did he understand the tragedy of a life spent this way, of what it must be like to earn one's paltry living as a symbol of inferiority? And did he realize that his privilege as an affluent white businessman (ironically he had just spent the day trying to sell a printing press to the Black Muslims for their newspaper *Mohammed Speaks*) was connected to the deprivation of this man and others like him?

But then my friend made a mistake that ended the game. In the heat 10
of argument, which until then had only been playfully challenging, he inadvertently mentioned his father. This stopped the victim cold and his eyes turned inward. "What about your father?" the businessman asked. My friend replied, "He had a hard life, that's all." "How did he have a hard life?" the businessman asked. Now my friend was on the defensive. I knew he did not get along with his father, a bitter man who worked nights in a factory and demanded that the house be dark and silent all day. My friend blamed his father's bitterness on racism, but I knew he had not meant to exploit his own pain in this silly "experiment." Things had gotten too close to home, but he didn't know how to get out of the situation without losing face. Now, caught in his own trap, he did what he least wanted to do. He gave forth the rage he truly felt to a white stranger in a public men's room. "My father never had a chance," he said with the kind of

anger that could easily turn to tears. "He never had a freakin' chance. Your father had all the goddamn chances, and you know he did. You sell print- ing presses to black people and make thousands and your father probably lives down in Fat City, Florida, all because you're white." On and on he went in this vein, using—against all that was honorable in him—his own profound racial pain to extract a flash of guilt from a white man he didn't even know.

He got more than a flash. The businessman was touched. His eyes became mournful, and finally he simply said, "You're right. Your people got a raw deal." He took a twenty dollar bill from his wallet and walked over and dropped it in the old man's tip plate. When he was gone my friend and I could not look at the old man, nor could we look at each other.

It is obvious that this was a rather shameful encounter for all concerned—my friend and I, as his silent accomplice, trading on our racial pain, tampering with a stranger for no reason, and the stranger then buying his way out of the situation for twenty dollars, a sum that was generous by one count and cheap by another. It was not an encounter of people but of historical grudges and guilts. Yet, when I think about it now twenty years later, I see that it had all the elements of a paradigm that I believe has been very much at the heart of racial policy-making in America since the 1960s.

My friend did two things that made this businessman vulnerable to his guilt—that brought his guilt into the situation as a force. First he put this man in touch with his own knowledge of his ill-gotten advantage as a white. The effect of this was to disallow the man any pretense of racial innocence, to let him know that, even if he was not the sort of white who used the word *nigger* around the dinner table, he still had reason to feel racial guilt. But, as disarming as this might have been, it was too abstract to do much more than crack open this man's vulnerability, to expose him to the logic of white guilt. This was the five-dollar, intellectual sort of guilt. The twenty dollars required something more visceral. In achieving this, the second thing my friend did was something he had not intended to do, something that ultimately brought him as much shame as he was doling out: He made a display of his own racial pain and anger. (What brought him shame was not the pain and anger, but his trading on them for what turned out to be a mere twenty bucks.) The effect of this display was to reinforce the man's knowledge of ill-gotten advantage, to give cred- ibility and solidity to it by putting a face on it. Here was human testimony, a young black beside himself at the thought of his father's racially con- stricted life. The pain of one man evidenced the knowledge of the other. When the businessman listened to my friend's pain, his racial guilt—nor- mally only one source of guilt lying dormant among others—was called out like a neglected debt he would finally have to settle. An ill-gotten advantage is not hard to bear—it can be marked up to fate—until it touches the genuine human pain it has brought into the world. This is the pain that hardens guilty knowledge.

Such knowledge is a powerful influence when it becomes conscious. What makes it so powerful is the element of fear that guilt always carries, the fear of what the guilty knowledge says about us. Guilt makes us afraid for ourselves, and thus generates as much self-preoccupation as concern for others. The nature of this preoccupation is always the redemption of innocence, the reestablishment of good feeling about oneself.

In this sense, the fear for the self that is buried in all guilt is a pressure   *15* toward selfishness. It can lead us to put our own need for innocence above our concern for the problem that made us feel guilt in the first place. But this fear for the self does not only inspire selfishness; it also becomes a pressure to *escape* the guilt-inducing situation. When selfishness and escapism are at work, we are no longer interested in the source of our guilt and, therefore, no longer concerned with an authentic redemption from it. Then we only want the look of redemption, the gesture of concern that will give us the appearance of innocence and escape from the situation. Obviously the businessman did not put twenty dollars in the tip plate because he thought it would uplift black Americans. He did it selfishly for the appearance of concern and for the escape it afforded him.

This is not to say that guilt is never the right motive for doing good works or showing concern, only that it is a very dangerous one because of its tendency to draw us into self-preoccupation and escapism. Guilt is a civilizing emotion when the fear for the self that it carries is contained—a containment that allows guilt to be more selfless and that makes genuine concern possible. I think this was the kind of guilt that, along with the other forces, made the 1964 Civil Rights Bill possible. But since then I believe too many of our social policies related to race have been shaped by the fearful underside of guilt.

Black power evoked white guilt and made it a force in American institutions, very much in the same way as my friend brought it to life in the businessman. Few people volunteer for guilt. Usually others make us feel it. It was the expression of black anger and pain that hardened the guilty knowledge of white ill-gotten advantage. And black power—whether from militant fringe groups, the civil rights establishment, or big city political campaigns—knew exactly the kind of white guilt it was after. It wanted to trigger the kind of white guilt in which whites fear for their own decency and innocence; it wanted the guilt of white self-preoccupation and escapism. Always at the heart of black power, in whatever form, has been a profound anger at what was done to blacks and an equally profound feeling that there should be reparations. But a sober white guilt (in which fear for the self is still contained) seeks a strict fairness—the 1964 Civil Rights Bill that guaranteed equality under the law. It is of little value when one is after more than fairness. So black power made its mission to have whites fear for their innocence, to feel a visceral guilt from which they would have to seek a more profound redemption. In such redemption was the possibility of black reparation. Black power upped the ante on white guilt.

With black power, all of the elements of the hidden paradigm that shape America's race-related social policy were in place. Knowledge of ill-gotten advantage could now be shown and deepened by black power into the sort of guilt from which institutions could only redeem themselves by offering more than fairness—by offering forms of reparation and compensation for past injustice. I believe this bent our policies toward racial entitlements at the expense of racial development. In 1964, one of the assurances Senator Hubert Humphrey and others had to give Congress to get the landmark Civil Rights Bill passed was that the bill would not in any way require employers to use racial preferences to rectify racial imbalances. But this was before the explosion of black power in the late 1960s, before the hidden paradigm was set in motion. After black power, racial preferences became the order of the day.

If this paradigm brought blacks entitlements, it also brought the continuation of the most profound problem in American society, the invisibility of blacks as a people. The white guilt that this paradigm elicits is the kind of guilt that preoccupies whites with their own innocence and pressures them toward escapism—twenty dollars in the plate and out the door. With this guilt, as opposed to the contained guilt of genuine concern, whites tend to see only their own need for quick redemption. Blacks then become a means to this redemption and, as such, they must be seen as generally "less than" others. Their needs are "special," "unique," "different." They are seen exclusively along the dimension of their victimization, so that they become "different" people with whom whites can negotiate entitlements but never fully see as people like themselves. Guilt that preoccupies people with their own innocence blinds them to those who make them feel guilty. This, of course, is not racism, and yet it has the same effect as racism since it makes blacks something of a separate species for whom normal standards and values do not automatically apply.

Nowhere is this more evident today than in American universities. At some of America's most elite universities administrators have granted concessions in response to black student demands (black power) that all but sanction racial separatism on campus—black "theme" dorms, black student unions, black yearbooks, homecoming dances, and so forth. I don't believe administrators sincerely believe in these separatist concessions. Most of them are liberals who see racial separatism as wrong. But black student demands pull administrators into the paradigm of self-preoccupied white guilt, whereby they seek a quick redemption by offering special entitlements that go beyond fairness. As a result, black students become all but invisible to them. Though blacks have the lowest grade point average of any racial group in American universities, administrators never sit down with them and "demand" in kind that black students bring their grades up to par. The paradigm of white guilt makes the real problems of black students secondary to the need for white redemption. It also cuts administrators off from their own values, which would most certainly discourage

20

racial separatism and encourage higher academic performance for black students. Lastly, it makes for escapist policies. There is no difference between giving black students a separate lounge and leaving twenty dollars in the tip plate on the way out the door.

The Responsive Reader

1. What is the basic contrast that Steele sees between racial attitudes when he grew up in the fifties and today? What brought the shift about? What to Steele was the symbolic significance of the civil rights legislation of the sixties? (How was the development of white guilt like the original biblical "fall" from innocence?)
2. What evidence does Steele see that the promise of the civil rights movement has not come true? Where does he think public policy took the wrong turn?
3. What makes the story of the tip for the restroom attendant a test case for Steele's view of race relations? How does it conform to his "paradigm" of black anger and white guilt? (Would you have interpreted the incident the same way Steele did?)
4. According to Steele, how have black militants traded on white guilt?
5. How or why, according to Steele, do racial preferences on and off campus have "the same effect as racism"?

Talking, Listening, Writing

6. Have you been the beneficiary of affirmative action? Or have you been disadvantaged by special preferences for others? What is your personal opinion regarding affirmative action to advance the cause of minorities who have experienced discrimination?
7. Steele endeared himself to white conservatives like the columnist George Will and alienated a large segment of the black community. Do you consider him a legitimate and effective voice for the concerns of African Americans?
8. Do you remember an earlier cycle when racial attitudes or race relations were different from what they are today? Work out a detailed comparison and contrast, drawing on vivid examples from your own experience and observation.

Collaborative Projects

9. Is there a consensus or a majority opinion on your campus concerning special admission procedures and programs designed to help minority students? Working with others, you could try to sample the opinions of students, counselors, people working in or enrolled in mentor programs, or teachers and students in special classes.

WHY THEY EXCEL
Fox Butterfield

> *Fox Butterfield won the National Book Award for his book* China: Alive
> in the Bitter Sea *(1982). He first became intrigued by the motivation and
> academic performance of Asian students when he was a young journalist in
> Taiwan. The young Vietnamese student he interviewed for the following
> article had left Vietnam ten years earlier and had not heard from her parents,
> who stayed behind, for three years. However, their admonitions to be a good
> daughter and a good student were still ringing in her ears. One of the sayings
> she remembered from her childhood said, "If you don't study, you will never
> become anything. If you study, you will become what you wish." In his article
> about why Asian students excel, Butterfield draws on a mix of personal
> experience, firsthand investigation, and expert opinion. Asians are often called
> the "model minority"—who work hard, study hard, and enter college and
> graduate in large numbers. How does this article support and explain the idea
> of the model minority?*

Thought Starters: How much of what you know about Vietnamese or
Chinese or other Asian students is based on personal contact or observation? How much is hearsay or media stereotype?

Kim-Chi Trinh was just 9 in Vietnam when her father used his   1
savings to buy a passage for her on a fishing boat. It was a costly and risky
sacrifice for the family, placing Kim-Chi on the small boat, among strangers, in hopes she would eventually reach the United States, where she
would get a good education and enjoy a better life. Before the boat reached
safety in Malaysia, the supply of food and water ran out.

Still alone, Kim-Chi made it to the United States, coping with a
succession of three foster families. But when she graduated from San Diego's Patrick Henry High School, she had a straight-A average and scholarship offers from Stanford and Cornell universities.

"I have to do well—it's not even a question," said the diminutive 19-
year-old, now a sophomore at Cornell. "I owe it to my parents in
Vietnam."

Kim-Chi is part of a tidal wave of bright, highly motivated Asian-
Americans who are surging into our best colleges. Although Asian-
Americans make up only 2.4 percent of the nation's population, by 1990
they had come to constitute 17.1 percent of the undergraduates at Har-

vard, 18 percent at the Massachusetts Institute of Technology and 27.3 percent at the University of California at Berkeley.

With Asians being the fastest-growing ethnic group in the country— *5* two out of five immigrants are now Asian—these figures will increase. At the University of California at Irvine, in a recent year, a staggering 35.1 percent of the undergraduates are Asian-American, but the proportion in the freshman class is even higher: 41 percent.

Why are the Asian-Americans doing so well? Are they grinds, as some stereotypes suggest? Do they have higher IQs? Or are they actually teaching the rest of us a lesson about values we have long treasured but may have misplaced—like hard work, the family and education?

Not all Asians are doing equally well. Poorly educated Cambodian and Hmong refugee youngsters need special help. And Asian-Americans resent being labeled a "model minority," feeling that is just another form of prejudice by white Americans, an ironic reversal of the discriminatory laws that excluded most Asian immigration to America until 1965.

But the academic success of many Asian-Americans has prompted growing concern among educators, parents and other students. Some universities have what look like unofficial quotas, much as Ivy League colleges did against Jews in the 1920s and '30s. Berkeley Chancellor Ira Heyman apologized for an admissions policy that, he said, had "a disproportionately negative impact on Asian-Americans."

I have wondered about the reason for the Asians' success since I was a fledgling journalist on Taiwan in 1969. That year, a team of boys from a poor, isolated mountain village on Taiwan won the annual Little League World Series at Williamsport, Pa. Their victory was totally unexpected. At the time, baseball was a largely unknown sport on Taiwan, and the boys had learned to play with bamboo sticks for bats and rocks for balls. But since then, teams from Taiwan, Japan or South Korea have won the Little League championship in 16 out of the 21 years. How could these Asian boys beat us at our own game?

Fortunately, the young Asians' achievements have led to a series of *10* intriguing studies. "There is something going on here that we as Americans need to understand," said Sanford M. Dornbusch, a professor of sociology at Stanford. Dornbusch, in surveys of 7000 students in six San Francisco-area high schools, found that Asian-Americans consistently get better grades than any other group of students, regardless of their parents' level of education or their families' social and economic status, the usual predictors of success. In fact, those in homes where English is spoken often, or whose families have lived longer in the United States, do slightly less well.

"We used to talk about the American melting pot as an advantage," Dornbusch said. "But the sad fact is that it has become a melting pot with low standards."

Other studies have shown similar results. Perhaps the most disturbing have come in a series of studies by a University of Michigan psychologist, Harold W. Stevenson, who has compared more than 7000 students in kindergarten, first grade, third grade and fifth grade in Chicago and Minneapolis with counterparts in Beijing; Sendai, Japan; and Taipei, Taiwan. On a battery of math tests, the Americans did worst at all grade levels.

Stevenson found no differences in IQ. But if the differences in performance are showing up in kindergarten, it suggests something is happening in the family, even before the children get to school.

It is here that the various studies converge: Asian parents are able to instill more motivation in their children. "My bottom line is, Asian kids work hard," said Professor Dornbusch.

In his survey of San Francisco-area high schools, for example, he   15
reported that Asian-Americans do an average of 7.03 hours of homework a week. Non-Hispanic whites average 6.12 hours, blacks 4.23 hours and Hispanics 3.98 hours. Asians also score highest on a series of other measures of effort, such as fewer class cuts and paying more attention to the teacher.

Don Lee, 20, is a junior at Berkeley. His parents immigrated to Torrance, Calif., from South Korea when he was 5, so he could get a better education. Lee said his father would warn him about the danger of wasting time at high school dances or football games. "Instead," he added, "for fun on weekends, my friends and I would go to the town library to study."

The real question, then, is how do Asian parents imbue their offspring with this kind of motivation? Stevenson's study suggests a critical answer. When the Asian parents were asked why they think their children do well, they most often said "hard work." By contrast, American parents said "talent."

"From what I can see," said Stevenson, "we've lost our belief in the Horatio Alger myth that anyone can get ahead in life through pluck and hard work. Instead, Americans now believe that some kids have it and some don't, so we begin dividing up classes into fast learners and slow learners, where the Chinese and Japanese believe all children can learn from the same curriculum."

The Asians' belief in hard work also springs from their common heritage of Confucianism, the philosophy of the 5th-century B.C. Chinese sage who taught that man can be perfected through practice. "Confucius is not just some character out of the past—he is an everyday reality to these people," said William Liu, a sociologist who directs the Pacific Asian-American Mental Health Research Center at the University of Illinois in Chicago.

Confucianism provides another important ingredient in the Asians'   20
success. "In the Confucian ethic," Liu continued, "there is a centripetal family, an orientation that makes people work for the honor of the family,

not just for themselves." Liu came to the United States from China in 1948. "You can never repay your parents, and there is a strong sense of guilt," he said. "It is a strong force, like the Protestant Ethic in the West."

Liu has found this in his own family. When his son and two daughters were young, he told them to become doctors or lawyers—jobs with the best guaranteed income, he felt. Sure enough, his daughters have gone into law, and his son is a medical student at UCLA, though he really wanted to be an investment banker. Liu asked his son why he picked medicine. The reply: "Ever since I was a little kid, I always heard you tell your friends their kids were a success if they got into med school. So I felt guilty. I didn't have a choice."

Underlying this bond between Asian parents and their children is yet another factor I noticed during 15 years of living in China, Japan, Taiwan and Vietnam. It is simply that Asian parents establish a closer physical tie to their infants than do most parents in the United States. When I let my baby son and daughter crawl on the floor, for example, my Chinese friends were horrified and rushed to pick them up. We think this constant attention is overindulgence and old-fashioned, but for Asians, who still live through the lives of their children, it is highly effective.

Yuen Huo, 22, a senior at Berkeley, recalled growing up in an apartment above the Chinese restaurant her immigrant parents owned and operated in Millbrae, Calif. "They used to tell us how they came from Taiwan to the United States for us, how they sacrificed for us, so I had a strong sense of indebtedness," Huo said. When she did not get all A's her first semester at Berkeley, she recalled, "I felt guilty and worked harder."

Here too is a vital clue about the Asians' success: Asian parents expect a high level of academic performance. In the Stanford study comparing white and Asian students in San Francisco high schools, 82 percent of the Asian parents said they would accept only an A or a B from their children, while just 59 percent of white parents set such a standard. By comparison, only 17 percent of Asian parents were willing to accept a C, against 40 percent of white parents. On the average, parents of black and Hispanic students also had lower expectations for their children's grades than Asian parents.

Can we learn anything from the Asians? "I'm not naïve enough to think   25 everything in Asia can be transplanted," said Harold Stevenson, the University of Michigan psychologist. But he offered three recommendations.

"To start with," he said, "we need to set higher standards for our kids. We wouldn't expect them to become professional athletes without practicing hard."

Second, American parents need to become more committed to their children's education, he declared. "Being understanding when a child doesn't do well isn't enough." Stevenson found that Asian parents spend many more hours really helping their children with homework or writing to their teachers. At Berkeley, the mothers of some Korean-American students move into their sons' apartments for months before graduate school entrance tests to help by cooking and cleaning for them, giving the students more time to study.

And, third, schools could be reorganized to become more effective—without added costs, said Stevenson. One of his most surprising findings is that Asian students, contrary to popular myth, are not just rote learners subjected to intense pressure. Instead, nearly 90 percent of Chinese youngsters said they actually enjoy school, and 60 percent can't wait for school vacations to end. These are vastly higher figures for such attitudes than are found in the United States. One reason may be that students in China and Japan typically have a recess after each class, helping them to relax and to increase their attention spans. Moreover, where American teachers spend almost their entire day in front of classes, their Chinese and Japanese counterparts may teach as little as three hours a day, giving them more time to relax and prepare imaginative lessons.

Another study, prepared for the U.S. Department of Education, compared the math and science achievements of 24,000 13-year-olds in the United States and five other countries (four provinces of Canada, plus South Korea, Ireland, Great Britain and Spain). One of the findings was that the more time students spent watching television, the poorer their performance. The American students watched the most television. They also got the worst scores in math. Only the Irish students and some of the Canadians scored lower in science.

"I don't think Asians are any smarter," said Don Lee, the Korean-American at Berkeley. "There are brilliant Americans in my chemistry class. But the Asian students work harder. I see a lot of wasted potential among the Americans." *30*

The Responsive Reader

1. Have you encountered the idea of the "model minority"? Do you remember any evidence, ideas, explanations? (Have you encountered challenges or rebuttals to this idea?)
2. The author dramatizes the issue by using Kim-Chi Trinh as a case in point. What key details and key ideas does the author want you to take in and remember?
3. How does the author use key statistics, expert testimony, and his "insider's" knowledge of the Confucian heritage to support his points?
4. What recommendations is Butterfield's article designed to support? Are they surprising or predictable? Which are strongest or most convincing? (Who has the last word in this article?)

Talking, Listening, Writing

5. Does this article change your ideas or preconceptions? Does it make you think? Why and how—or why not?

6. Do you want to take issue with all or part of this article? On what grounds? Where would you turn for supporting evidence?

7. What has shaped your own ideas about success and failure in our system of education? In your experience as a student, what have you learned about learning?

8. Some people support admission quotas to ensure fair representation of minority students in colleges and universities. Do you agree with them? Do you think there should be quotas to prevent *over*representation of groups like the Asian students described in Butterfield's article?

Collaborative Projects

9. Why do model students do well? Why do dropouts fail? How many dropouts are really pushouts—pushed out by educational policies or economic pressures that defeat them? How many dropouts drop back in for a second (or third) chance? You may want to focus on one of these questions. Working with a group, quiz students, teachers, counselors, or others in a position to know. Find some current articles or new reports. What conclusions do your explorations suggest? Is there a consensus among your sources?

MIXED LIKE ME

David Bernstein

> *David Bernstein was a twenty-six-year-old magazine editor in Washington, D.C., when he wrote the following essay. He was one of the "Generation X" or "twenty-something" group of writers included in a collection called* Next: Young American Writers on the New Generation *(1994). These writers were born after the great events that had shaped the outlook of an earlier generation: the traumas and divisions of the lost Vietnam war; the struggles and triumphs of the civil rights movement; the militant early years of the women's movement. Living in a post–Cold War world, many of these authors write about outgrowing the think schemes and stereotypes of the past. As Bernstein says, the opening statement of his essay might have sounded provocative thirty years ago; readers today may find it only mildly interesting and "move along." Because of his mixed ethnic parentage, Bernstein is in a unique position to reexamine this country's "way of thinking about race." What is his perspective on the future of race relations in America?*

Thought Starters: What do you think and know about "mixed marriages"? Has "intermarriage" been an issue in your family or among people you know? Are you aware of changing social attitudes on this topic?

I am a twenty-six-year-old man, half black and half Jewish, who   1
founded and edits a conservative magazine that deals with race relations and culture. Such a statement would have been extraordinary thirty years ago; today we treat it with mild interest and move along. No one would argue that my life has been typical—typical of the "black experience," of the "Jewish experience," or of any other dubious paradigm associated with a particular race or ethnicity. I have not overcome racism or poverty, and people become visibly disappointed when I tell them that my mixed background has not been a cause of distress, or any other difficulty for that matter.

However, my story may be of some interest. For better or worse, America is going to look more and more like me in the next century— that is to say, individuals are going to be walking embodiments of the melting pot. The argument over whether America is more like cheese dip or the multiculturalist "tossed salad" (Are you getting hungry yet?) will be made moot by the increasing incidence of mixed marriage and of the growing class of mutts like me who have more ethnicities than the former Yugoslavia.

My parents married in 1965, in Washington, D.C. If they had lived then in the comfortable suburb where they now reside, they would have been breaking the law—miscegenation, as marriage between blacks and whites was known in those days, was still illegal in Maryland. My mother was a native Washingtonian who, until her teen years, felt sorry for the few white people who lived near her, her mother, and two siblings; she thought they were albinos. Her parents—both of whom had moved from the country to Washington when they were teenagers—were separated when my mother was just a toddler. She was raised, along with an older sister and brother, in a small brownstone apartment in downtown D.C. Her brother, the oldest child, went off to fight in the Korean War, one of the first black airmen to participate in the integrated armed forces. While in Korea, he fell in love with and married a Korean girl. Meanwhile, my mother attended segregated public schools until senior high school, when she was in the first class that integrated Eastern Senior High School in the wake of the Supreme Court's *Brown* decision. After graduation, she opted not to attend college, because she didn't know what she wanted to do—and "didn't want to waste" my grandmother's money.

My father grew up in North Philadelphia, one of those old working-class neighborhoods where there were Jewish blocks, Italian blocks, Irish blocks, and so on. His parents were second-generation Americans: Grandpa Bernstein's family was from Poland; my grandmother's family from Leeds, England. (I understand the Blasky family still lives there, apparently running a successful wallpaper-hanging business.) My grandfather and my father's two brothers fought in World War II; my father, who was too young to go, became a paratrooper soon after the war ended. After leaving the Army in the early 1950s, he moved to Washington, where he and my mother eventually ended up working at the same furniture-rental place.

Despite the rich possibilities for mischief making presented by their union, my parents did not marry to make a political statement. While their contemporaries marched for civil rights and held sit-ins, they hung out with a mixed-race group of cool cats at various jazz nightclubs in downtown D.C. Most of these establishments were burned to the ground after Martin Luther King's assassination in 1968, bringing to an end that unique era of naive integration. Since those riots, race relations in this country have been tinged with guilt, fear, and lies.

In 1970, my father's company transferred him to the redneck mill town of Reading, Pennsylvania. My mother hated it; my father tolerated it; and I went about the business of growing up. I went to a mostly white private school and Monday afternoons attended Hebrew school with the children of Reading's prosperous and assimilated Jewish community. My Cub Scout group and summer camp were at the local Jewish community center, which had been bombed recently by Reading's prominent community of neo-Nazis.

It was also at the center that I was first called a "nigger." My mother had been preparing me my entire life for that to happen, but when it did,

I was hardly bothered at all. I actually felt sorry for the kid who shouted it at me during a softball game; he genuinely felt bad afterward and apologized about six times. (Even though it's out of sequence in our little narrative, I should recount the only other time I have been called a "nigger." A couple of years ago, I was riding on D.C.'s Metro with two white liberal friends when a white homeless person approached me and stated, "You niggers get all the jobs." My friends were horrified and silent. I laughed and told the bum that he was right; that was how it should be.)

We moved back to Washington in 1977. Again, I attended private school, this time at Georgetown Day School, a place founded in the 1940s as Washington's first integrated school. Despite the forty-year tradition, there were still not many blacks at GDS. The students were largely from well-to-do, secular Jewish families with traditions of liberal political activism. My family, though secular, was not well-to-do or politically active. My parents were somewhat liberal, but it was a liberalism of function rather than form; in other words, they might be considered budding neoconservatives. I inherited from my parents a healthy suspicion of conventional wisdom—which, in the case of my teachers and peers, was overwhelmingly on the left. By 1980, I was one of six kids in my junior-high class to vote for Ronald Reagan in our mock election.

My "political awakening" was just beginning. In high school I co-wrote a piece in the school newspaper on what it meant to be conservative, an awfully crafted piece of literature that nearly caused a riot, despite its (by my standards today) extremely mushy conservatism. I started to realize that you could make liberals mad just by saying the "c" word. On election day 1984, I wore a jacket and tie to school to celebrate President Reagan's impending victory. One friend didn't talk to me for a week.

It never dawned on me that, as a "person of color," I ought to be "mortally" opposed to this Reagan guy. All I ever heard come out of his mouth just sounded like good sense to me. I heard over and over again on TV that the man was a racist and that he was bad for black people. But what stuck with me from all this was that the people who repeated this charge were buffoons. Early on, the idea of race was not central to my view of politics. This would change rather sharply later on.

My freshman year in college was spent at Allegheny College in lovely Meadville, Pennsylvania. Within weeks, it was apparent to me and several of my friends there that the school was lousy. A group of us dedicated our lives to the idea of transferring out of that freezing mud hole of a campus. In one of our brainstorming sessions on how to make our transfer applications look beefier, we locked onto the idea of starting a "Conservative Club," which would be a forum for discussing ideas on the right. It sounded like fun, and more importantly, we would all be made vice presidents of the club, an ideal way to bolster our extracurricular résumés.

Once again, just using the word *conservative* nearly brought the campus down around our ears. Two of the conspirators in our résumé-building

10

scheme went before the student government in order to get the necessary recognition, supposedly just a formality. Forty-five minutes later, after shrieks of outrage from the so-called student leaders of this $13,000-a-year institution of higher learning, we were told that the student government was afraid to get involved in "neo-Nazi" groups and that we should come back in a month with a detailed statement of just what we stood for. Only one member of the SG stood up for us—a young woman who pointed out that on a campus with absolutely no political activity, people who showed some initiative to do something, anything, ought to be encouraged.

But this was a college where political discourse was typified by this statement from the school's chaplain: "We should divest from South Africa. Harvard and Princeton already have, and if we want to be as good as them, we must do so as well." In this kind of environment, which is now typical at liberal-arts colleges around the country, it should have come as no surprise that conservatism was associated with evil. It wasn't the last time that the supposed characteristics of conservatives like me—that we were narrow-minded, ignorant, and shrill—were to be embodied better by our critics.

I did finally escape from Allegheny College, going back home to the University of Maryland. At UM, I decided to make politics a full-time vocation. I worked in Washington afternoons and evenings at various political jobs, first at the Republican National Committee and later at a small, conservative nonprofit foundation. In between, I took a semester off to work for Senator Bob Dole's ill-fated presidential campaign. Returning to Maryland, I was soon elected president of the campus College Republicans, a position that occasionally put me at the center of campus political attention.

This was not because I was a vocal, articulate (some would say loud-mouthed) conservative but because I was a *black* conservative. Conservatives are a dime a dozen, smart ones are common, but a black one? "Nelly, wake the kids! They have to *see* this!"

Other conservatives loved having me around. After all, most of them were presumed to be Nazis from the get-go by the ultrasensitive P.C. crowd; having a black person say you're okay was temporary protection from the scholastic inquisition. Further, as a black conservative, I was thought to have special insight into why more blacks didn't identify with the Republican party. Again and again, I was asked how conservatives could find more blacks (or African-Americans, if the petitioner wanted to be sensitive). After a while, I think I actually began to believe that, somehow, I had special understanding of the souls of black folk, and with increasing confidence I would sound off about the political and social proclivities of African-Americans.

In a perverted way, liberals and left-radicals liked having me around as well—because I helped justify their paranoia. I was living proof that imperialist, racist forces were at work, dividing black people and turning us against one another. How else, they theorized, could a black person so obviously sell out both his race and the "progressive" whites who were the only thing standing between him and a right-wing lynch mob? The ardor (and obvious pleasure) with which they alternatively ignored and condemned me demonstrated their belief that I was more than just the opposition: I was a traitor, a collaborator in my own oppression. Finally, one particularly vitriolic black militant suggested in the school newspaper that black conservatives ought to be "neutralized." I took it personally.

And I got fired up. There comes a time in every conservative activist's life when he gets the heady rush of realization at how much fun (and how easy) it is to annoy liberals. Indeed, it was something I had been doing for years. People on the left, with their self-righteousness, humorless orthodoxies, and ultrasensitivity to their own and everyone else's "oppression" are only fun at parties if you get them pissed off. Naturally, then, it is something that conservatives spend a lot of time doing.

Rush Limbaugh, R. Emmett Tyrell, P. J. O'Rourke, hundreds of editors of conservative college newspapers like the *Dartmouth Review,* and thousands of College Republican activists turned the 1980s into one long laugh for conservatives at the expense of the P.C. crowd. The staleness of liberal beliefs, the inability of the campus activists to move beyond sloganeering to real thought, and the creation of a regime on campus by college professors and administrators that treats open discussion as anathema offered fertile ground for conservative humorists.

But it also allowed many conservatives to dismiss leftism as a political 20 force, and they were unprepared when it was resurrected as such in the person of Bill Clinton—thus in 1992, it was the right that too often degenerated into empty sloganeering. The intellectual stagnation of liberalism contributed to the intellectual sloth of too many conservatives, concerned more with one-liners than actually formulating policy.

I was no exception. I slipped easily into the world of leftist haranguing. I was always good for a sound bite in the school newspaper, and as a unique case—a black Jewish conservative—I had opportunities to comment with some built-in authority on a range of issues. Controversy with the Black Student Union? I would have a comment. Someone wants the university to divest from South Africa? I would be there with other conservatives holding a press conference presenting the other side. Controversy between Arab students and Jewish students? The College Republicans would uphold the Reagan tradition of unswerving support for Israel as long as I was in charge.

I tried not to lose sight of why I was doing this; that annoying liberals was just a means, not an end. But like every young right-winger, I'm sure that more than once I've annoyed just for annoyance's sake. There are worse sins, but this is the only one I'll admit to in print.

Since those heady college days, I have become a magazine editor. *Diversity & Division* looks at race relations in America from the perspective of young people, particularly of its black Jewish editor and white male managing editor. Do I still go after liberals? Yeah, sure. But the issues we talk about—those bearing on the future, on how we are all going to get along—are not very funny. And the things that leftists advocate on these issues, from radical multiculturalism to quotas, promise to make it next to impossible for us to survive as a multicultural society.

There are two lessons, I think, that my little autobiography teaches. First is my comfort in moving between worlds of different cultures and colors. The conventional wisdom about us mixed-race types, that we are alienated, never feeling comfortable in either culture, is baloney. I am black. I am Jewish. I am equally comfortable with people who identify themselves as either one, or neither one. Why? Because to me the most defining characteristic of who I am is not my race, ethnicity, religious beliefs, political party, or Tupperware club membership. Rather, I see myself as an individual first, part of the larger "human family," with all the suballegiances reduced to ancillary concerns.

This is obviously a very romantic and idealistic notion. It is also, equally as obviously, the only ideology that will allow us to overcome prejudice and bigotry and enable everyone to get along. In me, the melting pot the idea has become the melting pot the reality, with (I must immodestly say) reasonably positive results. My commonality with other people is not in superficial appeals to ethnic solidarity—it is far more fundamental. 25

That is why I am sickened by people who continue to insist that we must all cling to our ancestors' "cultures" (however arbitrarily defined at that moment) in order to have self-awareness and self-esteem. The notion of "self" should not be wrapped up in externalities like "culture" or "race"—unless you want to re-create the United States as Yugoslavia, Somalia, or any other such place where people's tribal identities make up their whole selves. Indeed, true self-awareness stands opposed to grouping human beings along arbitrary lines like race, gender, religion, weight, or preferred manner of reaching orgasm. Groupthink is primitive. It is not self-awareness; rather it is a refuge for those afraid of differences.

Those who preach about diversity believe that tolerance means not exulting one class of human being over another, by recognizing that every race and culture has made a contribution to modern civilization: a worthy goal, especially if this were true. But this way of thinking ignores a powerful truth, an obvious solution to the bigotry and suspicion that these sensitivity warriors say they are out to eliminate. The reality is that groups aren't equal; individuals are. If it is "self-evident that all men are created equal" isn't it even more self-evident that blacks and whites, men and women, Christians and Jews are created equal?

Granted, we haven't lived up to this absolute ideal. But we are beginning to see the implications of setting our aspirations below what we know to be the best. Here's the second lesson I think my story tells.

Despite my obvious distaste for the entire notion of group politics, I have become wrapped up in it. By editing a magazine that deals primarily with racial issues, I am not doing what I would most like to be doing. But I am doing what is expected. Under our phony system of racial harmony, college-educated blacks are expected to do something that is, well, black. Black academics are concentrated in Afro-American studies, sociology, and other "soft" fields where they can expound at length about the plight of the American Negro. Everyone, it seems, needs an expert on what it means to be black. Corporations need human-relations specialists to tell them about the "special needs" of black employees. Newspapers need "urban beat" reporters. Foundations, political parties, unions, and any other organizations you can name all need black liaisons to put them "in touch with the community." And, of course, conservatives need a magazine that reassures them that many of the ideas that they have about race relations are not evil and fascistic. These jobs are generally somewhat lucrative, fairly easy to do, and carry just one job requirement—you have to be black.

No one is forced to follow this course; there should be no whining   *30* about that. But in life, as in physics, currents flow along the path of least resistance. As long as it is easy to make a living as a professional race man, the best and brightest blacks will be siphoned off into this least-productive field in our service economy. The same is true, of course, of Hispanics, Asians, or whatever minority group is in vogue in a specific region or profession. Our educational system, our country's entire way of thinking about race, is creating a class of professionals whose entire raison d'être is to explore and explain—and thus perpetuate—the current regime. All the preaching of sensitivity, all the Afrocentric education, all the racial and ethnic solidarity in the world will not markedly improve race relations in America. Indeed, the smart money says that this obsession with our differences, however well-meaning, will make things much, much worse.

But this is a point that, blessedly, may well be rendered moot for the next generation. Intermarriage is the great equalizer; it brings people of different races together in a way that forced busing, sensitivity training, and affirmative action could never hope to—as individuals, on equal footing, united by common bonds of humanity. Four hundred years ago Shakespeare wrote of intermarriage:

> Take her, fair son, and from her blood raise up
>   Issue to me; that the contending kingdoms . . .
> May cease their hatred; and this dear conjunction
>   Plant neighbourhood and Christian-like accord
>   In their sweet bosoms . . .

Eventually, if all goes well, America's melting pot will be a physical reality, bringing with it the kind of healing Shakespeare had in mind. Let's just hope we don't file for an ethnic divorce before then.

The Responsive Reader

1. What is Bernstein's perspective on the strife-ridden racial legacy of the past? What glimpses do you get in his essay of racism or race-

related violence in the society around him? In his and his family's history, what was the role of miscegenation laws, segregation, and the movement toward integration?

2. Bernstein questions "dubious" paradigms, or theoretical models, associated with race or ethnicity. Where and how does he go counter to the reader's stereotypes and conventional expectations about race?

3. What were major factors in Bernstein's "political awakening"? Does his conservatism seem as wrong-headed to you as it did to many on campus? Why was his role as a black conservative of special interest to both conservatives and liberals?

4. Liberal-bashing has become a favorite conservative pastime in the days of Rush Limbaugh. What do you learn from Bernstein about its motivation or psychological workings? *Political correctness* became a buzzword as a conservative groundswell gained force. What are Bernstein's key criticisms of the "P.C. crowd"?

5. How or why does Bernstein rehabilitate the "melting pot" metaphor that many others have left behind? What does he see as the dangers of multiculturalism? What for him are the shortcomings of "group politics"?

Talking, Listening, Writing

6. On the basis of Bernstein's essay, what would you include in a capsule portrait of a young conservative? What are key positions or telltale features?

7. Have you seen evidence that harping on differences can be a mistake?

8. Do you think it inevitable that members of minority groups will turn politically conservative as they become affluent and move into the middle class?

9. Do you think of yourself as conservative, liberal, radical, or none of the above? Explain and defend your position.

Collaborative Projects

10. What statistics concerning race and ethnicity are kept at your school and in your community? Who collects them? Who uses them, and for what purpose? How are racial or ethnic criteria employed? What are the pitfalls in collecting and interpreting them? Your class may want to parcel out different aspects of this question to small groups.

EVERYDAY USE

Alice Walker

Alice Walker's novel The Color Purple *(1982) established her as a dominant voice in the search for a new black identity and black pride. In her Pulitzer Prize–winning novel, as in some of her short stories, her heroines are black women struggling to emerge from a history of oppression by white society and abuse by black males who "had failed women—and themselves." Walker's women find strength in bonding with other women, and they turn to the African past in the search for alternatives to our exploitative technological civilization. Walker's more recent novel,* The Temple of My Familiar *(1989), has been called a book of "amazing, overwhelming" richness, with characters "pushing one another towards self-knowledge, honesty, engagement" (Ursula K. Le Guin). Born in Eatonton, Georgia, Walker knew poverty and racism as the child of sharecroppers in the Deep South. While a student at Spelman College in Atlanta, she joined in the rallies, sit-ins, and freedom marches of the civil rights movement, which, she said later, "broke the pattern of black servitude in this country." She worked as a social worker for the New York City Welfare Department and as an editor for* Ms. *magazine. In the following story, the older generation holds on to its hard-won pride and independence, while members of a younger generation assert their break with the past by adopting Muslim names and African greetings. What do the quilts symbolize in the story? How do they bring the confrontation between the characters to a head?*

Thought Starters: Stereotyping lumps together diverse members of a group. Have you observed striking contrasts between members of the same ethnic, racial, or religious group?

---

for your grandmama

I will wait for her in the yard that Maggie and I made so clean and   *1*
wavy yesterday afternoon. A yard like this is more comfortable than most people know. It is not just a yard. It is like an extended living room. When the hard clay is swept clean as a floor and the fine sand around the edges lined with tiny, irregular grooves, anyone can come and sit and look up into the elm tree and wait for the breezes that never come inside the house.

Maggie will be nervous until after her sister goes: she will stand hopelessly in corners, homely and ashamed of the burn scars down her arms and legs, eyeing her sister with a mixture of envy and awe. She thinks her sister has held life always in the palm of one hand, that "no" is a word the world never learned to say to her.

You've no doubt seen those TV shows where the child who has "made it" is confronted, as a surprise, by her own mother and father, tottering in weakly from backstage. (A pleasant surprise, of course: What would they do if parent and child came on the show only to curse out and insult each other?) On TV mother and child embrace and smile into each other's faces. Sometimes the mother and father weep, the child wraps them in her arms and leans across the table to tell how she would not have made it without their help. I have seen these programs.

Sometimes I dream a dream in which Dee and I are suddenly brought together on a TV program of this sort. Out of a dark and soft-seated limousine I am ushered into a bright room filled with many people. There I meet a smiling, gray, sporty man like Johnny Carson who shakes my hand and tells me what a fine girl I have. Then we are on the stage and Dee is embracing me with tears in her eyes. She pins on my dress a large orchid, even though she has told me once that she thinks orchids are tacky flowers.

In real life I am a large, big-boned woman with rough, man-working 5
hands. In the winter I wear flannel nightgowns to bed and overalls during the day. I can kill and clean a hog as mercilessly as a man. My fat keeps me hot in zero weather. I can work outside all day, breaking ice to get water for washing; I can eat pork liver cooked over the open fire minutes after it comes steaming from the hog. One winter I knocked a bull calf straight in the brain between the eyes with a sledge hammer and had the meat hung up to chill before nightfall. But of course all this does not show on television. I am the way my daughter would want me to be: a hundred pounds lighter, my skin like an uncooked barley pancake. My hair glistens in the hot bright lights. Johnny Carson has much to do to keep up with my quick and witty tongue.

But that is a mistake. I know even before I wake up. Who ever knew a Johnson with a quick tongue? Who can even imagine me looking a strange white man in the eye? It seems to me I have talked to them always with one foot raised in flight, with my head turned in whichever way is farthest from them. Dee, though. She would always look anyone in the eye. Hesitation was no part of her nature.

"How do I look, Mama?" Maggie says, showing just enough of her thin body enveloped in pink skirt and red blouse for me to know she's there, almost hidden by the door.

"Come out into the yard," I say.

Have you ever seen a lame animal, perhaps a dog run over by some careless person rich enough to own a car, sidle up to someone who is ignorant enough to be kind to him? That is the way my Maggie walks.

She has been like this, chin on chest, eyes on ground, feet in shuffle, ever since the fire that burned the other house to the ground.

Dee is lighter than Maggie, with nicer hair and a fuller figure. She's a woman now, though sometimes I forget. How long ago was it that the other house burned? Ten, twelve years? Sometimes I can still hear the flames and feel Maggie's arms sticking to me, her hair smoking and her dress falling off her in little black papery flakes. Her eyes seemed stretched open, blazed open by the flames reflected in them. And Dee. I see her standing off under the sweet gum tree she used to dig gum out of; a look of concentration on her face as she watched the last dingy gray board of the house fall in toward the red-hot brick chimney. Why don't you do a dance around the ashes? I'd wanted to ask her. She had hated the house that much.

I used to think she hated Maggie, too. But that was before we raised the money, the church and me, to send her to Augusta to school. She used to read to us without pity; forcing words, lies, other folks' habits, whole lives upon us two, sitting trapped and ignorant underneath her voice. She washed us in a river of make-believe, burned us with a lot of knowledge we didn't necessarily need to know. Pressed us to her with the serious way she read, to shove us away at just the moment, like dimwits, we seemed about to understand.

Dee wanted nice things. A yellow organdy dress to wear to her graduation from high school; black pumps to match a green suit she'd made from an old suit somebody gave me. She was determined to stare down any disaster in her efforts. Her eyelids would not flicker for minutes at a time. Often I fought off the temptation to shake her. At sixteen she had a style of her own: and knew what style was.

I never had an education myself. After second grade the school was closed down. Don't ask me why: in 1927 colored asked fewer questions than they do now. Sometimes Maggie reads to me. She stumbles along good-naturedly but can't see well. She knows she is not bright. Like good looks and money, quickness passed her by. She will marry John Thomas (who has mossy teeth in an earnest face) and then I'll be free to sit here and I guess just sing church songs to myself. Although I never was a good singer. Never could carry a tune. I was always better at a man's job. I used to love to milk till I was hooked in the side in '49. Cows are soothing and slow and don't bother you, unless you try to milk them the wrong way.

I have deliberately turned my back on the house. It is three rooms, just like the one that burned, except the roof is tin; they don't make shingle roofs any more. There are no real windows, just some holes cut in the sides, like the portholes in a ship, but not round and not square, with rawhide holding the shutters up on the outside. This house is in a pasture, too, like the other one. No doubt when Dee sees it she will want to tear it down. She wrote me once that no matter where we "choose" to live, she will manage to come see us. But she will never bring her friends. Maggie and I thought about this and Maggie asked me, "Mama, when did Dee ever *have* any friends?"

She had a few. Furtive boys in pink shirts hanging about on washday   15 after school. Nervous girls who never laughed. Impressed with her they worshiped the well-turned phrase, the cute shape, the scalding humor that erupted like bubbles in lye. She read to them.

When she was courting Jimmy T she didn't have much time to pay to us, but turned all her faultfinding power on him. He *flew* to marry a cheap city girl from a family of ignorant flashy people. She hardly had time to recompose herself.

When she comes I will meet—but there they are!

Maggie attempts to make a dash for the house, in her shuffling way, but I stay her with my hand. "Come back here," I say. And she stops and tries to dig a well in the sand with her toe.

It is hard to see them clearly through the strong sun. But even the first glimpse of leg out of the car tells me it is Dee. Her feet were always neat-looking, as if God himself had shaped them with a certain style. From the other side of the car comes a short, stocky man. Hair is all over his head a foot long and hanging from his chin like a kinky mule tail. I hear Maggie suck in her breath. "Uhnnnh," is what it sounds like. Like when you see the wriggling end of a snake just in front of your foot on the road. "Uhnnnh."

Dee next. A dress down to the ground, in this hot weather. A dress   20 so loud it hurts my eyes. There are yellows and oranges enough to throw back the light of the sun. I feel my whole face warming from the heat waves it throws out. Earrings gold, too, and hanging down to her shoulders. Bracelets dangling and making noises when she moves her arm up to shake the folds of the dress out of her armpits. The dress is loose and flows, and as she walks closer, I like it. I hear Maggie go "Uhnnnh" again. It is her sister's hair. It stands straight up like the wool on a sheep. It is black as night and around the edges are two long pigtails that rope about like small lizards disappearing behind her ears.

"Wa-su-zo-Tean-o!" she says, coming on in that gliding way the dress makes her move. The short stocky fellow with the hair to his navel is all grinning and he follows up with "Asalamalakim, my mother and sister!" He moves to hug Maggie but she falls back, right up against the back of my chair. I feel her trembling there and when I look up I see the perspiration falling off her chin.

"Don't get up," says Dee. Since I am stout it takes something of a push. You can see me trying to move a second or two before I make it. She turns, showing white heels through her sandals, and goes back to the car. Out she peeks next with a Polaroid. She stoops down quickly and lines up picture after picture of me sitting there in front of the house with

Maggie cowering behind me. She never takes a shot without making sure the house is included. When a cow comes nibbling around the edge of the yard she snaps it and me and Maggie *and* the house. Then she puts the Polaroid in the back seat of the car, and comes up and kisses me on the forehead.

Meanwhile Asalamalakim is going through motions with Maggie's hand. Maggie's hand is as limp as a fish, and probably as cold, despite the sweat, and she keeps trying to pull it back. It looks like Asalamalakim wants to shake hands but wants to do it fancy. Or maybe he don't know how people shake hands. Anyhow, he soon gives up on Maggie.

"Well," I say. "Dee."

"No, Mama," she says. "Not 'Dee,' Wangero Leewanika Kemanjo!"   25

"What happened to 'Dee'?" I wanted to know.

"She's dead," Wangero said. "I couldn't bear it any longer, being named after the people who oppress me."

"You know as well as me you was named after your aunt Dicie," I said. Dicie is my sister. She named Dee. We called her "Big Dee" after Dee was born.

"But who was *she* named after?" asked Wangero.

"I guess after Grandma Dee," I said.   30

"And who was she named after?" asked Wangero.

"Her mother," I said, and saw Wangero was getting tired. "That's about as far back as I can trace it," I said. Though, in fact, I probably could have carried it back beyond the Civil War through the branches.

"Well," said Asalamalakim, "there you are."

"Uhnnnh," I heard Maggie say.

"There I was not," I said, "before 'Dicie' cropped up in our family,   35
so why should I try to trace it that far back?"

He just stood there grinning, looking down on me like somebody inspecting a Model A car. Every once in a while he and Wangero sent eye signals over my head.

"How do you pronounce this name?" I asked.

"You don't have to call me by it if you don't want to," said Wangero.

"Why shouldn't I?" I asked. "If that's what you want us to call you, we'll call you."

"I know it might sound awkward at first," said Wangero.   40

"I'll get used to it," I said. "Ream it out again."

Well, soon we got the name out of the way. Asalamalakim had a name twice as long and three times as hard. After I tripped over it two or three times he told me to just call him Hakim-a-barber. I wanted to ask him was he a barber, but I didn't really think he was, so I didn't ask.

"You must belong to those beef-cattle peoples down the road," I said. They said "Asalamalakim" when they met you, too, but they didn't shake hands. Always too busy: feeding the cattle, fixing the fences, putting up salt-lick shelters, throwing down hay. When the white folks poisoned some of the herd the men stayed up all night with rifles in their hands. I walked a mile and a half just to see the sight.

Hakim-a-barber said, "I accept some of their doctrines, but farming and raising cattle is not my style." (They didn't tell me, and I didn't ask, whether Wangero (Dee) had really gone and married him.)

We sat down to eat and right away he said he didn't eat collards and   45
pork was unclean. Wangero, though, went on through the chitlins and corn bread, the greens and everything else. She talked a blue streak over the sweet potatoes. Everything delighted her. Even the fact that we still used the benches her daddy made for the table when we couldn't afford to buy chairs.

"Oh, Mama!" she cried. Then turned to Hakim-a-barber. "I never knew how lovely these benches are. You can feel the rump prints," she said, running her hands underneath her and along the bench. Then she gave a sigh and her hand closed over Grandma Dee's butter dish. "That's it!" she said. "I knew there was something I wanted to ask you if I could have." She jumped up from the table and went over in the corner where the churn stood, the milk in it clabber by now. She looked at the churn and looked at it.

"This churn top is what I need," she said. "Didn't Uncle Buddy whittle it out of a tree you all used to have?"

"Yes," I said.

"Uh huh," she said happily. "And I want the dasher, too."

"Uncle Buddy whittle that, too?" asked the barber.   50

Dee (Wangero) looked up at me.

"Aunt Dee's first husband whittled the dash," said Maggie so low you almost couldn't hear her. "His name was Henry, but they called him Stash."

"Maggie's brain is like an elephant's," Wangero said, laughing. "I can use the churn top as a centerpiece for the alcove table," she said, sliding a plate over the churn, "and I'll think of something artistic to do with the dasher."

When she finished wrapping the dasher the handle stuck out. I took it for a moment in my hands. You didn't even have to look close to see where hands pushing the dasher up and down to make butter had left a kind of sink in the wood. In fact, there were a lot of small sinks; you could see where thumbs and fingers had sunk into the wood. It was beautiful light yellow wood, from a tree that grew in the yard where Big Dee and Stash had lived.

After dinner Dee (Wangero) went to the trunk at the foot of my bed   55
and started rifling through it. Maggie hung back in the kitchen over the dishpan. Out came Wangero with two quilts. They had been pieced by Grandma Dee and then Big Dee and me had hung them on the quilt frames on the front porch and quilted them. One was in the Lone Star pattern. The other was Walk Around the Mountain. In both of them were scraps of dresses Grandma Dee had worn fifty and more years ago. Bits and

pieces of Grandpa Jarrell's Paisley shirts. And one teeny faded blue piece, about the size of a penny matchbox, that was from Great Grandpa Ezra's uniform that he wore in the Civil War.

"Mama," Wangero said sweet as a bird. "Can I have these old quilts?"

I heard something fall in the kitchen, and a minute later the kitchen door slammed.

"Why don't you take one or two of the others?" I asked. "These old things was just done by me and Big Dee from some tops your grandma pieced before she died."

"No," said Wangero. "I don't want those. They are stitched around the borders by machine."

"That'll make them last better," I said.   60

"That's not the point," said Wangero. "These are all pieces of dresses Grandma used to wear. She did all this stitching by hand. Imagine!" She held the quilts securely in her arms, stroking them.

"Some of the pieces, like those lavender ones, come from old clothes her mother handed down to her," I said, moving up to touch the quilts. Dee (Wangero) moved back just enough so that I couldn't reach the quilts. They already belonged to her.

"Imagine!" she breathed again, clutching them closely to her bosom.

"The truth is," I said, "I promised to give them quilts to Maggie, for when she marries John Thomas."

She gasped like a bee had stung her.   65

"Maggie can't appreciate these quilts!" she said. "She'd probably be backward enough to put them to everyday use."

"I reckon she would," I said. "God knows I been saving 'em for long enough with nobody using 'em. I hope she will!" I didn't want to bring up how I had offered Dee (Wangero) a quilt when she went away to college. Then she had told me they were old-fashioned, out of style.

"But they're *priceless!*" she was saying now, furiously; for she has a temper. "Maggie would put them on the bed and in five years they'd be in rags. Less than that!"

"She can always make some more," I said. "Maggie knows how to quilt."

Dee (Wangero) looked at me with hatred. "You just will not under-   70
stand. The point is these quilts, *these* quilts!"

"Well," I said, stumped. "What would *you* do with them?"

"Hang them," she said. As if that was the only thing you *could* do with quilts.

Maggie by now was standing in the door. I could almost hear the sound her feet made as they scraped over each other.

"She can have them, Mama," she said, like somebody used to never winning anything, or having anything reserved for her. "I can 'member Grandma Dee without the quilts."

I looked at her hard. She had filled her bottom lip with checkerberry   75 snuff and it gave her face a kind of dopey, hangdog look. It was Grandma Dee and Big Dee who taught her how to quilt herself. She stood there with her scarred hands hidden in the folds of her skirt. She looked at her sister with something like fear but she wasn't mad at her. This was Maggie's portion. This was the way she knew God to work.

When I looked at her like that something hit me in the top of my head and ran down to the soles of my feet. Just like when I'm in church and the spirit of God touches me and I get happy and shout. I did something I never had done before: hugged Maggie to me, then dragged her on into the room, snatched the quilts out of Miss Wangero's hands and dumped them into Maggie's lap. Maggie just sat there on my bed with her mouth open.

"Take one or two of the others," I said to Dee.

But she turned without a word and went out to Hakim-a-barber.

"You just don't understand," she said, as Maggie and I came out to the car.

"What don't I understand?" I wanted to know.   80

"Your heritage," she said. And then she turned to Maggie, kissed her, and said, "You ought to try to make something of yourself, too, Maggie. It's really a new day for us. But from the way you and Mama still live you'd never know it."

She put on some sunglasses that hid everything above the tip of her nose and her chin.

Maggie smiled; maybe at the sunglasses. But a real smile, not scared. After we watched the car dust settle I asked Maggie to bring me a dip of snuff. And then the two of us sat there just enjoying, until it was time to go in the house and go to bed.

The Responsive Reader

1. What kind of person is the mother? What role do her daydreams play in the story? How does her initial self-portrait as the narrator, or person telling the story, prepare you for what happens later?
2. What is the contrasting history of the two sisters? What is most important in their earlier history?
3. What do Dee and her companion stand for in this story? Do you recognize their attitudes and way of talking?
4. How does the confrontation over the quilts bring things to a head? What is the history of the quilts and their symbolic meaning? How does the climactic ending resolve the conflict in this story?

Talking, Listening, Writing

5. If you had to choose a role model from this story, would you opt for the mother or for Dee? Defend your choice.

Collaborative Projects

6. Do you ever chafe at being a passive reader—who cannot enter into the story to help it steer one way or another? Write a passage in which one daughter or the other tells her side of the story. Or rewrite the ending the way you would have preferred the story to come out. Or write a sequel to the story bringing it up to date. Arrange for members of the class to share their imaginative efforts.

REFUGEE SHIP

Lorna Dee Cervantes

> *Lorna Dee Cervantes was born in San Francisco of Mexican descent and was a student at San Jose State University. She said in a poem addressed to her brother, "We were so poor . . . We were brilliant at wishing." Her poems often play on the contrast between an older generation with strong ties to an ethnic past and a younger generation living in the Americanized present. Cervantes published* Emplumada, *her first collection of poems, in 1981. She founded Mango Publications, a small press publishing books and a literary magazine.*

Thought Starters: What do you know about refugees? What do you know about boat people?

Like wet cornstarch, I slide   1
past my grandmother's eyes. Bible
at her side, she removes her glasses.
The pudding thickens.
Mama raised me without language,   5

I'm orphaned from my Spanish name.
The words are foreign, stumbling
on my tongue. I see in the mirror
My reflection: bronzed skin, black hair.

I feel I am a captive   10
aboard the refugee ship.
The ship that will never dock.
El barco que nunca atraca.

The Responsive Reader

1. In her poems, Cervantes casually shifts to Spanish words she heard in her childhood when she talks about the scenes and people of her youth. So then why does the speaker in the poem say that her mother raised her "without language"? Why do you think the mother did what she did? Why does the speaker feel "orphaned" from her Spanish name? (How can you be orphaned from a name?)
2. Why, right after talking about language, does the person speaking in the poem look at herself in the mirror? What's the point of what she sees?

3. Why does the poet feel trapped like a captive on a refugee ship? Why will the ship never dock? What do you know about refugees and refugee ships that would explain how the ship became a central symbol in this poem?
4. The last line of the poem repeats in Spanish the preceding line about the ship that will never dock. Why is it fitting that this idea is stated in both English and Spanish?

Talking, Listening, Writing

5. This poem spans three generations. What happened in the passage from one generation to another? Do you think this poet is alienated from her Hispanic or Latina heritage?
6. Linguists use the term *code-switching* for people shifting from one language to another. Have you observed people doing this? Is there any pattern to how and when they shift from one language to another?
7. Have you ever become estranged or alienated from a group to which you once belonged?

WRITING
WORKSHOP 5

Organizing Your Writing

How good are you at organizing your writing? Effective writers know how to lay things out. They present information and ideas in such a way that we say: "Now I see how this works." To organize your material, you may have to sort out a set of data—like statistics on temporary employment or teenage pregnancy. You may have to analyze the stages in a process to show us how to get from point A to point B. You may have to set up categories to show what goes with what. Looking at a problem, you may have to identify major factors that contribute to it and then show us how to deal with them.

These major organizing strategies prove useful again and again as you try to help readers make sense of a confusing situation. In organizing your writing, you will often ask yourself one or more questions like the following: What are the major steps in a process? (What does it take to produce the desired end result?) Do traditional classifications do justice to the current situation—or should we adjust our mental categories? Can we isolate some of the causes of a bad situation—and work toward a solution?

TRIGGERING Your ability to sort things out may be put to the test in situations like the following:

- Can you show people who dislike additive-laden supermarket food how to grow their own vegetables or bake their own bread?

- Do you feel that current talk about immigrants tends to lump together many different kinds of people? Can you show that legal status, voting rights, and entitlements vary greatly for different classifications of immigrants?

- Are you skeptical of politicians' claims about job creation and job growth? Can you show why the trend toward "temporary" work, without benefits, is likely to accelerate?

▪ If the city council is debating different plans for zoning or development, and if you are violently opposed to one of the alternatives, can you show the consequences of adopting plan A and of adopting plan B?

GATHERING If you want to shed light on a confusing situation, you have to start from a solid base of data. You will need substantial input before you try to explain how things fit together or how things work. For instance, immigration has resurfaced in recent political campaigns as a hot issue. Blue-collar workers are worried about immigrants taking their jobs. Politicians frighten taxpayers with stories about spiraling welfare costs for aliens. At some point, you may ask: Who are these people? Do they all fit the same stereotype? Or are there major kinds of immigrants representing different facets of the "new immigrant" population?

The following might be sample notes you type in (or jot down) during your material-gathering stage:

Several small businesses in this community are run by Korean grocers or liquor store owners. Both spouses and maybe older children work in the store. The store is open from early in the morning till late at night.

The local newspaper reports on a new city ordinance concerning day workers who everyone knows line up along a street every morning where employers pick them up for a day's work. Many of these workers are probably illegals. The city council is going to prohibit workers looking for temporary work from lining up along the street.

A pharmacy downtown is now run by a Vietnamese family. The business is a family operation. Little kids run around the store even late in the evening. Come to think of it, what used to be a dead part of town has come back to life with little stores, ethnic restaurants, and colorful shop signs.

I had high school friends whose parents were from Australia and worked in a high-tech company. They never took out citizenship papers and always talked about going back because of the threat of unemployment and poor health insurance.

Newspaper stories crop up about prominent politicians and wealthy Americans employing illegal nannies or gardeners and not paying social security taxes.

The immigration authorities raid sweatshops in New York City.

A visiting professor talks about visiting a migrant camp that is on no map and that the local sheriff said he knew nothing about (!). The people worked for local growers on a seasonal basis, living in shacks.

As you dig in, you may try to remember additional details and check out some of the newspaper stories. At the same time, you may start thinking in terms of three major categories. An early scratch outline might look something like this:

- *established immigrants*—many of these are legal immigrants who came as refugees or as relatives of earlier immigrants and are tax-paying, small-scale entrepreneurs
- *the migrant population*—many of these are illegals employed in sweatshops or by agribusiness as part of a black market economy; many live from day to day and from job to job
- *the in-between people*—many of these are professionals who work here when times are good but have not established permanent ties

When you present your classification of the "new immigrants" in your paper, you will try to flesh out each category with convincing real-life examples. Your readers will not have to agree with you, but you are giving them "a basis for discussion."

SHAPING Among the thinking and writing strategies that help you organize your papers, several prove useful again and again. For instance, you may trace the stages in a process, so you can show what leads to what. What is first, and what is the next step? You may classify, putting things that belong together in the same bin. What goes with what? You may analyze cause and effect: What are the consequences if we do A, and what will happen if we do B?

To get a handle on how something works, we often mark off stages. We trace a **process**—whether to help readers understand evolution or to help them raise chickens. Thinking in terms of major stages enables you to focus on one thing at a time—while yet seeing it as part of a larger whole. You do justice to what seems important during a particular phase without losing sight of the whole. Marie De Santis, in a later chapter of this book, charts the life cycle of the salmon somewhat as follows:

The Last of the Wild Salmon

PHASE ONE: THE SALMON RUN Salmon fight their way upstream, motivated by a powerful instinctual drive. In prodigious leaps, they overcome waterfalls and manmade obstacles.

PHASE TWO: THE SPAWNING GROUNDS Lacerated by their upstream fight, the salmon reach the spawning grounds. They lay and fertilize a myriad eggs.

PHASE THREE: NEW LIFE The parents die, but after an interval fingerlings are in evidence everywhere, which eventually begin their journey downstream.

PHASE FOUR: TRANSITION The young salmon stay in the delta—they live in a sweetwater environment for a time, until they are ready for the saltwater environment of the ocean.

PHASE FIVE: RETURN TO THE OCEAN The adult salmon live in the ocean for a number of years—until a powerful urge propels them to seek the spawning grounds of their birth, and the cycle begins anew.

Classification—sorting things out into categories—is a basic way of making sense of an array of data. We ask: What goes with what? Schools track students according to IQ, aptitude, or test results. Mortgage companies classify potential home buyers as low-risk, high-risk, and need-not-apply. To place people on a socioeconomic scale, sociologists used to rely on the traditional upper class-middle class-lower class scheme. Today, a sociologist might set up a more realistic scheme of classification like the following:

Are You Upwardly Mobile?

- upper class (families of large inherited wealth and the corporate elite)
- upper middle class (midlevel managers, professional people, successful business people)
- lower middle class (lower-echelon employees, office workers, teachers, nurses, owners of marginal businesses)
- underclass (dropouts, chronically unemployed, long-term welfare cases)

In trying to understand what goes on in our world, we often focus on **cause and effect**. Once we understand what caused a problem, we may be able to work toward a solution. Once we recognize the causes of a bad situation, we may be able to keep from repeating the same mistakes. For instance, why do both conservatives and feminists seem to have second thoughts about no-fault divorce?

No-fault divorce seemed to promise relief from vindictive court battles traumatizing the family members and enriching lawyers. However, experts found that in reality many women found themselves with insufficient child support, only a few years of hard-to-collect alimony, and a family home that had had to be sold so property could be divided. Many divorced women experienced a drastic decline in their standard of living. Why? Lenore J. Weitzman, a professor of sociology at Harvard, identified the causes somewhat as follows:

1 While treating women as theoretical equals, courts ignored the drastically unequal earning power of a man who had built a career and of a homemaker or part-time worker trying to enter the labor force after many years of marriage.

2 The "equal" division of property is in fact unequal if the property is divided between one person (usually the male) and three or four other people (the mother and children).

3 The elimination of misconduct as grounds for divorce eliminated the bargaining power that women used to have when men would make economic concessions in order to obtain the "innocent" partner's consent to a divorce.

4 Dividing tangible property such as money and real estate did not, at least at first, take into account such intangible assets as advanced degrees, pension rights, insurance entitlements, or business contacts.

A close look at cause and effect often offers clues on how to remedy a bad situation. If we can identify the most common causes of domestic violence, maybe we can institute educational programs or legal remedies that would help. If we can pinpoint the causes for high dropout rates in local schools, perhaps we can support remedial action.

REVISING In a first draft, you may have concentrated on getting your facts right or on working in different kinds of material. In a revision, you have a chance to ask yourself: Have I done enough to make my readers find their way? Will this paper make them say: "Now I see"? Here are questions you may want to keep in mind in reworking a paper:

• *Should you do more to show why your explanations matter?* You might be able to add a quote from an authority on nutrition testifying to the value of baking your own bread or raising free-range chickens. You might be able to show how a realistic estimate of the current immigrant population can help voters make informed decisions about welfare policy.

• *Should you do more to make your readers see your overall scheme?* Should you do more to give a preview or overview so that readers know how parts of your paper fit into the larger picture? Make sure they have a sense of what the whole process is as you close in on details. As you develop major categories, make sure readers see how these relate to one another.

• *Should you do more to bring in real-life examples or real people?* Categories you set up can easily remain lifeless and theoretical—"academic" in the bad sense.

• *Should you aim at more balanced treatment of different parts or stages?* Does any part of your paper seem too skimpy—because you were hurried, or because you did not have the right kind of support ready at the time?

A PAPER FOR PEER REVIEW In the following paper, how effectively has the student writer brought a familiar problem into focus? How clearly does he identify key factors contributing to the situation? How convincing are the answers or the solutions he suggests?

Why AIDS Education Has Failed

I remember walking into a locker room where students were crowding around a radio. "Magic Johnson has AIDS!" In the following months, AIDS awareness peaked all over the country. Magic Johnson's misfortune sparked an interest and a newfound curiosity in the youth of America, who felt they could relate to the basketball star. The media had specials on AIDS and on the HIV virus daily. Misconceptions were being answered about the virus and the disease.

Nevertheless, according to a recent article in the *New York Times*, the number of teenagers with AIDS increased 70 percent in the course of two years, and AIDS was the fifth leading cause of death among people 15 to 24 years old. Although many schools now require AIDS education, many teenagers continue to have unprotected sex. The blame for the failure of AIDS education can be placed on typically adolescent attitudes, on the attitudes of school boards and parents in local communities, and on the generally conservative nature of the political world.

Although studies show that as many as half of sexually active students use condoms, their main motivation is to avoid conception. Vivian Sheer, in an article in *Human Communication Research*, calls teenagers who put themselves at risk "sensation seekers" who like the immediate gratification that unprotected sex provides. Teenagers at this age feel immortal; the attitude is, "It will not happen to me." My own friends and acquaintances see condoms as a hassle; they "ruin an intimate mood, destroy spontaneity, and reduce the partner's sexual pleasure."

Often the community needs as much education as the students. Schools have been slow to address the medical, legal, and ethical issues raised by the presence of an HIV-infected student or even a faculty member. Although experts say that "comprehensive, open discussion about sexuality" is the most effective way of educating people about AIDS, this "open discussion" type of teaching has had to do battle against conservative communities. Parents as well as political leaders preach abstinence and the promotion of moral conduct as the answer. In the words of one school board member, children should be taught what is right and wrong; "they shouldn't be presented with options."

Advocates of sex education find themselves hampered by moralistic restrictions on explicit information about high-risk sexual practices and the effective use of condoms. Often the giving of explicit information is prohibited outright by a politically dominant faction. A surgeon general of the United States was forced from office for her outspoken discussion of adolescent sexuality and advocacy of condom use. Political leaders are more concerned with their image than with saving the lives of young people. I could find no evidence of a coordinated government effort that targets adolescents or collects research data concerning teenagers, a situation that one observer called "a national disgrace."

Nongovernment efforts like the AIDS education project for the National Coalition of Advocates for Students try to make people see the AIDS crisis from a public health perspective. How many lives must be put at risk before another superstar is infected and the media for a short time again keep the AIDS issue in the limelight? In the meantime, students are beginning to develop their own initiatives to protect themselves. In a high school in Massachusetts, students fought and negotiated for a year to make condoms available with counseling. In Connecticut, HIV testing was made available to students without a parent's consent. These battles fought and won show the maturity and capability of teenagers to deal with this topic and their desire to slow the epidemic down.

Topics for Analysis Papers (A Sampling)

1. Have you seen affirmative action at work? How does it work? What are typical issues or typical results?
2. Have you seen the local economy in your home town or your college town go through major stages? Have you observed different cycles—for better or for worse?
3. Bookstores do a brisk business selling books like *Internet for Dummies*. Write exceptionally clear and foolproof instructions for upgrading a computer, cruising the Internet, or a similar task.
4. Many different kinds of immigrants have come into the country in recent years. How would you sort them out, setting up major categories?
5. In recent decades, alternative living arrangements and lifestyles have come to compete with the traditional nuclear family. What are major current alternatives to the traditional family?
6. What is the ethnic or racial mix at your school? Can you sort out major groups? What sets them apart?
7. Teachers and parents worry about teenagers who seem alienated from what schools have to offer or who see no point in trying hard in school. To judge from your own experience or observation, what makes young people tune out teachers and school?
8. Many Americans seem to accept staggering divorce rates as a fact of life. Is it still worthwhile to look at major causes of divorce and talk about possible answers?
9. From what you have seen, what makes some people bigots? Why are some people more prejudiced or narrow-minded than others? What makes the difference—for instance, family, peers, school, media exposure?
10. What have you seen of programs to fight the spread of drugs among young people? Do they work? Why or why not?

6

Culture Wars: Constructing Gender

The legal subordination of one sex to another is wrong in itself and now one of the chief hindrances to human improvement.
—*John Stuart Mill*

Many cultures have had assumptions about what it means to be a man and what it means to be a woman. What parents, counselors, teachers, and employers expect of a young woman may steer her toward options very different from those open to a young man. How much is biology—how true is it that "biology is destiny"? How much is culture—with boys taught from the beginning to be tough and adventurous, and girls taught from the beginning to be dainty and play with dolls? How much is genetic; how much is learned?

In recent decades, there has been a seismic shift in how we think about gender roles and how we define "masculine" and "feminine" traits. Today we no longer take it for granted that the judge will be male and the court clerk female, the physician a man and the nurse a woman, the manager a male and the secretary a female, the college professor a male and the high school teacher someone's wife, and the police officer a male and the meter maid a maid. Medical schools and law schools enroll large numbers of female students, pointing to something closer to parity down the road. All-male "little-white-boys" businessmen's clubs and would-be macho military academies survive only in backwaters.

At the same time, the top-level executive suites and boardrooms of American business are still largely peopled by males. Congress remains largely a white male preserve. The coddled star athletes in the big-money sports are predominantly male. Women in "pink-collar" occupations are paid less than construction workers and truck drivers. Public school teachers, far from receiving "comparable pay" similar to that of other professionals, may find they are paid less than garbage collectors.

Whether or not women consciously identify with the feminist movement, they are likely to be involved in women's issues: There is growing

315

concern about widespread sexual abuse of women and children, with rape victims and women in battered women shelters demanding less cavalier treatment by law enforcement and the justice system. The integration of women into the military has led to widespread charges of sexual harassment and exploitation. Abortion rights are everywhere contested by male-dominated legislatures. For feminists, the mantra of "family values" is merely code for the male lords of creation trying to send their women back to baking cookies and chauffeuring their offspring as "soccer moms."

How do we become aware of the limits and opportunities that await us when we are identified according to such factors as gender, race, ethnicity, or sexual orientation? What chance do we have to shape our own destiny, to forge our own identity? In her feminist rereading of Charlotte Brontë's novel *Jane Eyre*, Adrienne Rich traces one young woman's journey toward self-realization. Young Jane exercises the limited options open to her as a poor young woman in nineteenth-century England. She goes to work as a governess in the mansion of Rochester, the gloomy aristocrat. When she finds he is married to a mentally ill woman, she refuses the temptation of an extramarital romance and leaves his employ. Later, she rejects the option of serving as a platonic helpmate to a high-minded missionary on his way to convert the heathens. She discovers female friends and teachers who think of other women not as rivals but as sisters. She finally marries the widowed Rochester when she can join in the union as a partner, as an equal.

How optimistic or how realistic is the scenario acted out in Brontë's novel? What chance do people in our culture have to transcend the barriers created by gender, ethnicity, or sexual orientation?

2 WOMEN CADETS LEAVE THE CITADEL

For several years, newspaper readers followed the ongoing saga of the Citadel military academy in South Carolina, a last holdout in the lost cause of trying to keep the military a bastion for would-be macho, tough hombre males. The academy fought a long and bitter battle against coeducation. Young women, and mothers and fathers of young women, looked at the pictures of male cadets whooping and hollering when they succeeded in driving the first woman who had breached the wall of segregation from their compound in 1995. The academy was a public institution supported with taxes raised regardless of the taxpayer's gender, but it took a court order to force gender integration on the males running the institution. The following newspaper story reports on the fate of the second wave of young women to enroll at the Citadel. The attorney for one of the two young women leaving the Citadel said, "somebody would have to be a moron" to let this happen. "They knew the eyes of the world were upon them."

Thought Starters: Colleges used to have Men's Faculty Clubs and Women's Faculty Clubs. The Student Union at the University of Michigan required women to enter through a side entrance. In some places, there are still all-male businessmen's clubs. Is such segregation by gender obsolete in our society?

When she enrolled at The Citadel just five months ago, Kim Messer   *1*
brimmed with the confidence of a young woman ready to meet a formidable challenge.

"I want the rigor of The Citadel as much as any guy wants it," she said in the days before she became one of the first women enrolled since the military college in Charleston, S.C., abandoned its male-only rule. "It's all a game. It's all mental, and your attitude when you go in there determines whether or not you are going to make it."

But yesterday her lawyer, Paul Gibson, announced that Messer and a second female cadet, Jeanie Mentavlos, would drop out after months of what they consider abuse at the hands of their student superiors.

In addition, Mentavlos' brother, Michael, a senior with a 4.0 average, said he would not return to the campus either. Instead, he will ask the school administration for permission to take elsewhere the three credits he lacks and to be allowed to graduate with honors from The Citadel this spring.

A Citadel spokesman told the Associated Press the school would have   *5*
no comment until a news conference today.

The departure of the two women leaves two females—Nancy Mace, of Goose Creek, S.C., and Petra Lovetinska, of Washington—as the only women in the corps of cadets, which numbers more than 1,700. Their parents report they are doing well, in both academics and military training.

Messer and Jeanie Mentavlos say they were assaulted and sexually harassed. The mistreatment intensified after they were excused by the Citadel's orthopedic surgeon from physical training because they suffered pelvic stress fractures, a fairly common occurrence in military training.

He said the women had reported being forced to listen to and sing obscene songs. Their sweatshirts, dampened with nail polish remover just below their breasts, were set on fire. Once, when one extinguished the flames, a superior ordered, "Light her up again," Gibson said. Setting freshmen on fire was something of a tradition within Echo Company, which has a reputation as being a hard-driving unit, Gibson said.

Once, a fellow "knob," as freshmen are called, was ordered to rub his clothed lower body against one of the women, Gibson said. Upperclassmen entered their rooms in the early hours of morning. Another time, they were forced to drink iced tea until they threw up.

Two seniors in Echo Company have been suspended and nine charged by school authorities. The results of a state Law Enforcement Division investigation into whether criminal laws were broken are expected in two weeks.

In her statement, Messer said she was no stranger to the military— her father is a retired master sergeant and she took part in ROTC in high school—yet life at The Citadel "bore little resemblance to the real military."

"The Citadel has a Fourth Class system that in theory is humane and fair," she said. "My company, at least, was run by a secret Fourth Class system that was neither."

Both women called on the new president, John Grinalds, a former headmaster of a boys' preparatory school, to correct the situation. Grinalds will take over mid-summer from the acting president, Clifton Poole. The former president, Claudius Watts, a staunch defender of the school's all-male policy, resigned last August as the school began coeducation.

The Responsive Reader

1. Do the two young women sound like promising or like unlikely candidates for a military academy to you? What did they have going for them? What was their attitude toward or expectation of the military?
2. Does what happened at the Citadel sound like a traditional kind of hazing or other initiation into all-male groups to you? Why or why not? (Is hazing obsolete in the culture at large?)

Talking, Listening, Writing

3. Do you think the "knobs" at the academy are especially backward, or do they represent a kind of sexism still widespread among young American males? (Is sexism on the rise or on the wane among young males?)

4. Traditional societies have had a special military caste with special traditions and codes of behavior. Do you think the nation needs special training institutions or elite units designed to inculcate a military mind-set or provide preparation for military service?

5. Do you think women should serve in the military? Do you think there should be restrictions on the capacities in which they can serve? Do you think women should be assigned combat duty?

Collaborative Projects

6. Is segregation by gender still legal for private groups and institutions? What is the status of all-male clubs? Have there been challenges to women-only groups or events? Working with a group, you may want to investigate recent test cases and legal developments.

THE INJUSTICE SYSTEM:
WOMEN HAVE BEGUN TO FIGHT

Patty Fisher

> *Patty Fisher is an editorial writer for a major newspaper in California. In the article that follows, she focuses on the explosive issue of rape as a test of attitudes toward women in our society. She buttresses personal observation and her close professional following of the news with an array of authoritative sources: a law professor and former public defender; statistics compiled by concerned organizations. She writes with the passion of intense personal involvement: She voices her concerns about her daughters; she shares the testimony of a friend.*

Thought Starters: Is our justice system rigged against victims of rape? Does our culture encourage or condone violence against women?

They called it "Brock's problem." Sen. Brock Adams, a respected   *1*
Democrat, was known to make sexual advances toward young women assistants. For years, his staff and close friends protected him, even after a woman told police he had drugged and molested her in his Washington apartment.

Then, the *Seattle Times* printed allegations from eight unnamed women that Adams raped, fondled, drugged or sexually harassed them over a period of 20 years. Before the day was over, Adams abruptly withdrew from his race for re-election.

So clean, so neat. No criminal charges, no trial, no witnesses. Just like that, the man's career is over, his reputation is shattered.

Vigilante justice, certainly. But if you believe the women's stories—and I do—it is justice nonetheless. And if you understand how the official justice system fails in cases of crimes against women, you see why women long ago abandoned the courts and began to fight against rape, spouse abuse and sexual harassment with whatever tools they could find.

The FBI has estimated that only one in 10 cases of rape is reported   *5*
to the police. Why don't women report these crimes? Some are afraid. Some are ashamed. All too many have learned that the system serves the interests of men and puts women victims on trial.

Cookie Ridolfi, a professor at Santa Clara University law school, worked for eight years as a public defender in Philadelphia. In most of the criminal cases she tried, her client was at a disadvantage, even though the burden of proof was on the prosecution.

"There is enormous bias against the defendant simply because he was arrested," she said. "Juries assume that he must have done something wrong."

Except in rape.

In a rape trial, the defense attorney has the edge. Instead of assuming the defendant is guilty, the jury assumes the victim either provoked the attack or made it up. "I can't think of one other criminal offense where the victim is blamed so routinely," she said.

It might be difficult for a man to see a situation short of Kafka in   *10*
which he, as an innocent victim, is blamed for the crime in court. But imagine this scenario:

A man is robbed at gunpoint. At the trial, he positively identifies the defendant as the one who followed him into a parking garage late at night and robbed him. The prosecution produces the man's credit cards and wedding ring, which were found on the defendant.

An open and shut case.

Until the defense attorney goes to work. The alleged victim, he says, is a liberal, guilt-ridden yuppie with a history of giving to homeless shelters. He spotted the defendant on the street, saw that he hadn't eaten all day and gave him his valuables. Only later, when he had to explain to his wife about his missing wedding ring, did he make up the story about being robbed.

The defense attorney points out inconsistencies in the victim's story: Why did he go into the garage alone that night when he knew it might be dangerous? Why didn't he leave his car and take a cab home? Why did he wear an expensive suit and flashy diamond ring unless he wanted to draw attention to his wealth? Why didn't he scream, fight or try to run away instead of docilely handing over his money?

There were no witnesses. There's plenty of room for reasonable   *15*
doubt. The jury returns a verdict of not guilty.

Preposterous? Only because juries don't assume that people give away their money and then lie about it later. But juries do assume that women have sex and then lie about it, file rape charges, lie to prosecutors and convince them to go to court.

Rape is a problem for the justice system in part because it is a unique crime. The act of sexual intercourse can be love or it can be rape, depending upon whether both parties consent to it. So the prosecution in a rape trial must prove the woman did not consent. That is difficult if the victim knew the rapist, which usually is the case; if there were no witnesses, which is nearly always the case; or if there are no bruises or other signs of struggle.

If the rapist had a gun or knife, if there was a group of assailants, or if the woman decided it was fruitless to struggle, the case comes down to her word against his. And traditionally, juries believe him and not her.

In ancient times, when women were regarded as the property of first their fathers and then their husbands, "consent" had nothing to do with rape. A man who deflowered a virgin not his wife was guilty of rape. He was ordered to marry the girl and pay her father the equivalent of what an intact virgin would have brought on the marriage market.

There was no such thing as rape of a married woman. If attacked, she was expected to fight to the death rather than give up her precious virtue (and her husband's good name). If she was unfortunate enough to live through the attack, she was guilty of adultery.

How far have we come? Only within the past 20 years have rape shield laws barred a victim's past sexual relations from being introduced as evidence in a rape trial. It remains more difficult to convict a man of raping a divorced woman than an "innocent" one.

Rape is not the only crime in which the system fails to treat women fairly. Wife beating wasn't even a crime until the 1800s. Today it is estimated that between 2 million and 6 million women are battered each year in this country by their husbands or boyfriends. Often their attempts to get protection from the justice system fail. And when they fight back and kill their abusers, the courts treat them more harshly than they do men who kill their wives or girlfriends.

According to statistics compiled by the National Clearinghouse for Battered Women, the average prison sentence for abusive men who kill their mates is two to six years. The average sentence for women who kill abusive men is 15 years.

Apparently juries make allowances for the remorseful man who kills in a momentary fit of rage, but not for the woman who pulls a gun on an unarmed man who has beaten her senseless for years and threatened to kill her.

Without the justice system to protect them, women have found ways to protect themselves. They taught their daughters to be "good" and follow the rules:

Never talk to strangers. Never walk alone at night. Never wear revealing clothes. Never let a boy kiss you on the first date.

But even "nice" girls get raped. In a San Jose courtroom recently, a man who confessed to raping more than 20 women said he attacked a Japanese exchange student because he thought she was flirting with him at a bus stop. "We stared at each other for a second," Gregory Smith told the jury. He apparently interpreted that one second as an invitation to follow her off the bus, drag her into a school playground, brutally rape and murder her.

Never look at strangers. Never take buses. Never leave the house. Of course there's always the chance you will be raped at home. Better get married so you'll have a man around to protect you.

Since Susan Brownmiller's landmark book on rape, *Against Our Will: Men, Women and Rape,* was published in 1975, women have recognized that fighting violence against women means more than avoiding dark alleys. Brownmiller dispelled the myth that women are better off if they submit to rapists. More women are taking self-defense classes and carrying guns. And they are fighting to change the system, through the courts, Congress and state legislatures.

Yet changing laws is only the first step in reforming the system. We 30 have to change attitudes. One attitude we have to change is the notion that when it comes to sex, "no" means "yes."

Men didn't make up the notion that "no" means "yes." Those parents who taught their daughters to be "good" fostered it. For generations, they raised girls to believe that only bad girls have sexual feelings. Consenting to sex or, heaven forbid, initiating it would be acknowledging "bad" feelings. What a way to mess with a normal adolescent's already fragile self-esteem.

For generations girls dealt with this dilemma by denying their sex drive. That was easy enough. Their boyfriends were willing to take all the necessary action, so the girls could feign resistance as a way of experimenting with sex without taking responsibility for it, without being bad girls.

Of course, once girls forfeited their integrity on the question of consent, it was difficult to get it back. Once boys got the word that "no" sometimes meant "yes," it was open season on resisting females.

Imagine a society in which when a woman says "no," a man stops. One man I spoke with suggested that in such a society there would be a lot less sex and a steep drop in the birth rate. I doubt it. I think that if men backed off from women who said no, more women would say yes.

It's hard to change 3,000 years of attitudes, but parents and teach- 35 ers, judges and lawmakers can help. We start by teaching little boys to respect the feelings—and words—of little girls. And what do we teach little girls?

I have two young daughters, and I want to protect them from harm just as my parents wanted to protect me. But the days are long gone when girls went directly from their father's house to their husband's.

I hope I can teach my daughters more than just how to avoid being alone with a man in an elevator. They will study karate as well as ballet. I want them to understand their own strength, the importance of knees and elbows, the power of a well-placed kick.

I want them to understand the difference between "no" and "yes." While I'll probably preach the virtue of "no," I hope I won't lead them to think that there is something wrong with them if they have sexual feelings.

I'll teach them that the justice system can be unjust. They should use the system, but not trust it, and work to reform it.

A woman was telling me about being raped many years ago. She was   *40*
young and naive, she said. He invited her to a party at his mother's fancy
apartment. When they got there she realized she was the party. The apartment was deserted. He showed her a gun and told her to do as he said.
She did.

She saw no point in calling the police. He was wealthy, she had gone
there on her own, he hadn't injured her. But she told the story to a friend,
a man, who was furious. He had some vague mob connections. He offered
to fix the guy for her. She declined.

"I figured somehow it was sort of my fault. I didn't think he deserved
to die."

Today, she says, she wishes she had told her friend to go ahead.
"What that man did to me was a crime."

Vigilante justice. It's not the best way, but sometimes it's the
only way.

The Responsive Reader

1. As Fisher writes, with charges of rape and sexual molestation, the
   case often comes down to the woman's word against the man's. Do
   you think it is true that in our society we are more likely to believe
   the man than the woman?
2. How does Fisher challenge entrenched attitudes? Do you think she
   is successful?
3. What historical background does Fisher provide for our current attitudes toward rape? How helpful or instructive is it? Does she shed
   new light for you on the psychological and cultural causes of rape
   and of society's treatment of rape? (What, for instance, are the problems with the concept of "consent"?)
4. What is Fisher's outlook or advice for the future? (Is she serious
   about her endorsement of vigilante justice at the end? Do you see
   her point?)

Talking, Listening, Writing

5. Have you personally observed or heard about abuse, molestation, or
   rape? How has what you saw or heard changed your thinking?
6. Do you think men's perspective on rape is basically different from
   women's? Why and how? Or why not?
7. Males today often feel on the defensive. Write a reply to Fisher's
   article from a male point of view or from the point of view of a
   woman trying to see the man's side.
8. Write an imaginary letter to a daughter or son on the issue of rape,
   sexual abuse, or sexual harassment.

Collaborative Projects

9. Collaborating with others, you may want to research widely publicized cases that have tested society's attitudes toward rape. Are attitudes changing? Are there new trends for the treatment of rape victims by law-enforcement officers and in court? You may want to look at cases of rape victims' charges believed or disbelieved by juries; you may want to examine reopenings of cases in which men were wrongfully convicted of rape.

ARE OPINIONS MALE?

Naomi Wolf

Naomi Wolf graduated from Yale, went to Oxford as a Rhodes scholar, and became a widely heeded new voice of feminism in the 90s. In her spectacularly successful The Beauty Myth: How Images of Beauty Are Used Against Women *(1990), she attacked "the icon of the anorexic fashion model" that drives out "most other images and stories of female heroines, role models, villains, eccentrics, buffoons, visionaries, sex goddesses, and pranksters." She marshaled a formidable array of statistics, insiders' testimony, and official reports in support of her charges against fashion magazines, the cosmetic surgery industry, the dieting industry, and other forces relentlessly promoting an ideal of female beauty that robs women of their sense of self-worth. As Gayle Greene said in a review of Wolf's book in* The Nation, *"The Beauty Myth not only sets women in competition with one another on a daily basis but sets younger women against older. . . . young people today are bombarded with more images of 'impossibly beautiful' women engaged in 'sexual posturing' than their grandmothers were in a lifetime." In her later book,* Fire With Fire: The New Female Power and How It Will Change the Twenty-First Century, *Wolf added her voice to those of writers who encourage women to move beyond "victim feminism," which leaves women with an "identity of powerlessness," to "power feminism," emphasizing positive action. In the following article, Wolf challenges the scarcity of women among the opinion makers who dominate the editorial pages and serious news programs.*

Thought Starters: What prominent women have shaped your opinions on social or political issues? When and where?

What is that vast silent wavelength out on the opinion superhighway? *1* It is the sound of women not talking.

Despite women's recent strides into public life, the national forums of debate—op-ed pages, political magazines, public affairs talk shows, newspaper columns—remain strikingly immune to the general agitation for female access. The agora of opinion is largely a men's club.

A simple count of the elite media bears out the charge. In 1992, the putative Year of the Woman, "Crossfire" presented fifty-five female guests, compared with 440 male guests. Of the print media, the most elite forums are the worst offenders: according to a survey conducted by Women, Men and Media, during a one-month period in 1992, 13 percent of the op-ed pieces published in *The Washington Post* were written by women; 16 percent of the articles on *The New York Times* op-ed page were by women. Over the course of the year, *The New Republic* averaged 14 percent female contributors; *Harper's,* less than 20 percent; *The Nation,* 23 percent; *The Atlantic Monthly,* 33 percent. *The National Interest* ran the remarkable ratio of eighty male bylines to one female. *The Washington Monthly* ran thirty-three women to 108 men; *National Review,* fifty-one female bylines to 505 male (and twelve of those female bylines belonged to one columnist, Florence King). Talk radio, an influential forum for airing populist grievances, counts fifty female hosts in its national association's roster that totals 900. Eric Alterman's book about opinion-makers, *Sound and Fury,* chronicles female pundits only in passing.

What is going on here? Is there an unconscious—or conscious—editorial bias against women's opinions? Or are opinions themselves somehow gendered male—does female socialization conspire against many women's ability or desire to generate a strong public voice?

The answer to the first question is an unhesitant yes: on the nuts- 5 and-bolts level of feminist analysis, women are being left out of the opinion mix because of passive but institutionalized discrimination on the part of editors and producers. General-interest magazines, newspapers and electronic forums tend to view public affairs as if they can be clothed exclusively in gray flannel suits, and rely on an insular Rolodex of white men.

In self-defense some male (and female) public opinion editors point to the allegedly "personal" way in which women tend to write about politics and express their public opinions. Women are accused of writing too much about their "feelings" and their "bodies"—as if such subjects were by nature ill-suited to respectable public discussion. And yes, this charge has some merit. But a double standard is at work here. Men, too, write about their feelings and bodies, but that discussion is perceived as being central and public. Though masculinists lay claim to passionless "objectivity," "logic" and "universality" as being the hallmarks of male debate, a glance shows how spurious is their position. What, after all, was the gays-in-the-military debate except a touchy-feely all-night boys-only slumber party, in which Dad—in the form of Sam Nunn—came downstairs to have a bull session with earnest youths lying on bunk beds? What were the snuggled-up military boys asked about but their feelings—feelings about being ogled, objectified, harassed; fears of seduction and even rape? Had it been young women interviewed in their dorm rooms about their fears of men, the whole exercise, cloaked in the sententious language of "national preparedness," would have been dismissed as a radical-feminist fiesta of victim-consciousness, encouraging oversensitive flowers to see sexual predators under every bed.

Indeed, the nationalism of German skinheads, the high melodrama of the World Cup and the recent convulsion of Japan-bashing—all of these are, on one level, complex sociopolitical developments; on another, they are a continuing global consciousness-raising session on vulnerability and self-esteem conducted primarily by men about men. One could read the Western canon itself as a record of men's deep feelings of alternating hope and self-doubt—whether it recounts Dick Diver destroying himself because his wife is wealthier than he, or King Lear raging on a heath at the humiliation of being stripped of his world.

So women and men often actually theorize about parallel experiences, but the author's maleness will elevate the language as being importantly public, while the author's femaleness stigmatizes it as being worthlessly private. Women writing about the stresses and failures of maternity, for instance, are deviating onto the literary mommy track, but when men write about the stresses and failures of paternity, they are analyzing "the plight of inner-city youths," "cultural breakdown" or "child abuse hysteria." A woman recounting her own experience of systematic oppression is writing a "confessional"; but when a man writes intensely personal, confessional prose—whether it is Rousseau in his *Confessions* or Bob Packwood in his diaries—he is engaged in pioneering enlightenment, or, even in William Safire's terms, acting as "a Pepysian diarist . . . [who] has kept voluminous notes on life as a lightning rod."

Of course, many women write about issues unmarked by gender, from city council elections to computer chips. But when women talk about politics, culture, science and the law in relation to female experience—i.e., rape statutes, fertility drugs, misogyny in film or abortion rights—they are perceived as talking about their feelings and bodies. Whereas when men talk about their feelings and bodies—i.e., free speech in relation to their interest in pornography, gun ownership in relation to their fear of criminal assault, the drive for prostate cancer research in relation to their fears of impotence, new sexual harassment guidelines in relation to their irritation at having their desire intercepted in the workplace—they are read as if they are talking about politics, culture, science and the law.

Thus, much of what passes for rational public debate is an exchange of subjective *male* impressions about *masculine* sensibilities and the *male* body—an exchange that appears "lucid" and "public" because men arrogate the qualities of transparency and generalization when discussing male emotions and the experiences of male flesh, but assign to women the qualities of opacity and particularity when they discuss their own. 10

The lack of media oxygen for women writers of opinion can strangle voice, putting them into an impossible double bind. Many women also write from a personal vantage point alone because they feel it is one realm over which they can claim authority. As Jodie Allen, an editor at *The Washington Post,* puts it, "When they sit down to write, they think, why should anyone listen to me? At least if I take it from the 'women's' point of view, they can't deny I'm a woman. It becomes a self-fulfilling prophecy." With the "public/male, private/female" split so schematized, many other women writers of opinion must assume "the female perspective," as if shouldering a heroic but cumbersome burden. They are forced, by the relative paucity of female pundits at the highest levels, to speak "for women" rather than simply hashing out the issues in a solitary way.

This extreme is represented sometimes by an Anna Quindlen, whose "maternal punditry" beats a lonely drum on the guy terrain of the *Times* op-ed page. The meager allocation of space for female pundits at the highest levels, what Quindlen calls "a quota of one," does indeed force the few visible women writers of opinion who take a feminist stance into becoming stoic producers of that viewpoint, counted upon to generate a splash of sass and color, a provocative readerly-writerly tussle, in the gray expanses of male perspectives and prose. Editors seem to treat these few female pundits as cans in six-packs marked, for instance, "Lyrical African American Women Novelists"; "Spunky White Female Columnists with Kids"; or, perhaps, the reliable category, "Feminists (Knee-Jerk to Loony)." As Quindlen once remarked, a newspaper editor explained that he could not syndicate her column because "we already run Ellen Goodman." Popular discourse treats such writers as sound bite producers when it needs someone to say "multiculturalism is good" or "rape is bad."

So the few "pundits of identity" achieve, in the minds of those who decide what ideas inhabit the op-ed pages and who should argue with whom about what, a hard-won commerce in the perspectives inflected by gender, or by gender and race. But few can hope to take for granted the sweet oxygen that any writer needs in order to flourish: space to speak for no one but oneself.

The other extreme of the female public voice is perhaps represented by a Jeane Kirkpatrick: a voice so Olympian, so neck-up and uninflected by the experiences of the female body, that the subtle message received by young female writers is: to enter public voice, one must abide by the no-uterus rule. This voice gives a publication the benefit of a woman's name on the title page, without the mess and disruption of women's issues entering that precious space. This is the message absorbed by the legions of young women I meet. Though many writers are avidly trying to seek it out, we still lack the space and encouragement to range from the personal to the political, from identity to universality, with the ease and unselfconsciousness assumed by men.

So women are left out, or included under conditions of constraint. But do we leave ourselves out of the public forum as well? When I have asked editors at *The New Republic, The Washington Post, Harper's* and *The New York Times* op-ed page about the gender imbalance in their forums, this is the overwhelming message. Women simply do not submit articles in the same numbers that men do. And this is accurate: during one randomly selected month at TNR (February 1992), eight women submitted unsolicited manuscripts, versus fifteen men; during another month (October 1993), the ratio was eight women to fifty-five men. According to Toby

Harshaw, staff member of *The New York Times* op-ed page, in the morning mail of November 8, of about 150 unsolicited manuscripts, the ratio of men to women was 10-to-1.

Why is this? Some editors argue that one reason for the imbalance is that women have not yet reached the highest echelons of public life: "Our biggest groups that submit are think tanks, lawyers, universities and government officials," says Harshaw. And the overwhelming majority of pieces from these groups, he notes, are by men. Yet while that argument has some validity, it cannot account for the extent of the imbalance: at the middle ranks of the law and the academy, women are reaching parity with men. What makes many women reluctant to write and submit opinion journalism, compared with men?

There is, I think, a set of deeply conditioned, internal inhibitions that work in concert with the manifest external discrimination to keep fewer women willing to submit opinion pieces, and to slug it out in public arenas. The problem is not, of course, that women can't write. They write, one can argue, with more facility than men do: women have dominated the novel—at least in its popular form—since its birth; and, if anything, social enculturation encourages girls to be more literary than most boys. No, the problem is that the traits required by writing opinion journalism or appearing on adversarial public affairs shows are often in conflict with what are deemed "appropriate" female speech patterns and behavior.

Dr. Deborah Tannen, the Georgetown University linguist, asserted that women and men often speak in different ways—women seek intimacy and consensus, she claims, while men seek status and independence. She notes that boys are raised to see boy-to-boy conflict as a way to express bonding, while girls are raised to avoid conflict in their play and enforce consensus. Psychologists Jean Baker Miller and Carol Gilligan suggest that women are more "relational" and men more "autonomous."

I don't agree with Miller or Gilligan that these tendencies are due to any primal psychic development; but women are surely encouraged to show such traits by virtue of social conditioning. And the act of writing an opinion piece—or appearing on "Crossfire"—calls for skills that are autonomous, contrarian and independent (not to say bloody-minded). Writing opinion journalism is a cranky, self-satisfied and, in traditionally feminine terms, extremely rude way to behave in public. The momentum to thrash out an opinion piece often begins with the conviction that others are wrong and that oneself is right, or that others are not saying the one thing that must be said. One is not *listening;* one is not set on enhancing others' well-being; one is certainly not demonstrating a "fusion of identity and intimacy," which pursuit Gilligan claims motivates women.

Unfortunately, you can't write strong, assertive prose if you are too   *20* anxious about preserving consensus; you can't have a vigorous debate if you are paralyzed with concern about wounding the sensitivities of your opposite number. Writing a bold declarative sentence that claims that the world is this way and not that, or that President Clinton should do X and is a fool to do Y, demands the assumption of a solitary, even arrogant, stance. In Gilliganesque "different voice" terms, it is lonely and emotionally unrewarding; it is, according to such theories, almost by definition an engagement in "masculine" values and patterns of speech.

Without a countervailing encouragement into speech, the social pressure on women to exhibit "connection" and suppress "autonomy" can inhibit many women's public assertiveness. Tannen describes English Professor Thomas Fox's observations of male and female freshman students' different approaches to writing analytical papers. He looked at a Ms. M. and a Mr. H. "In her speaking as well as her writing [to be read by the class]," Tannen reports, "Ms. M. held back what she knew, appearing uninformed and uninterested, because she feared offending her classmates. Mr. H. spoke with authority and apparent confidence because he was eager to persuade his peers. She did not worry about persuading; he did not worry about offending." But in Ms. M.'s papers that were to be read only by the professor—her "private" writing—Ms. M. was clear, forceful and direct. In this anecdote we see, essentially, that of the two, Mr. H., at 17, is being socialized to write opinion journalism and shout down interruptions on "The McLaughlin Group"; whereas Ms. M. is being socialized to write celebrity puff pieces in *Entertainment Weekly*.

Many women are raised to care—or to feel guilty if they don't care— about wounding the feelings of others. And yet, to write most purely out of herself, a writer must somehow kill off the inhibiting influence of the need for "connection." The woman writer of opinion must delve into what early feminists called "the solitude of self." When Camille Paglia claims that women have not produced great artists for the same reasons that they have not produced a Jack the Ripper, she touches, perhaps inadvertently, upon a real creative problem for women: fidelity to nothing but one's own voice can in fact depend upon a kind of radical solipsism, an ecstatic, highly unfeminine disregard for the importance of others if their well-being obtrudes upon the emergence of that transcendent vision.

Virginia Woolf returned often in her diaries to this theme, to the need to be impervious both to criticism and approval: "I look upon disregard or abuse as part of my bargain," Woolf wrote. "I'm to write what I like and they're to say what they like." Woolf's opinion of unsuccessful women's novels says volumes about the social disincentives many women face in writing damn-the-torpedoes opinion pieces: "It was the flaw in the center that had rotted them. [The novelist] had altered her values in deference to the opinions of others." And yet the world conspires against us, and within us, to have us do just that.

This internal dilemma is compounded by an external convention: even for the many women who are willing and eager to express strong opinions, conventions about how women are permitted to speak in print or on T.V. hem them in. The authoritative female voice asserting judgments about the real world is an unseemly voice. The globalizing tone that the conventions of opinion journalism or T.V. debate require involves an assumption of authority that women are actively dissuaded from claiming. A female writer of opinion at the *Post* concurs: "Op-ed language is the language of a certain level of abstraction; this is a language more often used by more men because more men are expert at it—you have to learn that language." As Professor Rhonda Garelick, who teaches French literary theory at the University of Colorado, put it to me, "It is just now becoming true for me that I can make 'sweeping' statements. But even as I make them, I am aware that it is an unusual verbal structure for me because I'm a woman. And I am always pleasurably surprised when they are accepted. The effect is good, but it is certainly something I am trained not to do by a lifetime of being a woman. I always opted for carefulness, precision, detail in what I said or wrote—but to take that leap [and write]: I must mean this large thing—that is disconcerting. And that's what opinion journalism is."

Since the authoritative voice can be so disconcerting for many   25
women to use, women writers often have turned to fiction to give safe cover to their longing to express their political points of view: *Jane Eyre* conceals a passionate outburst about feminism: *Uncle Tom's Cabin* sugarcoats an anti-slavery polemic. As Emily Dickinson warned, "Tell all the truth but tell it slant." A prominent feminist muckraker keeps on her refrigerator the motto, "Tell the truth and run."

We know as women that the act of "taking a position" in a sweeping way—"standing one's ground" above one's own byline, asserting one's view about the world of fact rather than fantasy—is a dangerous one, an act that will be met with punishment. When I have interviewed college women about their fears of leadership and public voice, they often use metaphors of punitive violence when describing their anxiety about expressing opinions in public: "having it blow up in my face"; "I'll be torn apart"; "ripped to shreds"; "they'll shoot me down."

Punishment—is that not too strong a word? This is the end of the twentieth century, after all; women no longer need to write under pseudonyms to conceal the force of their opinions. Yet when we look at what happens when women "take a stand," the common female fear of punishment for expressing an opinion suggests no phantom anxiety. A woman who enters public debate is indeed likely to be punished. A complex set of rules ensures it. Some involve ad feminam attacks: the absurd attacks on Chelsea Clinton's appearance that flitted across the public stage in the last year or so were in fact attacks on her mother, a message to all women contemplating entering public life that their children can be held hostage in retribution.

Others involve chivalry: when a woman tries to argue with men—as Rodham Clinton did in presenting her views on health care—the debate can be neatly sidestepped by labeling her "charming" and "disarming." These terms ensure that she cannot be seen to fight and win by virtue of her wits, for her potential adversaries preemptively "disarm" themselves— yield their weapons—and let themselves be "charmed"—go into a trance of delight that, presumably, mere reason cannot penetrate. Rodham Clinton's experience eerily re-evokes the debate-evasive reaction that Virginia Woolf anticipated after she finished the immensely (if elegantly) confrontational essay that became *A Room of One's Own:* "I forecast, then, that I shall get no criticism, except of the evasive, jocular kind . . . that the press will be kind and talk of its charm and sprightliness; Also I shall be attacked for a feminist and hinted at for a Sapphist. . . . I am afraid it will not be taken seriously."

Still others involve stigmatizing the woman's anger: if the female antagonist is less than universally admired (or doesn't happen to be married to the president), she is called "shrill," as Geraldine Ferraro was when she debated George Bush ("rhymes with rich"). Female radio personalities have told me that when they ask male guests tough questions, their listeners call in and tell them to stop being rude to the men. It was front-page news when, in a speech, President Clinton lost his temper at the press—something that a cool-headed leader is rightly expected not to do; but it was front-page news when his wife directed anger at the insurance industry—something that a leader in her position should do, if she is to serve her constituency well.

I do not believe that the "different voice" concerns lie deep in women; 30 granted permission to do so without punishment, as many women as men would write blustery, cantankerous prose and flock to the delights of public argument. Women do not lack the desire or ability to fight hard or write fiercely; we lack a behavioral paradigm that makes doing so acceptable.

When a woman does engage in public debate, she is often torn in two. She may be anguished by her own sense that her strong voice is in a state of conflict with her longing for approval and her discomfort with conflict. I feel this role conflict often myself: in a recent book, I argued hard with a certain writer's ideas; when I subsequently met her and liked her, I wanted to beg forgiveness—even though my views of her work had not changed. I feel a kind of terror when I am critical in public and experience a kind of nausea when I am attacked. The knowledge that another person and I publicly disagree makes me feel that I have left something unresolved, raw in the world; even if I "win"—especially if I win—I also lose, because I am guilty, in traditionally feminine terms, of a failure to create harmony and consensus; this bruise to identity manifests at the level of my sense of femininity.

Now I know that this anxiety is unhelpful, even retrograde; and it is directly at odds with my even stronger wish to enjoy the fray without this grief. But there it is. And if I, with my strong feminist upbringing, feel this sense of two drives in a state of absolute conflict when I enter public debate, I doubt that I can be alone. If a woman thinks of herself as someone who is warm and kind in private life, how can she also be a critic in public life, an agonist? This sense of role conflict can feel to many as if it is built in to women's participation in public life.

Women also lack any paradigm for expressing dissent with other women in a way that is perceived as a sign of respect. Men have rituals for expressing conflict as a form of honor, even of friendship; British male parliamentarians are famous for braying at one another and then joking over the urinal. But women lack any such social patterns. If a woman engages in hard debate with another woman, she is a "spoiler" or a "mud-slinger," as Liz Holtzman was accused of being when she attacked Ferraro in the 1992 Senate race; the fact that Senator Nancy Kassebaum *disagreed* with Senator Patty Murray about what to do with the Packwood investigation made news. Woman-to-woman argument is seen, even by women, as a breakdown of precious consensus, or a cat-fight, or a "betrayal of sisterhood"—a situation that can force women in public to suppress their legitimate differences of opinion; whereas man-to-man argument is understood as being the stuff of democracy.

Why is all this "subjective," "emotional" stuff a fit subject for the pages of a policy journal? Because the psychic disincentives for women to argue in public, or to write strong opinionated journalism, have profound implications for the health of democracy. Woolf wrote, "The effect of discouragement upon the mind of the artist should be measured." These psychological and social barriers to women's opinionated public speech make it literally not worth it, in many women's minds, to run for office, contradict an adversary or take a controversial public stance. If many women feel ridicule and hostility more acutely than men do, if they are uncomfortable with isolation, then ridicule, hostility and the threat of isolation can be—and are—standard weapons in the arsenal used to scare women away from public life.

In essence, certain kinds of forceful speech and interchange are de- *35* fined as male and prohibited to women, as a subtle but immensely effective means to maintain the world of opinion and policy-making as an all-male preserve. And then, in a vicious circle, many women pre-emptively internalize the barriers, which keeps them wary of storming their way into the marketplace of opinions.

The response to this state of affairs has to be a complex one. To begin with, editors and producers must root out their own often unwitting bias. They are welching on their commitment to inform citizens of a real range of views, leaving half the population ill-prepared to pursue their interests within the democratic process. They are also shortchanging us as a nation, for their unacknowledged warp in perspective leaves "women's issues" and female talking heads, no matter how pressing the topic nor how perspicacious the voices, to languish in the journalistic harem of women's magazines, crowded in among celebrity pets and the latest news on the French manicure. Because of this omission of "women's perspectives" and hard facts about women, we endure wildly off-the-mark debate and create faulty policy in a vacuum of information.

Further gender polarization is not the answer. Just as we are learning to integrate "male" and "female" perspectives about sexual harassment as we seek a newer, fairer social contract in the workplace, we must integrate "male" and "female" views and patterns of expression as we renegotiate the contract about what it is appropriate to say, and how it is appropriate to say it, in the forums of opinion.

The last solution to this dilemma, for all of us who are women still ambivalent about waging opinion, is internal: the only way forward is through. We must realize that public debate may starve the receptors for love and approval, but that it stimulates the synapses of self-respect. Let us shed the lingering sense that authority is something that others—male others—bestow upon us; whenever we are inclined to mumble invective into our coffee, let us flood the airwaves instead. Let's steal a right that has heretofore been defined as masculine: the right to be in love with the sound of one's own voice.

The Responsive Reader

1. What evidence does Wolf marshal that women are largely excluded from the "agora" or marketplace of public opinion? Which of her statistics are most striking or convincing?

2. How does she answer the charge that women's writing tends to be too personal and emotional, whereas men's writing stresses objectivity and logic?

3. What, according to Wolf, is wrong with both extremes of female punditry—the "female perspective" and the "no-uterus rule"?

4. Wolf often focuses on how women, and especially young women, internalize the subliminal signals sent them by our culture. What evidence does she give that women are reluctant to enter into the arena of public opinion?

5. What are key points in Wolf's contrast of the adversarial, assertive male style and a feminine rhetoric of consensus? What evidence or examples does she give for each? (What is "solipsism," and why does she call it "highly unfeminine"?)

6. Have you observed women being criticized or marginalized for being too active in the forum of public opinion?

Talking, Listening, Writing

7. Do you think it is true that "many women feel ridicule and hostility more acutely than men do"? Does the traditional "paradigm," or model, of female behavior hold women back in politics?

8. Does your local newspaper fit the pattern of female exclusion that Wolf describes? Are women largely confined to discussion of "women's issues"? What is their role or what are their assignments?

9. Do you think women should concentrate more on developing bonds of solidarity and sisterhood or on developing their own individual voices, feeling free to disagree with other women?

Collaborative Projects

10. Working with other students, you may want to establish an informal assertiveness index to measure how often and how vigorously female students at your school participate in class discussion compared with male students.

THE COMMUNITY OF MEN
Robert Bly

> *Robert Bly is an award-winning poet, storyteller, showman, translator, and guru who lives on a lake in Minnesota. He grew up as his mother's favorite and as the son of a kindly but distant alcoholic father. He has traveled around the country doing sold-out poetry readings that bring back the days when poetry, interwoven with song and story, was a communal experience that helped shape people's view of themselves and of the world. He became a leader of the men's movement with his book* Iron John *(1990), which looked in myth and popular tradition for heroic archetypal figures who could serve as inspiration and role models for the disoriented modern male. He explored rites of initiation that would bring young males closer to their natural and instinctual roots and turn the overmothered boy into a man. One reviewer of* Iron John: A Book about Men *said, "No poet in the United States in recent years has commanded so much attention. As a popularizer of archetypal psychology Bly has found a growing audience through public readings and lectures and more recently through a Bill Moyers television program which highlighted the wilderness 'gatherings' of men who have engaged with Bly on a ritualized variant of the 'talking cure'" (Stephen Kuusiso).*

Thought Starters: If you were to nominate a living contemporary as a role model for young boys, who would it be? How would you justify your choice?

We are living at an important and fruitful moment now, for it is clear   1
to men that the images of adult manhood given by the popular culture are worn out; a man can no longer depend on them. By the time a man is thirty-five he knows that the images of the right man, the tough man, the true man which he received in high school do not work in life. Such a man is open to new visions of what a man is or could be.

The hearth and fairy stories have passed, as water through fifty feet of soil, through generations of men and women, and we can trust their images more than, say, those invented by Hans Christian Andersen. The images the old stories give—stealing the key from under the mother's pillow, picking up a golden feather fallen from the burning breast of the Firebird, finding the Wild Man under the lake water, following the tracks of one's own wound through the forest and finding that it resembles the tracks of a god—these are meant to be taken slowly into the body. They continue to unfold, once taken in.

It is in the old myths that we hear, for example, of Zeus energy, that positive leadership energy in men, which popular culture constantly declares does not exist; from King Arthur we learn the value of the male mentor in the lives of young men; we hear from the Iron John story the importance of moving from the mother's realm to the father's realm; and from all initiation stories we learn how essential it is to leave our parental expectations entirely and find a second father or "second King."

The dark side of men is clear. Their mad exploitation of earth resources, devaluation and humiliation of women, and obsession with tribal warfare are undeniable. Genetic inheritance contributes to their obsessions, but also culture and environment. We have defective mythologies that ignore masculine depth of feeling, assign men a place in the sky instead of earth, teach obedience to the wrong powers, work to keep men boys, and entangle both men and women in systems of industrial domination that exclude both matriarchy and patriarchy.

Most of the language in my book speaks to heterosexual men but does not exclude homosexual men. It wasn't until the eighteenth century that people ever used the term homosexual; before that time gay men were understood simply as a part of the large community of men. The mythology as I see it does not make a big distinction between homosexual and heterosexual men.

We talk a great deal about "the American man," as if there were some constant quality that remained stable over decades, or even within a single decade.

The men who live today have veered far away from the Saturnian, old-man-minded farmer, proud of his introversion, who arrived in New England in 1630, willing to sit through three services in an unheated church. In the South, an expansive, motherbound cavalier developed, and neither of these two "American men" resembled the greedy railroad entrepreneur that later developed in the Northeast, nor the reckless I-will-do-without culture settlers of the West.

Even in our own era the agreed-on model has changed dramatically. During the fifties, for example, an American character appeared with some consistency that became a model of manhood adopted by many men: the Fifties male.

He got to work early, labored responsibly, supported his wife and children, and admired discipline. Reagan is a sort of mummified version of this dogged type. This sort of man didn't see women's souls well, but he appreciated their bodies; and his view of culture and America's part in it was boyish and optimistic. Many of his qualities were strong and positive, but underneath the charm and bluff there was, and there remains, much isolation, deprivation, and passivity. Unless he has an enemy, he isn't sure that he is alive.

The Fifties man was supposed to like football, be aggressive, stick up   *10*
for the United States, never cry, and always provide. But receptive space or
intimate space was missing in this image of a man. The personality lacked
some sense of flow. The psyche lacked compassion in a way that encouraged the unbalanced pursuit of the Vietnam war, just as, later, the lack of
what we might call "garden" space inside Reagan's head led to his callous-
ness and brutality toward the powerless in El Salvador, toward old people
here, the unemployed, schoolchildren, and poor people in general.

The Fifties male had a clear vision of what a man was, and what male
responsibilities were, but the isolation and one-sidedness of his vision were
dangerous.

During the sixties, another sort of man appeared. The waste and
violence of the Vietnam war made men question whether they knew what
an adult male really was. If manhood meant Vietnam, did they want any
part of it? Meanwhile, the feminist movement encouraged men to actually
look at women, forcing them to become conscious of concerns and suffer-
ings that the Fifties male labored to avoid. As men began to examine
women's history and women's sensibility, some men began to notice what
was called their *feminine* side and pay attention to it. This process continues
to this day, and I would say that most contemporary men are involved in
it in some way.

There's something wonderful about this development—I mean the
practice of men welcoming their own "feminine" consciousness and nurturing it—this is important—and yet I have the sense that there is something
wrong. The male in the past twenty years has become more thoughtful,
more gentle. But by this process he has not become more free. He's a nice
boy who pleases not only his mother but also the young woman he is
living with.

In the seventies I began to see all over the country a phenomenon
that we might call the "soft male." Sometimes even today when I look out
at an audience, perhaps half the young males are what I'd call soft. They're
lovely, valuable people—I like them—they're not interested in harming
the earth or starting wars. There's a gentle attitude toward life in their
whole being and style of living.

But many of these men are not happy. You quickly notice the lack   *15*
of energy in them. They are life-preserving but not exactly life-giving.
Ironically, you often see these men with strong women who positively
radiate energy.

Here we have a finely tuned young man, ecologically superior to his
father, sympathetic to the whole harmony of the universe, yet he himself
has little vitality to offer.

The strong or life-giving women who graduated from the sixties, so
to speak, or who have inherited an older spirit, played an important part
in producing this life-preserving, but not life-giving, man.

I remember a bumper sticker during the sixties that read "WOMEN SAY YES TO MEN WHO SAY NO." We recognize that it took a lot of courage to resist the draft, go to jail, or move to Canada, just as it took courage to accept the draft and go to Vietnam. But the women of twenty years ago were definitely saying that they preferred the softer receptive male.

So the development of men was affected a little in this preference. Nonreceptive maleness was equated with violence, and receptive maleness was rewarded.

Some energetic women, at that time and now in the nineties, chose   20 and still choose soft men to be their lovers and, in a way, perhaps, to be their sons. The new distribution of "yang" energy among couples didn't happen by accident. Young men for various reasons wanted their harder women, and women began to desire softer men. It seemed like a nice arrangement for a while, but we've lived with it long enough now to see that it isn't working out.

I first learned about the anguish of "soft" men when they told their stories in early men's gatherings. In 1980, the Lama Community in New Mexico asked me to teach a conference for men only, their first, in which about forty men participated. Each day we concentrated on one Greek god and one old story, and then late in the afternoons we gathered to talk. When the younger men spoke it was not uncommon for them to be weeping within five minutes. The amount of grief and anguish in these younger men was astounding to me.

Part of their grief rose out of remoteness from their fathers, which they felt keenly, but partly, too, grief flowed from trouble in their marriages or relationships. They had learned to be receptive, but receptivity wasn't enough to carry their marriages through troubled times. In every relationship something *fierce* is needed once in a while: both the man and the woman need to have it. But at the point when it was needed, often the young man came up short. He was nurturing, but something else was required—for his relationship, and for his life.

The "soft" male was able to say, "I can feel your pain, and I consider your life as important as mine, and I will take care of you and comfort you." But he could not say what he wanted, and stick by it. *Resolve* of that kind was a different matter.

In *The Odyssey*, Hermes instructs Odysseus that when he approaches Circe, who stands for a certain kind of matriarchal energy, he is to lift or show his sword. In these early sessions it was difficult for many of the younger men to distinguish between showing the sword and hurting someone. One man, a kind of incarnation of certain spiritual attitudes of the sixties, a man who had actually lived in a tree for a year outside Santa Cruz, found himself unable to extend his arm when it held a sword. He had learned so well not to hurt anyone that he couldn't lift the steel, even to catch the light of the sun on it. But showing a sword doesn't necessarily mean fighting. It can also suggest a joyful decisiveness.

The journey many American men have taken into softness, or recep-   25
tivity, or "development of the feminine side," has been an immensely
valuable journey, but more travel lies ahead.

The Responsive Reader

1. In recent years, males have come in for much negative criticism.
   How does Bly in his opening paragraphs acknowledge "the dark
   side of men"?
2. What are some models for the true American that Bly finds in the
   nation's early history? Do you recognize these early models of the
   typical American? (What is the meaning of *Saturnian* and *cavalier*?)
3. Do you recognize the fifties male as described by Bly? What are his
   key features? What are his strengths? What are his weaknesses?
4. Do you recognize the sixties male? What are his key qualities? What
   about the sixties male appeals to Bly? What does Bly think is
   lacking?
5. What is Bly's own vision of the ideal male? Do you recognize the
   mythical or literary precedents on which he draws?

Talking, Listening, Writing

6. Is the fifties man extinct? Do you identify with or feel attracted to
   the sixties man?
7. Are critics right who charge that Bly is merely in his own way
   rehabilitating the traditional patriarchal male?
8. Do you agree that our popular culture denies the existence of "positive leadership energy"? Is it true that we tend to debunk our
   leaders—cutting them down to size?
9. What would you include in your own portrait of the ideal male?

Collaborative Projects

10. Have images of American womanhood undergone a similar trans-
    formation as the images of manhood identified by Bly? Working
    with a group, you may want to prepare composite portraits of fifties
    woman, sixties woman, nineties woman.

THEIR DILEMMA AND MINE

Barbara Ehrenreich

Barbara Ehrenreich is an outspoken feminist who became one of the most effective voices of the women's movement. Counteracting the stereotype of feminism as a movement of upper-middle-class women with the money and leisure to attend conferences, she has called for a "next wave" of feminism concentrating on the rights and needs of working-class women still largely trapped in low-paid, low-regarded occupations. The articles in her collection The Worst Years of Our Lives *(1990) chronicled a "decade of greed," when worship of the bottom line began to supersede all considerations of human solidarity, community spirit, or "Judeo-Christian ethics." In a more recent collection,* The Snarling Citizen, *she probes such trends as the mindless worship of celebrity, the brutality of much American entertainment, and the confusion of physical fitness with virtue. Ehrenreich's voice has been heard in publications including* Ms., Mother Jones, *the* New York Times, *the* New Republic, *the* Nation, *and the* Atlantic Monthly. *In the following article, Ehrenreich castigates the arrogance of male-dominated legislatures in ruling on matters of paramount importance to women's lives and the lives of their children.*

Thought Starters: Are you tired of hearing arguments pro and con about abortion? Or has it been a live issue in your own life or in the lives of family and friends?

Quite apart from blowing up clinics and terrorizing patients, the   1
antiabortion movement can take credit for a more subtle and lasting kind of damage: it has succeeded in getting even prochoice people to think of abortion as a "moral dilemma," an "agonizing decision," and related code phrases for something murky and compromising, like the traffic in infant formula mix. In liberal circles, it has become unstylish to discuss abortion without using words like "complex," "painful," and the rest of the mealymouthed vocabulary of evasion. Regrets are also fashionable, and one otherwise feminist author writes recently of mourning, each year following her abortion, the putative birthday of her discarded fetus.

I cannot speak for other women, of course, but the one regret I have about my own abortions is that they cost money that might otherwise have been spent on something more pleasurable, like taking the kids to movies and theme parks. Yes, that is abortions, plural (two in my case)—a possibility that is not confined to the promiscuous, the disorderly, or the ignorant. In fact, my credentials for dealing with the technology of contraception are first rate: I have a Ph.D. in biology that is now a bit obsolescent but still good for conjuring up vivid mental pictures of zygotes and ova, and I was actually paid, at one point in my life, to teach other women about the mysteries of reproductive biology.

Yet, as every party to the abortion debate should know, those methods of contraception that are truly safe are not absolutely reliable no matter how reliably they are used. Many women, like myself, have felt free to choose the safest methods because legal abortion is available as a backup to contraception. Anyone who finds that a thoughtless, immoral choice should speak to the orphans of women whose wombs were perforated by Dalkon shields or whose strokes were brought on by high-estrogen birth-control pills.

I refer you to the orphans only because it no longer seems to be good form to mention women themselves in discussions of abortion. In most of the antiabortion literature I have seen, women are so invisible that an uninformed reader might conclude that fetuses reside in artificially warmed tissue culture flasks or similar containers. It must be enormously difficult for the antiabortionist to face up to the fact that real fetuses can only survive inside women, who, unlike any kind of laboratory apparatus, have thoughts, feelings, aspirations, responsibilities, and, very often, checkbooks. Anyone who thinks for a moment about women's role in reproductive biology could never blithely recommend "adoption, not abortion," because women have to go through something unknown to fetuses or men, and that is pregnancy.

From the point of view of a fetus, pregnancy is no doubt a good 5 deal. But consider it for a moment from the point of view of the pregnant person (if "woman" is too incendiary and feminist a term) and without reference to its potential issue. We are talking about a nine-month bout of symptoms of varying severity, often including nausea, skin discolorations, extreme bloating and swelling, insomnia, narcolepsy, hair loss, varicose veins, hemorrhoids, indigestion, and irreversible weight gain, and culminating in a physiological crisis which is occasionally fatal and almost always excruciatingly painful. If men were equally at risk for this condition—if they knew that their bellies might swell as if they were suffering from end-stage cirrhosis, that they would have to go for nearly a year without a stiff drink, a cigarette, or even an aspirin, that they would be subject to fainting spells and unable to fight their way onto commuter trains—then I am sure that pregnancy would be classified as a sexually transmitted disease and abortions would be no more controversial than emergency appendectomies.

Adding babies to the picture does not make it all that much prettier, even if you are, as I am, a fool for short, dimpled people with drool on their chins. For no matter how charming the outcome of a pregnancy that is allowed to go to term, no one is likely to come forth and offer to finance its Pampers or pay its college tuition. Nor are the opponents of abortion promising a guaranteed annual income, subsidized housing, national health insurance, and other measures that might take some of the terror out of parenthood. We all seem to expect the individual parents to shoulder the entire burden of supporting any offspring that can be traced to them, and, in the all-too-common event that the father cannot be identified or has skipped town to avoid child-support payments, "parent" means mother.

When society does step in to help out a poor woman attempting to raise children on her own, all that it customarily has to offer is some government-surplus cheese, a monthly allowance so small it would barely keep an adult male in running shoes, and the contemptuous epithet "welfare cheat." It would be far more reasonable to honor the survivors of pregnancy and childbirth with at least the same respect and special benefits that we give, without a second thought, to veterans of foreign wars.

But, you will object, I have greatly exaggerated the discomforts of pregnancy and the hazards of childbearing, which many women undergo quite cheerfully. This is true, at least to an extent. In my own case, the case of my planned and wanted pregnancies, I managed to interpret morning sickness as a sign of fetal tenacity and to find, in the hypertrophy of my belly, a voluptuousness ordinarily unknown to the skinny. But this only proves my point: a society that is able to make a good thing out of pregnancy is certainly free to choose how to regard abortion. We can treat it as a necessary adjunct to contraception, or as a vexing moral dilemma, or as a form of homicide—and whichever we choose, that is how we will tend to experience it.

So I will admit that I might not have been so calm and determined about my abortions if I had had to cross a picket line of earnest people yelling "baby-killer," or if I felt that I might be blown to bits in the middle of a vacuum aspiration. Conversely, though, we would be hearing a lot less about ambivalence and regrets if there were not so much liberal head-scratching going on. Abortions will surely continue, as they have through human history, whether we approve or disapprove or hem and haw. The question that worries me is: How is, say, a sixteen-year-old girl going to feel after an abortion? Like a convicted sex offender, a murderess on parole? Or like a young woman who is capable, as the guidance counselors say, of taking charge of her life?

This is our choice, for biology will never have an answer to that 10 strange and cabalistic question of when a fetus becomes a person. Potential persons are lost every day as a result of miscarriage, contraception, or someone's simple failure to respond to a friendly wink. What we can answer, with a minimum of throat clearing and moral agonizing, is the question of when women themselves will finally achieve full personhood: and that is when we have the right, unquestioned and unabrogated, to *choose* not to be pregnant when we decide not to be pregnant.

The Responsive Reader

1. Ehrenreich does not start her article by attacking antiabortionists gunning down receptionists or doctors and their unarmed bodyguards. Instead she takes issue with her "mealy-mouthed" fellow feminists and fellow liberals. What is her quarrel with them?
2. A key point in Ehrenreich's argument is that, while male politicians can exploit abortion as a wedge issue for stump speeches, for women like her it is a lived experience. What do you learn about her own firsthand experience with abortion, and how does she use that experience to support her arguments?
3. Is Ehrenreich right in claiming that women are practically "invisible" in antiabortion arguments? Do we care more about fetuses than people?
4. What does Ehrenreich do to emphasize the ironic contrast between the crusade to save the unborn and society's callous disregard for the millions of children already born but growing up in poverty, ignorance, and squalor?
5. "Pro-choice" and "pro-life" have become buzzwords in the ongoing controversy. For you, does Ehrenreich succeed in giving new meaning or urgency to the term *choice*?

Talking, Listening, Writing

6. In an interview, a leader of the pro-choice movement was quizzed about whether pro-choice advocates had anything in their arsenal to counter the pictures of aborted fetuses waved by antiabortion activists. Do you think Ehrenreich presents arguments that for her readers might have a similar emotional impact?

Collaborative Projects

7. In many American cities, the spectacle of citizen volunteers hustling a pregnant woman into an abortion clinic through a gauntlet of antiabortionists has become a familiar sight. After a spate of antiabortion killings, burnings, and bombings, some communities enacted ordinances to restrict the right of protesters to obstruct access and terrorize fellow citizens. A 1997 Supreme Court decision, however, seemed to come down on the side of the harassers in the name of free speech. Working with a group, you may want to investigate the current legal situation in your community or on the larger national scale.

AMERICA'S EMERGING GAY CULTURE

Randall E. Majors

> *Lesbians and gays are emerging from a long history during which they were forced to deny their identity. The struggle for recognition of gay rights continues in the military, in the Boy Scouts, and in campaigns to have gay rights ordinances enacted in communities and states. What kind of advocacy, what kind of political action, will further the cause of full acceptance of lesbians and gays in American society? Randall E. Majors, who teaches at California State University at Hayward, wrote the following article for a collection of readings on intercultural communication. He sees in the current movement toward a new sense of identity and solidarity in the gay community an affirmation of the "American vision of individual freedom and opportunity." How, according to this article, are gays "solidifying a unique sense of identity"?*

Thought Starters: What recent readings, movies, or television programs have influenced your perspective on the gay lifestyle or the gay community?

A gay culture, unique in the history of homosexuality, is emerging in   *1*
America. Gay people from all walks of life are forging new self-identity concepts, discovering new political and social power, and building a revolutionary new life style. As more people "come out," identify themselves as gay, and join with others to work and live as openly gay people, a stronger culture takes shape with each passing year.

There have always been homosexual men and women, but never before has there emerged the notion of a distinct "culture" based on being gay. A useful way to analyze this emerging gay culture is to observe the communication elements by which gay people construct their life styles and social institutions. Lesbians and gay men, hereafter considered together as gay people, are creating a new community in the midst of the American melting pot. They are building social organizations, exercising political power, and solidifying a unique sense of identity—often under repressive and sometimes dangerous conditions. The following essay is an analysis of four major communication elements of the American gay culture: the gay neighborhood, gay social groups, gay symbols, and gay meeting behavior. These communication behaviors will demonstrate the vibrancy and joy that a new culture offers the American vision of individual freedom and opportunity.

The Gay Neighborhood

Most cultural groups find the need to mark out a home turf. American social history has many examples of ethnic and social groups who create their own special communities, whether by withdrawing from the larger culture or by forming specialized groups within it. The utopian communities of the Amish or Shakers are examples of the first, and ghetto neighborhoods in large urban areas are examples of the latter.

This need to create a group territory fulfills several purposes for gay people. First, a gay person's sense of identity is reinforced if there is a special place that is somehow imbued with "gayness." When a neighborhood becomes the home of many gay people, the ground is created for a feeling of belonging and sharing with others. Signs of gayness, whether overt symbols like rainbow flags or more subtle cues such as merely the presence of other gay people on the street, create the feeling that a certain territory is special to the group and hospitable to the group's unique values.

How do you know when a neighborhood is gay? As with any generality, the rule of thumb is that "enough gay people in a neighborhood and it becomes a gay neighborhood." Rarely do gay people want to paint the streetlamps lavender, but the presence of many more subtle factors gives a gay character to an area. The most subtle cues are the presence of gay people as they take up residence in a district. Word spreads in the group that a certain area is starting to look attractive and open to gay members. There is often a move to "gentrify" older, more affordable sections of a city and build a new neighborhood out of the leftovers from the rush to the suburbs. Gay businesses, those operated by or catering to gay people, often develop once enough clientele is in the area. Social groups and services emerge that are oriented toward the members of the neighborhood. Eventually, the label of "gay neighborhood" is placed on an area, and the transformation is complete. The Castro area in San Francisco, Greenwich Village in New York, New Town in Chicago, the Westheimer district in Houston, and West Hollywood or Silver Lake in Los Angeles are examples of the many emergent gay neighborhoods in cities across America.

A second need fulfilled by the gay neighborhood is the creation of a meeting ground. People can recognize and meet each other more easily when a higher density of like population is established. It is not easy to grow up gay in America; gay people often feel "different" because of their sexual orientations. The surrounding heterosexual culture often tries to imprint on everyone sexual behaviors and expectations that do not suit gay natures. Because of this pressure, gay people often feel isolated and alienated, and the need for a meeting ground is very important. Merely knowing that there is a specific place where other gay people live and work and play does much to anchor the psychological aspect of gayness in a tangible, physical reality. A gay person's sense of identity is reinforced by knowing that there is a home base, or a safe place where others of a similar persuasion are nearby.

Gay neighborhoods reinforce individual identity by focusing activities and events for members of the group. Celebrations of group unity and pride, demonstrations of group creativity and accomplishment, and services to individual members' needs are more easily developed when they are centralized. Gay neighborhoods are host to all the outward elements of a community—parades, demonstrations, car washes, basketball games, petition signing, street fairs, and garage sales.

A critical purpose for gay neighborhoods is that of physical and psychological safety. Subcultural groups usually experience some degree of persecution and oppression from the larger surrounding culture. For gay people, physical safety is a very real concern—incidences of homophobic assaults or harassment are common in most American cities. By centralizing gay activities, some safeguards can be mounted, as large numbers of gay people living in proximity create a deterrence to violence. This may be informal awareness of the need to take extra precautions and to be on the alert to help other gay people in distress or in the form of actual street patrols or social groups, such as Community United Against Violence in San Francisco. A sense of psychological safety follows from these physical measures. Group consciousness raising on neighborhood safety and training in safety practices create a sense of group cohesion. The security inspired by the group thus creates a psychic comfort that offsets the paranoia that can be engendered by alienation and individual isolation.

Another significant result of gay neighborhoods is the political reality of "clout." In the context of American grassroots democracy, a predominantly gay population in an area can lead to political power. The concerns of gay people are taken more seriously by politicians and elected officials representing an area where voters can be registered and mustered into service during elections. In many areas, openly gay politicians represent gay constituencies directly and voice their concerns in ever-widening forums. The impact of this kind of democracy-in-action is felt on other institutions as well: police departments, social welfare agencies, schools, churches, and businesses. When a group centralizes its energy, members can bring pressure to bear on other cultural institutions, asking for and demanding attention to the unique needs of that group. Since American culture has a strong tradition of cultural diversity, gay neighborhoods are effective agents in the larger cultural acceptance of gay people. The gay rights movement, which attempts to secure housing, employment, and legal protection for gay people, finds its greatest support in the sense of community created by gay neighborhoods.

Gay Social Groups

On a smaller level than the neighborhood, specialized groups fulfill the social needs of gay people. The need for affiliation—to make friends, to share recreation, to find life partners, or merely to while away the time— *10* is a strong drive in any group of people. Many gay people suffer from an isolation caused by rejection by other people or by their own fear of being discovered as belonging to an unpopular group. This homophobia leads to difficulty in identifying and meeting other gay people who can help create a sense of dignity and caring. This is particularly true for gay teenagers who have limited opportunities to meet other gay people. Gay social groups serve the important function of helping gay people locate each other so that this affiliation need can be met.

The development of gay social groups depends to a large degree on the number of gay people in an area and the perceived risk factor. In smaller towns and cities, there are often no meeting places, which exacerbates the problem of isolation. In some small towns a single business may be the only publicly known meeting place for gay people within hundreds of miles. In larger cities, however, an elaborate array of bars, clubs, social groups, churches, service agencies, entertainment groups, stores, restaurants, and the like add to the substance of a gay culture.

The gay bar is often the first public gay experience for a gay person, and it serves as a central focus for many people. Beyond the personal need of meeting potential relationship partners, the gay bar also serves the functions of entertainment and social activity. Bars offer a wide range of attractions suited to gay people: movies, holiday celebrations, dancing, costume parties, live entertainment, free meals, boutiques, and meeting places for social groups. Uniquely gay forms of entertainment, such as drag shows and disco dancing, were common in gay bars before spreading into the general culture. Bars often become a very central part of a community's social life by sponsoring athletic teams, charities, community services, and other events as well as serving as meeting places.

The centrality of the bar in gay culture has several drawbacks, however. Young gay people are denied entrance because of age restrictions, and there may be few other social outlets for them. A high rate of alcoholism among urban gay males is prominent. With the spread of Acquired Immune Deficiency Syndrome (AIDS), the use of bars for meeting sexual partners has declined dramatically as gay people turn to developing more permanent relationships.

Affiliation needs remain strong despite these dangers, however, and alternative social institutions arise that meet these needs. In large urban areas, where gay culture is more widely-developed, social groups include athletic organizations that sponsor teams and tournaments; leisure activity clubs in such areas as country-and-western dance, music, yoga, bridge, hiking, and recreation; religious groups such as Dignity (Roman Catholic), Integrity (Episcopal), and the Metropolitan Community Church (MCC); volunteer agencies such as information and crisis hotlines and charitable organizations; and professional and political groups such as the Golden Gate Business Association of San Francisco or the national lobby group, the Gay Rights Task Force. A directory of groups and services is usually published in urban gay newspapers, and their activities are reported on and promoted actively. Taken together, these groups compose a culture that supports and nourishes a gay person's life.

Gay Symbols

Gay culture is replete with symbols. These artifacts spring up and constantly evolve as gayness moves from an individual, personal experience into a more complex public phenomenon. All groups express their ideas and values in symbols, and the gay culture, in spite of its relatively brief history, has been quite creative in symbol making.

The most visible category of symbols is in the semantics of gay establishment names. Gay bars, bookstores, restaurants, and social groups want to be recognized and patronized by gay people, but they do not want to incur hostility from the general public. This was particularly true in the past when the threat of social consequences was greater. In earlier days, gay bars, the only major form of gay establishment, went by code words such as "blue" or "other"—the Blue Parrot, the Blue Goose, the Other Bar, and Another Place.

Since the liberalization of culture after the 1960s, semantics have blossomed in gay place names. The general trend is still to identify the place as gay, either through affiliation (Our Place or His 'N' Hers), humor (the White Swallow or Uncle Charley's), high drama (the Elephant Walk or Backstreet), or sexual suggestion (Ripples, Cheeks, or Rocks). Lesbians and gay men differ in this aspect of their cultures. Lesbian place names often rely upon a more personal or classical referent (Amanda's Place or the Artemis Cafe), while hypermasculine referents are commonly used for gay male meeting places (the Ramrod, Ambush, Manhandlers, the Mine Shaft, the Stud, or Boots). Gay restaurants and nonpornographic bookstores usually reflect more subdued names, drawing upon cleverness or historical associations: Dos Hermanos, Women and Children First, Diana's, the Oscar Wilde Memorial Bookstore, and Walt Whitman Bookstore. More commonly, gay establishments employ general naming trends of location, ownership, or identification of product or service similar to their heterosexual counterparts. The increasing tendency of business to target and cater to gay markets strengthens the growth and diversity of gay culture.

A second set of gay symbols are those that serve as member-recognition factors. In past ages such nonverbal cues were so popular as to become mythical: the arched eyebrow of Regency England, the green carnation of Oscar Wilde's day, and the "green shirt on Thursday" signal of mid-century America. A large repertoire of identifying characteristics has arisen in recent years that serves the functions of recognizing other gay people and focusing on particular interests. In the more sexually promiscuous period of the 1970s, popular identifying symbols were a ring of keys worn on the belt, either left or right depending upon sexual passivity or aggressiveness, and the use of colored handkerchiefs in a rear pocket coded to

15

desired types of sexual activity. Political sentiments are commonly expressed through buttons, such as the "No on 64" campaign against the LaRouche initiative in California in 1986. The pink triangle as a political symbol recalls the persecution and annihilation of gay people in Nazi Germany. The lambda symbol, an ancient Greek referent, conjures up classical images of gay freedom of expression. Stud earrings for men are gay symbols in some places, though such adornment has evolved and is widely used for the expression of general countercultural attitudes. The rainbow and the unicorn, mythical symbols associated with supernatural potency, also are common signals of gay enchantment, fairy magic, and spiritual uniqueness to the more "cosmic" elements of the gay community.

Another set of gay symbols to be aware of are the images of gay people as portrayed in television, film, literature, and advertising. The general heterosexual culture controls these media forms to a large extent, and the representations of gay people in those media take on a straight set of expectations and assumptions. The results are stereotypes that often oversimplify gay people and their values and do not discriminate the subtleties of human variety in gay culture. Since these stereotypes are generally unattractive, they are often the target of protests by gay people. Various authors have addressed the problem of heterosexual bias in the areas of film and literature. As American culture gradually becomes more accepting of and tolerant toward gay people, these media representations become more realistic and sympathetic, but progress in this area is slow.

One hopeful development in the creation of positive gay role models   20
has been the rise of an active gay market for literature. Most large cities have bookstores that stock literature supportive of gay culture. A more positive image for gay people is created through gay characters, heroes, and stories that deal with the important issues of family, relationship, and social responsibility. This market is constantly threatened by harsh economic realities, however, and gay literature is not as well developed as it might be.

Advertising probably has done the most to popularize and integrate gay symbols into American culture. Since money making is the goal of advertising, the use of gay symbols has advanced more rapidly in ad media than in the arts. Widely quoted research suggests that gay people, particularly men, have large, disposable incomes, so they become popular target markets for various products: tobacco, body-care products, clothing, alcohol, entertainment, and consumer goods. Typical gay-directed advertising in these product areas includes appeals based upon male bonding, such as are common in tobacco and alcohol sales ads, which are attractive to both straight and gay men since they stimulate the bonding need that is a part of both cultures.

Within gay culture, advertising has made dramatic advances in the past ten years, due to the rise of gay-related businesses and products. Gay advertising appears most obviously in media specifically directed at gay markets, such as gay magazines and newspapers, and in gay neighborhoods.

Gay products and services are publicized with many of the same means as are their straight counterparts. Homoerotic art is widely used in clothing and body-care product ads. The male and female body are displayed for their physical and sexual appeal. This eroticizing of the body may be directed at either women or men as a desirable sexual object, and perhaps strikes at a subconscious homosexual potential in all people. Prominent elements of gay advertising are its use of sexuality and the central appeal of hypermasculinization. With the rise of sexual appeals in general advertising through double entendre, sexual punning, subliminal seduction, and erotic art work, it may be that gay advertising is only following suit in its emphasis on sexual appeals. Hugely muscled bodies and perfected masculine beauty adorn most advertising for gay products and services. Ads for greeting cards, billboards for travel service, bars, hotels, restaurants, and clothing stores tingle to the images of Hot 'N' Hunky Hamburgers, Hard On Leather, and the Brothel Hotel or its crosstown rival, the Anxious Arms. Some gay writers criticize this use of advertising as stereotyping and distorting of gay people, and certainly, misconceptions about the diversity in gay culture are more common than understanding. Gay people are far more average and normal than the images that appear in public media would suggest.

Gay Meeting Behavior

The final element of communication in the gay culture discussed here is the vast set of behaviors by which gay people recognize and meet one another. In more sexually active days before the concern for AIDS, this type of behavior was commonly called cruising. Currently, promiscuous sexual behavior is far less common than it once was, and cruising has evolved into a more standard meeting behavior that helps identify potential relationship partners.

Gay people meet each other in various contexts: in public situations, in the workplace, in gay meeting places, and in the social contexts of friends and acquaintances. Within each context, a different set of behaviors is employed by which gay people recognize someone else as gay and determine the potential for establishing a relationship. These behaviors include such nonverbal signaling as frequency and length of interaction, posture, proximity, eye contact, eye movement and facial gestures, touch, affect displays, and paralinguistic signals. The constraints of each situation and the personal styles of the communicators create great differences in the effectiveness and ease with which these behaviors are displayed.

Cruising serves several purposes besides the recognition of other gay   25
people. Most importantly, cruising is an expression of joy and pride in being gay. Through cruising, gay people communicate their openness and willingness to interact. Being gay is often compared to belonging to a universal—though invisible—fraternity or sorority. Gay people are generally friendly and open to meeting other gay people in social contexts

because of the common experience of rejection and isolation they have had growing up. Cruising is the means by which gay people communicate their gayness and bridge the gap between stranger and new-found friend.

Cruising has become an integral part of gay culture because it is such a commonplace behavior. Without this interpersonal skill—and newcomers to gay life often complain of the lack of comfort or ease they have with cruising—a gay person can be at a distinct disadvantage in finding an easy path into the mainstream of gay culture. While cruising has a distinctly sexual overtone, the sexual subtext is often a symbolic charade. Often the goals of cruising are no more than friendship, companionship, or conversation. In this sense, cruising becomes more an art form or an entertainment. Much as the "art of conversation" was the convention of a more genteel cultural age, gay cruising is the commonly accepted vehicle of gay social interaction. The sexual element, however, transmitted by double meaning, clever punning, or blatant nonverbal signals, remains a part of cruising in even the most innocent of circumstances.

In earlier generations, a common stereotype of gay men focused on the use of exaggerated, dramatic, and effeminate body language—the "limp wrist" image. Also included in this negative image of gay people was cross-gender dressing, known as "drag," and a specialized, sexually suggestive argot called "camp." Some gay people assumed these social roles because that was the picture of "what it meant to be gay," but by and large these role behaviors were overthrown by the gay liberation of the 1970s. Gay people became much less locked into these restraining stereotypes and developed a much broader means of social expression. Currently, no stereotypic behavior would adequately describe gay communication style—it is far too diverse and integrated into mainstream American culture. Cruising evolved from these earlier forms of communication, but as a quintessential gay behavior, cruising has replaced the bitchy camp of an earlier generation of gay people.

The unique factor in gay cruising, and the one that distinguishes it from heterosexual cruising, is the level of practice and refinement the process receives. All cultural groups have means of introduction and meeting, recognition, assessment, and negotiation of a new relationship. In gay culture, however, the "courtship ritual" or friendship ritual of cruising is elaborately refined in its many variants and contexts. While straight people may use similar techniques in relationship formation and development, gay people are uniquely self-conscious in the centrality of these signals to the perpetuation of their culture. There is a sense of adventure and discovery in being "sexual outlaws," and cruising is the shared message of commitment to the gay life style.

Conclusion

These four communication elements of gay culture comprise only a small part of what might be called gay culture. Other elements have been more widely discussed elsewhere: literature, the gay press, religion, politics, art, theater, and relationships. Gay culture is a marvelous and dynamic phenomenon, driven and buffeted by the energies of intense feeling and creative effort. Centuries of cultural repression that condemned gay people to disgrace and persecution have been turned upside down in a brief period of history. The results of this turbulence have the potential for either renaissance or cataclysm. The internalized fear and hatred of repression is balanced by the incredible joy and idealism of liberation. Through the celebration of its unique life style, gay culture promises to make a great contribution to the history of sexuality and to the rights of the individual. Whether it will fulfill this promise or succumb to the pressures that any creative attempt must face remains to be seen.

The Responsive Reader

1. What purpose does the creation of a gay neighborhood serve? What, for Majors, are some of the attitudes, activities, businesses, or civic efforts that give a gay character to an area? What does he say about the role of friendships, social groups, or institutions like the gay bar?
2. What does Majors say about the role of symbols in the gay lifestyle? How does he assess the ambivalent, two-sided role of the media in dealing with gays in our culture? (Are the media hostile to or supportive of the gay lifestyle?)
3. How or in what contexts does Majors touch on homophobia—the rejection, oppression, or persecution that gays experience? How, according to Majors, does it affect or shape their social behavior?
4. What, according to this article, are some of the stereotypes that gays are leaving behind as the result of gay liberation?

Talking, Listening, Writing

5. Are the purposes the gay neighborhood serves similar to or different from the purposes served by the "turf" staked out by other groups?
6. How does the struggle for gay rights compare with other struggles for civil rights? How is it similar to or different from the struggle for racial equality or for women's rights?
7. Is homophobia abating, holding steady, or increasing in our society? What is your prediction for the future?

Collaborative Projects

8. The issue of gays in the military has received much media attention. Why? What have been key developments? Who have been the key players in the controversy? What are the prospects for the future?

FORUM: *Gay Rights and Backlash*

Openly gay or lesbian Americans have become a familiar feature of American politics and entertainment. In sitcoms, the squirming of family and friends when introduced to the gay lover of one of theirs became a familiar joke. Tom Hanks played an AIDS victim treated shabbily by a homophobic establishment. Gay rights initiatives asked voters to ban discrimination against gays in housing and employment; at least one state (Hawaii) edged close to recognizing same-sex marriages. At the same time, fundamentalist ministers and conservative politicians mounted a counterattack against homosexuals as the favorite target of the American right. State legislatures rushed to pass laws declaring same-sex marriages invalid; a "Defense of Marriage Act" was sailing through Congress.

The two following articles represent voices from opposite ends of the spectrum. William Bennett is a liberal-bashing, gay-bashing, feminist-bashing conservative who marches under the banner of traditional values. He was President Reagan's secretary of education at a time when the Reagan administration was trying to abolish the U.S. Department of Education. He has published tracts like The Book of Virtues *to admonish Americans to adopt higher moral standards. According to* Harper's *magazine, the author of* The Book of Virtues *earned $1,800,000 in speaking fees in 1996. Richard Rodriguez first became known for his autobiographical* Hunger of Memory *(1982), in which he talked of immigrants and their children leaving their old-country language behind as a necessary rite of passage in the process of joining fully in the American experience. He has since become a media voice writing frequently about the fruitful tension between the Catholic, Spanish, mestizo tradition of Mexico and the Protestant Anglo tradition of North America. His* Days of Obligation: An Argument with My Mexican Father *was published in 1992.*

Thought Starters: What does the term "family values" bring to mind? Where do you hear or see it used, and by whom?

LOVE, MARRIAGE AND THE LAW

William J. Bennett

We are engaged in a debate which, in a less confused time, would   *1*
be considered pointless and even oxymoronic: the question of same-sex marriage.

But we are where we are. The Hawaii Supreme Court has discovered a new state constitutional "right"—the legal union of same-sex couples. Unless a "compelling state interest" can be shown against them, Hawaii will become the first state to sanction such unions. And if Hawaii legalizes same-sex marriages, other states might well have to recognize them because of the Constitution's Full Faith and Credit Clause. Some in Congress recently introduced legislation to prevent this from happening.

Now, anyone who has known someone who has struggled with his homosexuality can appreciate the poignancy, human pain and sense of exclusion that are often involved. One can therefore understand the effort to achieve for homosexual unions both legal recognition and social acceptance. Advocates of homosexual marriages even make what appears to be a sound conservative argument: Allow marriage in order to promote faithfulness and monogamy. This is an intelligent and politically shrewd argument. One can even concede that it might benefit some people. But I believe that overall, allowing same-sex marriages would do significant, long-term social damage.

Recognizing the legal union of gay and lesbian couples would represent a profound change in the meaning and definition of marriage. Indeed, it would be the most radical step ever taken in the deconstruction of society's most important institution. It is not a step we ought to take.

The function of marriage is not elastic; the institution is already   5
fragile enough. Broadening its definition to include same-sex marriages would stretch it almost beyond recognition—and new attempts to broaden the definition still further would surely follow. On what principled grounds could the advocates of same-sex marriage oppose the marriage of two consenting brothers? How could they explain why we ought to deny a marriage license to a bisexual who wants to marry two people? After all, doing so would be a denial of that person's sexuality. In our time, there are more (not fewer) reasons than ever to preserve the essence of marriage.

Marriage is not an arbitrary construct; it is an "honorable estate" based on the different, complementary nature of men and women—and how they refine, support, encourage and complete one another. To insist that we maintain this traditional understanding of marriage is not an attempt to put others down. It is simply an acknowledgment and celebration of our most precious and important social act.

Nor is this view arbitrary or idiosyncratic. It mirrors the accumulated wisdom of millennia and the teaching of every major religion. Among worldwide cultures, where there are so few common threads, it is not a coincidence that marriage is almost universally recognized as an act meant to unite a man and a woman.

To say that same-sex unions are not comparable to heterosexual marriages is not an argument for intolerance, bigotry or lack of compassion (although I am fully aware that it will be considered so by some). But it is an argument for making distinctions in law about relationships that are themselves distinct. Even Andrew Sullivan, among the most intelligent advocates of same-sex marriage, has admitted that a homosexual marriage contract will entail a greater understanding of the need for "extramarital outlets." He argues that gay male relationships are served by the "openness of the contract," and he has written that homosexuals should resist allowing their "varied and complicated lives" to be flattened into a "single, moralistic model."

But this "single, moralistic model" is precisely the point. The marriage commitment between a man and a woman does not—it cannot—countenance extramarital outlets. By definition it is not an open contract; its essential idea is fidelity. Obviously that is not always honored in practice. But it is normative, the ideal to which we aspire precisely because we believe some things are right (faithfulness in marriage) and others are wrong (adultery). In insisting that marriage accommodate the less restrained sexual practices of homosexuals, Sullivan and his allies destroy the very thing that supposedly has drawn them to marriage in the first place.

There are other arguments to consider against same-sex marriage— *10* for example, the signals it would send, and the impact of such signals on the shaping of human sexuality, particularly among the young. Former Harvard professor E. L. Pattullo has written that "a very substantial number of people are born with the potential to live either straight or gay lives." Societal indifference about heterosexuality would cause a lot of confusion. A remarkable 1993 article in the Washington Post supports this point. Fifty teen-agers and dozens of school counselors and parents from the local area were interviewed. According to the article, teen-agers said it has become "cool" for students to proclaim they are gay or bisexual—even for some who are not. Not surprisingly, the caseload of teen-agers in "sexual identity crisis" doubled in one year. "Everything is front page, gay and homosexual," according to one psychologist who works with the schools. "Kids are jumping on it . . . (counselors) are saying, 'What are we going to do with all these kids proclaiming they are bisexual or homosexual when we know they are not?'"

If the law recognizes homosexual marriages as the legal equivalent of heterosexual marriages, it will have enormous repercussions in many areas. Consider just two: sex education in the schools and adoption. The sex education curriculum of public schools would have to teach that heterosexual and homosexual marriage are equivalent. "Heather Has Two Mommies" would no longer be regarded as an anomaly; it would more likely become a staple of a sex education curriculum. Parents who want their children to be taught (for both moral and utilitarian reasons) the privileged status of heterosexual marriage will be portrayed as intolerant bigots; they will necessarily be at odds with the new law of matrimony and its derivative curriculum.

Homosexual couples will also have equal claim with heterosexual couples in adopting children, forcing us (in law at least) to deny what we know to be true: that it is far better for a child to be raised by a mother and a father than by, say, two male homosexuals.

The institution of marriage is already reeling because of the effects of the sexual revolution, no-fault divorce and out-of-wedlock births. We have reaped the consequences of its devaluation. It is exceedingly imprudent to conduct a radical, untested and inherently flawed social experiment on an institution that is the keystone in the arch of civilization. That we have to debate this issue at all tells us that the arch has slipped. Getting it firmly back in place is, as the lawyers say, a "compelling state interest."

GROWING ACCEPTANCE
BY FAMILY, FRIENDS

Richard Rodriguez

Does Supreme Court Justice Antonin Scalia wear boxers or briefs? *1* What do you think he does in the dark? And should we care?

In broad daylight, Scalia is a hefty fellow, a family man of (as some politicians like to say) "traditional values." Scalia is, to be sure, a brilliant legal scholar—or so he has long seemed to me. But last week, in a venomous opinion, the justice (echoing the traditional lament of the anti-Semite) informed us that homosexuals constitute a group with "disproportionate political power," "high disposable income" and "enormous influence in the American media."

Justice Scalia was petulant and in the minority. For last week, the Supreme Court (by a 6-3 ruling) struck down a provision of the Colorado Constitution that prohibits anti-gay discrimination laws. Arguing for the majority, Justice Anthony Kennedy observed that Colorado has no right to make homosexuals "unequal to everyone else."

As a homosexual man, I was relieved by the ruling. Though I do not forget that the Colorado provision, known as Amendment 2, was passed by 53 percent of that state's voters in 1992. Similar provisions are pending in Idaho, Oregon and Washington and are in effect locally in Florida, Oregon and Idaho.

Some very deep change is going on in America and it is as wide- *5* spread as it is surprising. Americans—men and women, married and not, young and old—are examining what it means to be sexual creatures.

Mama's decision to leave the kitchen, to be more than mother and wife, to work as an equal with men, may be the most revolutionary change of recent years. But the gay movement is the most inflammatory evidence of sexual meltdown. Gays, therefore, must be punished for the sins of the wife.

Justice Scalia provocatively chose a German word to describe what is happening in America: "*Kulturkampf*"—a culture war. What I see is an astonishing change. I meet homosexual men and women now in every corner of American life.

Everywhere people are "out" and, more remarkably, they are being accepted by their families and their friends and their coworkers. I know, like you, stories of parents who no longer speak to their children. But I am more impressed by the accommodation taking place throughout America.

I think of two Catholic families in California. They have been united in recent years by the love of two dying men—lovers dying of AIDS. There they all were—50 smiling faces in a Christmas photograph. Three or four generations, standing alongside the two thinning men. That is the way the sexual revolution is taking place—by the Christmas tree, within the very family that Pat Buchanan and Pat Robertson invoke for their own purposes as unchanging and rigid.

It is, paradoxically, because so many Americans are growing unafraid   10
of homosexuality that the counter-movement has grown. Homosexual activists tend to forget this. They incline to portray the gay movement as "counter-cultural."

I think, rather, that the politicians and religious leaders who parade under banners of TRADITION and FAMILY have become the counter-culture. And they know it. That was partly what Justice Scalia meant to imply: Homosexuals have power.

I am not being overly optimistic. I suspect that the great, perhaps even calamitous struggle in the next century will be a cultural war, pitting the secular against the fundamentalist.

In America, the sense of being in the minority has recently galvanized "traditionalists." "They got out the vote in Colorado." But they did so because they feel under threat. Much of America is no longer compliant to their will.

Do I think there will be more anti-gay legislation passed? Yes. Are we in for dangerous times? Yes. Do I think that there are many judges in America who will remain preoccupied by what I do in the dark?

But the other day I received a letter from my first-grade teacher, a   15
Catholic nun now in her 80's. "About your being gay," she writes, "I don't have any problem with it. I only pray that you will be a good man."

The Responsive Reader

1. What for Bennett is the essence of marriage as a traditional institution? What are the key values it represents? What in his praise of marriage seems idealized and what seems valid to you?

2. Bennett's "I'm-not-a-bigot" stance keeps him from repeating any vulgar abuse directed at gays by homophobes. How does he talk about gay people at the beginning of his article? Later in the article, what use does he make of familiar antigay charges such as their proselytizing for homosexuality among the impressionable young or their encouraging of promiscuity (or "less restrained sexual practices," in Bennett's words)?

3. Polemicists demonize trends they oppose by painting them as part of a threatened general breakdown of Western civilization. What are other items in Bennett's catalogue of societal evils that, like gay marriage, signal the decay (or "deconstruction") of traditional values? A "slippery slope" argument attacks people not for what they advocate but for what else the success of their advocacy might lead to. What other evils does Bennett envision as becoming possible once same-sex marriages open the door?

4. What evidence does Rodriguez give that "some very deep change is going on in America? Like Bennett, Rodriguez sees the change as part of a larger picture. How? How does Rodriguez size up the current legal and political developments, and how does he feel about them?

5. Like Bennett, Rodriguez tries to put down the opposition without lapsing into outright abuse. How does he describe Justice Scalia, and on what grounds does he criticize him?

6. The fundamentalist antigay crusade is often described as a rebellion of the "silent majority" against a current trend. How does Rodriguez try to change this perception? How does he explain the psychology of the "traditionalists"?

Talking, Listening, Writing

7. Do you think Bennett is a "bigot"? Do you think Rodriguez is "flaunting" his sexual orientation?

8. Have you seen evidence of an anti-gay backlash in your community or in society at large? Or have you seen evidence of growing tolerance or acceptance?

9. Do you think same-sex marriages are a threat from which the institution of marriage has to be protected?

Collaborative Projects

10. What is the current status of the movement to legalize same-sex marriages? What is the difference between recognizing same-sex marriages and recognizing homosexual couples as "domestic partners"? Working with a group, you may want to investigate current initiatives and legal or political developments.

HILLS LIKE WHITE ELEPHANTS
Ernest Hemingway

*Next to Mark Twain, Ernest Hemingway is known around the world as probably the most widely read and most American of American authors. His great novels—*The Sun Also Rises *(1926),* A Farewell to Arms *(1929), and* For Whom the Bell Tolls *(1940)—were read by millions. Some think that as writer of the modern short story he remains unsurpassed. Hemingway lives on in critical and media folklore as poster child of an obsolete macho mentality—an image he self-promoted as a bullfight aficionado, deep-sea fisherman, and Great White Hunter. (He killed himself with a shotgun blast to the head in Idaho.) However, there are no brainless Rambo types posturing as heroes in his fiction. Hemingway came away from volunteer service as an ambulance driver in Italy in World War I with a profound disillusionment with the windbag oratory of politicians and with glib talk about heroism and sacrifice. The men in his best-known novels and stories are often shell-shocked, physically maimed or emotionally crippled, wary of any kind of shallow talk, looking for some worthwhile definition of manhood in a violent, corrupt, hypocritical world. They often, like the two people in the following story, are expatriates—exiles who have left behind whatever roots or sense of belonging they once had.*

Thought Starters: What does the word *macho* bring to mind? Do you expect men to be less sensitive than women?

The hills across the valley of the Ebro were long and white. On this side there was no shade and no trees and the station was between two lines of rails in the sun. Close against the side of the station there was the warm shadow of the building and a curtain, made of strings of bamboo beads, hung across the open door into the bar, to keep out flies. The American and the girl with him sat at a table in the shade, outside the building. It was very hot and the express from Barcelona would come in forty minutes. It stopped at this junction for two minutes and went on to Madrid.

"What should we drink?" the girl asked. She had taken off her hat and put it on the table.

"It's pretty hot," the man said.

"Let's drink beer."

"Dos cervezas," the man said into the curtain.

"Big ones?" a woman asked from the doorway.

"Yes. Two big ones."

The woman brought two glasses of beer and two felt pads. She put the felt pads and the beer glasses on the table and looked at the man and the girl. The girl was looking off at the line of hills. They were white in the sun and the country was brown and dry.

"They look like white elephants," she said.

"I've never seen one," the man drank his beer. [10]

"No, you wouldn't have."

"I might have," the man said. "Just because you say I wouldn't have doesn't prove anything."

The girl looked at the bead curtain. "They've painted something on it," she said. "What does it say?"

"Anis del Toro. It's a drink."

"Could we try it?" [15]

The man called "Listen" through the curtain. The woman came out from the bar.

"Four reales."

"We want two Anis del Toro."

"With water?"

"Do you want it with water?" [20]

"I don't know," the girl said. "Is it good with water?"

"It's all right."

"You want them with water?" asked the woman.

"Yes, with water."

"It tastes like licorice," the girl said and put the glass down. [25]

"That's the way with everything."

"Yes," said the girl. "Everything tastes of licorice. Especially all the things you've waited so long for, like absinthe."

"Oh, cut it out."

"You started it," the girl said. "I was being amused. I was having a fine time."

"Well, let's try and have a fine time." [30]

"All right. I was trying. I said the mountains looked like white elephants. Wasn't that bright?"

"That was bright."

"I wanted to try this new drink. That's all we do, isn't it—look at things and try new drinks?"

"I guess so."

The girl looked across at the hills. [35]

"They're lovely hills," she said. "They don't really look like white elephants. I just meant the coloring of their skin through the trees."

"Should we have another drink?"

"All right."

The warm wind blew the bead curtain against the table.

"The beer's nice and cool," the man said. [40]

"It's lovely," the girl said.

"It's really an awfully simple operation, Jig," the man said. "It's not really an operation at all."

The girl looked at the ground the table legs rested on.

"I know you wouldn't mind it, Jig. It's really not anything. It's just to let the air in."

The girl did not say anything.

"I'll go with you and I'll stay with you all the time. They just let the air in and then it's all perfectly natural."

"Then what will we do afterward?"

"We'll be fine afterward. Just like we were before."

"What makes you think so?"

"That's the only thing that bothers us. It's the only thing that's made us unhappy."

The girl looked at the bead curtain, put her hand out and took hold of two of the strings of beads.

"And you think then we'll be all right and be happy."

"I know we will. You don't have to be afraid. I've known lots of people that have done it."

"So have I," said the girl. "And afterward they were all so happy."

"Well," the man said, "if you don't want to you don't have to. I wouldn't have you do it if you didn't want to. But I know it's perfectly simple."

"And you really want to?"

"I think it's the best thing to do. But I don't want you to do it if you don't really want to."

"And if I do it you'll be happy and things will be like they were and you'll love me?"

"I love you now. You know I love you."

"I know. But if I do it, then it will be nice again if I say things are like white elephants, and you'll like it?"

"I'll love it. I love it now but I just can't think about it. You know how I get when I worry."

"If I do it you won't ever worry?"

"I won't worry about that because it's perfectly simple."

"Then I'll do it. Because I don't care about me."

"What do you mean?"

"I don't care about me."

"Well, I care about you."

"Oh, yes. But I don't care about me. And I'll do it and then everything will be fine."

"I don't want you to do it if you feel that way."

The girl stood up and walked to the end of the station. Across on the other side, were fields of grain and trees along the banks of the Ebro. Far away, beyond the river, were mountains. The shadow of a cloud moved across the field of grain and she saw the river through the trees.

"And we could have all this," she said. "And we could have everything and every day we make it more impossible."

"What did you say?"

"I said we could have everything."

"We can have everything."

"No, we can't." 75

"We can have the whole world."

"No, we can't."

"We can go everywhere."

"No, we can't. It isn't ours any more."

"It's ours." 80

"No, it isn't. And once they take it away, you never get it back."

"But they haven't taken it away."

"We'll wait and see."

"Come on back in the shade," he said. "You mustn't feel that way."

"I don't feel any way," the girl said. "I just know things." 85

"I don't want you to do anything that you don't want to do—"

"Nor that isn't good for me," she said. "I know. Could we have
another beer?"

"All right. But you've got to realize—"

"I realize," the girl said. "Can't we maybe stop talking?"

They sat down at the table and the girl looked across at the hills on 90
the dry side of the valley and the man looked at her and at the table.

"You've got to realize," he said, "that I don't want you to do it if you
don't want to. I'm perfectly willing to go through with it if it means
anything to you."

"Doesn't it mean anything to you? We could get along."

"Of course it does. But I don't want anybody but you. I don't want
any one else. And I know it's perfectly simple."

"Yes, you know it's perfectly simple."

"It's all right for you to say that, but I do know it." 95

"Would you do something for me now?"

"I'd do anything for you."

"Would you please please please please please please please stop
talking?"

He did not say anything but looked at the bags against the wall of the
station. There were labels on them from all the hotels where they had
spent nights.

"But I don't want you to," he said, "I don't care anything about it." 100

"I'll scream," the girl said.

The woman came out through the curtains with two glasses of beer
and put them down on the damp felt pads. "The train comes in five
minutes," she said.

"What did she say?" asked the girl.

"That the train is coming in five minutes."

The girl smiled brightly at the woman, to thank her. *105*

"I'd better take the bags over to the other side of the station," the man said. She smiled at him.

"All right. Then come back and we'll finish the beer."

He picked up the two heavy bags and carried them around the station to the other tracks. He looked up the tracks but could not see the train. Coming back, he walked through the barroom, where people waiting for the train were drinking. He drank an Anis at the bar and looked at the people. They were all waiting reasonably for the train. He went out through the bead curtain. She was sitting at the table and smiled at him.

"Do you feel better?" he asked.

"I feel fine," she said. "There's nothing wrong with me. I feel fine." *110*

The Responsive Reader

1. Hemingway had a horror of big words and big speeches. How much of the talk in this story sounds like aimless chitchat? When do you first decide that something serious is going on? What is the issue? How do you know?
2. What kind of person is the man? What is his line of talk? What is his agenda? What do you think of him?
3. What kind of person is the woman? What is she looking for? How does she respond to the man's talk? Do you sympathize with her?

Talking, Listening, Writing

4. Do you think that in a different setting the same conversation could go on today? Or has the relationship between the sexes changed in basic ways?
5. If the two people in the story were able to express their true feelings, would they be able to deal better with the situation or improve their relationship? (Do you think people tend to be too tongue-tied and uncommunicative? Or do you think people tend to be too gushy and sentimental?)
6. The "war of the sexes" has been a major theme in the literature of the West. Do you think that the relationship between the sexes in our society is becoming too adversarial? Is there too much hostility between the sexes?

NADINE, RESTING ON HER NEIGHBOR'S STOOP

Judy Grahn

> *Judy Grahn is a feminist and lesbian poet who has published eight volumes of poetry, including* The Work of a Common Woman *(1978) and the* Queen of Swords. *She has also written books about poetry and language as well as a novel,* Mundane's World. *She founded the Women's Press Collective and has taught writing and mythology. In her cycle of poems devoted to the Helen myth, she takes it beyond the story of Helen of Troy, former Queen of Sparta, who as the "stolen queen" was "hated and blamed for the most famous war of western history and literature, the model war of Troy." Grahn makes Helen the archetypal creation goddess that appears in various forms in many early religions. Helen is the goddess of beauty and love, of the womb and the source of life, of life and fire. Grahn associates her with the tradition of the weaver, or webster, symbolized by the spider, from whose very body comes the cloth of life. The following is one of the poems in which Grahn pays tribute to "common women." How common is the "common woman" in the following poem? How does she challenge traditional definitions of femininity or womanhood?*

Thought Starters: Do the media today project images of ordinary women—women who are not fashion models, sex workers, or over-achievers in the world of business and law?

She holds things together, collects bail,   1
makes the landlord patch the largest holes.
At the Sunday social she would spike
every drink, and offer you half of what she knows,
which is plenty. She pokes at the ruins of the city   5
like an armored tank; but she thinks
of herself as a ripsaw cutting through
knots in wood. Her sentences come out
like thick pine shanks
and her big hands fill the air like smoke.   10
She's a mud-chinked cabin in the slums,
sitting on the doorstep counting
rats and raising 15 children,
half of them her own. The neighborhood
would burn itself out without her;   15
one of these days she'll strike the spark herself.

She's made of grease
and metal, with a hard head
that makes the men around her seem frail.
The common woman is as common as a nail.   *20*

The Responsive Reader

1. What are striking images or details in this poem that the reader is likely to remember?
2. Do you recognize this person? Does she seem like a real person to you?
3. Compare and contrast what you take to be a more traditional "feminine image" with Grahn's portrait of a "common woman."

Talking, Listening, Writing

4. What images of femininity or womanhood are dominant in our culture? How obsolete or how alive are such stereotypes as the homemaker, the cover girl, the beauty queen, the cheerleader, the dumb blonde, the sex bomb? What, if anything, has taken their place?
5. Have you encountered "strong women" in your own family or as part of your observation of friends, neighbors, coworkers, business associates?

Collaborative Projects

6. In a poem titled "They Say She Is Veiled," Grahn alludes to the myth of the earth goddess that anthropologists, psychoanalysts, and feminists have explored when searching for a stage of religion before the dominance of patriarchal male gods. Echoes of the earth mother tradition, for instance, survived in the cults of the goddess Ishtar and Cybele in the Middle East or of the Greek Demeter, or "grain mother," goddess of the harvest and of what is nurturing and life-sustaining in our world. Working with a group, you may want to investigate recent explorations of the earth mother tradition.

Thinking about Connections

Which of the women whose writing you have read in this volume comes close to Grahn's vision of a strong woman "that makes the men around her seem frail"?

WRITING
WORKSHOP 6

Comparing and Contrasting

Writers use comparison and contrast to make connections. They can help readers understand something new by showing in detail how it differs from something familiar. (Gentrification is different from earlier patterns of urban renewal—it does not raze existing structures. It renovates and upgrades them instead; it uses them to lure affluent buyers back to the city.) Purposeful comparison and contrast can help us put historical changes in perspective. It can help us make tricky choices between careers, mates, places to live, or political candidates.

TRIGGERING   Writers do not usually make comparisons merely as an intellectual exercise. They typically have an agenda. They compare with a purpose—to justify a preference, to influence our buying patterns or our votes, to nudge us toward needed change.

- A writer who contrasts the stark glass-and-steel highrises of Bauhaus (early modern) architecture with the curves, step patterns, and curlicues of postmodern buildings is not likely to be a neutral observer. He or she may consider the earlier style sterile and the newer style more imaginative and more human.

- It might be an eye-opener to compare the cost and trauma of an elderly relative's terminal illness under two different systems of health insurance. In this country—with a largely privately operated system of health insurance—the death of an elderly relative might leave a family bankrupt and in disarray. In a country like Canada or Germany, where health care is considered a citizen's right, all costs might be assumed by the publicly financed system of universal insurance.

GATHERING   For an informative comparison and contrast, the preliminary stock-taking is especially important. A key part of your prewriting may be **brainstorming** notes: You jot down features that might prove important as you chart similarities and differences. Suppose you are working on a paper that will show how changing gender roles have transformed traditional assumptions about marriage. The following might be your first jotting down of possibly relevant points:

TRADITIONAL	MODERN
church wedding	live together first
till death do us part	high divorce rate
virgin bride	family planning
subservient wife	both work
husband works	backyard weddings
take the good with the bad	equal relationships
husband handles finances	supportive, caring male
housewife cleans and cooks	share chores
wait on the husband	mixed marriages
sex on demand	marriage contract
talk about sex is taboo	mutual sex
marry your own kind	discuss problems
feminine wife	

Even while you jot down these items, you will be mentally making connections. Revealing contrasts emerge as you connect contrasting items: (traditional) the wife cooks and cleans/(modern) both share chores; (traditional) the husband works/(modern) both work; (traditional) subservient wife/(modern) equal partners. What other items should be linked to show a striking contrast between the old and the new?

SHAPING How would you organize the brainstorming notes about changing gender roles in the modern marriage? These notes might lead naturally to a **point-by-point** comparison. As each question is raised, the writer would first show the traditional answer and then the contrasting modern one. The following sequence might prove workable as an organizing strategy for the paper:

POINT ONE: Who supports the family financially? Who "provides"?

POINT TWO: Who is the dominant partner? Who is in charge?

POINT THREE: Who does the housekeeping?

POINT FOUR: What is the role of sex? (And what are the sex roles of the spouses?)

POINT FIVE: Who is considered an "eligible" marriage partner in the first place?

However, sometimes a **parallel-order** comparison might prove more workable or instructive. To give your readers a clear picture of two things you are comparing, you might decide to give them a complete, rounded picture of first the one and then the other. However, you help your readers see the connections. You take up key points in the same or very similar order—in parallel order. Here is the skeleton for a parallel-order comparison of two day-care centers:

It's Your Choice

preview

   . . . In the light of these findings, working parents can perhaps suspend some of their feelings of guilt and instead concentrate on the hardest task: finding the right place for their children. *Three important qualities to look for in a day-care center are a stable staff, the right activities, and an active role for the parents.*

EXAMPLE A
point 1

   I have worked at two different centers. The first one I consider a bad example. The staff changed every few months, mainly because we were paid minimum wage. The teachers who stayed did so because they did not feel qualified to work for a higher salary elsewhere. . . .

point 2

   The children's day was as follows: TV—inside play— outside play—lunch—nap—outside play—TV—parents' pick up. The main goal was to make the children follow the rules and keep quiet. I remember one small girl particularly who was a very active child. . . .

point 3

   Parents were not encouraged to participate; their role was to drop off the children and pick them up. . . .

EXAMPLE B
point 1

   The second school I worked at was quite different. There was a very low turnover of staff. . . .

point 2

   The children's schedule was as follows: Play—story time—work time—music—outside play—lunch—nap— independent work or play—story time—outside play—art— parents' pickup. . . .

point 3

   Parents joined in all the outside activities and often stopped for lunch with the children. Parents should be wary of any school that does not allow drop-in visits. . . .

   In a world of two-career or single-parent families, day care is going to be part of growing up for thousands of children. Instead of dropping a child off at the nearest center, parents must shop around to find a place designed to help children grow.

Make sure that your organizing strategy works for the job at hand. Instead of the classic point-by-point or parallel-order patterns, a strategy like the following may prove right for your topic:

- *You may want to start with strong but misleading similarities.* You then alert your reader to important differences that may not meet the eye.

- *You may want to start with deceptive surface differences.* (For instance, race relations today are different than they were in the days of overt, legalized segregation and officially condoned violence.) However, you might then go on to show that basic similarities remain, though their current version takes a more subtle form. (For instance, there is de facto segregation in the schools; minorities hit a "glass ceiling" on their way up the promotion ladder; etc.)

REVISING A comparison-and-contrast paper necessarily follows a more complicated plan than a paper that states a main point and then lines up supporting examples. As you reread and revise a first draft, see whether you have taken your readers with you—or whether you have lost them along the way. You may need stronger **transitions**—stronger signposts to keep pointing your readers in the right direction.

- *Spell out clearly the main point of your comparison.* Have you summed up in a unifying thesis what your paper as a whole is trying to show? You may also need a stronger conclusion to pull together various points you made along the way.

- *Give your readers a preview of the itinerary.* Try to word your thesis in such a way that it gives away your overall plan. Give your readers a hint: point-by-point? parallel-order? similarities first? (But avoid a stodgy "In-this-paper-I-plan-to-do-the-following" style.)

- *Strengthen your network of transitions.* Signal turning points. Signal similarities by phrases like *similarly, in parallel fashion, as an exact counterpart, pointing in the same direction,* or *along the same lines.* Signal contrasts by phrases like *however, by contrast, on the other hand, as the direct opposite,* or *providing a counterweight* (or *a counterpoint*).

What is the overall plan in the following sample paper? How does the plan become clear to the reader? How effectively has the student writer followed through?

Wolves Mate for Life—Do You?

It is believed that the wolf mates for life. Spring is the breeding season. Six to seven in a litter is usual, but there may be as many as fourteen. The pups are born with big blue eyes, which soon fade in color. The family remains together while the pups are young, even when the mother breeds in successive years, and all members help take care of the family.

This could be compared to the traditional marriages of earlier times— married for life with six to fourteen children, and the family was a unit— unlike some of today's modern marriages where divorce dismantles half of them. What are the differences between the old traditional marriage and the new modern one that is so prominent in today's society? Where do these differences lie? I believe the substantial differences lie in the three general areas of work, family, and education, each stemming from changes in economics, values, or morality (or the lack of it, depending upon your viewpoint).

My grandpa and grandma lived in the little town of Yuba City and carried on a very traditional marriage. My grandfather did all of the out-of-house work while Grandma preoccupied herself with the domestic duties such as cleaning, cooking, and taking care of the children. My grandfather was a farmer and grew fruit and nut trees. He "brought home the bacon," while Grandma did the frying. This was very common in the traditional marriage, for the husband to work and the wife to stay at home, but this isn't too often seen in today's society anymore.

Now we see the modern marriage as the only way to go. Because of the high cost of living both partners must work to support themselves. No longer can the husband deal with the outside job while his wife deals with the household. When I was younger my parents operated on a traditional-style marriage, but when I became a freshman in college, my mother went to work as an accountant. Our family could no longer live on what my father brought home, so my mother's joining the labor force was the only answer.

Family life in the traditional marriage is quite different from that in the modern marriage. My grandparents had three children—two boys and one girl. Having three or more children was not uncommon, but now in a modern marriage the third is usually "a mistake." My grandparents considered the family to be a very important institution and thus had many family activities together that brought closeness and harmony to the family. They often went camping at a cabin in Mt. Lassen, fed the ducks Wonder Bread at Ellis Lake, and played at the Sutter County park which had four swings, a set of monkey bars, a slide, and a merry-go-round. Vacations were also family-oriented. They would pack the car and drive to Oklahoma to visit family out there, singing "She'll be comin' round the mountain" as they traveled.

In the modern marriage, people often forget the importance of the family. Often there isn't even a whole family present. Half of today's marriages end in divorce, thus leaving a single parent somewhere with children to take care of, and that parent working to support the children usually has little or no time for family activities. Even when both parents are present, often work schedules conflict, and differing individual wants and needs come into play. Dad's been working all week and wants to watch baseball and relax on Saturday, Mom has to work 10 to 6:30, the older child has a book report due on Monday, but the little six-year-old wants to feed the ducks the stale bread with the family. It just doesn't work as well as it used to. Families are lucky if they get a one-week vacation together at Big Basin to camp in an overcrowded tent and fight off savage ants and blood-sucking mosquitoes, eat overripe fruit, and use outhouses that reek and have doors that never quite latch.

Education is something that the whole family participates in in a traditional marriage. Not only do the children learn at school, but they are also taught important things at home. My grandma taught her daughter to cook, embroider, can fruits and vegetables, iron, and churn butter. She taught all her kids manners and how to behave. My grandpa taught all his children how to grade fruit—know what is acceptable for market—drive the vehicles, milk the cows, even ride a bike, swim and dive, hunt, and fish. He also taught his sons how to work on mechanical vehicles, prune trees, irrigate, and breed the livestock. He also took time to help his children learn the value of money, by helping them open up a savings account. Other relatives taught the children also. An aunt taught the girl to crochet and her great-grandmother taught her to sew and quilt. The boys' great-grandfather taught them to carve things out of wood.

Things are quite different in the modern marriages we see today. The parents have little time for teaching in the home because of their work responsibilities. Education occurs at school and through peers and other sources, and children learn more on their own without the family than ever before. They attend driving school to learn how to drive, and the local Parks and Recreation Department takes care of the swim lessons. Relatives aren't usually involved as much as in a traditional marriage either. As *Ms.* magazine says, "Grandma is 61. She looks 45, is divorced, has a job selling real estate, and spends her weekends with a retired banker whose wife died three years ago."

Why have marriages changed? Why aren't families the self-sufficient, close, "all for one and one for all" units they used to be? I believe the change stems from economics. Society hardly allows that type of lifestyle anymore. Values have changed also, along with changes in morality. I don't believe people put as high a priority on marriage and family as they used to. Maybe divorce, suicide, emotional breakdowns, and child abuse would decrease if people valued marriage and family more, and looked back to some of the traditional marriage ways, and even took after the wolf and mated for life, as it used to be.

Topics for Comparison and Contrast Papers (A Sampling)

1. In movie or television fare, have you observed a change from "sex object" or stereotypically feminine female characters to "strong woman" characters?

2. Have you ever lived in a homogeneous neighborhood (with people of very similar backgrounds or social status)—but also in a more diverse, mixed neighborhood? Or, have you ever attended a school with a homogeneous student body—but also a school with a more diverse population? Write a paper working out the contrast between the two settings.

3. Have you ever converted from one religious or political group to another? Or have you had a chance to observe closely two such groups? How did they compare?

4. Have you experienced a major change in your lifestyle? Write a before-and-after paper on the subject.

5. Weigh the options on a topic like the following: What is preferable—a problem marriage or a divorce? What is preferable—single motherhood or an alternative?)

6. In the men you have a chance to observe, do you find both the macho and the sensitive male? What sets them apart?

7. Have you observed a difference in outlook and values between recent immigrants (or Americans from immigrant families) and other Americans?
8. In your family or in other areas of your experience, is there a generation gap? Have you observed a marked contrast in values or outlook between the older and the younger generation?
9. Do men and women feel differently about love?
10. Have you experienced the difference between blue-collar and white-collar jobs?

7

Media Watch: Image and Reality

*On the front page
of the daily fivestarfinal
***** Edition a child
is dying in the rubble
of newsprint.*

—*Olga Cabral*

The media have a vast potential for educating us and broadening our views. However, they also have a frightening power to manipulate our minds. As some people are alcohol-dependent, so many of us are media-dependent. We choose political leaders in campaigns conducted in large part in the newspapers and on television with a constant barrage of polls, sound bites, and attack ads. Often these campaigns are orchestrated by consultants and spin doctors who have no qualms about working both sides of the political street.

Our views on race relations may have been shaped by TV images of violence and riots in places that few viewers have actually visited. Our fears and doubts about child molestation, rape, and incest are aroused and fueled (and often again followed to fade) by the media. People who have never been in a courtroom get their ideas about how the justice system works from watching the O. J. Simpson trial on TV.

What we see and read on such subjects depends on editors' and network executives' judgment on what is newsworthy. Editorial and often marketing judgment decide what goes on page one and what is lost in the back pages. When the media focus on candidates for the Supreme Court or the presidency, the voter may learn more about their experiments with marijuana or the way they talk behind closed doors than about their stands on health insurance or abortion. For many viewers, the faces that people the small or the large screen—Madonna, Arnold Schwarzenegger, Michael Jackson, a favorite quarterback—are more real (not to mention interesting) than their coworkers or neighbors.

We know some of our world at first hand and much of it through the media. Viewers may know almost no African Americans personally but only media stereotypes: the smartass, wise-cracking tough street kid, male or female; the kindly, ever-smiling, and self-deprecating entertainer; the violent and self-destructing black male athlete in trouble with the law. The news may play out in loving detail the personal disasters, heroic rescues, and petty scandals that viewers love. However, it may provide little insight into the politics of race, immigration, education, the national debt, recession, sexism, mental health, or unemployment.

How do the media shape or distort our reality? Do they always skim the surface, in sound bites that allow for no real thinking? Are we always helpless "target audiences," or can we influence the steady stream of images and ideas that the media aim at us?

BOY KILLED AFTER SCHOOL

Patricia Jacobus

> All the news that's fit to print.
> Newspaper masthead

What do we expect of those who report the news? A past generation of journalists prided itself on the image of the fearless, objective reporter, whose credo was "Just the facts, Ma'am." Editorializing and pontificating were left to the editorial pages. A later wave of investigative journalism blurred the distinction between reporting and editorializing: It saw its mission as doing exposés of wrongdoing and corruption in high places. A still more recent definition of news has blurred the distinction between news and entertainment, often seeming to cater to its public's taste for mayhem, scandal, and gossip. In the words of Robert McNeil, one of the country's most respected journalists, "Those news shows—they're like circus barkers who have to exaggerate and hype to haul them into the tent." The following example of an everyday news report is by one of the near-anonymous reporters covering local news—a multiple-car crash on a fogged-in morning, a disoriented senior citizen lost when straying off a desert road, a violent incident at a local high school. How is this journalist doing her job? What is her job?

Thought Starters: Do you read the newspaper? When you do, what do you look for? Do you watch television news? Why?

He was a block from campus, walking home with a group of friends   1
from American High School, trying to avoid the pack of teenagers goading
him and his friends to rumble.

But 15-year-old Alejandro Cueva could not shake the youths who
jumped him from behind Tuesday after school, shortly before 3 p.m. As
one held back his arms, another plunged a knife into his heart, police said
yesterday.

Cueva collapsed to his death between two minivans on a car dealership's lot. His friend, Alejandro Campos, also 15, froze, unsure whether to
help the bleeding boy or flee as the others had. Before he reached a
decision, he was punched, kicked and stabbed, Sergeant Gus Arroyo said.

Campos was treated for a superficial stab wound to his side and was
released yesterday from Eden Medical Center, Arroyo said.

Police arrested three youths late Tuesday in connection with the stab-   5
bings. Their names have not been released because they are juveniles, but

they are described as a 16-year-old former student, a 17-year-old runaway who had stopped attending classes, and a 16-year-old student. They are being held in Juvenile Hall.

The stabbing apparently was in retaliation for a comment made during a first-period class Tuesday, when one youth harassed another about a hickey on his neck. When the boy responded, "Your mama gave it to me," an argument erupted. It continued during lunch and escalated after school.

Campos was not involved in the argument and just happened to be walking with the boy who made the final comment, police said. The intended victim fled before the fight started.

A sales manager at the Lincoln Mercury dealership where the fight took place said the crowd of 50 students who witnessed the stabbing showed no emotion and did nothing to intervene.

"I don't know how they could be so calloused," said Tom Callan. "I couldn't sleep last night thinking about that kid."

But Arroyo believes that the teenagers had no idea a killing was going   10
to take place. "At least I hope they didn't know," he said. "I think they were just there to watch some minor fight."

The suspects, stopped three blocks from the scene but released, were later brought to the police station by their parents. After they learned that one of the victims had died, they admitted to the stabbing, police said.

About eight officers and 12 parents roamed the campus yesterday making sure that no other fights broke out.

The killing came during the school's Spirit Week, with a rally yesterday, homecoming dance planned for Friday and the homecoming football game on Saturday.

During the rally, a group of Cueva's friends wearing black arm bands walked around the gym with a sign that they had painted in his memory. After the moment of silence, as the other students continued with their activities, the friends walked to a nearby field, sat cross-legged and hung their heads in prayer.

The school district sent nearly 20 bilingual counselors to console   15
Cueva's friends—most of whom are English-as-second-language students.

"These students are frustrated, upset and confused," said Arroyo, who spoke to the group in Spanish. "I told them to keep a level head and not make things worse."

Although police are downplaying race as a possible motive in the stabbing, the dead boy's family said they are convinced that the white suspects attacked Cueva because he was Mexican.

"All I know is a bunch of white guys stabbed my brother," said Karina Cueva, 13. "My brother always had a lot of problems at the school because the other students don't like Chicanos."

Alejandro was the oldest of Pedro and Cecilia Cueva's four children. He enjoyed running and playing basketball, his sister said in a telephone interview. The parents do not speak English.

The school has opened a trust fund for Cueva.   20

The Responsive Reader

1. Boil this news report down to its essentials. What for you are the bare facts? (Do you and your classmates disagree on what the basic facts are in this case?)
2. Do you think this has become a typical or normal incident in our society? Does the newspaper reporter treat it as if it were a normal occurrence?
3. We are often told that as human beings we can never be totally objective or impersonal like a machine. Does the reporter inject any personal interpretation or bias? Do you think anything important was left out? Could another reporter have told the story differently? How?

Talking, Listening, Writing

4. Is this incident an example of "senseless violence"? (What do we mean by that term?) Or is there a lesson to be learned from what happened here? What is it?
5. Has violence become the norm? Has our sensibility or sense of outrage become blunted by too much exposure to the kind of violence reported in this news story?
6. Many columns or editorials take off from a striking incident that brings a current issue into focus. Write a guest editorial for a newspaper or newsmagazine (or for your campus newspaper), taking off from the incident reported in this news story.

Collaborative Projects

7. Working with a group, check out recent newspaper reports of similar incidents. Compare and contrast them: What is similar? What is different? Is there a common pattern?

TALK TV: TUNING IN TO TROUBLE

Jeanne Albronda Heaton and Nona Leigh Wilson

> *In the view of many media watchers, the media landscape has been radically transformed by the emergence of talk shows as a medium rivaling rock stations, news channels, or movie channels in popularity. Talk show hosts, whether on radio or TV, go out of their way to broach provocative topics that will get people to talk—and talk they do, often spilling out unedited raw popular opinion very different from the scripted prose of commentators with expensive hairdos. What view of reality and of other people do we derive from tuning in to the talk show world? The authors of the following article on talk television focus on the way the shows shape women's image of themselves, of other women, and of men. For better or for worse, how do the shows shape women's views of relationships between men and women? Heaton is a practicing psychologist who also teaches psychology at Ohio University. Wilson teaches counseling and human resource development at South Dakota State University. Their essay is adapted from their book* Tuning In to Trouble: Talk TV's Destructive Impact on Mental Health *(1995).*

Thought Starters: Do you listen to talk radio or watch talk TV? When you do, do you think of callers or guests as weird or as representative ordinary people?

In 1967, *The Phil Donahue Show* aired in Dayton, Ohio, as a new daytime talk alternative. Donahue did not offer the customary "women's fare." On Monday of his first week he interviewed atheist Madalyn Murray O'Hair. Tuesday he featured single men talking about what they looked for in women. Wednesday he showed a film of a baby being born from the obstetrician's point of view. Thursday he sat in a coffin and interviewed a funeral director. And on Friday he held up "Little Brother," an anatomically correct doll without his diaper. When Donahue asked viewers to call in response, phone lines jammed.

For 18 years daytime talk *was* Donahue. His early guests reflected the issues of the time and included Ralph Nader on consumer rights, Bella Abzug on feminism, and Jerry Rubin on free speech. Never before had such socially and personally relevant issues been discussed in such a democratic way with daytime women viewers. But his most revolutionary contribution was in making the audience an integral part of the show's format. The women watching Donahue finally had a place in the conversation, and they were determined to be heard. The show provided useful infor-

1

mation and dialogue that had largely been unavailable to housebound women, affording them the opportunity to voice their opinions about everything from politics to sex—and even the politics of sex.

No real competition emerged until 1985, when *The Oprah Winfrey Show* went national. Her appeal for more intimacy was a ratings winner. She did the same topics Donahue had done but with a more therapeutic tone. Donahue seemed driven to uncover and explore. Winfrey came to share and understand. In 1987, Winfrey's show surpassed Donahue's by being ranked among the top 20 syndicated shows. Phil and Oprah made it easier for those who followed; their successors were able to move much more quickly to the top.

At their best, the shows "treated the opinions of women of all classes, races, and educational levels as if they mattered," says Naomi Wolf in her book *Fire with Fire*: "That daily act of listening, whatever its shortcomings, made for a revolution in what women were willing to ask for; the shows daily conditioned otherwise unheard women into the belief that they were entitled to a voice." Both Donahue and Winfrey deserve enormous credit for providing a platform for the voices of so many who needed to be heard, and for raising the nation's consciousness on many important topics, including domestic violence, child abuse, and other crucial problems. But those pioneering days are over. As the number of shows increased and the ratings wars intensified, the manner in which issues are presented has changed. Shows now encourage conflict, name-calling, and fights. Producers set up underhanded tricks and secret revelations. Hosts instruct guests to reveal all. The more dramatic and bizarre the problems the better.

While more air time is given to the problems that women face, the topics are presented in ways that are not likely to yield change. The very same stereotypes that have plagued both women and men for centuries are in full force. Instead of encouraging changes in sex roles, the shows actually solidify them. Women viewers are given a constant supply of the worst images of men, all the way from garden-variety liars, cheats, and con artists to rapists and murderers. 5

If there is a man for every offense, there is certainly a woman for every trauma. Most women on talk TV are perpetual victims presented as having so little power that not only do they have to contend with real dangers such as sexual or physical abuse, but they are also overcome by bad hair, big thighs, and beautiful but predatory "other" women. The women of talk are almost always upset and in need. The bonding that occurs invariably centers around complaints about men or the worst stereotypes about women. In order to be a part of the "sisterhood," women are required to be angry with men and dissatisfied with themselves. We need look no further than at some of the program titles to recognize the message. Shows about men bring us a steady stream of stalkers, adulterers, chauvinistic sons, abusive fathers, and men who won't commit to women.

The shows provide a forum for women to complain, confront, and cajole, but because there is never any change as a result of the letting loose, this supports the mistaken notion that women's complaints have "no weight," that the only power women have is to complain, and that they cannot effect real changes. By bringing on offensive male guests who do nothing but verify the grounds for complaint, the shows are reinforcing some self-defeating propositions. The idea that women should direct their energies toward men rather than look for solutions in themselves is portrayed daily. And even when the audience chastises such behavior, nothing changes, because only arguments and justifications follow.

On *The Jenny Jones Show* a woman was introduced as someone who no longer had sex with her husband because she saw him with a stripper. Viewers got to hear how the stripper "put her boobs in his face" and then kissed him. The husband predictably defended his actions: "At least I didn't tongue her." The next few minutes proceeded with insult upon insult, to which the audience "oohed" and "aahed" and applauded. To top it all off, viewers were informed that the offense in question occurred at the husband's birthday party, which his wife arranged, *stripper and all.* Then in the last few minutes a psychologist pointed out the couple weren't wearing rings and didn't seem committed. She suggested that their fighting might be related to some other problem. Her comments seemed reasonable enough until she suggested that the wife might really be trying to get her husband to rape her. That comment called up some of the most absurd and destructive ideas imaginable about male and female relationships—yet there was no explanation or discussion.

It is not that women and men don't find lots of ways to disappoint each other, or that some women and some men don't act and think like the women and men on the shows. The problem is talk TV's fixation on gender war, with endless portrayals of vicious acts, overboard retaliations, and outrageous justifications. As a result, viewers are pumped full of the ugliest, nastiest news from the front.

When issues affecting people of color are dealt with, the stereotypes 10 about gender are layered on top of the stereotypes about race. Since most of the shows revolve around issues related to sex, violence, and relationships, they tend to feature people of color who reflect stereotypical images—in a steady stream of guests who have children out of wedlock, live on welfare, fight viciously, and have complicated unsolvable problems. While there are less than flattering depictions of white people on these shows, white viewers have the luxury of belonging to the dominant group, and therefore are more often presented in the media in positive ways.

On a *Ricki Lake* show about women who sleep with their friends' boyfriends, the majority of the guests were African American and Hispanic women who put on a flamboyant display of screaming and fighting. The profanity was so bad that many of the words had to be deleted. The segment had to be stopped because one guest yanked another's wig off.

For many white viewers these are the images that form their beliefs about "minority" populations.

The shows set themselves up as reliable sources of information about what's really going on in the nation. And they often cover what sounds like common problems with work, love, and sex, but the information presented is skewed and confusing. Work problems become "fatal office feuds" and "back-stabbing coworkers." Problems concerning love, sex, or romance become "marraige with a 14-year-old," "women in love with the men who shoot them," or "man-stealing sisters." TV talk shows suggest that "marrying a rapist" or having a "defiant teen" are catastrophes about to happen to everyone.

Day in and day out, the shows parade all the myriad traumas, betrayals, and afflictions that could possibly befall us. They suggest that certain issues are more common than they actually are, and embellish the symptoms and outcomes. In actuality, relatively few people are likely to be abducted as children, join a Satanic cult in adolescence, fall in love with serial rapists, marry their cousins, hate their own race, or get sex changes in midlife, but when presented over and over again the suggestion is that they are quite likely to occur.

With their incessant focus on individual problems, television talk shows are a major contributor to the recent trend of elevating personal concerns to the level of personal rights and then affording those "rights" more attention than their accompanying responsibilities. Guests are brought on who have committed villainous acts (most often against other guests). The host and audience gratuitously "confront" the offenders about their wrongdoing and responsibilities. The alleged offenders almost always refute their accountability with revelations that they too were "victimized." On *Sally Jessy Raphael,* a man appeared with roses for the daughter he had sexually molested. He then revealed that he had been molested when he was five, and summed it up with "I'm on this show too! I need help, I'll go through therapy."

His sudden turnabout was not unusual. Viewers rarely see guests *15* admit error early in the show, but a reversal often occurs with just a few minutes remaining. This works well for the shows because they need the conflict to move steadily to a crescendo before the final "go to therapy" resolution. But before that viewers are treated to lots of conflict and a heavy dose of pseudo-psychological explanations that are really nothing more than excuses, and often lame ones at that. The guests present their problems, the hosts encourage them to do so with concerned questions and occasional self-disclosures, and the audience frequently get in on the act with their own testimonies. Anything and everything goes.

The reigning motto is "Secrets keep you sick." On a *Jerry Springer* show about confronting secrets, a husband revealed to his wife that he had been having an affair. Not only was the unsuspecting wife humiliated and speechless, but Springer upped the ante by bringing out the mistress, who kissed the husband and informed the wife that she loved them both. Conflict predictably ensued, and viewers were told this was a good idea because now the problem was out in the open. When Ricki Lake did a similar show, a man explained to his very surprised roommate that he had "finally" informed the roommate's mother that her son was gay, a secret the roommate had been hiding from his family.

Referring to these premeditated catastrophes as simply "disclosures" softens their edges and affords them a kind of legitimacy they do not deserve. On a program about bigamy, Sally Jessy Raphael invited two women who had been married to the same man at the same time to appear on the show. The man was also on, via satellite and in disguise. His 19-year-old daughter by one of the wives sat on the stage while these women and her father tore each other apart. Sally and the audience encouraged the fight with "oohs" and "aahs" and rounds of applause at the ever-increasing accusations. A "relationship therapist" was brought on to do the postmortem. Her most notable warning was that all this turmoil could turn the daughter "to women," presumably meaning that she could become a lesbian. The scenario was almost too absurd for words, but it was just one more show like so many others: founded on stereotypes and capped off with clichés. From the "catfight" to the "no-good father" to archaic explanations of homosexuality—cheap thrills and bad advice are dressed up like information and expertise.

These scenarios are often legitimized by the use of pseudopsychological explanations, otherwise known as psychobabble. This is regularly used as a "disclaimer," or as a prelude to nasty revelations, or as a new and more sophisticated way of reinforcing old stereotypes: "men are cognitive, not emotional," or "abused women draw abusive men to them." This not only leaves viewers with nothing more than platitudes to explain problems and clichés to resolve them, but it fails to offer guests with enormous conflicts and long histories of resentment and betrayals practical methods for changing their circumstances. The "four steps to get rid of your anger" may sound easy enough to implement, but what this kind of ready-made solution fails to acknowledge is that not all anger is the same, and certainly not everyone's anger needs the same treatment. Sometimes anger is a signal to people that they are being hurt, exploited, or taken advantage of, and it can motivate change.

Rather than encouraging discussion, exploration, or further understanding, psychobabble shuts it off. With only a phrase or two, we can believe that we understand all the related "issues." Guests confess that they are "codependents" or "enablers." Hosts encourage "healing," "empowerment," and "reclaiming of the inner spirit." In turn, viewers can nod knowingly without really knowing at all.

Talk TV initially had great potential as a vehicle for disseminating accurate information and as a forum for public debate, although it would be hard to know it from what currently remains. Because most of these 20 talks shows have come to rely on sensational entertainment as the means of increasing ratings, their potential has been lost. We are left with cheap shots, cheap thrills, and sound-bite stereotypes. Taken on its own, this combination is troubling enough, but when considered against the original opportunity for positive outcomes, what talk TV delivers is truly disturbing.

The Responsive Reader

1. Why do the authors see the early Phil Donahue show as a revolutionary departure? Was there a common pattern in choice of topics or of guests? What contribution did the early Oprah Winfrey show make? How did the two shows differ, and what did they have in common?
2. What is the difference between the pioneering early shows and today's fare? How did the shows change for the worse?
3. According to the authors, what is wrong with the way men are represented in today's shows? What is wrong with the way women are represented? What is wrong with the way people of color are represented? (Do you think the authors are too critical or negative?)
4. What function do the psychologists and counselors on these shows serve? On what grounds do the authors criticize the "experts" or "authorities"? (What is "psychobabble"?)

Talking, Listening, Writing

5. After watching several episodes of current shows, would you tend to agree with the authors or take issue with them? How or why?
6. Do you think media images or media talk have played a major role in shaping your own views on gender or race?

Collaborative Projects

7. Working with a group, you may want to tape several exchanges on a local talk radio show and analyze them for topics covered, people calling in, and the kind of interchange taking place.

THE IDIOT CULTURE

Carl Bernstein

Carl Bernstein, one of America's best-known journalists, worked his way up from errand boy to city desk clerk and eventually reporter and columnist. He already had a reputation as a maverick and iconoclast (or idol smasher) when he became involved in a developing story about a bungled break-in at the Watergate Apartments, the Democratic Party's headquarters building—a story that linked one of the burglars to President Nixon's reelection committee. Joining Bob Woodward, another Washington Post *reporter, Bernstein eventually traced responsibility for the burglary to close associates of President Nixon, forcing the president to resign in disgrace. The Watergate investigation, chronicled in Bernstein and Woodward's book* All the President's Men *(1974), was a triumph of exposé journalism, in which the press plays the role of the watchdog alerting the public to evildoing in high places. The hallmark of Bernstein and Woodward's investigative journalism was the dogged, persistent pursuit and verification of the facts in the face of official denial, stonewalling, and denunciation. In the article that follows, first published in 1992, Bernstein indicts a latter-day brand of sensation-mongering journalism for abandoning these high standards.*

Thought Starters: What recent scandals involving eminent public figures have you followed in some detail? What is your reaction—curiosity? outrage? boredom? cynicism?

It is now nearly a generation since the drama that began with the   *1*
Watergate break-in and ended with the resignation of Richard Nixon, a full twenty years in which the American press has been engaged in a strange frenzy of self-congratulation and defensiveness about its performance in that affair and afterward. The self-congratulation is not justified; the defensiveness, alas, is. For increasingly the America rendered today in the American media is illusionary and delusionary—disfigured, unreal, disconnected from the true context of our lives. In covering actually existing American life, the media—weekly, daily, hourly—break new ground in getting it wrong. The coverage is distorted by celebrity and the worship of celebrity; by the reduction of news to gossip, which is the lowest form of news; by sensationalism, which is always a turning away from a society's real condition; and by a political and social discourse that we—the press, the media, the politicians, *and* the people—are turning into a sewer.

The greatest felony in the news business today (as Woodward recently observed) is to be behind, or to miss, a major story; or more precisely, to seem behind, or to seem in danger of missing, a major story. So speed and quantity substitute for thoroughness and quality, for accuracy and context. The pressure to compete, the fear that somebody else will make the splash first, creates a frenzied environment in which a blizzard of information is presented and serious questions may not be raised; and even in those fortunate instances in which such questions are raised (as happened after some of the egregious stories about the Clinton family), no one has done the weeks and months of work to sort it all out and to answer them properly.

Reporting is not stenography. It is the best obtainable version of the truth. The really significant trends in journalism have not been toward a commitment to the best and the most complex obtainable version of the truth, not toward building a new journalism based on serious, thoughtful reporting. Those are certainly not the priorities that jump out at the reader or the viewer from Page One or "Page Six" of most of our newspapers; and not what a viewer gets when he turns on the 11 o'clock local news or, too often, even network news productions.

"All right, was it really the best sex you ever had?" Those were the words of Diane Sawyer, in an interview of Marla Maples on "Prime Time Live," a broadcast of ABC News (where "more Americans get their news from . . . than any other source"). Those words marked a new low (out of which Sawyer herself has been busily climbing). For more than fifteen years we have been moving away from real journalism toward the creation of a sleazoid info-tainment culture in which the lines between Oprah and Phil and Geraldo and Diane and even Ted, between the *New York Post* and *Newsday,* are too often indistinguishable. In this new culture of journalistic titillation, we teach our readers and our viewers that the trivial is significant, that the lurid and the loopy are more important than real news. We do not serve our readers and viewers, we pander to them. And we condescend to them, giving them what we think they want and what we calculate will sell and boost ratings and readership. Many of them, sadly, seem to justify our condescension, and to kindle at the trash. Still, it is the role of journalists to challenge people, not merely to amuse them.

We are in the process of creating, in sum, what deserves to be called 5 the idiot culture. Not an idiot *sub*-culture, which every society has bubbling beneath the surface and which can provide harmless fun; but the culture itself. For the first time in our history the weird and the stupid and the coarse are becoming our cultural norm, even our cultural ideal.

In New York we witnessed a primary election in which "Donahue," "Imus in the Morning," and the disgraceful coverage of the *New York Daily News* and the *New York Post* eclipsed *The New York Times, The Washington Post,* the network news divisions, and the serious and experienced political reporters on the beat. Even *The New York Times* has been reduced to naming the rape victim in the Willie Smith case; to putting Kitty Kelley on the front page as a news story; to parlaying polls as if they were policies.

I do not mean to attack popular culture. Good journalism *is* popular culture, but popular culture that stretches and informs its consumers rather than that which appeals to the ever descending lowest common denominator. If, by popular culture, we mean expressions of thought or feeling that require no work of those who consume them, then decent popular journalism is finished. What is happening today, unfortunately, is that the lowest form of popular culture—lack of information, misinformation, disinformation, and a contempt for the truth or the reality of most people's lives—has overrun real journalism.

Today ordinary Americans are being stuffed with garbage: by Donahue-Geraldo-Oprah freak shows (cross-dressing in the marketplace; skinheads at your corner luncheonette; pop psychologists rhapsodizing over the airways about the minds of serial killers and sex offenders); by the Maury Povich news; by "Hard Copy"; by Howard Stern; by local newscasts that do special segments devoted to hyping hype. In supposedly sophisticated New York, the country's biggest media market, there ran a craven five-part series on the 11 o'clock news called "Where Do They Get Those People . . . ?," a special report on where Geraldo and Oprah and Donahue get their freaks (the promo for the series featured Donahue interviewing a diapered man with a pacifier in his mouth).

The point is not only that this is trash journalism. That much is obvious. It is also essential to note that this was on an NBC-owned and -operated station. And who distributes Geraldo? The Tribune Company of Chicago. Who owns the stations on which these cross-dressers and transsexuals and skinheads and lawyers for serial killers get to strut their stuff? The networks, the Washington Post Company, dozens of major newspapers that also own television stations, Times-Mirror and the New York Times Company among others. And Ivana Trump, perhaps the single greatest creation of the idiot culture, a tabloid artifact if ever there was one, appeared on the cover of *Vanity Fair*. On the cover, that is, of Condé Nast's flagship magazine, the same Condé Nast/Newhouse/Random House whose executives will yield to nobody in their solemnity about their profession, who will tell you long into the night how seriously in touch with American culture they are, how serious they are about the truth.

Look, too, at what is on *The New York Times* best-seller list these 10 days. *Double Cross: The Explosive Inside Story of the Mobster Who Controlled America* by Sam and Chuck Giancana, Warner Books, $22.95. (Don't forget that $22.95.) This book is a fantasy pretty much from cover to cover. It is riddled with inventions and lies, with conspiracies that never happened, with misinformation and disinformation, all designed to line somebody's pockets and satisfy the twisted egos of some fame-hungry relatives of a mobster. But this book has been published by Warner Books, part of Time Warner, a conglomerate I've been associated with for a long time.

(*All the President's Men* is a Warner Bros. movie, the paperback of *All the President's Men* was also published by Warner Books, and I've just finished two years as a correspondent and contributor at *Time*.) Surely the publisher of *Time* has no business publishing a book that its executives and its editors know is a historical hoax, with no redeeming value except financial.

By now the defenders of the institutions that I am attacking will have cried the First Amendment. But this is not about the First Amendment, or about free expression. In a free country, we are free for trash, too. But the fact that trash will always find an outlet does not mean that we should always furnish it with an outlet. And the great information conglomerates of this country are now in the trash business. We all know pornography when we see it, and of course it has a right to exist. But we do not all have to be porn publishers; and there is hardly a major media company in America that has not dipped its toe into the social and political equivalent of the porn business in the last fifteen years.

Yes, we have always had a sensational, popular, yellow tabloid press; and we have always had gossip columns, even powerful ones like Hedda Hopper's and Walter Winchell's. But never before have we had anything like today's situation in which supposedly serious people—I mean the so-called intellectual and social elites of this country—live and die by (and actually believe!) these columns and these shows, and millions more rely upon them for their primary source of information. Liz Smith, *Newsday's* gossip columnist and the best of a bad lot, has admitted blithely on more than a few occasions that she doesn't try very hard to check the accuracy of many of her items, or even give the subjects of her column the opportunity to comment on what is being said about them.

The failures of the press have contributed immensely to the emergence of a talk-show nation, in which public discourse is reduced to ranting and raving and posturing. We now have a mainstream press whose news agenda is increasingly influenced by this netherworld. On the day that Nelson Mandela returned to Soweto and the allies of World War II agreed to the unification of Germany, the front pages of many "responsible" newspapers were devoted to the divorce of Donald and Ivana Trump.

Today the most compelling news story in the world is the condition of America. Our political system is in a deep crisis; we are witnessing a breakdown of the comity and the community that has in the past allowed American democracy to build and to progress. Surely the advent of the talk-show nation is a part of this breakdown. Some good journalism is still being done today, to be sure, but it is the exception and not the rule. Good journalism requires a degree of courage in today's climate, a quality now in scarce supply in our mass media. Many current assumptions in America—about race, about economics, about the fate of our cities—need to be challenged, and we might start with the media. For, next to race, the story of the contemporary American media is the great uncovered story in America today. We need to start asking the same fundamental questions about the press that we do of the other powerful institutions in this society—about who is served, about standards, about self-interest and its eclipse of the public interest and the interest of truth. For the reality is that the media are probably the most powerful of all our institutions today; and they are squandering their power and ignoring their obligation. They—or more precisely, we—have abdicated our responsibility, and the consequence of our abdication is the spectacle, and the triumph, of the idiot culture.

The Responsive Reader

1. In his two opening paragraphs, what key factors does Bernstein trace in the move away from "real journalism"?
2. Bernstein uses strong language—*gossip, sensationalism, trash, sleaze, pornography, yellow press*—throughout his indictment of the media. What examples does he give to substantiate his charges? Are his examples convincing? Are they representative? Do they remind you of similar examples from your own reading and viewing?
3. Bernstein admits that tabloid sensationalism and pornography have long been with us and will continue to be. Then what is the point he is making about their role today?
4. Bernstein charges that talk shows reduce public discourse "to ranting, raving, and posturing." Do you ever listen to talk shows? Try to reconstruct some typical exchanges between a talk show host and a caller. Do they deserve the kind of criticism that Woodward levels at these shows?

Talking, Listening, Writing

5. Study recent issues of a newspaper and of newsmagazines. Can you provide examples of celebrity worship? Can you provide examples of news that is not news but gossip? Can you provide examples of sensationalism?
6. In defense of the media, can you present some detailed examples of the media doing justice to "society's real condition" or "actually existing American life" as you know it?
7. Where do you draw the line between what is trivial and what is important?

Thinking about Connections

Naomi Wolf ("Are Opinions Male?") and Carl Bernstein ("The Idiot Culture") are insiders of the journalistic establishment in this country. How do their perspectives on American journalism compare?

EROTICA AND PORNOGRAPHY

Gloria Steinem

Gloria Steinem is America's most widely known and admired (not to mention attacked) feminist. She is the granddaughter of a prominent American suffragist, or suffragette—a woman fighting for women's right to vote. Steinem grew up in poverty in Toledo, Ohio, and went from there to Smith College. She came to New York to work as a journalist and in 1972 became a cofounder and editor of Ms. *magazine, the country's best-known feminist periodical, where the following article first appeared. She became an effective and influential lecturer, organizer, fund-raiser, and campaigner for the women's movement. Her apartment in New York City has been called "a stop on the underground railway" for international feminists. She published a collection of her essays,* Outrageous Acts and Everyday Rebellions, *in 1983, followed by a book about Marilyn Monroe,* Marilyn: Norma Jean. *In her best-selling* Revolution from Within: A Book of Self-Esteem *(1992), she turned from political activism to self-discovery and self-affirmation, searching for the "one true inner voice" that remains the constant in our changing roles, jobs, and relationships. In the following essay, Steinem tries to establish an essential distinction between acceptable and desirable "erotic" material and unacceptable pornography. What is the essence of the distinction she makes?*

Thought Starters: Have you observed anti-pornography campaigns? What form do they take? What results do they produce?

Human beings are the only animals that experience the same sex   *1*
drive at times when we can—and cannot—conceive.

Just as we developed uniquely human capacities for language, planning, memory, and invention along our evolutionary path, we also developed sexuality as a form of expression; a way of communicating that is separable from our need for sex as a way of perpetuating ourselves. For humans alone, sexuality can be and often is primarily a way of bonding, of giving and receiving pleasure, bridging differences, discovering sameness, and communicating emotion.

We developed this and other human gifts through our ability to change our environment, adapt physically, and in the long run, to affect our own evolution. But as an emotional result of this spiraling path away from other animals, we seem to alternate between periods of exploring our unique abilities to change new boundaries, and feelings of loneliness in the unknown that we ourselves have created; a fear that sometimes sends us back to the comfort of the animal world by encouraging us to exaggerate our sameness.

The separation of "play" from "work," for instance, is a problem only in the human world. So is the difference between art and nature, or an intellectual accomplishment and a physical one. As a result, we celebrate play, art, and invention as leaps into the unknown; but any imbalance can send us back to nostalgia for our primate past and the conviction that the basics of work, nature, and physical labor are somehow more worthwhile or even moral.

In the same way, we have explored our sexuality as separable from conception: a pleasurable, empathetic bridge to strangers of the same species. We have even invented contraception—a skill that has probably existed in some form since our ancestors figured out the process of birth—in order to extend this uniquely human difference. Yet we also have times of atavistic suspicion that sex is not complete—or even legal or intended-by-god—if it cannot end in conception.

No wonder the concepts of "erotica" and "pornography" can be so crucially different, and yet so confused. Both assume that sexuality can be separated from conception, and therefore can be used to carry a personal message. That's a major reason why, even in our current culture, both may be called equally "shocking" or legally "obscene," a word whose Latin derivative means "dirty, containing filth." This gross condemnation of all sexuality that isn't harnessed to childbirth and marriage has been increased by the current backlash against women's progress. Out of fear that the whole patriarchal structure might be upset if women really had the autonomous power to decide our reproductive futures (that is, if we controlled the most basic means of production), right-wing groups are not only denouncing prochoice abortion literature as "pornographic," but are trying to stop the sending of all contraceptive information through the mails by invoking obscenity laws. In fact, Phyllis Schlafly denounced the entire Women's Movement as "obscene."[1]

Not surprisingly, this religious, visceral backlash has a secular, intellectual counterpart that relies heavily on applying the "natural" behavior of the animal world to humans. That is questionable in itself, but these Lionel Tiger-ish studies make their political purpose even more clear in the particular animals they select and the habits they choose to emphasize.[2] The message is that females should accept their "destiny" of being sexually dependent and devote themselves to bearing and rearing their young.

[1][Phyllis Schlafly became known for her strong antifeminist views and her campaign against the Equal Rights Amendment.]

[2][Lionel Tiger is a Canadian-born anthropologist who has written about the relation between biology and culture and who looks with a critical eye at current patterns of marriage and divorce.]

Defending against such reaction in turn leads to another temptation: to merely reverse the terms, and declare that all nonprocreative sex is good. In fact, however, this human activity can be as constructive as destructive, moral or immoral, as any other. Sex as communication can send messages as different as life and death; even the origins of "erotica" and "pornography" reflect that fact. After all, "erotica" is rooted in *eros* or passionate love, and thus in the idea of positive choice, free will, the yearning for a particular person. (Interestingly, the definition of erotica leaves open the question of gender.) "Pornography" begins with a root meaning "prostitution" or "female captives," thus letting us know that the subject is not mutual love, or love at all, but domination and violence against women. (Though, of course, homosexual pornography may imitate this violence by putting a man in the "feminine" role of victim.) It ends with a root meaning "writing about" or "description of" which puts still more distance between subject and object, and replaces a spontaneous yearning for closeness with objectification and a voyeur.

The difference is clear in the words. It becomes even more so by example.

Look at any photo or film of people making love; really making love.   *10*
The images may be diverse, but there is usually a sensuality and touch and warmth, an acceptance of bodies and nerve endings. There is always a spontaneous sense of people who are there because they *want* to be, out of shared pleasure.

Now look at any depiction of sex in which there is clear force, or an unequal power that spells coercion. It may be very blatant, with weapons or torture or bondage, wounds and bruises, some clear humiliation, or an adult's sexual power being used over a child. It may be much more subtle: a physical attitude of conqueror and victim, the use of race or class difference to imply the same thing, perhaps a very unequal nudity, with one person exposed and vulnerable while the other is clothed. In either case, there is no sense of equal choice or equal power.

The first is erotic: a mutually pleasurable, sexual expression between people who have enough power to be there by positive choice. It may or may not strike a sense-memory in the viewer, or be creative enough to make the unknown seem real; but it doesn't require us to identify with a conqueror or a victim. It is truly sensuous, and may give us a contagion of pleasure.

The second is pornographic: its message is violence, dominance, and conquest. It is sex being used to reinforce some inequality, or to create one, or to tell us the lie that pain and humiliation (ours or someone else's) are really the same as pleasure. If we are to feel anything, we must identify with conqueror or victim. That means we can only experience pleasure through the adoption of some degree of sadism or masochism. It also means that we may feel diminished by the role of conqueror, or enraged, humiliated, and vengeful by sharing identity with the victim.

Perhaps one could simply say that erotica is about sexuality, but pornography is about power and sex-as-weapon—in the same way we have come to understand that rape is about violence, and not really about sexuality at all.

Yes, it's true that there are women who have been forced by violent   15
families and dominating men to confuse love with pain; so much so that they have become masochists. (A fact that in no way excuses those who administer such pain.) But the truth is that, for most women—and for men with enough humanity to imagine themselves into the predicament of women—true pornography could serve as aversion therapy for sex.

Of course, there will always be personal differences about what is and is not erotic, and there may be cultural differences for a long time to come. Many women feel that sex makes them vulnerable and therefore may continue to need more sense of personal connection and safety before allowing any erotic feelings. We now find competence and expertise erotic in men, but that may pass as we develop those qualities in ourselves. Men, on the other hand, may continue to feel less vulnerable, and therefore more open to such potential danger as sex with strangers. As some men replace the need for submission from childlike women with the pleasure of cooperation from equals, they may find a partner's competence to be erotic, too.

Such group changes plus individual differences will continue to be reflected in sexual love between people of the same gender, as well as between women and men. The point is not to dictate sameness, but to discover ourselves and each other through sexuality that is an exploring, pleasurable, empathetic part of our lives; a human sexuality that is unchained both from unwanted pregnancies and from violence.

But that is a hope, not a reality. At the moment, fear of change is increasing both the indiscriminate repression of all nonprocreative sex in the religious and "conservative" male world, and the pornographic vengeance against women's sexuality in the secular world of "liberal" and "radical" men. It's almost futuristic to debate what is and is not truly erotic, when many women are again being forced into compulsory motherhood, and the number of pornographic murders, tortures, and woman-hating images are on the increase in both popular culture and real life.

It's a familiar division: wife or whore, "good" woman who is constantly vulnerable to pregnancy or "bad" woman who is unprotected from violence. *Both* roles would be upset if we were to control our own sexuality. And that's exactly what we must do.

In spite of all our atavistic suspicions and training for the "natural"   20
role of motherhood, we took up the complicated battle for reproductive freedom. Our bodies had borne the health burden of endless births and poor abortions, and we had a greater motive for separating sexuality and conception.

Now we have to take up the equally complex burden of explaining that all nonprocreative sex is *not* alike. We have a motive: our right to a uniquely human sexuality, and sometimes even to survival. As it is, our bodies have too rarely been enough our own to develop erotica in our own lives, much less in art and literature. And our bodies have too often been the objects of pornography and the woman-hating, violent practice that it preaches. Consider also our spirits that break a little each time we see ourselves in chains or full labial display for the conquering male viewer, bruised or on our knees, screaming a real or pretended pain to delight the sadist, pretending to enjoy what we don't enjoy, to be blind to the images of our sisters that really haunt us—humiliated often enough ourselves by the truly obscene idea that sex and the domination of women must be combined.

Sexuality *is* human, free, separate—and so are we.

But until we untangle the lethal confusion of sex with violence, there will be more pornography and less erotica. There will be little murders in our beds—and very little love.

The Responsive Reader

1. According to Steinem, how has human sexuality evolved, and what human purposes does it (or should it) serve?
2. What is the key difference between "erotica" and pornography? Where do you think Steinem states it most clearly or persuasively? What are striking or convincing examples? What is the major recurrent theme in this essay?
3. How does Steinem relate her discussion to both traditional and current trends in our culture? How does she relate it to the sexual politics of the right and the left?

Talking, Listening, Writing

4. What do you take to be the dominant attitude toward sex in our culture? Is our society ready for the view of human sexuality that Steinem presents? Should it be?
5. Would you call Steinem's a distinctly feminist point of view? Would you call it a distinctly female point of view? (Does the reader have to be feminist to sympathize with her view? Does the reader have to be a woman?)
6. Where would *you* draw the line between acceptable and unacceptable material with sexual content? Is it possible to draw the line?
7. What is the difference between art and pornography?

Collaborative Projects

8. What is the current legal status of pornographic materials? As a possible research project, your class might want to choose an investigation of current legal definitions of pornography and their application.

FORUM: Hustler *and the First Amendment*

The Federal Government is without any power whatsoever under the Constitution to put any type of burden on free speech and the expression of ideas of any kind (as distinguished from conduct).
—Justice Hugo L. Black

It is no news that many women are defecting from the ranks of civil libertarians on the issue of obscenity.
—Susan Jacoby

Adopted as part of the Bill of Rights in 1791, the First Amendment to the U.S. Constitution stipulates that "Congress shall make no law . . . abridging the freedom of speech, or of the press." The classic dilemma of its supporters is that the amendment protects both what we admire and what we despise. The right of free speech protects neo-Nazis marching through Jewish neighborhoods, antiabortionists threatening to kill doctors, and rap artists singing cop-killer songs. The right of free speech protects Hustler *magazine, printing pictures of brutalized women and wallowing in bathroom humor. An Oliver Stone–produced movie (directed by Czech-born Milos Forman) celebrated the victory of* Hustler *publisher Larry Flynt when the Supreme Court squashed a libel suit by one of America's richest televangelists, who had protested against a crude satirical piece involving both incest and an outhouse. In a society where feminist crusades against the demeaning of women had sensitized many in the media and education to offensive material, the movie opened to dumbfounding critical acclaim. It was considered Oscar material until the film industry decided not to provoke further the censors on the right and the left. In Europe, the Larry Flynt movie won the Golden Bear Award at the 1997 Berlin Film Festival while religious groups in France protested violently against promotional posters they considered blasphemous.*

The following articles sample critical and editorial opinion on the Larry Flynt controversy. Feminists like Gloria Steinem, angry at the "fawning reviews" in mainstream publications, saw in the movie an expurgated, air-brushed pornographer whose truly ghastly, misogynous material was never shown on the screen. Defenders of the movie shared the absolutist position of "First Amendment junkies" (Susan Jacoby): If you give the censors an inch and allow them to ban the most offensive material, it won't be long before the censors come for you *at four in the morning. Of the writers represented here, Ellen Goodman is a widely admired columnist for the* Boston Globe *who calls herself a "First Amendment absolutist" while despising what Flynt stands for. Stanley Kauffmann of the* New Republic *reviews movies for connoisseurs of the art of the cinema—commenting, for instance, on the camera work, the actors' interpretation of their roles, or previous work of producers, directors, and actors. However, like other critics, he finally cannot escape facing up to the way a movie mirrors or distorts social reality. Hanna Rosin, also writing in the* New Republic, *tears into the moviemakers for claiming that they did not sentimentalize or whitewash Larry Flynt. However, she at the same time takes on basic issues raised by the controversy. For instance, are nudes art when viewed by sophisticates in a tony gallery but pornography when viewed by working-class males in a raunchy magazine?*

Thought Starters: Is freedom of speech an unconditional right? What about speech that incites hate or violence? Are photographs or paintings (and also parades and cross burnings) "speech"?

LARRY FLYNT'S BIG MAKEOVER

Ellen Goodman

I have long regarded Larry Flynt as the curse of the First Amendment. He's the catch that comes with the freedom of speech. The asterisk on the Constitution. 1

You want the freedom to say whatever you want? Fine, but you can't shut up the smutmeister. Nevertheless, there is one thing that Larry Flynt is not. My hero.

That brings us directly to "The People Vs. Larry Flynt," a film that opened with the most fawning reviews. This movie has morphed a curse into a hero with greater ease than it transformed Flynt into Woody Harrelson.

Director Milos Forman has fulfilled Flynt's last fantasy: "I would love to be remembered for something meaningful." This biopic cleans up Flynt's act to fit producer Oliver Stone's description of the pornographer as someone "in the rapscallion tradition of Mark Twain's Huckleberry Finn."

The cleanup takes place magically by making women disappear. The 5
love story of Larry and Althea edits down Flynt's relationships with other women and edits out his effects on all women. This movie about a pornographer is virtually devoid of questions surrounding pornography.

We do see Flynt at some drugged-out moments. But the average viewer can leave the darkened theater without knowing that Flynt had five wives, two of whom he trashed for promiscuity. Without knowing that he had, and neglected, five children, one of whom he refers to as a "lying little whacko."

But if "The People Vs. Larry Flynt" is now the text for the debate about free speech, tell it like it is. Anyone leaving the theater should be handed a copy of Hustler before they go off for their espresso and erudite conversations about Courtney Love's performance.

This is what's in the current Hustler:

Enough ads for phone sex to constitute a porn yellow pages.

Dozens of centers of centerfolds.

Women having sex with each other with large plastic male organs strapped on.

A feature called "How to Know if Your Girlfriend Is a Dog."

Enough racist cartoons to "balance" an article against neo-Nazis.

And don't leave out Nataly's sexual fantasy about occupying armies: "She knows that her only hope for survival is complete submission to their will—a price she is prepared to pay."

This is the porn that reduces a woman to the sum of her sexual parts.   10
The real porn that is degrading, desensitizing and arguably dangerous.

In the film, Larry says, "If the First Amendment can protect even a scumbag like me, then it will protect all of you, because I am the worst." But the irony is that the filmmakers don't present "the worst." It's as if they didn't trust the answer to the question they ask the public: "You may not like what he does, but are you prepared to give up his right to do it?" They don't show what he does.

For my own part, I accept the curse that comes with the First Amendment. When the Falwell case went to court, I wrote a friend-of-the-Flynt brief in this column. But I continue to regard him as an enemy. Those of us who are free speech absolutists believe absolutely that you fight speech with more speech. I don't truck with censors. But spare me those in Hollywood who turn the scumbag into the star.

THE MERCHANT OF VENUS

Stanley Kauffmann

"If the First Amendment will protect a scumbag like me, then it will   1
protect all of you. Because I'm the worst." Under this blazon *The People vs. Larry Flynt* (Columbia) advances. Flynt is the publisher of *Hustler* whose career in the porno-mag business and whose tangles because of it are the subject of Milos Forman's film. It's refreshing in these days of Moral Majorities, of religion as power tool, to see a film that defies those forces. That point is past argument. Now, if you like, let's believe that people will flock to this picture not because of its nudity and sex, but because we're all First Amendment absolutists.

Flynt was born in rural Kentucky and, we see, began in business as a boy, peddling moonshine with his brother. Next, in the early 1970s, in Ohio, he is running strip clubs with his brother while liberally sampling the stock in trade. He starts a newsletter to draw customers. The letter becomes *Hustler*, and Flynt becomes very rich. He meets, loves and eventually marries Althea Leasure, a bisexual underage stripper. They are devoted to each other, in their errant way, until she dies of AIDS and drugs.

Obscenity charges against Flynt come early and keep coming. With good legal counsel and with personal flamboyance, he wriggles through his troubles. (The real Flynt appears briefly as one of the judges trying the film's Flynt.) But troubles magnify when *Hustler* publishes raunchy jokes and cartoons about one of Flynt's most vociferous enemies, Jerry Falwell. Falwell sues; Flynt loses. Flynt appeals, and, after the usual judicial ascent, his appeal is heard by the Supreme Court, which in 1988 reverses the judgment, on First Amendment grounds.

Meanwhile, a personal horror has struck. A would-be assassin has shot Flynt and his lawyer, Alan Isaacman. Isaacman recovers completely, but Flynt is left paralyzed from the waist down. He is in agony and starts to hit drugs. (In sympathy Althea joins him.) Neurosurgery eliminates both his pain and any chance of recovery; he quits drugs. (Althea doesn't.) Flynt's assailant is still unknown, the film says. This fact, however, doesn't prevent the screenwriters, Scott Alexander and Larry Karaszewski, from showing him—indeed, showing how he trailed Flynt from courtroom to courtroom. (Why are they so sure it was a man? Mightn't a woman have wanted to murder Flynt for his treatment of her or for his general exploitation of women?)

The film isn't quite as daring as the man it's about. First, in the matter of nudity. Flynt keeps talking about vaginas. In one photo session he parts the legs of a reclining nude model. *Hustler* will corroborate this candor, but the film is more conservative: no vaginas. Second, the problematic material about Falwell that appeared in *Hustler*, including a cartoon of him having sex with his mother in an outhouse, does not appear in the film. If the film's reticence is because of the rating systems of the Motion Picture Association of America, this is a sour comment on the relative freedoms of the American press and screen—under the same First Amendment.

The film is further softened by some sentimental devices. When Althea dies—in her ornate bath, drugged out and drowned—Thomas Newman's music swells glutinously, with a wordless chorus behind it. (That chorus, soaring wordlessly over emotional peaks, must be the best-employed group in Movieland.) When Flynt returns home after his wife's funeral, he sees, in his mind's eye, flashbacks of their earlier days together, and we hear her voice on the soundtrack. *True Romance* invades *Hustler*.

Further, a trouble that couldn't be altered but that affects the climax. As Flynt himself implies in his scumbag aphorism, he is not the hero of his principal struggle. He is a victim, endangered, like the girl tied to the railroad track. The Supreme Court *en bloc* is the hero that rides to the rescue. It would be a mite difficult to create a climax out of nine justices doing research and conferring, but at the end of the film Flynt, dramatically speaking, is just someone waiting for help.

Forman, a Czech native who came to this country in 1969, . . . has done well here with his actors. Courtney Love plays Althea with sexual amplitude and moral abandon. Edward Norton, who impressed as the psychopath in *Primal Fear* and as Mr. Young Love in *Everyone Says I Love You*, gives Flynt's lawyer quiet strength. Donna Hanover, who is the wife of New York's mayor, is appealing as Ruth Carter Stapleton, the sister of Jimmy Carter. Stapleton is an evangelist who becomes friends with the Flynts before he is shot and who apparently develops a crush on him. At least Althea becomes jealous. James Cromwell strikes the right note as Charles Keating, the supporter of Falwell who later went to prison for involvement in a savings and loan scandal—and has just been released on legal technicalities.

Woody Harrelson plays Flynt viscerally and cleverly. In the shamefully underrated *Natural Born Killers*, Harrelson seethed and flamed as a young man who soars from the real into the surreal. Here, in a (relatively) more restrained role, he is a man who lives, in person and profession, by exaggerating the real.

Flynt, a postscript tells us, now publishes twenty-nine magazines.   10

LARRY FLYNT, SCUM CHIC

Hanna Rosin

> Words such as respectable, insightful, and icon are spilling from the   *1*
> tips of some decidedly unexpected tongues.
> —*from the introduction to an interview with Larry Flynt,*
> *publisher of* Hustler, *in the July 1996 issue*

James Carville, having run through his patter of Ken Starr jokes, suddenly grows somber. "Milos Forman lost his parents in the Holocaust," he says, introducing the Czech director who will introduce the new movie the Washington establishment has gathered to watch, *The People vs. Larry Flynt*. "The first thing a totalitarian state goes after is pornography, and when they do, the public applauds. It gets worse from there." Carville's wife, Mary Matalin, rests a fidgety hand on her fur coat. George Stephanopoulos stops throwing popcorn and catching it in his mouth. *The People vs. Larry Flynt* is meant to be consumed with grave import, and it is; the post-viewing crowd mingles in subdued tones. Carville, who has a largeish ranting role in the movie, says later that this reaction is a measure of his vehicle's subtle, nuanced nature. "Like they say in wine tasting, the movie had a long finish," he explains. "I can't imagine anyone going to see that movie and not stopping for a cup of coffee to talk about it."

The Christmas movie season is Hollywood's time for thinking large about large subjects. In the summer, it may be all sex, drugs and violence, but the winter solstice is a serious time, and it calls forth serious cinema about, well, sex, drugs and violence. But not pointless sex, drugs and violence. Sex, drugs and violence with a message—two thumbs up not from Joe Bob Briggs but from Frank Rich. This Christmas, pond scum is intellectually chic. Larry Flynt, once merely a millionaire publisher of vile, racist, scatological, pig-ugly and violently women-hating porn, has arrived, finally, at respectability's doorstep. Dredged from the sump just in time for *Hustler*'s twenty-fifth anniversary, the old slimemeister has been retrofitted as a hardscrabble defender of American freedoms. It's a transformation that longtime *Hustler* regulars watch with some awe. "I once wrote a couple of pieces for *Hustler*, and I used to dread that David Broder would see them," says Rudy Maxa, who covered the Flynt saga for *The Washington Post*. "It wasn't so chic back then. Now if I say at a dinner party I'm one of Larry Flynt's best friends, I get a lot of interest. I get a big kick out of it."

In between coast-to-coast signings for his new autobiography, *An Unseemly Man* ("I can't keep track of him," frets his agent), Flynt is juggling calls from "ABC, NBC, MTV, print press, magazines, it's absolutely overwhelming," she frets yet again. And the coverage is respectful, almost reverential: "the most timely and patriotic movie of the year," raves Frank Rich in *The New York Times*. Barry Hannah, in a breathless profile in *George* (which is holding a private screening) is nearly silenced by admiration: "Flynt and I are the same age, and when you see him you feel, in the fight for freedom, a relative coward." Hannah leaves us this question to ponder: "Was Flynt our hero?"

You don't have to be Catharine MacKinnon to smell something fishy here. It's not, as MacKinnon or William Bennett might argue, that Flynt's magazine should be boycotted for corrupting young minds. And it's not that he doesn't deserve credit for fighting and winning, in the 1988 Supreme Court decision *Falwell* v. *Flynt*, one of the most important freedom of the press cases since *New York Times* v. *Sullivan*. But our hero? In their desperation for a resounding liberal epiphany, the media seem to have swallowed Flynt's glossed-over image of himself. "We are talking about freedom!!" Woody Harrelson's Flynt screams at a group of reporters in one of the movie's endless portentous moments. "Doesn't anybody know what that means anymore?!" Script direction: "The reporters are silent. Larry is all choked up."

Crucial to the new Flynt mythology is faith in the movie's unstinting honesty; the idea that his new acolytes have bravely plumbed the abyss that is Larry Flynt's soul and have unflinchingly exposed this horror to the moviegoing public. "What makes this movie so effective is that it doesn't sentimentalize or airbrush Larry Flynt," writes Rich. Forman says he strove "not to glorify any of [Flynt's] life. I didn't try to cover the ugly side." The scriptwriters, Scott Alexander and Larry Karaszewski, are adamant on this point. "I don't think anyone will accuse us of whitewashing here," says Karaszewski. "As purists, we try to be honest."

Excuse me? What about, to start with the most obvious, the white-wash of shaving 200 pounds off Flynt and chiseling him into Woody Harrelson? "We knew we needed a real star because the subject matter was so strange," admits Alexander. "The studio would not have been comfortable if we had gone with Tom Arnold."

There must have been many things that made the studio uncomfortable. The movie opens with a barefoot and freckled 10-year-old Larry peddling moonshine to the locals in eastern Kentucky (script direction: "Larry is backwards, dirt poor, barely educated, yet bursting with Huckleberry Finn industriousness"). Soon he parlays his entrepreneurial vigor into a series of go-go clubs. The clubs are skanky, but they are also just this side of cool. He pays his girls well and treats them with respect, except for the occasional pat on the bum. He loves girls; in fact, it's because the female body is the most beautiful of God's creations that he wants to share it with his fellow man. The central drama is the love story of Larry and Althea, his soulmate and muse. It's a story about what a mischievous but good-hearted young man has to do to make it in a tough world, and what he learns along the way about liberty, the Constitution and the inalienable rights of man. Basically, it's an updated Capra flick: *Mr. Juggs Goes to Washington*.

In the movie, *Hustler* is almost accidentally in the nudie business (which is, by the way, presented as pretty innocent). Its real mission is social progress. It is engaged in the noble task of "breaking taboos": publishing nude pictures of Jackie O., a cartoon of Dorothy and the Tin Man having sex, and interracial orgies. And it is engaged, too, in the artist's calling of showing life as it is: *Playboy*'s hairless bunnies are replaced by working girls spreading it all under the bright lights. "God made the genitals. Who are we to say they aren't beautiful?" asks Woody/Flynt.

But what distinguishes *Hustler* is not its bare-all daring—the adult 10 section of any newsstand is full of lesser-known titles brimming with genitalia—but its relentless depiction of sex as beastly and of sexual creatures as beasts. Sex in *Playboy* is a barefoot romp in the park. Sex in *Hustler* is a freak show. The magazine's pictorials are violent, depressing and perverse. The objects of sexual desire are often chosen precisely for their unwholesomeness. They mock and debase the very idea of the female body as sacred: women smeared with excrement, 300-pound women, women with penises—a horror house of Diane Arbus rejects. *Hustler*'s preferred sex toy is a pile of shit. There is a running joke ad called "Butt-wiper Beer—the King of Smears," showing a woman's firm, sexy behind with diarrhea dripping down her leg. Couples have sex by smelly urinals, a man masturbates while watching a fat woman pee. As Flynt writes in the

September 1994 issue: "the desire to prick a pompous inflated bimbo is perfectly natural." (Yes, and so also to deflate a pompous prick.)

Flynt's venomous, bestial depiction of the world is not limited to women. What fits least well with the image of Flynt as liberal icon is the unbridled racism in *Hustler,* also left out of the movie. The magazine's pages are filled with pictures of fat-lipped black men—Negroes, actually—stuttering in semi-literate English or waving their oversized manhoods. In one, a smirking Louis Farrakhan chomps on watermelon while watching two white women make it. In another, a Negro picking cotton in the antebellum South waxes prophetic: "Payback's a comin'," he says. "Two hundred years from now we'll sell 'em drugs and make their daughters hos. Then they'll be our slaves."

So what? Art is complex. Truth is ugly. The way of progressivism is not for the faint of heart. And so on. But the idea of Flynt as a man whom good liberals must regard as heroic falls apart for another reason: the facts of Flynt's own life. When, as noted in the movie, Flynt described himself as a "scumbag," it was rare modesty. Flynt has led the sort of life that gives sordid a bad name. If all you knew about Flynt came from Milos Forman, you would get the impression that Althea was the only woman he married. You would also get the impression that he passed most of his days winning over juries with impassioned speeches on the First Amendment. In fact, Althea was the fourth of Flynt's five wives. And the story of Flynt's serial marriages is an unenlightening one. Flynt's bootstrap autobiography maintains a calm, sentimental tone throughout ("I made a lot of mistakes . . ."), except when it comes to his ex-wives. First there's Mary, a blonde he met at a bar in Dayton. Only after they were married did he learn, to his horror, that he was "the only one in the place who hadn't screwed her!" Then there's Peggy, the girl-next-door type. She turned out to have "the morals of an alley cat."

One viewer of *The People vs. Larry Flynt* who knew a bit about the subject beforehand is Tonya Flynt-Vega, who is 31 and one of five children whom Flynt fathered but didn't live with. This summer, Flynt-Vega publicly accused her father of sexually abusing her. Flynt, calling his daughter "a habitual liar," has denied the accusation. His daughter won't divulge the details, making it impossible to know what really happened. But she says some of her other stories ring painfully true. Like the time Flynt sent her and her mother, who were living in public housing, a Christmas card with $500. Inside was a picture of Santa exposing himself to a little girl. Flynt says he never sent the card. "This movie makes *Hustler* into a coffee-table magazine," Flynt-Vega says. "It lifts my father up as some kind of American hero, like Jesse James or Bonnie and Clyde. He's very manipulative, and he's just bought himself a respectable place in history."

Flynt's angry daughter is right about the movie. Forman's supposedly harsh examination of Flynt's life is really as soft and gauzy as a *Playboy* bunny shot. Even the fact that Flynt was a drug addict is presented with apologies. There is a brief interlude where an increasingly haggard and bloated Flynt ingests handfuls of pills and watches his wife do the same, but, as we learn later, it was only to dull the pain after he was shot. As soon as the pain is over he quits, "cold turkey." The movie ends with a teary, grieving Flynt, watching home videos of his dearly departed Althea. Forman excuses himself for his dishonesty. Artistic license and all that. "Bio pics are boring," he says, explaining why he left certain incidents out. But what Forman chose to omit is the central (and, incidentally, more interesting) truth of Flynt's life, and what he chose to include works to mitigate against that truth, in favor of what's politically apt.

As it happens, Forman's airbrushing of Flynt works against the core 15 intellectual defense of Flyntism. Flynt's worshipers argue that accepting the grim, grubby reality of Flynt is the whole point. Flynt (and *Hustler*), they say, is the authentic voice of working-class America. "If you had a provocative magazine and it appealed to more educated people, it was all right," writes philosopher/movie star James Carville in the latest issue of *Hustler*. "But for blue-collar people to have this was less desirable. One thing to ponder. Are the masses entitled to as much provocative art and provocative magazines as the elites are?" Carville's view is shared by a certain breed of feminist, the vampish kind that gets a thrill from seeing Camille Paglia surrounded by her bodyguards. One such person is Laura Kipnis, who has just published *Bound and Gagged: Pornography and the Politics of Fantasy in America*, with a chapter devoted to *Hustler*. The author's photo shows a dreamy-eyed Kipnis leaning back on a Turkish pillow, her hair tousled, her billowy blouse wrinkled and undone.

Kipnis upbraids her feminist colleagues for one of their most "formative blind spots": class. *Hustler*, she argues, "rants madly" against privilege, making it "by far the most openly class antagonistic mass-circulation periodical of any genre." She chalks up its grossness to "Rabelaisian transgression," a triumph of carnivalesque inversions: "the out-of-control, unmannerly body is precisely what threatens the orderly operation of the status quo." And we would all see its value if we gave up our prudish "insistence . . . [on] high-minded language."

But to accept Flynt's vision of the working class is, to say the least, condescending. Flynt invents a cast of blue-collar characters—buck-toothed sex maniacs, peeping Toms—and then spits on them. His working class has no aspirations outside the four walls of their truck beds. They mock American institutions and dream of nothing more than they already possess. Flynt actually disdains the working class, and his disdain shows in his lifestyle. He wheels around his mansion in an $85,000 gold-plated wheelchair and marvels at his French provincial and eighteenth-century English antiques, Persian rugs and faux Old Masters. He likes to brag to reporters that his average reader is 28 and has a median income of $50,000. He thought they were Joe Lunchbox types but was surprised in a recent survey to find he had more highly educated readers. "Ph.D.s must be more open-minded," he says. Thus, *The People vs. Larry Flynt*.

That Milos Forman should have an exaggerated impression of Flynt's heroism is understandable. After all, he points out, the two brutal regimes he lived through, the Nazis and the communists, "started with crusades against perverts." But for Frank Rich or Barry Hannah to repeat this mantra is stunningly empty. After all, Larry Flynt's story does not prove America is a dangerous place, but the opposite. There has never really been anything close to a real threat to Larry Flynt's liberty or his peculiar pursuit of happiness. Each time a narrow-minded Southern judge fined him or threw him in jail, the decision was overturned on appeal. He warns, and others repeat, that he was sentenced to twenty-five years. But he only served a few days, and, as he gloated at the time, his circulation skyrocketed. The court case on which Forman's entire movie is based was not even a censorship case. The very title of the movie is a lie. The case wasn't *The People* v. *Larry Flynt*. It was *Falwell* v. *Flynt*. It wasn't, in other words, an effort by the state to censor free speech. It was a libel case (much like the libel case Flynt plans to pursue against his daughter), an effort by one citizen, the Reverend Jerry Falwell, to prove that another citizen, Larry Flynt, had lied about him in publishing a parody interview in which Falwell talks about having sex with his mother. Flynt didn't go to court to stop the totalitarians from starting down the slippery slope of censorship. He went to court to protect his bank account. In doing so, he accidentally protected the right of free speech. That's not particularly brave or heroic. The real protectors of American rights are rather boring. They're a few dour justices and the Constitution that guides them. But that wouldn't make much of a movie.

The Responsive Reader

1. How does Goodman show that her "absolute" commitment to the First Amendment has been more than just talk? On the other hand, what are her key objections to the Larry Flynt movie?
2. What seems important in the capsule bio Kauffmann provides of the movie's hero? Does any of it put the controversy over the movie in a new light? Does any of it seem particularly relevant to the First Amendment issue? What is Kauffmann's criticism of the film's "reticence"? of its "sentimental devices"? of its weak climax? Does Kauffmann take a stand on the moral questions raised by the movie and its subject?
3. How does Rosin mock the pretensions of the moviemakers? What for her are major ingredients in the sanitized, whitewashed picture the movie presents? How convincing is her evidence that Flynt treats sex as bestial and disgusting; that he is guilty of racism that "fits least

well with the image of Flynt as a liberal icon"; and that the movie glosses over Flynt's sordid personal life? (For you, how relevant is Flynt's personal history to the controversy?)

Talking, Listening, Writing

4. If Flynt's story is seen as an American biography, what does it say to you about our society? What does it say about our legal system?
5. Most of the critics mention or allude to the director's experience with repression and censorship under totalitarian regimes. Why does it matter one way or the other?
6. A recent news story reported that one in five publications available on military bases is an adult magazine. Would you support a ban on the sale of such publications there? Why or why not?
7. Is there truth to the charge that social class plays a role in the crusade against pornography? Is it true that overtly sexy or kinky material is acceptable in art museums and in ads for high fashion (or jeans) but not in cheap magazines or videos?

Collaborative Projects

8. In a recent issue of a national publication for English teachers, several teachers with years of experience and good teaching records each told the story of being fired as the result of censorship pressures. Who practices censorship in American schools—when, where, and why? Working with a group, you may want to investigate recent test cases.

A BLACK JOURNALIST URGES O. J. TO ADMIT THE TRUTH

Gregory Clay

> *The murder of Nicole Brown Simpson (ex-wife of football star O. J. Simpson) and her escort Ronald Goldman set off one of the great media feeding frenzies of all time. O. J.'s flight in his white Bronco, pursued at a respectful distance by police cars from the Los Angeles police department; the tape of a 911 call by a frantic Nicole gasping "He'll kill me" and the photograph of her battered face; the bloody glove retrieved from behind O. J.'s mansion; the claims and counterclaims concerning the blood splattered at the murder scene and across the defendant's belongings; the bloody footprints left by the murderer's expensive Italian shoes—all these became familiar ingredients in one of the most widely watched crime shows in media history. The twelve million-dollar defense attorneys trooping each morning into the courtroom; the outmatched prosecutors; and the rogue cop who denied but was later found guilty of using the N-word—all these became familiar faces and household names and were signed to megabuck book contracts. When the "not guilty" verdict was announced, black students were shown on television as cheering wildly while white audiences listened in stunned silence. Johnny Cochran, who his colleague Robert Shapiro said had played the "race card" to sway a mostly black jury, became a television star on Court TV. The Brown and Goldman families sued in a subsequent civil trial for damages, and even though the judge in the second trial banned the television cameras, a mesmerized public remained glued to the proceedings. (The networks agonized over whether to break into the president's State of the Union address to announce the guilty verdict in the second trial.) Many observers explained the difference between the two verdicts by pointing to the mostly black jury in the first trial and the all-white jury in the second trial. In the following article, a black journalist working for the Knight-Ridder newspapers crosses the color line to take an inside look at the role of race in O. J. Simpson's life and in the O. J. trials.*

Thought Starters: During jury selection, a judge will often ask prospective jurors whether they will weigh police testimony as impartially as any other. The judge may also ask if the defendant's race would make any difference. How would you respond to these two questions?

It's time for O. J. Simpson to go tell it on the mountain. Time to come clean.

It's time for Simpson—1968 Heisman Trophy winner, first NFL 2,000-yard rusher, No. 1 American pariah—to erase the facade and tell the truth that he killed two people on June 12, 1994.

It's time for him to admit his demagoguery, his preying upon the passions of the black community to further his own selfish, misguided cause. Examine O. J. now, and examine O. J. in the 1960s, the period known for the civil rights movement.

In June 1969, O. J. was on top of the world. He had won the Heisman seven months earlier at USC, was making movies and television appearances on such shows as "Medical Center" while he was a rookie contract holdout with the Buffalo Bills, who selected him in the NFL draft that spring.

During a visit to New York that June, O. J. talked to sportswriter   5
Robert Lipsyte of the *New York Times*. (Remember, this is 1969, so there is some antiquated word usage.)

Simpson said:

> My biggest accomplishment is that people look at me like a man first, not a black man. I was at a wedding, my wife and a few friends were the only Negroes there, and I overheard a lady say, 'Look, there's O. J. Simpson and some niggers.'
>
> Isn't that weird? That sort of thing hurts me, even though it's what I strive for, to be a man first. Maybe it's money, a class thing. The Negro is always identified with poverty. But then you think of Willie Mays as black, but not Bill Cosby.
>
> So it's more than just money. As black men, we need something up there all the time for us, but what I'm doing is not for principles or black people. No, I'm dealing first for O. J. Simpson, his wife and his baby.

The wife, at that time, was Marguerite, and the baby was Arnelle.   10
Still, it seems he almost revels in this perceived class distinction of O. J. on one side of the fence and other black people on the other side.

With that, it seems so ironically strange and unsettling that someone like O. J. Simpson would end up creating such a wide racial divide in this nation.

Now look at the O. J. of the 1990s. He's giving speeches in sold-out black churches in Washington, D.C., where during a "love and support rally," black supporters were hailing Simpson as "our friend and brother." O. J. is holding anti-gang rallies at his Rockingham mansion in Los Angeles. He's talking about racism in the criminal justice system, talking about unequal treatment of black folk, talking about black men—namely himself—being vilified and white women—namely his slain ex-wife Nicole—being deified.

In reality, the only obvious unfairness that Simpson has faced was in 1967, when overrated UCLA quarterback Gary Beban won the Heisman Trophy.

Recall this is the man who previously was on the other side of that aforementioned fence. He's what I call a "convenient black person." In other words, if it's convenient to be black for his own motives, then he's black. If it's not convenient, then he's something else. It is very convenient now for O. J. to be black. Man, is it ever.

Many white folk have basically disowned him, and many black folk   *15* have come to his aid. O. J. is the biggest demagogue in the black community. When Simpson's butt was caught in the wringer, he suddenly became a black person.

The closest parallel is Supreme Court Associate Justice Clarence Thomas, who once appeared to try to distance himself from black folk. But when Thomas was being investigated for alleged sexual harassment against Anita Hill, Thomas made that infamous comment: "This is akin to a high-tech lynching of uppity blacks." Suddenly! Voila! That comment alone made many black people reduce Thomas to the level of most-hated black person in America.

In a tangential point, Thomas probably will be the focus of a potentially volatile debate when the National Association of Black Journalists holds its annual convention in Washington, D.C. The issue will be: Do we invite Justice Thomas as a news-maker speaker? If it were someone like Supreme Court Justice Thurgood Marshall, the matter would be a no-brainer, but this time—well, we'll see.

Simpson has figured out how to play black people like a drum. It's his discovery issue. He discovered that when you talk about race and racism in the United States, black folk tend to perk up. He's appealing to black folk's emotions and passions, thus a demagogue. And many black folk are falling for it.

That's the real shame in this. We should not be the ones pushing him to martyrdom. Remember, when Mike Tyson was released from prison, some black leaders foolishly hailed the convicted boxer as the next Malcolm X.

O. J., in a sense, lives in a prison without walls. He knows that black   *20* folk are all that he has left. Despite that smidgen of comfort, he will never work at a real occupation in this country again.

NBC Sports knows it would be network suicide to rehire him as a commentator. The Hertz rental car company dumped him soon after he was accused of the double homicide.

There would be boycotts, protests and demonstrations from advertising clients and viewers alike if O. J. returned to NBC's NFL pre-game show.

And, despite all the rhetoric and vocal support, no black-owned corporation, such as Black Entertainment Television, will hire him either.

In the criminal trial, Simpson's celebrity won out. The only thing that the first trial proved was former detective Mark Fuhrman's racist ways, even though the LAPD largely pandered to Simpson's desires (listen to the audiotape of the Bronco chase).

After his acquittal in the criminal trial, the victims' families felt   *25*
no sense of closure. Thus, the civil case. You can't blame Fred and Kim
Goldman for filing wrongful-death and battery suits for compensatory and
punitive damages. I would have done the same thing if Simpson had killed
my wife or sister or mother. If you feel the system fails, you must take
alternative action. That's a constitutional right.

O. J. was arguably the greatest running back who ever played in the
NFL. He was pretty to watch, he broke records, he had style. He was
the Juice.

I once admired O. J., not so much because of his ability to juke a
Dolphins defensive back or a Steelers linebacker, but because of where he
came from and where he ended up—that is, before 1994.

O. J. grew up in the Potrero Hill public housing project in San
Francisco. He was stricken with rickets as a child and associated with
street-gang hoodlums as a teenager. His mother, Eunice, too poor to afford
sophisticated medical care, fashioned home-made braces for his legs out of
scrap metal.

Simpson overcame many obstacles to find a measure of success,
which is so important because black men, the most stereotyped segment
of society, are often confronted with more than their fair share of hurdles
and put-downs in society.

O. J. used his lofty status to effectively become the first black person   *30*
to cross over into the lucrative world of commercial endorsements.

Before O. J. in the mid-1970s, the only place black people, especially
athletes, could hawk even the most obscure products was in the black
media, such as Ebony or Black Enterprise magazines.

O. J. made it cool and fashionable to run through airports for Hertz
on national television. Simpson, with his charming personality and articulate
style, was the precursor to the TV appearances of Shaquille O'Neal, Deion
Sanders, Bo Jackson, Michael Jordan, Grant Hill and Scottie Pippen.

He has thrown it away. Much of the public considers him a double
murderer who escaped prison. If the evidence used against him were found
against me, I would be eating my last Big Mac before heading to the
California gas chamber.

I wouldn't have a chance even to think about becoming a golfing
fanatic or demagogue, much less actually doing it. Much less a demagogue
with ulterior motives.

O. J., in the words of that revered spiritual, go tell it on the mountain.   *35*

The Responsive Reader

1. What portrait does Clay paint of Simpson's early history and accomplishments? Does he give a sympathetic account? How was Simpson
   a pioneer, setting precedents for other African Americans? Why does

Clay consider Simpson's past accomplishments not an extenuating but an aggravating circumstance?

2. How, according to Clay, did Simpson prey "upon the passions of the black community"? What does Clay mean when he calls Simpson a "convenient black person"?

3. Clay distances himself from two other prominent African Americans —Supreme Court Justice Clarence Thomas and boxing champion Mike Tyson. Why and how?

4. What is Clay's attitude toward some of the other players in the Simpson drama—the LAPD (the Los Angeles Police Department), the Goldman family, corporate sponsors?

Talking, Listening, Writing

5. A private university invited three of Simpson's original defense attorneys—Johnny Cochran, Robert Shapiro, Gerald Uelmen— to a symposium to talk about the media and the law. From what you saw or have read about the O. J. Simpson story, what conclusions did you yourself draw about the media and the law?

6. Do you think that the media coverage of the O. J. Simpson case helped widen the racial divide in this country?

7. Some other countries severely restrict the media in covering sensational court cases. In this country, some judges ban television or use gag orders to limit media access to lawyers and witnesses. Do you think the glare of sensational publicity interferes with the pursuit of justice? Or should the public's right to know be paramount?

8. Many observers saw race as the deciding factor in the O. J. story. Others emphasized the role of money, and still others focused on the incompetence of a bungling law enforcement system. Which of the three do you think may have been most important or decisive?

Collaborative Projects

9. Working with a group, you may want to investigate the role of the media in another famous court case that turned into a media circus, for instance the Dr. Shepherd trial or the Rodney King case.

SISTER FROM ANOTHER PLANET PROBES THE SOAPS

Andrea Freud Loewenstein

> *The ancient art of satire holds our human weaknesses and vices up to ridicule. The satirist's art is like a funhouse mirror that exaggerates our short-comings for all to see. It employs humor as a weapon to shame us into acting more responsible or humane. Satire may be gentle and affectionate, but it may also turn cutting and bitter when ignorance, deviousness, or callousness offend the satirist's standards of acceptable behavior. The women's movement, some-times stereotyped as humorless, is increasingly providing a stage for women's satirical humor. (*Women's Glibber: State-of-the-Art Women's Humor *appeared in 1993.) In the following example of feminist satire, a contributor to* Ms. *magazine directs her satirical barbs at a time-honored American insti-tution. She has a visitor from outer space marvel at the strange rituals of court-ship and "copulation" in the universe of the soaps. Andrea Freud Loewen-stein is the author of* The Worry Girl, *published by a women's press in the United Kingdom. This collection of interconnected stories, with its echoes of an Austrian Jewish past and the Holocaust, has been described as re-creating "the sorrows and terrors that inform a Jewish child's dreams." Loewenstein's study* Loathsome Jews and Engulfing Women *was published by New York University Press.*

Thought Starters: Why do people watch soap operas? Is it true that soap opera plots and a soap opera mentality are increasingly infiltrating prime-time television?

Dear Professor:

Enclosed is my research paper. As you may remember, I attended every one of your lectures (I float at a right angle in the front row; last Thursday I was an iridescent green with ocher spots) on that most fascinating subject, the human species North Americanus Soapus. For my research project, I viewed several weeks' worth of documentary videotapes from four different "Soaps," chosen because they were among the most widely watched programs in the Earthling year 1993, with some 50 million viewers combined. I will hereafter refer to the humanoids whose acquaintance I made in "The Young and the Restless," "The Bold and the Beautiful," "All My Children," and "Gen-eral Hospital," as "Soapoids."

The name "Soaps," by the way, appears to derive from the obsessional recurrence of the cleanliness theme in the "commercials," which occur at rhyth-

1

mic intervals throughout the tapes. These are short, ritualized hymns of thanksgiving and praise to selected objects of worship, such as toilet bowl cleaners and vaginal deodorants.

I must admit that during the first week of viewing, in which I used all 17 of my sensors, I was unable to distinguish one Soapoid from another. The only distinction I was immediately able to make was between male and female—the Soapoids' preoccupation with ritual ownership of the opposite sex causes them to go to amazing lengths to signal gender distinction. These signals include the compulsory arrangement and selective removal of facial and head hair, distinctive body coverings, and (for the adult female) symbolic facial markings and mutilations.

This species, in contrast to our own, is subdivided into a mere two   5 fixed gender groupings: male and female. Contrary to the lecture in which you informed us that occasionally both male and female choose to couple with their own kind and that those humanoids tend to be ostracized by the majority, I observed no variation in gender identity or object choice. On the contrary, all of my sample were hostile toward their own gender, whom they perceived as rivals in their never-ending fight to possess the opposite sex. Although this goal appears to be the Soapoids' overwhelming motivational force, the humans in my sample spent almost no time actually copulating. Instead, their main behavior consisted of endless discussions of, preparations for, and references to the act.

Nevertheless, copulation, when it does occur, often leads to trouble and confusion, even for the viewer. I spent a great deal of time attempting to determine the name of the young woman from *All My Children* who works in a police station, is the daughter of one of the two possible fathers of Mimi's unborn child, and nosily looked up information to determine the date of conception. Since the records revealed that she had copulated with both men during the same week, Mimi was forced to confess and call off her wedding the day it was scheduled. I never did get the young woman's name.

Copulation does allow the females to exert ownership over the males. You had informed us that males are the dominant gender, and that their inability to express their feelings verbally leads to frequent acts of violence. I regret to inform you that this conclusion is no longer valid. Soapoid males are quite gentle and verbally expressive. Their preferred behavior consists of lengthy expositions on their feelings toward the females. The male is especially prone to elaborate courtship rituals in preparation for copulation. These include the repetition of such submissive phrases as: "I love you so much," "You're my whole life," and "You were amazing last night, darling!" In one typical behavior, a male in *The Bold and the Beautiful* prepared for intercourse by placing at least 20 floating water lilies containing small lit candles in a pool of water upon which floated an inflatable rubber raft, the intended scene of sexual activity.

The far more complex females are the actual aggressors. In a lecture, you had mentioned that some women, referred to as "feminists," join with one another toward a common goal. No such movement was evident in this sample. In fact, the females' most favored posture was the standoff, a highly aggressive position in which two women position themselves from one to two feet apart and emit such statements as "I hated you the first time I saw you." This is accompanied by a full range of physical expressions, including crossing of the arms, curling of the lip, and advancing in a menacing manner.

Unlike the male, the female can be classified into several subtypes, all arranged around the notions of "good" and "evil." These inborn tendencies emerge at puberty, apparently along with the mammary glands. The Good Female mitigates her natural dominance by an exaggerated concern for the welfare and nourishment of "her" male. She is especially solicitous of his title—Writer, Actor, Businessman, Doctor, Lawyer, or Policeman— and is always ready to abandon her own title to have more time to support his efforts. In *The Young and the Restless,* for example, Nikki, a Businesswoman, repeatedly interrupts her own work to service Cole, a Writer who is also a Groomer of Horses. Attired in a series of low-cut red evening gowns, she waits on him at his workplace in the horse stable, serving him champagne and caviar, assuring him that publishers from the mythical city of New York will turn his novel into a "best-seller."

It is important to note, however, that these work titles are symbolic. 10 Soapoids, who possess a limited will to action and often require several hours of "processing" conversation to accomplish a simple task, must limit themselves to the all-important Preparation for Copulation. They have neither the time nor the energy to engage in actual "work." (The now meaningless title *General Hospital* indicates that Soapoids did work at one time.)

Good Females can be recognized by their wide-open, forward-gazing eyes, modest demeanor, and light pink lip-paint. In old age they become wrinkled. Evil Females, on the other hand, remain slim, highly polished, and brightly painted throughout life, a certain tautness of the facial skin being the only visible sign of aging. The Evil Females' characteristics include unfaithfulness, sexual rapacity, and the need to manipulate others. Most Evil Females confine their ambition to collecting a large number of men, but a few exhibit a further will to power through the ownership of Titles, Land, Factories, Businesses, or Patents. These women, whom I call Controllers, have destroyed the lives of generations of Soapoids.

In your lecture on racial and ethnic diversity, you brought us almost to jellification with your tale of the oppression of darker-hued or "African American" humanoids at the hands of the lighter ones whom you labeled the subspecies "European American." I am happy to inform you that no such oppression exists among modern-day Soapoids. In fact, there seems to be no difference between the darker and lighter types. All hues mix and converse on terms of perfect equality and good-will and hold titles of equal symbolic significance. Dark-skinned females (who exhibit a wide range of coloration, unlike the more muted light-skinned humanoids) wear their head hair in the same fashion as all other females—raised two or three inches from the head, then flowing to the shoulders. Darker and lighter humanoids do not mate, and appear to have no desire to do so. Whether this is because of the force of taboo or physical incompatibility cannot be determined at this juncture. It should be noted, however, that none of the African American females had attained the status of Controller, perhaps because they lack the necessary icy blue eyes.

Saul, an elderly male from *The Bold and the Beautiful,* speaks with an accent, wears a pink shirt, highly ornamented necktie, and thick spectacles; he appears to be a eunuch. My ethnosensor identified him as a member of the subspecies "Jew." Whether these characteristics are an honest reflection of this identity is hard for me to determine—he was the only member of the group in this sample. Maria from *All My Children* was identified as a member of the subspecies "Latina"; as far as I can tell from my viewing, this group is notable for wavy head hair and the ability to ride a Horse without a saddle. Unlike African Americans, these Latinas appear able to mate with the "European Americans."

The photographs you showed us of the unsavory dwelling places (known as "Ghettos") of some humanoids also appear to be out of date. As of now, all Soapoids inhabit spacious, carefully color-coordinated cubes, filled with plastic flowers and bright modular furniture, in which they engage in their activities of arguing, preparing for copulation, and discussing their feelings for one another. Since eating, cleaning, and evacuation are not part of these sequences (being reserved for the "commercials"), no rooms are provided for these activities. It is unclear whether this is by choice or necessity (perhaps the atmosphere outside these cubes is not pure enough to breathe).

No analysis of Soapoid society would be complete without a mention of the interlacing "commercials." These mini-documentaries demonstrate the Soapoids' unique ability to encapsulate and split off areas of behavior and their need to control their errant bodies. The mini-docs also provide a neat solution for any scholars who may, thus far in my narrative, have been puzzled by the absence of ingestion and excretion in the lives of these living organisms. All such functions are reserved for the mini-docs, during which Soapoids frantically ingest prepackaged slimness-controlling nourishments and rid their cubes, their eating utensils, their garments, and their bodies of all superfluous liquids and imperfections. "Dirty on the outside!" exclaims a voice-over as a female handles her mate's garment in horror. "Uh oh, what about the inside!" A typical hour in the lives of Soapoids contains countless mini-docs that utilize not only a cleaning fluid that will purify garments on the inside, but also: a garment that can absorb the excretions of even the most wiggly of infant young; a tablet that cleans the excreting instrument by providing 2,000 flushes; another tablet to be ingested by the enemy species Cockroach; and yet another to be taken by the female Soapoid in order to soften her stools and ease excretion.

The lower body of the female seems to be especially in need of such devices. A sequence that begins with the frightening words "Out of control!" introduces tablets that will "take control" of diarrhea in one day. The vaginal area is serviced by a pellet that cures yeast infections, a deodorant designed to "intercede" between the female's odor and her undergarments, and—for those who would seem to have the opposite problem—an ointment for vaginal dryness. Is it because the female Soapoid's vagina is the seat of her dominance over the male, and thus the location of her power, that it requires such constant servicing? Or is the female's verbal aggression yet another mark of her need to "stay in control" of her wayward body?

I end this paper with a confession: I entered my research project with a certain amount of bias against humanoids, whom I had been taught to regard as primitive, quarrelsome creatures, frozen in their limited natures and bodily forms, unable to regulate their own lives and affairs. But slowly, I grew increasingly susceptible to the charm of these beings. Before long, I found myself growing impatient with the time spent in my ordinary occupations. As I went about my daily tasks, I couldn't wait to join those beings who, never challenging, always predictable, asked nothing more from me than to watch them. Now that the viewing is over, I feel empty.

As I beam this paper to your neurotransmitters and project it into the ozone, it is with both fondness and regret that, amid the busy whirl of my life, I pause to remember the Soapoids, a matriarchal people whose lives drag out in long luxurious segments lived within color-coordinated cubes, and who relegate the more messy business of life to quick one-minute segments, thus freeing themselves for a stress-free, germ-free, moisture-controlled existence.

The Responsive Reader

1. What trappings of research and science fiction help make this space visitor's field trip to the land of the humanoids humorous?
2. What is exaggerated and what is true to life in the visitor's naive observations of gender distinctions and gender roles? As here observed, what is revealing and funny about the treatment of sex in the soaps? about the treatment of "courtship"? What are some telling satirical touches on these subjects in this space traveler's log?
3. Does the episode about Mimi's intended marriage and unborn child from *All My Children* ring true? What does it show about the moral universe of the soaps?
4. What are Loewenstein's targets when she satirizes the treatment of race, ethnicity, or class differences in soapland?
5. How does life in the soaps go counter to what the visitor had been taught about the impact of feminism in the real human world? How

else does the humanoid world of the soaps contradict what the visitor had been led to expect?

Talking, Listening, Writing

6. How much in the soaps as described here mirrors life? How much is fantasy? What kind of fantasy is it? Why is it so popular? What if anything is its central appeal?
7. Many college students reportedly are avid followers of the soap operas. What would you say or write in defense of the soaps? Or, what would you say or write to wean people from this kind of entertainment?
8. Do male humor and female humor reflect different ways of looking at the world? Is what is funny to men often not funny to women, and vice versa?

Collaborative Projects

9. Working with a group, study typical plots of current soaps and examine what they show about the emotional and moral world of soap opera.

THE DEATH OF MARILYN MONROE
Sharon Olds

Sharon Olds is a widely published American poet who with uninhibited candor takes on the topics of a new generation: bad parenting, sex without love, sex with love, and the wars between mothers and daughters. In the following poem, Olds offers her own perspective on the myth of Marilyn Monroe, "goddess of the silver screen / the only original American queen" (Judy Grahn). In the popular imagination, Norma Jean or Marilyn Monroe, stereotypical sex bomb and dumb blonde, became the ultimate Hollywood creation. A male admirer called her "every man's love affair," whose voice "carried such ripe overtones of erotic excitement and yet was the voice of a little child" (Norman Mailer). Feminist writers have tried to rediscover the human being behind the stereotype, who "tried, I believe, to help us see that beauty has its own mind" (Judy Grahn).

Thought Starters: What memories and associations does mention of Marilyn Monroe bring to mind? What do you remember about her career, her movies, her private life, her suicide?

The ambulance men touched her cold   1
body, lifted it, heavy as iron,
onto the stretcher, tried to close the
mouth, closed the eyes, tied the
arms to the sides, moved a caught   5
strand of hair, as if it mattered,
saw the shape of her breasts, flattened by
gravity, under the sheet,
carried her, as if it were she,
down the steps.   10

These men were never the same. They went out
afterwards, as they always did,
for a drink or two, but they could not meet
each other's eyes.

                    Their lives took   15
a turn—one had nightmares, strange
pains, impotence, depression. One did not
like his work, his wife looked

different, his kids. Even death
seemed different to him—a place where she   *20*
would be waiting,

And one found himself standing at night
in the doorway to a room of sleep, listening to
a woman breathing, just an ordinary
woman   *25*
breathing.

The Responsive Reader

1. Poets often make us notice realities that to others might seem merely routine. In the account of the ambulance crew collecting the body, what details are striking, different, gripping, or unexpected?
2. Why did the death have such an impact on the ambulance men? How did it affect them and why?

Talking, Listening, Writing

3. A persona is an assumed identity that may serve as a mask hiding the real person. Have you ever discovered the private person or human being behind a public persona or media creation?
4. Has popular entertainment left the stereotype of the Hollywood blonde behind? Are other stereotypical females evident in the media today?

Collaborative Projects

5. Macho Norman Mailer and Gloria Steinem, a leading feminist, have both published books about Marilyn Monroe. What accounts for the wide range of perspectives on her life, work, and person? Your class may want to farm out different treatments of the Marilyn Monroe legend to members of a group and then have them compare notes and pool their resources.

WRITING
WORKSHOP 7

Weighing Pro and Con

Thinking the matter through often means sorting out the pro and con. When we face a thorny issue, we weigh arguments for and against. We lean to one side, but then we listen to those who disagree, and we find that there is something to be said for the other side. Ideally, after giving due weight to opposing views, we reach a balanced conclusion. We give others the benefit of the doubt, so that we don't make up our minds prematurely, in ignorance of crucial facts. We listen to dissenting voices so that fair-minded listeners or readers cannot accuse us of being one-sided, of having a closed mind.

Of course, no one is ever likely to have a totally open mind. Even open-minded people are likely to have at least tentative commitments on most serious subjects. They incline one way or the other on tax monies for public transportation, on affirmative action in college admissions, on health services for illegal immigrants, on smoking bans for restaurants, or on mandatory helmets for bicycle riders. (You might want to poll the people in your class on how many would vote for and how many against on these and perhaps other debatable issues.) However, the test of a thinking, rational person is the willingness to consider alternative views and to judge them on their merits.

Weighing the pro and con is not just a matter of helping you make up your own mind. To convince a fair-minded person, you need to show that you have looked at relevant evidence—without sweeping unwanted facts under the sofa. If readers suspect that you are prone to slant the evidence, you may lose your credibility. The more experienced your readers are, the more likely they are to be wary of being manipulated by someone who knows more than they do but is not telling.

Writing that honestly weighs the pro and con invites the reader to share in an intellectual journey. Writer and reader together embark on a journey of discovery. They look at the conflicting evidence together, trying to sort it out and make sense of it. Ideally, writer and reader will arrive at the same or similar conclusion. Readers then do not have to feel that they were browbeaten or bamboozled or manipulated. Pro-and-con writing gives you a chance to show that you respect your reader's intelligence.

TRIGGERING Many people's minds are set on controversial subjects. (Sometimes they seem set in cement.) Such people often voice their opinions confidently, sometimes at the top of the voice. But many other people are genuinely challenged by issues where there is something to be said on both sides. Here are some issues that you may want to think and write about:

- Traditionally, Americans have prided themselves on their opposition to censorship. However, we encounter situations that test our commitment to freedom of speech. Do we have to protect hate literature circulated by neo-Nazis, rap songs endorsing the killing of cops, or art that seems blasphemous to religious groups? Where do we draw the line? Or is there a line? What do we learn from listening to those who radically oppose and those who seem to endorse censorship?

- Most Americans endorse equal educational opportunity. However, what happens when those students reach college age whose previous schooling has been hampered by poverty, a violent environment, substandard schools with burnt-out teachers and no money for up-to-date textbooks? Do we apply the same admission standards to them as to preppies? Or do we make allowance—and how? Do we "water down" our standards and our curriculum?

- Traditionally, Americans have prided themselves on freedom of choice. If someone continues to smoke in spite of health warnings, it is that person's choice. However, nonsmokers who inhale secondary smoke in offices, restaurants, or airplanes did not make that choice. Do smokers have rights, and how do we balance them off with those of nonsmokers?

GATHERING As with any other substantial paper, so with your pro-and-con paper, input has to come before output. You need to explore the issue—listening, reading, taking notes. Try to develop the mental habits that will help you profit from the play of pro and con:

- *Learn to listen to people you think are wrong.* (The natural impulse is to ridicule them or shout them down.) What are they actually saying? *Why* do they disagree with you? What do they know that you don't know? What do they value that you disregard—and why?

- *Try playing the devil's advocate.* To come to know an opposing view from the inside, try to present your opponents' position as if you were on their side.

- *Look for the informed impartial observer.* Listen to some voices that do *not* represent the opposing factions. Is there someone who is knowledgeable but above the fray? Can you find someone who might care but not have an axe to grind? Much of what you encounter will be "facts" and arguments presented by interested parties or by PR people promoting an agenda. Who might be unbiased and yet be in a position to know?

To help you explore the pro and con on an issue, you might want to participate in a group writing activity. Different members of the class would suggest arguments to be lined up in two separate pro and con columns on the board. Or your class might want to stage a mock debate, with opposing speakers presenting arguments that members of the class would have to ponder in their pro-and-con papers.

SHAPING As with other kinds of papers, there is no "one-size-fits-all" formula for writing a pro-and-con paper. To start getting your material under control, try lining up pro and con arguments in two separate facing columns. Preparing these two contrasting lists will help clarify the issue for you. It will at the same time be a big step toward structuring your paper.

Here is a tentative lining up of the pro and con on the issue of drug testing on the job: As a condition of employment, should people in sensitive occupations agree to submit to unannounced testing for illegal drugs? (Which side do you find yourself on when looking over these notes? Or are you torn between the two opposed positions?)

PRO	CON
1. Pilots, engineers, and operators of heavy equipment literally take others' lives into their hands.	1. The "war on drugs" makes no distinction between recreational drug users and addicts.
2. Drug users are responsible for absenteeism, low productivity, and high injury rates on the job.	2. The tests are notoriously inaccurate (sesame seeds cause false positives) and ruin the careers of people falsely accused.
3. "Recreational" drug users support a murderous drug trade responsible for unprecedented levels of crime.	3. Employers become agents of a police state, poisoning employer-employee relations.
4. Drug users in prestigious occupations are the worst possible role models for endangered American youth.	4. Drug testing undermines basic American traditions of due process and protection against self-incrimination.
5. Testing is above-board and better than snooping and spying.	5. We already have too much government meddling in people's private lives.

By looking at what you have on each side of the issue, you can decide what organizational strategy might be more effective: presenting the position of each side in its entirety—or presenting the pro and con point by point.

Should you present and explain major arguments on one side first—and then look at those on the opposing side? This way the inner logic of each opposing position might become clear. Your readers would see how major planks in each opposing position are related, how they fit together.

Or should you present one argument on one side at one time—and then immediately show what the other side would say in return? This way your readers could share in the excitement of the debate. They could become involved in the give-and-take of assertion and rebuttal.

REVISING In spite of your good intentions, a first draft is still likely to be too one-sided. It is likely to be too polemical—pushing your own side of the argument while giving a nod to the other (with too many barbs at those who disagree with you). Try the following to make your paper read more like a true weighing of the options:

 ▪ *Try to apply the equal time rule.* The treatment of the other side is likely to be too brief—or too biased. A rule of thumb: Are the arguments for given roughly as much space as the arguments against?

 ▪ *Lower the emotional thermostat.* Use your revision to tone down heated statements—to make your treatment more objective, more balanced. A sentence like "Again our First Amendment rights are encroached upon, ignored, and violated by the pro-censorship forces" is not likely to make the other side listen to your arguments (it is going to make them mad).

 ▪ *Edit out outright invective or abuse.* Check for terms like *extremists, lunatic fringe, safety nazis, gun nuts, femlibbers*—all such expressions generate more heat than light. (If any such appear in your paper, make sure to show that you are merely *quoting* them and that they are not yours.)

Study the following sample student paper. How successful is it? How good a model does it make?

Warning: Material May Not Be Suitable for Members of Congress

We drink the vomit of priests, make love with the dying whore.
We suck the blood of the beast and hold the key to death's door.

This song by a heavy metal band shows the kind of lyrics that have brought organizations like the Parents' Music Resource Center (PMRC) into the censorship arena. With the aim of fighting explicit lyrics promoting violence, racism, suicide, sexual abuse, drugs, and alcohol, the PMRC has supported numerous bills mandating the labeling and censorship of offending recording artists and their albums. An in-house legal research service advised the U.S. Congress in 1987 that it has the "constitutional authority to regulate explicit sound recording lyrics and restrict minors' access to them." Albert Gore, then Democratic senator from Tennessee, went on record as saying that he would be "looking to find if there is some constitutional means to regulate lyrics." Phyllis Pollack, the executive director of Music in Action, an anti-censorship group, replied that "this is very dangerous, strange stuff. We've always said that the issue is not rock music; it's trying to take away freedom of speech. Once they convince people that censorship is O.K. in rock, they'll move on to other media."

The basic argument of the groups asking for warning labels on offensive recordings is that parents have the responsibility to bring up their children in a way that is acceptable to the parents' moral and ethical beliefs. Parents cannot exercise this responsibility when material diametrically opposite to their religious and moral views is everywhere easily accessible to their children. As one supporter of the labeling laws explained, our thoughts are influenced by the words and images we put in our minds. We should try to supply our minds with input that will promote healthy thoughts, "which in turn will produce healthy lives." Many supporters of warning labels for offensive material are members of the Christian right who attribute the rise of teenage suicides, teenage sex, and violence in our society to the constant presence of sex and violence in the media.

In rebuttal, defenders of rock musicians have challenged the alleged links between teen murderers or suicide victims and the rock lyrics that are being made the "scapegoat." As Jean Dixon, member of Congress from Missouri, said, there must have been something terribly wrong with these children before they listened to any particular song. The proposed laws would require large warning stickers or parental advisory labels on certain albums. Who would make the decisions? Retailers are not experts on the political and religious ideologies involved. More than one skeptic has warned, "a sticker may just entice kids to buy a record." Warning labels might actually encourage people to purchase records they otherwise would pass by.

As with similar issues, charges and countercharges are heated. Pro-censorship groups freely use terms like "filth" and "garbage of the mind." Anti-censorship forces call their opponents "book burners." What is the answer?

We are not going to control our children's minds. We cannot dictate what they can see and hear and think. The best we can hope for is open and honest communication between parents and their children. I agree we must help create positive images for our children. I also agree that there is much offensive or borderline material in today's popular music. However, if there is to be any labeling of recordings, it should be worked out on a voluntary basis by representatives of the industry and the artists concerned. The Federal, state, and local governments should keep their hands off. The basic challenge is to provide some voluntary system of rating, similar to the one used for movies. The music industry professionals should create their own system of labeling while protecting the free speech rights of their artists.

QUESTIONS How and how well does the student writer set up the issue? Do you think both sides are fairly represented in this paper? Are you willing to accept the writer's solution as a balanced, rational conclusion? Do you think the paper as a whole leads up to it effectively? Why or why not?

Topics for Pro-and-Con Papers (A Sampling)

1. Are efforts to protect or bring back predators—coyotes, wolves, grizzlies—wrong-headed?
2. Should college bookstores take from the shelves materials (magazines, calendars) accused of being sexist or exploitative of women?
3. Are the courts justified in banning school prayer? (Do they have the right to ban invocations at ceremonies at public colleges or universities?)
4. Should colleges have special admission standards for members of minorities? (Should they lower their requirements for special groups?)
5. Should public funds be used to support art that is offensive to the majority? (Study test cases like exhibits supported in part by funds from the National Endowment for the Arts and criticized vehemently by conservative groups.)
6. Should anything be done to stem the flood of violence in movies and television programs?
7. Are the private lives and past histories of political candidates fair game for the news media? Or do public figures have a right to privacy?
8. Do people teaching minority literature have to be members of minorities themselves? (Is a white teacher qualified to teach a course in African American literature, for instance?)
9. Are you in favor of sting operations, or do they constitute entrapment? (For instance, is the government or the post office justified in conducting sting operations to combat child pornography?)
10. Do smokers have rights?

8

Role Models:
In Search of Heroes

*When I hear the people praising greatness, then I know that I too
shall be recognized; I too when my time comes shall achieve.*
                                                    —*from the Chippewa*

*I never heard my friends say they wanted to be like their fathers when
they grew up. Why would we want that when we knew our fathers
were catching hell. That would be like saying we wanted to catch hell,
too. If anything, we wanted to be the opposite of our fathers. . . .
There is nothing more dangerous and destructive in a household than
a frustrated, oppressed black man.*
                                                    —*Nathan McCall*

Where do we expect young Americans to look for role models to
admire or to imitate? To encourage young people to collect inspirational
stamps, the U.S. Post Office recently offered stamps in four categories:
"Presidents," "Athletes," "Inventors," and "Heroes." On the promotional
poster, the example of a hero was Paul Bunyan with his axe. In real life,
teachers, social workers, and parents looking for role models for young
Americans have found heroic figures harder to identify.

Our society finds it hard to worship heroes—or to find heroes to
worship. Americans have a tradition of debunking or iconoclasm (or idol-
smashing). Historians scour the history books "in search of heroes to lay
low" (Mark Leyner). Biographers or offspring of famous people lay bare
the private traumas and meannesses behind the glamorous façade. The
media thrive on scandal. Political leaders spend millions investigating one
another, trying to prove the other side guilty of influence peddling and
illegal activities.

The idols the media glorify often have feet of clay: Celebrities endorse products they don't use. The heroes of financial newsletters and the
Wall Street Journal are cost-cutting executives who engineer mass layoffs
and downgrade the jobs of the remaining employees. A skater who a few

years earlier was implicated in the knee-bashing (with a steel pipe) of an Olympic rival again skated for money raised by promoters with dubious standards of sportsmanship.

Nevertheless, people who are struggling or faced with barriers have a need for someone to admire, to look up to, to emulate. They look for role models that can symbolize for them their hopes and aspirations. Eve Merriam said in her poem dedicated to Elizabeth Blackwell, who braved centuries of precedent to become a female M.D., "don't let it darken, / the spark of fire; / keep it aglow." Amelia Earhart, before she left on the flight around the world from which she did not return, wrote a letter that said:

> Please know that I am quite aware of the hazards. I want to do it because I want to do it. Women must try to do things as men have tried. When they fail, their failure must be but a challenge to others.

Thousands of Americans each year visit the Martin Luther King Memorial in Atlanta to remind themselves of the eloquence and vision of the preacher who spoke of his dream that "the rough places will be made plain, and the crooked places will be made straight, and the glory of the Lord shall be revealed, and all flesh shall see it together."

In our diverse culture, what role models do we have who are not athletes, generals, or astronauts? What do we hear when we do not merely put people we admire on a pedestal but listen to what they have to say?

A BLACK ATHLETE LOOKS
AT EDUCATION
Arthur Ashe

> *Arthur Ashe was one of the first African Americans to achieve an international reputation in tennis, until then often thought of as a sport for white people with money and social aspirations. Althea Gibson had been the first black woman to win the English Wimbledon tournament in 1957 and 1958. Ashe defeated the seemingly invincible Jimmy Connors for the Wimbledon title in men's tennis in 1975. Ashe was ranked first in the world at the time, but injuries and finally a heart attack cut short his career. He used his influence as a sports celebrity to promote civil rights causes; he helped get South Africa banned from the Davis Cup because of the government's apartheid policies. The following is one of the articles he wrote for the* New York Times *and the* Washington Post, *often trying to convince "not only black athletes but young blacks in general to put athletics in its proper place." Ashe said about this article, "Some teacher probably read it and put it on the bulletin board. . . . The people who have the problems may not read it, but the ones who are in a position to influence them will." Do you think the kind of advice Ashe gives in this article influences people?*

Thought Starters: Have you ever read or heard enough about an outstanding athlete to make you feel you knew the person behind the media image?

Since my sophomore year at UCLA, I have become convinced that   1
we blacks spend too much time on the playing fields and too little time in the libraries. Consider these facts: for the major professional sports of hockey, football, basketball, baseball, golf, tennis and boxing, there are roughly only 3170 major league positions available (attributing 200 positions to golf, 200 to tennis and 100 to boxing). And the annual turnover is small.

There must be some way to assure that those who try but don't make it to pro sports don't wind up on street corners or in unemployment lines. Unfortunately, our most widely recognized role models are athletes and entertainers—"runnin'" and "jumpin'" and "singin'" and "dancin'."

Our greatest heroes of the century have been athletes—Jack Johnson, Joe Louis, and Muhammad Ali. Racial and economic discrimination forced us to channel our energies into athletics and entertainment. These were the ways out of the ghetto, the ways to get that Cadillac, those regular shoes, that cashmere sport coat.

Somehow, parents must instill a desire for learning alongside the desire to be Walt Frazier. Why not start by sending black professional athletes into high schools to explain the facts of life?

I have often addressed high school audiences and my message is always the same: "For every hour you spend on the athletic field, spend two in the library. Even if you make it as a pro athlete, your career will be over by the time you are 35. You will need that diploma."

Have these pro athletes explain what happens if you break a leg, get a sore arm, have one bad year or don't make the cut for five or six tournaments. Explain to them the star system, wherein for every star earning millions there are six or seven others making $15,000 or $20,000 or $30,000. Invite a bench-warmer or a guy who didn't make it. Ask him if he sleeps every night. Ask him whether he was graduated. Ask him what he would do if he became disabled tomorrow. Ask him where his old high school athletic buddies are.

We have been on the same roads—sports and entertainment—too long. We need to pull over, fill up at the library and speed away to Congress and the Supreme Court, the unions and the business world.

I'll never forget how proud my grandmother was when I graduated from UCLA. Never mind the Davis Cup. Never mind the Wimbledon title. To this day, she still doesn't know what those names mean. What mattered to her was that of her more than thirty children and grandchildren, I was the first to be graduated from college, and a famous college at that. Somehow, that made up for all those floors she scrubbed all those years.

The Responsive Reader

1. Where does Ashe state his central thesis? How does he echo or reinforce it? How does he support it with examples, explanations, statistics?
2. Does Ashe look at the larger political or cultural context of the issue? Does he try to get at underlying causes?

Talking, Listening, Writing

3. Do you think this article persuaded its intended audience? Why or why not?
4. Some observers say that the lionizing of black athletes and entertainers perpetuates damaging stereotypes: African Americans can succeed only as ballplayers, singers, or comedians. Others answer that successful athletes from nonwhite backgrounds give both nonwhite and white youngsters people from other backgrounds to admire. Widely admired athletes thus help break down the barriers of preju-

dice. What do you think? How would you defend your stand on this issue?

5. In 1992 Ashe announced at a news conference that he had been infected with the AIDS virus, apparently as the result of a blood transfusion during open-heart surgery. He made the announcement reluctantly, after *USA Today* confronted him with a rumor of his condition and asked him to confirm or deny. Anna Quindlen examined the questions of journalistic ethics involved when she wrote in her column in the *New York Times:*

> Anyone who tries to make readers believe the questions are simple ones, who automatically invokes freedom of the press and the public's right to know, is doing a disservice to America's newspapers. . . . Naming rape victims. Outing gay people. The candidate's sex life. The candidate's drug use. Editors are making decisions they have never made before, on deadline, with competitors breathing down their necks. . . . Like victims of rape, perhaps the victims of this illness deserve some special privacy. . . . The white light of the press and the closed doors of our homes are two of the most deeply prized assets of our lives as Americans. It just so happens that they are often in direct opposition.

Toward the end of her column, Quindlen asked: "Need we know the medical condition of every public figure? . . . What are the parameters?" How would you answer the questions raised by her column?

Collaborative Projects

6. Critics attack the passive role of the audience in the popular spectator sports, which the fans follow from their seats in the stadium or from the couch in front of the small screen. On your campus or in your community, is there a trend away from spectator sports and toward more active participation in sports? Working with other students, you may want to organize an investigation or survey to find answers to this question.

LARGER THAN LIFE

Jenny Lyn Bader

The following long essay is an entry Eric Liu included in his collection
Next: Young American Writers on the New Generation *(1994). Liu*
focused on the way a new generation of "twentysomethings" look at the
world—what they believe in, what "their aspirations and anxieties" are. Are
young people today career-obsessed? Or, according to an alternate stereotype,
are they drifters with no clear goals? Are they "spoiled whiners"? When
Jenny Lyn Bader published the following essay about role models and heroes,
she was a twenty-four-year-old writer living in New York City. Two years
earlier, her play Shakespeare's Undiscovered One Act *had premiered at*
the Village Gate theater. She has worked as a theater director, book editor,
and writer for the National Law Journal *and the* New York Times. *In*
this essay, Bader takes the long way around in approaching her subject. She
takes us to the Austrian-Hungarian empire, where her grandmother grew up
and which perished in the upheaval of World War I; she alludes to legendary
heroes of the distant past, like the Germanic warrior Beowulf; she mentions
the mythical blind poet Homer, who chronicled the exploits of prehistoric
Greek heroes in the war of Troy. But she also keeps mentioning figures that
could serve as role models for a later generation: Harriet Tubman, Mahatma
Gandhi, Eleanor Roosevelt, Martin Luther King, John F. Kennedy, Nelson
Mandela, Ann Richards.

Thought Starters: Is there someone—historical or political figure, artist,
sports personality, celebrity—that you admire or would call your hero?

When my grandmother was young, she would sometimes spot the   *1*
emperor Franz Josef riding down the cobbled roads of the Austro-Hungarian
Empire.

She came of age so long ago that the few surviving photographs are
colored cream and chestnut. Early on, she saw cars replace horses and
carriages. When she got older, she marveled at the first televisions. Near
the end of her life, she grew accustomed to remote control and could spot
prime ministers on color TV. By the time she died, the world was freshly
populated by gadgetry and myth. Her generation bore witness to the rise
of new machinery created by visionaries. My generation has seen machinery break down and visionaries come under fire.

As children, we enjoyed collecting visionaries, the way we collected
toys or baseball cards. When I was a kid, I first met Patrick Henry and

Eleanor Roosevelt, Abraham Lincoln and Albert Einstein. They could always be summoned by the imagination and so were never late for play dates. I thought heroes figured in any decent childhood. I knew their stats.

Nathan Hale. Nelson Mandela. Heroes have guts.

Michelangelo. Shakespeare. Heroes have imagination.   5

They fight. Alexander the Great. Joan of Arc.

They fight for what they believe in. Susan B. Anthony. Martin Luther King.

Heroes overcome massive obstacles. Beethoven, while deaf, still managed to carry an unforgettable tune. Homer, while blind, never failed to give an excellent description. Helen Keller, both deaf and blind, still spoke to the world. FDR, despite his polio, became president. Moses, despite his speech impediment, held productive discussions with God.

They inspire three-hour movies. They make us weepy. They do the right thing while enduring attractive amounts of suffering. They tend to be self-employed. They are often killed off. They sense the future. They lead lives that make us question our own. They are our ideals, but not our friends.

They don't have to be real. Some of them live in books and legends.   10
They don't have to be famous. There are lower-profile heroes who get resurrected by ambitious biographers. There are collective heroes: firefighters and astronauts, unsung homemakers, persecuted peoples. There are those whose names we can't remember, only their deeds: "you know, that woman who swam the English Channel," "the guy who died running the first marathon," "the student who threw himself in front of the tank at Tiananmen Square." There are those whose names we'll never find out: the anonymous benefactor, the masked man, the undercover agent, the inventor of the wheel, the unknown soldier. The one who did the thing so gutsy and terrific that no one will ever know what it was.

Unlike icons (Marilyn, Elvis) heroes are not only sexy but noble, too. Unlike idols (Gretzky, Streisand), who vary from fan to fan, they are almost universally beloved. Unlike icons and idols, heroes lack irony. And unlike icons and idols, heroes are no longer in style.

As centuries end, so do visions of faith—maybe because the faithful get nervous as the double zeroes approach and question what they've been worshiping. Kings and queens got roughed up at the end of the eighteenth century; God took a beating at the end of the nineteenth; and as the twentieth century draws to a close, outstanding human beings are the casualties of the moment. In the 1970s and 1980s, Americans started feeling queasy about heroism. Those of us born in the sixties found ourselves on the cusp of that change. A sweep of new beliefs, priorities, and headlines has conspired to take our pantheon away from us.

Members of my generation believed in heroes when they were younger but now find themselves grasping for them. Even the word *hero* sounds awkward. I find myself embarrassed to ask people who their heroes are, because the word just doesn't trip off the tongue. My friend Katrin sounded irritated when I asked for hers. She said, "Oh, Jesus . . . Do people still have heroes?"

We don't. Certainly not in the traditional sense of adoring perfect people. Frequently not at all. "I'm sort of intrigued by the fact that I don't have heroes right off the top of my head," said a colleague, Peter. "Can I get back to you?"

Some of us are more upset about this than others. It's easy to tell   15
which of us miss the heroic age. We are moved by schmaltzy political speeches, we warm up to stories of pets saving their owners, we even get misty-eyed watching the Olympics. We mope when model citizens fail us. My college roommate, Linda, remembers a seventh-grade class called "Heroes and She-roes." The first assignment was to write about a personal hero or she-ro. "I came home," Linda told me, "and cried and cried because I didn't have one. . . . Carter had screwed up in Iran and given the malaise speech. Gerald Ford was a nothing and Nixon was evil. My parents told me to write about Jane Fonda the political activist and I just kept crying."

Not everyone feels sentimental about it. A twentyish émigré raised in the former Soviet Union told me: "It's kind of anticlimactic to look for heroes when you've been brought up in a culture that insists on so many heroes. . . . What do you want me to say? Lenin? Trotsky?" Even though I grew up in the relatively propaganda-free United States, I understood. The America of my childhood insisted on heroes, too.

Of all the myths I happily ate for breakfast, the most powerful one was our story of revolution. I sang about it as early as kindergarten and read about it long after. The story goes, a few guys in wigs skipped town on some grumpy church leaders and spurned a loopy king to branch out on their own. The children who hear the story realize they don't have to believe in oldfangled clergy or a rusty crown—but they had better believe in those guys with the wigs.

I sure did. I loved a set of books known as the "Meet" series: *Meet George Washington, Meet Andrew Jackson, Meet the Men Who Sailed the Seas,* and many more. I remember one picture of an inspired Thomas Jefferson, his auburn ponytail tied in a black ribbon, penning words with a feather as a battle of banners and cannon fire raged behind him.

A favorite "Meet" book starred Christopher Columbus. His resistance to the flat-earth society of his day was engrossing, especially to a kid like me who had trouble trying new foods let alone seeking new land masses. I identified with his yearning for a new world and his difficulty with finding investors. Standing up to the king and queen of Spain was like convincing your parents to let you do stuff they thought was idiotic. Now, my allowance was only thirty-five cents a week, but that didn't mean I wasn't going to ask for three ships at some later date.

This is pretty embarrassing: I adored those guys. The ones in the   20
white powder and ponytails, the voluptuous hats, the little breeches and

cuffs. They were funny-looking, but lovable. They did outrageous things without asking for permission. They invented the pursuit of happiness.

I had a special fondness for Ben Franklin, statesman and eccentric inventor. Inventions, like heroes, made me feel as though I lived in a dull era. If I'd grown up at the end of the nineteenth century, I could have spoken on early telephones. A few decades later, I could have heard the new sounds of radio. In the sixties, I could have watched black-and-white TVs graduate to color.

Instead, I saw my colorful heroes demoted to black and white. Mostly white. By the time I finished high school, it was no longer hip to look up to the paternalistic dead white males who launched our country, kept slaves and mistresses, and massacred native peoples. Suddenly they weren't visionaries but oppressors, or worse—objects. Samuel Adams became a beer, John Hancock became a building, and the rest of the guys in wigs were knocked off one by one, in a whodunit that couldn't be explained away by the fact of growing up.

The flag-waving of my youth, epitomized by America's bicentennial, was a more loving homage than I know today. The year 1976 rolled in while Washington was still reeling from Saigon, but the irony was lost on me and my second-grade classmates. The idea of losing seemed miles away. We celebrated July fourth with wide eyes and patriotic parties. Grown-ups had yet to tell themselves (so why should they tell us?) that the young nation on its birthday had suffered a tragic defeat.

Historians soon filled us in about that loss, and of others. Discovering America was nothing compared to discovering the flaws of its discoverers, now cast as imperialist sleaze, racist and sexist and genocidal. All things heroic—human potential, spiritual fervor, moral resplendence—soon became suspect. With the possible exception of bodybuilding, epic qualities went out of fashion. Some will remember 1992 as the year Superman died. Literally, the writers and illustrators at *D.C. Comics* decided the guy was too old to keep leaping buildings and rescuing an aging damsel in distress. When rumors circulated that he would be resurrected, readers protested via calls to radio shows, letters to editors, and complaints to stores that they were in no mood for such an event.

A monster named Doomsday killed Superman, overcoming him not 25 with Kryptonite but with brute force. Who killed the others? I blame improved modes of character assassination, media hype artists, and scholars. The experts told me that Columbus had destroyed cultures and ravaged the environment. They also broke the news that the cowboys had brazenly taken land that wasn't theirs. In a way, I'm glad I didn't know that earlier; dressing up as a cowgirl for Halloween wouldn't have felt right. In a more urgent way, I wish I had known it then so I wouldn't have had to learn it later.

Just fifteen years after America's bicentennial came Columbus's quincentennial, when several towns canceled their annual parades in protest of his sins. Soon other festivities started to feel funny. When my aunt served corn pudding last Thanksgiving, my cousin took a spoonful, then said drily that the dish was made in honor of the Indians who taught us to use corn before we eliminated them. Uncomfortable chuckles followed. Actually, neither "we" nor my personal ancestors had come to America in time to kill any Native Americans. Yet the holiday put us in the same boat with the pilgrims and anchored us in the white man's domain.

I am fascinated by how we become "we" and "they." It's as if siding with the establishment is the Alka-Seltzer that helps us stomach the past. To swallow history lessons, we turn into "we": one nation under God of proud but remorseful Indian killers. We also identify with people who look like us. For example, white northerners studying the Civil War identify both with white slaveholders and with northern abolitionists, aligning with both race and place. Transsexuals empathize with men and women. Immigrants identify with their homeland and their adopted country. Historians proposing a black Athena and a black Jesus have inspired more of such bonding.

I'll admit that these empathies can be empowering. I always understood the idea of feeling stranded by unlikely role models but never emotionally grasped it until I watched Penny Marshall's movie *A League of Their Own*. For the first time, I appreciated why so many women complain that sports bore them. I had enjoyed baseball before but never as intensely as I enjoyed the games in that film. The players were people like me. Lori Petty, petite, chirpy, wearing a skirt, commanded the pitcher's mound with such aplomb that I was moved. There's something to be said for identifying with people who remind us of ourselves, though Thomas Jefferson and Lori Petty look more like each other than either of them looks like me. I'll never know if I would've read the "Meet" books with more zeal if they'd described our founding mothers. I liked them as they were.

Despite the thrill of dames batting something on the big screen besides their eyelashes, the fixation on look-alike idols is disturbing for those who get left out. In the movie *White Men Can't Jump*, Wesley Snipes tells Woody Harrelson not to listen to Jimi Hendrix, because "White people can't hear Jimi." Does this joke imply that black people can't hear Mozart? That I can admire Geena Davis's batting but never appreciate Carlton Fisk? Besides dividing us from one another, these emotional allegiances divide us from potential heroes too, causing us to empathize with, say, General Custer and his last stand instead of with Sitting Bull and the victorious Sioux.

Rejecting heroes for having the wrong ethnic credentials or sex organs says less about our multicultural vision than our lack of imagination. By focusing on what we are instead of who we can become, by typecasting and miscasting our ideals—that's how we become "we" and "they." If heroes are those we'd like to emulate, it does make sense that they resemble us. But the focus on physical resemblance seems limited and racist.

Heroes should be judged on their deeds, and there are those with plenty in common heroically but not much in terms of ethnicity, nationality, or gender. Just look at Harriet Tubman and Moses; George Washington and Simón Bolívar; Mahatma Gandhi and Martin Luther King; Murasaki and Milton; Cicero and Ann Richards. Real paragons transcend nationality. It didn't matter to me that Robin Hood was English—as long as he did good, he was as American as a barbecue. It didn't matter to Queen Isabella that Columbus was Italian as long as he sailed for Spain and sprinkled her flags about. The British epic warrior Beowulf was actually Swedish. Both the German hero Etzel and the Scandinavian hero Atli were really Attila, king of the Huns. With all this borrowing going on, we shouldn't have to check the passports of our luminaries; the idea that we can be like them not literally but spiritually is what's uplifting in the first place.

The idea that we can never be like them has led to what I call jealousy journalism. You know, we're not remotely heroic so let's tear down anyone who is. It's become hard to remember which papers are tabloids. Tell-all articles promise us the "real story"—implying that greatness can't be real. The safe thing about *Meet George Washington* was that you couldn't actually meet him. Today's stories and pictures bring us closer. And actually meeting your heroes isn't the best idea. Who wants to learn that a favorite saint is really just an egomaniac with a publicist?

Media maestros have not only knocked public figures off their pedestals, they've also lowered heroism standards by idealizing just about everyone. Oprah, Geraldo, and the rest turn their guests into heroes of the afternoon because they overcame abusive roommates, childhood disfigurement, deranged spouses, multiple genitalia, cheerleading practice, or zany sexual predilections. In under an hour, a studio audience can hear their epic sagas told.

While TV and magazine producers helped lead heroes to their graves, the academic community gave the final push. Just as my peers and I made our way through college, curriculum reformers were promoting "P.C." agendas at the expense of humanistic absolutes. Scholars invented their own tabloidism, investigating and maligning both dead professors and trusty historical figures. Even literary theory helped, when deconstructionists made it trendy to look for questions instead of answers, for circular logic instead of linear sense, for defects, contradictions, and the ironic instead of meaning, absolutes, and the heroic.

It was the generations that preceded ours who killed off our heroes. 35 And like everyone who crucified a superstar, these people thought they were doing a good thing. The professors and journalists consciously moved in a positive direction—toward greater tolerance, openness, and realism—eliminating our inspirations in the process. The death of an era of hero worship was not the result of the cynical, clinical materialism too often identified with my generation. It was the side effect of a complicated cultural surgery, of an operation that may have been necessary and that many prescribed.

So with the best of intentions, these storytellers destroyed bedtime stories. Which is too bad for the kids, because stories make great teachers.

Children glean by example. You can't tell a child "Be ingenious," or "Do productive things." You can tell them, "This Paul Revere person jumped on a horse at midnight, rode wildly through the dark, figured out where the mean British troops were coming to attack the warm, fuzzy, sweet, great-looking colonists, and sent messages by code, igniting our fight for freedom," and they'll get the idea. America's rugged values come gift wrapped in the frontier tales of Paul Bunyan, Daniel Boone, Davy Crockett—fables of independence and natural resources. Kids understand that Johnny Appleseed or Laura Ingalls Wilder would never need a Cuisinart. Pioneer and prairie stories convey the fun of roughing it, showing kids how to be self-reliant, or at least less spoiled.

Children catch on to the idea of imitating qualities, not literal feats. After returning his storybook to the shelf, little Billy doesn't look around for a dragon to slay. Far-off stories capture the imagination in an abstract but compelling way, different from, say, the more immediate action-adventure flick. After watching a James Bond film festival, I might fantasize about killing the five people in front of me on line at the supermarket, while legends are remote enough that Columbus might inspire one to be original, but not necessarily to study Portuguese or enlist in the navy. In tales about conquerors and cavaliers, I first flirted with the idea of ideas.

Even Saturday-morning cartoons served me as parables, when I woke up early enough to watch the classy Superfriends do good deeds. Sure, the gender ratio between Wonder Woman and the gaggle of men in capes seemed unfair, but I was rapt. I wonder whether I glued myself to my television and my high expectations with too much trust, and helped to set my own heroes up for a fall.

Some heroes have literally been sentenced to death by their own followers. *Batman* subscribers, for example, were responsible for getting rid of Batman's sidekick, Robin. At the end of one issue, the Joker threatened to kill the Boy Wonder, and readers could decide whether Robin lived or died by calling one of two "900" numbers. The public voted overwhelmingly for his murder. I understand the impulse of those who dialed for death. At a certain point, eternal invincibility grows as dull and predictable as wearing a yellow cape and red tights every day of the year. It's not human. We get fed up.

My generation helped to kill off heroism as teenagers, with our language. We used heroic words that once described brave deeds—*excellent, amazing, awesome*—to describe a good slice of pizza or a sunny day. In our everyday speech, *bad* meant good. *Hot* meant cool. In the sarcastic slang of street gangs in Los Angeles, *hero* currently means traitor, specifically someone who snitches on a graffiti artist. 40

Even those of us who lived by them helped shatter our own myths, which wasn't all negative. We discovered that even the superhero meets his match. Every Achilles needs a podiatrist. Every rhapsodically handsome leader has a mistress or a moment of moral ambiguity. We injected a dose of reality into our expectations. We even saw a viable presidential candidate under a heap of slung mud, a few imperfections, an alleged tryst or two.

We're used to trysts in a way our elders aren't. Our parents and grandparents behave as if they miss the good old days when adulterers wore letter sweaters. They feign shock at the extramarital exploits of Thomas Jefferson, Frank Sinatra, JFK, Princess Di. Their hero worship is a romance that falters when beloved knights end up unfaithful to their own spouses. People my age aren't amazed by betrayal. We are suspicious of shining armor. Even so, tabloid sales escalate when a Lancelot gives in to temptation—maybe because the jerk who cheats on you somehow becomes more attractive. Other generations have gossiped many of our heroes into philanderers. The presumptuous hero who breaks your heart is the most compelling reason not to get involved in the first place.

Seeing your legends discredited is like ending a romance with someone you loved but ultimately didn't like. However much you longed to trust that person, it just makes more sense not to. Why pine away for an aloof godlet who proves unstable, erratic, and a rotten lover besides? It's sad to give up fantasies but mature to trade them in for healthier relationships grounded in reality.

We require a new pantheon: a set of heroes upon whom we can rely, who will not desert us when the winds change, and whom we will not desert. It's unsettling, if not downright depressing, to go through life embarrassed about the identity of one's childhood idols.

Maybe we should stick to role models instead. Heroes have become quaint, as old-fashioned as gas-guzzlers—and as unwieldy, requiring too much investment and energy. Role models are more like compact cars, less glam and roomy but easier to handle. They take up less parking space in the imagination. Role models have a certain degree of consciousness about their job. The cast members of "Beverly Hills 90210," for example, have acknowledged that they serve as role models for adolescents, and their characters behave accordingly: they refrain from committing major crimes; they overcome inclinations toward substance abuse; they see through adult hypocrisy; and any misdemeanors they do perpetrate are punished. For moral mediators we could do better, but at least the prime-time writing staff is aware of the burden of having teen groupies.

Heroes don't have the luxury of staff writers or the opportunity to endorse designer jeans. Hercules can't go on "Nightline" and pledge to stop taking steroids. Prometheus can't get a presidential pardon. Columbus won't have a chance to weep to Barbara Walters that he didn't mean to endanger leatherback turtles or monk seals or the tribes of the Lucayas. Elizabeth I never wrote a best-seller about how she did it her way.

Role models can go on talk shows, or even host them. Role models may live next door. While a hero might be a courageous head of state, a saint, a leader of armies, a role model might be someone who put in a three-day presidential bid, your local minister, your boss. They don't need

45

their planes to go down in flames to earn respect. Role models have a job, accomplishment, or hairstyle worth emulating.

Rather than encompassing the vast kit and caboodle of ideals, role models can perform a little neat division of labor. One could wish to give orders like Norman Schwarzkopf but perform psychoanalysis like Lucy Van Pelt, to chair a round-table meeting as well as King Arthur but negotiate as well as Queen Esther, to eat like Orson Welles but look like Helen of Troy, and so forth. It was General Schwarzkopf, the most tangible military hero for anyone my age, who vied instead for role-model status by claiming on the cover of his book: *It Doesn't Take a Hero*. With this title he modestly implies that anyone with some smarts and élan could strategize and storm as well as he has.

Role models are admirable individuals who haven't given up their lives or livelihoods and may even have a few hang-ups. They don't have to be prone to excessive self-sacrifice. They don't go on hunger strikes; they diet. They are therefore more likely than heroes to be free for lunch, and they are oftener still alive.

Heroism is a living thing for many of my contemporaries. In my informal poll, I not only heard sob stories about the decline of heroes, I also discovered something surprising: the ascent of parents. While the founding fathers may be passé, actual mothers, fathers, grands, and great-grands are undeniably "in." An overwhelming number of those I polled named their household forebears as those they most admired. By choosing their own relatives as ideals, people in their twenties have replaced impersonal heroes with the most personal role models of all. Members of my purportedly lost generation have not only realized that it's time to stop believing in Santa Claus, they have chosen to believe instead in their families—the actual tooth fairy, the real Mr. and Mrs. Claus. They have stopped needing the folks from the North Pole, the guys with the wigs, the studs and studettes in tights and capes. 50

In a way it bodes well that Superman and the rest could be killed or reported missing. They were needed to quash the most villainous folks of all: insane communists bearing nuclear weapons, heinous war criminals, monsters named Doomsday. The good news about Superman bleeding to death was that Doomsday died in the struggle.

If the good guys are gone, so is the world that divides down the middle into good guys and bad guys. A world without heroes is a rigorous, demanding place, where things don't boil down to black and white but are rich with shades of gray; where faith in lofty, dead personages can be replaced by faith in ourselves and one another; where we must summon the strength to imagine a five-dimensional future in colors not yet invented. My generation grew up to see our world shift, so it's up to us to steer a course between naïveté and nihilism, to reshape vintage stories, to create stories of spirit without apologies.

I've heard a few. There was one about the woman who taught Shake-speare to inner-city fourth graders in Chicago who were previously thought to be retarded or hopeless. There was the college groundskeeper and night watchman, a black man with a seventh-grade education, who became a contracts expert, wrote poetry and memoirs, and invested his salary so wisely that he bequeathed 450 acres of mountainous parkland to the university when he died. There was the motorcyclist who slid under an eighteen-wheeler at full speed, survived his physical therapy only to wind up in a plane crash, recovered, and as a disfigured quadriplegic started a business, got happily married, and ran for public office; his campaign button bore a caption that said "Send me to Congress and I won't be just another pretty face. . . ."

When asked for her heroes, a colleague of mine spoke of her great-grandmother, a woman whose husband left her with three kids in Galicia, near Poland, and went to the United States. He meant to send for her, but the First World War broke out. When she made it to America, her hus-band soon died, and she supported her family; at one point she even ran a nightclub. According to the great-granddaughter, "When she was ninety she would tell me she was going to volunteer at the hospital. I would ask how and she'd say, 'Oh, I just go over there to read to the old folks.' The 'old folks' were probably seventy. She was a great lady."

My grandmother saved her family, too, in the next great war. She did $_{55}$ not live to see the age of the fax, but she did see something remarkable in her time, more remarkable even than the emperor riding down the street: she saw him walking down the street. I used to ask her, "Did you really see the emperor Franz Josef walking down the street?"

She would say, "Ya. Walking down the street." I would laugh, and though she'd repeat it to amuse me, she did not see what was so funny. To me, the emperor was someone you met in history books, not on the streets of Vienna. He was larger than life, a surprising pedestrian. He was probably just getting some air, but he was also laying the groundwork for my nos-talgia of that time when it would be natural for him to take an evening stroll, when those who were larger than life roamed cobblestones.

Today, life is larger.

The Responsive Reader

1. When Jacqueline Kennedy Onassis died, a *Time* writer said she was one of the few women's names instantly recognizable to everyone. Bader includes a number of women's names in her "pantheon" (or "assembly of the gods") of traditional heroes: Eleanor Roosevelt, Joan of Arc, Susan B. Anthony, Helen Keller, and Jane Fonda. Do any of these names have a special meaning for you? Who were they, and what do they stand for? Do they have something in common?

2. An icon is an instantly recognizable image with a large symbolic meaning. In what sense is Marilyn Monroe or Elvis Presley an icon in our culture? We worship an idol uncritically, but it may turn out to be a false god (it may have feet of clay). How and why does Bader distinguish among heroes, icons, and idols?
3. Who were the objects of Bader's childhood hero worship? What were the sources that fueled it? What did she adore about Columbus, Franklin, and other "dead white males"?
4. What happened to Bader's childhood heroes? When and how did Americans start "feeling queasy about heroism"? What according to Bader were major causes for our modern debunking of heroes or deflating of reputations? What role did or does "jealousy journalism" play?
5. What for Bader is the difference between a hero and a role model? Does she make the distinction meaningful for you?

Talking, Listening, Writing

6. Have you personally experienced a "twilight of heroes"? Have you gone through a cycle of idealism and disillusionment similar to that lived by this author?
7. Do you believe that sometimes the real heroes are unsung, near-anonymous people?
8. Do you have role models? Who and what are they?

Collaborative Projects

9. Media people are often accused of being cynical. Working with a group, examine current news coverage and commentary for evidence that would help you substantiate or refute this charge.

Thinking about Connections

Of the authors whose work you have read in this volume, who could be your choice as a role model, a culture hero, or simply an admirable person? Explain and defend your choice.

FAD OF THE MOMENT: STARVING SCHOOLS

Stephanie Salter

> If you can read this, thank a teacher.
> Bumpersticker

Most ordinary Americans have little contact with the celebrities fawned over by the media: star athletes endorsing rent-a-cars or cereals; entertainers with a retinue of hangers-on and groupies; "hard-nosed," cost-cutting executives with huge bonuses; generals. If we are lucky, however, we encounter in the course of our lives some of the unsung heroes: A student remembers her dying grandmother and the nurse that befriended and comforted her to the end. A family remembers the policewoman that calmed an apparently suicidal family member and finally broke down a bathroom door to save a life. Students remember the teacher who drove late at night to the correctional facility to take an exam to a fellow student who had been arrested, hoping to give him a chance to rejoin the class. In the following selection, a newspaper columnist pays tribute to one of the unsung heroes. At the time she wrote the column, teachers had for years been getting a bad press: The governor of the state was on record as announcing that teachers were "only interested in their fat paychecks." A candidate for the country's highest office had devoted his few references to the subject of education to tearing into "militant teachers unions" and teachers' addiction to costly frills and fads.

Thought Starters: Can you recall the media giving the celebrity treatment to someone who would qualify as a teacher, scholar, or intellectual? Can you remember an article, TV program, or movie about an educator that you might have considered as a role model?

Sitting in the shabby classroom in which Therese Hickey will teach   *1*
math and science to 34 Everett Middle School sixth-graders, I look for
signs of what Bob Dole called the educational "fads of the moment."

In his acceptance speech for the Republican presidential nomination,
Dole said these fads are the reason we are "the biggest education spenders
and among the lowest of education achievers of the leading industrial
nations." Public school students "are being forced to absorb" the fads, he
said, and thus "we are not educating all of our children."

I see a little gray mouse scurry across Hickey's classroom floor. Could that be a fad? The cabinets were full of them a couple of weeks ago, Hickey says.

What about the 11 work tables, which Hickey says are so scarce they are fairly worth their weight in gold these days in many San Francisco schools? Are they a fad of the moment? What about the window blind that has been ripped and inoperable for three years?

"When I came here, that window was broken. The wind blew so   5 hard, the only way to shield the kids was to use the blind as a wind block," said Hickey. "It took more than a month before the (San Francisco Unified School) District could get someone out to replace the glass. The blind finally ripped."

If Hickey wants a new blind any time soon, she knows she has to buy and install it herself. Just as she knew that, if she wanted to cover the grimy, scarred walls of her third-floor classroom—this year—she had to do that herself.

So she did, with the help of a couple of students who didn't mind giving up some of their waning summer vacation.

"I got the paint and rollers for $29," said Hickey, with a hint of bargain hunter's pride. "I could get in trouble for it though; it's against the rules. The district is supposed to send people out to do things like this. It's just, they're so backed up. I couldn't wait any longer. It was too dirty."

In her 11th year as a teacher, Hickey herself is an enemy of education, according to Dole. She belongs to an organization he blasted as harshly in his speech as he did violent criminals.

Hickey is a member of a teachers' union, as are 95 percent of the   10 public school teachers in California. So are more than 3 million women and men nationwide.

Although Dole tried to have it both ways—"I say this not to teachers but their unions . . ."—teachers like Therese Hickey didn't see the difference. His insults felt decidedly personal.

"If education were a war, you would be losing it," Dole scolded. "If it were a business, you would be driving it into bankruptcy. If it were a patient, it would be dying."

Why? Because teachers' unions don't buy the Republican dream of "open competition" in education. Because union members believe that vouchers for school "choice" will do nothing for most public schools but destroy them. Especially vulnerable: urban schools like Everett, which draws most of its students from Mission District working-class or poor families.

Last school year, teaching language arts and social studies as well as math and science, Hickey saw her students' test scores rise three points in reading skills and 13 points in math.

The fact that Hickey chooses to work from 7 a.m. to 5 or 6 p.m.   15 might explain part of the increase. Another factor might be that, on a

$38,000 annual salary, she spent about $700 of her own money for supplemental teaching supplies.

Then there were special projects like the African American History Gala that Hickey and her colleagues helped Everett students to put on. Nowhere in the official budget was there money or a month-and-a-half of after-school time for that.

"I don't want you to get the idea that the district is at fault or that Everett is a bad school," said Hickey. "They aren't. The district does the best it can with the money it gets. The teachers and administrators here are wonderful. So are the students. I taught in East Oakland before I moved over here. I can't tell you how much *those* kids meant to me. For a lot of kids, school is one of the few places in the world they can go where people do care about them."

In March, Examiner education writer Venise Wagner analyzed California public school teachers' salaries. Taking inflation into account, she found that in all but three of the 88 largest districts, entry level teachers make less money now than they did in 1987. At the top of the salary scale, teachers make less in all but 12 of the 88.

If, as Dole contends, the teachers' unions have such a stranglehold on education funding, they sure have a funny way of demonstrating their power in California.

Then again, perhaps shows of power are like "fads of the moment"— 20 in the eye of the beholder.

Looking for answers, I peer out of the tall windows of Therese Hickey's classroom. It isn't easy. In three years, they have been washed once on the outside.

The Responsive Reader

1. What to you are striking details in Salter's account of the condition of the school? Do you think these conditions are typical or representative?
2. What for Salter is admirable about the teacher who is the subject of her column?

Talking, Listening, Writing

3. Everyone agrees that teachers can have a tremendous impact—inspirational or traumatic—on a young person's life. Have your own experiences with teachers been good or bad? Can you put your finger on key qualities that for you make good teachers outstanding or bad teachers bad?
4. If you were to nominate an individual or a group for an "Unsung Heroes" award, what would be your choice? What would you say in your tribute?

5. Teachers often feel that they are made scapegoats for the problems of American education. Who would be *your* scapegoat?

Collaborative Projects

6. Working with a group, you may want to explore questions like the following: Should teachers be unionized? What are key arguments for and against? What is the history of teachers' unions? What is their role in current politics and their influence in American education?

THE DECLINE OF FATHERHOOD

David Popenoe

Much current writing about the changing American family assumes that the traditional two-parent family is rapidly becoming a thing of the past. Millions of American children are not living with their fathers, and more than half of them have never been in the father's home. Politicians and pundits who preach "family values" (even if they themselves are veterans of nasty divorces) call this trend toward fatherlessness the single most harmful demographic trend of this generation—blaming it for adolescent pregnancy, child sexual abuse, and soaring juvenile crime. How important is the father to the intellectual, emotional, and moral growth of a child? In particular, how important is it for young males to have a male role model in the immediate family? David Popenoe is a professor of sociology at Rutgers University who believes that government policies should be designed to favor married, child-rearing couples. He sees the phenomenon of the absent father as part of a larger ominous picture including "rising crime rates, growing personal and corporate greed, deteriorating communities, and increasing confusion over moral issues." The following is the first part of an article he published in the Spring 1996 Wilson Quarterly.

Thought Starters: Is it true that fathers have been getting a bad press in recent years? How much do the media dwell on deadbeat dads, child-molesting dads, or emotionally absent fathers?

The decline of fatherhood is one of the most basic, unexpected, and extraordinary social trends of our time. Its dimensions can be captured in a single statistic: In just three decades, between 1960 and 1990, the percentage of U.S. children living apart from their biological fathers more than doubled, from 17 percent to 36 percent. By the turn of the century, nearly 50 percent of American children may be going to sleep each evening without being able to say good night to their dads.

No one predicted this trend, few researchers or government agencies have monitored it, and it is not widely discussed, even today. But the decline of fatherhood is a major force behind many of the most disturbing problems that plague American society: crime and delinquency; teenage pregnancy; deteriorating educational achievement; depression, substance abuse, and alienation among adolescents; and the growing number of women and children living in poverty. The current generation of children may be the first in our nation's history to be less well off—psychologically, socially, economically, and morally—than their parents were at the same age. The United States, observes Senator Daniel Patrick Moynihan, "may be the first society in history in which children are distinctly worse off than adults."

Even as this calamity unfolds, our cultural view of fatherhood itself is changing. Few people doubt the fundamental importance of mothers. But fathers? More and more, the question of whether fathers are really necessary is being raised. Fatherhood is said by many to be merely a social role that others—mothers, partners, stepfathers, uncles and aunts, grandparents—can play.

There was a time in the past when fatherlessness was far more common than it is today, but death was to blame, not divorce, desertion, and out-of-wedlock births. In early-17th-century Virginia, only an estimated 31 percent of white children reached age 18 with both parents still alive. That figure climbed to 50 percent by the early 18th century, to 72 percent by the start of the 20th century, and close to its current level by 1940. Today, well over 90 percent of America's youngsters turn 18 with two living parents. Almost all of today's "fatherless" children have fathers who are alive, well, and perfectly capable of shouldering the responsibilities of fatherhood. Who would have thought that so many men would relinquish them?

Not so long ago, social scientists and others dismissed the change in the cause of fatherlessness as irrelevant. Children, it was said, are merely losing their parents in a different way than they used to. You don't hear that very much anymore. A surprising finding of recent research is that it is decidedly worse for a child to lose a father in the modern, voluntary way than through death. The children of divorced and never-married mothers are less successful in life by almost every measure than the children of widowed mothers. The replacement of death by divorce as the prime cause of fatherlessness is a monumental setback in the history of childhood. 5

Until the 1960s, the falling death rate and the rising divorce rate neutralized each other. In 1900 the percentage of American children living in single-parent families was 8.5 percent. By 1960 it had increased to just 9.1 percent. Virtually no one during those years was writing or thinking about family breakdown, disintegration, or decline.

Indeed, what is most significant about the changing family demography of the first six decades of the 20th century is this: Because the death rate was dropping faster than the divorce rate was rising, more children were living with both of their natural parents by 1960 than at any other time in world history. The figure was close to 80 percent for the generation born in the late 1940s and early 1950s. But then the decline in the death rate slowed, and the divorce rate skyrocketed. "The scale of marital breakdowns in the West since 1960 has no historical precedent that I know of," says Lawrence Stone, a noted Princeton University family historian. "There has been nothing like it for the last 2,000 years, and probably longer."

Consider what has happened to children. Most estimates are that only about 50 percent of the children born during the 1970–84 "baby bust" period will still live with their natural parents by age 17—a staggering drop from nearly 80 percent.

In theory, divorce need not mean disconnection. In reality, it often does. A large survey conducted in the late 1980s found that about one in five divorced fathers had not seen his children in the past year and that fewer than half of divorced fathers saw their children more than several times a year. A 1981 survey of adolescents who were living apart from their fathers found that 52 percent hadn't seen them at all in more than a year; only 16 percent saw their fathers as often as once a week—and the fathers' contact with their children dropped off sharply over time.

The picture grows worse. Just as divorce has overtaken death as the   10 leading cause of fatherlessness, out-of-wedlock births are expected to surpass divorce in the 1990s. They accounted for 30 percent of all births by 1991; by the turn of the century they may account for 40 percent (and 80 percent of minority births). And there is substantial evidence that having an unmarried father is even worse for a child than having a divorced father.

Across time and cultures, fathers have always been considered essential—and not just for their sperm. Indeed, no known society ever thought of fathers as potentially unnecessary. Marriage and the nuclear family—mother, father, and children—are the most universal social institutions in existence. In no society has the birth of children out of wedlock been the cultural norm. To the contrary, concern for the legitimacy of children is nearly universal.

In my many years as a sociologist, I have found few other bodies of evidence that lean so much in one direction as this one: On the whole, two parents—a father and a mother—are better for a child than one parent. There are, to be sure, many factors that complicate this simple proposition. We all know of a two-parent family that is truly dysfunctional—the proverbial family from hell. A child can certainly be raised to a fulfilling adulthood by one loving parent who is wholly devoted to the child's well-being. But such exceptions do not invalidate the rule any more than the fact that some three-pack-a-day smokers live to a ripe old age casts doubt on the dangers of cigarettes.

The collapse of children's well-being in the United States has reached breathtaking proportions. Juvenile violent crime has increased from 18,000 arrests in 1960 to 118,000 in 1992, a period in which the total number of young people in the population remained relatively stable. Reports of child neglect and abuse have quadrupled since 1976, when data were first collected. Since 1960, eating disorders and depression have soared among adolescent girls. Teen suicide has tripled. Alcohol and drug abuse among teenagers, although it has leveled off in recent years, continues at a very high rate. Scholastic Aptitude Test scores have declined more than 70 points, and most of the decline cannot be accounted for by the increased academic diversity of students taking the test. Poverty has shifted from the elderly to the young. Of all the nation's poor today, 38 percent are children.

One can think of many explanations for these unhappy developments: the growth of commercialism and consumerism, the influence of television and the mass media, the decline of religion, the widespread availability of guns and addictive drugs, and the decay of social order and neighborhood relationships. None of these causes should be dismissed. But the evidence is now strong that the absence of fathers from the lives of children is one of the most important causes.

What do fathers do? Partly, of course, it is simply being a second 15
adult in the home. Bringing up children is demanding, stressful, and often exhausting. Two adults can support and spell each other; they can also offset each other's deficiencies and build on each other's strengths.

Beyond that, fathers—men—bring an array of unique and irreplaceable qualities that women do not ordinarily bring. Some of these are familiar, if sometimes overlooked or taken for granted. The father as protector, for example, has by no means outlived his usefulness. And he is important as a role model. Teenage boys without fathers are notoriously prone to trouble. The pathway to adulthood for daughters is somewhat easier, but they still must learn from their fathers, as they cannot from their mothers, how to relate to men. They learn from their fathers about heterosexual trust, intimacy, and difference. They learn to appreciate their own femininity from the one male who is most special in their lives (assuming that they love and respect their fathers). Most important, through loving and being loved by their fathers, they learn that they are worthy of love.

Recent research has given us much deeper—and more surprising— insights into the father's role in child rearing. It shows that in almost all of their interactions with children, fathers do things a little differently from mothers. What fathers do—their special parenting style—is not only highly complementary to what mothers do but is by all indications important in its own right.

For example, an often-overlooked dimension of fathering is play. From their children's birth through adolescence, fathers tend to emphasize play more than caretaking. This may be troubling to egalitarian feminists, and it would indeed be wise for most fathers to spend more time in caretaking. Yet the fathers' style of play seems to have unusual significance. It is likely to be both physically stimulating and exciting. With older children it involves more physical games and teamwork that require the competitive testing of physical and mental skills. It frequently resembles an apprenticeship or teaching relationship: Come on, let me show you how.

Mothers generally spend more time playing with their children, but mothers' play tends to take place more at the child's level. Mothers provide the child with the opportunity to direct the play, to be in charge, to proceed at the child's own pace. Kids, at least in the early years, seem to prefer to play with daddy. In one study of 2 1/2-year-olds who were given a choice, more than two-thirds chose to play with their fathers.

The way fathers play affects everything from the management of 20 emotions to intelligence and academic achievement. It is particularly important in promoting the essential virtue of self-control. According to one expert, "Children who roughhouse with their fathers . . . usually quickly learn that biting, kicking, and other forms of physical violence are not acceptable." They learn when enough is enough.

Children, a committee assembled by the Board on Children and Families of the National Research Council concluded, "learn critical lessons about how to recognize and deal with highly charged emotions in the context of playing with their fathers. Fathers, in effect, give children practice in regulating their own emotions and recognizing others' emotional clues." A study of convicted murderers in Texas found that 90 percent of them either didn't play as children or played abnormally.

At play and in other realms, fathers tend to stress competition, challenge, initiative, risk taking, and independence. Mothers, as caretakers, stress emotional security and personal safety. On the playground, fathers will try to get the child to swing higher than the person on the next swing, while mothers will worry about an accident. It's sometimes said that fathers express more concern for the child's long-term development, while mothers focus on the child's immediate well-being. It is clear that children have dual needs that must be met. Becoming a mature and competent adult involves the integration of two often-contradictory human desires: for *communion*, or the feeling of being included, connected, and related, and for *agency*, which entails independence, individuality, and self-fulfillment. One without the other is a denuded and impaired humanity, an incomplete realization of human potential.

For many couples, to be sure, these functions are not rigidly divided along standard female-male lines, and there may even be a role reversal. But the exceptions prove the rule. Gender-differentiated parenting is so important that in child rearing by gay and lesbian couples, one partner commonly fills the male role while the other fills the female role.

It is ironic that in our public discussion of fathering, it's seldom acknowledged that fathers have a distinctive role to play. Indeed, it's far more often said that fathers should be more like mothers (and that men generally should be more like women—less aggressive, less competitive). While such things may be said with the best of intentions, the effects are perverse. After all, if fathering is no different from mothering, males can easily be replaced in the home by women. It might even seem better. Already viewed as a burden and obstacle to self-fulfillment, fatherhood thus comes to seem superfluous and unnecessary as well.

We know that fathers have a surprising impact on children. Fathers' involvement seems to be linked to improved quantitative and verbal skills, improved problem-solving ability, and higher academic achievement. Several studies have found that the presence of the father is one of the determinants of girls' proficiency in mathematics. And one pioneering study found that the amount of time fathers spent reading was a strong predictor of their daughters' verbal ability.

For sons, who can more directly follow their fathers' example, the results have been even more striking. A number of studies have uncovered a strong relationship between father involvement and the quantitative and mathematical abilities of their sons. Other studies have found a relationship between paternal nurturing and boys' verbal intelligence.

How fathers produce these intellectual benefits is not yet clear. No doubt it is partly a matter of the time and money a man brings to his family. But it is probably also related to the unique mental and behavioral qualities of men; the male sense of play, reasoning, challenge, and problem solving, and the traditional male association with achievement and occupational advancement.

Men also have a vital role to play in promoting cooperation and other "soft" virtues. We don't often think of fathers as teachers of empathy, but involved fathers, it turns out, may be of special importance for the development of this character trait, essential to an ordered society of law-abiding, cooperative, and compassionate adults. Examining the results of a 26-year longitudinal study, a trio of researchers at McGill University reached a "quite astonishing" conclusion: The single most important childhood factor in developing empathy is paternal involvement in child care. Fathers who spent time alone with their children more than twice a week— giving meals, baths, and other basic care—reared the most compassionate adults.

It is not yet clear why fathers are so important in instilling this quality. Perhaps merely by being with their children they provide a model for compassion. Perhaps it has to do with their style of play or mode of reasoning. Perhaps it is somehow related to the fact that fathers typically are the family's main arbiter with the outside world. Or perhaps it is because mothers who receive help from their mates have more time and

energy to cultivate the soft virtues. Whatever the reason, it is hard to think
of a more important contribution that fathers can make to their children.

Men, too, suffer grievously from the growth of fatherlessness. The   *30*
world over, young and unattached males have always been a cause for social
concern. They can be a danger to themselves and to society. Young unattached men tend to be more aggressive, violent, promiscuous, and prone
to substance abuse; they are also more likely to die prematurely through
disease, accidents, or self-neglect. They make up the majority of deviants,
delinquents, criminals, killers, drug users, vice lords, and miscreants of
every kind. Senator Moynihan put it succinctly when he warned that a
society full of unattached males "asks for and gets chaos."

The Responsive Reader

1. What would you include in a statistical digest of figures on the
   changing "demography" of the American family that Popenoe presents in the first few pages? What figures are most predictable or
   familiar? Which statistics for you are startling or thought-provoking?
   What has happened to the "nuclear family"?
2. What support does Popenoe offer for his claim that "the collapse of
   children's well-being in the United States has reached breathtaking
   proportions"?
3. What are key ideas in Popenoe's discussion of the father's role in a
   child's play? Does he convince you that some or all of that role is
   "gender-specific"?
4. In what other areas does Popenoe see a need for the "array of unique
   and irreplaceable qualities" that fathers bring to a child's development?

Talking, Listening, Writing

5. Are fathers necessary? Do you think father and mother should be
   equal partners in parenting? Or do you agree with Popenoe that
   fathers have a special, important "masculine" role to play?
6. Whether or not the fatherless family is bound to be bad for a child
   is a subject of vigorous current debate. In a reply to Popenoe's article,
   Judith Stacey, a professor of sociology and women's studies at the
   University of California at Davis, said: "The evidence resoundingly
   supports the idea that a high-conflict marriage injures children more
   than divorce does. Instead of protecting children, the current assault
   on no-fault divorce endangers them by inviting more parental conflict, desertion, and fraud." To judge from your own experience and
   that of friends and relatives, is a high-conflict marriage with a father
   present better or worse than a family situation without one?
7. Alix Kates Shulman, who says that all her novels were centered
   on the mother-child relationship, has written, "Mothering is so

unsupported in our society that every attempt to raise a child is a complex juggling act. . . . In the end, I think all you can do, feminist or not, is try to raise your children lovingly as best you can, pass on what you know, and keep your fingers crossed." Do you agree that mothering is unsupported in our society?

Collaborative Projects

8. Working with a group, you may want to ask: Is there a movement to reconsider no-fault divorce? Who is behind it? What are the arguments?

IN SEARCH OF OUR MOTHERS' GARDENS

Alice Walker

> *Alice Walker is the author of the novel* The Color Purple *and the short story "Everyday Use" (p. 296). She has written and lectured widely on the relationship between black and white men and women, and between her own writing and the work of African American writers—Jean Toomer, Zora Neale Hurston—who were her role models and inspiration. She has taught creative writing and black literature at colleges including Jackson State College, Wellesley, and Yale. Many of Walker's essays, articles, and reviews were collected in her* In Search of Our Mothers' Gardens *(1983). In the title essay, she paid tribute to women of her mother's and grandmother's generations. They channeled the creative and spiritual energies that were denied other outlets into their rich gardens and into the "fanciful, inspired, and yet simple" quilts they fashioned from "bits and pieces of worthless rags." How does Walker answer her two basic questions: "What did it mean for a black woman to be an artist in our grandmothers' time?" What does it mean to be "an artist and black woman" today?*

Thought Starters: Does great art or "fine art" depend on the patronage of people with power and wealth? Is art only for the well-to-do?

I described her own nature and temperament. Told how they needed a larger life for their expression.... I pointed out that in lieu of proper channels, her emotions had overflowed into paths that dissipated them. I talked, beautifully I thought, about an art that would be born, an art that would open the way for women the likes of her. I asked her to hope, and build up an inner life against the coming of that day.... I sang, with a strange quiver in my voice, a promise song. (Jean Toomer, "Avey," *Cane*)

(The poet speaking to a prostitute who falls asleep while he's talking)[1]

When the poet Jean Toomer walked through the South in the early twenties, he discovered a curious thing: black women whose spirituality

[1][Jean Toomer (1894–1967) was born in Washington, D.C., and published *Cane*, a collection of poems and stories, in 1923.]

was so intense, so deep, so *unconscious* that they were themselves unaware of the richness they held. They stumbled blindly through their lives: creatures so abused and mutilated in body, so dimmed and confused by pain, that they considered themselves unworthy even of hope. In the selfless abstractions their bodies became to the men who used them, they became more than "sexual objects," more even than mere women: they became "Saints." Instead of being perceived as whole persons, their bodies became shrines: what was thought to be their minds became temples suitable for worship. These crazy Saints stared out at the world, wildly, like lunatics—or quietly, like suicides; and the "God" that was in their gaze was as mute as a great stone.

Who were these Saints? These crazy, loony, pitiful women?

Some of them, without a doubt, were our mothers and grandmothers.

In the still heat of the post-Reconstruction South, this is how they   5
seemed to Jean Toomer: exquisite butterflies trapped in an evil honey, toiling away their lives in an era, a century, that did not acknowledge them, except as "the *mule* of the world." They dreamed dreams that no one knew—not even themselves, in any coherent fashion—and saw visions no one could understand. They wandered or sat about the countryside crooning lullabies to ghosts, and drawing the mother of Christ in charcoal on courthouse walls.

They forced their minds to desert their bodies and their striving spirits sought to rise, like frail whirlwinds from the hard red clay. And when those frail whirlwinds fell, in scattered particles, upon the ground, no one mourned. Instead, men lit candles to celebrate the emptiness that remained, as people do who enter a beautiful but vacant space to resurrect a God.

Our mothers and grandmothers, some of them: moving to music not yet written. And they waited.

They waited for a day when the unknown thing that was in them would be made known; but guessed, somehow in their darkness, that on the day of their revelation they would be long dead. Therefore to Toomer they walked, and even ran, in slow motion. For they were going nowhere immediate, and the future was not yet within their grasp. And men took our mothers and grandmothers, "but got no pleasure from it." So complex was their passion and their calm.

To Toomer, they lay vacant and fallow as autumn fields, with harvest time never in sight: and he saw them enter loveless marriages, without joy; and become prostitutes, without resistance; and become mothers of children, without fulfillment.

For these grandmothers and mothers of ours were not Saints, but   10
Artists; driven to a numb and bleeding madness by the springs of creativity in them for which there was no release. They were Creators, who lived lives of spiritual waste, because they were so rich in spirituality—which is the basis of Art—that the strain of enduring their unused and unwanted talent drove them insane. Throwing away this spirituality was their pathetic

attempt to lighten the soul to a weight their work-worn, sexually abused bodies could bear.

What did it mean for a black woman to be an artist in our grand-mothers' time? In our great-grandmothers' day? It is a question with an answer cruel enough to stop the blood.

Did you have a genius of a great-great-grandmother who died under some ignorant and depraved white overseer's lash? Or was she required to bake biscuits for a lazy backwater tramp, when she cried out in her soul to paint watercolors of sunsets, or the rain falling on the green and peaceful pasturelands? Or was her body broken and forced to bear children (who were more often than not sold away from her)—eight, ten, fifteen, twenty children—when her one joy was the thought of modeling heroic figures of rebellion, in stone or clay?

How was the creativity of the black woman kept alive, year after year and century after century, when for most of the years black people have been in America, it was a punishable crime for a black person to read or write? And the freedom to paint, to sculpt, to expand the mind with action did not exist. Consider, if you can bear to imagine it, what might have been the result if singing, too, had been forbidden by law. Listen to the voices of Bessie Smith, Billie Holiday, Nina Simone, Roberta Flack, and Aretha Franklin, among others, and imagine those voices muzzled for life. Then you may begin to comprehend the lives of our "crazy," "Sainted" mothers and grandmothers. The agony of the lives of women who might have been Poets, Novelists, Essayists, and Short-Story Writers (over a pe-riod of centuries), who died with their real gifts stifled within them.

And, if this were the end of the story, we would have cause to cry out in my paraphrase of Okot p'Bitek's great poem:

> O, my clanswomen
> Let us all cry together!
> Come,
> Let us mourn the death of our mother,
> The death of a Queen
> The ash that was produced
> By a great fire!
> O, this homestead is utterly dead
> Close the gates
> With *lacari* thorns,
> For our mother
> The creator of the Stool is lost!
> And all the young women
> Have perished in the wilderness!

But this is not the end of the story, for all the young women—our *15* mothers and grandmothers, *ourselves*—have not perished in the wilderness. And if we ask ourselves why, and search for and find the answer, we will know beyond all efforts to erase it from our minds, just exactly who, and of what, we black American women are.

One example, perhaps the most pathetic, most misunderstood one, can provide a backdrop for our mothers' work: Phillis Wheatley, a slave in the 1700s.[2]

Virginia Woolf, in her book *A Room of One's Own*, wrote that in order for a woman to write fiction she must have two things, certainly: a room of her own (with key and lock) and enough money to support herself.[3]

What then are we to make of Phillis Wheatley, a slave, who owned not even herself? This sickly, frail black girl who required a servant of her own at times—her health was so precarious—and who, had she been white, would have been easily considered the intellectual superior of all the women and most of the men in the society of her day.

Virginia Woolf wrote further, speaking of course not of our Phillis, that "any woman born with a great gift in the sixteenth century [insert "eighteenth century," insert "black woman," insert "born or made a slave"] would certainly have gone crazed, shot herself, or ended her days in some lonely cottage outside the village, half witch, half wizard [insert "Saint"], feared and mocked at. For it needs little skill and psychology to be sure that a highly gifted girl who had tried to use her gift for poetry would have been so thwarted and hindered by contrary instincts [add "chains, guns, the lash, the ownership of one's body by someone else, submission to an alien religion"], that she must have lost her health and sanity to a certainty."

The key words, as they relate to Phillis, are "contrary instincts." For *20* when we read the poetry of Phillis Wheatley—as when we read the novels of Nella Larsen or the oddly false-sounding autobiography of that freest of all black women writers, Zora Hurston—evidence of "contrary instincts" is everywhere.[4] Her loyalties were completely divided, as was, without question, her mind.

But how could this be otherwise? Captured at seven, a slave of wealthy, doting whites who instilled in her the "savagery" of the Africa they "rescued" her from . . . one wonders if she was even able to remember her homeland as she had known it, or as it really was.

Yet, because she did try to use her gift for poetry in a world that made her a slave, she was "so thwarted and hindered by . . . contrary

[2][Phillis Wheatley (c. 1753–1794), an African slave, wrote *Poems on Various Subjects, Religious and Moral*, published in 1773.]

[3][Virginia Woolf (1882–1941) was a leading British novelist and critic whose best-known novels are *Mrs. Dalloway* (1925) and *To the Lighthouse* (1927).]

[4][Zora Neale Hurston (1901–1960) wrote *Mules and Men*, a collection of black legend and folklore. Her novels include *Their Eyes Were Watching God*, which Alice Walker has praised for its "sense of black people as complete, complex, *undiminished* human beings."]

instincts, that she . . . lost her health. . . ." In the last years of her brief life, burdened not only with the need to express her gift but also with a penniless, friendless "freedom" and several small children for whom she was forced to do strenuous work to feed, she lost her health, certainly. Suffering from malnutrition and neglect and who knows what mental agonies, Phillis Wheatley died.

So torn by "contrary instincts" was black, kidnapped, enslaved Phillis that her description of the "Goddess"—as she poetically called the Liberty she did not have—is ironically, cruelly humorous. And, in fact, has held Phillis up to ridicule for more than a century. It is usually read prior to hanging Phillis's memory as that of a fool. She wrote:

> The Goddess comes, she moves divinely fair,
> Olive and laurel binds her *golden* hair.
> Wherever shines this native of the skies,
> Unnumber'd charms and recent graces rise. [My italics]

It is obvious that Phillis, the slave, combed the "Goddess's" hair every morning; prior, perhaps, to bringing in the milk, or fixing her mistress's lunch. She took her imagery from the one thing she saw elevated above all others.

With the benefit of hindsight we ask, "How could she?"   25

But at last, Phillis, we understand. No more snickering when your stiff, struggling, ambivalent lines are forced on us. We know now that you were not an idiot or a traitor; only a sickly little black girl, snatched from your home and country and made a slave; a woman who still struggled to sing the song that was your gift, although in a land of barbarians who praised you for your bewildered tongue. It is not so much what you sang, as that you kept alive, in so many of our ancestors, *the notion of song.*

Black women are called, in the folklore that so aptly identifies one's status in society, "the *mule* of the world," because we have been handed the burdens that everyone else—*everyone* else—refused to carry. We have also been called "Matriarchs," "Superwomen," and "Mean and Evil Bitches." Not to mention "Castraters" and "Sapphire's Mama." When we have pleaded for understanding, our character has been distorted; when we have asked for simple caring, we have been handed empty inspirational appellations, then stuck in the farthest corner. When we have asked for love, we have been given children. In short, even our plainer gifts, our labors of fidelity and love, have been knocked down our throats. To be an artist and a black woman, even today, lowers our status in many respects, rather than raises it: and yet, artists we will be.

Therefore we must fearlessly pull out of ourselves and look at and identify with our lives the living creativity some of our great-grandmothers were not allowed to know. I stress *some* of them because it is well known that the majority of our great-grandmothers knew, even without "know-ing" it, the reality of their spirituality, even if they didn't recognize it beyond what happened in the singing at church—and they never had any intention of giving it up.

How they did it—those millions of black women who were not Phillis Wheatley, or Lucy Terry or Frances Harper or Zora Hurston or Nella Larsen or Bessie Smith; or Elizabeth Catlett, or Katherine Dunham, either—brings me to the title of this essay, "In Search of Our Mothers' Gardens," which is a personal account that is yet shared, in its theme and its meaning, by all of us. I found, while thinking about the far-reaching world of the creative black woman, that often the truest answer to a question that really matters can be found very close.

In the late 1920s my mother ran away from home to marry my father.   *30* Marriage, if not running away, was expected of seventeen-year-old girls. By the time she was twenty, she had two children and was pregnant with a third. Five children later, I was born. And this is how I came to know my mother: she seemed a large, soft, loving-eyed woman who was rarely impatient in our home. Her quick, violent temper was on view only a few times a year, when she battled with the white landlord who had the mis-fortune to suggest to her that her children did not need to go to school.

She made all the clothes we wore, even my brothers' overalls. She made all the towels and sheets we used. She spent the summers canning vegetables and fruits. She spent the winter evenings making quilts enough to cover all our beds.

During the "working" day, she labored beside—not behind—my father in the fields. Her day began before sunup, and did not end until late at night. There was never a moment for her to sit down, undisturbed, to unravel her own private thoughts; never a time free from interruption—by work or the noisy inquiries of her many children. And yet, it is to my mother—and all our mothers who were not famous—that I went in search of the secret of what has fed that muzzled and often mutilated, but vibrant, creative spirit that the black woman has inherited, and that pops out in wild and unlikely places to this day.

But when, you will ask, did my overworked mother have time to know or care about feeding the creative spirit?

The answer is so simple that many of us have spent years discovering it. We have constantly looked high, when we should have looked high—and low.

For example: in the Smithsonian Institution in Washington, D.C.,   *35* there hangs a quilt unlike any other in the world. In fanciful, inspired, and yet simple and identifiable figures, it portrays the story of the Crucifixion. It is considered rare, beyond price. Though it follows no known pattern of quilt-making, and though it is made of bits and pieces of worthless rags, it is obviously the work of a person of powerful imagination and deep spiritual feeling. Below this quilt I saw a note that says it was made by "an anonymous Black woman in Alabama, a hundred years ago."

If we could locate this "anonymous" black woman from Alabama, she would turn out to be one of our grandmothers—an artist who left her mark in the only materials she could afford, and in the only medium her position in society allowed her to use.

As Virginia Woolf wrote further, in *A Room of One's Own*:

> Yet genius of a sort must have existed among women as it must have existed among the working class. [Change this to "slaves" and "the wives and daughters of sharecroppers."] Now and again an Emily Brontë or a Robert Burns [change this to "a Zora Hurston or a Richard Wright"] blazes out and proves its presence. But certainly it never got itself on to paper. When, however, one reads of a witch being ducked, of a woman possessed by devils [or "Sainthood"], of a wise woman selling herbs [our root workers], or even a very remarkable man who had a mother, then I think we are on the track of a lost novelist, a suppressed poet, of some mute and inglorious Jane Austen. . . . Indeed, I would venture to guess that Anon, who wrote so many poems without signing them, was often a woman. . . .

And so our mothers and grandmothers have, more often than not anonymously, handed on the creative spark, the seed of the flower they themselves never hoped to see: or like a sealed letter they could not plainly read.

And so it is, certainly, with my own mother. Unlike "Ma" Rainey's songs, which retained their creator's name even while blasting forth from Bessie Smith's mouth, no song or poem will bear my mother's name. Yet so many of the stories that I write, that we all write, are my mother's stories. Only recently did I fully realize this: that through years of listening to my mother's stories of her life, I have absorbed not only the stories themselves, but something of the manner in which she spoke, something of the urgency that involves the knowledge that her stories—like her life— must be recorded. It is probably for this reason that so much of what I have written is about characters whose counterparts in real life are so much older than I am.

But the telling of these stories, which came from my mother's lips as 40 naturally as breathing, was not the only way my mother showed herself as an artist. For stories, too, were subject to being distracted, to dying without conclusion. Dinners must be started, and cotton must be gathered before the big rains. The artist that was and is my mother showed itself to me only after many years. This is what I finally noticed:

Like Mem, a character in *The Third Life of Grange Copeland*, my mother adorned with flowers whatever shabby house we were forced to live in. And not just your typical straggly country stand of zinnias, either. She planted ambitious gardens—and still does—with over fifty different varieties of plants that bloom profusely from early March until late November. Before she left home for the fields, she watered her flowers, chopped up the grass, and laid out new beds. When she returned from the fields she might divide clumps of bulbs, dig a cold pit, uproot and replant roses, or prune branches from her taller bushes or trees—until night came and it was too dark to see.

Whatever she planted grew as if by magic, and her fame as a grower of flowers spread over three counties. Because of her creativity with her flowers, even my memories of poverty are seen through a screen of blooms—sunflowers, petunias, roses, dahlias, forsythia, spirea, delphiniums, verbena . . . and on and on.

And I remember people coming to my mother's yard to be given cuttings from her flowers; I hear again the praise showered on her because whatever rocky soil she landed on, she turned into a garden. A garden so brilliant with colors, so original in its design, so magnificent with life and creativity, that to this day people drive by our house in Georgia—perfect strangers and imperfect strangers—and ask to stand or walk among my mother's art.

I notice that it is only when my mother is working in her flowers that she is radiant, almost to the point of being invisible—except as Creator: hand and eye. She is involved in work her soul must have. Ordering the universe in the image of her personal conception of Beauty.

Her face, as she prepares the Art that is her gift, is a legacy of respect   45
she leaves to me, for all that illuminates and cherishes life. She has handed down respect for the possibilities—and the will to grasp them.

For her, so hindered and intruded upon in so many ways, being an artist has still been a daily part of her life. This ability to hold on, even in very simple ways, is work black women have done for a very long time.

This poem is not enough, but it is something, for the woman who literally covered the holes in our walls with sunflowers:

They were women then
My mama's generation
Husky of voice—Stout of
Step
With fists as well as
Hands
How they battered down
Doors
And ironed
Starched white
Shirts
How they led
Armies
Headragged Generals
Across mined

Fields
Booby-trapped
Kitchens
To discover books
Desks
A place for us
How they knew what we
Must know
Without knowing a page
Of it
Themselves.

Guided by my heritage of a love of beauty and a respect for strength—in search of my mother's garden, I found my own.

And perhaps in Africa over two hundred years ago, there was just such a mother; perhaps she painted vivid and daring decorations in oranges and yellows and greens on the walls of her hut; perhaps she sang—in a voice like Roberta Flack's—*sweetly* over the compounds of her village; perhaps she wove the most stunning mats or told the most ingenious stories of all the village story-tellers. Perhaps she was herself a poet—though only her daughter's name is signed to the poems that we know.

Perhaps Phillis Wheatley's mother was also an artist.   *50*

Perhaps in more than Phillis Wheatley's biological life is her mother's signature made clear.

The Responsive Reader

1. How would you sum up the central lesson or inspiration that Walker draws from her look at the past?
2. Which of the writers and singers whose memory Walker invokes do you recognize? What use does she make of the quotations from the African American writer Jean Toomer and the British novelist Virginia Woolf?
3. Walker has made her readers revise more conventional judgments of writers like Zora Neale Hurston, for instance. How does she want her readers to revise stereotyped views of Phillis Wheatley? What is the meaning of Wheatley's story for her?
4. What use does Walker make of her own family history in this essay? What makes her mother a role model for her?

Talking, Listening, Writing

5. Have people who played a central role in your own past been good role models? Or have they been negative examples? Where have you looked for or found sources of inspiration—in the family, in school, in church, among friends?

6. Has art or music played a major role in your own life? Does any traditional or modern art have spiritual or vital significance for you? What outlets for creative energy or talent have you encountered outside conventional art?
7. Have school books or the media presented believable role models for you or for others with similar background or of the same generation?
8. Write a tribute to someone who has made a major contribution to your life or to the shaping of your personality.

Collaborative Projects

9. Who are the heroes for students of differing ethnic or cultural backgrounds? What role models do young people with minority backgrounds recognize? How do they explain their choices? What difficulties or disappointments do they encounter in the search for heroes? Work with others to find and interpret answers to these questions.

I HAVE A DREAM
Martin Luther King, Jr.

The Reverend Martin Luther King, Jr., gave his "I Have a Dream" speech in August 1963 after he led 200,000 people in a march on Washington, D.C., to commemorate the one-hundredth anniversary of Lincoln's proclamation freeing the slaves. King was born in Atlanta, Georgia, and became a Baptist minister like his father. He was the pastor of the Dexter Avenue Baptist Church in Montgomery, Alabama, when Rosa Parks challenged the blacks-to-the-back-of-the-bus rule of the city's bus system. King organized the boycott that brought the segregated transit system to its knees and marked the birth of the civil rights movement. He founded the Southern Christian Leadership Conference, preaching the philosophy of nonviolent revolution in books like Letter from a Birmingham Jail *(1963) and* Why We Can't Wait *(1964). The movement he led brought about the 1964 Civil Rights Act and the 1965 Voting Rights Act and ended a century of legally sanctioned segregation. King was kept under surveillance as a suspected Communist sympathizer by the FBI under its notorious director, J. Edgar Hoover. He was struck down in Memphis on April 4, 1968, by the bullet of a cowardly assassin, who went to jail without revealing the identity of the instigators, if any, who put him to work. The Martin Luther King Memorial in Atlanta, Georgia, has become a shrine for visitors who remember King's courage and vision and will not forget. Like no other black leader before or after him, King stirred the consciences of white Americans. Why or how?*

Thought Starters: For you, is the civil rights movement ancient history? Or do its goals and commitments have meaning for you today?

Five score years ago, a great American, in whose symbolic shadow   *1*
we stand, signed the Emancipation Proclamation. This momentous decree came as a great beacon light of hope to millions of Negro slaves who had been seared in the flames of withering injustice. It came as a joyous daybreak to end the long night of captivity.

But one hundred years later, we must face the tragic fact that the Negro is still not free. One hundred years later, the life of the Negro is still sadly crippled by the manacles of segregation and the chains of discrimination. One hundred years later, the Negro lives on a lonely island of poverty in the midst of a vast ocean of material prosperity. One hundred years later, the Negro is still languishing in the corners of American society and finds himself an exile in his own land. So we have come here today to dramatize an appalling condition.

In a sense we have come to our nation's capital to cash a check. When the architects of our republic wrote the magnificent words of the Constitution and the Declaration of Independence, they were signing a promissory note to which every American was to fall heir. This note was a promise that all men would be guaranteed the unalienable rights of life, liberty, and the pursuit of happiness.

It is obvious today that America has defaulted on this promissory note insofar as her citizens of color are concerned. Instead of honoring this sacred obligation, America has given the Negro people a bad check; a check which has come back marked "insufficient funds." But we refuse to believe that the bank of justice is bankrupt. We refuse to believe that there are insufficient funds in the great vaults of opportunity of this nation. So we have come to cash this check—a check that will give us upon demand the riches of freedom and the security of justice. We have also come to this hallowed spot to remind America of the fierce urgency of *now*. This is no time to engage in the luxury of cooling off or take the tranquilizing drugs of gradualism. *Now* is the time to make real the promises of Democracy. *Now* is the time to rise from the dark and desolate valley of segregation to the sunlit path of racial justice. *Now* is the time to open the doors of opportunity to all of God's children. *Now* is the time to lift our nation from the quicksands of racial injustice to the solid rock of brotherhood.

It would be fatal for the nation to overlook the urgency of the moment and to underestimate the determination of the Negro. This sweltering summer of the Negro's legitimate discontent will not pass until there is an invigorating autumn of freedom and equality. 1963 is not an end, but a beginning. Those who hope that the Negro needed to blow off steam and will now be content will have a rude awakening if the nation returns to business as usual. There will be neither rest nor tranquility in America until the Negro is granted his citizenship rights. The whirlwinds of revolt will continue to shake the foundations of our nation until the bright day of justice emerges. 5

But there is something I must say to my people who stand on the warm threshold which leads into the palace of justice. In the process of gaining our rightful place we must not be guilty of wrongful deeds. Let us not seek to satisfy our thirst for freedom by drinking from the cup of bitterness and hatred. We must forever conduct our struggle on the high plane of dignity and discipline. We must not allow our creative protest to degenerate into physical violence. Again and again we must rise to the majestic heights of meeting physical force with soul force. The marvelous new militancy which has engulfed the Negro community must not lead us to a distrust of all white people, for many of our white brothers, as evidenced by their presence here today, have come to realize that their destiny is tied up with our destiny and their freedom is inextricably bound to our freedom. We cannot walk alone.

And as we walk, we must make the pledge that we shall march ahead. We cannot turn back. There are those who are asking the devotees of civil rights, "When will you be satisfied?" We can never be satisfied as long as the Negro is the victim of the unspeakable horrors of police brutality. We can never be satisfied as long as our bodies, heavy with the fatigue of travel, cannot gain lodging in the motels of the highways and the hotels of the cities. We cannot be satisfied as long as the Negro's basic mobility is from a smaller ghetto to a larger one. We can never be satisfied as long as a Negro in Mississippi cannot vote and a Negro in New York believes he has nothing for which to vote. No, no, we are not satisfied, and will not be satisfied until justice rolls down like waters and righteousness like a mighty stream.

I am not unmindful that some of you have come here out of great trials and tribulations. Some of you have come fresh from narrow jail cells. Some of you have come from areas where your quest for freedom left you battered by the storms of persecution and staggered by the winds of police brutality. You have been the veterans of creative suffering. Continue to work with the faith that unearned suffering is redemptive.

Go back to Mississippi, go back to Alabama, go back to South Carolina, go back to Georgia, go back to Louisiana, go back to the slums and ghettos of our northern cities, knowing that somehow this situation can and will be changed. Let us not wallow in the valley of despair.

I say to you today, my friends, that in spite of the difficulties and   10
frustrations of the moment I still have a dream. It is a dream deeply rooted in the American dream.

I have a dream that one day this nation will rise up and live out the true meaning of its creed: "We hold these truths to be self-evident; that all men are created equal."

I have a dream that one day on the red hills of Georgia the sons of former slaves and the sons of former slaveowners will be able to sit down together at the table of brotherhood.

I have a dream that one day even the state of Mississippi, a desert state sweltering with the heat of injustice and oppression, will be transformed into an oasis of freedom and justice.

I have a dream that my four little children will one day live in a nation where they will not be judged by the color of their skin but by the content of their character.

I have a dream today.   15

I have a dream that one day the state of Alabama, whose governor's lips are presently dripping with the words of interposition and nullification, will be transformed into a situation where little black boys and black girls will be able to join hands with little white boys and white girls and walk together as sisters and brothers.

I have a dream today.

I have a dream that one day every valley shall be exalted, every hill and mountain shall be made low, the rough places will be made plain, and the crooked places will be made straight, and the glory of the Lord shall be revealed, and all flesh shall see it together.

This is our hope. This is the faith with which I return to the South. With this faith we will be able to hew out of the mountain of despair a stone of hope. With this faith we will be able to transform the jangling discords of our nation into a beautiful symphony of brotherhood. With this faith we will be able to work together, to pray together, to struggle together, to go to jail together, to stand up for freedom together, knowing that we will be free one day.

This will be the day when all of God's children will be able to sing   20
with new meaning

> My country, 'tis of thee,
> Sweet land of liberty,
>   Of thee I sing:
> Land where my fathers died,
> Land of the pilgrims' pride,
> From every mountain-side
>   Let freedom ring.

And if America is to be a great nation this must become true. So let freedom ring from the prodigious hilltops of New Hampshire. Let freedom ring from the mighty mountains of New York. Let freedom ring from the heightening Alleghenies of Pennsylvania!

Let freedom ring from the snowcapped Rockies of Colorado!

Let freedom ring from the curvaceous peaks of California!

But not only that; let freedom ring from Stone Mountain of Georgia!

Let freedom ring from Lookout Mountain of Tennessee!   25

Let freedom ring from every hill and molehill of Mississippi. From every mountainside, let freedom ring.

When we let freedom ring, when we let it ring from every village and every hamlet, from every state and every city, we will be able to speed up that day when all of God's children, black men and white men, Jews and Gentiles, Protestants and Catholics, will be able to join hands and sing in the words of the old Negro spiritual, "Free at last! free at last! thank God almighty, we are free at last!"

The Responsive Reader

1. King in this speech invokes many of the weighty words that have played a role in the history of race relations in this country. What meanings, memories, and associations cluster around words like *emancipation, segregation, gradualism, brotherhood, militancy, civil rights, police brutality, the American dream, interposition,* or *nullification*? (Which of these do you have to look up? What do you learn from your dictionary or other reference source?)

2. King was speaking to a double audience: His aim was to mobilize the aspirations of African Americans and to appeal to the consciences of the white majority. How does he appeal to shared values by using historical documents, the Bible, or Negro spirituals?
3. Where does King speak most directly for or to "my people"? Where does he most eloquently voice their grievances? What warnings does he address to them?
4. What principles does King appeal to in speaking to white Americans? How does he link the civil rights struggle and the American dream?

Talking, Listening, Writing

5. Although King preached nonviolent revolution, he also said: "A riot is the language of the unheard." Is the philosophy of nonviolence alive today? Or has it been left behind by events?
6. King exhorts members of American minorities who believe they have "nothing for which to vote." After the 1992 riots in South Central Los Angeles, the black congresswoman from the district said, "A third of my people vote." Do you believe that in today's America the individual vote makes a difference? Why or why not?
7. Among people you know best, is racism alive or on the wane? Is there such a thing as "reverse racism"?

Collaborative Projects

8. What African American leaders, national or local, receive prominent media coverage today? Working with a group, you may want to study the media coverage of the current black leadership. For instance, look at news reports, editorials and columns, magazine articles, and documentary coverage of protest activities. What are recurrent images, familiar criticisms, or prevalent attitudes?

Thinking about Connections

Compare King's dream for a better future with the vision of the future in Harvey Milk's "A City of Neighborhoods."

MISTER TOUSSAN

Ralph Ellison

> *Ralph Ellison, born in Oklahoma City, became famous for his novel* Invisible Man *(1952). One reviewer said about this book that it "has been viewed as one of the most important works of fiction in the twentieth century, has been read by millions, influenced dozens of younger writers, and established Ellison as one of the major American writers" of his time. Ellison's semi-autobiographical hero embarked on an archetypal journey of a Southern black in search of his true identity. He experienced segregated schools in the South. He rebelled against white coworkers considering him inferior ("Were they all Ph.D.s?"). In the big Northern city, he first tried to deny and then came to accept his southern roots—grits and hot yams and all ("I yam what I yam!"). He watched political groups—Communists, black nationalists— trying to use him for their own purposes. Everywhere he felt no one saw him as a human being in his own right. He was typed as a member of a racial group—he was invisible as his own person. In the following short story, two young boys are learning pride in who they are. The "Mister Toussan" of the title is Toussaint L'Ouverture (1743–1803), who led the people of Haiti in their fight against French colonial rule. Napoleon was rising to power as emperor of France at the time.*

Thought Starters: What do you know about the colonial history of the Caribbean?

> Once upon a time
> The goose drink wine
> Monkey chew tobacco
> And he spit white lime.
> *—Rhyme used as a prologue
>   to Negro slave stories*

"I hope they all gits rotten and the worms git in 'em," the first boy said.   1

"I hopes a big windstorm comes and blows down all the trees," said the second boy.

"Me too," the first boy said. "And when old Rogan comes out to see what happened I hope a tree falls on his head and kills him."

"Now jus' look a-yonder at them birds," the second boy said, "they eating all they want and when we asked him to let us git some off the ground he had to come calling us names and chasing us home!"

"Doggonit," said the second boy, "I hope them birds got poison in   5
they feet!"

The two small boys, Riley and Buster, sat on the floor of the porch,
their bare feet resting upon the cool earth as they stared past the line on
the paving where the sun consumed the shade, to a yard directly across the
street. The grass in the yard was very green and a house stood against it,
neat and white in the morning sun. A double row of trees stood alongside
the house, heavy with cherries that showed deep red against the dark green
of the leaves and dull dark brown of the branches. They were watching an
old man who rocked himself in a chair as he stared back at them across
the street.

"Just look at him," said Buster. "Ole Rogan's so scared we gonna git
some of his ole cherries he ain't even got sense enough to go in outa the sun!"

"Well, them birds is gitting theirs," said Riley.

"They mockingbirds."

"I don't care what kinda birds they is, they sho in them trees."   10

"Yeah, old Rogan don't see *them*. Man, white folks ain't got no
sense."

They were silent now, watching the darting flight of the birds into
the trees. Behind them they could hear the clatter of a sewing machine:
Riley's mother was sewing for the white folks. It was quiet and, as the
woman worked, her voice rose above the whirring machine in song.

"Your mamma sho can sing, man," said Buster.

"She sings in the choir," said Riley, "and she sings all the leads in
church."

"Shucks, I know it," said Buster. "You tryin' to brag?"   15

As they listened they heard the voice rise clear and liquid to float
upon the morning air:

> I got wings, you got wings,
> All God's chillun got a-wings
> When I git to heaven gonna put on my wings
> Gonna shout all ovah God's heaven.
> Heab'n, heab'n
> Everybody talkin' bout heab'n ain't going there
> Heab'n, heab'n, Ah'm gonna fly all ovah God's heab'n. . . .

She sang as though the words possessed a deep and throbbing meaning for her, and the boys stared blankly at the earth, feeling the somber,
mysterious calm of church. The street was quiet and even old Rogan had
stopped rocking to listen. Finally the voice trailed off to a hum and became
lost in the clatter of the busy machine.

"Sure wish I could sing like that," said Buster.

Riley was silent, looking down to the end of the porch where the
sun had eaten a bright square into the shade, fixing a flitting butterfly in
its brilliance.

"What would you do if you had wings?" he said.   20

"Shucks, I'd outfly an eagle, I wouldn't stop flying till I was a million, billion, trillion, zillion miles away from this ole town."

"Where'd you go, man?"

"Up north, maybe to Chicago."

"Man, if I had wings I wouldn't never settle down."

"Me, neither. With wings you could go anywhere, even up to the   25
sun if it wasn't too hot. . . ."

". . . I'd go to New York. . . ."

"Even around the stars . . ."

"Or Dee-troit, Michigan . . ."

"You could git some cheese off the moon and some milk from the Milky Way. . . ."

"Or anywhere else colored is free. . . ."   30

"I bet I'd loop-the-loop. . . ."

"And parachute. . . ."

"I'd land in Africa and git me some diamonds. . . ."

"Yeah, and them cannibals would eat you too," said Riley.

"The heck they would, not fast as I'd fly away. . . ."   35

"Man, they'd catch you and stick soma them long spears in you!" said Riley.

Buster laughed as Riley shook his head gravely: "Boy, you'd look like a black pin cushion when they got through with you," said Riley.

"Shucks, man, they couldn't catch me, them suckers is too lazy. The geography book says they 'bout the most lazy folks in the whole world," said Buster with disgust, "just black and lazy!"

"Aw naw, they ain't neither," exploded Riley.

"They is too! The geography book says they is!"   40

"Well, my ole man says they ain't!"

"How come they ain't then?"

"'Cause my ole man says that over there they got kings and diamonds and gold and ivory, and if they got all them things, all of 'em cain't be lazy," said Riley. "Ain't many colored folks over here got them things."

"Sho ain't, man. The white folks won't let 'em," said Buster.

It was good to think that all the Africans were not lazy. He tried to   45
remember all he had heard of Africa as he watched a purple pigeon sail down into the street and scratch where a horse had passed. Then, as he remembered a story his teacher had told him, he saw a car rolling swiftly up the street and the pigeon stretching its wings and lifting easily into the air, skimming the top of the car in its slow, rocking flight. He watched it rise and disappear where the taut telephone wires cut the sky above the curb. Buster felt good. Riley scratched his initials in the soft earth with his big toe.

"Riley, you know all them African guys ain't really that lazy," he said.

"I know they ain't," said Riley, "I just tole you so."

"Yeah, but my teacher tole me, too. She tole us 'bout one of them African guys named Toussan what she said whipped Napoleon!"

Riley stopped scratching the earth and looked up, his eyes rolling in disgust:

"Now how come you have to start lying?"   50

"Thass what she said."

"Boy, you oughta quit telling them things."

"I hope God may kill me."

"She said he was a *African*?"

"Cross my heart, man. . . ."   55

"Really?"

"Really, man. She said he come from a place named Hayti."

Riley looked hard at Buster and seeing the seriousness of the face felt the excitement of a story rise up within him.

"Buster, I'll bet a fat man you lyin'. What'd that teacher say?"

"Really, man, she said that Toussan and his men got up on one of   60
them African mountains and shot down them peckerwood soldiers fass as they'd try to come up. . . ."

"Why good-a-mighty!" yelled Riley.

"Oh boy, they shot 'em down!" chanted Buster.

"Tell me about it, man!"

"And they throwed 'em all off the mountain. . . ."

". . . Goool-leee! . . ."   65

". . . And Toussan drove 'em cross the sand. . . ."

". . . Yeah! And what was they wearing, Buster? . . ."

"Man, they had on red uniforms and blue hats all trimmed with gold, and they had some swords, all shining what they called sweet blades of Damascus. . . ."

"Sweet blades of Damascus! . . ."

". . . They really had 'em," chanted Buster.   70

"And what kinda guns?"

"Big, black cannon!"

"And where did ole what-you-call-'im run them guys? . . ."

"His name was Toussan."

"Toussan! Just like Tarzan . . ."   75

"Not *Taar*-zan, dummy, *Toou*-zan!"

"Toussan! And where'd ole Toussan run 'em?"

"Down to the water, man . . ."

". . . To the river water . . ."

". . . Where some great big ole boats was waiting for 'em. . . ."   80

". . . Go on, Buster!"

"An' Toussan shot into them boats. . . ."

". . . He shot into 'em. . . ."

"With his great big cannons . . ."

". . . Yeah! . . ."   85

". . . Made a-brass . . ."

". . . Brass . . ."

". . . An' his big black cannonballs started killin' them pecker-woods. . . ."

". . . Lawd, Lawd . . ."

". . . Boy, till them peckerwoods hollowed 'Please, please, Mister Tous-   90
san, we'll be good!'"

"An' what'd Toussan tell em, Buster?"

"'Boy,' he said in his big deep voice, 'I oughta drown all a-you.'"

"An' what'd the peckerwoods say?"

"They said, 'Please, Please, Please, Mister Toussan . . .'"

". . . 'We'll be good,'" broke in Riley.   95

"Thass right, man," said Buster excitedly. He clapped his hands and kicked his heels against the earth, his black face glowing in a burst of rhythmic joy.

"Boy!"

"And what'd ole Toussan say then?"

"He said in his deep voice: 'You all peckerwoods better be good, 'cause this is sweet Papa Toussan talking and my men is crazy 'bout white meat!'"

"Ho, ho, ho!" Riley bent double with laughter. The rhythm still   100
throbbed within him and he wanted the story to go on and on. . . .

"Buster, you know didn't no teacher tell you that lie," he said.

"Yes she did, man."

"That teacher said there was really a guy like that what called hisself Sweet Papa Toussan?"

Riley's voice was unbelieving and there was a wistful expression in his eyes which Buster could not understand. Finally he dropped his head and grinned.

"Well," he said, "I bet thass what ole Toussan said. You know how   105
grown folks is, they cain't tell a story right, 'cepting real old folks like grandma."

"They sho cain't," said Riley. "They don't know how to put the right stuff to it."

Riley stood, his legs spread wide, and stuck his thumbs in the top of his trousers, swaggering sinisterly.

"Come on, watch me do it now, Buster. Now I bet ole Toussan looked down at them white folks standing just about like this and said in a soft easy voice: 'Ain't I done begged you white folks to quit messin' with me? . . .'"

"Thass right, quit messing with 'im," chanted Buster.

"'But naw, you-all had to come on anyway. . . .'"   110

". . . Jus' 'cause they was black . . ."

"Thass right," said Riley. "Then ole Toussan felt so bad and mad the tears come a-trickling down. . . ."

". . . He was really mad."

"And then, man, he said in his big bass voice: 'white folks, how come you-all cain't let us colored alone?'"

". . . An' he was crying. . . ."   115

". . . An' Toussan tole them peckerwoods: 'I been beggin' you-all to quit bothering us. . . .'"

". . . Beggin' on his bended knees! . . ."

"Then, man, Toussan got real mad and snatched off his hat and started stompin' up and down on it and the tears was tricklin' down and he said: 'You-all come tellin' me about Napoleon. . . .'"

"They was tryin' to make him scared, man. . . ."

"Toussan said: 'I don't care about no Napoleon. . . .'"   120

". . . Wasn't studyin' 'bout him. . . ."

". . . Toussan said: 'Napoleon ain't nothing but a man!' Then Toussan pulled back his shining sword like this, and twirled it at them peckerwoods' throats so hard it z-z-z-zinged in the air!"

"Now keep on, finish it, man," said Buster. "What'd Toussan do then?"

"Then you know what he did, he said: 'I oughta beat you pecker-woods!'"

"Thass right, and he did it too," said Buster. He jumped to his feet and   125
fenced violently with five desperate imaginary soldiers, running each through with his imaginary sword. Buster watched from the porch, grinning.

"Toussan musta scared them white folks almost to death!"

"Yeah, thass 'bout the way it was," said Buster. The rhythm was dying now and he sat back upon the porch, breathing tiredly.

"It sho is a good story," said Riley.

"Heck, man, all the stories my teacher tells us is good. She's a good ole teacher—but you know one thing?"

"Naw; what?"   130

"Ain't none of them stories in the books! Wonder why?"

"You know why, ole Toussan was too hard on them white folks, thass why."

"Oh, he was a hard man!"

"He was mean. . . ."

"But a good mean!"   135

"Toussan was clean. . . ."

". . . He was a good, clean mean," said Riley.

"Aw, man, he was sooo-preme," said Buster.

"Riiiley!!"

The boys stopped short in their word play, their mouths wide.   140

"Riley I say!" It was Riley's mother's voice.

"Ma'am?"

"She musta heard us cussin'," whispered Buster.

"Shut up, man. . . . What you want, Ma?"

"I says I wants you-all to go around in the backyard and play, you   145

keeping up too much fuss out there. White folks says we tear up a neighborhood when we move in it and you-all out there jus' provin' them out
true. Now git on round in the back."

"Aw, ma, we was jus' playing, ma. . . ."

"Boy, I said for you-all to go on."

"But, ma . . ."

"You hear me, boy!"

"Yessum, we going," said Riley. "Come on, Buster."   *150*

Buster followed slowly behind, feeling the dew upon his feet as he
walked upon the shaded grass.

"What else did he do, man?" Buster said.

"Huh? Rogan?"

"Heck, naw! I mean Toussan."

"Doggone if I know, man—but I'm gonna ask that teacher."   *155*

"He was a fightin' son-of-a-gun, wasn't he, man?"

"He didn't stand for no foolishness," said Riley reservedly. He
thought of other things now, and as he moved along he slid his feet easily
over the short-cut grass, dancing as he chanted

> Iron is iron,
> And tin is tin,
> And that's the way
> The story . . .

"Aw come on man," interrupted Buster. "Let's go play in the
alley. . . ."

And that's the way . . .

"Maybe we can slip around and git some cherries," Buster went on. *160*

". . . the story ends," chanted Riley.

The Responsive Reader

1. In much of his fiction, Ellison has fought racial stereotypes. How
   does he do so in this story?
2. The boys in this story delight in word play, in playing games with
   words. Can you describe their way of talking, their use of language?
3. What is the role of the mother in the story?

Talking, Listening, Writing

4. The boys claim that stories like the ones about Toussaint are not in
   their school books. Should they be?
5. Are treatments of black history in the media too downbeat? Are
   blacks or other minorities too often associated in the viewers' or
   readers' minds with problems or trouble?

6. Have you observed or participated in recent efforts to help African Americans or members of other groups to overcome a sense of inferiority and to feel pride? What are these efforts? How successful are they?

Collaborative Projects

7. You may want to do some background reading for a capsule portrait of, or short tribute to, one of the following famous people: Paul Laurence Dunbar, Harriet Tubman, Frederick Douglass, Sojourner Truth, William E. B. DuBois, Marian Anderson, Paul Robeson, Leontyne Price, Mahalia Jackson, Alexander Haley, Thurgood Marshall, Lorraine Hansberry, Cicely Tyson. (You may want to start with but also go beyond entries in encyclopedias or biographical dictionaries.)

FLIGHT (for Amelia Earhart)

Pamela Alexander

> *In the following poem, the poet pays tribute to a pioneering flyer whose achievements made her name a household word around the world. Amelia Earhart became famous when an airplane was still "a thing of wood and wire." Charles Lindbergh had been lionized by newspapers, governments, and adoring crowds after his daredevil solo flight across the Atlantic. Earhart had participated in air races, set speed and altitude records, and had been a crew member on one of the early transatlantic flights. A crowning achievement of her career was meant to be a flight around the world in her Electra plane. The plane with her and her navigator disappeared over the Pacific in July 1937, on the last leg of that flight.*

Thought Starters: Do you think women should compete with men as race car drivers, test pilots, mountain climbers?

A series of white squares, each   1
an hour's flying time, each with instructions
in pencil: the organized adventure. "Carelessness
offends the spirit of Ulysses." She suspends herself,
as he did, in the elements, finds   5
reason turns to motion, caution to design.
"One ocean led naturally to
another." The earth led naturally to the sky
after a look at a thing of wood and wire
at the state fair in Des Moines, after the sting   10
of snow blown from the skis of training planes
near Philadelphia.
           The rumble of the red and gold
Electra wakes the air, shakes stars
down their strings until   15
they hang outside the cockpit, close enough
to touch. The squares, short days,
take turns showing her senses
what to do. The fragrance of blooming
orange orchards carries to considerable   20
altitudes. "No one has seen a tree
who has not seen it from the air, with
its shadow." Lake Chad is huge, shallow,

brightened by the wings of cranes and maribou
storks. The Red Sea is blue; the White and Blue Niles 25
green; the Amazon delta a party of currents,
brown and yellow, distinct. Beyond
the clutter of sensations, the shriek and clatter
of tools at landing fields, she prepares
herself, like the engine, for 30
one thing. Flight
above the wine-dark shining flood
is order, makes the squares
come and go, makes the plane
a tiny gear that turns the world. "Of all those things 35
external to the task at hand, we clutch
what we can."
                    She leaves the plane briefly to join
a crowd of Javanese walking up a beautiful mountain.
They laugh and talk, they carry baskets 40
and various loads on poles. "Sometime
I hope to stay somewhere as long as I like." For
the last long passage she abandons personal items,
souvenirs; also the parachute, useless over the Pacific.
The plane staggers with the weight of fuel. 45
The squares arrive,
live in her,
subside. The plane
is lighter, then
light. The last square has 50
an island in it, but does not
show her where.

The Responsive Reader

1. What is paradoxical about the phrase "the organized adventure"?
   What do you know about Ulysses, and what role does he play in the
   poem?
2. What concrete details and striking images re-create for you the sights,
   sounds, and sensations of the journey? (How does the rumble of the
   plane shake "stars down their strings"? How does the flight make the
   plane "a tiny gear that turns the world"?)
3. The squares of the flight plan and the limited amount of fuel play a
   central role in this poem. How and where?

Talking, Listening, Writing

4. Do today's media build up inspirational female sports or adventure
   figures comparable to Earhart? Have you admired someone like

Martina Navratilova, Wilma Rudolph, or Nancy Kerrigan? What do you know about her achievements and the person behind the media image? What accounts for the person's celebrity status? How much is athletic achievement? How much is personality? How much is media hype?

5. While working as a career counselor, Earhart told one group of young women, "A girl must nowadays believe completely in herself as an individual. She must realize at the outset that a woman must do the same job better than a man to get as much credit for it." Is this still true today?

Collaborative Projects

6. Elizabeth Blackwell, Madame Curie, and Margaret Mead are other pioneering women who made their way in what was once considered men's domain. Work with a group to prepare biographical portraits of these and other legendary female role models for presentation to the class.

WRITING
WORKSHOP 8

Arguing from Principle

As rational, objective people, we pride ourselves on our ability to approach a subject with an open mind. We feel capable of looking at the evidence and drawing logical conclusions. Three major reasoning patterns help writers structure papers that present a strong argument:

- The **inductive**, generalizing kind of reasoning is the most easily demonstrated of the procedures that our minds use to process information. The inductive think scheme, moving from fact to inference, has for centuries been the model for Western science. (Early scientists took in such facts as that the moon is kept in orbit around Earth, that pens fall to the floor and not to the ceiling, that apples drop to the ground instead of flying off toward the sky. They concluded that there was an all-pervading physical force—gravity—that pulled material objects toward one another.)

- The playing off of **pro and con** mirrors the way a public consensus takes shape on many debatable issues. By listening to both sides, we can hope to weed out what is clearly self-serving, partisan, or extreme in order to find common ground. We move from statement to counterstatement and, ideally, to a balanced conclusion.

- Much formal, structured argument follows a third reasoning pattern. Much of our reasoning follows the opposite of the inductive procedure. **Deduction**, or deductive reasoning, spells out something that we believe—something that we already accept as true. It then shows how the general principle applies to a specific situation. (The two kinds of reasoning work together if we first develop general physical laws or patterns of behavior and then use them to predict behavior in a specific situation. For instance, if the law of gravity holds true, a space module passing Venus or Mars should be pulled toward the planet or deflected into an orbit around the planet.)

Deductive reasoning moves from the general to the specific. It invokes principles that we expect the reader to share. It then applies these to the situation in question. Many arguments concerning values or behavior follow a deductive pattern:

- If all human beings, regardless of race, are created equal, then slavery is evil.

- If we believe in the sanctity of life, and if life begins at conception, then abortion is a sin.

- If the foundation of democracy is an educated citizenry, then providing universal public education is a civic duty.

- If all Americans are equal before the law, then the offspring of a senator or a corporation president should not get a special exemption from military service.

As you can see, many such arguments hinge on the initial *if*—the initial assumption, or **premise**. If the premise does not hold true, the argument does not convince. (If the masses are not intelligent enough to make informed political decisions, we are off the hook as far as free universal public education is concerned. We may then settle for minimal vocational training for those who need only basic skills and the ability to follow instructions.)

TRIGGERING As with other kinds of reasoning, we may think about the principles at stake in a current issue at least in part to make up our own minds. But more often we use an appeal to principle to bring others around to our point of view. We invoke basic principles when defending our position on public education, drunken driving laws, Christmas displays on public property, welfare reform, military service, or capital punishment.

In his famous "I Have a Dream" speech, Martin Luther King, Jr., invoked basic principles of the American political tradition: In the country of the free, one large segment of the population should not be denied the freedom to live, eat, and go to school where they choose. In a country founded on the principle of human dignity, a large number of fellow citizens should not be subjected to demeaning restrictions and exclusions. In the words of President Lincoln, a country cannot be half free.

GATHERING To appeal effectively to shared values, you might need to invoke precedents and established legal principles. For instance, what is the history of our protections for freedom of speech? (Why were printers and journalists in the colonies concerned about their freedom to print? What are the roots of First Amendment rights in earlier British history? Where in modern times have censorship forces been especially odious and repressive?) On our obligation to the poor, you might want to quote an eloquent statement by a widely respected leader, or you might present a modern rereading of a parable from the New Testament. On an unpopular law, you might present impressive evidence of public opinion.

Perhaps you want to appeal to the principle of compassion in arguing against "heroic" medical procedures that needlessly prolong the suffering of the terminally ill. Your reading notes for the paper might include entries like the following:

> Public opinion polls show that most Americans oppose the use of "heroic measures" to keep patients alive when there is no hope of recovery. A Louis Harris poll found that 82% supported the idea of withdrawing feeding tubes if it was the patient's wish. . . .
>
> In many cases, the family and the staff agree that the patient in question "derives no comfort, no improvement, and no hope of improvement" from further medical treatment. . . .
>
> Many Americans linger in a hopeless twilight zone between life and imminent death. Recent studies show the tremendous financial burden and the anguish suffered by their families. . . .

SHAPING A classic pattern for an argument from principle first dramatizes the current situation that raised the issue. It then spells out the principle (or principles) involved, presented in such a way that the argument will speak strongly to the shared values of the intended audience. Then the writer applies the principle (or principles) to specific authentic examples.

What are the principles invoked in the following paper? Do you think they will command the assent or at least the respect of the intended readers? How authentic or convincing do the test cases or key examples seem to you? How do *you* react to this paper as a reader?

Thou Shalt Not

As we hear about prayer vigils and last-minute pleas protesting the current spate of executions, we realize that an issue that has lain dormant for many years is again dividing the citizens into hostile camps. The weakness of the passionate last-minute appeals for clemency played up by the media is that they tend to focus on the special circumstances of the individual case. A murderer was the victim of child abuse. A rapist suffered brain damage. By focusing on the individual history of those waiting on death row, we run the danger of losing sight of the basic principles at stake when a civilized society reinstitutes capital punishment.

In spite of strong current arguments in favor of the death penalty, capital punishment violates basic principles underlying the American system of justice. Most basic to our legal system is the commitment to even-handed justice. We believe that equal crimes should receive equal punishment. However, the death penalty has always been notorious for its "freakish unfairness." Some murderers walk the streets again after three or five or seven years, whereas others—because of ineffectual legal counsel, a vindictive prosecutor, or a harsh judge—join the inmates waiting out their appeals on death row. In one celebrated case, two partners in crime were convicted of the same capital crime on identical charges. One was executed; the other is in prison and will soon be eligible for parole. In the words of one study, "Judicial safeguards for preventing the arbitrary administration of capital punishment are not working." Judges and juries apply widely different standards.

We believe that all citizens are equal before the law. Justice should be blind to wealth, race, or ethnic origin. However, poor defendants are many times more likely to receive the death penalty than wealthy ones, protected by highly paid teams of lawyers whose maneuvers stymie the prosecution and baffle the jury. Minority defendants convicted of capital crimes have a much higher statistical chance of being executed than white defendants. A black person killing a white person is more likely to receive the death penalty than a white person killing a black person.

Fairness demands that the judicial system make provision for correcting its own mistakes. If someone has been unjustly convicted, there should be a mechanism for reversing the verdict and setting the person free. No one doubts that there are miscarriages of justice. Citizens of Northern Ireland convicted as terrorists are set free after many years because of evidence that they were framed and their confessions coerced by the police. Victims withdraw rape charges; witnesses admit to mistaken identification of suspects. A convict confesses on his deathbed to a crime for which someone else was convicted.

However, in the case of the death penalty, any such correction of error is aborted. We are left with futile regrets, like the prosecutor who said, "Horrible as it is to contemplate, we may have executed the wrong man."

REVISING When we write with special conviction, we are likely to come on strong. We may use emotional language. We are often impatient with the opposition. We may sound very sure—probably too sure—of ourselves. Give yourself time to reread a paper that you wrote in the heat of passion. Rereading the paper in the sober light of next morning, you have a chance to take some of the heat and steam out of the argument. You have a chance to make sure the argument stands on its merits. In revising your paper, consider advice like the following:

• *Do not invoke large abstractions like Science or History or Common Sense.* "Science says . . ." is a weak argument, because specific scientists make limited assertions—and often scientists disagree among themselves. (Quote specific scientists, and try to show that they are recognized authorities or people in the mainstream of current scientific opinion.) Remember that common sense told people that Earth was flat.

• *Try not to dismiss (or brush off) opposing points of view.* People who feel insulted or ignored are not likely to listen attentively—and perhaps change their minds. (Not everyone who more or less reluctantly endorses the reinstatement of the death penalty is a fascist, a sadist, a vigilante, or a believer in primitive eye-for-an-eye justice.)

• *Tone down passages that make you sound bigoted or prejudiced.* ("The average criminal is a brutal individual who deserves exactly what he got."

"To rid our streets of violent crime, we should lock up violent criminals and throw the key away.")

■ *Strengthen logical links.* Signal turns in the argument. Use the transitions that are needed to hold an argument together. Insert a strategic *therefore* or *consequently* to signal that you are drawing a logical conclusion. Use *however* or *nevertheless* to signal that you are raising a major objection. Use links like *on the one hand* and *on the other hand* to show that you are playing off the pro and con.

Topics for Papers Arguing from Principle (A Sampling)

1. Should a college assure parity in funding for men's and women's sports? Why or why not? If you answer in the affirmative, how would parity be achieved?
2. Should women receive equal pay not only for the same jobs but also for jobs of "comparable worth"? What principles are involved?
3. Does society have the right to deny welfare payments to unwed teenage mothers? What principles are at stake?
4. Should employers have the right to hire permanent replacements for striking workers? (Are there limits to the right to strike?)
5. Should employers have the right to ban romantic relationships among employees? On what grounds?
6. Do traditional tests or qualifying exams work against equal opportunity for candidates from other than conventional white, middle-class backgrounds? What principles are at stake?
7. In awarding custody of children in divorce cases, should the courts give preference to the mother? Why or why not?
8. Should colleges terminate their relationship with the ROTC? What are the principles at stake?
9. Should the military have the right to ban gays and lesbians?
10. Does the United States have a humanitarian obligation to accept refugees escaping from war, poverty, or repression?

9

Language: Bond or Barrier?

An education for freedom (and for the love and intelligence which are at once the conditions and the results of freedom) must be, among other things, an education in the proper uses of language.

—*Aldous Huxley*

Languages are far-reaching realities. They go far beyond those political and historical structures we call nations.

—*Octavio Paz*

Language is the greatest human invention. It gives us more than neutral information of the kind that could be stored in a computer—or recited by a computerized voice. Words do not just give directions ("This way to the center of the city"). They tell us something about the speaker— as if a telephone while carrying a message were to tell us whether it liked its job. *Bureaucrat, politician, schoolmarm, welfare cheat, redneck,* and *woman driver* are not neutral labels like *detergent* or *soap*. They give vent to the speaker's feelings. They carry messages of dislike, of antagonism—they say "I am not as dense or conniving or bigoted as you are."

Many of the following selections raise a crucial question about language: Is it boon or bane in relationships between individuals or groups? Does it further human understanding? Or does it serve to muddy the waters or poison the wells? We like to think of language as a bond. It helps people to break out of their isolation, to break down the wall of separateness. In the prehistoric past, it enabled human beings to band together, to make plans, to coordinate their efforts. Language enables us to offer other human beings help and comfort. ("Be of good cheer; we will not abandon you" is chalked on a message board held up on a rescue vessel to comfort the people on a shipwrecked ship in one of Walt Whitman's poems.) However, language also carries messages of rejection, condescension, and contempt, as with words like *stud, slut, young punk, dirty foreigner, greaser, dago,* and other racial or ethnic slurs too ugly to mention. Language often reinforces divisions; it serves to outgroup people who are "not one of us." Language is the medium of love, but it is also the medium of quarrels, of hate propaganda, of incitement to violence.

Many people in our modern world have been suspicious of language— wary of its potential for abuse. Others have maintained their faith in the capacity of language to help human beings communicate. The critic Margaret Laurence said about the Nigerian novelist Chinua Achebe, author of *Things Fall Apart*,

> In Ibo villages, the men working on their farm plots in the midst of the rain forest often shout to one another—a reassurance, to make certain the other is still there, on the next cultivated patch, on the other side of the thick undergrowth. The writing of Chinua Achebe is like this. It seeks to send human voices through thickets of our separateness.

TALK IN THE INTIMATE RELATIONSHIP: HIS AND HERS

Deborah Tannen

Deborah Tannen is a language scholar who says her marriage broke up because of a classic breakdown in communication: She employed a literal style, trying to say exactly what she meant, whereas her husband used the indirect style of people who hint at what they want and expect other people to pick up the hints. Tannen, who studied at Berkeley under linguists focusing on language as an interactive social medium, reached a large public with two books on the undercurrents and hidden messages in how people talk: You Just Don't Understand: Women and Men in Conversation *and* That's Not What I Meant: How Conversational Style Makes or Breaks Relationships. *Her focus is on the* meta*messages we send—the messages that* go *beyond what we say outright. Literal-minded people miss much of the subtext of communication—what lies below surface meanings. The mere fact that people bother to talk to us already sends a message (they care enough to give us some of their time), just as their* refusal *to talk to us also sends a message. Tannen's most recent book is* Talking from 9 to 5 *(1994), on the role of language in the workplace. A reviewer of the book said that much of the secret of her success is "that she is writing about the single most common social activity in the world; everyone talks, although not everyone reads, writes, or reasons." Dr. Tannen's scholarly essays have been collected in* Gender and Discourse, *published by Oxford University Press.*

Thought Starters: Is it true that as far as language goes, boys and girls "grow up in different worlds"? Is a conversation between a man and a woman truly "cross-cultural" communication?

Male-female conversation is cross-cultural communication. Culture is   1
simply a network of habits and patterns gleaned from past experience, and women and men have different past experiences. From the time they're born, they're treated differently, talked to differently, and talk differently as a result. Boys and girls grow up in different worlds, even if they grow up in the same house. And as adults they travel in different worlds, reinforcing patterns established in childhood. These cultural differences include different expectations about the role of talk in relationships and how it fulfills that role.

Everyone knows that as a relationship becomes long-term, its terms change. But women and men often differ in how they expect them to change. Many women feel, "After all this time, you should know what I want without my telling you." Many men feel, "After all this time, we should be able to tell each other what we want."

These incongruent expectations capture one of the key differences between men and women. Communication is always a matter of balancing conflicting needs for involvement and independence. Though everyone has both these needs, women often have a relatively greater need for involvement, and men a relatively greater need for independence. Being understood without saying what you mean gives a payoff in involvement, and that is why women value it so highly.

If you want to be understood without saying what you mean explicitly in words, you must convey meaning somewhere else—in how words are spoken, or by metamessages. Thus it stands to reason that women are often more attuned than men to the metamessages of talk. When women surmise meaning in this way, it seems mysterious to men, who call it "women's intuition" (if they think it's right) or "reading things in" (if they think it's wrong). Indeed, it could be wrong, since metamessages are not on record. And even if it is right, there is still the question of scale: How significant are the metamessages that are there?

Metamessages are a form of indirectness. Women are more likely to   5
be indirect, and to try to reach agreement by negotiation. Another way to understand this preference is that negotiation allows a display of solidarity, which women prefer to the display of power (even though the aim may be the same—getting what you want). Unfortunately, power and solidarity are bought with the same currency: Ways of talking intended to create solidarity have the simultaneous effect of framing power differences. When they think they're being nice, women often end up appearing deferential and unsure of themselves or of what they want.

When styles differ, misunderstandings are always rife. As their differing styles create misunderstandings, women and men try to clear them up by talking things out. These pitfalls are compounded in talks between men and women because they have different ways of going about talking things out, and different assumptions about the significance of going about it.

Sylvia and Harry celebrated their fiftieth wedding anniversary at a mountain resort. Some of the guests were at the resort for the whole weekend, others just for the evening of the celebration: a cocktail party followed by a sit-down dinner. The manager of the dining room approached Sylvia during dinner. "Since there's so much food tonight," he said, "and the hotel prepared a fancy dessert and everyone already ate at the cocktail party anyway, how about cutting and serving the anniversary cake at lunch tomorrow?" Sylvia asked the advice of the others at her table. All the men agreed: "Sure, that makes sense. Save the cake for tomorrow." All the women disagreed: "No, the party is tonight. Serve the cake tonight." The men were focusing on the message: the cake as food. The women were thinking of the metamessage: Serving a special cake frames an occasion as a celebration.

Why are women more attuned to metamessages? Because they are more focused on involvement, that is, on relationships among people, and it is through metamessages that relationships among people are established and maintained. If you want to take the temperature and check the vital signs of a relationship, the barometers to check are its metamessages: what is said and how.

Everyone can see these signals, but whether or not we pay attention to them is another matter—a matter of being sensitized. Once you are sensitized, you can't roll your antennae back in; they're stuck in the extended position.

When interpreting meaning, it is possible to pick up signals that 10 weren't intentionally sent out, like an innocent flock of birds on a radar screen. The birds are there—and the signals women pick up are there—but they may not mean what the interpreter thinks they mean. For example, Maryellen looks at Larry and asks, "What's wrong?" because his brow is furrowed. Since he was only thinking about lunch, her expression of concern makes him feel under scrutiny.

The difference in focus on messages and metamessages can give men and women different points of view on almost any comment. Harriet complains to Morton, "Why don't you ask me how my day was?" He replies, "If you have something to tell me, tell me. Why do you have to be invited?" The reason is that she wants the metamessage of interest: evidence that he cares how her day was, regardless of whether or not she has something to tell.

A lot of trouble is caused between women and men by, of all things, pronouns. Women often feel hurt when their partners use "I" or "me" in a situation in which they would use "we" or "us." When Morton announces, "I think I'll go for a walk," Harriet feels specifically uninvited, though Morton later claims she would have been welcome to join him. She felt locked out by his use of "I" and his omission of an invitation: "Would you like to come?" Metamessages can be seen in what is not said as well as what is said.

It's difficult to straighten out such misunderstandings because each one feels convinced of the logic of his or her position and the illogic—or irresponsibility—of the other's. Harriet knows that she always asks Morton how his day was, and that she'd never announce, "I'm going for a walk," without inviting him to join her. If he talks differently to her, it must be that he feels differently. But Morton wouldn't feel unloved if Harriet didn't ask about his day, and he would feel free to ask, "Can I come along?," if she announced she was taking a walk. So he can't believe she is justified in feeling responses he knows he wouldn't have.

These processes are dramatized with chilling yet absurdly amusing authenticity in Jules Feiffer's play *Grown Ups*. To get a closer look at what happens when men and women focus on different levels of talk in talking things out, let's look at what happens in this play.

Jake criticizes Louise for not responding when their daughter, Edie, 15
called her. His comment leads to a fight even though they're both aware
that this one incident is not in itself important.

Jake: Look, I don't care if it's important or not, when a kid calls its
mother the mother should answer.
Louise: Now I'm a bad mother.
Jake: I didn't say that.
Louise: It's in your stare.
Jake: Is that another thing you know? My stare?

Louise ignores Jake's message—the question of whether or not she responded when Edie called—and goes for the metamessage: his implication
that she's a bad mother, which Jake insistently disclaims. When Louise
explains the signals she's reacting to, Jake not only discounts them but is
angered at being held accountable not for what he said but for how he
looked—his stare.

As the play goes on, Jake and Louise replay and intensify these
patterns:

Louise: If I'm such a terrible mother, do you want a divorce?
Jake: I do not think you're a terrible mother and no, thank you, I do
not want a divorce. Why is it that whenever I bring up any difference
between us you ask me if I want a divorce?

The more he denies any meaning beyond the message, the more she blows
it up, the more adamantly he denies it, and so on:

Jake: I have brought up one thing that you do with Edie that I don't
think you notice that I have noticed for some time but which I have deliberately not brought up before because I had hoped you would notice it for
yourself and stop doing it and also—frankly, baby, I have to say this—I
knew if I brought it up we'd get into exactly the kind of circular argument
we're in right now. And I wanted to avoid it. But I haven't and we're in it,
so now, with your permission, I'd like to talk about it.
Louise: You don't see how that puts me down?
Jake: What?
Louise: If you think I'm so stupid why do you go on living with me?
Jake: Dammit! Why can't anything ever be simple around here?!

It can't be simple because Louise and Jake are responding to different levels
of communication. As in Bateson's example of the dual-control electric
blanket with crossed wires, each one intensifies the energy going to a
different aspect of the problem. Jake tries to clarify his point by over-
elaborating it, which gives Louise further evidence that he's condescending
to her, making it even less likely that she will address his point rather than
his condescension.

What pushes Jake and Louise beyond anger to rage is their different perspectives on metamessages. His refusal to admit that his statements have implications and overtones denies her authority over her own feelings. Her attempts to interpret what he didn't say and put the metamessage into the message makes him feel she's putting words into his mouth—denying his authority over his own meaning.

The same thing happens when Louise tells Jake that he is being manipulated by Edie:

Louise: Why don't you ever make her come to see you? Why do you always go to her?

Jake: You want me to play power games with a nine year old? I want her to know I'm interested in her. Someone around here has to show interest in her.

Louise: You love her more than I do.

Jake: I didn't say that.

Louise: Yes, you did.

Jake: You don't know how to listen. You have never learned how to listen. It's as if listening to you is a foreign language.

Again, Louise responds to his implication—this time, that he loves Edie more because he runs when she calls. And yet again, Jake cries literal meaning, denying he meant any more than he said.

Throughout their argument, the point to Louise is her feelings—that Jake makes her feel put down—but to him the point is her actions—that she doesn't always respond when Edie calls:

Louise: You talk about what I do to Edie, what do you think you do to me?

Jake: This is not the time to go into what we do to each other.

Since she will talk only about the metamessage, and he will talk only about the message, neither can get satisfaction from their talk, and they end up where they started—only angrier:

Jake: That's not the point!

Louise: It's *my* point.

Jake: It's hopeless!

Louise: Then get a divorce.

American conventional wisdom (and many of our parents and English teachers) tell us that meaning is conveyed by words, so men who tend to be literal about words are supported by conventional wisdom. They may not simply deny but actually miss the cues that are sent by how words are spoken. If they sense something about it, they may nonetheless discount what they sense. After all, it wasn't said. Sometimes that's a dodge—a plausible defense rather than a gut feeling. But sometimes it is a sincere conviction. Women are also likely to doubt the reality of what they sense. If they don't doubt it in their guts, they nonetheless may lack the arguments to support their position and thus are reduced to repeating, "You said it. You did so." Knowing that metamessages are a real and fundamental part of communication makes it easier to understand and justify what they feel.

An article in a popular newspaper reports that one of the five most   20
common complaints of wives about their husbands is "He doesn't listen to me anymore." Another is "He doesn't talk to me anymore." Political scientist Andrew Hacker noted that lack of communication, while high on women's lists of reasons for divorce, is much less often mentioned by men. Since couples are parties to the same conversations, why are women more dissatisfied with them than men? Because what they expect is different, as well as what they see as the significance of talk itself.

First, let's consider the complaint "He doesn't talk to me."

One of the most common stereotypes of American men is the strong silent type. Jack Kroll, writing about Henry Fonda on the occasion of his death, used the phrases "quiet power," "abashed silences," "combustible catatonia," and "sense of power held in check." He explained that Fonda's goal was not to let anyone see "the wheels go around," not to let the "machinery" show. According to Kroll, the resulting silence was effective on stage but devastating to Fonda's family.

The image of a silent father is common and is often the model for the lover or husband. But what attracts us can become flypaper to which we are unhappily stuck. Many women find the strong silent type to be a lure as a lover but a lug as a husband. Nancy Schoenberger begins a poem with the lines "It was your silence that hooked me, / so like my father's." Adrienne Rich refers in a poem to the "husband who is frustratingly mute." Despite the initial attraction of such quintessentially male silence, it may begin to feel, to a woman in a long-term relationship, like a brick wall against which she is banging her head.

In addition to these images of male and female behavior—both the result and the cause of them—are differences in how women and men view the role of talk in relationships as well as how talk accomplishes its purpose. These differences have their roots in the settings in which men and women learn to have conversations: among their peers, growing up.

Children whose parents have foreign accents don't speak with ac-   25
cents. They learn to talk like their peers. Little girls and little boys learn how to have conversations as they learn how to pronounce words: from their playmates. Between the ages of five and fifteen, when children are learning to have conversations, they play mostly with friends of their own sex. So it's not surprising that they learn different ways of having and using conversations.

Anthropologists Daniel Maltz and Ruth Borker point out that boys and girls socialize differently. Little girls tend to play in small groups or, even more common, in pairs. Their social life usually centers around a best friend, and friendships are made, maintained, and broken by talk—

especially "secrets." If a little girl tells her friend's secret to another little girl, she may find herself with a new best friend. The secrets themselves may or may not be important, but the fact of telling them is all-important. It's hard for newcomers to get into these tight groups, but anyone who is admitted is treated as an equal. Girls like to play cooperatively; if they can't cooperate, the group breaks up.

Little boys tend to play in larger groups, often outdoors, and they spend more time doing things than talking. It's easy for boys to get into the group, but not everyone is accepted as an equal. Once in the group, boys must jockey for their status in it. One of the most important ways they do this is through talk: verbal display such as telling stories and jokes, challenging and sidetracking the verbal displays of other boys, and withstanding other boys' challenges in order to maintain their own story—and status. Their talk is often competitive talk about who is best at what.

Feiffer's play is ironically named *Grown Ups* because adult men and women struggling to communicate often sound like children: "You said so!" "I did not!" The reason is that when they grow up, women and men keep the divergent attitudes and habits they learned as children—which they don't recognize as attitudes and habits but simply take for granted as ways of talking.

Women want their partners to be a new and improved version of a best friend. This gives them a soft spot for men who tell them secrets. As Jack Nicholson once advised a guy in a movie: "Tell her about your troubled childhood—that always gets 'em." Men expect to *do* things together and don't feel anything is missing if they don't have heart-to-heart talks all the time.

If they do have heart-to-heart talks, the meaning of those talks may be opposite for men and women. To many women, the relationship is working as long as they can talk things out. To many men, the relationship isn't working out if they have to keep working it over. If she keeps trying to get talks going to save the relationship, and he keeps trying to avoid them because he sees them as weakening it, then each one's efforts to preserve the relationship appear to the other as reckless endangerment.

If talks (of any kind) do get going, men's and women's ideas about how to conduct them may be very different. For example, Dora is feeling comfortable and close to Tom. She settles into a chair after dinner and begins to tell him about a problem at work. She expects him to ask questions to show he's interested; reassure her that he understands and that what she feels is normal; and return the intimacy by telling her a problem of his. Instead, Tom sidetracks her story, cracks jokes about it, questions her interpretation of the problem, and gives her advice about how to solve it and avoid such problems in the future.

All of these responses, natural to men, are unexpected to women, who interpret them in terms of their own habits—negatively. When Tom comments on side issues or cracks jokes, Dora thinks he doesn't care about what she's saying and isn't really listening. If he challenges her reading of what went on, she feels he is criticizing her and telling her she's crazy, when what she wants is to be reassured that she's not. If he tells her how to solve the problem, it makes her feel as if she's the patient to his doctor—a metamessage of condescension, echoing male one-upmanship compared to the female etiquette of equality. Because he doesn't volunteer information about his problems, she feels he's implying he doesn't have any.

His way of responding to her bid for intimacy makes her feel distant from him. She tries harder to regain intimacy the only way she knows how—by revealing more and more about herself. He tries harder by giving more insistent advice. The more problems she exposes, the more incompetent she feels, until they both see her as emotionally draining and problem-ridden. When his efforts to help aren't appreciated, he wonders why she asks for his advice if she doesn't want to take it. . . .

When women talk about what seems obviously interesting to them, their conversations often include reports of conversations. Tone of voice, timing, intonation, and wording are all re-created in the telling in order to explain—dramatize, really—the experience that is being reported. If men tell about an incident and give a brief summary instead of re-creating what was said and how, the women often feel that the essence of the experience is being omitted. If the woman asks, "What exactly did he say?," and "How did he say it?," the man probably can't remember. If she continues to press him, he may feel as if he's being grilled.

All these different habits have repercussions when the man and the woman are talking about their relationship. He feels out of his element, even one down. She claims to recall exactly what he said, and what she said, and in what sequence, and she wants him to account for what he said. He can hardly account for it since he has forgotten exactly what was said—if not the whole conversation. She secretly suspects he's only pretending not to remember, and he secretly suspects that she's making up the details.   35

One woman reported such a problem as being a matter of her boyfriend's poor memory. It is unlikely, however, that his problem was poor memory in general. The question is what types of material each person remembers or forgets.

Frances was sitting at her kitchen table talking to Edward, when the toaster did something funny. Edward began to explain why it did it. Frances tried to pay attention, but very early in his explanation, she realized she was completely lost. She felt very stupid. And indications were that he thought so too.

Later that day they were taking a walk. He was telling her about a difficult situation in his office that involved a complex network of interrelationships among a large number of people. Suddenly he stopped and said, "I'm sure you can't keep track of all these people." "Of course I can," she said, and she retraced his story with all the characters in place, all the details right. He was genuinely impressed. She felt very smart.

How could Frances be both smart and stupid? Did she have a good memory or a bad one? Frances's and Edward's abilities to follow, remember, and recount depended on the subject—and paralleled her parents' abilities to follow and remember. Whenever Frances told her parents about people in her life, her mother could follow with no problem, but her father got lost as soon as she introduced a second character. "Now who was that?" he'd ask. "Your boss?" "No, my boss is Susan. This was my friend." Often he'd still be in the previous story. But whenever she told them about her work, it was her mother who would get lost as soon as she mentioned a second step: "That was your tech report?" "No, I handed my tech report in last month. This was a special project."

Frances's mother and father, like many other men and women, had   40
honed their listening and remembering skills in different arenas. Their experience talking to other men and other women gave them practice in following different kinds of talk.

Knowing whether and how we are likely to report events later influences whether and how we pay attention when they happen. As women listen to and take part in conversations, knowing they may talk about them later makes them more likely to pay attention to exactly what is said and how. Since most men aren't in the habit of making such reports, they are less likely to pay much attention at the time. On the other hand, many women aren't in the habit of paying attention to scientific explanations and facts because they don't expect to have to perform in public by reciting them—just as those who aren't in the habit of entertaining others by telling jokes "can't" remember jokes they've heard, even though they listened carefully enough to enjoy them.

So women's conversations with their women friends keep them in training for talking about their relationships with men, but many men come to such conversations with no training at all—and an uncomfortable sense that this really isn't their event.

Most of us place enormous emphasis on the importance of a primary relationship. We regard the ability to maintain such relationships as a sign of mental health—our contemporary metaphor for being a good person.

Yet our expectations of such relationships are nearly—maybe in fact—impossible. When primary relationships are between women and men, male-female differences contribute to the impossibility. We expect partners to be both romantic interests and best friends. Though women and men may have fairly similar expectations for romantic interests, obscuring their differences when relationships begin, they have very different ideas about how to be friends, and these are the differences that mount over time.

In conversations between friends who are not lovers, small misunder-   45
standings can be passed over or diffused by breaks in contact. But in the context of a primary relationship, differences can't be ignored, and the pressure cooker of continued contact keeps both people stewing in the juice of accumulated minor misunderstandings. And stylistic differences are

sure to cause misunderstandings—not, ironically, in matters such as sharing values and interests or understanding each other's philosophies of life. These large and significant yet palpable issues can be talked about and agreed on. It is far harder to achieve congruence—and much more surprising and troubling that it is hard—in the simple day-to-day matters of the automatic rhythms and nuances of talk. Nothing in our backgrounds or in the media (the present-day counterpart to religion or grandparents' teachings) prepares us for this failure. If two people share so much in terms of point of view and basic values, how can they continually get into fights about insignificant matters?

If you find yourself in such a situation and you don't know about differences in conversational style, you assume something's wrong with your partner, or you for having chosen your partner. At best, if you are forward thinking and generous minded, you may absolve individuals and blame the relationship. But if you know about differences in conversational style, you can accept that there are differences in habits and assumptions about how to have conversation, show interest, be considerate, and so on. You may not always correctly interpret your partner's intentions, but you will know that if you get a negative impression, it may not be what was intended—and neither are your responses unfounded. If he says he really is interested even though he doesn't seem to be, maybe you should believe what he says and not what you sense.

Sometimes explaining assumptions can help. If a man starts to tell a woman what to do to solve her problem, she may say, "Thanks for the advice but I really don't want to be told what to do. I just want you to listen and say you understand." A man might want to explain, "If I challenge you, it's not to prove you wrong; it's just my way of paying attention to what you're telling me." Both may try either or both to modify their ways of talking and to try to accept what the other does. The important thing is to know that what seem like bad intentions may really be good intentions expressed in a different conversational style. We have to give up our conviction that, as Robin Lakoff put it, "Love means never having to say 'What do you mean?'"

The Responsive Reader

1. Tannen once said that readers of her work reported an "Aha!" response. They found that what they thought was their personal problem was actually part of a larger pattern. Did you have an "Aha!" response to any part of this selection? Can you give examples from your own experience for the clashing assumptions or expectations that Tannen ascribes to men and women?
2. What are key examples that Tannen gives for the difficulties of communication between men and women? How real or convincing do they seem to you? (How convincing are the examples from

the Feiffer play?) Do you interpret the examples the same way she does?

3. How does Tannen explain how misunderstandings "intensify" or escalate?

4. How familiar are the stereotypes about males that Tannen claims are widespread in our culture and shape male behavior? How strong are they?

5. Is there hope for miscommunicating couples? What is the gist of the positive advice, explicit or implied, that Tannen would give to couples who have trouble communicating?

Talking, Listening, Writing

6. There is much debate over what is truly gender-specific in our culture. Do you think Tannen exaggerates the differences between the talking styles of the sexes? Where and how?

7. Tannen has challenged the feminist claim that men dominate women in conversation. Is it true that men tend to interrupt women, cutting them off or brushing off their opinions? Or are women right who claim that "men never talk"?

8. Have you ever rebelled against a style of talking expected of you? Have you ever found yourself using language that was not "you"? What was the occasion or situation? What was the problem? What was the outcome?

Collaborative Projects

9. Working alone or in a group, you may want to investigate the "women's language" of fashion sections or society pages. Or you may want to study the "men's language" of the sports pages. Or you may want to work out significant contrasts between the two.

CULTURAL ETIQUETTE: A GUIDE
Amoja Three Rivers

Ms. *magazine published the following article as part of a series on race and women. The editors called it a "creative attempt to shed some light— and levity—on the serious task of dispelling racial myths and stereotypes." The author is a cofounder of the Accessible African Herstory Project and was described by the editors of* Ms. *as a "lecturer, herstorian, and craftswoman." Much of the article focuses on how language—ready-made phrases, loaded words—channel or distort our thinking. The article provides a guide to words that can raise hackles or short-circuit communication—in short, make people see red. This article should make you think about the power of words to shape our thinking and our views of other people.*

Thought Starters: Whatever the color of their skin, people tend to be thin-skinned when they encounter words that they perceive to be slurs on their group, religion, or background. Are there ways of talking about a group with which you identify that you find embarrassing or offensive?

Cultural Etiquette is intended for people of all "races," nationalities, and creeds, not necessarily just "white" people, because no one living in Western society is exempt from the influences of racism, racial stereotypes, race and cultural prejudices, and anti-Semitism. I include anti-Semitism in the discussion of racism because it is simply another manifestation of cultural and racial bigotry.

All people are people. It is ethnocentric to use a generic term such as "people" to refer only to white people and then racially label everyone else. This creates and reinforces the assumption that whites are the norm, the real people, and that all others are aberrations.

"Exotic," when applied to human beings, is ethnocentric and racist.

While it is true that most citizens of the U.S.A. are white, at least four fifths of the world's population consists of people of color. Therefore, it is statistically incorrect as well as ethnocentric to refer to us as minorities. The term "minority" is used to reinforce the idea of people of color as "other."

A cult is a particular system of religious worship. If the religious practices of the Yorubas constitute a cult, then so do those of the Methodists, Catholics, Episcopalians, and so forth.

A large radio/tape player is a boom-box, or a stereo or a box or a large metallic ham sandwich with speakers. It is not a "ghetto blaster."

Everybody can blush. Everybody can bruise. Everybody can tan and get sunburned. Everybody.

Judaism is no more patriarchal than any other patriarchal religion.

Koreans are not taking over. Neither are Jews. Neither are the Japanese. Neither are the West Indians. These are myths put out and maintained by the ones who really have.

All hair is "good" hair. Dreadlocks, locks, dreads, natty dreads, et cetera, is an ancient traditional way that African people sometimes wear their hair. It is not braided, it is "locked." Locking is the natural tendency of African hair to knit and bond to itself. It locks by itself, we don't have to do anything to it to make it lock. It is permanent; once locked, it cannot come undone. It gets washed just as regularly as anyone else's hair. No, you may not touch it, don't ask.

One of the most effective and insidious aspects of racism is cultural genocide. Not only have African Americans been cut off from our African tribal roots, but because of generations of whites pitting African against Indian, and Indian against African, we have been cut off from our Native American roots as well. Consequently, most African Native Americans no longer have tribal affiliations, or know for certain what people they are from.

Columbus didn't discover diddly-squat.

Slavery is not a condition unique to African people. In fact, the word "slave" comes from the Slav people of Eastern Europe. Because so many Slavs were enslaved by other people (including Africans), their very name came to be synonymous with the condition.

Native Americans were also enslaved by Europeans. Because it is almost impossible to successfully enslave large numbers of people in their own land, most enslaved Native Americans from the continental U.S. were shipped to Bermuda, and the West Indies, where many intermarried with the Africans.

People do not have a hard time because of their race or cultural background. No one is attacked, abused, oppressed, pogromed, or enslaved because of their race, creed, or cultural background. People are attacked, abused, oppressed, pogromed, or enslaved because of racism and anti-Semitism. There is a subtle but important difference in the focus here. The first implies some inherent fault or shortcoming within the oppressed person or group. The second redirects the responsibility back to the real source of the problem.

Asians are not "mysterious," "fatalistic," or "inscrutable."

Native Americans are not stoic, mystical, or vanishing.

Latin people are no more hot-tempered, hot-blooded, or emotional than anyone else. We do not have flashing eyes, teeth, or daggers. We are lovers pretty much like other people. Very few of us deal with any kind of drugs.

Middle Easterners are not fanatics, terrorists, or all oil-rich.

Jewish people are not particularly rich, clannish, or expert in money matters.

Not all African Americans are poor, athletic, or ghetto-dwellers.

Most Asians in the U.S. are not scientists, mathematicians, geniuses, or wealthy.

Southerners are no less intelligent than anybody else.

It is not a compliment to tell someone: "I don't think of you as Jewish/Black/Asian/Latina/Middle Eastern/Native American." Or "I think of you as white."

Do not use a Jewish person or person of color to hear your confes-   25
sion of past racist transgressions. If you have offended a particular person, then apologize directly to that person.

Also don't assume that Jews and people of color necessarily want to hear about how prejudiced your Uncle Fred is, no matter how terrible you think he is.

If you are white and/or gentile, do not assume that the next Jewish person or person of color you see will feel like discussing this guide with you. Sometimes we get tired of teaching this subject.

If you are white, don't brag to a person of color about your overseas trip to our homeland. Especially when we cannot afford such a trip. Similarly, don't assume that we are overjoyed to see the expensive artifacts you bought.

Words like "gestapo," "concentration camp" and "Hitler" are only appropriate when used in reference to the Holocaust.

"Full-blood," "half-breed," "quarter-blood." Any inference that a   30
person's "race" depends on blood is racist. Natives are singled out for this form of bigotry and are denied rights on that basis.*

"Scalping": a custom also practiced by the French, the Dutch, and the English.*

Do you have friends or acquaintances who are terrific except they're really racist? If you quietly accept that part of them, you are giving their racism tacit approval.

As an exercise, pretend you are from another planet and you want an example of a typical human being for your photo album. Having never heard of racism, you'd probably pick someone who represents the majority of the people on the planet—an Asian person.

How many is too many? We have heard well-meaning liberals say things like "This event is too white. We need more people of color." Well, how many do you need? Fifty? A hundred? Just what is your standard for personal racial comfort?

People of color and Jewish people have been so all their lives. Fur-   35
ther, if we have been raised in a place where white gentiles predominate, then we have been subjected to racism/anti-Semitism all our lives. We are therefore experts on our own lives and conditions. If you do not under-

*Reprinted with permission from *The Pathfinder Directory*, by Amylee, Native American Indian Resource Center. [Author's note]

stand or believe or agree with what someone is saying about their own oppression, do not automatically assume that they are wrong or paranoid or oversensitive.

It is not "racism in reverse" or "segregation" for Jews or people of color to come together in affinity groups for mutual support. Sometimes we need some time and space apart from the dominant group just to relax and be ourselves. If people coming together for group support makes you feel excluded, perhaps there's something missing in your own life or cultural connections.

The various cultures of people of color often seem very attractive to white people. (Yes, we are wonderful, we can't deny it.) But white people should not make a playground out of other people's cultures. We are not quaint. We are not exotic. We are not cool.

Don't forget that every white person alive today is also descended from tribal peoples. If you are white, don't neglect your own ancient traditions. They are as valid as anybody else's, and the ways of your own ancestors need to be honored and remembered.

"Race" is an arbitrary and meaningless concept. Races among humans don't exist. If there ever was any such thing as race, there has been so much constant crisscrossing of genes for the last 500,000 years that it would have lost all meaning anyway. There are no real divisions between us, only a continuum of variations that constantly change, as we come together and separate according to the movement of human populations.

Anyone who functions in what is referred to as the "civilized" world 40 is a carrier of the disease of racism.

Does reading this guide make you uncomfortable? Angry? Confused? Are you taking it personally? Well, not to fret. Racism has created a big horrible mess, and racial healing can sometimes be painful. Just remember that Jews and people of color do not want or need anybody's guilt. We just want people to accept responsibility when it is appropriate, and actively work for change.

The Responsive Reader

1. The writer attacks stereotypes about hot-blooded Latins, inscrutable Asians, athletic blacks, rich Jews, Middle Eastern terrorists, and others. Which of these stereotypes have you encountered—where and how? Have they shaped your own thinking?
2. What are the author's objections to the terms *minority, exotic, cult, half-breed, reverse racism,* and *race* itself? What other uses of language does she ask you to reconsider? How serious or valid do her objections seem to you?
3. When conversations turn on sensitive subjects, it is easy to say the wrong thing. What advice does this guide to etiquette give for conversations with people from different ethnic or cultural backgrounds?

What pitfalls does Three Rivers warn against? How helpful or valid are her warnings?

4. The author uses weighty words like *ethnocentric, anti-Semitism, bigotry, genocide.* What do these words mean to you? How does the author use them?

5. The writer defends herself against the charge of being oversensitive— do you think she is?

Talking, Listening, Writing

6. The author says that "no one living in Western society is exempt from the influences of racism." Do you agree?

7. At the end, Three Rivers asks, "Does reading this guide make you uncomfortable? Angry? Confused? Are you taking it personally?" What are your answers to these questions?

8. What has been your own experience with the power of language to hurt people, to divide them, or to hold them back?

Collaborative Projects

9. Many colleges have considered speech codes aimed at hate speech or offensive language. Working with a group, investigate the history and the pros and cons of such initiatives.

BILINGUALISM: ASSIMILATION IS MORE THAN ABCs

Jorge R. Mancillas

> Even the most acculturated Mexican–American writer faces the
> dilemma of straddling two languages and two cultures.
>
> Alejandro Portes

*Like millions of immigrants and children of immigrants, Jorge R. Mancillas
speaks English as a second language. He came to this country from Ensenada
in Mexico and wrote the following article in 1993 while an assistant professor
of anatomy and cell biology at the UCLA School of Medicine. He takes a
stand on an issue of special concern in areas with large Spanish-speaking
school populations, such as New York City, Miami, Texas, or California.
What should the schools do for students whose proficiency in English is
limited or nonexistent? The traditional policy had been immersion (or, more
informally, sink or swim). Everyone was taught all subjects in English, and
the use of any other language even during recess was discouraged or banned
outright. This policy was once credited with turning the children of Jewish,
Polish, German, Armenian, or Czech immigrants into Americans after a
few years of schooling. In the seventies and eighties, with high dropout rates
for ESL (English as a second language) students, a different policy was
mandated by the federal government. Bilingual education provides instruction in subjects like reading, math, geography, or history in the students'
original language, to keep them from falling behind while they are still
learning English. Bilingual education has come in for much criticism: It has
been charged with perpetuating the linguistic and cultural separation of immigrant children. It has had to grapple with inadequate funding, a shortage
of bilingual teachers, and the proliferation of foreign languages among our
school populations, ranging from Spanish to Vietnamese, Chinese, Tagalog,
Lebanese, and Russian.*

Thought Starters: Do you know people who are bilingual? How many
of your classmates are bilingual? What is meant by "bilingual education"?

Imagine going from a working-class neighborhood in Ensenada to   1
the University of California at Berkeley. Having graduated from high
school with the Mexican equivalent of a 4.0 GPA, having studied English
and worked in my hometown's tourist industry, and having passed the

TOEFL (Test of English as a Foreign Language) without difficulties, I sat in my first lecture at Berkeley full of confidence and excitement.

I had just been exposed to the United States' dual immigration policy. For the first time in my life, I had been treated courteously by immigration officials: With a letter of acceptance from one of the world's most prestigious universities, my expected contribution to Mexico's brain drain was greeted with the prompt dispensation of a student visa. Now, sitting in the front row of a large lecture hall, I opened my notebook as the professor began to speak. A few minutes later, I was devastated.

Engaging in conversation with tourists at a hotel desk and passing the TOEFL were quite different from trying to grasp complex concepts in psychology delivered at the pace required by 10-week quarter terms. I was lost. Trying to absorb the material from the 600-page psychology textbook was no easier.

Still, that was the easiest part. I also had to fulfill the English 1A requirement, for which we had to read a text and write a report at the end of each week. Assigned reading for the first two weeks: Theodore Roszak's "The Making of the Counter-Culture" and Norman Mailer's "Miami and the Siege of Chicago." Quite a tall order for a boy who had grown up in Ensenada. It was more than the language that I was "deficient" in; it was the implied understanding of the culture and politics.

Sitting in the back of the classroom, I struggled for two quarters as I had never struggled before in my life, and I barely managed to maintain a C average. My self-esteem was shattered. I forged ahead, however, understanding very well what the educational opportunity that I had before me meant to my future prospects. By the time I graduated, my grade average was up to an A, although my overall average was much lower due to the impact of the first quarters. 5

Years later, I find myself part of the faculty at the UCLA School of Medicine and the director of a research laboratory affiliated with UCLA's Brain Research Institute. Had I not been able to overcome the hurdles of my first few months at Berkeley, emotional as well as practical—and I almost didn't—my life and any contribution I may be able to make to society would have been very different.

This experience comes to mind when I hear arguments about bilingual education for the substantial proportion of children with limited English proficiency in the Los Angeles Unified School District. It is easy for me to understand the experience of children finding themselves in a new culture, wanting and struggling to master the English language but lagging behind in other subjects while they do. By the time they learn English— and almost invariably they do—they are behind academically; they are left with gaps in their academic development. Even worse, their self-esteem has suffered considerably, for at that tender age, their sense of self-worth is shaped to a large degree by their perception of how they measure up in comparison to, and in the eyes of, their peers.

Why would we want to academically disable and emotionally impair thousands of children instead of providing them with the mechanisms that allow for a healthy transition to their adopted culture?

The Mexican government's recent contribution of school texts and bilingual teachers to the LAUSD was born of compassion for Spanish-speaking children. It also was influenced by the government's intelligent understanding of Mexico's need to respond to ongoing changes in contemporary society; the Mexican educators who will be exposed to the U.S. educational system and culture will be a valuable resource upon returning to their country.

Children with limited English proficiency must be seen, like other *10* children, as a valuable resource, not as a hindrance or a burden. If we help them to integrate successfully into the mainstream while preserving their original language and cultural skills, they will be the bridge-builders this country needs to succeed in the global community.

This is a priceless resource: a new generation of Americans committed to preserving and strengthening a democratic and pluralistic U.S. society, but also having a birthright familiarity with Latin American, Asian or Middle Eastern societies. Think of what these children might contribute in an age of revolutions in communications and development that we, today, can hardly imagine.

Against this possibility, the alternative is ludicrous: to create a large population of school dropouts, hostile to the mythical "mainstream American culture" to which, they are made to feel, they have nothing to contribute because they are culturally and linguistically deficient.

Those who oppose bilingual education are propelled more by fear of others and insecurity about their own capabilities, identity, and culture. To follow them is to go against the current of history and embark on a futile attempt to become culturally insular and ethnically "clean." Our only other choice is to embrace change and learn the value of diverse expressions of the human experience as a strong basis for our place in the global society of the 21st Century. From that perspective, the monetary cost of bilingual education is trivial and a sound investment in the future.

The Responsive Reader

1. Advocates of bilingual education stress the adverse effect that English-only instruction has on students' overall academic performance and on their self-image or self-esteem. What light does Mancillas' experience throw on this issue?

2. What for Mancillas are the social costs of failure to integrate second-language students "successfully into the mainstream"?

3. A much-debated question is whether bilingual education should be a "transition" to full English proficiency or whether students should at the same time "maintain" their first language and culture. What is

Mancillas' answer to this question? What are the reasons for the stand he takes?

Talking, Listening, Reading

4. What has been your own experience or what has shaped your own views on the issue of bilingualism? Is it an issue in schools you know?
5. Mancillas uses or alludes to buzzwords that have played a prominent role in public discourse in recent years: ethnic cleansing, pluralism, diversity, a global perspective. Why and where does he use them and with what effect?

Collaborative Projects

6. Mancillas wrote his essay at a time when critics were mounting an attack on the bilingual education program in the Los Angeles Unified School District, one of the largest in the country and a district with one of the largest ESL populations. Has bilingual education been an issue in your area or your state? Working with a group, explore questions like the following: Why is bilingual education such an emotion-charged issue? Who are key players on either side? What are major arguments pro and con? What evidence or what facts are being used to back up conflicting claims? What are the prospects for the future?

EBONICS: OPENING PANDORA'S BOX

Toni Cook

> Most African Americans speak standard English in a business or
> school setting, or when they are around white people they do
> not know, and then slip into some form of Black English among
> the home folks. The transition is so fluid and unthinking that
> many African Americans may not even know it's happening,
> just as Mexicans can flow back and forth between Spanish and
> English within the same conversation. Most African Americans
> are bilingual (or bidialectal, depending on one's point of view
> on the language question).
>
> —J. Douglas Allen-Taylor

*Millions of Americans have always been bilingual. They spoke the Italian,
Polish, Chinese, or Yiddish they brought from across the sea—or the Spanish
their ancestors spoke in what was once part of Mexico. They learned American
English as a second language, allowing them to function and do business
beyond the circle of their family and friends or tightly knit ethnic group. Their
children often did not learn English till they went to school. Other millions
of Americans have always been bidialectal. They spoke a rural dialect or
downhome variety of English at home and with their friends, and they learned
to speak and write standard English as the language of school and office, of
the media and public life. The school board in the predominantly African
American city of Oakland in California caused a huge media flap when it
called the Black English spoken by many of its students "Ebonics" and said
it should be recognized as a separate language showing the influence of African
roots. Soon amended or "clarified," the school board's resolution called for
"maintaining the richness and legitimacy" of the students' "primary language" while teaching them standard English. The Oakland initiative caused
an outpouring of criticism and denunciation—with reactions ranging from
vicious racist humor on the Internet to the embarrassed statements of establishment blacks distancing themselves from "bad English." Hundreds of articles
and editorials revealed the extent to which language is still a taboo-ridden
subject and a divisive force in our society.*

*In the following interview, Toni Cook, a member of the Oakland school
board, talks candidly about the background of the resolution, the thinking
that went into it, and the political and pedagogical implications of the resulting controversy. Toni Cook has B.A. and M.A. degrees with honors from
UCLA. She has served as associate dean at Howard University and as
national director of advance for Jesse Jackson's presidential campaign in 1984.
Cook was one of the Oakland school board members asked to testify before a
Senate committee scrambling to keep federal money from being spent on programs that would "respect and embrace" the home language of African American students.*

Thought Starters: Are you bidialectal? Are you bilingual? Where and when do you use a home language or a first language different from the standard English of school and office? Can you give your classmates some samples?

Q: Other than making a lot of people mad, what have you done   *1*
here?

A: I've sounded a bell that everyone is talking about. We got a call from Amsterdam, and another one from South Africa. I'm finding that more people are becoming anywhere from supportive to understanding about this.

Q: Has anyone given you serious trouble?

A: Someone called from a radio talk show and played real raw, racist stuff live and on air. My reaction to the first flood of phone calls (on my answering machine) was to deep-six every call.

Q: Why?   *5*

A: I was broadsided by the controversy. I didn't get home (from the board meeting) until 2 a.m. and I didn't listen to any news the next day because I didn't think anything we did was newsworthy. I'm just thinking, "I can't function." So I get up and make the call (to my job at the San Francisco Housing Authority): "I'm not coming." Then Edgar, our board's assistant, calls and says, "Can you come over?" I said, "Edgar, I'm trying to put a lie together about why I'm not going to work." He said, "All hell has broken loose on the resolution." I said, "What resolution?" He said, "The one put out by the African American task force. The mayor's on a rampage."

Q: Why was (Mayor) Elihu Harris so mad?

A: I used to work for Elihu. He could be mad at anything! And when I got there, he had already gone off to (Superintendent) Carolyn Getridge. And he asked me, "Do you know what you have done? I'm getting calls from everybody in the world! This is embarrassing to Oakland! You all have adopted a policy that's going to teach black English!"

I said, "Elihu, I know you're cheap, but do you have television? Did you watch the school board meeting last night? We meant you no ill will in terms of your challenges with the city. But our kids are being ridiculed if they speak standard English—'Ugh, you talk like a white girl!' So this is the problem we're faced with, and this is how we're going to deal with it." Elihu kind of calmed down a little and began to focus on why we did it like we did it.

Q: What did you do and why did you do it?   *10*

A: I asked the superintendent to form a task force to look at the performance of African American kids. Since I've been on the board, dropout rates, suspensions, expulsions, truancy—all have gone up for African American kids. But enrollment in the gifted and talented program and presence in college-bound, honors and advanced-placement classes were not proportionate to black enrollment, which is 53 percent.

Q: What about special education?

A: Of 5,000 kids in that, 71 percent are African American. And they were in there for "causing disruption."

Q: Aren't special education classes supposed to be for students who are disabled or have learning disabilities?

A: Yes. And you have to have a referral to be placed in the program. *15* The referrals disproportionately were because of a "language deficiency."

Q: What's that?

A: When you really dug down, it's that they weren't writing or speaking standard English. We found there were white and black teachers making referrals. And white and black principals—disproportionately black—saying yes. So when the task force began to talk with teachers, it was like, "Well, we don't have any strategies for these kids." The only one they had was the (state's) Standard English Proficiency Program for a few teachers who got that training.

Q: So what did you do?

A: You know, there's an old guy who comes to the board meetings named Oscar Wright. He came to every board meeting until his wife died about a year ago. And he would stand with those trembling hands and talk about the performance of African American kids—test scores, truancy— and he said, "I see having four black board members has made no difference in what these kids are doing."

And we hung our heads, because it was true! We had a crisis situation *20* and we kept coming up with old ways. Or ways that were so homogenized they didn't really wake anybody up.

Q: You're saying that test scores will go up as African American students begin speaking standard English?

A: Yes. Which ultimately means—more critically—that they can go from high school to college if that's their choice. You can no longer drop your kid off in kindergarten and expect to pick him up in the 12th grade with a diploma that means he's ready for college. We should quit making these promises that we're going to do that by adding health programs, and all those other kinds of things. That is not about education. I know they need all that, but there isn't any education strategy here. When it's directed to African American kids, it's basically the assumption that we have to control them before we can educate them.

Q: You don't feel that way?

A: No.

Q: How can you teach a kid who's out of control—whether threat- *25* ening a teacher or just making noise?

A: Teachers need the teaching and learning tools to know how to communicate with these youngsters to capture their attention. We have some kids with a proven record of suspension in the third grade, and they're going like this (waves wildly) in the math class! I've seen that at some of our schools in the deepest parts of the flatlands.

Q: Are you saying their teachers caught their attention because they spoke ebonics?

A: What they knew was how to hear the child, listen to the child, correct the child, and make the child feel good about being corrected. These are teachers who have been through our Standard English Proficiency Program.

Q: Give me an example.

A: Well, I go to classes to read to the kids. Everybody knows Dr. Seuss, so I made the presumption that I could read a page and the child would read a page. I found two things: Either the kids could not read, or they could read, but the words they pronounced were definitely not on that piece of paper.

Q: What were they saying?

A: *-ing*'s left off of words, consonants left off words, and you begin to think: "Does this kid have dyslexia? Half the word is falling off." And then I went to Prescott Elementary, and I noticed that in (teacher) Carrie Secret's class, where most of the kids are from the housing projects, they were excited about learning. They could read, and tell you what they had read, had great diction, good reasoning skills. And this was the third grade.

Q: You're saying that the kids in this class had better diction than kids in other classes with the same background?

A: Yes. And I began to ask Carrie Secret, "What are you doing differently?" She told me about the Standard English Proficiency Program. So when a kid did not make the *-ing* sound, or left off a consonant or made a word singular when it should be plural, or plural when it should be singular, Carrie would repeat back to the young people until they began to hear the correct word.

Q: How did she do it?

A: The child says, "I'm going wif my mother." Or, "I'm goin home." She says, "Where?" And the child says, "I'm going to go home."

Q: When you heard children speaking standard English, you were thrilled. You're sounding like the critics of your own ebonics resolution.

A: Standard English is (necessary) to go to a four-year college, to being accepted in an apprenticeship program, to understanding the world of technology, to communicating. We owe it to our kids to give them the best that we've got.

Q: There's great disagreement over black English as a language, language "pattern" or just street slang. What is black English?

A: All I know is that it's not slang. The linguists call that "lazy

30

35

40

English." But our children come to school with this language pattern. Go back to what they call the Negro spiritual: "I'm going to lay my 'ligion down." That was the code song that got you your ticket on the Underground Railroad. It's the way the words were used. So they might have thought we were old dumb slaves, but it served a purpose. It was communication.

Q: Do some parents and children resist speaking standard English because they really see it as white English?

A: I don't think they consciously resist. My youngest daughter has had that criticism: "You talk like a white girl." It's another way of saying, "How come you don't sound like us?" It hurts to be accused of that. When I was a girl, it was a goal to speak standard English, not a ridicule. I have no idea how that changed.

Q: Why don't children automatically know standard English, since they hear it all the time on television and at school?

A: Two things. African Americans whose economic status and exposure is closer to that of the Huxtables have the exposure to work with the youngsters, and teach them about the "two-ness" of the world they're involved in. But some schools are located in very depressed areas, have a primary population of African Americans on a fixed income. They see very little, the young people are exposed to very little, and there isn't a whole lot of reason in the home—this is just my guess—to adopt the behavior of duality.

Q: Do you believe that the language pattern of black English is genetic? 45

A: It's ancestral. "Genetic" doesn't say "in your blood, in your biology." It says, "in the beginning!"

Q: Following that logic, why don't other ethnic groups use the grammar of their immigrant ancestors?

A: No other group in America, outside the Native American, ever had to grope (as we did) with the new language. If you didn't get off the Good Ship Lollypop speaking English, learning it was exacerbated by the fact that you had to sneak to teach yourself. Then if you stay together in an isolated, segregated environment, the language pattern persists over time.

Q: And yet there are millions of African Americans who speak with no trace of ebonics.

A: And there are an awful lot of second- and third-generation Chinese who speak perfect English, but when they go home to grandmother, they make the switch. 50

Q: And many African Americans don't. Is this an issue of class?

A: In some instances, it is class. You know, having come from a family of educators, it was a symbol of your ability to speak the King's English. I remember my mother telling me the tragedy is that as those kids became comfortable with the tools of the middle class, one of which was language, they began to turn their backs on their parents. They were embarrassed about their language style.

Q: This is the traditional immigrant experience. What's unusual is for children to cling to the language patterns of their elders.

A: Here is where it's confusing to some, but to others, I think they have ulterior motives.

Q: What's the ulterior motive?

A: The English Only campaign. We talked informally among the school board members. Be careful, don't get caught up in the English Only campaign.

Q: And the ulterior motive is the anti-affirmative action movement?

A: The funding is from the same platform. Right-wing America. It used to be that we'd just simply say it was racism. But now they are so sophisticated that it's about being anti-black, anti-Jewish, anti-immigrant, anti anything that's not Christian. Anti-urban, anti-female, I mean they just kind of took everybody and just threw us all over there together. We have no allies over there. None whatsoever.

Q: If nothing else, you've gotten them to add anti-ebonics to the list. But you've also gotten many people on your side, haven't you?

A: I'd love to be able to tell you how we plotted and planned to become the topic of everybody's conversation in the world. That's dishonest. It took me by surprise.

Q: You had been very opposed to changing any of the controversial wording in your resolution—that ebonics is "genetically based," for instance, and that students will be taught "in ebonics." Yet you changed your mind. What happened?

A: Sometimes you have to look: Are you winning the battle but losing the war? The African American Task Force met (for about 10 hours) last week and got no closure on the word "genetics." Then Oscar Wright, the old man of the group, said, "If removal of this word will heal the pain of the African American community, then remove the word." When that old man gave the word, we moved on. I felt fine about that. I would have stayed on course, but the village said to do things differently.

Q: Did you grow up speaking ebonics?

A: No, but I heard it. You've got to think about coming up in a segregated time. In 1954, when the school desegregation decision came, I was 10. But the more I think about it, the more I think about how blessed I've been. Both of my parents had graduate degrees. My dad was a dentist. My mom was a linguist with the National Security Agency. We were never quite sure what she really did. We knew she spoke perfect Russian. We used to say Mom was a spy for the FBI. And we always thought that Mommy was the smartest thing we ever saw.

Q: So language and politics were always entwined in your family?

A: Everyone in my family, whether it was Mom or Dad, they were always crusaders. You never earned the right to snub your nose at anybody based on speech patterns. I remember a time we went down the street, and a drunk said something to my sister Twink, and she laughed. Mom gave her a backhand, and said, "That man meant nothing but to be kind. Go back and say: 'How do you do, sir?'" She was serious. My mother was 4-foot-9, and 89 pounds, boy. And she spoke perfect English.

Q: Did you send your own children to private schools?

A: Both (religious and public) schools. I have two girls. Arlene, 31, is teaching in San Francisco. Leslie will be 33 this year. They got exposed to some things in all environments. But only in California was the diversity. Here they've got everybody. I like that. This is real.

Q: California's diversity is unusual even in America, isn't it?

A: But that's the advantage. That's the gift. If we are really taking   70
pride in the diversity, is it not important that we know something about everything that makes us Americans? Because the tragedy is that really, multicultural curricula in our schools are predicated in the philosophy of, "Can't we all get along?"

I don't care whether we all get along. I care whether you respect me and know something about me.

Q: Why is that the job of teachers? Why isn't that the job of parents and neighbors and friends?

A: It's all of our jobs. But I think what this (ebonics issue) does is show we are a long way from being a multicultural society. Somehow, talking about anything African American makes people very tight-lipped and angry, and wondering, "Am I being politically correct?" Our prejudice comes out.

Q: Or our ignorance?

A: Yeah. If you ever want to see how segregated our schools are, go   75
to the teachers' lounge. Very segregated. We are all operating from a state of ignorance.

Q: How will the Oakland school board pay for expanding this program to teach standard English?

A: The program is now paid for by federal Title I money. So we'll move money from other Title I programs that are less effective, and into this one, which makes more sense. And we'll evaluate how well it's going.

Q: In Los Angeles, school board member Barbara Boudreaux said she will try to get federal funding if the board approves her ebonics resolution. Will Oakland do the same?

A: It's a useless fight. Those bilingual kids don't get enough money already. Besides, those are federally mandated funds. When you start using those funds for other than what the law mandates, you get into a very dangerous zone called "supplanting." That is not our goal.

Q: And that's illegal?   80

A: Hell, yes.

Q: Was your resolution a trial balloon for bilingual funds that Riley did not go for?

A: No. There was never any intent on the part of the board to ask for bilingual funds. No. The intent is to expand the Standard English Proficiency Program.

Q: Why did you and the board make it so difficult for the public to get copies of your resolution? The board seemed to be hiding it.

A: I know, I looked for it on the Web site and I didn't see it, either. I don't understand why.

Q: Is it because the resolution didn't stand on its own until the board prepared to change its controversial wording on Wednesday?

A: For me it always stood on its own. But it was getting to be ugly—which black leader can we find to kick y'all in the butt now? They were not focusing on the problems of kids that brought us to this point.

While Rome is burning, we're trying to figure out whether the song we're singing is politically correct. But now that we've gotten past the wordsmithing, it's time to roll up our sleeves and do the work. We've got a class that is getting ready to graduate and may not even have a grade-point average of 1.8! Rome is burning, folks. It's burning! I don't know how much more pitiful we've got to get.

The Responsive Reader

1. How does Cook sketch out the concerns that led the school board to adopt the controversial resolution? What were typical student attitudes toward language in her district? What were typical attitudes of teachers and administrators? What is Cook's view of the connection between poor academic performance on the one hand and students' and teachers' attitudes toward language on the other?
2. Some of the critics of the Oakland resolution called Black English "slang." What is Cook's answer? What is your own definition of slang, and what to you are typical current examples?
3. What does Cook mean by the "two-ness" of the world of her students? What does she mean by the "behavior of duality"? Why do some African American students learn it while others don't?
4. How would you describe Cook's basic attitude toward standard English? What was her own experience with standard English? What did her parents teach her about language? How were language and politics always entwined in her upbringing?
5. According to Cook, what makes the relationship of African Americans to the English language different from that of immigrant groups from non-English language backgrounds? Why does she think, for instance, that language issues are different for the many Asian students in her area of California?
6. Charges of racism started flying both ways in the controversy. What "ulterior motives" does Cook identify or suspect on the part of people who attacked the initiative? How does she think the

politics of racism have changed from earlier days of crude, overt antiblack prejudice? (What do you know about the English Only movement?)

Talking, Listening, Writing

7. Do you know people who are or were embarrassed by the language of their parents, family, or neighborhood? Are you?
8. Dialect differences are a staple target in racist and ethnic jokes. Some disk jockeys and talk show hosts apparently used the Ebonics controversy as an occasion to trot out parodies and caricatures of Black English. What has been your observation of language differences as the butt of the joke?

Collaborative Projects

9. During the flowering of African American literature early in the twentieth century, poets at times used a solemn formal English, the way Arna Bontemps does in the following opening lines of "Southern Mansion":

> Poplars are standing there still as death
> And ghosts of dead men
> Meet their ladies walking

However, poets also used the downhome language of black folk in poems like Sterling A. Brown's "Sister Lou." How is the language of the following excerpt from the poem different from the speech patterns of standard English? What features do you think also occur in the nonstandard speech of rural white dialect? Which features do you think are specific to "Black English"?

> Honey
> Don't be feared of them pearly gates.
> Don't go 'round to de back,
> No mo' dataway
> Not evah no mo'.

> Let Michael tote yo' burden
> An' yo' pocketbook an' evah thing
> 'Cept yo' Bible.
> While Gabriel blows somp'n
> Solemn but loudsome
> On dat horn of his'n.

> Honey
> Go Straight on to de Big House,
> An' speak to yo' God
> Widout no fear or tremblin'. . . .

Then, when you gits de chance,
Always rememberin' yo' raisin',
Let 'em know youse tired
Jest a mite tired.

Jesus will find yo' bed for you
Won't no servant evah bother wid yo' room.
Jesus will lead you
To a room wid windows
Openin' on cherry trees an' plum trees
Bloomin' everlastin'.

Working with a group, you may want to research dialect literature
in English and prepare a festival of poetry from Black English or
other dialect sources, including perhaps scenes from the works of
playwrights like August Wilson or ntozake shange.

FORUM: *Black English and Standard English*

In the Ebonics controversy, the voices of language scholars and teachers concerned about the failure of traditional methods were at first largely drowned out. (In the words of one African American commentator, for a while "it was hard to sort everything out, what with all the hollering and the blood and the hum of the chainsaws.") Finally people talking candidly about their own experiences with becoming bilingual or bidialectal or with teaching bilingual or bidialectal students were beginning to be heard. Assumptions like the following have long been shared by linguists and language scholars:

▪ *Calling the Spanish, rural dialect, or Black English that students bring to school inferior, ignorant, or illiterate is counterproductive. It does not create large numbers of students with perfect accents but has in the past created large numbers of hostile dropouts.*

▪ *Speakers of nonstandard varieties of English do not make up mistakes as they go along but follow the rules of their own dialect. For instance, rural whites used to say, "The book is hisn," but not, "It's hisn book." Features like multiple negatives—from Chaucer's "He never yet no villainy ne said" to the blues singer's "I ain't got nobody"—have been part of the English language for centuries, although they are no longer used in standard English.*

▪ *Effective teaching methods copy modern methods of foreign-language instruction that stress exposure and "immersion" rather than constant correction. They may rely on "contrastive analysis" pointing up the differences between the home dialect and the prestige dialect.*

▪ *Slaves brought from Africa developed Creole or Creolized languages with vocabulary items (like* gumbo*) and speech patterns indebted to African languages. Gullah, spoken in the isolated islands off the shore of Georgia and South Carolina, has often been described as the African American dialect closest to becoming a separate language, "distinct from English in that it stirs a generous gumbo of African words into the European, and that it employs many distinctly non-English rules of grammar" as well as a completely distinct rhythm pattern. Among linguists, the extent of African influence in Black English is a matter of dispute.*

Lolis Eric Elie is a teacher who published his comments in the Times Picayune *in New Orleans, a city that is like Oakland—an economically depressed area with a large African American population and an embattled educational system. Ira Eisenberg is a free-lance journalist and substitute teacher a few miles down the freeway from the Oakland schools. Angelo Figueroa is a Latino columnist who went to school in a predominantly black neighborhood in Detroit and who now works for a newspaper in San Jose, another city with a large minority population.*

NAYSAYERS MISS POINT

Lolis Eric Elie

If you're a linguist, Ebonics is a complicated issue. You have to deter-   1
mine whether it's a language or a dialect, whether it's primarily of African
or European origin, whether it started before or after the Civil War.

For most of us, the issue is less complicated. We just have to decide
whether the research linguists have conducted can help students grasp standard English.

Many commentators have dismissed the potential importance of
Ebonics as a teaching tool because they don't agree with scholars who
argue that Ebonics is an African language with an English vocabulary.

I don't know enough about linguistics to give an informed opinion
on these findings. But I do know that many teachers are convinced that a
knowledge of Ebonics can help us educate our children.

SECOND-LANGUAGE STIGMA

Perhaps the biggest misunderstanding in the Ebonics debate is the be-   5
lief that African-American students would be taught standard English as a
second language. Critics have railed against this because it implies that Ebonics-
speaking students are a special, marginal category among Americans.

But the idea of applying the methodology of second-language
instruction is not the same as denying the Americanness of students of
African descent.

The point is that, for decades, scholars have been developing techniques for teaching people to speak foreign languages. Some of the techniques, if applied to students who speak variations on standard English,
might prove more effective than the one-size-fits-all approach commonly
taken.

Generally, American students are taught the "right" and "wrong"
way to speak and write English. The problem, some teachers say, is that
many Ebonics speakers don't hear anything "wrong" with the way they
speak, so they resist "correction."

According to Mary Hoover, one of the linguists advising the Oakland
Unified School District, studies have shown that Ebonics speakers perform
better when they are taught through comparison and contrast.

Rather than tell students that their grammar is "wrong," Hoover   10
suggests we teach them that there are more appropriate ways to express
themselves in the classroom or workplace context.

For example, if a student said, "Don't nobody know nothing about
that," Hoover would say, "That's a perfectly good serial negation in
Ebonics." Then she'd teach the student to translate that statement into
standard English.

TEACHERS GRASP PROBLEMS

Mary Gehman teaches freshman composition, remedial English and English as a second language at Delgado Community College. She is sensitive to the problem of stigmatizing American students. Yet her experience has taught her that many Americans in her remedial classes, regardless of their race, have problems grasping standard English. The problems are similar to those faced by her foreign-born students. For Ebonics speakers, the problem is most acute.

"The majority of the people ending up in developmental classes are Ebonics speakers, but we don't have any specific books or programs to deal with them," she said. "Through the years, I've fashioned grammar exercises on my own that I can use for those students. They are similar to the things that are used in English-as-a-second-language courses."

Many commentators have ignored the research on Ebonics and taken offense at the idea of teaching American students as if English were not their primary language.

Many teachers have said that they don't care what the teaching meth-   15
ods are called, as long as they are effective.

I agree with the teachers.

THE PRESS AND THE EBONICS STORY

Ira Eisenberg

By now it should be clear to all but the hopelessly uninformed and   1
the irredeemably bigoted that Oakland's decision to recognize black English as a distinctive "language" got a bum rap.

The Oakland school board's Task Force on the Education of African-American Students may have made some unfortunate choices of words, but it most certainly did not advocate substituting "ebonics" for the teaching of standard English in public school classrooms.

Nor was their report, unanimously adopted by the Oakland school board, an attempt to excuse or explain away the poor academic performance of inner-city black children by declaring their street lingo equal to standard English.

But you'd hardly know these things from the misinformation disseminated by the putatively liberal news media and gleefully amplified by their wicked step-siblings, the right-wing radio talkmeisters.

As a result, we were treated to the bizarre spectacle of Jesse Jackson   5
and other black leaders denouncing the Oakland Unified School District for degrading the culture, demeaning the intelligence of black children and debasing performance standards in order to make themselves look good.

In the immortal words of Paul Newman in "Cool Hand Luke," what we have here is a failure to communicate, and this time the messengers have no one to blame but themselves. Superficial, knee-jerk journalism has roiled the ugly currents of racism that simmer just beneath the surface of our society.

Ten years ago, Oakland launched a pilot program called Standard English Proficiency, or SEP. Now a regular part of the curriculum in about 20 of its elementary schools, SEP is premised on the recognition that African-American children isolated by poverty often come to school unable to communicate in anything other than the parlance of the ghetto. SEP's aim is to make these kids proficient in the language of the upwardly mobile by teaching them to translate their mother tongue into standard English.

All the school board really did was proclaim its intention to expand SEP district-wide. And as Oakland schools Superintendent Carolyn Getridge has reiterated to anyone willing to listen, "This is about improving English proficiency skills." Teachers, not students, would be instructed in the syntax and vocabulary of ebonics. Instead of just putting kids down for using black English, teachers would be trained to help them "decode their language" into the vernacular of the larger culture. A similar effort has been under way in the Los Angeles public schools for six years now, and educators there say it works.

If labeling the jargon these at-risk kids speak "ebonics" helps Oakland get more money for their SEP program, more power to them. Federal Education Secretary Richard Riley's pre-emptive rejection of the idea makes that appear unlikely. But maybe he'll follow Jackson's lead and rethink his hasty and ill-considered judgment. For anyone who's spent time in any inner-city classroom knows that most of these kids are neither stupid nor lazy.

Lately, I've been teaching high school English in San Leandro, a *10* working-class community adjoining Oakland. More than half of my students are African American, and while those with a command of standard English may be the ones succeeding academically, they aren't always the smartest or most creative.

One day, while waiting for the bell to ring, the black students in one of my classes started playing a game. They set up a rhythmic chant— "Shaboola, shaboola, shaboola ya ya"—and took turns inventing stanzas in time with the rhythm they'd established to create a hip hop song, or "rap."

The stanzas were four lines of verse in which the last two lines rhymed, not unlike the quatrains of a Shakespearean sonnet. Yet the vocabulary and sentence structure were typically ebonic, as unlike contemporary standard English as arcane language of the Elizabethan bards. These 10th-graders, including some at the bottom of the grade curve, were creating poetry just for the spontaneous fun of it. Yet they'd be the last to recognize their own potential. After all, even Jesse Jackson has put down their utterances as so much garbage.

What a stupid, tragic waste.

EBONICS PLAN IS WORTH A LISTEN

Angelo Figueroa

If you're like me, you probably never heard of the word Ebonics.   *1*
Well, the word will probably become part of our collective lexicon.

Ebonics, as I understand it, is a word to describe black vernacular or
more simply, the way some black people talk. The term derives from the
words ebony and phonics.

Oakland public school officials made national headlines when they
declared that Ebonics is so radically different from English that it merits
special recognition. The district wants to train Oakland teachers to understand Ebonics so they can use it as a springboard to teach black students
standard English.

Now, I suspect that many of you—or least the guy who called me   *5*
Friday to rant about the issue—believe that this is insane.

Why should tax dollars be used to teach teachers how to use a frac-
tured form of English?

I can understand the stick-to-the-basics sentiment, but don't agree
with it.

How, for example, is our average school teacher supposed to translate
something like this if they don't understand it:

> *Yo, what up, dog? What it be like? I's fixin' to scoop you in my hoopty*
> *so we can jet to Jerome's crib and kick it. I likes to listen to some mad tunes,*
> *if Jerome's moms don't be trippin, all-ight?*

While this may be a hack's example of Ebonics and common street   *10*
slang, this fact remains: Black kids who grow up in the inner-city speak in
a distinct dialect that makes learning standard English a major challenge.

I grew up in a predominantly black neighborhood in Detroit. I
learned the street slang and sentence structure that everyone else around
me employed.

Spanish was my first language, adding to my language confusion.

Fortunately, I've always loved to read and learned standard English
more from books than grammar classes. Otherwise, I wouldn't be writing
this column.

For many kids, the language barrier created by a mixture of slang and
Ebonics places them at a disadvantage when they have to work or study
outside their communities. Many are so intimidated, in fact, that they
simply drop out—out of school and the mainstream.

That's why I applaud the Oakland school system if the goal is to   *15*
make teachers aware of Ebonics so that they can help students overcome
its potentially crippling impact.

Some may counter that it would be better if the black community simply abandoned black English. But that's like expecting Latinos to stop speaking Spanish because a law making English the official language is passed.

It's not realistic.

Black folks have been speaking a different dialect and using different phrasing to express themselves since the days of slavery. There's nothing wrong with that. If there were, Texans and New Yorkers would have been forced to take diction classes long ago.

Language isn't static. It's constantly evolving. Ebonics and street slang add spice to our language and give its speakers a sense of cultural identity they can be proud of.

But let's be clear about one thing: Ebonics and slang don't play in the boardroom. In other words, it doesn't work in a marketplace where standard English rules. 20

Both blacks and Latinos must recognize that mastering English is vital to their success in the United States.

That's the way it be's whether we likes it or not.

The Responsive Reader

1. What according to Elie is the core issue of the Ebonics controversy as far as teachers are concerned? (Why are some of the concerns of linguists side issues for him?) What can or should teachers learn from teachers of foreign languages?

2. According to Eisenberg, how did the Oakland initiative get a "bum rap"? What are "putative" liberal news media? And how are right-wing radio talk show hosts "their wicked step-siblings"? What do you learn from Eisenberg about the Standard English Proficiency pilot program and its connection with the Oakland initiative? How does Eisenberg try to counteract the racist stereotype that inner-city kids are "stupid" or "lazy"?

3. How does Figueroa's own experience give him a special insider's perspective on the controversy? A major issue was whether or not the challenges facing Spanish-speaking students and students with Black English are similar. What do you think is Figueroa's answer? How would you sum up his position on the relation between "dialects" or "vernaculars" and standard English? What should be the teachers' goals? What methods might work?

Talking, Listening, Writing

4. Does it sound to you as if both sides in the controversy accuse each other of "stigmatizing" the students? Why or how? Why would the students be "stigmatized," and what could or should be done about it?

5. Have you had any experience with foreign language learning? Did you think it was modern, productive, or effective?

6. Some Americans retain a first language or downhome dialect; others seem to leave it behind at least in part more quickly than others. (And some rediscover a first language or dialect as they go back to their roots.) To judge from your own experience or observation, what makes the difference? Do you think of a first language or downhome dialect as a liability or as an asset?

Collaborative Projects

7. Is it true that earlier in American history it was against the law to teach slaves to read and write? Working with a group, you may want to explore the early history of efforts to bring literacy to slaves and ex-slaves.

RETURN OF THE CLICHÉ EXPERT

Roger Angell

> *Some people sound like a commercial that has been run too many times.*
> *They speak and write in clichés—tired and predictable phrases that sound as*
> *if they came to the speaker all ready-made and strung together ready for use:*
> a run for their money, throw in the towel, only the tip of the iceberg,
> the window of opportunity, the cutting edge, *and* the bottom line.
> *Some of these may at one time have been clever or imaginative, but they have*
> *lost their flavor, like stale bread. To say it in the language of clichés:* To be
> brutally frank, and not to put too fine a point upon it, the bloom is
> off such expressions (to coin a phrase), and in this day and age they
> are far from being a sure winner in the hearts and minds of men and
> women from all walks of life, and in the final analysis, when all is said
> and done, they do more harm than good. *The* New Yorker *magazine*
> *for many years ran a feature with the cliché expert parodying contemporaries*
> *who fall back on trite, ready-made expressions rather than using fresh lan-*
> *guage to communicate some fresh thinking of their own. Recently, the cliché*
> *expert returned to take stock of the buzzwords of a new, proactive, computer-*
> *literate generation.*

Thought Starters: How aware are you of changing fashions in the way
people use words? Do you or your friends use expressions like, "You don't
want to go there," or, "It doesn't get any better than this"? Do you ever
say, "No problema"? Does anyone anymore say, "You've made my day"?

Q: Good morning, Mr. Arbuthnot. It's a pleasure to see you again, 1
and to hear further testimony from you on the subject of clichés.

A: Wrong man. You're thinking of my uncle, Dr. Magnus Arbuthnot, who is no longer with us. Bought the farm, checked out, fumed out,
popped off, slipped his cable, went over the pass, hit the throughway. I
mean, he's gone-zo. I'm Chip Arbuthnot, his heir. His *spiritual* heir.

Q: But you are here to give us your views on current and established
clichés, are you not?

A: No way.

Q: You're not? 5

A: I'm here to share my views.

Q: I see. And you are an expert in the field, are you not?

A: Arguably.

Q: You wish to argue with the court?

A: No, I'm arguably an expert. The adverb allows me to say some-   *10*
thing and then partly take it back.

Q: I think I understand.

A: Don't worry about it. This stuff isn't written in stone.

Q: You're very kind.

A: There's a reason for that.

Q: I can almost guess what it is. It's on the tip of my tongue.   *15*

A: I'm a people person.

Q: I knew it! Now, Mr. Arbuthnot, may I ask a strange question? What's that on your head?

A: This is my other hat.

Q: Your *other* hat?

A: This is the hat I wear when I'm being the cliché expert. When   *20*
I'm doing something else, I wear a different other hat, not this one.

Q: Hmm. Are you telling us that being a cliché expert is not a full-time occupation?

A: As if. Get a grip.

Q: You must be a busy man, holding so many demanding jobs.

A: None of this is rocket science. But, yes, my plate is full.

Q: And you must have to maintain a constant schedule of travels to   *25*
different parts of the country, if not the world, to keep up with regional as well as occupational clichés, is that not the case?

A: Been there, done that.

Q: Tell me, do most people know when they're speaking in clichés? Or is that a dumb question?

A: I'm not comfortable with it. If I said it was a no-brainer, I'd be sending the wrong message. Let's say that some folks who think they're pushing the envelope conversationwise ain't.

Q: Mr. Arbuthnot, are there specific occupations that produce a greater preponderance of clichés in daily human intercourse than others do?

A: "Daily human intercourse" is very fine. Congratulations.   *30*

Q: Shall I repeat the question?

A: No, because I'm going to pass. This is a slippery slope.

Q: What about the sexes? Are women more likely than men to—

A: Whoa. Back off, Mister. Don't go there. It's a no-win situation.

Q: Oh, I'm sorry.   *35*

A: You're putting me between a rock and a hard place.

Q: I didn't mean to upset you. I apologize.

A: You mean you empathize.

Q: That's what I meant to say.

A: You feel my pain.   *40*

Q: Yes, I do, I do!

A: Historically, you have concerns.

Q: That's right!

A: Unless I miss my guess, you're also pro-active.

Q: Yup.   45

A: At the same time, you're a very private person.

Q: Absolutely. How did you know?

A: Trust me, it's easy. All you have to do is listen to your inner child.

Q: So any of us can become a cliché expert—is that what you're saying?

A: How did we end up here? Hello?   50

Q: Oop, I'm going too fast again, aren't I? Just *using* clichés doesn't do the trick—is that right?

A: No. You have to talk the talk and walk the walk.

Q: But of course. I wish we could go on with this and perhaps find out how you got to ask all the questions, instead of the court. But our time is up. I hope you've enjoyed our little meeting.

A: You've made my day.

Q: You have enlightened us all.   55

A: It doesn't get any better than this.

Q: Thank you, Mr. Arbuthnot.

A: No problema.

The Responsive Reader

1. How up-to-date are you on buzzwords and current clichés? Have you heard people talk about wearing different hats? When do people talk about a *no-win situation*? What do people mean when they use the terms *no-brainer, counter-intuitive, pushing the envelope, or a full plate*?

2. People may pick up new buzzwords because they fit in well with the way they think or with their personal agendas. Who uses the expression *the bottom line*—when, where, and for what purpose? When do people use expressions like, "It's not written in stone," or, "This is not rocket science"? Why do they say, "I'm not comfortable with it"? What signal do they give when they say, "We have concerns"? What purposes does the expression *slippery slope* serve? What's the difference between giving your views and sharing your views? Why does Angell think there is something wrong with the term *arguably*?

Talking, Listening, Writing

3. Do you use one kind of language when you are trying to impress people and another kind of language when relaxing with your friends? Can you give examples of the two contrasting ways of saying things?

Collaborative Projects

4. The language of politics and political campaigns is shot through with buzzwords and clichés. For instance, when and why did politicians start to talk about a color-blind society? When and how did "preferences" get to be a dirty word? Working with a group, you may want to investigate current trends in political rhetoric.

THE LESSON
Toni Cade Bambara

*Toni Cade Bambara has been described as a "dancer, teacher, critic, editor, activist, and writer." She was born and educated in New York City, with degrees from Queens and City College. She started writing in the politically active sixties and has published two volumes of short stories—*Gorilla, My Love *(1972) and* The Sea Birds Are Still Alive *(1977)—and a novel,* The Salt Eaters *(1980). Critics commenting on her work have focused on her blend of politics and sexual politics; on the role of gender, family, and community in her stories; and on her awareness of the subjective, personal quality of the world we construct for ourselves. The following story, about black kids from a poor neighborhood coming downtown, makes us see affluent white society through their eyes. It thus turns the tables on the affluent majority, whose spokespersons endlessly study and analyze and report on the children of the poor. A major part of the contrast between the two worlds is set up by the tough street language of the young people, with the story told in what one editor has called "uncondescending, witty, poetic Black English."*

Thought Starters: How much of your perception of people's personalities is shaped by the way people talk?

Back in the days when everyone was old and stupid or young and   *1*
foolish and me and Sugar were the only ones just right, this lady moved
on our block with nappy hair and proper speech and no makeup. And
quite naturally we laughed at her, laughed the way we did at the junk man
who went about his business like he was some big-time president and his
sorry-ass horse his secretary. And we kinda hated her too, hated the way
we did the winos who cluttered up our parks and pissed on our handball
walls and stank up our hallways and stairs so you couldn't halfway play
hide-and-seek without a goddamn gas mask. Miss Moore was her name.
The only woman on the block with no first name. And she was black as
hell, cept for her feet, which were fish-white and spooky. And she was
always planning these boring-ass things for us to do, us being my cousin,
mostly, who lived on the block cause we all moved North the same time
and to the same apartment then spread out gradual to breathe. And our
parents would yank our heads into some kinda shape and crisp up our
clothes so we'd be presentable for travel with Miss Moore, who always
looked like she was going to church, though she never did. Which is just
one of the things the grownups talked about when they talked behind her

back like a dog. But when she came calling with some sachet she'd sewed up or some gingerbread she'd made or some book, why then they'd all be too embarrassed to turn her down and we'd get handed over all spruced up. She'd been to college and said it was only right that she should take responsibility for the young ones' education, and she not even related by marriage or blood. So they'd go for it. Specially Aunt Gretchen. She was the main gofer in the family. You got some ole dumb shit foolishness you want somebody to go for, you send for Aunt Gretchen. She been screwed into the go-along for so long, it's a blood-deep natural thing with her. Which is how she got saddled with me and Sugar and Junior in the first place while our mothers were in a la-de-da apartment up the block having a good ole time.

So this one day Miss Moore rounds us all up at the mailbox and it's pure-dee hot and she's knockin herself out about arithmetic. And school suppose to let up in summer I heard, but she don't never let up. And the starch in my pinafore scratching the shit outta me and I'm really hating this nappy-head bitch and her goddamn college degree. I'd much rather go to the pool or to the show where it's cool. So me and Sugar leaning on the mailbox being surly, which is a Miss Moore word. And Flyboy checking out what everybody brought for lunch. And Fat Butt already wasting his peanut-butter-and-jelly sandwich like the pig he is. And Junebug punchin on Q.T.'s arm for potato chips. And Rosie Giraffe shifting from one hip to the other waiting for somebody to step on her foot or ask her if she from Georgia so she can kick ass, preferably Mercedes'. And Miss Moore asking us do we know what money is, like we a bunch of retards. I mean real money, she say, like it's only poker chips or monopoly papers we lay on the grocer. So right away I'm tired of this and say so. And would much rather snatch Sugar and go to the Sunset and terrorize the West Indian kids and take their hair ribbons and their money too. And Miss Moore files that remark away for next week's lesson on brotherhood. I can tell. And finally I say we oughta get to the subway cause it's cooler and besides we might meet some cute boys. Sugar done swiped her mama's lipstick, so we ready.

So we heading down the street and she's boring us silly about what things cost and what our parents make and how much goes for rent and how money ain't divided up right in this country. And then she gets to the part about we all poor and live in the slums, which I don't feature. And I'm ready to speak on that, but she steps out in the street and hails two cabs just like that. Then she hustles half the crew in with her and hands me a five-dollar bill and tells me to calculate 10 percent tip for the driver. And we're off. Me and Sugar and Junebug and Flyboy hangin out the window and hollering to everybody, putting lipstick on each other cause Flyboy a faggot anyway, and making farts with our sweaty armpits. But I'm mostly trying to figure how to spend this money. But they all fascinated with the meter ticking and Junebug starts laying bets as to how much it'll read when Flyboy can't hold his breath no more. Then Sugar lays bets as to how much it'll be when we get there. So I'm stuck. Don't nobody want to go for my plan, which is to jump out at the next light and run off to the first bar-b-que we can find. Then the driver tells us to get the hell out cause we there already. And the meter reads eighty-five cents. And I'm stalling to figure out the tip and Sugar say give him a dime. And I decide he don't need it bad as I do, so later for him. But then he tries to take off with Junebug foot still in the door so we talk about his mama something ferocious. Then we check out that we on Fifth Avenue and everybody dressed up in stockings. One lady in a fur coat, hot as it is. White folks crazy.

"This is the place," Miss Moore say, presenting it to us in the voice she uses at the museum. "Let's look in the windows before we go in."

"Can we steal?" Sugar asks very serious like she's getting the ground   5
rules squared away before she plays. "I beg your pardon," say Miss Moore, and we fall out. So she leads us around the windows of the toy store and me and Sugar screamin, "This is mine, that's mine, I gotta have that, that was made for me, I was born for that," till Big Butt drowns us out.

"Hey, I'm goin to buy that there."

"That there? You don't even know what it is, stupid."

"I do so," he say punchin on Rosie Giraffe. "It's a microscope."

"Whatcha gonna do with a microscope, fool?"

"Look at things."   10

"Like what, Ronald?" ask Miss Moore. And Big Butt ain't got the first notion. So here go Miss Moore gabbing about the thousands of bacteria in a drop of water and the somethinorother in a speck of blood and the million and one living things in the air around us is invisible to the naked eye. And what she say that for? Junebug go to town on that "naked" and we rolling. Then Miss Moore ask what it cost. So we all jam into the window smudgin it up and the price tag say $300. So then she ask how long'd take for Big Butt and Junebug to save up their allowances. "Too long," I say. "Yeh," adds Sugar, "outgrown it by that time." And Miss Moore say no, you never outgrow learning instruments. "Why, even medical students and interns and," blah, blah, blah. And we ready to choke Big Butt for bringing it up in the first damn place.

"This here costs four hundred eighty dollars," says Rosie Giraffe. So we pile up all over her to see what she pointin out. My eyes tell me it's a chunk of glass cracked with something heavy, and different-color inks dripped into the splits, then the whole thing put into a oven or something. But for $480 it don't make sense.

"That's a paperweight made of semi-precious stones fused together under tremendous pressure," she explains slowly, with her hands doing the mining and all the factory work.

"So what's a paperweight?" asks Rosie Giraffe.

"To weigh paper with, dumbbell," say Flyboy, the wise man from   15
the East.

"Not exactly," say Miss Moore, which is what she say when you warm or way off too. "It's to weigh paper down so it won't scatter and make your desk untidy." So right away me and Sugar curtsy to each other and then to Mercedes who is more the tidy type.

"We don't keep paper on top of the desk in my class," say Junebug, figuring Miss Moore crazy or lyin one.

"At home, then," she say. "Don't you have a calendar and pencil case and a blotter and a letter-opener on your desk at home where you do your homework?" And she know damn well what our homes look like cause she nosys around in them every chance she gets.

"I don't even have a desk," say Junebug. "Do we?"

"No. And I don't get no homework neither," says Big Butt. ₂₀

"And I don't even have a home," say Flyboy like he do at school to keep the white folks off his back and sorry for him. Send this poor kid to camp posters, is his specialty.

"I do," says Mercedes. "I have a box of stationery on my desk and a picture of my cat. My godmother bought the stationery and the desk. There's a big rose on each sheet and the envelopes smell like roses."

"Who wants to know about your smelly-ass stationery," say Rosie Giraffe fore I can get my two cents in.

"It's important to have a work area all your own so that . . ."

"Will you look at this sailboat, please," say Flyboy, cuttin her off and ₂₅ pointin to the thing like it was his. So once again we tumble all over each other to gaze at this magnificent thing in the toy store which is just big enough to maybe sail two kittens across the pond if you strap them to the posts tight. We all start reciting the price tag like we in assembly. "Hand-crafted sailboat of fiberglass at one thousand one hundred ninety-five dollars."

"Unbelievable," I hear myself say and am really stunned. I read it again for myself just in case the group recitation put me in a trance. Same thing. For some reason this pisses me off. We look at Miss Moore and she lookin at us, waiting for I dunno what.

"Who'd pay all that when you can buy a sailboat set for a quarter at Pop's, a tube of glue for a dime, and a ball of string for eight cents? It must have a motor and a whole lot else besides," I say. "My sailboat cost me about fifty cents."

"But will it take water?" say Mercedes with her smart ass.

"Took mine to Alley Pond Park once," say Flyboy. "String broke. Lost it. Pity."

"Sailed mine in Central Park and it keeled over and sank. Had to ask ₃₀ my father for another dollar."

"And you got the strap," laugh Big Butt. "The jerk didn't even have a string on it. My old man wailed on his behind."

Little Q.T. was staring hard at the sailboat and you could see he wanted it bad. But he too little and somebody'd just take it from him. So what the hell. "This boat for kids, Miss Moore?"

"Parents silly to buy something like that just to get all broke up," say Rosie Giraffe.

"That much money it should last forever," I figure.

"My father'd buy it for me if I wanted it." 35

"Your father, my ass," say Rosie Giraffe getting a chance to finally push Mercedes.

"Must be rich people shop here," say Q.T.

"You are a very bright boy," say Flyboy. "What was your first clue?" And he rap him on the head with the back of his knuckles, since Q.T. the only one he could get away with. Though Q.T. liable to come up behind you years later and get his licks in when you half expect it.

"What I want to know is," I says to Miss Moore though I never talk to her, I wouldn't give the bitch that satisfaction, "is how much a real boat costs? I figure a thousand'd get you a yacht any day."

"Why don't you check that out," she says, "and report back to the 40 group?" Which really pains my ass. If you gonna mess up a perfectly good swim day least you could do is have some answers. "Let's go in," she say like she got something up her sleeve. Only she don't lead the way. So me and Sugar turn the corner to where the entrance is, but when we get there I kinda hang back. Not that I'm scared, what's there to be afraid of, just a toy store. But I feel funny, shame. But what I got to be shamed about? Got as much right to go in as anybody. But somehow I can't seem to get hold of the door, so I step away from Sugar to lead. But she hangs back too. And I look at her and she looks at me and this is ridiculous. I mean, damn, I have never ever been shy about doing nothing or going nowhere. But when Mercedes steps up and then Rosie Giraffe and Big Butt crowd in behind and shove, and next thing we all stuffed into the doorway with only Mercedes squeezing past us, smoothing out her jumper and walking right down the aisle. Then the rest of us tumble in like a glued-together jigsaw done all wrong. And people lookin at us. And it's like the time me and Sugar crashed into the Catholic church on a dare. But once we got in there and everything so hushed and holy and the candles and the bowin and the handkerchiefs on all the drooping heads, I just couldn't go through with the plan. Which was for me to run up to the altar and do a tap dance while Sugar played the nose flute and messed around in the holy water. And Sugar kept givin me the elbow. Then later teased me so bad I tied her up in the shower and turned it on and locked her in. And she'd be there till this day if Aunt Gretchen hadn't finally figured I was lyin about the boarder takin a shower.

Same thing in the store. We all walkin on tiptoe and hardly touchin the games and puzzles and things. And I watched Miss Moore who is steady watchin us like she waitin for a sign. Like Mama Drewery watches the sky and sniffs the air and takes note of just how much slant is in the bird formation. Then me and Sugar bump smack into each other, so busy gazing at the toys, specially the sailboat. But we don't laugh and go into our fat-lady bump-stomach routine. We just stare at that price tag. Then

Sugar run a finger over the whole boat. And I'm jealous and want to hit her. Maybe not her, but I sure want to punch somebody in the mouth.

"Watcha bring us here for, Miss Moore?"

"You sound angry, Sylvia. Are you mad about something?" Givin me one of them grins like she tellin a grown-up joke that never turns out to be funny. And she's lookin very closely at me like maybe she planning to do my portrait from memory. I'm mad, but I won't give her that satisfaction. So I slouch around the store bein very bored and say, "Let's go."

Me and Sugar at the back of the train watchin the tracks whizzin by large then small then getting gobbled up in the dark. I'm thinkin about this tricky toy I saw in the store. A clown that somersaults on a bar then does chin-ups just cause you yank lightly at his leg. Cost $35. I could see me askin my mother for a $35 birthday clown. "You wanna who that costs what?" she'd say, cocking her head to the side to get a better view of the hole in my head. Thirty-five dollars could buy new bunk beds for Junior and Gretchen's boy. Thirty-five dollars and the whole household could go visit Granddaddy Nelson in the country. Thirty-five dollars would pay for the rent and the piano bill too. Who are these people that spend that much for performing clowns and $1000 for toy sailboats? What kinda work they do and how they live and how come we ain't in on it? Where we are is who we are, Miss Moore always pointin out. But it don't necessarily have to be that way, she always adds then waits for somebody to say that poor people have to wake up and demand their share of the pie and don't none of us know what kind of pie she talking about in the first damn place. But she ain't so smart cause I still got her four dollars from the taxi and she sure ain't gettin it. Messin up my day with this shit. Sugar nudges me in my pocket and winks.

Miss Moore lines us up in front of the mailbox where we started   *45* from, seem like years ago, and I got a headache for thinkin so hard. And we lean all over each other so we can hold up under the draggy-ass lecture she always finishes us off with at the end before we thank her for borin us to tears. But she just looks at us like she readin tea leaves. Finally she say, "Well, what did you think of F. A. O. Schwarz?"

Rosie Giraffe mumbles, "White folks crazy."

"I'd like to go there again when I get my birthday money," says Mercedes, and we shove her out the pack so she has to lean on the mailbox by herself.

"I'd like a shower. Tiring day," say Flyboy.

Then Sugar surprises me by sayin, "You know, Miss Moore, I don't think all of us here put together eat in a year what that sailboat costs." And Miss Moore lights up like somebody goosed her. "And?" she say, urging Sugar on. Only I'm standin on her foot so she don't continue.

"Imagine for a minute what kind of society it is in which some   *50* people can spend on a toy what it would cost to feed a family of six or seven. What do you think?"

"I think," say Sugar pushing me off her feet like she never done before, cause I whip her ass in a minute, "that this is not much of a democracy if you ask me. Equal chance to pursue happiness means an equal crack at the dough, don't it?" Miss Moore is besides herself and I am disgusted with Sugar's treachery. So I stand on her foot one more time to see if she'll shove me. She shuts up, and Miss Moore looks at me, sorrowfully I'm thinkin. And somethin weird is goin on, I can feel it in my chest.

"Anybody else learn anything today?" lookin dead at me. I walk away and Sugar has to run to catch up and don't even seem to notice when I shrug her arm off my shoulder.

"Well, we got four dollars anyway," she says.

"Uh hunh."

"We could go to Hascombs and get half a chocolate layer and then   55
go to the Sunset and still have plenty money for potato chips and ice cream sodas."

"Un hunh."

"Race you to Hascombs," she say.

We start down the block and she gets ahead which is O.K. by me cause I'm going to the West End and then over to the Drive to think this day through. She can run if she want to and even run faster. But ain't nobody gonna beat me at nuthin.

The Responsive Reader

1. A key feature of the tough street language in this story is the use of profanity. Where and how is it used in this story? Is it offensive?
2. Suppose you were working as an amateur linguist, recording key features of the black dialect in this story. What are some of the features you would note?
3. What role does Miss Moore play in the story? Does your view of her change as the story develops?
4. What is the "lesson" the kids or the readers learn when the story reaches its turning point as the group comes to the toy store? Where does the story go after the climactic episode in the store?
5. What do you think is the relationship between the author and the girl telling the story? (What do you think is the distance between the author and the person speaking in the story?)

Talking, Listening, Writing

6. What would be your usual view of the kids you listen to in this story? Does the story change your assumptions or preconceptions as you see them through the eyes of one of their own? What do you think of their behavior, their thinking, their humor?
7. Why do people talk tough? Do you think the girl talking in this story might be playing a public role, with a different personality under the tough surface?

8. What do you think of the contrast between wealth and poverty in our society? Where have you observed it?

Collaborative Projects

9. You may want to participate in a story-telling session where several participants try telling a personal story or an anecdote leading up to "Ain't nobody gonna beat me at nuthin" or a similar punch line.

A GATHERING OF DEAFS

John Heaviside

> Researchers like Oliver Sacks have written about the heightened sensitivity, or acuteness of other senses, that people who are color-blind or have other impairments may develop to compensate for what we normally see as deficiencies. Authors writing about the Deaf community have written about the hearing-impaired not as medical cases or people with disabilities but as people who share a rich culture, historically conditioned and transmitted across generations. In that culture, signed languages (sign languages or gesture languages) play a central role. Authors writing about the structure and uses of American Sign Language (ASL) have stressed the "linguistic richness" of the languages of the deaf, describing them as "rich systems with complex structures that reflect their long histories." John Heaviside wrote the following poem about the deaf as a student and published it in the Olivetree Review, a publication devoted to student work at Hunter College of the City University of New York.

Thought Starters: What do you know about or what experience have you had with alternative language or writing systems like braille or ASL?

By the turnstiles   1
in the station
where the L train greets
the downtown six there was
a congregation of deafs   5
passing forth
a jive wild
and purely physical
in a world dislocated
from the subway howling   10
hard sole shoe stampede
punk rock blasted radio
screaming, pounding, honking
they gather in community
lively and serene, engaging   15
in a dexterous conversation

An old woman
of her dead husband tells

caressing the air
with wrinkled fingers that demonstrate the story with   *20*
delicate, mellifluous motion
she places gentle configurations before the faces of the group

A young Puerto Rican
describes a fight with his mother emphasizing each word
with abrupt, staccato movements jerking his elbows   *25*
and twisting his wrists
teeth clenched and lips pressed
he concluded the story
by pounding his fist
into his palm   *30*

By the newsstand
two lovers express emotion
caressing the air
with syllables
graceful and slow   *35*
joining their thoughts
by the flow of fingertips

The Responsive Reader

1. How does the world of sound acquire negative connotations in this poem? How does it set the scene for the contrasting world of the deaf?
2. What do you learn from this poem about the signed language of the deaf as a language? What are key features it shares with spoken language? How is it different?
3. What are the usual meanings of *serene, dexterous, mellifluous, staccato, congregation*? How does the poet transpose these words to the culture of the deaf?
4. Why or how did the poet select the "speakers" that he asks us to focus on in this poem?

Talking, Listening, Writing

5. What has been your experience with people with impaired sight, hearing, or mobility? How much do you know from firsthand experience or observation? How much is hearsay or stereotype?
6. What is the reaction of people in our society to the hearing-impaired? How are attitudes in our society changing toward people with disabilities? How much progress has society made toward recognizing the needs and rights of the disabled?

Collaborative Projects

7. Many colleges now employ interpreters who translate oral instruction into signed language. If you can, arrange for such a person to
come and speak to your class about the language of the deaf.

WRITING
WORKSHOP 9

Writing to Define

Definition stakes out the territory a term covers. Sometimes it simply fills in a blank in the reader's mind. If you suspect that some of your readers do not know the term *recidivism*, you may briefly explain it as the pattern of released convicts becoming repeat offenders. More often, however, definition is needed to give exact meaning to terms that on closer inspection turn out to be vague, slippery, or misleading.

To define means to draw the line. Who is poor in our society? It depends on where we draw the "poverty line." Who is a "qualified applicant" for a job or a promotion? It depends on the criteria of the people who do the hiring. (They are sometimes second-guessed by an arbitration board or by the courts.) What is obscene in our society depends on how explicit the treatment of sex has to become before viewers or readers stop saying "This is sexy!" and start saying, "This is sick!" Ultimately, what is obscene in our society depends on where the members of the United States Supreme Court draw the line.

TRIGGERING Definition becomes an issue whenever someone says: "Just a minute—what exactly do we mean by this word?" The French philosopher Voltaire said, "Before you start arguing with me, define your terms!" Here are some typical situations where a writer might say: "Time out to define a key term!"

- *You may have to pin down the meaning of a catch-all label.* What for you is the core meaning of *conservative, liberal, radical, feminist,* or *activist*? People you label liberals or feminists or conservatives may resist a label that commits them to more than they bargained for. A person who says, "I'm not a feminist, but . . ." often turns out to be a feminist—in the sense of someone promoting women's causes and standing up for women's rights. However, the person might not want to buy into other positions the label might imply—whether a generally negative view of men, or a commitment to aggressive legal or political tactics. Your definition of such a term can highlight the common core, telling the reader: "This is what the term basically means. Much else is optional!"

▪ *You may have to pin down the exact meaning of a catch phrase.* Definition makes sure that words do not remain "just words." The more sweeping and uplifting the terms are, the easier it is for everyone to pay lip service to them. Everyone today is an "equal opportunity employer." What does that mean? What equal opportunities can two students have if one struggled to stay in school in a violence-prone neighborhood and the other grew up with good schools, regular homework, and much help from well-educated parents? If you commit yourself to "equal opportunity," how are you going to ensure the legendary "level playing field"? Are you going to provide the kind of second chance (or third chance) without which "equal opportunity" remains just words?

▪ *You may have to reexamine slippery categories.* The boxes you are expected to check on a questionnaire may make you ask: "What do you mean?" Is a person with two French and two Hawaiian grandparents of "European descent"? Is a person with an Irish father and an African American mother white or black? Who is white or black in our society is a matter of definition.

GATHERING You may be tempted to start a definition paper by saying, "*Webster's Dictionary* defines *equity* as the practice of being fair and equal." Noah Webster, of course, is dead, and several publishers of dictionaries have appropriated his name to help peddle their wares. (So what reference book are you quoting?) Moreover, the dictionary definition is often a **circular definition**: It tells us that being equitable means being fair but does nothing to show what that means in practice.

To make your readers see what a key word means in practice, ask yourself questions like the following: Who uses the word? In what situations? For what purpose? Are there several main uses? How are they related? Is there a common denominator? What do you think is the prevailing or most useful meaning of the term? What are possible abuses or dishonest uses?

Here are some categories a student might set up to collect material for a definition of the term *feminism*. Such categories serve as a **discovery frame**, charting a program for a systematic stock-taking of relevant material:

> What popular associations and misunderstandings cluster around the term? What stereotypes do you hear invoked on talk shows, for instance?
>
> What is the history of the movement—what famous names and events come to mind?
>
> How do the media reflect changing definitions of gender roles? (Do commercials, action movies, or soap operas feature more independent, less vulnerable women than they used to?)
>
> Where have feminist issues played a role in my own experience?

What related terms (*women's liberation*, *emancipation*, *sexism*, *patriarchy*) cluster around the term?

What is the core meaning of the term? What is the common denominator?

SHAPING Strategies for presenting an **extended definition**—a definition in depth of a much-used important term—will vary.

▪ You may want to set your paper in motion by focusing on a common misunderstanding of the term—and then correcting it. You lead from the misuse or misunderstanding of the term to what you consider its true meaning. You then give several examples of situations where your definition fits especially well.

▪ You may want to focus on providing a historical perspective. For instance, you might trace key meanings of the term *democracy* from its original Greek meaning—"rule by the people"—to modern times. You move from the *direct* democracy of ancient Greece (with the whole electorate voting on major decisions) to the *representative* democracy of modern times (voting on major issues by proxy). From there, you move to the participatory, "town meeting" kind of democracy advocated by those who feel that democratic institutions have become too isolated from the people.

▪ You may want to examine several key examples of affirmative action to find what they have in common. Or you may want to focus on one extended **case history** that puts possible definitions of the term to the test.

What is the overall plan in the following student paper? What problems of definition does the writer recognize? What is the core definition that emerges from the paper?

Dem's Fightin' Words!

When does ordinary name-calling turn into offensive slurs? Where do we draw the line when people use racial epithets or demeaning language directed at other groups? What do we do about it?

"Faggot! Hope you die of AIDS! Can't wait till you die!" These words were shouted, not by an ignorant twelve-year-old, but by Keith R., a law student at Stanford University. Weeks later, when confronted, he said he had used offensive language on purpose in order to test the limits of freedom of speech at Stanford. Others doubt that his use of language was an experiment; they say it closely coincided with opinions he had expressed in *The Stanford Review*.

When dealing with abusive individuals like R., the natural impulse is to legislate, to pass ordinances, to enforce guidelines. If we could only ban offensive language, expel the offender, or shut down an offending magazine, we would get rid of the problem. Many colleges have tried this tack by instituting "Fighting Words" rules. Responding to the pain felt by the victims of racism, sexism, and homophobia, these schools have as necessary amended their constitutions to forbid certain offensive expressions. Violators may be reprimanded or even expelled. At Dartmouth, for instance, a student was called on the carpet for asking in class whether it was possible to "cure" homosexuals.

The objection to such rules is that they inevitably have what lawyers call "a chilling effect" on the free expression of ideas. These rules inevitably pose a problem of definition: Where do we draw the line? Who decides what is offensive, and to whom? Stanford's "Speech Code" made a brave attempt to minimize the problem by being very specific. It read in part: "Speech or other expression constitutes harassment or personal vilification if it: (1) intends to insult or stigmatize an individual or group of individuals on the basis of sex, race, color, handicap, religion, sexual orientation, or national or ethnic origin; (2) is addressed directly to the individual; (3) makes use of insulting or fighting words or gestures."

Nevertheless, drawing the line between offensive speech and legitimate expression is not easy. How would this rule apply to the speeches of Malcolm X, who for a time referred to whites as "white devils"? On the other hand, what set of rules could stop a person like Keith R. from being personally offensive? He could have expressed his hostility by gestures instead of words—a wink, a leer, a walk, humming a few bars of "Here Comes the Bride."

The British writer Christopher Isherwood (who often referred to himself as Christopher Swisherwood) insisted on using words like *faggot* and *queer*. He said that by using them and making them ordinary, he could help take away their power to insult and to hurt. Would Mr. Isherwood be censored today on Stanford's green and pleasant lawn? No, say supporters of the Speech Code, because his use of language was not intended to offend. But this puts the censors into the business of judging the intent of an expression— looking into people's heads to judge what made them say what they said. Who is going to say if an expression was used insultingly, kiddingly, or ignorantly?

At Stanford, the reaction to the incident was a petition condemning R.'s behavior, signed by almost five hundred students and faculty members. At the law school, a large poster read: "Exercise your right of free speech. Tell this law student what you think of his behavior. It may be legal, but it isn't right." This has to be the definition of offensive language in a free society: What bigots and racists say may be offensive, but they have the right to say it, and we have the right and duty to talk back to them. That is what free speech is all about.

If you take away the bigot's right to shout "Faggot!" you may also be taking away my right to say: "Shut up, you creep!" You may be taking away my right to call a religious fanatic a bigot or my gun-toting neighbor a redneck. Bad ideas and bad language cannot be legislated against; they must be driven out by better ideas.

Topics for Definition Papers (A Sampling)

1. What kind of group qualifies as a "minority"? Who decides? (For instance, do white ethnics count as minority groups? Are Jews a minority group?)

2. What is meant by terms like the "culture of victimization" or "victimology"? Why have such terms become widely used? What controversies revolve around them?

3. What does *macho* mean? Who uses the term, and why? How do you react to it?

4. What is meant by "welfare dependency"? Who uses the term, and why?

5. Is the term *feminine* obsolete? Does anyone still want to be "feminine"?

6. Is there such a thing as an "ideal marriage"? (Or does it exist only in reruns of fifties television shows or movies?)

7. When does a sexual encounter qualify as "date rape"?

8. Where would you draw the line between popular culture and high culture?

9. Is there such a thing as "reverse racism" or "reverse discrimination"?

10. What is homophobia, and how widespread is it in our society?

10

Violence:
Living at Risk

Our feelings are no longer a matter of tenderness, dreams, or
hope; everything is aimed at the gut.

—*Christine Ockrent*

The American culture of drive-by shootings, homicidal youth gangs, drug vendettas, serial killers, celebrity murders, and mass cult suicides has a global resonance: In countries that pride themselves on a tradition of law and order, young killers appear out of nowhere, without a psychiatric history or any intelligible motive. In a mansion in Switzerland, 48 bodies are found, sacrificed to the apocalyptic vision of a messianic leader. Media phenomena like *Natural Born Killers* or the latest Schwarzenegger movie travel around the globe, reinforcing what a French journalist called the "culture of brutality."

Violence is an integral part of our historical and cultural legacy. The twentieth century brought wars deploying an unprecedented technology of mass destruction. A generation of young men was killed in the trench warfare of World War I. In World War II, civilian casualties—from scorched-earth policies, bombings, and campaigns of extermination—rivaled the numbers of those killed in combat. Many Americans first came here as refugees—from Germany, Russia, Southeast Asia—carrying with them the scars, physical and psychological, of repression, starvation, and genocide. Young Americans (many from minority backgrounds) were sent to fight in North Africa, Italy, France, and the Pacific in World War II; in Korea, in Vietnam, and in Iraq. Thousands of veterans suffer from the disabilities and traumas left in the wake of their war experience overseas.

At home, American cities have rates of violent crime and murder unprecedented in the developed countries of the West. Serial murders and gang wars are features of our news and entertainment. Americans live in fear of violence. Often that fear pits members of different racial or ethnic groups against one another. Are we going to live in a society where a white police officer is assumed to be the enemy of a black citizen? Are we going to live in communities where a Korean grocer and a customer from the barrio regard one another with hatred and distrust?

Have Americans come to accept violence as an inevitable fact of life? Do we have any blueprints for making ours a safer world?

EMOTIONS CLOUDING RATIONAL DECISIONS

Steven Musil

> *College campuses are no longer refuges from a violent outside world. Emergency phones and escort services are an attempt to provide some minimal security after spates of rapes in dorms or assaults in parking lots. Students working a few blocks from college campuses witness shootouts in fast-food restaurants or convenience stores. Steven Musil was an editor for a student newspaper when he wrote the following editorial about the loss of a friend. Like other writers of editorials and newspaper columns, he shares his thoughts and feelings, but these are grounded in what he knows. He writes as a witness—someone who took in and cared about something that for many newspaper readers was just a statistic.*

Thought Starters: What has been your closest brush with violence? What were your thoughts and feelings?

"An eye for an eye and the whole world goes blind."—Ghandi

The following is an open letter to a lost friend.

Dear Dennis,

It has been two-and-a-half years since we last spoke. I'm sorry that I 1 haven't written to you before but I wasn't sure where to send this. I haven't seen you since two days before your funeral and I'm sure you must have many questions. First off, you probably know by now that Tony was your killer. Last week, a jury found him guilty and sentenced him to life in prison without the possibility of parole.

All the articles in the newspaper got me thinking about the whole mess again. I watched some of the trial downtown and a couple days ago I visited your memorial in front of Chili's. It has been hard to forget lately.

Many of us who were working at Chili's at the time of the murder were hoping for the death sentence. We wanted to see him die in the gas chamber for what he did to you. Some of us even felt sorry for him before we realized that he murdered you. The autopsy reported that you were shot once in the back of the head with a sawed-off .22-caliber rifle and then twice in the face after you fell to the floor.

The coroner said that you probably didn't know what was happening and you died instantly without suffering. Is that true? The sheriff found the rifle and about $1,600 in cash in his apartment on the day of your funeral. I was one of the last to be told.

The jury "let him off" because he had "no prior convictions of violent crimes or anything of that sort," according to the jury foreman. 5

Everyone at Chili's liked you Dennis. Even Tony. He testified that he was in a confused, cocaine-induced trance and needed the money to cover some debts. He said that he knew he would have to kill whoever was in the restaurant at the time. You weren't even scheduled to work that day, but were doing another manager a favor. I'm thankful no one else was there.

It just seemed so unfair. You were so young. So nice, so gentle. I regret the hard time we gave you at the Fourth of July party the night before. Do you remember? We were kidding you because you were the only married manager without children. The night before you died you said that it was time to have a child.

They closed the store for a couple of days for the investigation and to clean up. With all the extra time, some of the cooks decided to go camping, stay together. We had a real hard time dealing with it so we just took off. We ended up on a beach south of Santa Cruz. We bought a couple cases of beer, built a bonfire and toasted your memory all night until the sun came up the next day.

That night we made a pact to visit the campsite every year in your honor. A year later, I was the only one that returned. Many of those people don't work at Chili's anymore and are hard to get a hold of. I'm sure they haven't forgotten you.

It touched some people so that they revised their personal stance on 10 capital punishment. After your murder there were people stating that they had rethought the issue and now supported the death penalty, gun control, and assorted other related causes. I admit that I too made my gun control decision based on the emotional aftershock. I'm not sure if someone can make a rational decision of such importance based on an emotionally traumatic event.

Anyway, I don't have a lot of room to write to you. I have to tell you that I'm putting this behind me and you probably won't hear from me again. Know that we haven't forgotten you just because we are going on with our lives. Somehow I think you would have wanted it that way. Take care of yourself.

Your friend,
Steven

The Responsive Reader

1. What are the bare facts in this case? What are allegations, theories, or excuses?
2. What does this "letter to a lost friend" accomplish? What did it do for the writer? What does it do for the reader?

Talking, Listening, Writing

3. Who or what is to blame? What if anything can be done to help prevent a similar tragedy? Does this editorial make you rethink your position regarding the "death penalty, gun control, and assorted other related causes"?

4. Musil says, "I'm not sure if someone can make a rational decision . . . based on an emotionally traumatic event." Don't we have a right to be emotional about events like the one that is the occasion for this editorial? Shouldn't we be emotional? What would a "rational" reaction be to what happened in this case?

5. A tired joke has it that when the students at one college were asked whether they were concerned about apathy concerning social issues, 87% responded: "I don't care." Do you think students of your generation or on your campus are guilty of apathy?

6. Write your own personal response to the author of this "letter to a lost friend."

Collaborative Projects

7. For one of several possible research projects related to issues in this chapter, you might choose to collaborate with others to find out about the movement toward victims' rights. What are reasons, initiatives, accomplishments? What are possible roadblocks, pitfalls, objections?

VIOLENCE KILLS MORE U.S. KIDS

One way to look at the rampant violence in America is to say that violence is a fact of life. What can you do—other than staying out of risky situations, all the while knowing that murderous violence may erupt in places once considered safe? Another way to look at violence is to say that violence happens because society allows it to happen and that, compared with other nations, our society has an incredibly dismal record in trying to ensure safety of life and limb. While officials have in recent years talked about falling crime rates overall, the rise in juvenile crime and in violence affecting the young seems to be going counter to the trend. How does the following newspaper story "put the issue in perspective"?

Thought Starters: Are you aware of current statistics about homicides and suicides? Are you alarmed about rising juvenile crime?

Nearly three of four child slayings in the industrialized world occur in the United States, federal health officials said yesterday.

American children are five times more likely to be killed: The homicide rate is 2.57 out of every 100,000 children under age 15. That compares with an overall rate of 0.51 in the 25 other countries surveyed, according to the federal Centers for Disease Control and Prevention.

In releasing an extraordinary international scorecard of youth violence, the center found that the United States has the highest rates of childhood homicide, suicide and firearms-related deaths of any of the world's 26 richest nations.

The suicide rate alone for children 14 and younger is double that of the rest of the industrialized world, the agency said. The U.S. rate is 0.55 out of every 100,000 children, compared with 0.27 for the rest of the industrialized world.

And deaths caused by firearms amount to 1.66 out of every 100,000 children in the United States, compared with 0.14 in the other nations.

The statistics show that the epidemic of violence that has hit younger and younger children in recent years is confined almost exclusively to the United States, where the rate of juvenile crime over the past decade has grown at a far faster clip than that for adults. Many nations, which were asked for statistics from the most recent year they had available, reported that they had no homicides involving children under 15.

The center gave no explanation for the huge gap between the rates of violent death for American children and those of other countries, although other criminologists have attributed the explosion of youth crime here to among other things a growing faction of children who are unsupervised or otherwise at risk.

Etienne Krug, the medical epidemiologist who conducted the study, said some researchers have suggested that the high rate of violent death among American children might be associated with the low level of funding for social programs in the United States. Other theories, he said, blame the prevalence of American violence on the high number of working women, the high divorce rate and the social acceptability of violence in the United States.

Handgun control groups blame much of the problem on the presence of more than 200 million handguns in American homes. Slightly less than half of all American households own firearms, many of them are pistols, and many are kept loaded, according to Stephen Teret, director of the Johns Hopkins Center for Gun Policy and Research.

Teret said that American society has high levels of violence in general, and that when that is combined with the presence of handguns, tragedy can result.

Teret said the deep causes of violence in society—such as racism, poverty and unequal opportunity—are very hard to change. He said, "It is much easier to change the design of a gun to make it child-proof, or the availability of a gun," than to attack the "biggest hardest problems in American society."

The federal study was conducted to determine whether the increase in violent deaths that has been so marked in the United States since 1950 has occurred elsewhere. The officials studied death rates of children under age 15 in the largest industrialized nations, selected because they were economically comparable and considered likely to maintain the most accurate records.

The study found:

- As childhood death rates from pneumonia, influenza, cancer and other diseases fell since 1950 in the United States, childhood homicide rates tripled and suicide rates quadrupled.
- Of 2,872 violent deaths among children 14 and younger in the 26 countries in a single year (generally 1993), 1,994 were homicides.
- Boys were more likely to be murdered than girls, and of the total homicides in the world, 73 percent, or 1,464, occurred among U.S. children.
- Almost 600 young children committed suicide in 1994, 54 percent of them Americans.
- Children committed suicide using methods other than firearms at about the same rate in the United States as in the other 25 countries.

The Responsive Reader

1. Do you think the statistics in this news story would shake up even the jaded reader? Why or why not? What for you is new or disturbing here? What is old news?
2. Are you surprised by the suicide statistics? Have you read or heard about a suicide epidemic among America's young? Have you seen any firsthand evidence of it?
3. When it comes to pointing to the causes of rampant violence affecting the young, this report is full of phrases like "might be," "others have claimed that," and "it has been suggested that." What possible causes are hinted at here? Which do you think are most important? What do you know about them?
4. Is there any hint in this newspaper story of suggested remedies or attempts at prevention? Or does the article strike you as fatalistic?

Talking, Listening, Writing

5. Are you or people you know well fatalistic about violence? Do you take precautions?
6. For a student newspaper, write a column that discusses a current news story involving violence and tries to spell out the lessons to be learned from it.

Collaborative Projects

7. For further reading, you may want to study the role violence plays in the columns of one widely read columnist, such as George Will, Ellen Goodman, Anna Quindlen, or a widely read local writer. Check a series or a sampling of columns spread over a period of several weeks or months. Do you find recurrent themes or often repeated arguments? How influential do you think are the columnist's opinions or advice?

WHY HANDGUNS MUST BE OUTLAWED

Nan Desuka

In spite of attempts to place restrictions on the free sale—being sold like groceries—of lethal weapons, more guns are in circulation (and in use) in the United States than in any other country in the world. American citizens, and especially young Americans, are killed by firearms at a rate unheard of in civilized countries. One city councillor trying to get a gun control ordinance passed discovered that anyone, regardless of criminal record or medical history, could buy a gun but that the local sheriff tried to screen out angry wives who might use the guns to shoot their husbands. The councillor's initiative, like many before and after, was defeated after an organized campaign by the National Rifle Association. Nan Desuka, the author of the following article on gun control, was born in Japan but came to the United States with her parents when she was two. She knows how to listen, how to take in what people on the other side of an issue have to say.

Thought Starters: Is there any point in listening one more time to arguments about gun control? Are they going to change anyone's mind? Is anything going to be done?

"Guns don't kill people—criminals do." That's a powerful slogan, *1*
much more powerful than its alternate version, "Guns don't kill people—people kill people." But this second version, though less effective, is much nearer to the whole truth. Although accurate statistics are hard to come by, and even harder to interpret, it seems indisputable that large numbers of people, not just criminals, kill, with a handgun, other people. Scarcely a day goes by without a newspaper in any large city reporting that a child has found a gun, kept by the child's parents for self-protection, and has, in playing with this new-found toy, killed himself or a playmate. Or we read of a storekeeper, trying to protect himself during a robbery, who inadvertently shoots an innocent customer. These killers are not, in any reasonable sense of the word, criminals. They are just people who happen to kill people. No wonder the gun lobby prefers the first version of the slogan, "Guns don't kill people—criminals do." This version suggests that the only problem is criminals, not you or me, or our children, and certainly not the members of the National Rifle Association.

Those of us who want strict control of handguns—for me that means the outlawing of handguns, except to the police and related service units—have not been able to come up with a slogan equal in power to "Guns don't kill people—criminals do." The best we have been able to come up with is a mildly amusing bumper sticker showing a teddy bear, with the words "Defend your right to arm bears." Humor can be a powerful weapon (even in writing *on behalf* of gun control, one slips into using the imagery of force), and our playful bumper sticker somehow deflates the self-righteousness of the gun lobby, but doesn't equal the power (again the imagery of force) of "Guns don't kill people—criminals do." For one thing, the effective alliteration of "*c*riminals" and "*k*ill" binds the two words, making everything so terribly simple. Criminals kill; when there are no criminals, there will be no deaths from guns.

But this notion won't do. Despite the uncertainty of some statistical evidence, everyone knows, or should know, that only about 30 percent of murders are committed by robbers or rapists. For the most part the victims of handguns know their assailants well. These victims are women killed by jealous husbands, or they are the women's lovers; or they are drinking buddies who get into a violent argument; or they are innocent people who get shot by disgruntled (and probably demented) employees or fellow workers who have (or imagine) a grudge. Or they are, as I've already said, bystanders at a robbery, killed by a storekeeper. Or they are children playing with their father's gun.

Of course this is not the whole story. Hardened criminals also have guns, and they use them. The murders committed by robbers and rapists are what gave credence to Barry Goldwater's quip, "We have a crime problem in this country, not a gun problem." But here again the half-truth of a slogan is used to mislead, used to direct attention away from a national tragedy. Different sources issue different statistics, but a conservative estimate is that handguns annually murder at least 15,000 Americans, accidentally kill at least another 3,000, and wound at least another 100,000. Handguns are easily available, both to criminals and to decent people who believe they need a gun in order to protect themselves from criminals. The decent people, unfortunately, have good cause to believe they need protection. Many parts of many cities are utterly unsafe, and even the tiniest village may harbor a murderer. Senator Goldwater was right in saying there is a crime problem (that's the truth of his half-truth), but he was wrong in saying there is not also a gun problem.

Surely the homicide rate would markedly decrease if handguns were   5 outlawed. The FBI reports that more than 60 percent of all murders are caused by guns, and handguns are involved in more than 70 percent of these. Surely many, even most, of these handgun killings would not occur if the killer had to use a rifle, club, or knife. Of course violent lovers, angry drunks, and deranged employees would still flail out with knives or baseball bats, but some of their victims would be able to run away, with few or no injuries, and most of those who could not run away would nevertheless survive, badly injured but at least alive. But if handguns are outlawed, we are told, responsible citizens will have no way to protect themselves from criminals. First, one should remember that at least 90 percent of America's burglaries are committed when no one is at home. The householder's gun, if he or she has one, is in a drawer of the bedside table, and the gun gets lifted along with the jewelry, adding one more gun to the estimated 100,000 handguns annually stolen from law-abiding citizens. (See Shields, *Guns Don't Die—People Do*.) Second, if the householder is at home, and attempts to use the gun, he or she is more likely to get killed or wounded than to kill or deter the intruder. Another way of looking at this last point is to recall that for every burglar who is halted by the sight of a handgun, four innocent people are killed by handgun accidents.

Because handguns are not accurate beyond ten or fifteen feet, they are not the weapons of sportsmen. Their sole purpose is to kill or at least to disable a person at close range. But only a minority of persons killed with these weapons are criminals. Since handguns chiefly destroy the innocent, they must be outlawed—not simply controlled more strictly, but outlawed—to all except to law-enforcement officials. Attempts to control handguns are costly and ineffective, but even if they were cheap and effective stricter controls would not take handguns out of circulation among criminals, because licensed guns are stolen from homeowners and shopkeepers, and thus fall into criminal hands. According to Wright, Rossi, and Daly, authors of *Under the Gun*, about 40 percent of the handguns used in crimes are stolen, chiefly from homes that the guns were supposed to protect.

The National Rifle Association is fond of quoting a University of Wisconsin study that says, "gun control laws have no individual or collective effect in reducing the rate of violent crime." Agreed—but what if handguns were not available? What if the manufacturer of handguns is severely regulated, and if the guns may be sold only to police officers? True, even if handguns are outlawed, some criminals will manage to get them, but surely fewer petty criminals will have guns. It is simply untrue for the gun lobby to assert that all criminals—since they are by definition lawbreakers—will find ways to get handguns. For the most part, if the sale of handguns is outlawed, guns won't be available, and fewer criminals will have guns. And if fewer criminals have guns, there is every reason to believe that violent crime will decline. A youth armed only with a knife is less likely to try to rob a store than if he is armed with a gun. This commonsense reasoning does not imply that if handguns are outlawed crime will suddenly disappear, or even that an especially repulsive crime such as rape will decrease markedly. A rapist armed with a knife probably has a sufficient weapon. But *some* violent crime will almost surely decrease. And the decrease will probably be significant if in addition to outlawing handguns, severe mandatory punishments are imposed on a person who is found to possess one, and even severer mandatory punishments are imposed on a person who uses one while committing a crime. Again, none of this activity will solve "the crime problem," but neither will anything else, including the "get tough with criminals" attitude of Senator Goldwater. And of course any attempt to reduce crime (one cannot realistically talk of "solving" the crime problem) will have to pay attention to our systems of bail, plea bargaining, and parole, but outlawing handguns will help.

What will the cost be? First, to take "cost" in its most literal sense, there will be the cost of reimbursing gun owners for the weapons they surrender. Every owner of a handgun ought to be paid the fair market value of the weapon. Since the number of handguns is estimated to be between fifty million and ninety million, the cost will be considerable, but it will be far less than the costs—both in money and in sorrow—that result from deaths due to handguns.

Second, one may well ask if there is another sort of cost, a cost to our liberty, to our constitutional rights. The issue is important, and persons who advocate abolition of handguns are blind or thoughtless if they simply brush it off. On the other hand, opponents of gun control do all of us a disservice by insisting over and over that the Constitution guarantees "the right to bear arms." The Second Amendment in the Bill of Rights says this: "A well-regulated militia being necessary to the security of a free State, the right of the people to keep and bear arms shall not be infringed." It is true that the founding fathers, mindful of the British attempt to disarm the colonists, viewed the presence of "a well-regulated militia" as a safeguard of democracy. Their intention is quite clear, even to one who has not read Stephen P. Halbrook's *That Every Man Be Armed*, an exhaustive argument in favor of the right to bear arms. There can be no doubt that the framers of the Constitution and the Bill of Rights believed that armed insurrection was a justifiable means of countering oppression and tyranny. The Second Amendment may be fairly paraphrased thus: "*Because* an organized militia is necessary to the security of the State, the people have the right to possess weapons." But the owners of handguns are not members of a well-regulated militia. Furthermore, nothing in the proposal to ban handguns would deprive citizens of their rifles or other long-arm guns. All handguns, however, even large ones, should be banned. "Let's face it," Guenther W. Bachmann (a vice president of Smith and Wesson) admits, "they are all concealable." In any case, it is a fact that when gun control laws have been tested in the courts, they have been found to be constitutional. The constitutional argument was worth making, but the question must now be regarded as settled, not only by the courts but by anyone who reads the Second Amendment.

Still, is it not true that "If guns are outlawed, only outlaws will have guns"? This is yet another powerful slogan, but it is simply not true. First, we are talking not about "guns" but about handguns. Second, the police will have guns—handguns and others—and these trained professionals are the ones on whom we must rely for protection against criminals. Of course

10

the police have not eradicated crime; and of course we must hope that in the future they will be more successful in protecting all citizens. But we must also recognize that the efforts of private citizens to protect themselves with handguns has chiefly taken the lives not of criminals but of innocent people.

The Responsive Reader

1. Where does Desuka take her stand on this controverted issue? How is her stance similar to or different from other positions on this issue that you know?
2. Desuka uses the "Yes, but" technique—taking in carefully what other people have to say, agreeing with them in part, but then trying to show that their arguments are only half-truths. What slogans does she take on that often cloud this issue? How does she deal with them?
3. On an issue where emotions often drown out rational argument, Desuka makes a special effort to show that she is well informed. Where and how does she use authoritative sources? How does she use and interpret statistics? Do you interpret them the same way?
4. How does Desuka deal with the "constitutional argument"? How does she make you reread the language of the Second Amendment?

Talking, Listening, Writing

5. What for you are Desuka's strongest arguments? Which seem to you weakest? (Where is she most persuasive, where least?)
6. What do you know about the National Rifle Association? Where and how does this author take on the NRA? With what success?
7. Do you think there are other, more effective ways to support gun control? Are there precedents of successful gun control initiatives?
8. Write a "Yes, but" reply to Desuka's arguments.

Collaborative Projects

9. Collaborating with others, you may want to study news reports in your area over a period of time to determine the role different kinds of firearms play in local crime.

A PEACEFUL WOMAN EXPLAINS WHY SHE CARRIES A GUN

Linda M. Hasselstrom

For a time it seemed that the argument over gun control had divided the American public into two camps. Debate seemed polarized: Liberals were asking citizens to hand in their guns as a first step toward a safer, saner world. Conservatives seemed to be defending the constitutional right of citizens to assemble arsenals of lethal weapons for armed resistance against an evil government. In recent years, however, women especially have been rethinking their attitude toward guns as the symbol of a violence-prone civilization. Increasingly, law enforcement seemed incompetent to protect women from battering abuse and homicidal violence. Linda M. Hasselstrom originally wrote the following widely read call for women's self-reliance and self-defense for the High Country News, *a regional Rocky Mountain publication. She is from the grasslands of western South Dakota near the Black Hills. Her family had homesteaded in the late 1800s in the "vast emptiness" of the South Dakota prairie along with other Swedes and Norwegians. She has worked as a cattle rancher, saying that "someone who pays attention to the messages the natural world sends can bring cattle home the day before a blizzard nine times out of ten." A poet and environmental activist, she for years operated her own small press, named Lame Johnny after a horse thief.*

Thought Starters: What advice does local enforcement give to women concerned about safety? Is it helpful? Is it useless? Does it reflect a male point of view?

I am a peace-loving woman. But several events in the past 10 years have convinced me I'm safer when I carry a pistol. This was a personal decision, but because handgun possession is a controversial subject, perhaps my reasoning will interest others.

I live in western South Dakota on a ranch 25 miles from the nearest town: for several years I spent winters alone here. As a free-lance writer, I travel alone a lot more than 100,000 miles by car in the last four years. With women freer than ever before to travel alone, the odds of our encountering trouble seem to have risen. Distances are great, roads are deserted, and the terrain is often too exposed to offer hiding places.

A woman who travels alone is advised, usually by men, to protect herself by avoiding bars and other "dangerous situations," by approaching her car like an Indian scout, by locking doors and windows. But these precautions aren't always enough. I spent years following them and still found myself in dangerous situations. I began to resent the idea that just because I am female, I have to be extra careful.

A few years ago, with another woman, I camped for several weeks in the West. We discussed self-defense, but neither of us had taken a course in it. She was against firearms, and local police told us Mace was illegal. So we armed ourselves with spray cans of deodorant tucked into our sleeping bags. We never used our improvised Mace because we were lucky enough to camp beside people who came to our aid when men harassed us. But on one occasion we visited a national park where our assigned space was less than 15 feet from other campers. When we returned from a walk, we found our closest neighbors were two young men. As we gathered our cooking gear, they drank beer and loudly discussed what they would do to us after dark. Nearby campers, even families, ignored them: rangers strolled past, unconcerned. When we asked the rangers point-blank if they would protect us, one of them patted my shoulder and said, "Don't worry, girls. They're just kidding." At dusk we drove out of the park and hid our camp in the woods a few miles away. The illegal spot was lovely, but our enjoyment of that park was ruined. I returned from the trip determined to reconsider the options available for protecting myself.

At that time, I lived alone on the ranch and taught night classes in town. Along a city street I often traveled, a woman had a flat tire, called for help on her CB radio, and got a rapist who left her beaten. She was afraid to call for help again and stayed in her car until morning. For that reason, as well as because CBs work best along line-of-sight, which wouldn't help much in the rolling hills where I live, I ruled out a CB.

As I drove home one night, a car followed me. It passed me on a narrow bridge while a passenger flashed a blinding spotlight in my face. I braked sharply. The car stopped, angled across the bridge, and four men jumped out. I realized the locked doors were useless if they broke the windows of my pickup. I started forward, hoping to knock their car aside so I could pass. Just then another car appeared, and the men hastily got back in their car. They continued to follow me, passing and repassing. I dared not go home because no one else was there. I passed no lighted houses. Finally they pulled over to the roadside, and I decided to use their tactic: fear. Speeding, the pickup horn blaring, I swerved as close to them as I dared as I roared past. It worked: they turned off the highway. But I was frightened and angry. Even in my vehicle I was too vulnerable.

Other incidents occurred over the years. One day I glanced out a field below my house and saw a man with a shotgun walking toward a pond full of ducks. I drove down and explained that the land was posted. I politely asked him to leave. He stared at me, and the muzzle of the shotgun began to rise. In a moment of utter clarity I realized that I was alone on the ranch, and that he could shoot me and simply drive away. The moment passed: the man left.

One night, I returned home from teaching a class to find deep tire ruts in the wet ground of my yard, garbage in the driveway, and a large gas tank empty. A light shone in the house: I couldn't remember leaving it on. I was too embarrassed to drive to a neighboring ranch and wake someone up. An hour of cautious exploration convinced me the house was safe, but once inside, with the doors locked, I was still afraid. I kept thinking of how vulnerable I felt, prowling around my own house in the dark.

My first positive step was to take a kung fu class, which teaches evasive or protective action when someone enters your space without permission. I learned to move confidently, scanning for possible attackers. I learned how to assess danger and techniques for avoiding it without combat.

I also learned that one must practice several hours every day to be good at kung fu. By that time I had married George: when I practiced with him, I learned how *close* you must be to your attacker to use martial arts, and decided a 120-pound woman dare not let a six-foot, 220-pound attacker get that close unless she is very, very good at self-defense. I have since read articles by several women who were extremely well trained in the martial arts, but were raped and beaten anyway. 10

I thought back over the times in my life when I had been attacked or threatened and tried to be realistic about my own behavior, searching for anything that had allowed me to become a victim. Overall, I was convinced that I had not been at fault. I don't believe myself to be either paranoid or a risk-taker, but I wanted more protection.

With some reluctance I decided to try carrying a pistol. George had always carried one, despite his size and his training in martial arts. I practiced shooting until I was sure I could hit an attacker who moved close enough to endanger me. Then I bought a license from the county sheriff, making it legal for me to carry the gun concealed.

But I was not yet ready to defend myself. George taught me that the most important preparation was mental: convincing myself I could actually *shoot a person*. Few of us wish to hurt or kill another human being. But there is no point in having a gun—in fact, gun possession might increase your danger—unless you know you can use it. I got in the habit of rehearsing, as I drove or walked, the precise conditions that would be required before I would shoot someone.

People who have not grown up with the idea that they are capable of protecting themselves—in other words, most women—might have to work hard to convince themselves of their ability, and of the necessity. Handgun ownership need not turn us into gunslingers, but it can be part of believing in, and relying on, *ourselves* for protection.

To be useful, a pistol has to be available. In my car, it's within instant reach. When I enter a deserted rest stop at night, it's in my purse, with my hand on the grip. When I walk from a dark parking lot into a motel, it's 15 in my hand, under a coat. At home, it's on the headboard. In short, I take it with me almost everywhere I go alone.

Just carrying a pistol is not protection; avoidance is still the best approach to trouble. Subconsciously watching for signs of danger, I believe I've become more alert. Handgun use, not unlike driving, becomes instinctive. Each time I've drawn my gun—I have never fired it at another human being—I've simply found it in my hand.

I was driving the half-mile to the highway mailbox one day when I saw a vehicle parked about midway down the road. Several men were standing in the ditch, relieving themselves. I have no objection to emergency urination, but I noticed they'd dumped several dozen beer cans in the road. Besides being ugly, cans can slash a cow's feet or stomach.

The men noticed me before they finished and made quite a performance out of zipping their trousers while walking toward me. All four of them gathered around my small foreign car, and one of them demanded what the hell I wanted.

"This is private land. I'd appreciate it if you'd pick up the beer cans."

"What beer cans?" said the belligerent one, putting both hands on 20 the car door and leaning in my window. His face was inches from mine, and the beer fumes were strong. The others laughed. One tried the passenger door, locked; another put his foot on the hood and rocked the car. They circled, lightly thumping the roof, discussing my good fortune in meeting them and the benefits they were likely to bestow upon me. I felt very small and very trapped and they knew it.

"The ones you just threw out," I said politely.

"I don't see no beer cans. Why don't you get out here and show them to me, honey?" said the belligerent one, reaching for the handle inside the door.

"Right over there," I said, still being polite. "—there, and over there." I pointed with the pistol, which I'd slipped under my thigh. Within one minute the cans and the men were back in the car and headed down the road.

I believe this incident illustrates several important principles. The men were trespassing and knew it: their judgment may have been impaired by alcohol. Their response to the polite request of a woman alone was to use their size, numbers, and sex to inspire fear. The pistol was a response in the same language. Politeness didn't work: I couldn't match them in size or number. Out of the car, I'd have been more vulnerable. The pistol just changed the balance of power. It worked again recently when I was driving in a desolate part of Wyoming. A man played cat-and-mouse with me for 30 miles, ultimately trying to run me off the road. When his car passed mine with only two inches to spare, I showed him my pistol, and he disappeared.

When I got my pistol, I told my husband, revising the old Colt 25 slogan, "God made men *and women*, but Sam Colt made them equal."

Recently I have seen a gunmaker's ad with a similar sentiment. Perhaps this is an idea whose time has come, though the pacifist inside me will be saddened if the only way women can achieve equality is by carrying weapons.

We must treat a firearm's power with caution. "Power tends to corrupt, and absolute power corrupts absolutely," as a man (Lord Acton) once said. A pistol is not the only way to avoid being raped or murdered in today's world, but, intelligently wielded, it can shift the balance of power and provide a measure of safety.

The Responsive Reader

1. Why was Hasselstrom dissatisfied with the advice she was given about how to avoid danger? What alternatives did she check out before she turned to guns? What were her conclusions?
2. What about where and how she lived put Hasselstrom especially at risk? What are the key points she is trying to make about the incidents she describes? Do you think these are "isolated incidents" or parts of a familiar pattern of male behavior?
3. How concerned is Hasselstrom about the "intelligent" use of guns? What does she think it takes for women to use guns successfully for protection? What warnings or advice does she have for other women?

Talking, Listening, Writing

4. The incidents that Hasselstrom reports took place in an isolated rural setting. Do you think her arguments could apply equally in a crowded urban environment? Why or why not?
5. Do you think that safeguards or precautions could be developed to limit the use of guns to self-defense or to make them safer for their owners and their families?
6. Are there still men who think that female victims of rape or male violence probably "asked for it"?

FEDERAL OFFENSE

Wendy Kaminer

> *Lawyer and social critic Wendy Kaminer's most recent book is* It's All the Rage: Crime and Culture *(Addison Wesley, 1995). She is also the author of* Women Volunteering *and* A Fearful Freedom *(two books about women and women's rights) and* I'm Dysfunctional, You're Dysfunctional, *a critique of the personal development tradition. A fellow at Radcliffe College, she has written about law, politics, and culture for publications including* The Atlantic Monthly, *where she is a contributing editor,* The New York Times Book Review, *and* The Village Voice. *Kaminer is known as a sharp critic of popular psychology and self-help books, who has questioned the tendency to seek simple formulaic solutions to complicated problems as well as the false intimacy fostered by the talk-show culture. Regarding the confessional tone of the talk show, she has written, "Never have so many known so much about people for whom they cared so little." In the essay that follows—abridged from a longer article that first appeared in the June 1994 issue of* The Atlantic Monthly *and is included in* It's All the Rage—*she attacks the demagoguery that has taken the place of informed debates about crime and public safety. Most citizens who "are spared firsthand experience with corrections and courts," she writes, learn about the criminal justice system from "Amy Fisher docudramas, TV cop shows and crime stories, and talk show palaver about sensational cases." At the risk of being labeled a "bleeding-heart liberal," in this excerpt she questions the stampede toward "tough" mandatory sentencing schemes that sometimes lead to the long-term imprisonment of relatively petty offenders.*

Thought Starters: Have you had a chance to learn about the criminal justice system from firsthand experience or observation? Or have your views been shaped by "talk shows and the cases on Court TV"?

If a conservative is a liberal who has been mugged, a liberal is a conservative who has been arrested. Hollywood liberals buy guns. The former Reagan Administration official Lyn Nofziger, who was prosecuted in the Wedtech scandal, gives thanks to the American Civil Liberties Union. Ideology can be sorely tested by experience.

The politics of crime control is, therefore, sometimes a simple matter of arithmetic. There are, of course, more crime victims than criminal defendants, particularly among the voting public, so there are likely to be more conservatives than liberals on the subject of crime—many more.

Polling data indicate that nearly 80 percent of the American public supports the death penalty in the absence of an alternative such as life without parole, and this in turn suggests that nearly 80 percent of Americans fear being murdered more than they fear being convicted of murder.

Conservative approaches to crime thus have a natural advantage over liberal ones—an advantage that has been decisive during the recent years of intense social anxiety. Liberalism held sway briefly during the 1960s, at least until the Nixon law-and-order campaign of 1968, not because crime was down (it rose sharply) but, in part, because hope was up. Hope fueled the War on Poverty, the civil-rights movement, and feminism; even the angriest protests of the Vietnam War reflected hope for the possibility of peace.

Today hope seems as out-of-date as beehive hairdos, reaching improbably toward the sky. The hopeful notion that prisons might rehabilitate people has long been dismissed as naive, displaced by a belief in retributive justice and the demand that prisons serve as places of near permanent exile for the incorrigible among us. Some liberals still protest America's uniquely high incarceration rate, tirelessly pointing out that we imprison more people per capita than any other country in the world, but a majority of Americans favor building more prisons, despite their cost, and believe that sentencing practices are excessively lenient.

At the state and federal levels the answer to violent crime has been the three-time-loser statute, imposing mandatory life sentences without parole on repeat violent offenders, without much regard for the nature of their crimes or their characters. In Washington, which became by referendum the first state to enact a three-time-loser law, qualifying "violent" felonies include drunk driving, promoting prostitution, and petty theft. One unintended consequence of this law may be an increase of violence on the streets: preliminary anecdotal reports from the police suggest that when cornered, offenders may shoot their way out rather than surrender and face life in prison. Three-time-loser laws have also been widely criticized as arbitrary and as burdensome to the nation's prisons and courts. (Such laws are bound to increase the number of trials, since people aren't likely to plead to life imprisonment, resulting in still more delays throughout the system.) Nevertheless, the drive to imprison more people for longer periods of time seems unstoppable, fueled not just by fury and fear but by a sense of resignation. It is as if all we can do is warehouse people until they die or are too old and decrepit to threaten anyone on the outside again.

Adopting violence-prevention programs, as Attorney General Janet Reno has advocated, requires hope that the federal government in partnership with localities can treat the social pathologies that give rise to crime. Indeed, the assumption that there are identifiable, treatable connections between these pathologies—for example, the neglect and abuse of children—and crime reflects the hopeful notion that violent people are made, not born, and can sometimes be unmade, if intervention comes early enough.

Along with faith in the curative powers of good government, programs to treat and prevent violent behavior reflect faith in the malleability of human beings and the capacity of distressed people and communities for self-improvement.

Despite his sunniness about America, Ronald Reagan presented a much darker view of criminality, which still holds popular appeal. There are no social solutions to crime, Reagan asserted in 1981, because crime is not a social problem; "it's a problem of the human heart." Reagan cited what he viewed as a dual liberal fallacy about crime—the conviction that ameliorating poverty might reduce crime and the assumption that "there [is] nothing permanent or absolute about man's nature."

This bleak vision of crime as an unchangeable fact of life, implicitly equating crime with original sin, dismisses liberalism as utopian. Government can respond to the symptoms with arrest and incarceration, but only God can treat the disease, Reagan implied.

The public-policy expert James Q. Wilson offered a more thoughtful, less biblical variation on this theme in his landmark book *Thinking About Crime*, in which he chided liberals for seeking to treat the root causes of crime. In 1968 John Lindsay, then the mayor of New York City, gave a typical definition of these causes: "the poverty that grips over thirty million of our citizens." Lindsay added, "If we are to eliminate the crime and violence in this country, we must eliminate the hopelessness, futility, and alienation from which they spring." It's not that social reasons for crime don't exist, Wilson wrote, but they are practically impossible to address. "The more we understand the causes of crime, the more we are drawn into the complex and subtle world of attitudes, predispositions, and beliefs, a world in which planned intervention is exceptionally difficult." In Wilson's view, the liberal fallacy was the notion that "no problem is adequately addressed unless its causes are eliminated."

Wilson argued that policy is most effective when it focuses on objective matters like the costs and benefits of crime, not the realm of "the subjective and the familial." He posited criminals as essentially rational human beings who would be deterred from committing crimes when the associated costs became impractical. 10

It's impossible to know how many violent offenders weigh the consequences of their actions. (It's likely that many who do engage in cost-benefit analyses never get past assuming they won't be arrested.) Certainly thirteen-year-old boys with guns and a wide range of neurotics, psychotics, and apparently sane, smart killers like Gary Gilmore tend to act impulsively, without regard for harsh sentencing laws. Nor would the prospect of a prison sentence necessarily deter a young male for whom imprisonment has become a rite of passage or a haven from the street: "three hots and a cot." A sentence might not even distress his parents. One Boston defense attorney remembers the first time the mother of a client encouraged her not to free him from prison. "At least I'll know where he is," she said.

The poignancy of this appeal, and the threatened destruction of several young generations, may force liberals and conservatives alike to reconsider some of their most basic assumptions. "Those mothers in the ghetto love their children," Senator Orrin Hatch asserts, with all the force of revelation, and he acknowledges that poverty is related to crime (as is a welfare system that "does not stimulate the desire to make something of yourself"). "Some people become locked in poverty and become embittered in the process," Hatch says. "That's why drugs are so rampant in our society. Kids in the ghetto can make more money pushing drugs than working for the minimum wage." Meanwhile, Jesse Jackson is preaching self-help, an ethic of individual and communal responsibility, and telling African-Americans to "look inward to go forward." . . .

The new talk about crime control has not, however, been a prelude to new programs. The Senate's $23 billion crime bill, promising more prisons and police officers, longer sentences, and some fifty new federal death penalties, was passed in a few frenzied weeks after state and local elections that seemed to crystallize voters' concern about crime.

"If someone came to the Senate floor and said we should barbwire the ankles of anyone who jaywalks, I think it would pass," Senator Joseph Biden said, shortly after voting with ninety of his colleagues to impose mandatory life sentences on people with the bad luck or bad judgment to commit their third "violent" felony on federal property. This bill would have particularly harsh effects on Native Americans who live on federally owned reservations, but it would not affect the majority of offenders nationwide. The small number to whom it could apply would be bound to include people who were more hapless than vicious, given the expansive definitions of "violent" incorporated in the bill.

Three-time-loser laws need not, of course, be written this stupidly. 15 (The House offered a narrower, smarter law.) But the more narrowly these laws are drafted, the more redundant they may be. Violent crimes already carry lengthy sentences, and many states have career-criminal laws that impose strict mandatory terms on repeat felony offenders. (In the states that have career-criminal laws, crime rates have generally stayed in line with those in the rest of the country.) The problem that is supposed to be addressed by three-time-loser laws—the early release of violent felons—might best be solved not by inflexible life sentences but by more rational allocations of prison space, decreases in the sentences of nonviolent offenders, and increases in strictly supervised alternatives to prison. More felons are put back on the street by prison overcrowding than by soft-hearted judges or legislators—creatures more mythic than real.

If, however, it is easy to imagine an arguably reasonable, narrowly drawn three-time-loser law, it is practically impossible to imagine state or federal legislators actually drafting one. Limiting the application of a three-time-loser law also limits its political appeal. A legislator who voted to allow for the release of geriatric prisoners after twenty-five or thirty years, or to exempt from the list of qualifying felonies burglaries or robberies in which no one is harmed, would probably be labeled soft on crime. And the recent history of congressional action on sentences demonstrates that lawmakers are less concerned with reducing crime than with signaling their concern about it.

Congress has traditionally committed itself to the promise of strict, sure sentencing, with little regard for consequences or facts. Consider federal sentencing laws. From 1984 to 1990 Congress every two years demonstrated its toughness on crime by enacting mandatory minimum sentences for various drug and firearms offenses, including drug offenses committed near schools, violent crimes (defined broadly) or drug crimes involving the use of a firearm (the firearm triggers a mandatory sentence in addition to the sentence for the underlying offense), the possession of more than five grams of crack cocaine, and any degree of involvement in a drug conspiracy.

These laws have had no demonstrable effect on drug- or gun-related violence, but they have greatly increased the number of people taking up space in federal prisons for nonviolent, low-level drug offenses. According to one study, in the year ending September 1992, more than 3,000 drug offenders with no record of violent crime in the previous fifteen years were sentenced to minimum terms of at least five years. From 1984 to 1990 the proportion of people sent to federal prison for drug offenses rose 12 percent, while the proportion of people sentenced for violent crimes and property offenses declined, according to a study by the Federal Judicial Center. Today more than 60 percent of all federal prisoners are serving time for drug offenses, including the simple possession of marijuana or cocaine.

These statistics are hardly news to legislators or policymakers, and stories about people spending five to ten years in federal prison for playing minimal roles in drug conspiracies have begun to appear in the mainstream press. Last November, *The New York Times* featured the case of a twenty-four-year-old man serving ten years in a federal prison because he agreed to help a federal undercover agent find someone selling LSD at a Grateful Dead concert. Relatives of people like this have formed a lobbying group, Families Against Mandatory Minimums, headed by Julie Stewart, whose brother is serving five years for a first offense—growing marijuana at home. Critics of mandatory minimums range from Janet Reno to Orrin Hatch. Hatch does not oppose mandatory minimums in principle, but he acknowledges that they have been "overused" for low-level, nonviolent crimes. Reno has been critical of mandatory minimums (though her criticisms do not appear to have had much effect on Administration policy).

There is also strong opposition to mandatory sentencing from federal judges, both Republican and Democratic appointees. In one survey a majority of judges and a majority of probation officers, in addition to most defense attorneys, viewed mandatory minimums unfavorably, as did about a third of federal prosecutors.

Widespread, bipartisan dissatisfaction with mandatory minimums, however, is not likely to effect any meaningful reform. Senator Biden, who does not generally support mandatory minimums, considers proposals to reform them utterly unrealistic: "I can count: eighty percent of the Congress and eighty-five percent of the public still believes the misinformed rhetoric about sentencing."

Much of what people don't know about mandatory minimums is included in a 1991 report on them by the U.S. Sentencing Commission, which gently recommended their repeal. The Sentencing Commission was established by Congress in 1984 and charged with promulgating guidelines for sentences in federal cases. This represented a revolution in sentencing which was initially sparked by liberal protests about undue sentence disparity resulting from the broad discretion exercised by judges and parole boards.

A bill to establish a commission had been introduced by Senator Ted Kennedy in 1975. It took nearly ten years for Kennedy's bill to pass the Senate, and by the time the commission was established, the political climate had changed considerably. As Kate Stith and Steve Koh point out in a 1993 article in the *Wake Forest Law Review*, sentence reform was "conceived by liberal reformers as an anti-imprisonment and antidiscrimination measure, but finally born as part of a more conservative law-and-order crime control measure."

Federal sentencing guidelines are stringent and are generally reviled by defense attorneys. They are also quite rigid and complex. Judges are required to rely on a sentencing table, established by the commission, which lists generic offense-severity levels in a vertical column and offenders' characteristics (mainly criminal histories) horizontally, creating a grid on which the judge locates the appropriate sentence range, which is fairly narrow. Judges are not supposed to consider mitigating factors, such as a defendant's family and community ties, employment history, or emotional and mental state. Sentencing becomes a technical task, not one requiring thinking or judgment. Judges have only limited discretion to depart from the guidelines, which have thus always been quite controversial. (The guidelines were challenged on constitutional grounds but upheld by the Supreme Court in 1989.) Still, sentencing guidelines don't eliminate all judicial discretion from sentencing, as the mandatory minimums do. If Congress had stopped at establishing the Sentencing Commission and not gone on to enact so many new mandatory minimums, it would have avoided much of the controversy about sentencing today.

The establishment of a sentencing commission, however, isn't nearly *25* as dramatic an anti-crime measure as the passage of mandatory-minimum statutes carrying sentences of many years. So, in the same year that Congress empowered the commission to create sentencing guidelines, it enacted new mandatory minimums for drug offenses. This wasn't quite a revolution in sentencing. . . . According to the Sentencing Commission, nearly 60,000 offenders were sentenced under mandatory minimums from 1984 to 1990; of the sixty mandatory-minimum statutes only four accounted for 94 percent of these cases, which related to drug offenses or carrying a firearm during a drug-related or violent crime. Of the nearly 7,000 defendants sentenced in fiscal year 1990 under mandatory minimums, 91 percent were primarily drug offenders.

There are, then, essentially two federal sentencing systems in place. People who are not charged under statutes carrying mandatory sentences are sentenced under the commission guidelines. Since the guidelines are stringent, mandatory minimums seem at best redundant when applied to serious cases. At worst, and quite often, they're arbitrary and excessively harsh.

"Pathetic cases come along," Judge Stephen Breyer remarked in a speech to the American Bar Association. "No one will ever formulate a system of law for which you don't have to have exceptions." Breyer tells the story of a bank-robbery case involving "a man with the IQ of a seven-year-old who got a toy gun, went to a bank, got seventy dollars to get an operation for his dog, his best friend in the world, turned himself in to the FBI, and the dog died anyway. What should we do? Give him life?"

As Judge Breyer's story suggests, mandatory minimum sentences hold people strictly liable for their acts, regardless of any mitigating circumstances, which is another way of saying that mandatory minimums preclude individualized determinations of accountability—which is another way of saying they're un–American.

Virtually all of us act immorally if not illegally at least on occasion. We'd like to believe that if we ever get caught or feel compelled to confess, we'll be judged not simply by what we've done but by why we did it and who we are. In other words, we want our acts to be judged in the context of motivation and personal history, and a concept of character that involves more than our worst offenses. People do sometimes commit bad acts for good reasons, which means that guilt—and especially sentences—ought to be determined by considering the actor as well as the act. Two people may behave similarly under different circumstances, calling for different standards of accountability. A retarded man who holds up a bank with a toy gun in order to save his dog ought to be treated more leniently than, say, a successful college student who holds up a bank with a toy gun in order to buy a new car. Even in hard cases involving felony assaults or homicides, motive and character should play some role in sentencing. A woman who shoots her husband because he has been beating her and her children for several years seems less culpable than a woman who shoots her husband for money. Imposing the same mandatory sentence in both cases would be imposing punishment without regard to guilt.

It's not surprising that people who bring a sense of justice to the   *30*
system of mandatory minimums often find themselves at odds with the
law. Judge Breyer observes that mandatory-minimum-sentencing schemes
encourage disrespect and disregard for the law among the people charged
with enforcing it. "You cannot tell human beings to do things they think
are totally unfair. They won't do it. They'll figure a way out." The judge
may be constrained from imposing a lesser sentence, but "the prosecutor
won't prosecute, the juries won't convict." In fact, according to Breyer,
many federal prosecutors are using their discretion not to prosecute under
mandatory minimums. Mandatory-minimum statutes do not eliminate discretion or disparities in sentencing. They shift discretion from judges to
prosecutors.

Pursuant to mandatory-minimum-sentencing laws, prosecutors essentially decide how defendants will be sentenced when they decide how
defendants will be charged. This clear usurpation of judicial authority is
justified as a way of providing prosecutors with an important bargaining
tool: they use the threat of indictment under a mandatory-minimum statute to persuade defendants to cooperate and inform. . . .

If Congress were genuinely interested in truth in sentencing, it would
make clear to the public how erratically and arbitrarily mandatory minimums are enforced. It would point out that federal sentencing guidelines
already call for very tough sentences for serious crimes. It would explain
that defendants are not faceless or fungible: they and their circumstances
vary, even when they are charged with the same crime, and judges must
have at least limited discretion to vary their sentences.

But there are so few ways for Congress to demonstrate toughness
on crime. The Senate passed new mandatory minimums in 1993, with
no apparent opposition from the Administration. As Orrin Hatch con-
cedes, "Mandatory minimums are a political response to violent crime.
Let's be honest about it. It's awfully difficult for politicians to vote against
them."

The Responsive Reader

1. In her opening paragraphs, what is Kaminer's perspective on "the
   politics of crime control"? (How is it "sometimes a simple matter of
   arithmetic"?) Can you elaborate on the three ways of looking at the
   purposes of the prison system that she briefly mentions: rehabilitation, retribution, and "permanent exile"?
2. For Kaminer, what are major weaknesses or drawbacks of the current
   movement toward harsher mandatory sentences and "three-strikes-
   and-you're-out" legislation? What are unintended side effects?
3. How does Kaminer contrast basic liberal and conservative assumptions about human nature, about the social roots of crime, and about
   the deterrent effect of punishment?

4. Where in the essay do you get glimpses of the individual human beings affected by the current "get tough" policies?
5. What positive alternatives to the current trend does Kaminer present or imply? What modifications of current laws does she recommend?

Talking, Listening, Writing

6. Do you personally incline to the conservative or liberal side of this argument? What has shaped your views on this issue?
7. Why does the distinction between "violent" and "nonviolent" crimes become a major issue in this article? Where do *you* draw the line?

Collaborative Projects

8. What is the history or record of "three-strikes-and-you're-out" in your state?

TOUR OF DUTY

Larry Heinemann

> *The Vietnam War was a traumatic chapter in this country's history. It shaped the outlook of a generation of Americans—whether they were actually sent to Vietnam or whether they joined the growing antiwar protest at home. In the following essay, a Vietnam War veteran writes as an eyewitness who shared the "blunt and heartfelt bitterness" of those who felt they "had been lied to and used by arrogant and selfish men." Prize-winning author Larry Heinemann was born in Chicago in 1944. He graduated from Columbia College and later came back there to teach writing. He said almost twenty years after the war, "I have been thinking and talking and reading about the war since I got back in 1968." He had served as a sergeant in the infantry, and he published his novel, Close Quarters, based on his experience, in 1977. In the following excerpt from an article first published in 1985, he reported on his interviews with other veterans. When he published this article, he said, "Tens of thousands of GIs got chewed up in Vietnam, and there are tens of thousands on whom the war still chews."*

Thought Starters: Is the Vietnam War ancient history for the current generation of young Americans? What ideas, assumptions, or memories do you as a reader bring to the subject?

During World War I, the Allied military, and the British especially, weren't interested in attributing the soldiers' responses to battle and butchery to any unmanly newfangled psychological or emotional causes. Rather, it was believed that the very shock, the concussion, from an artillery round had an irresistible effect upon the body itself. "Shell shock" seemed a perfectly reasonable explanation for what happened to the men in the trenches.

During World War II, the troops suffered "combat fatigue"—the boys were just tired. World War II veterans did not escape the effects associated with delayed stress. The psychiatric casualties were 300 percent higher in the early years of World War II than in World War I. But the way soldiers fought in World War II, and the way they stopped fighting after it, were different from what happened in Vietnam—and this difference would prove crucial. During World War II, a unit trained together and shipped overseas together. You humped North Africa, Italy and Sicily, then France and Germany, or you island-hopped from Tarawa and Guadalcanal and Peleliu to Iwo Jima and Okinawa. You were in for the duration, as the saying went. After the war, waiting to be shipped home, you had time to share the sympathetic support of men with whom you had a particular intimacy not often permitted in this culture. (It wasn't "buddies," the dead-flat, shopworn newspaper cliché that trivialized a complex and powerful relationship. "Buddy-up" was something you did at Boy Scout camp, when everyone would mosey down to the lake for a swim. Boy Scout camp may be many things, but it ain't the straight-leg, ground-pounding infantry.)

Waiting, you got to work some of the war out of your system; to release the grief for men long dead; to feel keenly, perhaps for the first time, your survivor's guilt; to feel as well the sharp personal guilt for murdering prisoners, say, or for shelling villages good and hard that you later discovered were filled with women and children, or for firebombing Dresden; to recognize the delight you took in destruction (what the Bible calls "lust of the eye") and the warm, grim satisfaction of your firm and bitter anger. Waiting, you had time for crying jags, public and private; you had time for fistfights to settle old scores once and for all. By the time your ship docked, you had worked much of the stress out of your system, though the annual depressions (usually coinciding with anniversaries), the periodic screaming, thrashing nightmares (vivid and colorful recollections of the worst times of your life), and the rest would linger for years— delayed stress (though no one yet called it by that name)—a permanent fixture in your life.

In the Vietnam War, everyone served a one-year tour—the assumption being that any dipstick could keep his buttons buttoned *that* long— though you could volunteer to stay as long as you liked. (United States Marine Corps esprit dictated that every Marine would serve one year and one month. *Semper Fi*, Mac.) But the one-year tour created a reverberating and lingering turmoil of emotional problems unlike anything known after World War II.

Vietnam was a war of individuals. You went through Basic Training   5 with one group, Advanced Individual Training with another. You shipped overseas with a planeload of total strangers, and when you reached your outfit—a rifle company out in the middle of nowhere, say—the astonishment on your face and the bright sheen of your uniform pegged you as a 'cruit, the newbee, the fucking new guy.

You have never seen those people before in your life. Everyone avoids you (dumb guys never last, we used to say). At the very least, you have replaced a highly experienced and valuable man whose tour was up. He was as smooth as silk when he took the point, and no John Wayne. You, on the other hand, have hardly seen an M-16 and do not know your ass from a hole in the ground. The heat and humidity are withering, and you're so exhausted by ten in the morning, pouring sweat, that when they call a break in place you can't even stand up to piss.

As you begin your tour, the short-timers finish theirs, mount their choppers and leave, and are never heard from again; other FNGs arrive.

Your first firefight is a bloody, nasty mess, and it is a pure wonder you are not killed. Slowly you become accustomed to the weather and the work— the *grinding*, backbreaking humps, the going over the same ground day in and day out, aboard choppers and on foot. More short-timers leave; more FNGs arrive. This is the ugliest, most grueling, and most spiritless work you have ever done. But you soon discover you're a pretty good tunnel rat or booby-trap man, or especially canny and efficient on night ambush. You come to know the ground around your base camp and fire-bases like the back of your hand. In camp, on standdown, you smoke dope in earnest; you drink like a fish; you party with a serious frenzy.

More short-timers leave; more FNGs arrive. With every firefight the men around you drop like flies. You endure jungle rot, heat exhaustion, crabs and head lice, and an endless diarrhea from the one-a-day malaria pills. You take your five-day R&R in Bangkok, a culinary and sexual rampage. When you get back to the field more short-timers have disappeared; more FNGs have replaced them. You are sprayed with Agent Orange; the dust is in your hair, in your water, on your food. They send you to sharpshooter school; you return with an M-14 with scope and carrying case and a $500 pair of field glasses—the company sniper. You can draw a bead and drop a VC—man, woman, or child—in his tracks at 500 meters, and he never knows what hit him. You have many kills. More short-timers leave; more FNGs arrive. You are promoted to sergeant and made a squad leader. Your platoon leader, an ROTC first lieutenant, admires and trusts you: you will go anywhere and do anything. Humping is a snap, and you live in the midst of an alien ease.

The firefights and ambushes are bloody and nasty, businesslike massacres with meat all over everything. The one-year tour is the topic of endless conversation; you know exactly when your tour will end, and *that* is what keeps you going. You don't care about anything but finishing your tour—you just don't care.

Then one morning you wake up and it is finally your turn—not a   10 day too soon, you understand. You say your goodbyes, hop in your chopper, and leave. You will never see or hear of these men again. The next morning you hitch a ride to the airfield in time to catch the plane to Saigon. You have hacked it, but you are exhausted. Your body is as tight as a drum. The plane finally comes: a Boeing 707. The replacements file off and you and your fellow passengers walk across the tarmac, and load up—a ritual unbelievably ordinary and benign.

On the plane you sit in a space both anonymous and claustrophobic, more glad and more guilty than tongue can tell. Sick, lame or lazy, blind, crippled or crazy—you just want out. The plane ride is nineteen hours of canned music and beach-blanket movies. At Oakland Army Terminal you're mustered out—given a bum's rush of a physical and a new baggy, smelly uniform, and issued your outstanding pay in greenback cash. You are free to go.

Your entire family meets you at the airport and takes you home to the house where you grew up. Yesterday or the day before you were surrounded by men who humped guns and grenades, up to their eyeballs in bloody murder (mean and evil sons-of-bitches, you bet). Now you're dumped into a maelstrom—walk/don't-walk lights, Levi's and daytime TV; mom and dad and the dog on the couch—that bears no relationship to anything you're accustomed to. You're with people who love you, but they don't have the faintest inkling how to help you. You want to sit and tell them what happened—what you saw, what you did, what you became—but more often than not they don't want to hear about it. Your father, a World War II Marine, perhaps, shrugs his shoulders and, struggling with his own residual delayed stress, says, Everybody did those things, grow up, forget it (it's all right). But you sit in that clean kitchen, smelling the eggs and bacon, and warming your hands on a cup of coffee, and it is not all right.

And no "validating" ritual—no parade or Vietnam War memorial—will make it so.

And make no mistake: if you have any healthy impulses left at all, you want to find a woman and take her to bed. Skip the date; skip the dinner; skip the movie. You want to feel good in your body and re-establish those powerful human feelings. Maybe you manage it, but just as likely you don't: some women refuse to date veterans, and then brag to them about it.

You get your old job back (it's the law) stocking shelves at the A&P. The work is easy and dull, and the money's decent, but the petty harassment is galling. The boss doesn't want you around, the way you *stare* when the customers ask their endlessly stupid questions. You drift from job to job. Sometimes, as soon as you mention you're a veteran, the clerk behind the counter tells you to beat it; they don't need junkies and they don't need freaks.

You cannot concentrate. You begin having nightmares; you jerk out of sleep, pouring sweat. You drink to anesthetize yourself against the dreams and the daydream flashbacks (drunks don't dream very well). You try to stay up as long as you can. You know you will dream about the night you shivved that wounded VC who kept waving his hands in your face, shaking his head and whispering man to man, "No, no," while he squirmed against your knife with all his might.

You cannot stand crowds or people walking too close behind you. You discover an abrupt and furious temper; you startle into a crouch at the damnedest things. You become self-destructive, picking fights and driving your car crazily. There is the nagging thought that you didn't do enough, that you never should have left Vietnam. Everyone you came to trust has disappeared from your life, dead by now, for all you know. How does that make you feel? You withdraw into isolation. Why put up with the grief?

15

The Responsive Reader

1. Why does Heinemann start with a discussion of earlier wars? What essential contrasts is he setting up?
2. Heinemann sets out to make you understand veterans who felt misunderstood, stereotyped, or rejected. What is his major point or central thesis? Does he succeed in making you understand the way the veterans felt?
3. What are the major way stations or mileposts in the author's "tour of duty"?
4. What is the mix of personal experience and other sources in this essay?

Talking, Listening, Writing

5. Many people would prefer to forget the war experience and move on to the challenges of the present. Do you agree or disagree with them, and why?
6. How does Heinemann use slang or obscenities? Do you find his use of language offensive?
7. Write about a traumatic period in your life or in the life of someone close to you.
8. During and after the Vietnam War, there was much protest activity designed to keep army recruiters or ROTC units off campus. What arguments would you present to support or reject such initiatives?

Collaborative Projects

9. How does our society treat its veterans? Working with a group, you may want to research one limited area of this larger subject. For instance, choose the treatment or reception of the veterans of the Gulf War; the story of the Vietnam War Memorial in Washington, D.C.; medical or counseling services for Vietnam veterans; the reception of American prisoners of war returning from Vietnam; or the treatment of Vietnam veterans in the media.

CAMBODIAN BOYS DON'T CRY

Rasmey Sam

Many Americans first came to this country as refugees. They fled from repression, revolution, famine, or war. They made it to a ship going to America barely ahead of the kaiser's or the tsar's police. Like the Irish during the great famine, they left a country in which there seemed to be no hope of freedom or even survival. They crossed a border to temporary safety before the Gestapo sealed off the last routes of escape. Like many of the boat people leaving Vietnam after the war, some perished in the attempt. Some were turned back, sometimes to prison or death. Some spent years in crowded refugee camps—unwanted, undesirable. Many others, finally, found sanctuary and a chance to start a new life. The student who wrote the following essay in a basic writing class in an American college is the survivor of the genocide in Cambodia, a small country in Southeast Asia that was nominally neutral during the Vietnam War. But the American government accused the Vietnamese Communists of using Cambodia as a staging area and conducted heavy bombing raids. When the Americans lost the war, the Cambodian Communist guerrillas, the Khmer Rouge, took over the country.

Thought Starters: How much do you know about the "killing fields" of Cambodia? Do you know refugees from revolution or war?

Cambodia is a small country that is about the size of the state of   *1*
Missouri; it is a land of great contrasts. One still sees in the people and in their ways of living an awareness of an ancient heritage of greatness. Cambodians have pride in their language: pride in their music, dancing, visual arts, and pride in being Cambodian.

Cambodia came prominently to the attention of United States policy makers in the early 1970s, when the United States actively supported the noncommunist Lon Nol government against the communist Khmer Rouge regime. Cambodia again became an important issue after 1978, when the Soviet Union backed a Vietnamese invasion that toppled the Khmer Rouge regime.

I was a little boy eating some greasy chicken, on a dark, cloudy summer night when suddenly the air became calm and cool. The countryside was silent as if there were no people there. Some people were heading to their homes from a hard day of work. The breeze was starting to pick up and leaves were falling from the tall, healthy trees to the ground in my front yard. It seemed like the rain was coming toward our direction. It was only about six o'clock, but it seemed like almost midnight. The restless insects were starting to make extremely loud noises across the innocent, quiet villages. The insects seemed to cry horribly loud as the night went on. Maybe the insects were crying for the rain to come down, or maybe it was just something else. The clouds became thicker and thicker all over my house and the beautiful, small countryside. The wooden houses in the village were clustered together so as to help each other survive better. The houses had roofs made of dried palm tree leaves that were tied together to provide protection from rain. The sound of lightning was almost like the sound of guns shooting toward my house, while the white light flashed all over the villages. As I sat down on the rocker in front of my parents' house and gazed at the rice fields, I wondered what could possibly happen that night. The fields fascinated me. Low earthen dikes divided them into a pattern like irregular checkerboards, with paddies instead of squares, and trees rose here and there where dikes met. As I watched the darkness and the lightning, my imagination began to wonder about a ghost that I dreamed of the previous night. My body suddenly started to chill. Without wasting any more time, I got up and ran inside the house.

It was ten till eleven o'clock when, suddenly, a heavy sound exploded approximately a quarter of a mile away from my house. It seemed like my whole house was moving. I had never heard anything like this before. I was very curious to see what was going on out there. Since the filthy dogs started to bark and chickens cackled, the village seemed to become a jungle. Standing in front of the house, I immediately looked to my left, and, sure enough, there was a big fire flashing all over the village. It looked to me as if the village was on fire. While I stood there wondering what could possibly cause the fire to burn the village, there were two more bombs dropped right after one another as close as fifty yards away from my back yard. As I watched a small house of wood and palm trees, I noticed that part of its back was destroyed. As I stood alone in front of the house, the images of violence burned harder and harder. My heart started to pound. I was nervous and panicked through the whole event. The night of the countryside was filled with light and burning fire. The people were screaming for help. The bombs continually exploded while the sounds of the guns were so loud that my ears hurt. I began to cry for my parents, but I didn't remember where they were. Because of the sound of explosions, I was unable to hear my parents call me. Although all my family was inside the house, my parents were trying to find where I was. Somehow, I was running to my next door neighbor's house. In a short time, the village became a war zone. The airplanes, helicopter and tanks were all over the countryside. People were hit by bombs left and right. The bodies of my neighbors were lying all over their walkways. The moment the bombs were dropped, I could feel the ground move. Suddenly, a dark cloudy summer night became a lightning war zone. My father finally found me and took me inside the bomb shelter.

Two days later, the Cambodian communist government that called   5
itself the Khmer Rouge took over Cambodia. The war was finally ended
and many people were anguished to know about our new government.
The symbol of the red flag was rising everywhere. People were wondering
how this communist government was going to control people and the
country. The soldiers were everywhere, and everything seem confused. As
the people began to settle down and start their new lives, the Khmer
Rouge government forced people to go to work every day and every
night. They gave us very little food and there was nothing we could do
about it. Whenever we received a small amount of rice, we ate it gladly.
Human life had no meaning and people were treated like animals. Some
people couldn't work because they were hungry or sick. The Khmer
Rouge government punished them and shot them.

As I remember, on one cold winter season, the rains were constantly
dropping down every day and night. I was forced to stay in a boys' home
that was almost falling apart. I was sick and hungry while lying down on
the wet dirt floor. No one was allowed to take care of me, not even my
parents. That didn't matter anyway, because I was separated from my parents the day the Khmer Rouge took over the power. It was almost three
years since I saw my parents, but I could never forget. When the rain
season brought its heavy storms, teams of men and women transplanted
the seedlings to the rest of the paddies. One day I was working behind a
skinny woman with long black hair, brown eyes and a black torn outfit. It
seemed as though the wind could easily have blown her away. She seemed
as if she was thinking of something that made her appear worried. She
turned around and looked straight into my eyes and said "Rasmey son." I
was confused and didn't realize it was my mother. I slowly looked up to
my mother's face and stood there with a somber smile—I didn't have any
word to say. I was shocked; my heart began to pound inside of me. My
tears started to drip down my sweaty face as fast as I could blink. My
skinny, skeleton-body became weaker and weaker from staring into her
crying eyes. Being a lonely boy who was standing in the mud that was
overcrowded with blood-sucking leeches, I could barely hold my body
straight up from excitement. I finally got to see my beloved mother whom
I had admired and respected for so long. I thought it was just a dream. But
either way, I am grateful to have a vivid picture of her in my mind. I didn't
want the Khmer Rouge to see, and I quickly walked away to another rice
field and continued to work.

I can't remember the day or month when one of the leaders of the
Khmer Rouge came and dragged me to work. I was so sick and hungry
that I didn't care what he would do to me. He kicked me while I was
lying down and pointed his gun toward my head and said "either you go
to work, or I'll shoot you right now." I had no choice but with my long
skeleton's body, I got up slowly and went to work with the rest of the
people.

During the next four years, three to four million innocent hard working people were murdered by the Khmer Rouge. Many houses, automobiles, trees and many more things were destroyed during the war under the Khmer Rouge's power. My father, grandfather, sister and many other close relatives were killed by the Khmer Rouge. The picture of one of the most beautiful countries in South East Asia became the jungle of the killing field. The skeletons and the bodies of the innocent human beings were lying all over the rice fields and the bushes. I found myself believing, for at least a few moments at a time, that the Khmer Rouge had done it, that the people of Cambodia had nothing left, except the memories of the most brutal, inhumane and senseless killings that ever happened; it will stay with them—forever.

It was a happy day when I learned that my mother, two brothers and one sister were still alive. The country was now under Vietnamese rule and my surviving family in no danger of being killed, since this new communist government was non-violent.

I am a student in Cal State San Bernardino, but nothing has shaped   10
my life as much as surviving the Khmer Rouge regime. I am a survivor of the Cambodian holocaust. That's who I am.

The Responsive Reader

1. Can you identify with the student telling this story? Why or why not?
2. How much does the writer reveal of his feelings? Do you think he is holding back some of what he thinks and feels?

Talking, Listening, Writing

3. When something defeats our attempts at understanding, we may give up and call it senseless or irrational. Is there any rational explanation for what happened to Rasmey's people?
4. People in the West have become jaded by reports of upheavals in distant countries and by the flood of refugees asking for asylum. Assuming your vote counted, would you have voted to admit people like Rasmey Sam to the United States? Why or why not?

Collaborative Projects

5. Social scientists and psychologists have studied the physical and psychological scars of survivors of holocaust or genocide. For further reading, you may want to study the published testimony of survivors. (Or conduct some firsthand interviews if you can.) What do survivors remember? How do survivors cope? What do they want us to learn from their experience?

THE BUCK PRIVATE (*SOLDADO RAZO*)
Luis Valdez

> If you can sing, dance, walk, march, hold a picket sign,
> play a guitar or harmonica or any other instrument, you can
> participate! No acting experience required.
> —from a recruiting leaflet for the *Teatro Campesino*

Luis Valdez (born 1940) founded the Teatro Campesino, *which has been honored in both the United States and Europe. (A campesino is someone who works in the fields.) Valdez himself was working in the fields by the time he was six years old, with the much interrupted schooling of the children of America's migrant workers. He eventually accepted a scholarship at San Jose State University and graduated with a B.A. in English in 1964. The theater group that Valdez founded in 1965 began by performing actos— short, one-act plays—in community centers, church halls, and in the fields in California. Under his leadership, the* Teatro Campesino *explored the lives of urban Chicano youth, Mexican Indian legend and mythology, and materials from Third World sources. At the beginning of his play* Los Vendidos (The Sellouts, *1967), a secretary from the governor's office comes to Honest Sancho's Used Mexican lot to look for a suave, not-too-dark Chicano to become a token Mexican American at social functions in the state capital. In 1987, Valdez wrote and directed the movie* La Bamba, *a biography of the Chicano rock 'n' roll singer Ritchie Valens. His PBS production of* Corridos: Tales of Passion and Revolution, *with Linda Ronstadt, won the Peabody Award.* Soldado Razo, *or* The Buck Private, *was first performed by the* Teatro Campesino *in 1971.*

Thought Starters: What is the history of minorities in the American military? Have the least privileged in our society borne a disproportionate share of the burden of defending it?

Characters

Johnny	The Mother
The Father	Cecilia
Death	The Brother

DEATH (*enters singing*). I'm taking off as a private, I'm going to join the   *1*
ranks . . . along with the courageous young men who leave behind
beloved mothers, who leave their girlfriends crying, crying, crying

their farewell. Yeah! How lucky for me that there's a war. How goes it, bro? I am death. What else is new? Well, don't get paranoid because I didn't come to take anybody away. I came to tell you a story. Sure, the story of the Buck Private. Maybe you knew him, eh? He was killed not too long ago in Vietnam.

[JOHNNY *enters, adjusting his uniform.*]

DEATH. This is Johnny, The Buck Private. He's leaving for Vietnam in the morning, but tonight—well, tonight he's going to enjoy himself, right? Look at his face. Know what he's thinking? He's thinking (Johnny *moves his lips*) "Now, I'm a man!"

[THE MOTHER *enters.*]

DEATH. This is his mother. Poor thing. She's worried about her son, like all mothers. "Blessed be God," she's thinking; (The Mother *moves her mouth*) "I hope nothing happens to my son." (The Mother *touches* Johnny *on the shoulder.*)

JOHNNY. Is dinner ready, mom?

MOTHER. Yes, son, almost. Why did you dress like that? You're not   5
leaving until tomorrow.

JOHNNY. Well, you know. Cecilia's coming and everything.

MOTHER. Oh, my son. You're always bringing girlfriends to the house but you never think about settling down.

JOHNNY. One of these days I'll give you a surprise, ma. (*He kisses her forehead. Embraces her.*)

DEATH. Oh, my! What a picture of tenderness, no? But, watch the old lady. Listen to what she's thinking. "Now, my son is a man. He looks so handsome in that uniform."

JOHNNY. Well, mom, it's getting late. I'll be back shortly with Cecilia,   10
okay?

MOTHER. Yes, son, hurry back. (*He leaves.*) May God take care of you, mom's pride and joy.

[JOHNNY *re-enters and begins to talk.*]

DEATH. Out in the street, Johnny begins to think about his family, his girl, his neighborhood, his life.

JOHNNY. Poor mom. Tomorrow it will be very difficult for her. For me as well. It was pretty hard when I went to boot camp, but now? Vietnam! It's a killer, man. The old man, too. I'm not going to be here to help him out. I wasn't getting rich doing fieldwork, but it was something. A little help, at least. My little brother can't work yet because he's still in school. I just hope he stays there. And finishes. I never liked that school stuff, but I know my little brother digs it. He's smart too—maybe he'll even go to college. One of us has got to make it in this life. Me—I guess I'll just get married to Cecilia and have a bunch of kids. I remember when I first saw her at the Rainbow Ballroom. I couldn't even dance with her because I had had a few beers. The next week was pretty good, though. Since then. How long ago was that? June . . . no, July. Four months. Now I want to get hitched. Her parents don't like me, I know. They think I'm a good for nothing. Maybe they'll feel different when I come back from Nam. Sure, the War Veteran! Maybe I'll get wounded and come back with tons of medals. I wonder how the dudes around here are going to think about that? Damn neighborhood—I've lived here all my life. Now I'm going to Vietnam. *(Taps and drum)* It's going to be a drag, man. I might even get killed. If I do, they'll bring me back here in a box, covered with a flag . . . military funeral like they gave Pete Gomez . . . everybody crying . . . the old lady—*(Stops)* What the hell am I thinking, man? Damn fool! *(He freezes.)*

[DEATH *powders* JOHNNY'S *face white during the next speech.*]

DEATH. Foolish, but not stupid, eh? He knew the kind of funeral he wanted and he got it. Military coffin, lots of flowers, American flag, women crying, and a trumpet playing taps with a rifle salute at the end. Or was it goodbye? It doesn't matter, you know what I mean. It was first class all the way. Oh, by the way, don't get upset about the makeup I'm putting on him, eh? I'm just getting him ready for what's coming. I don't always do things in a hurry, you know. Okay, then, next scene. (Johnny *exits.*)

[JOHNNY *goes on to* CECILIA'S *and exits.*]

DEATH. Back at the house, his old man is just getting home.   15

[THE FATHER *enters.*]

FATHER. Hey, old lady, I'm home. Is dinner ready?

[THE MOTHER *enters.*]

MOTHER. Yes, dear. Just wait till Juan gets home. What did you buy?
FATHER. A sixpack of Coors.
MOTHER. Beer?
FATHER. Well, why not? Look—This is my son's last night.   20
MOTHER. What do you mean, his last night? Don't speak like that.
FATHER. I mean his last night at home, woman. You understand—hic.
MOTHER. You're drunk, aren't you?
FATHER. And if I am, what's it to you? I just had a few beers with my buddy and that's it. Well, what is this, anyway . . . ? It's all I need, man. My son's going to war and you don't want me to drink. I've got to celebrate, woman!
MOTHER. Celebrate what?   25

FATHER. That my son is now a man! And quite a man, the twerp. So don't pester me. Bring me some supper.

MOTHER. Wait for Juan to come home.

FATHER. Where is he? He's not here? Is that so-and-so loafing around again? Juan? Juan?

MOTHER. I'm telling you he went to get Cecilia, who's going to have dinner with us. And please don't use any foul language. What will the girl say if she hears you talking like that?

FATHER. To hell with it! Who owns this damn house, anyway? Aren't I *30* the one who pays the rent? The one who buys the food? Don't make me get angry, huh? Or you'll get it. It doesn't matter if you already have a son who's a soldier.

MOTHER. Please. I ask you in your son's name, eh? Calm down. (*She exits.*)

FATHER. Calm down! Just like that she wants me to calm down. And who's going to shut my trap? My son the soldier? My son . . .

DEATH. The old man's thoughts are racing back a dozen years to a warm afternoon in July. Johnny, eight years old, is running toward him between the vines, shouting: "Paaa, I already picked 20 trays, paaapá!"

FATHER. Huh. Twenty trays. Little bugger.

[THE BROTHER *enters.*]

BROTHER. Pa, is Johnny here? *35*

DEATH. This is Johnny's little brother.

FATHER. And where are you coming from?

BROTHER. I was over at Polo's house. He has a new motor scooter.

FATHER. You just spend all your time playing, don't you?

BROTHER. I didn't do anything. *40*

FATHER. Don't talk back to your father.

BROTHER (*shrugs*). Are we going to eat soon?

FATHER. I don't know. Go ask your mother.

[THE BROTHER *exits.*]

DEATH. Looking at his younger son, the old man starts thinking about him. His thoughts spin around in the usual hopeless cycle of defeat, undercut by more defeat.

FATHER. That boy should be working. He's already fourteen years old. *45* I don't know why the law forces them to go to school till they're sixteen. He won't amount to anything, anyway. It's better if he starts working with me so that he can help the family.

DEATH. Sure, he gets out of school and in three or four years, I take him the way I took Johnny. Crazy, huh?

[JOHNNY *returns with* CECILIA.]

JOHNNY. Good evening, pa.

FATHER. Son! Good evening. What's this? You're dressed as a soldier?

JOHNNY. I brought Cecilia over to have dinner with us.

FATHER. Well, have her come in, come in.   50

CECILIA. Thank you very much.

FATHER. My son looks good, doesn't he?

CECILIA. Yes, sir.

FATHER. Damn right. He's off to be a buck private. (*Pause*) Well, let's see . . . uh, son, would you like a beer?!

JOHNNY. Yes, sir, but couldn't we get a chair first? For Cecilia?   55

FATHER. But, of course. We have all the modern conveniences. Let me bring one. Sweetheart? The company's here! (*He exits.*)

JOHNNY. How you doing?

CECILIA. Okay. I love you.

DEATH. This, of course, is Johnny's girlfriend. Fine, ha? Too bad he'll never get to marry her. Oh, he proposed tonight and everything—and she accepted, but she doesn't know what's ahead. Listen to what she's thinking. (Cecilia *moves her mouth.*) "When we get married I hope Johnny still has his uniform. We'd look so good together. Me in a wedding gown and him like that. I wish we were getting married tomorrow!"

JOHNNY. What are you thinking?   60

CECILIA. Nothing.

JOHNNY. Come on.

CECILIA. Really.

JOHNNY. Come on, I saw your eyes. Now come on, tell me what you were thinking.

CECILIA. It was nothing.   65

JOHNNY. Are you scared?

CECILIA. About what?

JOHNNY. My going to Vietnam.

CECILIA. No! I mean . . . yes, in a way, but I wasn't thinking that.

JOHNNY. What was it?   70

CECILIA (*Pause*). I was thinking I wish the wedding was tomorrow.

JOHNNY. Really?

CECILIA. Yes.

JOHNNY. You know what? I wish it was too. (*He embraces her.*)

DEATH. And, of course, now he's thinking too. But it's not what she was   75
thinking. What a world!

[THE FATHER *and* THE BROTHER *enter with four chairs.*]

FATHER. Here are the chairs. What did I tell you? (*To* The Brother) Hey, you, help me move the table, come on.

JOHNNY. Do you need help, pa?

FATHER. No, son, your brother and I'll move it. (*He and* The Brother *move imaginary table into place.*) There it is. And your mom says you should start sitting down because dinner's ready. She made tamales, can you believe that?

JOHNNY. Tamales?

BROTHER. They're Colonel Sanders, eeehh.   80

FATHER. You shut your trap! Look ... don't pay attention to him, Cecilia; this little bugger, uh, this kid is always saying stupid things, uh, silly things. Sit down.

MOTHER (*entering with imaginary bowl*). Here come the tamales! Watch out because the pot's hot, okay? Oh, Cecilia, good evening.

CECILIA. Good evening, ma'am. Can I help you with anything?

MOTHER. No, no, everything's ready. Sit down, please.

JOHNNY. Ma, how come you made tamales? (Death *begins to put some*   85
more makeup on Johnny's *face.*)

MOTHER. Well, because I know you like them so much, son.

DEATH. A thought flashes across Johnny's mind: "Too much, man. I should go to war every day." Over on this side of the table, the little brother is thinking: "What's so hot about going to war—tamales?"

BROTHER. I like tamales.

FATHER. Who told you to open your mouth? Would you like a beer, son?

JOHNNY (*nods*). Thanks, dad.   90

FATHER. And you, Cecilia?

CECILIA (*surprised*). No, sir, uh, thanks.

MOTHER. Juan, don't be so thoughtless. Cecilia's not old enough to drink. What are her parents going to say? I made some Kool-Aid, sweetheart; I'll bring the pitcher right out. (*She exits.*)

DEATH. You know what's going through the little brother's mind? He is thinking: "He offered her a beer! She was barely in the eighth grade three years ago. When I'm 17 I'm going to join the service and get really drunk."

FATHER. How old are you, Cecilia?   95

CECILIA. Eighteen.

DEATH. She lied, of course.

FATHER. Oh, well, what the heck, you're already a woman! Come on son, don't let her get away.

JOHNNY. I'm not.

MOTHER (*re-entering*). Here's the Kool-Aid and the beans.   100

JOHNNY. Ma, I got an announcement to make. Will you please sit down?

MOTHER. What is it?

FATHER (*to* The Brother). Give your chair to your mother.

BROTHER. What about my tamale?

MOTHER. Let him eat his dinner.   105

FATHER (*to* The Brother). Get up!

JOHNNY. Sit down, Mom.

MOTHER. What is it, son? (*She sits down.*)

DEATH. Funny little games people play, ha? The mother asks, but she already knows what her son is going to say. So does the father. And even little brother. They are all thinking: "He is going to say: Cecilia and I are getting married!"

JOHNNY. Cecilia and I are getting married!   *110*

MOTHER. Oh, son!

FATHER. You don't say!

BROTHER. Really?

MOTHER. When, son?

JOHNNY. When I get back from Vietnam.   *115*

DEATH. Suddenly a thought is crossing everybody's mind: "What if he doesn't come back?" But they shove it aside.

MOTHER. Oh, darling! (*She hugs Cecilia.*)

FATHER. Congratulations, son. (*He hugs Johnny.*)

MOTHER (*hugging Johnny*). My boy! (*She cries.*)

JOHNNY. Hey, mom, wait a minute. Save that for tomorrow. That's   *120*
enough, ma.

FATHER. Daughter. (*He hugs Cecilia properly.*)

BROTHER. Heh, Johnny, why don't I go to Vietnam and you stay here for the wedding? I'm not afraid to die.

MOTHER. What makes you say that, child?

BROTHER. It just came out.

FATHER. You've let out too much already, don't you think?   *125*

BROTHER. I didn't mean it! (The Brother *exits.*)

JOHNNY. It was an accident, pa.

MOTHER. You're right; it was an accident. Please, sweetheart, let's eat in peace, ha? Juan leaves tomorrow.

DEATH. The rest of the meal goes by without any incidents. They discuss the wedding, the tamales, and the weather. Then it's time to go to the party.

FATHER. Is it true there's going to be a party?   *130*

JOHNNY. Just a small dance, over at Sapo's house.

MOTHER. Which Sapo, son?

JOHNNY. Sapo, my friend.

FATHER. Don't get drunk, okay?

JOHNNY. Oh, come on, dad, Cecilia will be with me.   *135*

FATHER. Did you ask her parents for permission?

JOHNNY. Yes, sir. She's got to be home by eleven.

FATHER. Okay. (Johnny *and* Cecilia *rise.*)

CECILIA. Thank you for the dinner, ma'am.

MOTHER. You're very welcome.   *140*

CECILIA. The tamales were really good.

JOHNNY. Yes, ma, they were terrific.

MOTHER. Is that right, son? You liked them?

JOHNNY. They were great. (*He hugs her.*) Thanks, eh?

MOTHER. What do you mean thanks? You're my son. Go then, it's *145* getting late.

FATHER. Do you want to take the truck, son?

JOHNNY. No thanks, pa. I already have Cecilia's car.

CECILIA. Not mine. My parents' car. They loaned it to us for the dance.

FATHER. It seems like you made a good impression, eh?

CECILIA. He sure did. They say he's more responsible now that he's in *150* the service.

DEATH (*to audience*). Did you hear that? Listen to her again.

CECILIA (*repeats sentence, exactly as before*). They say he's more responsible now that he's in the service.

DEATH. That's what I like to hear!

FATHER. That's good. Then all you have to do is go ask for Cecilia's hand, right, sweetheart?

MOTHER. God willing. *155*

JOHNNY. We're going, then.

CECILIA. Good night.

FATHER. Good night.

MOTHER. Be careful on the road, children.

JOHNNY. Don't worry, mom. Be back later. *160*

CECILIA. Bye!

[JOHNNY *and* CECILIA *exit.* THE MOTHER *stands at the door.*]

FATHER (*sitting down again*). Well, old lady, little Johnny has become a man. The years fly by, don't they?

DEATH. The old man is thinking about the Korean War. Johnny was born about that time. He wishes he had some advice, some hints, to pass on to him about war. But he never went to Korea. The draft skipped him, and somehow, he never got around to enlisting. (The Mother *turns around.*)

MOTHER (*She sees* Death). Oh, my God! (*Exit*)

DEATH (*ducking down*). Damn, I think she saw me. *165*

FATHER. What's wrong with you? (The Mother *is standing frozen, looking toward the spot where* Death *was standing.*) Answer me, what's up? (*Pause*) Speak to me! What am I, invisible?

MOTHER (*solemnly*). I just saw Death.

FATHER. Death? You're crazy.

MOTHER. It's true. As soon as Juan left, I turned around and there was Death, standing—smiling! (The Father *moves away from the spot inadvertently.*) Oh, Blessed Virgin Mary, what if something happens to Juan.

FATHER. Don't say that! Don't you know it's bad luck? *170*

[*They exit.* DEATH *re-enters.*]

[*The Greyhound Bus Depot.*]

DEATH. The next day, Johnny goes to the Greyhound Bus Depot. His mother, his father, and his girlfriend go with him to say goodbye. The Bus Depot is full of soldiers and sailors and old men. Here and there, a drunkard is passed out on the benches. Then there's the announcements: THE LOS ANGELES BUS IS NOW RECEIVING PASSENGERS AT GATE TWO, FOR KINGSBURG, TULARE, DELANO, BAKERSFIELD AND LOS ANGELES, CONNECTIONS IN L.A. FOR POINTS EAST AND SOUTH.

[JOHNNY, FATHER, MOTHER, *and* CECILIA *enter.* CECILIA *clings to* JOHNNY.]

FATHER. It's been several years since I last set foot at the station.
MOTHER. Do you have your ticket, son?
JOHNNY. Oh, no, I have to buy it.
CECILIA. I'll go with you.   *175*
FATHER. Do you have money, son?
JOHNNY. Yes, pa, I have it.

[JOHNNY *and* CECILIA *walk over to* DEATH.]

JOHNNY. One ticket, please.
DEATH. Where to?
JOHNNY. Vietnam. I mean, Oakland.   *180*
DEATH. Round trip or one way?
JOHNNY. One way.
DEATH. Right. One way. (*Applies more makeup.*)

[JOHNNY *gets his ticket and he and* CECILIA *start back toward his parents.* JOHNNY *stops abruptly and glances back at* DEATH, *who has already shifted positions.*]

CECILIA. What's wrong?
JOHNNY. Nothing. (*They join the parents.*)   *185*
DEATH. For half an hour then, they exchange small talk and trivialities, repeating some of the things that have been said several times before. Cecilia promises Johnny she will be true to him and wait until he returns. Then it's time to go: THE OAKLAND-VIETNAM EXPRESS IS NOW RECEIVING PASSENGERS AT GATE NUMBER FOUR. ALL ABOARD PLEASE.
JOHNNY. That's my bus.
MOTHER. Oh, son.
FATHER. Take good care of yourself then, okay, son?
CECILIA. I love you, Johnny. (*She embraces him.*)   *190*
DEATH. THE OAKLAND-VIETNAM EXPRESS IS IN THE FINAL BOARDING STAGES. PASSENGERS WITH TICKETS ALL

ABOARD PLEASE. AND THANKS FOR GOING GREY-
HOUND.

JOHNNY. I'm leaving, now.

[*Embraces all around, weeping, last goodbyes, etc.* JOHNNY *exits. Then parents exit.* THE MOTHER *and* CECILIA *are crying.*]

DEATH (*sings*). *Goodbye, Goodbye*
           Star of my nights
           A soldier said in front of a window
           I'm leaving, I'm leaving
           But don't cry, my angel
           For tomorrow I'll be back . . .

So Johnny left for Vietnam, never to return. He didn't want to go and yet he did. It never crossed his mind to refuse. How can he refuse the government of the United States? How could he refuse his family? Besides, who wants to go to prison? And there was the chance he'd come back alive . . . wounded maybe, but alive. So he took a chance—and lost. But before he died he saw many things in Vietnam; he had his eyes opened. He wrote his mother about them.

[JOHNNY *and* THE MOTHER *enter at opposite sides of the stage.* JOHNNY *is in full battle gear. His face is now a skull.*]

JOHNNY. Dear mom.

MOTHER. Dear son.   *195*

JOHNNY. I am writing this letter.

MOTHER. I received your letter.

JOHNNY. To tell you I'm okay.

MOTHER. And I thank the heavens you're all right.

JOHNNY. How's everybody over there?   *200*

MOTHER. Here, we're all doing fine, thank God.

JOHNNY. Ma, there's a lot happening here that I didn't know about before. I don't know if I'm allowed to write about it, but I'm going to try. Yesterday we attacked a small village near some rice paddies. We had orders to kill everybody because they were supposed to be V-C's, communists. We entered the small village and my buddies started shooting. I saw one of them kill an old man and an old lady. My sergeant killed a small boy about seven years old, then he shot his mother or some woman that came running up crying. Blood was everywhere. I don't remember what happened after that but my sergeant ordered me to start shooting. I think I did. May God forgive me for what I did, but I never wanted to come over here. They say we have to do it to defend our country.

MOTHER. Son what you are writing to us makes me sad. I talked to your father and he also got very worried, but he says that's what war is like. He reminds you that you're fighting communists. I have a candle lit and everyday I ask God to take good care of you wherever you are and that he return you to our arms healthy and in one piece.

JOHNNY. Ma, I had a dream the other night. I dreamed I was breaking into one of the hooches, that's what we call the Vietnamese's houses. I went in firing my M–16 because I knew that the village was controlled by the gooks. I killed three of them right away, but when I looked down it was my pa, my little brother and you, mother. I don't know how much more I can stand. Please tell Sapo and all the dudes how it's like over here. Don't let them . . .

[DEATH *fires a gun, shooting* JOHNNY *in the head. He falls.* THE MOTHER *screams without looking at* JOHNNY.]

DEATH. Johnny was killed in action November 1965 at Chu Lai. His *205* body lay in the field for two days and then it was taken to the beach and placed in a freezer, a converted portable food locker. Two weeks later he was shipped home for burial.

[DEATH *straightens out* JOHNNY'S *body. Takes his helmet, rifle, etc.* THE FATHER, THE MOTHER, THE BROTHER, *and* CECILIA *file past and gather around the body. Taps plays.*]

The Responsive Reader

1. Death plays a major role in Mexican folklore and custom. What is the role of Death in this play? What is the role of the soldier's family?
2. Does this play make a political statement about the war? Where and how?
3. In your judgment, would this play appeal primarily to Mexican Americans? Or does it have universal appeal?
4. How do you relate to the humor in this play? What are its targets? How does it affect the tone of the play?

Talking, Listening, Writing

5. Are the people in this play too passive in their acceptance of what is in store for them?
6. Have people in our society become jaded about the arguments of antiwar or pacifist groups? What would you say to a group of people to make them pay renewed attention to warnings about war? Or what would you answer if someone approached you with a plea to join an antiwar group?
7. Have you lost someone close to you as the result of war, illness, accident? Write a tribute to the person.

Collaborative Projects

8. Valdez' text is well suited for a mini-production designed to bring the play to life for an audience and help them get into the spirit of

the play. (One class production changed the GI in the Valdez play to a young woman and the war to the "Desert Storm" war against Iraq.) You and your classmates may want to organize a group project to stage your own reenactment of the Valdez play.

WRITING
WORKSHOP 10

Writing to Persuade

Persuasion is the art of changing the reader's mind—and changing the reader's ways. A persuasive writer does not just want readers to say, "This is good to know," or "I sympathize with your problem," or "I have had the same experience myself." Much persuasive writing tries to influence behavior. It instigates action—a sale, a contribution, a vote. However, much persuasive writing also aims at a change of attitude—a different attitude toward women in the workplace, a raised consciousness about sexual harassment, or a more active concern about homophobia among gay-bashing young males.

TRIGGERING Persuasive writing often has a special urgency. It serves a personal need or agenda. People who are concerned or aggrieved feel they need to make their voices heard so that something will be done.

- *Much persuasive writing asks us to help correct specific abuses.* When a family member or close friend has been killed by a drunk driver, people may want to transform their impotent rage into corrective action. They may join an organization pressuring legislators for stiffer penalties and tougher enforcement. They may join in letter-writing campaigns, writing letters to newspapers, local officials, or their representatives in Congress.

- *Much persuasive writing enlists our support for the good cause.* For people who live in a crime-ridden, drug-infested society, issues like gun control are not academic questions. People write about issues like gun control, prison reform, or AIDS counseling because they want us to care.

- *Much persuasive writing aims at a change of heart.* Writers may plead with their readers when they see their group or society at large taking a wrong turn. They plead for a return to traditional values, or an end to the degradation of our natural environment, or compassion for the down and out.

- *Much persuasive writing is advocacy.* It asks us to help defend people accused or to support an official or candidate. It aims at clearing someone's name or bringing the guilty to justice.

GATHERING What kind of material will sway your readers? If you respect their intelligence, you will make sure you know relevant facts, understand arguments pro and con, and respect the right of others to disagree. However, although your writing will have to be intellectually respectable, it will also have to *move* your readers. It will have to arouse their concern; it will have to activate their loyalties or sympathy. It will have to break through the crust of apathy. Look at the kinds of materials that persuasive writers use to reach and influence their intended audience:

- *Persuasive writers establish their authority.* You will have to show your involvement and commitment. You will have to show you know enough about the subject; you have earned the right to speak up. As with other kinds of papers, you may want to start by taking stock of your own relevant experiences, memories, thoughts, and feelings. Suppose you want to plead for heightened awareness of rape as a major social issue in our society. The following might be your **cluster** charting associations that the term *rape* brings to mind:

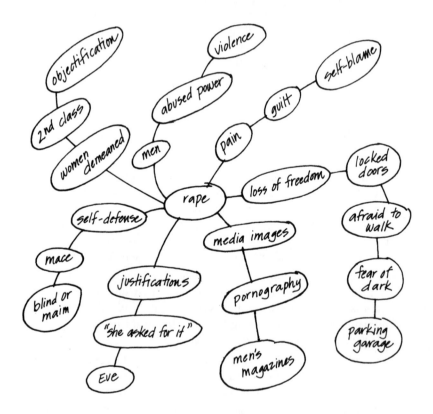

What kind of paper might this cluster generate? What major points would it touch on?

- *Persuasive writers dramatize the issue.* They may start with a dramatic incident that will shake up the blasé reader. Even frightening statistics may remain impersonal and colorless; they cannot compete with the impact of a real-life story like the following:

I remember being awakened at about four o'clock in the morning. My parents told me they were leaving for the hospital—my brother-in-law had been shot. He had been at a small all-night store that night buying some milk. A quarrel started in the store. As he stepped out to avoid the whole scene, a car pulled up with three men inside. One of the men in the car shot him, putting a bullet through his head. Art is now partially paralyzed in his left leg and arm, and he has restricted speech and vision.

Because there is little or no restriction on the purchase or use of guns, innocent people are killed or maimed every day. . . .

- *Persuasive writers appeal to shared values.* They compile examples and statistics that will arouse the indignation or activate the loyalties of the reader. Look at the following skeleton of a paper attacking the huge damage awards assessed against businesses and individuals accused of negligence. What are the standards or values that the writer appeals to in each successive section of the paper?

Are You Insured?

Courts are going out of their way to do away with traditional standards of fairness and shared responsibility. Increasingly, courts are disallowing the traditional defense of contributory negligence. One case involved a man who strapped a refrigerator on his back and ran a stunt footrace. One of the straps failed, and he collected $1 million from the strap manufacturer.

Little attention is paid to the limited financial resources of small businesses or of individuals. The costs of litigation and the enormous damage awards are driving small companies to the wall. . . .

The effects on the pharmaceutical industry are especially harmful. Liability for rare side effects is driving many manufacturers out of the vaccine market, even in cases where medical opinion agrees that the good the vaccines do far outweighs the possible harm. Vaccines (such as those for diphtheria and tetanus) for children are steadily climbing in price. . . .

Who benefits from the inflation of damage awards? The big winners (in case you had any doubts) are the lawyers. A Rand study found that a typical court case costs $380,000, of which $125,000 went to the defense lawyers, $114,000 to the plaintiff's lawyers, and $141,000 in net compensation to the plaintiff.

- *Persuasive writers often use a key example to clinch an argument.* They discuss a test case in graphic detail. A reader who is already predisposed to think of tests as culturally biased is likely to remember a striking example like the following:

Consider this question from a standardized group IQ test. "No garden is without its _____." The desired answer is one of these five:
"sun-rain-tool-work-weeds." A child who happens to know the expression will recognize the missing word (weeds) and complete the
sentence "correctly." If he doesn't have that piece of information,
he'll have to figure out the answer. He might explain to a tester, "It
isn't 'tools' because I once planted a garden with my hands." But
there is no tester to tell. He might continue, "I don't know how to
choose between sun and rain, so I won't use either one." Again
there's no tester to hear his reasoning. "So it's either 'work' or
'weeds.'" Another pause. "Well, if a gardener worked hard, maybe
he wouldn't have any weeds—but, if he doesn't work at all, he won't
have any garden!" Triumphantly, the clever, logical, analytical young
mind has selected—the wrong answer!

When a computer grades that test, "work" will simply be
marked wrong, and no one will be there to explain the thought
process to the computer. Nor will anyone point out the differences
between the child who has personal experience with gardens and
the child whose closest contact may be the city park, ten blocks
away from his fire escape.   *Arlene Silberman, "The Tests That Cheat Our
Children," McCall's*

▪ *Persuasive writers exploit the weaknesses of the opposition.* They look for
contradictions. They look for a contrast between public pronouncements
and actual practice. The author of the following excerpt took aim at an
ironic discrepancy he saw between enlightened humanitarian ideals and
personal behavior:

Among trendy young professionals in our major cities, there is
no stigma attached to using cocaine. In particular, the hip lawyers,
doctors, movie stars, and so on who use the drug are not deterred,
or even bothered much, by the mere fact that it happens to be illegal.
But perhaps they will be receptive to a more fashionable approach.
After all, many cocaine consumers are the same sort of people who
will boycott lettuce or grapes because farm workers are underpaid,
or a cosmetic because the company tortures rabbits, or tuna to protest the killing of dolphins. . . .

Murder is as much a part of cocaine culture as tiny silver
spoons and rolled-up hundred-dollar bills. There is seldom a major
coke bust that doesn't also turn up an arsenal of automatic weapons.
In a recent year in Miami, the cocaine capital of the Northern
Hemisphere, a quarter of the city's 614 murders were committed
with machine guns.   *David Owen, "Boycott Cocaine," Harper's*

SHAPING A basic strategy in much persuasive writing—as in advertising and propaganda—is insistence. Often a writer will pile on graphic
examples, keeping after the reader. Sooner or later, even a reluctant reader

may begin to say: "I see what you mean. I didn't realize things were this bad or the needs this great."

To make your plea as effective as possible, try to spell out the heart of your message in pointed, memorable language:

Of all the drug problems afflicting our society, heroin is the most deadly. Once addicted, the user needs cash to feed the habit. The males steal and rob. The women become shoplifters and prostitutes.

Remember that much effective persuasion builds to a climax. The writer leads up to a high point or saves an especially telling example for the last. A paper pleading for allowing the terminally ill to "go in peace" took up in turn the traditions of the medical profession and the cases of a hypothetical comatose patient, a brain-dead accident victim, and a patient with terminal cancer. But the paper saved for the end the case of a person close to the student writer:

My grandmother asked what I would do when it came time for her to die. I told her I would weep for her and be very sad, but I would remember how she lived. For me, this means that I could not let her linger in a life in between with machines and tubes. I must respect her wishes concerning how she wants to die. She must be able to go in peace the way she plans, not the way a doctor plans. She chose the way she lived, and with my help she will choose the way she dies.

REVISING Pleas written in the heat of passion or indictments written in the first flush of anger are best allowed to cool a day or two. Remember that a strong plea may seem shrill and biased when sent out unedited. When revising a persuasive paper, consider advice like the following:

- *Focus your enthusiasm or channel your anger.* Do not scatter your shots. Do not flail out indiscriminately at miscellaneous abuses or multiple villains. Make sure your paper does not read like a mere inventory of grievances. Concentrate on worthy targets, and do them justice.

- *Do not make weighty charges lightly.* Use strong words like *corruption* or *deceit* only after due deliberation and when you are sure of your target. Accusations made without the necessary backup often backfire.

- *Reconsider strongly charged language.* When we are passionately committed to a cause, we naturally use emotional language. But consider that wildly enthusiastic language can seem immature or overdone. Abusive language can weaken your cause when it alienates fair-minded readers. Revise any labels that might be considered condescending or offensive.

- *Revise* ad hominem *attacks.* In other words, be wary of using arguments directed "against the person." Broad hints about an opponent's divorce, troubled private life, or medical history may gain an advantage, but they may also alienate fair-minded people. Do without remarks about a person's baldness, obesity, accent, or limp.

How persuasive is the following sample paper? How much depends on the audience? What is the overall pattern or strategy adopted by the writer? Does anything in the paper have a special effect on you?

Justice

Three years ago I signed up to be a Big Sister to an eight-year-old girl through the Big Brothers/Big Sisters agency of the county. When the caseworker matched me with Sonia she warned me that Sonia's mother had decreed two topics as taboo for Sonia: sex and her father. I could somewhat understand the mother's prudery about sex, although I disagreed with it. But I was surprised and intrigued when the caseworker told me that Sonia's father was in a state prison, sentenced to death. I pitied the girl, wondering how she felt about having a father who brought her shame.

Sonia has rarely mentioned sex, so that part of the agreement was easy to keep. However, although I never brought up the subject of her father, I discussed how she felt about him whenever she wanted to discuss him. After about three months of seeing each other, Sonia told me that she had been to the movie *Pinocchio* as a very little girl but she didn't remember it. She explained that she had fallen asleep in the car and her father had carried her into the theater, held her as she slept through the movie, and carried her out again. I was astonished that she had a warm memory of trusting a man who had raped and brutally killed two teenage girls. Then she said that she liked visiting him in jail because she and her brothers got to eat a lot at the prison. I didn't discourage her from talking; I was discovering that she loved her father and was not ashamed of him.

Not only does Sonia love her father, but she has the same need to idealize him as all children need to admire their parents. I remember being moved once when she startled me as we were driving downtown by pointing to a tall building and exclaiming, "There's my daddy's cell." I was confused, so I asked her to explain. She told me that he wasn't there at that time but he had spent some time in jail in the city and she remembered visiting him there. She had pointed with pride to a building she associated with her father, just as another child might say excitedly, "There's my daddy's office." I realized that her father, a vicious killer, was loved and needed. If capital punishment is reinstated in the state, she will lose her father and she will have to shift through an immense burden of conflicting feelings—grief, anger, shame, confusion. His death would help no one. His victims are already dead and his death can't bring them back. Perhaps their relatives want justice, but his death is not justice. It would simply be vengeance. By killing him, we can't bring back the innocent; we can only hurt more innocent people.

I have always been opposed to capital punishment. I believe that, as a society, our role is to care for and protect each other. When one of our members hurts others, we remove him or her from the rest. But killing that person as punishment seems to be sinking to a low level of ethics. Policies of vengeance and "an eye for an eye" morality serve only to escalate violence. We forbid people from killing each other, yet as a legal institution, society dictates that killing is acceptable only when it deems it necessary, as in times of war and as punishment for crimes. I believe that if, as a society, we refuse to accept violence among ourselves and refuse to punish the violent with death, we are carrying out a commitment to peace and non-violence.

Sonia has two pictures hanging in her bedroom that her father painted for her while imprisoned. One is of an Indian girl and the other of an eagle flying above a canyon. Sonia has told me that her father has painted a mural at the prison, as well. Perhaps she idealizes him in her ignorance; most people are guilty of idealizing imperfect people. Yet Sonia will be faced with the much harder job of reconciling her love for her father with the reality that he is a criminal. Most children only have to realize that their caretakers aren't strong, all-knowing, and perfect. To increase this child's pain for the sake of saving tax dollars or of satisfying the understandable, but impossible to achieve, needs for revenge that some people have, would be tragic. Allowing Sonia's father to live would save his family more pain, and it would allow our society to rise above ethics based on violence and revenge.

Topics for Persuasion Papers (A Sampling)

1. Write a fund-raising letter to help support a cause to which you are committed. Or, write a letter in defense of someone unjustly accused.
2. Have there been recent initiatives concerning gun control in your community or state? Write a persuasive paper designed to influence votes on this issue.
3. Do you have strong feelings about the "right to die"? Present your position, trying to persuade those who might disagree.
4. Do you feel strongly about an issue like child abuse, domestic violence, rape prevention, the treatment of rape victims, or marital rape? Write a paper designed to arouse readers who in your opinion are too unconcerned or uncommitted on the issue.
5. What would you say to young people who have gang affiliations or who might get involved in youth gangs?
6. Write a letter to officials in which you call for stricter supervision of, or more official support for, the local police.
7. Can you persuade skeptical readers that talk about family values is more than election year rhetoric?
8. Are we as a society becoming too callous about the poor, the homeless, or the sick? How would you appeal to your reader's conscience?
9. What needs to be done to lessen violence in our communities? Try to persuade a skeptical or disillusioned reader.
10. Should anything be done to counteract Americans' addiction to violent sports or violent entertainment?

11

Environment: Participating in Nature

Once we live no longer beneath our mothers' hearts, it is the earth with which we form the same dependent relationship, relying completely on its cycles and elements, helpless without its protective embrace.

—*Louise Erdrich*

There is power in an antelope, but not in a goat or in a sheep, which holds still while you butcher it, which will eat your newspaper if you let it. There was a great power in a wolf, even in a coyote. You have made him into a freak—a toy poodle, a Pekingese, a lap dog.

—*John (Fire) Lame Deer*

A central goal of Western culture has been to tame and control nature. Progress meant advances in freeing humanity from hunger and disease. It meant release from back-breaking toil in the fields to wrest meager crops from the earth. Without technology, one of its defenders has said, a human being would be a naked ape—at the mercy of droughts, floods, blights, and epidemics. Cities would cease to exist, with bands of survivors roaming the countryside and plundering and scrounging for food.

In recent times, however, many voices have expressed second thoughts about the blessings of our technological civilization. Our technology, our modern lifestyle, has increasingly isolated us from contact with the natural world. Air-conditioned buildings isolate us from the changing winds and the fresh air. We walk on asphalt and concrete rather than on sand or grass. We fly over prairies and rivers and mountains with the windows closed, watching a Hollywood movie. The toxic byproducts of our technological civilization are poisoning the rivers, the oceans, the air.

Many have turned to other cultural traditions to search for a different sense of the relationship between humanity and nature. Other cultures have envisioned a more organic relation between human civilization and the natural world. They have or had a better sense of the interdependence of creatures. Some cultures have taught human beings to look at all living things with reverence. Their myths or religious traditions kept people in touch with their roots in the natural world.

In recent years, an active ecological movement has tried to reverse the trend toward the heedless exploitation and destruction of our natural environment. Environmental activists have tried to block floating factories that were decimating fish populations or to stop logging companies that were clear-cutting ancient forests. Politicians and self-styled "hard-nosed" business leaders have begun to reckon with those agitating to preserve the wilderness or crusading for clean water and clean air.

Is it true that Western industrial civilization is at war with nature and is bound to destroy our natural environment? Is it possible for people in the modern world to live in harmony with nature?

LISTENING TO THE AIR
John (Fire) Lame Deer and Richard Erdoes

In the lore of the West, Native Americans have been seen through chang-ing prisms reflecting contradictory images. They were often seen as "savages" needing the blessings of Western culture to become civilized and fully human. However, they have also been seen as people living close to nature, with a respect for the land and for the animals that nourished them, and with a reverence for the life-giving forces of the natural world that the exploitative, technocratic, technology-dominated white culture had lost. John (Fire) Lame Deer, who published Lame Deer, Seeker of Visions *with Richard Erdoes in 1972, is one of many voices asking other Americans to reexamine their assumptions about the superiority of the dominant white civilization. Richard Erdoes, an illustrator and photographer, met Lame Deer when on an assign-ment for* Life *magazine on a Sioux reservation. Lame Deer mentions the Washita Massacre in what is now Oklahoma (1868), the Sand Creek Mas-sacre in Colorado (1864), and the battle at Wounded Knee in South Dakota (1890)—encounters in which the U.S. Cavalry or local militia broke the resistance of the Cheyenne and the Sioux, killing men, women, and children. Lame Deer compares these massacres to the killings at My Lai in Vietnam, where American GIs "wasted" several hundred Vietnamese, many of them women and their children.*

Thought Starters: Do you feel cut off from nature? How do you feel about poodles or Pekingese dogs? How do you feel about wolves or coyotes?

Let's sit down here, all of us, on the open prairie, where we can't see   *1* a highway or a fence. Let's have no blankets to sit on, but feel the ground with our bodies, the earth, the yielding shrubs. Let's have the grass for a mattress, experiencing its sharpness and its softness. Let us become like stones, plants, and trees. Let us be animals, think and feel like animals.

Listen to the air. You can hear it, feel it, smell it, taste it. *Woniya waken*—the holy air—which renews all by its breath. *Woniya, woniya waken*—spirit, life, breath, renewal—it means all that. *Woniya*—we sit to-gether, don't touch, but something is there; we feel it between us, as a presence. A good way to start thinking about nature, talk about it. Rather talk to it, talk to the rivers, to the lakes, to the winds as to our relatives.

You have made it hard for us to experience nature in the good way by being part of it. Even here we are conscious that somewhere out in those hills there are missile silos and radar stations. White men always pick the few unspoiled, beautiful, awesome spots for the sites of these abominations. You have raped and violated these lands, always saying, "Gimme, gimme, gimme," and never giving anything back. You have taken 200,000 acres of our Pine Ridge reservation and made them into a bombing range. This land is so beautiful and strange that now some of you want to make it into a national park. The only use you have made of this land since you took it from us was to blow it up. You have not only despoiled the earth, the rocks, the minerals, all of which you call "dead" but which are very much alive; you have even changed the animals, which are part of us, part of the Great Spirit, changed them in a horrible way, so no one can recognize them. There is power in a buffalo—spiritual, magic power—but there is no power in an Angus, in a Hereford.

There is power in an antelope, but not in a goat or in a sheep, which holds still while you butcher it, which will eat your newspaper if you let it. There was great power in a wolf, even in a coyote. You have made him into a freak—a toy poodle, a Pekingese, a lap dog. You can't do much with a cat, which is like an Indian, unchangeable. So you fix it, alter it, declaw it, even cut its vocal cords so you can experiment on it in a laboratory without being disturbed by its cries.

A partridge, a grouse, a quail, a pheasant, you have made them into 5 chickens, creatures that can't fly, that wear a kind of sunglasses so that they won't peck each other's eyes out, "birds" with a "pecking order." There are some farms where they breed chickens for breast meat. Those birds are kept in low cages, forced to be hunched over all the time, which makes the breast muscles very big. Soothing sounds, Muzak, are piped into these chicken hutches. One loud noise and the chickens go haywire, killing themselves by flying against the mesh of their cages. Having to spend all their lives stooped over makes an unnatural, crazy, no-good bird. It also makes unnatural, no-good human beings.

That's where you fooled yourselves. You have not only altered, declawed, and malformed your winged and four-legged cousins; you have done it to yourselves. You have changed men into chairmen of boards, into office workers, into time-clock punchers. You have changed women into housewives, truly fearful creatures. I was once invited into the home of such a one.

"Watch the ashes, don't smoke, you stain the curtains. Watch the goldfish bowl, don't breathe on the parakeet, don't lean your head against the wallpaper; your hair may be greasy. Don't spill liquor on that table: it has a delicate finish. You should have wiped your boots; the floor was just varnished. Don't, don't, don't . . ." That is crazy. We weren't made to endure this. You live in prisons which you have built for yourselves, calling them "homes," offices, factories. We have a new joke on the reservation: "What is cultural deprivation?" Answer: "Being an upper-middle-class white kid living in a split-level suburban home with a color TV."

Sometimes I think that even our pitiful tar-paper shacks are better than your luxury homes. Walking a hundred feet to the outhouse on a clear wintry night, through mud or snow, that's one small link with nature. Or in the summer, in the back country, leaving the door of the privy open, taking your time, listening to the humming of the insects, the sun warming your bones through the thin planks of wood; you don't even have that pleasure anymore.

Americans want to have everything sanitized. No smells! Not even the good, natural man and woman smell. Take away the smell from under the armpits, from your skin. Rub it out, and then spray or dab some nonhuman odor on yourself, stuff you can spend a lot of money on, ten dollars an ounce, so you know this has to smell good. "B.O.," bad breath, "Intimate Female Odor Spray"—I see it all on TV. Soon you'll breed people without body openings.

I think white people are so afraid of the world they created that they don't want to see, feel, smell, or hear it. The feeling of rain and snow on your face, being numbed by an icy wind and thawing out before a smoking fire, coming out of a hot sweat bath and plunging into a cold stream, these things make you feel alive, but you don't want them anymore. Living in boxes which shut out the heat of the summer and the chill of winter, living inside a body that no longer has a scent, hearing the noise from the hi-fi instead of listening to the sounds of nature, watching some actor on TV having a make-believe experience when you no longer experience anything for yourself, eating food without taste—that's your way. It's no good. 10

The food you eat, you treat it like your bodies, take out all the nature part, the taste, the smell, the roughness, then put the artificial color, the artificial flavor in. Raw liver, raw kidney—that's what we old-fashioned full-bloods like to get our teeth into. In the old days we used to eat the guts of the buffalo, making a contest of it, two fellows getting hold of a long piece of intestines from opposite ends, starting chewing toward the middle, seeing who can get there first; that's eating. Those buffalo guts, full of half-fermented, half-digested grass and herbs, you didn't need any pills and vitamins when you swallowed those. Use the bitterness of gall for flavoring, not refined salt or sugar. *Wasna*—meat, kidney fat, and berries all pounded together—a lump of that sweet *wasna* kept a man going for a whole day. That was food, that had the power. Not the stuff you give us today: powdered milk, dehydrated eggs, pasteurized butter, chickens that are all drumsticks or all breast; there's no bird left there.

You don't want the bird. You don't have the courage to kill honestly—cut off the chicken's head, pluck it and gut it—no, you don't want this anymore. So it all comes in a neat plastic bag, all cut up, ready to eat, with no taste and no guilt. Your mink and seal coats, you don't want to know about the blood and pain which went into making them. Your idea of war—sit in an airplane, way above the clouds, press a button, drop the bombs, and never look below the clouds—that's the odorless, guiltless, sanitized way.

When we killed a buffalo, we knew what we were doing. We apologized to his spirit, tried to make him understand why we did it, honoring with a prayer the bones of those who gave their flesh to keep us alive, praying for their return, praying for the life of our brothers, the buffalo nation, as well as for our own people. You wouldn't understand this and that's why we had the Washita Massacre, the Sand Creek Massacre, the dead women and babies at Wounded Knee. That's why we have Song My and My Lai now.

To us life, all life, is sacred. The state of South Dakota has pest-control officers. They go up in a plane and shoot coyotes from the air. They keep track of their kills, put them all down in their little books. The stockmen and sheepowners pay them. Coyotes eat mostly rodents, field mice and such. Only once in a while will they go after a stray lamb. They are our natural garbage men cleaning up the rotten and stinking things. They make good pets if you give them a chance. But their living could lose some man a few cents, and so the coyotes are killed from the air. They were here before the sheep, but they are in the way; you can't make a profit out of them. More and more animals are dying out. The animals which the Great Spirit put here, they must go. The man-made animals are allowed to stay— at least until they are shipped out to be butchered. That terrible arrogance of the white man, making himself something more than God, more than nature, saying, "I will let this animal live, because it makes money"; saying, "This animal must go, it brings no income, the space it occupies can be used in a better way. The only good coyote is a dead coyote." They are treating coyotes almost as badly as they used to treat Indians.

The Responsive Reader

1. What is Lame Deer's advice to help us get closer to our natural roots? Does it make sense?
2. What, for you, are the major charges in Lame Deer's indictment of white civilization? Can you explain his charges? Are they fair?
3. The buffalo and the coyote play a major role in Native American tradition. What role do they play in this account?

Talking, Listening, Writing

4. Have you observed, or participated in, attempts to bring people closer to unspoiled countryside and animals in the wild? What did you learn from your observations or experiences?
5. What would you say in defense of domesticated animals and pets?
6. Do you agree with people who say that the extermination or displacement of the Native American tribes was "inevitable"—no dif-

ferent from other nations' striking out in search of new lands for their people?

Collaborative Projects

7. How much has been preserved of Native American myth or folklore (and by whom)? How accessible is it? What light does it shed on the relationship of the tribes to nature, to the land, to the animals? (For instance, what is the role of the coyote in Native American lore?) Working with a group, try to find answers to questions like these. Your group may want to prepare a presentation of poems, songs, and stories from authentic Native American sources.

THE LAST OF THE WILD SALMON

Marie de Santis

We tend to be armchair ecologists who know the threatened wildlife of our planet mostly from television specials. The author of the following article knows the life of the oceans and rivers from close personal observation. De Santis worked for eight years as a commercial fisherwoman and the captain of her own boat. She told her story of the lure of the sea and of the hard work and dangers faced by those who make a living from the sea in her book Neptune's Apprentice *(1984). In the following excerpt from her book* California Currents *(1985), she pays tribute to the wild salmon who are endangered by the destruction of their spawning grounds and the obstacles that dams and polluted or diverted rivers present to their age-old journey upstream. She hated to see the wild salmon replaced by artificially bred fish "no more suited to the stream than a poodle is to the woods." She addressed her book to those who "wish to continue living in a world with real animals" and who want future generations to "see more than the broken spirits of the animals of the zoo."*

Thought Starters: What animal would you choose as the best symbol of the threatened life on our endangered planet?

In a stream so shallow that its full body is no longer submerged in   1
the water, the salmon twists on its side to get a better grip with its tail. Its gillplate is torn, big hunks of skin hang off its sides from collisions with rocks, there are deep gouges in its body, and all around for miles to go there is only the cruelty of more jagged rocks and less and less water to sustain the swim. Surely the animal is dying!

And then the salmon leaps like an arrow shot from a bow; some urge and will and passion ignores the animal body and focuses on the stream.

Of all the extremes of adaptation to the ocean's awful toll on the young, none is more mythic in proportion than the salmon's mighty journey to the mountain streams: a journey that brings life to meet death at a point on a perfect circle, a return through miles of narrowing waters to the exact gravel-bedded streamlet of its birth. A journey to spawning and death, so clear in its resemblance to the migrations of the sperm to the egg as to entwine their meanings in a single reflection.

On every continent of the northern hemisphere, from the temperate zone to the arctic, there is hardly a river that hasn't teemed with the salmon's spawn: the Thames, the Rhine, the rivers of France and Spain, Kamchatka and Siberia, Japan (which alone has more than 200 salmon rivers) and the arctic streams of Greenland. From the Aleutians to Monterey Bay, through the broadest byways to the most rugged and narrow gorge, the salmon have made their way home. There are many journeys for which the salmon endure more than 1000 miles.

As soon as the ice melts on the Yukon, the king salmon enter the river's mouth, and for a month, the fish swim against the current, 50 miles a day for a total of 1500. And like every other salmon on its run, the king salmon fasts completely along the way. In other rivers, salmon scale vertical rocks up to 60 feet high, against hurtling waterfalls.

The salmon gets to spawn once in life, and maybe that's reason enough. The salmon's instinct to return to the place of its birth is so unmodifiable and of such purity as to have inspired hundreds of spiritual rites in as many societies of human beings.

The salmon arrives battered and starved, with a mate chosen along the way, and never has passion seemed less likely from two more wretched-looking beings. But, there in the gravel of the streamlet, the female fans out a nest with the sweep of her powerful tail and the male fends off intruders. The nest done, the two fish lie next to each other suspended in the water over the nest; their bodies quiver with intense vibrations, and simultaneously they throw the eggs and the sperm. Compared with the millions of eggs thrown by a cod in a stream, the salmon need throw only 2000 to 5000. Despite the predators and other hazards of the stream, these cold mountain waters are a sanctuary compared with the sea. For the next two or three days, the pair continue nesting and spawning until all the eggs are laid. Then the salmon, whose journey has spanned the ocean and the stream, lies by the nest and dies.

Soon the banks of the streams are stacked with ragged carcasses, and the animals of the woods come down for a feast. The stream lies quiet in the winter's deepening cold. But within a month two black eyes appear through the skin of each egg. And two weeks later, the water is again alive with the pulsing of millions of small fish feeling the first clumsy kicks of their tails. The fingerlings stay for a while, growing on the insects and larvae that have been nurtured by the forest. Then, one day, they realize what that tail is for and begin their descent to the sea, a journey mapped in their genes by the parents they left behind.

The young salmon arrive in the estuary facing the sea, where they linger again and learn to feed on shrimp, small crustaceans and other creatures of the brine. Here, also, their bodies complete an upheaval of internal and external changes that allow them to move on to the saltier sea. These adaptations require such extraordinary body transformations that when the same events occur on the stage of evolution they take millions and millions of years. In the life of the salmon, the changes take place in only a matter of months. One of life's most prohibitive barriers—that between fresh and salt water—is crossed, and the salmon swim back and forth, in and out of the sea, trying it on for size.

Then one day, the youngsters do not return. The stream is only a dis-   *10*
tant memory drifting further and further back in the wake of time, only
different—a memory that will resurrect and demand that its path be retraced.

So accessible is the salmon's life in the stream that more is known
about the reproduction of this fish than any other ocean animal. With the
ease of placing cameras underwater, there isn't any aspect of this dramatic
cycle that hasn't been captured in full color in some of the most spectacular
film footage ever made.

But once the salmon enters the sea, the story of its life is a secret as
deep and dark as the farthest reaches of the ocean it roams. The human
eye with its most sophisticated aids, from satellite to sonar, has never caught
more than a glance of the salmon at sea. Extensive tagging programs have
been carried out, but they tell us little more than that the salmon is likely
to be found anywhere within thousands of miles of its origins, and even
this is only a sliver of the picture because the tags are recovered only when
the salmon is caught by fishermen, who work solely within the narrow
coastal zone. Along with a few other pelagic fishes, like the tuna, that
claim vast stretches of sea for their pasture, the salmon's life remains one of
the most mysterious on earth.

The Responsive Reader

1. What makes the stage of the salmon's life cycle that she describes at
   the beginning the symbolic high point for the author?
2. What are the major stages of the salmon's life journey? What are key
   events or striking details at each stage?

Talking, Listening, Writing

3. For you, does the salmon's life cycle make a good symbolic representation of life on this planet? Why or why not?
4. What plant or animal with an especially rich or varied life cycle have
   you studied or do you know well? Trace it in rich authentic detail,
   emphasizing major stages.
5. Do people, institutions, or ideas have life cycles similar to those de
   Santis observed in the natural world? Focus on one central example,
   and bring it to life for your reader.

Collaborative Projects

6. How successful is the struggle to restore life to lakes and streams poisoned by pollution? What have been notable successes and notable
   failures? What in particular is the current status of attempts to save
   the wild salmon? For a possible research project, work with a group
   to collect and collate data from authoritative sources.

Thinking about Connections

Is the attitude toward nature in this article similar to or different from the attitude toward nature that John (Fire) Lame Deer talks about in "Listening to the Air"?

HEARTS OF OAK

John Vidal

> *The environmentalist movement knows no frontiers. Green parties in the U.S. and in other parts of the world are united in a common cause. Greenpeace volunteers have risked their lives to stop nuclear tests scheduled by the French government in the South Pacific. They have tried to block the operations of Japanese fishing fleets trapping dolphin along with tuna. German ecologists fight pitched battles with police over bulldozers that destroy green spaces in the way of airport expansion or over the transport of radioactive materials to contested storage sites. For many ecologists, saving the forests has become a powerful rallying cry. One of the photographs accompanying the following article showed a protester trapped at the top of a tall birch tree, treed like a raccoon, while a hardhat with a chainsaw was making his way up the trunk of the tree, cutting away the branches as he went along. The protesters were trying to block the cutting down of trees to make way for a bypass through a historic stretch of British countryside. In spite of their efforts, more than 10,000 trees were felled, and 788 people were arrested. Protesters were making plans for Phase Two when actual construction work on the road was scheduled to start. They were planning mass trespassing and "pixie work"— the British term for monkey-wrenching.*

Thought Starters: Have you ever protested against anything? Have you ever joined in an organized protest? What was the issue? What was the result?

It's a bone-chilling midnight in late March, and the only way I can climb the 150-foot Corsican pine tree in Reddings Copse is to "prusik"— to grapple my way up a long rope using two loops of string barely thicker than shoelaces as moveable handholds. I move, fist over fist, toward a square of candlelight showing through a trapdoor 100 feet above me, gingerly bypassing the coils of barbed wire and a precarious bucket of urine. One last heave and I'm in the lowest tree house, a shelter built of old pallets, doors, and beams and hung with hooks, chains, ropes, locks, handcuffs— for people to grab on to when the bailiffs arrive. Here, way above where birds nest, there's no sight of ground.

Thirty feet above us in this, the highest tree for miles around, is a second tree house, and at the very tip of the pine a defiant Union Jack and a rainbow pennant fly from a ladder. From here you can see most of the southern English county of Berkshire. In the dawn mists it's a landscape out of King Arthur: rickety little wooden bridges, old water meadows, oak copses, a slow river. Running through it all is a nine-mile-long, hundred-yard-wide scar of mud and broken trees—the route of the Newbury bypass.

The plan to carve a four-lane highway through this quintessential English landscape has enraged conservationists and the young. Tree house occupations have been an accepted mode of environmental dissent in Britain since a 1994 road protest in London. What's different at Newbury is the sheer size of the action: The first protester started living in the trees more than six months ago and now there are scores of camps, with hundreds of people in tree houses or in "benders" made of bent hazelwood and plastic sheeting on the frozen ground. Some tree houses, like "the Mothership" at the Kennet River camp, stretch across nine or ten trees and have separate kitchens and sleeping areas. Others are no more than "twigloos," fragile nests for one or two people in the highest branches.

This protest is as passionate and sometimes as dangerous as any war or genocide I've covered in 12 years with *The Guardian* of London. The police have warned that they will arrest us on sight if we're found in the trees; attorneys say we risk prison and a criminal record; and the guards say—off the record—that they'll injure us if they can. Worse, one false step on the ice at 100 feet and we will plummet to our deaths.

Tonight this pine will sleep about 15 people. The last defenders will   5
arrive at about 3 a.m. Then we'll drape ourselves around the trunk and huddle next to each other in blankets and sleeping bags donated by well-wishers. A small woodstove will burn, and there will be little sleep as the wind gets up and a light snow drifts in to melt in clouds of breath.

The route of the bypass, which goes within half a mile of the sites of two 17th-century English Civil War battles—the First and Second Battles of Newbury—was picked years ago when the environment wasn't as high on the British political agenda. Now the European Union is supporting the bypass as the last link in a motorway chain that will run from the south of France to Scotland. But it goes through what are supposed to be two of the best-protected nature sites in Britain (protected by the national government, which can rescind the protection when it purchases the land, as it did here) and through land given in trust to the nation. There has been no environmental impact survey. The scheme has united Britain's disparate environmental groups, archaeologists, climbers, walkers, and civil libertarians. The busy market town of Newbury is divided.

But the actual protesters at the site—300 self-styled "eco-warriors" in more than 30 camps along the route—are not your typical middle-class environmentalists. Many in the trees tonight are misfits who live on the margins of the British economy. Greg, who oils his dreadlocks with the sap of fallen pine trees, is an air force officer training dropout. Howie is a neotribal nomad by choice. Balin, a local man, has spent 16 days and nights slung heroically under a tripod made of scaffolding bars. There's also a former art dealer, a philosophy student, a poet, an EU political officer. Local villagers provide the ground support for the camps, opening their homes to the protesters and bringing food and drink. Much of the protest is playful. Bagpipes, flutes, and drums resound. Protesters have dressed up (and been arrested) in cow costumes. One man covers himself in oil so the police can't grab hold of him.

It is first light and the battle has begun. Through the mists emerge 100 policemen and 300 guards, escorting a giant cherrypicker that can reach 200 feet. They are followed by three giant front-end loaders, one carrying fire in its bucket. "It's like Verdi," says one man. "More like a siege," cries another. "They've brought their own damn hell torch."

The protesters screech like Amazonian howler monkeys, raining insults down on their adversaries. "We'd rather die than live like you!" shouts one woman. Within an hour climbers have cut the rope and wire walkways that run between the tree houses. There have been hand to hand fights in five nearby oak trees. Twelve people have been bundled onto mechanical platforms, brought down, and arrested.

Now it's our turn. Greg cuts the only rope down the tree as a state- 10 ment that no one will descend willingly. Mick from Liverpool is at the top of the tree bellowing oaths. "This land is ours," he cries. "Ours," repeats the echo.

The platform of the cherrypicker approaches. The workers test the lower tree house defenses, approaching from below, then from above, clipping the barbed wire and lopping the lower branches as they go. Jim shoves a mop at the chain saw operator to jam up his machine. Rachel hurls paint. Ralph is out on a branch with no safety harness, daring the bailiffs to remove him.

The cherrypicker moves closer, cutting through a hail of rice and flour. The workers begin to saw through the branches that the tree house is roped to. A terrible *crack* shudders the whole tree. There are screams of protest. Now they are cutting within six, within three feet of us. The noise is deafening. Fear mounts.

The battle lasts all morning. Suddenly the platform soars upward, to the top of the tree. The bailiffs detach and carry off the rainbow flag and the Union Jack. Then they leave us in peace.

The protesters have won a round: A bulldozer has accidentally pushed a small oak tree onto the largest machine and damaged it. The guards and police march off with their machinery, and the action moves on to the next camp, where eight trees are occupied. By nightfall 20 more people will have been brought down, arrested, and ordered to keep well away from the battleground. (Miraculously, there have only been two serious injuries in more than two months' high drama.)

The pine stands, its lower branches shorn, its defenses down. The *15*
bailiffs say they will be back for us tomorrow. The tree people put the
kettle on and bring out the drums. "Every cup of tea is a victory," says
Howie. "This is the start of the eco-wars," says Cat. The party will last
through the night.

The Responsive Reader

1. Environmental awareness has become a cliché, with many people
   and organizations at least paying lip service. What makes the protesters described in this article different? What kind of people are
   they? What for you was startling or provocative about their methods
   or their behavior?
2. References to the Union Jack and to the historic battle sites remind
   readers that this confrontation is taking place in Britain and not the
   United States. Do you think the same thing could have happened
   more or less the same way in the United States? Why or why not?

Talking, Listening, Writing

3. In reading about events like this protest, or seeing photographs or
   television coverage, many readers have a gut reaction impelling them
   to take sides with one side or the other. Do you find yourself taking
   sides? Why and how?
4. Do you think protests like the one described in this article do any
   good? Why or why not?

Collaborative Projects

5. Ecological activists have for years been involved in skirmishes with
   conservative European governments. For instance, Greenpeace was
   accused of sinking a French ship, and the French government was
   accused of engineering the sinking of a Greenpeace vessel. Battles
   between helmeted riot police and swarming groups of protesters are
   a regular feature of German television news. Working with a group,
   you may want to prepare a report on recent confrontations.

THE FEMINIZATION OF EARTH FIRST!

Judi Bari

> *For many people in the western United States, a powerful symbol of our threatened natural heritage is the giant redwood trees (*Sequoia sempervirens*) that reach a height of 360 feet. Many of those still standing were already growing at the time of the birth of Christ. In an ominous note, Merriam Webster's Collegiate Dictionary (tenth edition) calls the redwood a "commercially important" timber tree, and for years ecologists and nature lovers have done battle with the logging interests to save the remaining stands of original growth. (Ronald Reagan, then governor of California, once said that if you have seen one redwood you have seen them all.) In the following article from* Ms. *magazine, a committed feminist and social activist talks about the "Redwood Summer," with radical ecologists blocking logging roads and living off the ground in the trees in a last-ditch attempt to save the remnants of the ancient forests. Bari and a close associate had been receiving death threats, and a pipe bomb exploded in their car, injuring her severely. At the instigation of the FBI, local police arrested her as a suspected terrorist who allegedly had been transporting explosives, but no charges were ever filed. At the time of Bari's death of cancer in 1997, her lawsuit charging false arrest and violation of her civil rights was still pending. Rearguard actions to save the remaining old-growth forests of the Northwest were continuing to make headlines.*

Thought Starters: What has been your experience or contact with the ecology movement? Do you think you would have joined in the efforts to save the redwood trees?

It is impossible to live in the redwood region without being profoundly affected by the massive destruction of this once-magnificent ecosystem. Miles and miles of clearcuts cover our bleeding hillsides. Ancient forests are being strip-logged to pay off corporate junk bonds. Log trucks fill our roads, heading to the sawmills with loads ranging from 1,000-year-old redwoods, one tree trunk filling an entire logging truck, to six-inch-diameter baby trees that are chipped for pulp.

So it is not surprising that I, a lifelong activist, would become an environmentalist. What is surprising is that I, a feminist, single mother, and blue-collar worker, would end up in Earth First!, a "no compromise" direct action group with the reputation of being beer-drinking ecodudes.

Little did I know that combining the feminist elements of collectivism and nonviolence with the spunk and outrageousness of Earth First! would spark a mass movement. And little did I know that I would pay for our success by being bombed and nearly killed, and subjected to a campaign of hatred and misogyny.

I was attracted to Earth First! because its activists were the only people willing to put their bodies in front of the bulldozers and chain saws to save the trees. They were also funny and irreverent, and they played music. But it was the philosophy of Earth First! that ultimately won me over. This philosophy, known as biocentrism or deep ecology, states that the Earth is not just here for human consumption. All species have a right to exist for their own sake, and humans must learn to live in balance with the needs of nature instead of trying to mold nature to fit the needs of humans.

I see no contradiction between deep ecology and ecofeminism, but Earth First! was founded by five men, and its principal spokespeople have all been male. As in all such groups, there have always been competent women doing the real work behind the scenes. But they have been virtually invisible behind the public Earth First! persona of "big man goes into big wilderness to save big trees." I certainly objected to this. Yet despite the image, the structure of Earth First! was decentralized and nonhierarchical, so we could develop any way we wanted in our local northern California group.

In many ways the northwest timber country resembles Appalachia   5 more than California. It is sparsely populated and set in mountainous terrain. Some of the more isolated communities are located hours away from the nearest sheriff, and have become virtually lawless areas, with a wild West mentality. The economy is dominated by a few large timber corporations. Louisiana-Pacific, Georgia-Pacific, and Maxxam are the most powerful, and in our impoverished rural communities local government, police, schools, and others all bow to the economic blackmail of King Timber. The town of Scotia, one of the last actual company towns in the U.S., is owned and operated by Maxxam, and you are not allowed to rent a house in Scotia unless you work for the company.

For years the strategy of Earth First!, under male leadership, had been based on individual acts of daring. "Nomadic action groups" of maybe ten people would travel to remote areas and bury themselves in logging roads, chain themselves to heavy equipment, or sit in trees. There were certainly brave and principled women who engaged in these actions. But by and large, most of the people who had the freedom for that kind of travel and risk-taking were men.

I have nothing against individual acts of daring. But the flaw in this strategy is the failure to engage in long-term community-based organizing. There is no way that a few isolated individuals, no matter how brave, can bring about the massive social change necessary to save the planet. So we began to organize with local people, planning our logging blockades around local issues. And we began to build alliances with progressive timber workers based on our common interests against the big corporations. As our success grew, more women and more people with families and roots in the community began calling themselves Earth First!ers in our area.

But as our exposure and influence grew, so did the use of violence against us. At one demonstration a 50-year-old nonviolent woman was punched so hard her nose was broken. In another incident, my car was rammed Karen Silkwood–style by the same logging truck that we had blockaded less than 24 hours earlier. In both these cases, as in other instances of violence against us, local police refused even to investigate our assailants.

Earth First! had never initiated any violence. But I felt we needed a much more explicit nonviolence code in the face of an increasingly volatile situation on the front lines. So, drawing on the lessons of the civil rights movement, we put out a nationwide call for Freedom Riders for the Forest to come to northern California and engage in nonviolent mass actions to stop the slaughter of the redwoods. We called the campaign Redwood Summer and, as it became clear that we were sucessfully drawing national interest, the level of repression escalated again.

I began to receive a series of increasingly frightening death threats, *10* obviously written on behalf of Big Timber. The most frightening was a photo of me with a rifle scope and cross hairs superimposed on my face and a yellow ribbon (the timber industry's symbol) attached. My complaints to the local police and to the county board of supervisors were ignored. Finally, on May 24, 1990, as I was driving through Oakland on a concert tour to promote Redwood Summer, a bomb exploded under my car seat. I remember my thoughts as it ripped through me. I thought, this is what men do to each other in wars.

The bomb was meant to kill me, and it nearly did. It shattered my pelvis and left me crippled for life. My organizing companion, Darryl Cherney, who was riding with me in the car, was slightly injured. Then, adding to the outrage, police and the FBI moved in immediately and arrested Darryl and me, saying that it was our bomb and we were knowingly carrying it. For eight weeks they slandered us in the press, attempting to portray us as violent and to discredit Redwood Summer, until they finally admitted there was no evidence against us.

There were indications in advance that the attack on me was specifically misogynist. One of the death threats described Earth First!ers as "whores, lesbians, and members of NOW." But soon after the bombing a letter was received that left no doubt. It was signed "The Lord's Avenger," and it took credit for the bombing. It described the bomb in exact detail and explained in chilling prose why the Lord's Avenger wanted me dead.

It was not just my "paganism" and defense of the forest that outraged him. The Lord's Avenger also recalled an abortion clinic defense I had led years ago, and quoted Timothy 2:11: "Let the woman learn in silence with all subjection. But I suffer not a woman to teach, nor to usurp authority over the man, but to be in silence."

Meanwhile, out in the forest, Redwood Summer went on without me. Before the bombing I was one of very few women leaders in Earth First! But after the bombing it was the women who rose to take my place. Redwood Summer was the feminization of Earth First!, with three quarters of the leadership made up of women. Our past actions had drawn no more than 150 participants. But 3,000 people came to Redwood Summer, blocking logging operations and marching through timber towns in demonstrations reminiscent of civil rights protests against the Klan in the South. Despite incredible provocation, and despite the grave violence done to me, Earth First! maintained our nonviolence throughout the summer.

Being the first women-led action, Redwood Summer has never got- 15 ten the respect it deserves from the old guard of Earth First! nationally. But it has profoundly affected the redwood region. The 2,000-year-old trees of Headwaters Forest, identified, named, and made an issue of by Earth First!, are now being preserved largely due to our actions. And the movement here, recently renamed Ecotopia Earth First!, is probably the only truly gender-balanced group I have ever worked in.

I recently attended a workshop in Tennessee on violence and harassment in the environmental movement. As the 32 people from all over the country shared their stories, I was struck by the fact that the most serious acts of violence had all been done to women. This is no surprise because it is the hatred of the feminine, which is the hatred of life, that has contributed to the destruction of the planet. And it is the strength of women that can restore the balance we need to survive.

The Responsive Reader

1. Does Bari succeed in making the loss of the redwoods seem urgent to you? What images or details in her account are most likely to overcome the apathy of readers?
2. Bari says that the activists of Earth First! used to be mainly male. What does she admire them for; why or how does she criticize them?
3. The struggle to save the redwoods is often presented as a struggle between "ecofreaks" and logging workers who need jobs. What is Bari's take on the economic dimension of the struggle? What are her views of the workers and the corporations?
4. What did Bari see as her special role or contribution as a woman? What does she mean by the "feminization" of the movement? What does she say about the role of misogyny in the attacks on her and her associates?

Talking, Listening, Writing

5. Can you see yourself as a radical ecologist? (Or would you limit yourself mainly to making contributions to genteel organizations like the Sierra Club?) Where do you draw the line?
6. Where do you stand on the issue of violence or nonviolence in efforts to bring about social change?
7. Where do *you* think the emphasis or the priorities should be in the effort to save the environment?

Collaborative Projects

8. A recent article in *Time* magazine concluded that "green sentiment is again a powerful political force." Working with a group, you may want to investigate a test case like the controversies over logging in the Headwaters redwood groves in California or in Alaska's Tongass National Forest or over clear-cutting in the north woods of Maine. What is involved in the struggle of environmental organizations, corporate interests, and political alliances "over the future of huge tracts of forest land that lie before the logger's axe"?

SAVING NATURE, BUT ONLY FOR MAN

Charles Krauthammer

> *Charles Krauthammer is a conservative columnist who is a frequent contributor to* Time. *As the 500th anniversary of Columbus' voyage to the New World was approaching, Krauthammer published a* Time *essay titled "Hail Columbus, Dead White Male." As is his custom, he skewered what he considers the intellectual fashions of the "politically correct" American left: He attacked the "sentimental" glorification of the natives by writers "singing of the saintedness of the Indians in their pre-Columbian Eden, a land of virtue, empathy, ecological harmony." In the* Time *essay that follows, Krauthammer raises the familiar question of the economic cost of our current commitment to ecology and urges the setting of priorities.*

Thought Starters: Has the environmental movement made a difference? Has it created a backlash?

Environmental sensitivity is now as required an attitude in polite   1
society as is, say, belief in democracy or aversion to polyester. But now that
everyone from Ted Turner to George Bush, Dow to Exxon has professed
love for Mother Earth, how are we to choose among the dozens of conflicting proposals, restrictions, projects, regulations and laws advanced in
the name of the environment? Clearly not everything with an environmental claim is worth doing. How to choose?

There is a simple way. First, distinguish between environmental luxuries and environmental necessities. Luxuries are those things it would be
nice to have if costless. Necessities are those things we must have regardless.
Then apply a rule. Call it the fundamental axiom of sane environmentalism: Combatting ecological change that directly threatens the health and
safety of people is an environmental necessity. All else is luxury.

For example: preserving the atmosphere—stopping ozone depletion
and the greenhouse effect—is an environmental necessity. In April scientists reported that ozone damage is far worse than previously thought.
Ozone depletion not only causes skin cancer and eye cataracts, it also de-
stroys plankton, the beginning of the food chain atop which we humans sit.

The reality of the greenhouse effect is more speculative, though its
possible consequences are far deadlier: melting ice caps, flooded coastlines,
disrupted climate, parched plains and, ultimately, empty breadbaskets. The
American Midwest feeds the world. Are we prepared to see Iowa acquire
New Mexico's desert climate? And Siberia acquire Iowa's?

Ozone depletion and the greenhouse effect are human disasters. They   *5*
happen to occur in the environment. But they are urgent because they
directly threaten man. A sane environmentalism, the only kind of environmentalism that will win universal public support, begins by unashamedly
declaring that nature is here to serve man. A sane environmentalism is
entirely anthropocentric: it enjoins man to preserve nature, but on the
grounds of self-preservation.

A sane environmentalism does not sentimentalize the earth. It does
not ask people to sacrifice in the name of other creatures. After all, it is
hard enough to ask people to sacrifice in the name of other humans.
(Think of the chronic public resistance to foreign aid and welfare.) Ask
hardworking voters to sacrifice in the name of the snail darter, and, if they
are feeling polite, they will give you a shrug.

Of course, this anthropocentrism runs against the grain of a contemporary environmentalism that indulges in earth worship to the point of
idolatry. One scientific theory—Gaia theory—actually claims that Earth is
a living organism. This kind of environmentalism likes to consider itself
spiritual. It is nothing more than sentimental. It takes, for example, a highly
selective view of the benignity of nature. My nature worship stops with
the April twister that came through Kansas or the May cyclone that killed
more than 125,000 Bengalis and left 10 million (!) homeless.

A nonsentimental environmentalism is one founded on Protagoras'
maxim that "Man is the measure of all things." Such a principle helps us
through the thicket of environmental argument. Take the current debate
raging over oil drilling in a corner of the Alaska National Wildlife Refuge.
Environmentalists, mobilizing against a bill working its way through the
U.S. Congress to permit such exploration, argue that Americans should be
conserving energy instead of drilling for it. This is a false either/or proposition. The U.S. does need a sizable energy tax to reduce consumption.
But it needs more production too. Government estimates indicate a nearly
fifty-fifty chance that under the ANWR lies one of the five largest oil
fields ever discovered in America.

The U.S. has just come through a war fought in part over oil. Energy
dependence costs Americans not just dollars but lives. It is a bizarre senti-
mentalism that would deny oil that is peacefully attainable because it risks
disrupting the calving grounds of Arctic caribou.

I like the caribou as much as the next man. And I would be rather   *10*
sorry if their mating patterns are disturbed. But you can't have everything.
And if the choice is between the welfare of caribou and reducing an oil
dependency that gets people killed in wars, I choose man over caribou
every time.

Similarly the spotted owl in Oregon. I am no enemy of the owl. If it
could be preserved at no or little cost, I would agree: the variety of nature
is a good, a high aesthetic good. But it is no more than that. And sometimes aesthetic goods have to be sacrificed to the more fundamental ones.

If the cost of preserving the spotted owl is the loss of livelihood for 30,000 logging families, I choose family over owl.

The important distinction is between those environmental goods that are fundamental and those that are merely aesthetic. Nature is our ward. It is not our master. It is to be respected and even cultivated. But it is man's world. And when man has to choose between his well-being and that of nature, nature will have to accommodate.

Man should accommodate only when his fate and that of nature are inextricably bound up. The most urgent accommodation must be made when the very integrity of man's habitat—e.g., atmospheric ozone—is threatened. When the threat to man is of a lesser order (say, the pollutants from coal- and oil-fired generators that cause death from disease but not fatal damage to the ecosystem), a more modulated accommodation that balances economic against health concerns is in order. But in either case the principle is the same: protect the environment—because it is man's environment.

The sentimental environmentalists will call this saving nature with a totally wrong frame of mind. Exactly. A sane—a humanistic—environmentalism does it not for nature's sake but for our own.

The Responsive Reader

1. What is the essence of Krauthammer's "sane environmentalism"? What are the test cases that help him expound his thesis? (What does he mean by "anthropocentrism"?)
2. What is Krauthammer's basic philosophical difference with what he calls "sentimental" environmentalism?

Talking, Listening, Writing

3. Prepare an oral presentation or write an essay to support or rebut Krauthammer's position. Support your point of view with detailed examples or cases in point.

Collaborative Projects

4. Scientists like Carl Sagan sounded the alarm concerning the loss of the protective ozone layer in the atmosphere and the resultant global warming—the "greenhouse effect." What is the current state of scientific knowledge concerning global warming? Has there been preventive action by this country or other nations? Your class may want to farm out different aspects of this issue for research by small groups.

THE MONKEY WARS

Deborah Blum

> *Do animals have rights? Do they have the right to be protected against extermination, against wretched conditions, or against torture in medical experiments? The animal rights movement has led many to rethink their relationship with the animal world. It has led to crusades to rehabilitate and protect animals of the wild like the wolf and the coyote. Animal rights activists have challenged the unnatural conditions under which chickens and calves, for instance, are raised for food. They have made zookeepers reexamine the unnatural conditions under which animals are confined. In particular, the animal rights movement has focused attention on the suffering and destruction of animals in medical and military research. In the words of one activist, "A rabbit's right not to have oven cleaner poured into its eye is inherent. It exists whether the state recognizes it or not." Deborah Blum is a science writer who was trained at the University of Wisconsin and went to California to write first for the* Fresno Bee *and then for the* Sacramento Bee. *She first became interested in the ethics of animal experiments when apes used for laboratory experiments contracted the Ebola virus, which has proved deadly to patients and medical personnel in Africa. Her "Monkey Wars" series of articles won her the Pulitzer Prize.*

Thought Starters: Do animal trainers and pet owners have the right to do with animals as they please? Should we be concerned about how chickens or calves are raised to be butchered? Are zoos inhumane?

On the days when he's scheduled to kill, Allen Merritt summons up   1
his ghosts.

They come to him from the shadows of a 20-year-old memory. Eleven human babies, from his first year out of medical school. All born prematurely. All lost within one week when their lungs failed.

"We were virtually helpless," said Merritt, now head of the neonatal intensive care unit at the University of California-Davis Medical Center.

"There's nothing worse than being a new physician and standing there watching babies die. It's a strong motivator to make things different."

On this cool morning, he needs that memory. The experiment he's   5
doing is deceptively simple: a test of a new chemical to help premature babies breathe. But it's no clinical arrangement of glass tubes. He's trying the drug on two tiny rhesus monkeys, each weighing barely one-third of a

pound. At the end of the experiment, he plans to cut their lungs apart, to
see how it worked.

Even his ghosts don't make that easy. Nestled in a towel on a surgical
table, eyes shut, hands curled, the monkeys look unnervingly human. "The
link between people and monkeys is very close," Merritt said. "Much
closer than some people would like to think. There's a real sense of sadness,
that we can only get the information we need if we kill them."

Once, there was no such need to justify. Once, American researchers
could go through 200,000 monkeys a year, without question. Now, the
numbers are less—perhaps 20,000 monkeys will die every year, out of an
estimated 40,000 used in experiments. But the pressures are greater.

These days, it seems that if researches plan one little study—slicing
the toes off squirrel monkeys, siphoning blood from rhesus macaques, hiding baby monkeys from their mothers—they face not just questions, but
picket signs, lawsuits and death threats phoned in at night.

The middle ground in the war over research with monkeys and apes
has become so narrow as to be nearly invisible. And even that is eroding.

Intelligent, agile, fast, but not fast enough, these non-human primates
are rapidly being driven from the planet, lost to heavy trapping and vanishing rain forests. Of 63 primate species in Asia—where most research monkeys come from—only one is not listed as vulnerable.

Primate researchers believe they are making the hard choice, using
non-human primates for medical research because they must, because no
other animal so closely mirrors the human body and brain. During the
1950s, American scientists did kill hundreds of thousands of monkeys for
polio research, using the animals' organs to grow virus, dissecting their
brains to track the spread of the infection. But out of those experiments
came a polio vaccine. Using monkeys, scientists have created vaccines for
measles, learned to fight leprosy, developed anti-rejection drugs that make
organ transplants possible.

Outside the well-guarded laboratory wall, that choice can seem less
obvious. Animal rights advocates draw a dark description of research. They
point out that AIDS researchers have used endangered chimpanzees, without, so far, managing to help people dying of the disease. Further, conservationists fear that the research is introducing dangerous infection into the
country's chimpanzee breeding program, badly needed to help counter the
loss of wild animals.

"They're guzzling up money and animals, and for what?" asked
Shirley McGreal, head of the non-profit International Primate Protection
League. "Why not use those resources in helping sick people, why infect
healthy animals?"

Her argument is that of animal advocates across the country—that
scientists are sacrificing our genetic next-of-kin for their own curiosity,
dubious medical gains and countless tax dollars.

No one is sure exactly how much money scientists spend experimenting on monkeys, although the National Institutes of Health alone allocates almost $40 million annually to its primate research programs, including one in Davis. Overall, more than half of NIH's research grants—approaching $5 billion—involve at least some animal research. 15

Rats and mice are the most abundant, some 15 million are used in experiments every year. But primates are the most expensive; monkeys cost a basic $1,000, chimpanzees start at $50,000.

For people such as McGreal, these are animals in a very wrong place. McGreal's long-term goal for monkeys is simple: out of the laboratory, back into what remains of the rain forests.

"I used to think that we could persuade those people to understand what we do," said Frederick King, director of the Yerkes Regional Primate Research Center in Atlanta. "But it's impossible. And that's why I no longer describe this as a battle. I describe it as a war."

The rift is so sharp that it is beginning to reshape science itself.

"Science has organized," marveled Alex Pacheco, founder of the 20 country's most powerful animal rights group, People for Ethical Treatment of Animals. "Researchers are out-lobbying us and outspending us. They've become so aggressive that it puts new pressure on us. We're going to have to fight tougher too."

In the past year, researchers have made it clear just how much they dislike the role of victim. If Pacheco wants to call scientists "sadistic bastards"—which he does frequently—then Fred King is more than ready to counter with his description of PETA: "Fanatic, fringe, one of the most despicable organizations in the country."

But beyond name-calling, the research community is realizing its political power. Its lobbyists are pushing for laws that would heavily penalize protesters who interfere with research projects. And this year, to the fury of animal rights groups, primate researchers were able to win a special exemption from the public record laws, shielding their plans for captive monkey care.

For researchers, the attention focused on them is an almost dizzying turn-about. Not so long ago, they could have hung their monkey care plans as banners across streets and no one would have read them.

"When I first started, 20 years ago, monkeys were $25 each," said Roy Henrickson, chief of lab animal care at the University of California, Berkeley. "You'd use one once and you'd throw it away. I'd talk to lab vets who were under pressure about dogs and I'd say, I'm sure glad I'm in nonhuman primates. Nobody cares about them."

He can date the change precisely, back to 1981, the year Pacheco 25 went undercover in the laboratory of Edward Taub. Taub was a specialist in nerve damage, working in Silver Springs, Md. To explore the effects of ruined nerves, he took 17 rhesus monkeys and sliced apart nerves close to the spinal column, crippling their limbs. Then he studied the way they coped with the damage.

Pacheco left the laboratory with an enduring mistrust of scientists and an armload of inflammatory photographs: monkeys wrenched into vices, packed into filthy cages. Monkeys who, with no feeling in their hands, had gnawed their fingers to the bone. Some of the wounds were oozing with infection, darkening with gangrene.

Many believe those battered monkeys were the fuse, lighting the current, combative cycle of animal rights. In the fury over the Silver Springs monkeys, Pacheco was able to build People for Ethical Treatment of Animals into a national force, and across the country, the movement gained power. Today, membership in animal advocacy groups tops 12 million; the 30 largest organizations report a combined annual income approaching $70 million.

And primate researchers have suddenly found themselves under scrutiny of the most hostile kind.

There are experiments, such as Allen Merritt's work to salvage premature infants, that the critics will sometimes reluctantly accept. The compound that Merritt is testing on young monkeys is a kind of lubricant for the lungs, a slippery ooze that coats the tissues within, allowing them to flex as air comes in and out.

Without the ooze—called surfactant—the tissues don't stretch. They *30* rip. The problem for premature babies is that the body doesn't develop surfactant until late in fetal development, some 35 weeks into a pregnancy. Although aritifical surfactants are now available, Merritt doesn't believe they're good enough. Two-thirds of the tiniest premature babies, weighing less than a pound at birth, still die as their lungs shred. He's trying to improve the medicine.

"There could be a scientific defense for doing that, even though it's extremely cruel," said Elliot Katz, head of In Defense of Animals, a national animal rights group, headquartered in San Rafael.

But Katz finds most of the work indefensible. He can rapidly cite examples of a different sort: a U.S. Air Force experiment, which involved draining 40 percent of the blood from rhesus macaques and then spinning them on a centrifuge, to simulate injured astronauts; a New York University study of addiction in which monkeys were strapped into metal boxes and forced to inhale concentrated cocaine fumes.

Last year, animal advocates rallied against a proposed study at the Seattle center, a plan to take 13 baby rhesus macaques from their mothers and try to drive them crazy through isolation, keeping them caged away from their mothers and without company. The scientists acknowledged that they might drive the monkeys to self-mutilation; rhesus macaques do badly in isolation, rocking, pulling out their hair, sometimes tearing their skin open.

This year, protesters have been holding candlelight vigils outside the home of a researcher at a Maryland military facility, the Uniformed Services University of the Health Sciences. That project involves cutting the toes from kittens and young squirrel monkeys and then, after they've wobbled into adjustment, killing them to look at their brains.

In both cases, there are scientific explanations. The Washington scientists wanted to analyze the chemistry of a troubled brain, saying that it could benefit people with mental illness. The Maryland researchers are brain-mapping, drafting a careful picture of how the mind reorganizes itself to cope with crippling injury.

But these are not—and may never be—explanations acceptable to those crusading for animal rights. "This is just an example of someone doing something horrible to animals because he can get paid for it," said Laurie Raymond, of Seattle's Progressive Animal Welfare Society, which campaigned against the baby monkey experiment and takes credit for the fact that it failed to get federal funding.

Researchers are tired of telling the public about their work, documenting it in public records—and having that very openness used against them. The Washington protesters learned about the baby monkey experiment through a meeting of the university's animal care committee—which is public. The Maryland work came to light through a listing of military funded research—which is public.

When the U.S. Department of Agriculture, which inspects research facilities annually, complained about the housekeeping at the Tulane Regional Primate Research Center in Louisiana, the director wrote the agency a furious letter. Didn't administrators realize that the report was public—and made scientists look bad?

"The point I am making is that USDA, without intending to do so, is playing into the hands of the animal rights/anti-vivisectionists whose stated goal is to abolish animal research," wrote center head Peter Gerone, arguing that the complaints could have been handled privately. "If you are trying to placate the animal rights activists by nitpicking inspections . . . you will only serve to do us irreparable harm."

When Arnold Arluke, a sociologist at Boston's Northeastern University, spent six years studying lab workers and drafted a report saying that some actually felt guilty about killing animals, he found himself suddenly under pressure. "I was told putting that information out would be like giving ammunition to the enemy," he said.

He titled his first talk "Guilt Among Animal Researchers." The manager of the laboratory where he spoke changed "guilt" to stress. When he published that in a journal, the editors thought that stress was too controversial. They changed the title to "Uneasiness Among Lab Workers." When he gave another talk at a pharmaceutical company, he was told uneasiness was too strong. They changed the title to "How to Deal with Your Feelings." Arluke figures his next talk will be untitled.

"People in animal research don't even want to tell others what they do," he said. "One woman I talked to was standing in line at a grocery store, and when she told the person next to her what she did, the woman started yelling at her: 'You should be ashamed of yourself.'"

And when new lab animal care rules were published this year, it was clear that researchers were no longer willing to freely hand over every record of operation.

The new regulations resulted from congressional changes in 1985 to the Animal Welfare Act. They included a special provision for the care of laboratory primates; legislators wanted scientists to recognize that these were sociable, intelligent animals.

The provision—perhaps the most controversial in the entire act— 45
was called "psychological well-being of primates." When the USDA began drafting rules, in response to the new law, it received a record 35,000 letters of comment. And 14,000 consisted of a written shouting match over how to make primates happy. It took six years before the agency could come up with rules that the research community could accept.

Originally, the USDA proposed firm standards: Laboratories would have to give monkeys bigger cages, let them share space, provide them with puzzles and toys from a list.

Researchers argued that was unreasonable: Every monkey species was different, the rigid standards might satisfy one animal and make another miserable. Now, each institution is asked to do what it thinks best for its monkeys; USDA inspectors will be free to study, criticize and ask for changes in those plans.

But animal rights groups will not. Research lobbyists persuaded the USDA to bypass the federal Freedom of Information Act; the president of the American Society of Primatologists told the agency that making the plans public would be like giving a road map to terrorists. Under the new rules, the plans will be kept at the individual institutions rather than filed with the federal government, as has been standard practice. That makes them institutional property—exempted from any requests for federal records.

Tom Wolfle, director of the Institute for Laboratory Animal Resources in Washington, D.C., the federal government's chief advisory division on animal issues, said the research community simply needed some clear space. "The idea was to prevent unreasonable criticism by uninformed people," he said.

Advocacy groups have sued the government over the new rules, say- 50
ing they unlawfully shut the public out of research that it pays for. "In the end, they just handed everything back to the researchers and said, here, it's all yours," said Christine Stevens, an executive with the non-profit Animal Welfare Institute.

Stevens, daughter of a Michigan physiology researcher, finds this the ultimate contradiction, as well as "foolish and short-sighted." She thinks that science, of all professions, should be one of open ideas.

On this point, she has some unlikely allies. Frederick King, of Yerkes, no friend to the animal rights movement, is also unhappy with the research community's tendency to withdraw. "I don't know about the law," he said. "But our plans for taking care of our primates will be open.

"We are using taxpayers' money. In my judgment, we have an obligation to tell the public what we're about. And the fact that we haven't done that, I think, is one of the greatest mistakes over the last half-century, hell, the last century, that scientists have made."

Against that conflict, Allen Merritt's decision to make public an experiment in which he kills monkeys was not an easy one. His wife worried that anti-research fanatics would stalk their home. His supervisors worried that animal lovers would be alienated; one administrator even called the Davis primate center, suggesting that Merritt's work should not be publicly linked to the medical school's pediatrics department.

But Merritt, like King, believes that his profession will only lose if it remains hidden from the public. "People need to understand what we're doing. If I were to take a new drug first to a nursery, and unforeseen complications occurred, and a baby died—who would accept that?"

So, on a breezy morning, he opens the way to the final test of lung-lubricating surfactants that he will do this year, a 24-hour-countdown for two baby monkeys. Those hours are critical to whether these drugs work. If human premature babies last from their first morning to the next one, their survival odds soar.

The tiny monkeys—one male, one female—taken by C-section, are hurried into an intensive care unit, dried and warmed with a blow drier, put onto folded towels, hooked up to ventilators, heart monitors, intravenous drip lines. During the experiment, they will never be conscious, never open their eyes.

"OK, let's treat," Merritt says. His technician gently lifts the tube from the ventilator, which carries oxygen into the monkey's lungs. A white mist of surfactant fills the tube, spraying into the lungs. And then, through the night, the medical team watches and waits.

The next morning, they decide to kill the female early. An intravenous line going into her leg is starting to cause bleeding problems. The monkey is twitching a little in her unconsciousness, as if in pain. Merritt sees no point in dragging her through the experiment's official end.

But the male keeps breathing. As the sun brightens to midday, the scientists inject a lethal dose of anesthesia. Still, the monkey's chest keeps moving, up and down, up and down with the push of the ventilator. But, behind him, the heart monitor shows only a straight green line.

For a few seconds, before they shut the machines down and begin the lung dissection, Allen Merritt stands quietly by the small dead monkey, marshaling the ghosts of the babies he couldn't save, a long time ago.

The Responsive Reader

1. How does the opening anecdote raise the central issue in Blum's article? How does her story about the researcher and the two tiny monkeys bring the central dilemma into focus? Does she seem biased against the researcher? Why or why not?
2. Like other current crusades—antismoking, antiabortion—the campaign against animal experiments has often been intensely emotional. What do you learn hear about the polarization of opinion on the issue? Do you feel you can understand the point of view of both sides? Is there any middle ground?
3. Horror stories about tortured animals have played a major role in the crusade against animal experiments. What role do they play in this article? Do they sway your reaction one way or the other?
4. How much room does Blum give to the economics of animal research? How big are the stakes? How much room does Blum give to scientific explanations? How much would a layperson need to know to understand the scientific arguments involved?
5. To judge from this article, what has been the role of the government in this controversy?

Talking, Listening, Writing

6. Where do you stand on the issue of animal experiments? Would you approve of baboons or other apes being maimed and killed in the search for the answer to a killer virus? Would you approve of monkeys being mutilated in the search for therapies for traumatic injuries? Would you approve of trying out more effective new military weapons on animal targets?

Collaborative Projects

7. Working with a group, you may want to search computer indexes for current media coverage of topics like animal experiments, primate research, or medical research and animal rights. What have been recent developments? What is the current state of the controversy?

THE SNOW WALKER

Farley Mowat

> *Farley Mowat was a Canadian ethnologist—a student of cultures different from our own. When Mowat was fourteen, a great-uncle introduced him to Canada's vast Arctic territories. After serving in the Canadian army in World War II, Mowat lived for two years among the Ihalmuit tribe of the Eskimo, or Inuit, of the North. His* People of the Deer *(1952) was highly critical of the Canadian government's treatment of the dying tribe. In* Never Cry Wolf, *Mowat championed the cause of a species threatened with extinction. The following is the lead story of his* The Snow Walker *(1975), a collection of stories about the native peoples of the Arctic. The story makes us reexamine one of the cherished myths of Western civilization—the myth of European cultures bringing the blessings of civilization to the backward peoples of the world. In this story, what is the life of the native peoples before the arrival of the white man? What is their relationship with nature? What does the arrival of white civilization bring for the peoples of the North?*

Thought Starters: What have you read about the native peoples of the Arctic?

After death carried the noose to Angutna and Kipmik, their memory   *1*
lived on with the people of the Great Plains. But death was not satisfied and, one by one, he took the lives of the people until none was left to remember. Before the last of them died, the story was told to a stranger and so it is that Angutna and Kipmik may cheat oblivion a little while longer.

It begins on a summer day when Angutna was only a boy. He had taken his father's kayak and paddled over the still depths of the lake called Big Hungry until he entered a narrow strait called Muskox Thing. Here he grounded the kayak beneath a wall of looming cliffs and climbed cautiously upward under a cloud-shadowed sky. He was hunting for *Tuktu*, the caribou, which was the source of being for those who lived in the heart of the tundra. Those people knew of the sea only as a legend. For them seals, walrus and whales were mythical beasts. For them the broad-antlered caribou was the giver of life.

Angutna was lucky. Peering over a ledge he saw three caribou bucks resting their rumbling bellies on a broad step in the cliffs. They were not sleeping, and one or other of them kept raising his head to shake off the black hordes of flies that clung to nostrils and ears, so Angutna was forced to crawl forward an inch or two at a time. It took him an hour to move twenty yards, but he moved with such infinite caution that the bucks remained unaware of his presence. He had only a few more yards to crawl before he could drive an arrow from his short bow with enough power to kill.

Sunlight burst suddenly down through the yielding grey scud and struck hot on the crouched back of the boy and the thick coats of the deer. The warmth roused the bucks and one by one they got to their feet. Now they were restless, alert, and ready to move. In an agony of uncertainty Angutna lay still as a rock. This was the first time he had tried to stalk Tuktu all by himself, and if he failed in his first hunt he believed it would bode ill for his luck in the years ahead.

But the burst of sunlight had touched more than the deer and the   *5*
boy. It had beamed into a cleft in the cliffs overhanging the ledge where it had wakened two sleeping fox pups. Now their catlike grey faces peered shortsightedly over the brilliant roll of the lake and the land. Cloudy black eyes took in the tableau of the deer and the boy; but in their desire to see more, the pups forgot the first precept of all wild things—to see and hear but not to be seen or heard. They skittered to the edge of the cleft, shrilling a mockery of the dog fox's challenge at the strange beasts below.

The bucks turned their heavy heads and their ears flopped anxiously until their eyes found the pups scampering back and forth far over their heads. They continued to watch the young foxes, and so they did not see the boy move rapidly closer.

The hard twang of the bow and the heavy thud of an arrow striking into flesh came almost together. The deer leapt for the precipitous slope leading to the lake, but one of them stumbled, fell to his knees, and went sliding down on his side. In a moment Angutna was on him. The boy's copper knife slipped smoothly between the vertebrae in the deer's neck, and the buck lay dead.

The curiosity of the pups had now passed all bounds. One of them hung so far out over the ledge that he lost his balance. His hind legs scrabbled furiously at the smooth face of the rocks while his front feet pushed against air. The rocks thrust him away and he came tumbling in a steep arc to pitch into the moss almost at Angutna's feet.

The pup was too stunned to resist as the boy picked him up by the tail. Angutna put a tentative finger on the small beast's head, and when it failed to snap at him he laughed aloud. His laughter rang over the hills to the ears of the mother fox far from her den; it speeded the flight of the two surviving bucks, and rose to the ears of a high-soaring raven.

Then the boy spoke to the fox: *10*

"*Ayee!* Kipmik—Little Dog—we have made a good hunt, you and I. Let it be always this way, for surely you must be one of the Spirits-Who-Help."

That night in his father's skin tent Angutna told the tale of the hunting. Elder men smiled as they listened and agreed that the fox must indeed be a good token sent to the boy. Tethered to a tent pole, the pup lay in a little grey ball with his ears flat to his head and his eyes tightly shut, hoping with all his small heart that this was only a dream from which he would wake to find solace at the teats of his mother.

Such was the coming of the white fox into the habitations of men. In the days that followed, Angutna shared most of his waking hours with Kipmik who soon forgot his fears; for it is in the nature of the white fox to be so filled with curiosity that fear can be only a passing thing.

While the pup was still young enough to risk falling into the lean jaws of the dogs that prowled about the camp, he was kept tethered at night; but during the days, fox and boy travelled the land and explored the world that was theirs. On these expeditions the pup ran freely ahead of the boy over the rolling plains and hills, or he squatted motionless on the precarious deck of a kayak as Angutna drove the slim craft across the shining lakes.

Boy and fox lived together as one, and their thoughts were almost as one. The bond was strong between them for Angutna believed the fox was more than a fox, being also the embodiment of the Spirit-Who-Helps which had attached itself to him. As for Kipmik, perhaps he saw in the boy the shape of his own guardian spirit. 15

The first snows of the year came in late September and soon after that Kipmik shed the sombre grey fur of youth and donned the white mantle of the dog fox. His long hair was as fine as down and the white ruff that bordered his face framed glistening black eyes and the black spot of his nose. His tail was nearly as long and as round as his body. He was small compared to the red foxes who live in the forests, but he was twice as fleet and his courage was boundless.

During the second winter they spent together, Angutna came of age. He was fifteen and of a strength and awareness to accept manhood. In the time when the nights were so long they were almost unbroken, Angutna's father spoke to the father of a young girl named Epeetna. Then this girl moved into the snowhouse of Angutna's family and the boy who was now a man took her to wife.

During the winters life was lived without much exertion in the camps of the barrenland people for the deer were far to the south and men lived on the fat and meat they had stored up from the fall slaughter. But with the return of the snowbirds, spring and the deer came back to the plains around the Big Hungry and the camps woke to new and vigorous life.

In the spring of the first year of his marriage, Angutna went to the deer-hunting places as a full-fledged hunter. With him went the white fox. The two would walk over the softening drifts to reach rocky defiles that channelled the north-flowing deer. Angutna would hide in one of the ravines while the fox ran high up on the ridges to a place where he could overlook the land and see the dark skeins of caribou approaching the ambush. When the old doe leading a skein approached the defile, she would look carefully around and see the little white shadow watching from above. Kipmik would bark a short greeting to Tuktu, and the herd would move fearlessly forward believing that, if danger lurked, the fox would have barked a cry of alarm. But Kipmik's welcoming bark was meant for the ears of Angutna, who drew back the arrow on the bent bow and waited.

Angutna made good hunts during that spring and as a result he was sung about at the drum dances held in the evenings. The fox was not forgotten either, and in some of the songs the boy and the fox were called the Two Who Were One, and that name became theirs.

In the summer, when the deer had passed on to the fawning grounds far to the north, the fox and the boy sought other food. The Two Who Were One took the kayak down the roaring rivers that debouched over the scarred face of the plains, seeking the hiding places of the geese that nested in that land. After midsummer the adult geese lost their flight quills and had to stay on the water, and at such times they became very shy. The kayak sought out the backwaters where the earthbound geese waited in furtive seclusion for the gift of flight to return.

While Angutna concealed himself behind rocks near the shore, Kipmik would dance on the open beach, barking and squealing like a young pup. He would roll on his back or leap into the air. As he played, the geese would emerge from their hiding places and swim slowly toward him, fascinated by this peculiar behaviour in an animal they all knew so well. They had no fear of the fox for they knew he would not try to swim. The geese would come closer, cackling to one another with necks outstretched in amazement. Then Angutna's sling would whir and a stone would fly with a angry hiss. A goose would flap its wings on the water and die.

It was an old trick Kipmik played on the geese, one used by foxes since time began . . . but only Kipmik played that game for the benefit of man.

So the years passed until there were two children in the summer tent of Angutna—a boy and a girl who spent long hours playing with the soft tail of the fox. They were not the only young to play with that white brush. Every spring, when the ptarmigan mated on the hills and the wild dog foxes barked their challenges as an overtone to the sonorous singing of the wolves, unrest would come into the heart of the fox that lived in the houses of men.

On a night he would slip away from the camp and be gone many days. When he returned, lean and hungry, Angutna would feed him special tidbits and smilingly wish good luck to the vixen secreted in some newly dug den not far away. The vixen never ventured into the camp, but Kipmik saw to it that she and her pups were well fed, for Angutna did not begrudge the fox and his family a fair share of the meat that was killed.

20

25

Sometimes Angutna followed the fox into the hills to the burrow. Then Angutna might leave a fresh fish at its mouth, and he would speak kindly to the unseen vixen cowering within. "Eat well, little sister," he would say.

As the years slipped by, stories of the Two Who Were One spread through the land. One of them told of a time when Angutna and his family were camped alone by the lake called Lamp of the Woman. It was a very bad year. In midwinter there was an unbroken month of great storms and the people used up all the meat stored near the camp but the weather was too savage to permit the men to travel to their more distant caches. The people grew hungry and cold, for there was no more fat for the lamps.

Finally there came a day without wind. Angutna hitched up his team and set out for a big cache lying two days' travel to the west. The dogs pulled as hard as their starved muscles would let them while the fox, like a white wraith, flitted ahead, choosing the easiest road for the team. The sled runners rasped as if they were being hauled over dry sand, for the temperature stood at fifty or sixty degrees below freezing.

On the second day of the journey the sun failed to show itself and there was only a pallid grey light on the horizon. After a while the fox stopped and stared hard into the north, his short ears cocked forward. Then Angutna too began to hear a distant keening in the dark sky. He tried to speed up the dogs, hoping to reach the cache, which lay sheltered in a deep valley, before the storm broke. But the blizzard exploded soon after, and darkness fell with terrible swiftness as this great gale, which had swept a thousand miles south from the ice sea, scoured the frozen face of the plains. It drove snow before it like fragments of glass. The drifting granules swirled higher and higher, obscuring the plodding figures of man, fox and dogs.

Kipmik still moved at the head of the team but he was invisible to Angutna's straining, snowcaked eyes, and many times the anxious white shadow had to return to the sled so that the dogs would not lose their way. Finally the wind screamed to such a pitch that Angutna knew it would be madness to drive on. He tried to find a drift whose snow was firm enough for the making of a snowhouse, but there was none at hand and there was no time to search. Turning the sled on its side facing the gale, he dug a trench behind it with his snowknife—just big enough for his body. Wrapping himself in his robes he rolled into the trench and pulled the sled over the top of the hole.

The dogs curled abjectly nearby, noses under their tails, the snow *30* drifting over them, while Kipmik ran among them snapping at their shoulders in his anxiety to make them continue on until some shelter was found. He gave up when the dogs were transformed into white, inanimate mushrooms. Then the fox ran to the sled and burrowed under it. He wormed in close, and Angutna made room so that he might share the warmth from the little body beside him.

For a day and a night nothing moved on the white face of the dark plains except the snow ghosts whirling before the blast of the gale. On the second day the wind died away. A smooth, curling drift shattered from within as Angutna fought free of the smothering snows. With all the haste his numbed body could muster, he began probing the nearby drifts seeking the dogs who were sealed into white tombs from which they could no longer escape by themselves.

He had little need of the probe. Kipmik ran to and fro, unerringly sniffing out the snow crypts of the dogs. They were all uncovered at last, and all were alive but so weak they could barely pull at the sled.

Angutna pressed on. He knew that if no food was found soon, the dogs would be finished. And if the dogs died, then all was lost, for there would be no way to carry the meat from the cache back to the camp. Mercilessly Angutna whipped the team on, and when the dogs could no longer muster the strength to keep the sled moving, he harnessed himself into the traces beside them.

Just before noon the sun slipped over the horizon and blazed red on a desolate world. The long sequence of blizzards had smoothed it into an immense and shapeless undulation of white. Angutna could see no landmarks. He was lost in that snow desert, and his heart sank within him.

Kipmik still ran ahead but for some little while he had been trying 35
to swing the team to a northerly course. Time after time he ran back to Angutna and barked in his face when the man persisted in trudging into the west. So they straggled over that frozen world until the dogs could go no farther. Angutna killed one of the dogs and fed it to the others. He let them rest only briefly, for he was afraid a new storm would begin.

The sun was long since gone and there were no stars in the sky when they moved on; therefore Angutna did not notice as, imperceptibly, Kipmik turned the team northward. He did not notice until late the next morning when the dawn glow showed him that all through the long night they had been travelling into the north.

Then Angutna, who was a man not given to rage, was filled with a terrible anger. He believed it was all finished for him and his family. He seized his snowknife from the sled and with a great shout leapt at the fox, his companion of so many years.

The blow would have sliced Kipmik in two but, even as he struck, Angutna stumbled. The blade hissed into the snow and the fox leapt aside. Angutna stayed on his knees until the anger went from him. When he rose to his feet he was steadfast once more.

"*Ayorama!*" he said to the fox who watched him without fear. "It cannot be helped. So, Little Pup, you will lead us your way? It is a small matter. Death awaits in all directions. If you wish, we will seek death to the north."

It is told how they staggered northward for half a day, then the fox 40
abandoned the man and the dogs and ran on ahead. When Angutna caught

up to Kipmik it was to find he had already tunnelled down through the snow to the rocks Angutna had heaped over a fine cache of meat and fat in the fall.

A year or so later a great change came to the world of the plains dwellers. One winter day a sled drove into the camps by the Big Hungry and a man of the sea people came into the snowhouses. Through many long nights the people listened to his wondrous tales of life by the salt water. They were particularly fascinated by his accounts of the wonders that had been brought to that distant land by a white man come out of the south. Their visitor had been commissioned by the white man to acquaint the plains people with the presence of a trading post on the eastern edge of the plains, and to persuade them to move closer to that post and to trap furs for trade.

The idea was much talked about and there were some who thought it would be a good thing to go east for a winter, but most of the people were opposed. By reason of his renown as a hunter, Angutna's opinions carried weight and one night he spoke what was in his mind.

"I think it is to be remembered that we have lived good lives in this land, knowing little evil. Is it not true that *Tuktoriak* has fed and clothed us from before the time of the father's fathers? *Eeee!* It is so. And if we turn from the Deer Spirit now to seek other gifts, who can say what he may do? Perhaps he will be angry and speak to his children, the deer, and bid them abandon our people. And then of what value would be the promises made by this man on behalf of the Kablunait? . . . Those promises would be dead sticks in our hands."

So spoke Angutna, and most agreed with him. Still, when the stranger departed, there were two families who went with him. These returned before the snows thawed in the spring and they brought such wealth as a man could hardly credit: rifles, steel knives, copper kettles and many such things.

But they also brought something they did not know they were bringing.   45

It was a sickness that came into men's lungs and squeezed the life from their bodies. It was called the Great Pain and it flung itself on the plains people like a blazing wind. In one season it killed more than half of those who lived in that land.

Panic struck many of the survivors who, believing the land was now cursed, fled to the east to seek help from the white man. From him they learned a new way of life, becoming trappers of fur and eaters of white man's food. And, instead of Tuktu, the beast they now pursued was Terriganiak—the white fox. During all time that had been, the plains people had known the white fox as a friend in a land so vast and so empty that the bark of the fox was often the only welcoming sound. Since time began, foxes and men had shared that land and there had been no conflict between them. Now men turned on Terriganiak and lived by the sale of his skin.

For a time Angutna and a few other men and their families tried to continue living the old life in the old places, but hunger came more often upon them and one autumn the deer failed to appear at all. Some said this was because of the great slaughter of deer resulting from the new rifles in the hands of all northern people, Indian and Innuit; but Angutna believed it was due to the anger of Tuktoriak. In any event, the last few people living on the inland plains were forced to follow those who had already fled to the east and become trappers of fox.

When the survivors of that long trek came to the snowhouses which stood a few miles away from the house of the trader at the mouth of the River of Seals, they expected to be greeted with warmth and with food, for it had always been the law of the land that those who have food and shelter will share with those who have not.

Disappointment was theirs. White foxes, too, were scarce that 50 winter and many traps stood empty. Those people who had chosen to live by the fox were nearly as hungry as the people who journeyed out of the west.

Angutna built a small snowhouse for his family, but it was a dark place filled with dark thoughts. There was no fuel for the lamps and almost no fuel for the belly. Angutna, who had once been such a great hunter, was now forced to live on the labours of others because, even if he had so wished, he could not have trapped foxes. He could not have done so because Terriganiak was his Spirit-Who-Helps and, for him, the lives of all foxes were sacred. Other men went to their traps and, when they were lucky, caught foxes whose pelts they bartered for food. Sometimes a portion of that food was given to Angutna's wife; but Angutna had nothing to give in return.

The new way of life was as hard for Kipmik as for Angutna. The fox who had always been free now lay, day and night, tethered to a stick driven into the floor of the snowhouse. All around that place steel traps yawned for his kind and there were many men with rifles who, to help feed their families, would not have hesitated to put a bullet through him, for although Kipmik was growing old, his pelt was still thicker, softer and longer than that of any fox that had ever been seen before.

As the winter drew on, the remaining foxes deserted that part of the country and then hunger was the lot of all who had tried to live by the fox. There were no more gifts to the family of Angutna, who had himself become so emaciated that he could do little but sit like a statue in his cold house, dreaming of other times, other days. Sometimes his gaze would fix on the curled ball of white fur that was Kipmik, and his lips would move, but silently, for he was addressing a plea to the Spirit-Who-Helps. Sometimes the fox would raise its head and stare back into the eyes of the man, and perhaps he too was pleading . . . for the freedom that once had been his.

The trader heard about the fabulous fox who lived in the houses of men and one day he drove his dogs to the camps of the people to see for himself whether the stories were true. He entered Angutna's snowhouse, and as soon as he saw Kipmik curled up on the floor he wished to possess that magnificent pelt.

It distressed him to see the big, staring eyes and the swollen bellies of   55
Angutna's children. He felt pity for the people who were starving that winter. But what could he do? He did not own the food that lay in his storehouse. It belonged to the company that employed him, and he could not part with a pound unless there was payment in fur.

Angutna greeted the visitor with a smile that tautened the skin that was already stretched too tightly over the broad bones of his face. Even though he be in despair, a man must give a good greeting to those who visit his house. It was otherwise with the fox. Perhaps he smelled the death stink from the skins of so many of his kind this stranger had handled. He pulled away to the side of the snowhouse as far as his tether would reach and crouched there like a cat facing a hound.

The white man spoke of the hard times that lay on the people; of the shortage of foxes and the absence of deer. Then he turned to look at Kipmik again.

"That is a fine fox you have there. I have never seen better. If you will sell it to me, I can pay . . . as much as three sacks of flour and, yes, this I can do, ten, no, fifteen pounds of fat."

Angutna still smiled, and none knew the thoughts that swirled behind the masked face. He did not answer the white man directly, but spoke instead of trivial things while he wrestled with himself in his mind: food . . . food enough to ensure that his wife and children would live until spring. Perhaps he even believed his Spirit-Who-Helps had something to do with the miraculous hope the white man extended. Who will know what he thought?

The trader knew better than to say anything more about Kipmik, but   60
when he went outside to his waiting sled he ordered his Eskimo helper to take a small bag of flour into Angutna's snowhouse. Then he returned to his trading post at the mouth of the River of Seals.

That night the woman, Epeetna, made a small fire of willow twigs in the tunnel entrance and she and her children ate unleavened bread made of flour and water. She passed a cake of it to Angutna where he sat unmoving on the sleeping ledge, but he did not taste it. Instead he threw it to the fox. Kipmik bolted it down, for he too was starving. Then Angutna spoke, as it seemed, to himself.

"This is the way it must be."

Epeetna understood. The woman let her hair loose so that it hung down over her face. The acrid smoke from the fire clouded the four figures sitting on the high ledge. The small flames gave hardly enough light for

Angutna to see what he was doing, but his fingers needed no light as he
carefully plaited the Noose of Release.

When it was finished, Angutna slipped Kipmik's tether, and the fox
leapt up to the ledge and stood with its paws braced against the chest of
the man—free once again. The black eyes were fixed on the eyes of the
man, in wonder perhaps, for the fox had never seen tears in those eyes
before. Kipmik made no move when the noose fell over his neck. He
made no move until Angutna spoke.

"Now, Little Pup, it is time. You will go out onto the plains where   65
the deer wait our coming."

And so Kipmik passed into that country from which nothing returns.

Next morning when the trader opened his door he found the frozen
pelt of the fox suspended from the ridge of his porch by a strangely plaited
noose. The pelt swayed and spun in the breath of the wind. The trader
was delighted, but he was uneasy too. He had lived in that land long
enough to know how little he knew. He wasted no time ordering his
helper to load the promised food on a sled and take it to the snowhouse
of Angutna.

The payment was received by Epeetna. Angutna could not receive it,
for the Noose of Release was drawn tight at his throat. He had gone to
join the one he had lost.

His grave still stands on the bank of the River of Seals. It is no more
than a grey cairn of rocks with the decayed weapons of a hunter scattered
among the quiet stones. Inside the grave lies Angutna, and beside him lies
the fox who once lived in the houses of men.

The two are still one.   70

The Responsive Reader

1. What does Mowat want the reader to learn about the setting, the
   climate, and the relation of Angutna and his people to the cycles of
   the seasons and the habits of the wildlife?
2. Does Mowat seem to romanticize the life of Angutna's people or his
   relationship with the fox?
3. What changes does the arrival of white men bring for Angutna's
   people? Which are physical? Which relate to ways of living and
   thinking? How do Angutna and his people interpret them and react
   to them?
4. What is the role of the white trader in this story? Is he the villain?

Talking, Listening, Writing

5. At the end of his conversation with Angutna, the trader "knew better than to say anything more." Epeetna "understood" but said little.

If Angutna had felt the need to share his thoughts and feelings at the end, what might he have said?

6. If the white trader could have had the last word, what do you think he might have said in reply to Angutna? (Your class may want to stage an imaginary dialogue between the two.)

7. What to you is the most essential difference between the native life-style that Mowat re-creates in this story and the outlook and way of life brought by the white traders?

Collaborative Projects

8. What is the current status of the people Mowat wrote about? What can you find out about recent developments in Canada's treatment of the indigenous tribes of the North?

DREAMS OF THE ANIMALS

Margaret Atwood

Margaret Atwood is the Canadian writer best known in the United States. Atwood was born in Ottawa and studied at the University of Toronto and at Harvard. She has published much poetry and short fiction and is the author of novels including The Edible Woman *(1969),* The Handmaid's Tale *(1985),* Cat's Eye *(1989), and* The Robber Bride *(1993). The Hand- maid's Tale was made into a chilling dystopian, anti-Utopian movie in which a traditional sexist, patriarchal society has turned into a grotesque caricature of itself. Atwood has written about survival as a major theme in Canadian literature, focusing on the struggle to survive in a harsh, unforgiving natural environment.*

Thought Starters: Do young people today still grow up thinking of animals as cuddly, lovable pets? Or do they grow up with a sense of what animals are like in the wild?

Mostly the animals dream   1
of other animals   each
according to its kind

      (though certain mice and small rodents
      have nightmares of a huge pink   5
      shape with five claws descending)

: moles dream of darkness and delicate
mole smells

frogs dream of green and golden
frogs   10
sparkling like wet suns
among the lilies

red and black
striped fish, their eyes open
have red and black striped   15
dreams   defense, attack, meaningful
patterns

birds dream of territories
enclosed by singing.

Sometimes the animals dream of evil   *20*
in the form of soap and metal
but mostly the animals dream
of other animals.

There are exceptions:

      the silver fox in the roadside zoo   *25*
      dreams of digging out
      and of baby foxes, their necks bitten

      the caged armadillo
      near the train
      station, which runs   *30*
      all day in figure eights
      its piglet feet pattering,
      no longer dreams
      but is insane when waking;

      the iguana   *35*
      in the petshop window on St. Catherine Street
      crested, royal-eyed, ruling
      its kingdom of water-dish and sawdust

      dreams of sawdust

The Responsive Reader

1. How does Atwood describe the animals of the wild? What are striking or unexpected details? Is there any common pattern or connecting thread in the animals she selects and the way she talks about
   them?
2. How does Atwood describe the animals in captivity? Is there a
   common pattern? What images or details is her reader likely to
   remember?
3. Atwood often offers a harsh criticism of the way we behave as human
   beings. How would you spell out or sum up the criticism she offers
   in this poem of the way human beings treat their cousins of the
   animal kingdom?

Talking, Listening, Writing

4. People writing about animals or making movies about them are
   often accused of making them seem too much like human beings—
   ascribing to them human feelings and patterns of behavior. (The
   animals then become too *anthropomorphic*—made over in the image
   of humankind.) Do you think Atwood would have to plead guilty to
   this charge? Why or why not?

5. Do you think of some animals as beautiful and of others as repulsive? Are any such distinctions part of the natural scheme of things? Or are we merely applying our own limited human standards to the rest of creation?

6. Do you think the current movement to reintroduce wolves or other predatory animals into areas where they have long been absent is misguided?

WRITING
WORKSHOP 11

The Investigative Paper

Many writing classes now feature investigative papers—shorter, informal research papers—as an alternative to the full-length, formal library paper. Such investigative papers can help bridge the gap between the short, informal, weekly or biweekly paper and a full-fledged, documented research paper—which checks out a whole range of available material and gives full publishing information for readers who may want to verify your sources. Emphasis in the shorter investigative paper can be on the basic research skills—treating the paper first of all as a writing project, with the emphasis on tracking down, evaluating, and bringing together reliable information and informed opinion.

Honest writing results from a process of investigation. The writer has gone through a process of fact-gathering, of checking things out. In some kinds of writing, the emphasis on investigation, on finding out, is especially strong. Journalists serving as watchdogs on big government or big business are not satisfied with press releases or campaign handouts. They aim at getting out the real story. They dig and probe; they believe in the public's right to know. Historians and biographers try to unearth the truth behind official pronouncements. They try to get at the real human being behind the idealized public figure that has become a national monument. Students of current issues try to find out what is behind the buzzwords—"the white backlash," "victimology," "the men's movement," "Ebonics," "mainstreaming the disabled."

TRIGGERING   Investigative writing is triggered when someone says: "There is more to this than meets the eye. The truth is worth ferreting out." Situations like the following might set you to work as an investigative writer:

- A watchdog group charges that local industry continues to discharge toxic materials into local waterways in violation of state and federal law. Spokespersons for concerned companies state that their firms are in compliance with applicable legislation. What is the truth?

- A political figure talks to an audience of developers about costly restrictions on logging, mandated to preserve the habitat of an endangered species. He claims that environmentalist legislation restricting logging has added between three thousand and five thousand dollars to the cost of the homes they are building. How much of this is true? What is the economic cost of protecting endangered species? Who is in a position to make informed estimates?

■ What was behind the huge media flap about Ebonics or "Black English"? Who were the leading critics, and what were their arguments? What did language scholars and teachers say? How did leaders in the African American community line up in the controversy?

■ What progress has been made toward making insurers cover mental illnesses as illnesses? What is the story of recent legislative battles? Who carried the ball? Who fought the initiatives? What was the final result?

GATHERING As an investigative writer, you may find yourself playing detective. For instance, the headlines about extending insurance coverage to people with mental illnesses may turn out to be mostly media hype. You may have to check out what disillusioned original supporters of the legislation actually said. You may have to check out what spokespersons for groups like the Mental Health Alliance said. In the final legislation, what were the compromises and the ifs and buts buried in the fine print? Here are some hints for the apprentice sleuth:

■ *Check out relevant background.* Read up on the subject. Here are a student writer's notes on some promising sources for a paper on the "men's movement":

Review of Robert Bly's book *Iron John* in *Fremont News*.
　　Bly has focused attention on the complicated nature of what it means to be masculine and on recent changes in male identity. The "men's movement" is part of a larger trend toward redefining gender roles and reexamining male and female sexuality.

Jack Balswick, *The Inexpressive Male*.
　　The book explains why men are "inexpressive" and unable to communicate their feelings as women do. It offers suggestions on how men can overcome their fear of intimacy.

John Gray, *Men Are from Mars, Women Are from Venus*.
　　Gray writes about how to make a relationship between a man and a woman work by recognizing distinct characteristics of the male and the female.

Mark Simpson, *Male Impersonators: Men Performing Masculinity*.
　　Simpson explores the whole concept of masculinity, touching on topics like body building, skinheads, and pornography. He says that the men's

movement is sought out by both straight and gay men who feel alienated from a macho culture.

▪ *Listen to the people involved.* Listen to the stories of people whose lives have been affected. Establish them as authorities. When you investigate current efforts to weaken tough drunk-driving laws, you might introduce one of your key sources as follows:

> Three years ago a 23-year-old man, with a blood alcohol nearly three times the 0.10 legal limit, crashed head-on into a car carrying Jackie Masso, her husband Patrick, her daughter Patty, and a friend at 4:30 in the afternoon. Today Jackie Masso faces two to three more operations on her legs. Her husband must get his lungs pumped about three times a year because of congestive heart failure, and her 21-year-old daughter, after having her crushed nose broken and reset two times, faces yet more plastic surgery.
>
> Masso got MADD. She and her husband are copresidents of the local chapter of Mothers Against Drunk Driving, which has 400–600 paying members and 1,000 on a mailing list.
>
> Masso said she has noticed something in the many courtrooms where she has sat with families who have had a son or daughter killed or badly injured. She has noticed that the drunken drivers with multiple offenses always tend to blame their car, the weather, or the other driver—but never themselves.
>
> "I've never heard a drunken driver say he's sorry," she said.

▪ *Pay attention to insiders' information.* Pay close attention when your sources cite internal memos and informal letters rather than official press releases. Listen carefully to people recalling informal conversations, rather than to public relations handouts prepared for a public meeting.

▪ *Pay special attention to candid interviews.* Listen when people who feel misrepresented or slighted try to tell their side of the story.

SHAPING Many investigative papers start by documenting a public misunderstanding, a questionable official version, or misleading media stereotypes. Typically, the writer's assumption is that there is another side to the story. The paper will thus often play off an unauthorized, unofficial version against the established or familiar view. It may then sift testimony for and against the "revisionist" hypothesis. Finally, the paper may try to present a balanced conclusion.

Often an investigative paper will try to reenact the excitement of the search, of the hunt. It may create an air of mystery by first hints of something misrepresented or amiss. It may build suspense as the paper examines additional clues. It may lead up to a climax where a clinching admission or discovery provides the high point.

The following might be a working outline for an investigative paper:

the official version

first hints: discrepancies in official accounts

clues leading to an alternative version of events

a clinching discovery

a belated revision of the official account

REVISING   The feedback you receive for your paper from peer reviewers or from your instructor will vary. The following is an exceptionally complete **running commentary** by an instructor on a paper investigating health insurance for mental illness. To judge from this commentary, what were the strengths of the paper? What needed work?

1. Introduction: Your startling opening statistics should wake up the apathetic reader. However, they need to be attributed to somebody. Who said this? What is the credibility of the source?

2. Thesis: The point that a "huge step" has been taken toward equal treatment of physical and "mental" illness, in spite of the last-ditch resistance of the insurance companies, comes through loud and clear. (The rest of your paper follows up your thesis extremely well.)

3. Backup of thesis: Explanation of the traditional "stigma" attached to mental illness and contrasting medical definitions of mental illness really back up your thesis. Good sources here. (But I would leave out the dictionary definition, which seems routine and has no real punch.)

4. Organization: The key point that mental illness is "treatable" leads naturally to a look at current new medications. But you seem to take a detour when talking about the drugs. Make it clearer that you basically *endorse* the new developments but that you are also sounding a warning that the drug-happy American public might expect too much from "miracle drugs"?

5. The part of your paper examining the restriction and denial of medical treatment as the result of a for-profit health care system is very strong. You make excellent use of a local authority at your own college. You explain well the economics of the shift from fee-for-service to managed care. Some of your readers might need more explanation of what "managed care" is all about?

6. The personal connection: Your stories about people you know about personally add much to your paper. As one of your peer reviewers says, "The suicide stories are very shaking and dramatic."

7. The section on the legislative battles to ensure insurance coverage for mental illness seems exceptionally informative and well-balanced, with well-deserved credit to advocates like Senator Domenici. However, you do a good job of showing how the fine print makes the

apparent victory for his side just a limited first step. (Perhaps you should also identify by name some of the people who fought the legislation—so that voters who care about health issues can remember.)

8. Conclusion: Good circling back to the story of your friend's brother. Good and memorable punchline. Good work.

Some cautions and suggestions tend to come up again and again in readers' comments on investigative papers. Revision gives you a chance to rewrite your paper to sidestep familiar pitfalls:

- *Check the credibility of your sources.* Be wary of what is clearly biased or partisan testimony. Readers may not be impressed by a flack's defense of agency policy, a fired employee's disgruntled remarks, or a CEO's lauding the integrity of the company's balance sheet.

- *Guard against charges of having slanted the evidence.* If you filter out all doubt or disagreement, your readers will start reading your tract as one-sided propaganda. Many will discount it accordingly. Take on and try to rebut major objections that are likely to arise in your readers' minds. For instance, make sure you cite both management and workers when investigating a labor dispute.

- *Give facts and credible testimony a chance to speak for themselves.* There is a strong temptation to call evildoers the names they deserve. Some writers keep up a steady drumfire of labels like *inexcusable, self-interested, incompetent, maniacal, capricious, greedy for profits*, and *using political ploys*. Save weighty words and serious charges for places where you have clearly earned the right to use them. Support them by careful presentation of evidence.

- *Watch out for innuendo.* Innuendos or insinuations are damaging charges that are never openly made but only hinted at—and therefore not really supported or defended. ("Politician X attended the same fund raiser as alleged mobster Y." Yes? What are you hinting or implying?)

A PAPER FOR PEER REVIEW The following is a paper investigating the "men's movement"—ridiculed by some but taken seriously by others. How and how well does the paper bring the issue into focus? How or how well does the student writer establish her authority? How would you chart the organizing strategy of the paper? What use does the student writer make of key sources? How informative is the paper? Is more than one side heard? How do you react to the paper?

Walk like a Man, Talk like a Man?

Another thing I learned—if you cry the audience won't. A man can cry for his horse, for his dog, for another man, but he cannot cry for a woman. A strange thing. He can cry at the death of a friend

or pet. But where he's supposed to be boss, with his children or wife, something like that, he better hold 'em back and let them cry.
—John Wayne

Feminism and the women's movement have focused on defining the woman's role and helping women's advancement in the community. Adrienne Rich, a noted feminist poet, has said: "This drive of self-knowledge, for women, is more than a search for identity: it is part of our refusal of the self-destructiveness of male dominated society." This emphasis on and attention to women has allowed them to discover their role and self-identity in the family, the workplace, as well as the community at large.

However, with all the focus on what it means to be a woman in society, the new question that arises is, "What does it mean to be a man today?" Are men feeling lost and confused as to what their own role in our culture ought to be? In recent years, masculinity or the male sex role in society has become a popular topic of discussion. Books on masculinity—*Be A Man*; *The Limits of Masculinity*; *Men Are from Mars, Women Are from Venus*—have climbed the best-seller lists. Television talk shows have dealt with what the ideal male should be. Gatherings have been held for men to discuss what it means to be a man today. The Men's Movement, parallel to the Women's Liberation Movement, was established in order to deal with this new problem facing young males.

The conflict seems to be that young men do not have good and influential role models in our present society because there is such an ambiguity when it comes to defining this idea of the "ideal" male. Robert Bly, an award-winning poet and author of *Iron John*, says, "It is clear that the images of adult manhood given by the popular culture are worn out; a man can no longer depend on them." Should men maintain the tough, stone-hearted, protector image of the past, or should they follow the current trend of openly expressing their feelings and being in touch with their nurturing, feminine side?

Jack Balswick, author of *The Inexpressive Male*, writes that men have traditionally been defined as "independent, task-oriented, aggressive, and inexpressive—meaning they do not verbally express their feelings." The inability to express one's feelings openly or freely is most commonly associated with men of past generations. Alan Buczynski, author of *Iron Bonding*, states, "The notion prevails that men's emotional communication skills are less advanced than those of chimpanzees—that we can no more communicate with one another than can earthworms." Balswick says that men are "ill-suited for roles that call for a high degree of nurturant caring." Because of this lack of nurturant caring, whether it be with children, parents, or significant others, men are not mentally equipped to share their emotional burdens without feeling a sense of alienation or ridicule. One of my father's good male friends summarizes the problem by saying, "When I was growing up, if you were too open with your feelings and emotions, people thought you were weird or effeminate."

A closely related traditional trait of men is that they are hostile and aggressive by nature. According to Karen Huffman, author and researcher of *Psychology in Action*, "one of the clearest and most consistent findings in gender studies is greater physical aggressivenes in males." From an early age, boys are given toy weapons and are more interested in mock fighting and rough-and-tumble play. Typical role models in film and television—John Wayne, Arnold Schwarzenegger, Sylvester Stallone—help young and impressionable males acquire these idiosyncrasies. How many action films have you seen where the hero breaks down emotionally and has a cathartic moment, in which he discusses his fears and insecurities? Instead, these men are portrayed as vigilantes and heroes, who ultimately take the law into their own hands.

In a Clint Eastwood blockbuster, the hero, known as the "meanest sonofabitch in the West," had left his violent past behind but had to decide whether or not to put on his gun belt and seek revenge for the rape of a prostitute. When I saw this film, the audience, mostly men, cheered when the protagonist decided to be the gunslinging hero. As Mark Simpson, author of *Male Impersonators*, sees it, when he "becomes a killer again, he becomes a man." These macho-male role models tend to acquire the beautiful female as well, both on screen and off.

These qualities of the tough and aggressive man are learned through cognitive growth and identification with the same-sex parent. According to Freud's social-learning theory, boys learn how to be masculine by watching and imitating the social behavior of their father or any male that is a dominant figure in their lives. Professor Manita, from the college psychology department, supports Freud's theory by saying, "Young boys are taught that they need to be either aggressive or submissive based upon observing their same-sex parent." Balswick maintains that this theory is also one of the main explanations for male inexpressiveness. He says, "The gist is that males are not rewarded, and are even punished, for expressions of emotion or any other behaviors that could be considered feminine."

School is another social institution that can powerfully influence young men's attitude towards traditional masculinity. For example, in Andrew Tolson's book *The Limits of Masculinity*, he talks about the all-male boarding school that he attended as a young boy. He says, "The school transmitted, as a sanctioned part of their experience, a notion of 'manhood,' which remained the ideological reference point for the training of 'gentlemen.'" This notion of manhood was enshrined in the school's ten commandments, which was an instructional bible for these young boys to follow. The following are some of these commandments:

> Without big muscles, strong will, and proper collars there is no salvation.
>
> I must play games with all my heart, with all my soul and with all my strength.
>
> Enthusiasm, except for games, is in bad taste.
>
> I must show no emotion and not kiss my mother in public.

With all this in mind, it would be easy to conclude that "men are from Mars and women are from Venus." However, these traditional dividing lines are increasingly becoming blurred. Bly states it best when he says that "by the time a man is thirty-five he knows that the images of the right man, the tough man, the true man which he received in high school do not work in life." One reason is that women now find it more socially acceptable, politically correct, as well as sexually appealing for men to deny their brutish and aggressive tendencies and follow the archetype of the "sensitive" male. By sensitive male, I mean that he must be in touch with his nurturing feminine side, which allows him to express his emotions and insecurities. According to a survey published in the February '96 edition of *Young and Modern* magazine, 85% of the women polled preferred to date a sensitive male rather than a stud. Part of the explanation behind this may be that our current culture deems that communication is the essential element to any successful relationship.

Are we saying that men should now forget about the past role models and traditional notions of manhood that were once deemed acceptable and follow the archetype of the modern sensitive male?

Freud once observed that the concept of masculinity is among the most confused that occurs in science. The point he was most tenacious about was that despite traditional assumptions about masculinity, it never exists in a pure state. He went on to say that "layers of emotion coexist and contradict each other. Each personality is a shade-filled, complex structure, not a transparent unit." Freud believed that men had both masculine and feminine qualities from a biological and psychological standpoint. Carl Jung was another psychoanalyst who argued that an imperative task of gender development was integrating the man's masculine and feminine characteristics to produce a fully functioning person.

If men are innately given both feminine and masculine traits, one can only imagine how challenging it must be to try to find a balance between them. This has been a central question for the men's movement. Its main goal is to address the current crisis in masculinity through workshops and consciousness-raising groups. Robert Bly, who became the "self-styled spiritual" leader of the men's movement with his book *Iron John*, argues that young men today have gone too far in expressing their feminine side. He says, "They are too eager to please women, with the result that they are out of touch with the 'deep masculine,' the 'warrior' who is an essential part of the psyche." He goes on to say:

> There's something wonderful about this development—I mean the practice of men welcoming their own 'feminine' consciousness and nurturing it—this is important—and yet I have the sense that there is something wrong. The male in the past twenty years has become more free. He's a nice boy who pleases not only his mother but also the young woman he is living with. But many of these men are not happy. You quickly notice the lack of energy in them. They are life-preserving but not exactly life-giving.
>
> Here we have a finely tuned young man, ecologically superior to his father, sympathetic to the whole harmony of the universe, yet he himself has little vitality to offer.

How far does Bly want young men to go back toward the "violently non-feminine behavior of maladjusted males," in the words of Mark Simpson, author of *Male Impersonators*? In order to escape the fate of the feminized male, must they "employ the threat of violence and show the sword"? According to Simpson, "Tens of thousands of American males have attended weekends in the forest based around [Bly's] Wild Man masculinity and the need to counteract the 'feminization' of modern men."

In an ideal world, I would say that men should be secure in both their masculine and feminine traits in order to maintain a sense of balance and truly find happiness in their lives. However, we have seen that this sentiment is a lot easier said than actually carried out. Instead, I feel that it would be more realistic to say that men should stay true to whichever side (whether it be their masculine or feminine traits) they feel instinctively comfortable with, despite current redefining of the sex roles. In society, it is only natural for differences to exist, and this is not necessarily an unfavorable attribute. In fact, differences are good and should be looked upon from a positive perspective.

Topics for Investigative Papers (A Sampling)

1. Is there any hope for lakes and rivers in your area or state? Or are they terminally polluted?
2. Are toxic dumps a danger in your community or state? Who is responsible?
3. Who is concerned about the academic performance of college athletes? Is it true that many don't graduate? What is being done about it?
4. Why do insurance companies treat "physical" and "mental" illnesses differently? What's behind the current movement to have insurers cover people with mental illnesses? How successful has it been?
5. What was at the center of the Ebonics or "Black English" controversy? Was it a local issue or one that has been an issue in other places? What explains the large outpouring of criticism? What do language scholars and teachers say? What was the role of the black leadership?
6. Who employs illegal aliens? In your area, are there sweatshops, migrant camps, illegal nannies or cleaning women?
7. Are there employment barriers for minorities or for women in local police and fire departments? Who or what is responsible?
8. In your community or larger area, are there charges of police brutality? Are they justified? Are they exaggerated? How are they dealt with, and by whom?
9. What is the record of the U.S. government concerning efforts to safeguard the variety of living species?
10. Are people who warn against ecological catastrophes alarmists? Focus on one widely debated threat: acid rain, water shortages for urban areas in the West, global warming, runaway population growth in underdeveloped countries.

12

Uncertain Future: Dream or Nightmare

I guess so many things are happening today that we're too busy to do anything but look, talk, and think about all of it. We don't have time to remember the past, and we don't have the energy to imagine the future.

—*Andy Warhol*

Since the time of the Greek philosopher Plato 2,500 years ago, writers projecting our common future have written Utopias. Literally, a Utopia is a place that exists "nowhere"—only in our dreams. Often these Utopias were imaginary commonwealths where human beings had outgrown their tendencies toward selfishness, conflict, and war. They had learned to live in harmony, to share the wealth, to marry sagely and raise their children without traumas. They had learned to follow wise leaders—or to do without leaders altogether.

However, gradually apprehension and disillusionment seeped in: Writers wrote *dys*topias—the opposite of books projecting an ideal future state. Dystopias took readers to nightmare worlds where people were faceless nobodies in beehive societies. All pleasure or satisfaction came from artificial stimulants. Books were likely to be banned, and their owners persecuted. Big Brother (or the big master computer) did the thinking for everybody. A ghastly newspeak channeled everyone's language into officially approved ways to talk.

Aldous Huxley's novel *Brave New World* (1932) was read by millions of readers as one of the first great modern dystopias—in which the perennial human dream of a perfect utopian future had been turned inside out. His society of the future was populated by happy zombies manipulated by the all-pervasive media. Giving up on the Utopian dream of a society in which all are created equal, Huxley's *Brave New World* featured an elaborate caste structure with the alphas at the top and the epsilons at the bottom. Stoned on a synthetic happiness drug, the people at the lower levels of the social heap accepted their lot.

How optimistic or how pessimistic are we as Americans about the society of the future? What kind of world are we going to leave for future generations? What are our projections for the future state of technology, economic warfare, women's rights, racial divisions, or health catastrophes like AIDS?

BARDS OF THE INTERNET

Philip Elmer-Dewitt

Students of communication often focus not so much on what we say but on how we communicate. In the words of the Canadian futurist Marshall McLuhan, "The medium is the message." The invention of writing (in the Near East several thousand years ago) made possible a wider sharing of knowledge, a durable record of the past, and sustained arguments about this life and the next. The invention of the printing press by the German printer Gutenberg in the fifteenth century ushered in the print age, which made possible mass literacy, mass education, and popular religious movements centered on the Good Book rather than on a select priesthood. Television, in the eyes of some critics, is reducing all political dialogue to the level of the sound bite or the attack ad. What's ahead for the future?

The author of the following article is a trend watcher for Time *magazine who explores the ways e-mail and other forms of electronic networking are shaping the way a new generation is going to think and write. While radio and television were widely seen as spelling the end of the print age, the coming of the personal computer has paradoxically sent millions back to keyboards and made modern-day scribblers out of most of us. What kind of "written speech" is shaping up as a major form of communication for the future?*

Thought Starters: Has the computer changed your own writing habits? Has it changed your reading habits?

One of the unintended side effects of the invention of the telephone   *1*
was that writing went out of style. Oh, sure, there were still full-time scribblers—journalists, academics, professional wordsmiths. And the great centers of commerce still found it useful to keep on hand people who could draft a memo, a brief, a press release or a contract. But given a choice between picking up a pen or a phone, most folks took the easy route and gave their fingers—and sometimes their mind—a rest.

Which makes what's happening on the computer networks all the more startling. Every night, when they should be watching television, millions of computer users sit down at their keyboards; dial into CompuServe, Prodigy, America Online or the Internet; and start typing—e-mail, bulletin-board postings, chat messages, rants, diatribes, even short stories and poems. Just when the media of McLuhan were supposed to render obsolete the medium of Shakespeare, the online world is experiencing the greatest boom in letter writing since the 18th century.

"It is my overwhelming belief that e-mail and computer conferencing are teaching an entire generation about the flexibility and utility of prose," writes Jon Carroll, a columnist at the *San Francisco Chronicle*. Patrick Nielsen Hayden, an editor at Tor Books, compares electronic bulletin boards with the "scribblers' compacts" of the late 18th and early 19th centuries, in which members passed letters from hand to hand, adding a little more at each turn. David Sewell, an associate editor at the University of Arizona, likens netwriting to the literary scene Mark Twain discovered in San Francisco in the 1860s, "when people were reinventing journalism by grafting it onto the tall-tale folk tradition." Others hark back to Tom Paine and the Revolutionary War pamphleteers, or even to the Elizabethan era, when, thanks to Gutenberg, a generation of English writers became intoxicated with language.

But such comparisons invite a question: If online writing today represents some sort of renaissance, why is so much of it so awful? For it can be very bad indeed: sloppy, meandering, puerile, ungrammatical, poorly spelled, badly structured and at times virtually content free. "HEY!!!1!" reads an all too typical message on the Internet, "I THINK METALLICA IZ REEL KOOL DOOD!1!!!"

One reason, of course, is that e-mail is not like ordinary writing. *5* "You need to think of this as 'written speech,'" says Gerard Van der Leun, a literary agent based in Westport, Connecticut, who has emerged as one of the preeminent stylists on the Net. "These things are little more considered than coffeehouse talk and a lot less considered than a letter. They're not to have and hold; they're to fire and forget." Many online postings are composed "live" with the clock ticking, using rudimentary word processors on computer systems that charge by the minute and in some cases will shut down without warning when an hour runs out.

That is not to say that with more time every writer on the Internet would produce sparkling copy. Much of the fiction and poetry is second-rate or worse, which is not surprising given that the barriers to entry are so low. "In the real world," says Mary Anne Mohanraj, a Chicago-based poet, "it takes a hell of a lot of work to get published, which naturally weeds out a lot of the garbage. On the Net, just a few keystrokes sends your writing out to thousands of readers."

But even among the reams of bad poetry, gems are to be found. Mike Godwin, a Washington-based lawyer who posts under the pen name "mnemonic," tells the story of Joe Green, a technical writer at Cray Research who turned a moribund discussion group called rec.arts.poems into a real poetry workshop by mercilessly critiquing the pieces he found there. "Some people got angry and said if he was such a god of poetry, why didn't he publish his poems to the group?" recalls Godwin. "He did, and blew them all away." Green's *Well Met in Minnesota*, a mock-epic account of a face-to-face meeting with a fellow network scribbler, is now revered on the Internet as a classic. It begins, "The truth is that when I met Mark

I was dressed as the *Canterbury Tales*. Rather difficult to do as you might suspect, but I wanted to make a certain impression."

The more prosaic technical and political discussion groups, meanwhile, have become so crowded with writers crying for attention that a Darwinian survival principle has started to prevail. "It's so competitive that you have to work on your style if you want to make any impact," says Jorn Barger, a software designer in Chicago. Good writing on the Net tends to be clear, vigorous, witty, and above all brief. "The medium favors the terse," says Crawford Kilian, a writing teacher at Capilano College in Vancouver, British Columbia. "Short paragraphs, bulleted lists and one-liners are the units of thought here."

Some of the most successful netwriting is produced in computer conferences, where writers compose in a kind of collaborative heat, knocking ideas against one another until they spark. Perhaps the best examples of this are found on the WELL, a Sausalito, California, bulletin board favored by journalists. The caliber of discussion is often so high that several publications—including the *New York Times* and the *Wall Street Journal*—have printed excerpts from the WELL.

Curiously, what works on the computer networks isn't necessarily   *10* what works on paper. Netwriters freely lace their prose with strange acronyms and "smileys," the little faces constructed with punctuation marks and intended to convey the winks, grins, and grimaces of ordinary conversations. Somehow it all flows together quite smoothly. On the other hand, polished prose copied onto bulletin boards from books and magazines often seems long-winded and phony. Unless they adjust to the new medium, professional writers can come across as self-important blowhards in debates with more nimble networkers. Says Brock Meeks, a Washington-based reporter who covers the online culture for *Communications Daily*: "There are a bunch of hacker kids out there who can string a sentence together better than their blue-blooded peers simply because they log on all the time and write, write, write."

There is something inherently democratizing—perhaps even revolutionary—about the technology. Not only has it enfranchised thousands of would-be writers who otherwise might never have taken up the craft, but it has also thrown together classes of people who hadn't had much direct contact before: students, scientists, senior citizens, computer geeks, grassroots (and often blue-collar) bulletin-board enthusiasts, and most recently the working press.

"It's easy to make this stuff look foolish and trivial," says Tor Books' Nielsen Hayden. "After all, a lot of everyone's daily life is foolish and trivial. I mean, really, smileys? Housewives in Des Moines who log on as VIXEN?"

But it would be a mistake to dismiss the computer-message boards or to underestimate the effect a lifetime of dashing off e-mail will have on a generation of young writers. The computer networks may not be Brook

Farm or the Globe Theatre, but they do represent, for millions of people, a living, breathing life of letters. One suspects that the Bard himself, confronted with the Internet, might have dived right in and never logged off.

The Responsive Reader

1. What is the author's account of the state of the art of writing and its uses before the onset of the computer age?
2. What effect is computer networking having on the way people communicate? According to the author, what effect, good or bad, is the rediscovery of written language in the computer age having on the style of writing?
3. What is "democratizing" about the new technology?

Talking, Listening, Writing

4. What has been your own experience with e-mail or electronic networking? Can you serve as a guide to a part of the new world of communication described by the author? (Try to provide samples of communications to share with others.)
5. What evidence have you seen that computers increasingly shape, manage, and control our lives?

Collaborative Projects

6. Working with a group, investigate the amounts of time your fellow students devote to competing claims on their attention: watching television, listening to recorded music, using the computer. What conclusions can you draw about how today's communication technologies are structuring the lives of the current generation?

AMERICAN CAPITALISM NEEDS A HEART TRANSPLANT

Lester Thurow

> *Futurologists everywhere see a trend toward multinational megacorporations that are largely beyond the control of individual governments or the voters. Corporate giants wed in multibillion-dollar mergers; "takeover artists" move in on large companies and acquire them in often hostile takeovers. Lester Thurow of MIT's Sloan School of Management is an economist who has written many books and articles about the American economy to educate the common reader. The following excerpt is from Chapter 9 of his* Head to Head: The Coming Economic Battle Among Japan, Europe, and America *(1992). He here focuses on corporate raiders who raise huge sums through junk bonds or other means, seduce the stockholders with inflated prices for their shares, skim off huge profits and lawyers' and consultants' fees, and finally leave the companies weakened or gutted, saddled with crippling interest payments on a huge debt. How does it work? Why does it work? Why should the reader care? The chapter from which the following selection is taken cites over ninety sources, ranging from the* Wall Street Journal *and* New York Times *to the British* Economist *and* Financial Times. *Marshaling the information gleaned from his wide-ranging reading, Thurow tries to make business people, voters, and political leaders understand basic economic issues: global competition, trade deficits, the high-tech future.*

Thought Starters: What evidence have you seen that big corporations are becoming more impersonal—cut off from direct human contact with their employees or their customers?

American capitalism is rich in financial investors of every size and variety, from the man on the street to the giant pension funds to the get-rich-quick speculators and takeover artists. In the 1980s financial Vikings were everywhere raiding everyone. If the merger and takeover wars had tightened up efficiency, a case could have been made for the merger wars, but productivity was falling at the end of the decade. Like the real Vikings who laid waste to so many vegetable gardens that they were eventually forced to become farmers if they did not want to starve, the financial Vikings were temporarily driven out of business by their own excesses. But their temporary demise is not enough.

Put bluntly, American capitalism needs a heart transplant. The financial traders who have become the heart of American capitalism need to be taken out and replaced by real capitalists who can become the heart of an American industrial rebirth. What America lacks is genuine, old-style capitalists—those big investors of yesteryear who often invented the technologies they were managing and whose personal wealth was inextricably linked to the destiny of their giant companies. It misses them. Men like Henry Ford; Thomas J. Watson, of IBM; and J. P. Morgan were at the heart of the system that produced the greatest economic power and the highest standard of living in history.

Old-fashioned corporations were run by individual capitalists—a shareholder with enough stock to dominate the board of directors and to dictate policy; a shareholder who usually was also the chief executive officer. Owning a majority or controlling interest, the old-fashioned capitalist did not have to concentrate his attention on reshuffling financial assets to fight off the raids of the financial Vikings. He was an industrialist who made his living by producing new products or by producing old products more cheaply. He was in control. But he was also locked into his corporation. He couldn't look to get rich by selling out for a quick profit—dumping his large stock holdings on the market would have simply depressed the price of his stock and cost him his job as one of the captains of American industry. His wealth, job, ego, and prestige were all locked up with the success or failure of his corporation. He had no choice but to work to improve the long-run efficiency and productivity of his company.

Today, with very few exceptions, old-fashioned capitalists are gone and cannot be brought back to life. In the aggregate, financial institutions such as pension funds, foundations, or mutual funds own 60 to 70 percent of most publicly listed companies. Collectively, they own the company, but individually, there are limits to how much of any one company they can own (usually no more than 10 percent), and how actively they can intervene in the decision making of the companies in which they do own stock (they cannot sit on the board of directors of any firm in which they have substantial holdings, since this would give them inside information). Minority shareholders are, in the aggregate, majority shareholders. By law, the institutions are essentially forced to be traders and speculators. They cannot be active builders that seek to strengthen a company's long-run competitive position. They cannot act as real capitalists who control what they own.

Minority shareholders have agendas very different from those of the dominant capitalist. Since they do not have the clout to change business decisions, strategies, or incumbent managers with their voting power, they can only enhance their wealth by buying and selling shares in accordance with what they think is going to happen to short-term profits. As a result, earnings per share, judged on a quarterly basis, become the dominant factor in determining whether the institutional investors will buy, sell, or keep a stock. Hundreds of millions of shares change hands every day in a game that has nothing to do with beliefs about long-term success or failure, or with plans to convert failure into success.

As the financial institutions grew to their present size, they could make money by being better informed than the individual shareholders whose shares they were acquiring. But as they came to own a majority of the shares in the market, they were essentially buying and selling from each other. What one financial institution gained, another lost. Their only options were to buy stock-market averages (a dull option that does not yield high returns or take talented people to implement it) or to participate in the financial wars.

For these minority-majority institutional shareholders, the takeover game was simply the only money-making game in town. Opportunities existed to make a lot of money quickly. It was a game far better than the zero-sum game they were playing with each other on the stock market. America's laws could even be interpreted as saying that institutional investors that did not want to participate in the takeover game had to sell out to others who did. If a takeover artist offered a pension fund more for its shares than their current stock-market value and the fund did not sell out, perhaps it could be sued for not living up to its fiduciary responsibilities to maximize stock-market values for the benefit of future pension recipients. To ignore such short-run profit-making opportunities might actually be illegal. Recently, the financial institutions have organized to prevent management from adopting defense mechanisms such as poison pills to stop takeovers, since these devices undercut the value of the shares the institutions hold.

In the absence of dominant shareholders, corporations are effectively run by their professional managers. Unlike founding fathers, the professional chief executive officers (CEOs) of large corporations usually reach that exalted position just a few years before they retire. Long-run careers at the top are very unusual. As a short-term CEO, they not surprisingly organize compensation packages for themselves that emphasize bonuses and salaries keyed to current profits or sales. These short-run compensation packages are unfortunately completely congruent with the short-run perspective of the institutional shareholders. Neither the manager nor the shareholder expects to be around very long.

For both managers and minority shareholders, mergers and acquisitions—the takeover game—represent an almost irresistible path to glory. The managers of acquiring companies can double sales and profits (and, hence, their own salaries and bonuses, which are tied to those sales and profits) with a stroke of a pen—and without risking a cent of their own personal money. If a firm's own economic crop of new or cheaper products were homegrown, the crop probably wouldn't ripen before the incumbent manager retired. Rome could not be built in a day, but in the 1980s its economic equivalent could be bought in a single day.

Those who rise to the top from finance, a large fraction of American   *10* CEOs, may in fact know far more about fighting the financial wars than they know about running their own companies. It is what they are good at. It is what they have been trained to do. Attack or be attacked! Some managers will, of course, lose in the takeover games, but those on the losing side have the solace of multimillion-dollar golden parachutes.

Financial takeovers are always justified on the grounds that they will enhance productivity and competitiveness, but the promised leaner and meaner corporations do not seem to emerge. No one can know for sure how today's mergers will be performing fifteen years from now, but we do know that the last conglomerate merger wave in the late 1960s and early 1970s did not lead to firms with superior performance. The whole process looked much like a random walk—some winners, some losers—on average, average.

The short-run results of the current wave of financial activities are only too clear. Productivity growth is lower at the end of the decade than it was at the beginning of the decade. Firms ended up loaded with too much debt, having too few free funds to invest in new products, new processes, or research and development. With all of that debt, they became more risk-averse—less willing to bet on new activities. In many cases they simply could not bet on the future, since the company had effectively already been bet.

Firms become financially weaker and more vulnerable to collapse in recessions. The 1991 recession was the first big test of the merger wave of the 1980s. Would the firms that were affected by those activities be able to survive a downturn in revenue, given their needs to make huge interest payments? Until a recovery is well under way, we won't know the exact extent of the damage, but midway through the process, for too many the answer is already no. A list of the firms in bankruptcy that in the 1980s participated in the merger wars would go on for many pages.

Those who argue for the virtues of the takeover movement do so on the basis that it enriches the shareholders and that firms exist *solely* to serve the interests of the shareholders. There is no doubt that the enrichment part of the argument is true, but the question remains whether firms exist solely to serve the interests of the shareholders. Shareholders' rights are not in fact paramount.

In the dicta of Adam Smith, the individual search for profits would 15
always promote the nation's economic growth. But in practice a problem developed. Too often, Adam Smith's "invisible hand" became the hand of a pickpocket. Free unfettered markets had a habit of discovering very profitable but nonproductive activities. Practical experience taught that profit maximizing did not necessarily lead to output maximizing.

In the midnineteenth century, the railroads used their monopoly over the means of transportation to divert the fruits of others' productive energies to themselves by setting transportation prices that extracted monopoly rents. The railroad barons were profit maximizers, but their profit maximizing did not lead to a larger economic pie. Quite the reverse; it led to a smaller economic pie. There was simply more money to be made extracting monopoly rents than there was to be made in operating better transportation systems. In response, the United States created the Interstate

Commerce Commission to refocus the attention of railroad entrepreneurs on running better railroads than on economically raping the rest of society.

Later, the robber barons in steel, oil, and copper discovered that man-made monopolies were as good as those made by technology. Establishing monopolies and raising prices were far more profitable than increasing efficiency and production. In engaging in these activities, the corporation was fulfilling its private obligation to maximize profits and shareholder wealth, but it was not meeting its social obligation of being a vehicle for maximizing national growth and a higher standard of living for everyone. Again, society refocused the profit-making ambitions of the robber barons with the Sherman Antitrust Act of 1890 and the Clayton Antitrust Act of 1914. The new laws were designed to insure that the name of the game was not simply to make money, but to make money by building a better or cheaper product.

Present laws are often the equivalent of shooting oneself in the foot. General Motors, for example, is permitted to engage in a joint venture with Toyota that will effectively attack Ford and Chrysler, whereas it would not be permitted to engage in a joint venture with Ford to repel the Japanese auto invasion. Antitrust limitations that apply to two American firms do not apply to an American and a Japanese firm, although there is now a world, not an American, market for cars.

Private firms exist in our society because Americans have collectively decided that private firms are in general the best way to promote economic growth and to expand the output available to everyone—shareholder and nonshareholder alike. If private firms fail to serve this social function, they will be redirected, as they have been in the past, with new sets of rules and regulations that will hopefully once again set them off on productive paths.

What has to be done, however, is not simply to deregulate or to *20* make minor changes in antitrust laws. The entire regulatory framework governing finance and industry must be altered so that the biggest profits and highest incomes are paid to those who expand productivity and output rather than to those who rejiggle financial assets. The financial Vikings, today's counterpart to yesterday's robber barons, need to be reined in so as to refocus their attention on production, just as those earlier robber barons needed to refocus on production rather than monopoly profits.

The Responsive Reader

1. For Thurow, what sets apart old-fashioned entrepreneurial capitalism and the go-go capitalism of the eighties and nineties?
2. Who are the key players in the takeover game? What role do the institutional investors play? What role do the managers play? How does Thurow characterize the "financial Vikings"?
3. How successful is Thurow in explaining the mechanisms involved? What comparisons or analogies do you find especially helpful? What questions would you ask him if you could?

Talking, Listening, Writing

4. Does Thurow confirm or change your idea of what capitalism is?
5. How would you explain a basic economic issue that should vitally concern ordinary voters? For instance, you might shed light on hostile takeovers, the budget deficit, structural unemployment, the migration of jobs to low-wage locations, the decline of labor unions, or the role of small business.

Collaborative Projects

6. Participate in staging a debate between critics and defenders of the takeover artists or "financial Vikings."

CANDID CAMERA: CORPORATE SNOOPING 101

Mark Frankel

"Big Brother is watching you": In the heyday of totalitarian governments, citizens learned to express their private opinions only in whispers and out of hearing of hidden microphones and government spies. Communist governments in Eastern Europe maintained a huge surveillance apparatus, listening in on telephone conversations, opening letters, and filing the reports of an army of informers. Americans had their own horror stories: a President who kept an "enemies list"; the FBI snooping on suspected subversives and on the Reverend Martin Luther King, Jr. Today, Americans are learning to look over their shoulders and to try to shield their private communications from a new kind of snoop: The Big Boss is using state-of-the-art technology to monitor employees' work habits, bathroom breaks, union activities, and private communications. Mark Frankel is a writer for Newsweek International *in New York. He looks at surveillance techniques with the jaundiced eyes of a journalist—a member of a profession that has always been a premier target of those who read with the informer's eye and listen with the informer's ear.*

Thought Starters: Have you ever felt you were being watched? Have you ever felt the pressure to watch your language, your moves, or your contacts with other people? Have you ever felt someone was keeping track, keeping a file, or compiling a dossier?

I used to think professional snoops were all variations on Harry Caul, the paranoid, guilt-ridden wiretapper of Francis Ford Coppola's *The Conversation.* But W. T. "Ted" Sandin clearly loves his work. With the infectious enthusiasm of a high-school camera club faculty adviser, the middle-aged Sandin runs Video Systems Inc., one of the country's leading manufacturers and distributors of covert video surveillance hardware. At Surveillance Expo '95, which brought several hundred private investigators and corporate security specialists (plus a smattering of Armani-clad Middle Eastern and Latin American gentlemen too discreet to expose their affiliations) to the McLean Hilton in Virginia last summer, Sandin was among the top draws. About three dozen conferees paid $100 each to attend his seminar on how to spy on other people in the electronic age.

He did not disappoint. Reminding his scribbling pupils that "surveillance means only extension of the eye," Sandin spent four hours demonstrating a collection of eye-popping miniature video cameras, each seemingly tinier than the last. The smallest was a black-and-white TV camera barely larger than a piece of Bazooka bubble gum. Attached to a tiny transmitter powered by a common 9-volt battery, such minicams can be hidden almost anywhere in a typical office or factory, Sandin explained. Light switches, exit signs or room thermostats are just a few of the possibilities for camouflage. "Be creative," he exhorted us.

In the name of personal security, Americans have already learned to accept and ignore video cameras in the public spaces they routinely pass through: parking lots, elevators, bank lobbies and hotel stairways. (According to STAT Resources, a Massachusetts research firm, an estimated $2.1 billion will be spent on closed-circuit video gear this year alone.) Now they may have to learn to accept them in the workplace as well. Propelled by concerns with worker productivity, industrial espionage, personal security, drugs on the job and skyrocketing insurance liability, corporate America is increasingly resorting to secret monitoring of its employees. An August 1994 report by the Geneva-based International Labor Organization concluded that "Monitoring and surveillance techniques available as a result of advances in technology make methods of control more pervasive than ever before and raise serious questions of human rights."

Consider a few recent cases. In Phoenix, Arizona, Freddy Craig, a longtime elementary school principal, stumbled upon a video camera hidden in the ceiling of his suburban school office—as well as one secreted in the school shower he often used after jogging. The cameras had been installed by the newly hired school district superintendent, who claimed that Craig was under investigation for unspecified "misconduct" with his students' parents. The charges proved groundless.

In Elmira, New York, a former McDonald's restaurant manager went to court seeking $2 million from the burger chain, as well as the local franchise, for invasion of privacy. In addition to overseeing the deep fryer and griddle, the plaintiff, Michael Huffcut, had been conducting an extramarital affair with another McDonald's employee. Huffcut's suit charged that not only did his former restaurant supervisor obtain copies of the romantic messages the illicit lovers left for each other on their office voice mail, he also played the recordings for Huffcut's wife.

Several years ago, the Boston Sheraton Hotel installed a hidden camera in the employees' locker room in what management claimed was an effort to crack a drug ring—and what lawyers for the hotel workers describe as a heavy-handed attempt to discourage union activity.

The threat is not limited to videocams and voice mail. Service industries place millions of workers in front of computer terminals where their performance is easily monitored by remote. Desktop computers, fax machines, pagers, computer networks, cellular phones and e-mail have become as ubiquitous as styrofoam coffee cups in most offices. While employees have been introduced to these contraptions with soothing talk about "personal passwords" and "private files," workers' privacy is easily shredded. In one of the few surveys of corporate electronic privacy policies, conducted by *MacWorld* magazine in 1993, of 301 U.S. companies polled, more than one in five had searched their employees' computer files, voice mail, e-mail or other digital network communications. "Users naturally assume that, because they have private passwords, only they can enter their e-mail and private files, . . . but even the most insignificant network managers can override passwords and enter files," says Charles Pillar, who conducted the survey.

While researching this article, I struck up an e-mail correspondence with a New York-based high-tech surveillance specialist who told me about his work:

> For a cellular phone interception system, I charge $2,500 to $4,000. This allows the employer to monitor all employees' cellular phone conversations or simply to keep a log of the times and length of calls and any numbers called, etc. It is not actually necessary to listen in on the conversations; they can be logged into a computer. The employer can thus see who has been using these phones for personal use to make $2-a-minute personal calls to the kids. . . .
>
> I've been called to do phone interception work a lot, especially with telemarketer and service representative type workers where the boss monitors the line to make sure that the employees don't have a nasty tone with the customers. . . .
>
> For computer modem interception, I usually charge $3,000. It allows an employer to passively monitor a particular telephone line and intercept the modem data that's going through [it]. The employer can, in effect, see everything that the employee types into his computer and that appears on his screen.

Most American workers assume that their privacy on the job is ensured by constitutional safeguards. Unfortunately, they are wrong. While the Fourth Amendment protects citizens against unreasonable search and seizure by the state, it does not touch private employers, who are free to run their businesses—and spy on their employees—as they please. Current federal privacy laws are case studies in half-measures. While the 1986 Electronic Communications Act prohibits eavesdropping on telephones without a warrant or permission, it provides a loophole that permits companies to monitor employees' calls "for business purposes." And, while privacy laws vary widely from state to state, cutting-edge gizmos such as mini-video cameras are so new they slip between existing wiretap statutes and labor regulations.

Privacy advocates, labor unions and groups such as 9 to 5, the working women's lobby, have long sought national standards that would regulate workplace surveillance. In the last Congress, Senator Paul Simon and Representative Pat Williams introduced such legislation, the Privacy for Con-   *10* sumers and Workers Act. But the U.S. Chamber of Commerce and the National Association of Manufacturers (NAM) opposed the bill fiercely, and it died in committee. Privacy advocates have all but given up on trying to pass a meaningful piece of legislation this session.

Until Congress puts on the brakes, video cameras and other means of workplace surveillance will only get cooler, and more insidious. Back at the Surveillance Expo, Ted Sandin proudly demonstrated the latest thing: body video. Wearing a tiny camera hidden in a pair of plastic sunglasses, he strutted about the stage. In the audience, we watched, mesmerized, as an image of ourselves jiggled on a nearby video monitor. Sandin promised that as marvelous as this micro-gadgetry seemed, even niftier stuff was coming down the pike. After all, he reminded us, "This is a consumer-driven marketplace."

The Responsive Reader

1. What was "eye-boggling" for the author about state-of-the-art surveillance technology? What for you were some of the most striking examples of sophisticated gadgetry?
2. Is there a common thread in Frankel's case histories of aggrieved parties? Does the right to privacy seem to apply equally to all of them? (*Is* there a right to privacy?)
3. What are the motives of employers employing surveillance technology? Which of their aims or justifications seem most important to you? Which methods or procedures seem to you most defensible?
4. To judge from this article, who tries to protect employees' and private citizens' rights, and why? Who fights them? (Do you find yourself taking sides? With whom or against whom?)

Talking, Listening, Writing

5. Many of our constitutional safeguards were developed to protect Americans against a tyrannical government. Do Americans tend to be paranoid about an intrusive government but naive and helpless when it comes to exploitation or manipulation by private interests? Do Americans tend to be more wary of Big Government than of Big Business?
6. What do you know about consumer groups, consumer advocacy, or other attempts to provide a counterweight to the economic and political power of corporations?

Collaborative Projects

7. Working with a group, you may want to investigate recent legislation or lawsuits involving the right to privacy.

OUR CHILDREN ARE OUR FUTURE— UNFORTUNATELY THEY'RE BIGOTS

Richard Cohen

During the era of the civil rights movement, many Americans believed in progress toward better race relations. They envisioned a future where African Americans and other minorities would emerge from poverty and deprivation to become fully integrated into American life. However, in the eighties and nineties, trend watchers like the Washington Post *columnist who wrote the following selection noticed a growing backlash against official policies of toler- ance, integration, and affirmative action. "Forced busing" to achieve better racial balance in the schools proved bitterly divisive and contributed to "white flight" from public education. The media sensationalized racial incidents like the beating by Los Angeles police of the black motorist Rodney King or the killing of a black youth by a white mob in Bensonhurst. Journalists started to give prominent treatment to racial incidents on college campuses. Is the nation backsliding where the fight against racism is concerned?*

Thought Starters: Would you call your campus integrated or divided along ethnic and racial lines? Can you cite incidents that point to racial animosity or racial harmony? Do your friends and acquaintances sound prejudiced to you?

There's hardly a politician in the land who, when children are men- tioned, does not say they are our future. That's true, of course—and noth- ing can be done about it—but the way things are going we should all be worried. A generation of bigots is coming of age.   *1*

The evidence for that awful prognostication can be found in a recent public opinion survey conducted for the Anti-Defamation League by the Boston polling firm of Marttila & Kiley—two outfits with considerable credentials in the field of public opinion research. For the first time, a trend has been reversed. Up to now, opinion polls have always found that the more schooling a person has, the more likely he is to be tolerant. For that reason, older people—who by and large have the least education— are the most intolerant age group in the nation.

But no longer. The ADL found a disturbing symmetry: Older and younger white Americans share the same biases. For instance, when white people were asked if blacks prefer to remain on welfare rather than work, 42 percent of the respondents 50 years old and over said the statement was "probably true." Predictably, the figure plummeted to 29 percent for those 30 to 49. But then it jumped to 36 percent for respondents under 30.

Similarly, a majority of younger respondents thought blacks "complain too much about racism" (68 percent) and "stick together more than others" (63 percent). For both statements, the young had a higher percentage of agreement than any other age category. The pattern persisted for the other questions as well—questions designed to ferret out biased attitudes. In the words of Abraham Foxman, the ADL's national director, the generation that's destined to run this country is either racist or disposed to racism to a degree that he characterized as "a crisis." It's hard to disagree with him.

What's going on? The short answer is that no one knows for sure. But some guesses can be ventured and none of them is comforting. The first and most obvious explanation has to do with age itself: The under 30 generation is pathetically ignorant of recent American history. Younger people apparently know little about—and did not see on television—the civil rights struggles of the 1950s and 1960s, everything from the police dogs of Birmingham to the murder of civil rights workers. They apparently do not understand that if blacks tend to see racism everywhere, that's because in the recent past, it *was* everywhere and remains the abiding American sickness.

But historical ignorance is not the only factor accounting for the ADL's findings. Another, apparently, is affirmative action. It has created a category of white victims, either real or perceived, who are more likely than other whites to hold prejudicial views. For instance, the ADL asked, "Do you feel you have ever been a victim of reverse discrimination in hiring or promotion?" Only 21 percent said yes. But the percentage rose to 26 percent for college graduates and 23 percent for people with postgraduate degrees. Since the ADL found that "about one third" of the self-described victims of reverse discrimination fell into the "most prejudiced" category, these numbers are clearly worth worrying about. Too many of the American elite are racially aggrieved—although possibly some of them were bigoted in the first place.

One could argue that not all of the statements represent proof of bigoted attitudes. For instance, white college students who witness voluntary self-segregation on the part of black students—demands for their own dorms, for instance—have some reason to think that blacks "stick together more than others." Nevertheless, the data strongly suggest that progress on racial attitudes is being reversed—with contributions from both races. Worse, this is happening at a time when the economic pie is shrinking and competition for jobs increasing. If the economic trend continues, racial intolerance is likely to grow.

No one I spoke with at either the Anti-Defamation League or at Marttila & Kiley thought their findings were definitive or could offer concrete explanations. But the numbers conform to what you and I know—or think we do—about racial friction on the nation's campuses and a growing uneasiness about affirmative action. After all, most of those programs were instituted during a period of sustained economic growth, a boom time especially for college graduates, when jobs were plentiful. That's no longer the case.

Given the ADL's findings, it's clear that something has to be done. It's nothing less than a calamity that a generation has come of age without a deep appreciation of the recent history of African Americans. At the same time, black leaders who advocate or condone separatism had better appreciate the damage they are doing. And finally, affirmative action programs, as well-intentioned as they may be, need to be re-examined—and without critics automatically being labeled as racist. No doubt these programs have done some good. But there's a growing body of evidence—of which the ADL poll is only the latest—that they also do some bad.

The Responsive Reader

1. According to this columnist, how does the survey he cites reverse traditional assumptions about intolerance?
2. What test questions did the survey use to determine whether young people were "disposed to racism"? Which to you seem most relevant or important? Would you challenge any of them? Does Cohen question any of them?
3. Why and how, as in other similar discussions, does affirmative action become a central issue in this column?

Talking, Listening, Writing

4. Cohen concludes "that something has to be done." What? How useful or convincing are his suggestions?
5. Do you agree that racism is on the rise in our society? What evidence can you cite to support your opinion?
6. Do you or institutions or organizations you know have a concrete program for addressing the problem Cohen examines?

Collaborative Projects

7. Working with a group, explore questions like the following: How much attention do people pay to opinion polls? How much confidence do they place in them? What role have opinion polls played in recent elections or policy decisions by officials?

FEDERAL FOOLISHNESS
AND MARIJUANA

Jerome P. Kassirer

"Death with Dignity" became a watchword in the nineties. Surveys revealed that large numbers of terminal patients were kept alive by a depersonalized medical technology, often in severe pain, and against their own express wishes, against the wishes of family, and against the better judgment of nursing staff most directly involved with dying patients. As part of the movement to honor the rights and needs of dying patients, states started to pass laws allowing the medical use of marijuana to alleviate the extreme retching nausea or severe discomfort many terminal patients are subjected to as the result of chemotherapy or other medical interventions. Ample legal precedent exists: In two world wars, morphine was used to alleviate the hellish pain suffered by severely wounded veterans. The Virginia legislature passed a law in 1979 allowing doctors to prescribe marijuana to treat glaucoma and to help cancer patients cope with the side effects of chemotherapy. Nevertheless, politicians afraid of being labeled soft on drugs started a campaign to criminalize the patients and compassionate doctors or family. In the following editorial, the editor-in-chief of the New England Journal of Medicine, *the most prestigious medical journal in the country, published since 1812 by the Massachusetts Medical Society, weighs in on the subject of medical marijuana. In the words of a newspaper editor, the* Journal's *"editorials and commentaries by medical specialists have long played a major role in debates over health policy controversies." Dr. Kassirer is a kidney specialist formerly on the faculty at Tufts University Medical Center in Boston.*

Thought Starters: From your reading or firsthand observation, what do you know about living wills, hospices, or Dr. Kevkorian?

The advanced stages of many illnesses and their treatments are often   *1*
accompanied by intractable nausea, vomiting or pain. Thousands of patients with cancer, AIDS and other diseases report they have obtained striking relief from these devastating symptoms by smoking marijuana. The alleviation of distress can be so striking that some patients and their families have been willing to risk a jail term to obtain or grow the marijuana.

Despite the desperation of these patients, within weeks after voters in Arizona and California approved propositions allowing physicians in their states to prescribe marijuana for medical indications, federal officials, including the president, the secretary of health and human services, and the attorney general sprang into action. At a news conference, Health and Human Services Secretary Donna E. Shalala gave an organ recital of the parts of the body that she asserted could be harmed by marijuana and warned of the evils of its spreading use. Attorney General Janet Reno announced that physicians in any state who prescribed the drug could lose the privilege of writing prescriptions, be excluded from Medicare and Medicaid reimbursement, and even be prosecuted for a federal crime. General Barry R. McCaffrey, director of the Office of National Drug Control Policy, reiterated his agency's position that marijuana is a dangerous drug and implied that voters in Arizona and California had been duped into voting for these propositions. He indicated that it is always possible to study the effects of any drug, including marijuana, but that the use of marijuana by seriously ill patients would require, at the least, scientifically valid research.

I believe that a federal policy that prohibits physicians from alleviating suffering by prescribing marijuana for seriously ill patients is misguided, heavy-handed and inhumane. Marijuana may have long-term adverse effects and its use may presage serious addictions, but neither long-term side effects nor addiction is a relevant issue for such patients. It is also hypocritical to forbid physicians to prescribe marijuana while permitting them to use morphine and meperidine to relieve extreme dyspnea (difficulty breathing) and pain. With both these drugs, the difference between the dose that relieves symptoms and the dose that hastens death is very narrow; by contrast, there is no risk of death from smoking marijuana. To demand evidence of therapeutic efficacy is equally hypocritical. The noxious sensations that patients experience are extremely difficult to quantify in controlled experiments. What really counts for a therapy with this kind of safety margin is whether a seriously ill patient feels relief as a result of the intervention, not whether a controlled trial "proves" its efficacy.

Paradoxically, dronabinol, a drug that contains one of the active ingredients in marijuana (tetrahydrocannabinol), has been available by prescription for more than a decade. But it is difficult to titrate the therapeutic dose of this drug, and it is not widely prescribed. By contrast, smoking marijuana produces a rapid increase in the blood level of the active ingredients and is thus more likely to be therapeutic. Needless to say, new drugs such as those that inhibit the nausea associated with chemotherapy may well be more beneficial than smoking marijuana, but their comparative efficacy has never been studied.

Whatever their reasons, federal officials are out of step with the public. Dozens of states have passed laws that ease restrictions on the prescribing of marijuana by physicians, and polls consistently show that the public favors the use of marijuana for such purposes. Federal authorities should rescind their prohibition of the medicinal use of marijuana for seriously ill patients and allow physicians to decide which patients to treat. The government should change marijuana's status from that of a Schedule I drug (considered to be potentially addictive and with no current medical use) and regulate in accordingly. To ensure its proper distribution and use, the government could declare itself the only agency sanctioned to provide the marijuana. I believe that such a change in policy would have no adverse effects. The argument that it would be a signal to the young that "marijuana is OK" is, I believe, specious.

This proposal is not new. In 1986, after years of legal wrangling, the Drug Enforcement Administration (DEA) held extensive hearings on the transfer of marijuana to Schedule II. In 1988, the DEA's own administrative-law judge concluded: "It would be unreasonable, arbitrary, and capricious for DEA to continue to stand between those sufferers and the benefits of this substance in light of the evidence in this record." Nonetheless, the DEA overruled the judge's order to transfer marijuana to Schedule II, and in 1992, it issued a final rejection of all requests for reclassification.

Some physicians will have the courage to challenge the continued proscription of marijuana for the sick. Eventually, their actions will force the courts to adjudicate between the rights of those at death's door and the absolute power of bureaucrats whose decisions are based more on reflexive ideology and political correctness than on compassion.

The Responsive Reader

1. What are the key points in Kassirer's support for his thesis that "a federal policy that prohibits physicians from alleviating suffering by prescribing marijuana for seriously ill patients is misguided, heavy-handed and inhumane"? What is the problem with asking for more research? What is the problem with drugs providing alternative therapy? What are the key arguments in favor of using marijuana?
2. What according to Kassirer is the history of the "legal wrangling" over the issue?
3. As Kassirer sees it, what does the future hold? How does he sum up the choice that will confront the courts, politicians, and voters?

Talking, Listening, Writing

4. Gary Trudeau in his *Doonesbury* cartoon had a series about local cops refusing to shut down a clinic dispensing medical marijuana; "They had to send Republicans in!" Do you think controversies like the ones about medical marijuana or assisted suicide tend to polarize the public along predictable liberal vs. conservative lines? Why, or why not?
5. What would you say in a letter to the editor in response to Kassirer's editorial?

6. Would you "risk a jail term" to relieve the insufferable pain of a dying patient?

Collaborative Projects

7. Kübler-Ross was among the pioneers objecting to doctors playing God and using a runaway medical technology in indefinitely prolonging the death agonies of patients. Working with a group, you may want to investigate current thinking and current controversies on the subject of death with dignity.

SISTERHOOD WAS POWERFUL

Laura Shapiro

> *Some of the most widely read, reviewed, and discussed books of our time have been manifestos of the women's movement, starting with the early classics: Betty Friedan's* The Feminine Mystique, *Germaine Greer's* The Female Eunuch, *or Simone de Beauvoir's* The Second Sex. *More recently, Naomi Wolf's* The Beauty Myth *and Susan Faludi's* Backlash *(both 1991) attracted intensive media attention. In the following article, a reviewer for* Newsweek *examines a more recent crop of books about the feminist movement. Some are books of soul-searching or recrimination as the women's movement tries to chart a course into an uncertain future. Many reflect a sense that the movement has lost momentum or is searching for new directions. The authors address such issues as women's failure to translate numbers into votes for candidates committed to women's issues; the perception of the feminist movement as dominated by radical advocates of gay and lesbian rights; or the charge that feminists tend to be well-educated and middle-class, out of touch with working-class women.*

Thought Starters: What images, slogans, or associations do terms like *feminism* or *women's liberation* bring to mind? Have your own ideas about feminism or what it means to be a feminist changed over time? How or why?

In 1968 Susan Douglas and her college roommate wrote across their windows in fluorescent paint, "The more I see of men, the more I like dogs." Strictly speaking, this was high jinks, not politics, Douglas acknowledges in *Where the Girls Are* (340 pages. Times Books. $23), an analysis of growing up female in postwar America. But as a curtain raiser for the women's movement, Douglas's fluorescent message—with its excess, its flamboyance and its hard kernel of truth—perfectly captured the spirit of those early years. Barriers toppled, new frontiers seemed to open daily; it was exhilarating, it was unstoppable. The whole world was watching.

And today? Nearly three decades of revolution later, it seems as though the whole world is kvetching. Despite victories that include two Supreme Court justices and the first Disney heroine in history who'd rather read than get married, complaints about the women's movement are piling up. According to a spate of new books, the problem with the movement is that it's all about lesbians. Or abortion. Or political correctness. Or anything, runs the criticism, except ordinary women struggling with jobs and families.

No question about it, some of these complaints have merit. The excesses of feminist correctness are detailed with relish by Christina Hoff Sommers in *Who Stole Feminism?* (320 pages. Simon & Schuster. $23), likely to be the most talked-about manifesto since Susan Faludi's *Backlash*. Sommers, a philosophy professor at Clark University in Worcester, Mass., collected much of her evidence at feminist conferences, traditionally places where the worst inanities of the movement swarm like gnats. She describes conferences breaking up into grievance groups—Jewish women, Asian-American women, fat women, old women—as well as the inevitable sub-groups ("The Jewish women discovered they were deeply divided: some accepted being Jewish; others were seeking to recover from it"). Then there were the campfire-type songs, the healing rituals, the group hugs and the victim testimonials.

But on the substantive issues driving feminism today, Sommers is dead serious. She sees what she calls gender feminism in the ascendancy, a movement devoted to nurturing femaleness in various treacly ways, at the expense of "equity feminism," dedicated to achieving equal rights. Such phony issues as date rape and self-esteem preoccupy gender feminists, according to Sommers; they're also busy transforming academia. "While male students are off studying . . . engineering and biology, women in feminist classrooms are sitting around being 'safe' and 'honoring' feelings," she writes.

There is enough truth in Sommers's accusations to make them im- *5* portant, but not enough to make them completely convincing. Her analysis of rape statistics, for instance, indicates that they may indeed be inflated; but her definition of rape—a gender-blind crime of violence, nothing misogynistic about it—is ludicrous. And while she skillfully attacks two widely publicized studies purporting to show that girls lack self-esteem and get less attention from teachers than boys do, it's hard to go along with her conclusion that girls are doing just fine. Teen-pregnancy rates, eating disorders, and disappointing scores on standardized tests tell another story.

Sherrye Henry also finds the current movement beset by radicals out of touch with ordinary women in *The Deep Divide* (452 pages. Macmillan. $25). Henry, a long-time radio-talk-show host in New York, ran for the state senate in 1990 and lost. The defeat inspired her to investigate a compelling (certainly to her) question: why don't women support feminist candidates? (In 1992 several feminists were elected to Congress, but Henry notes that dozens more lost.) She turned up some provocative data.

Through polling and focus groups, Henry learned that many women just don't get it. Even though they suffer the indignities and injustices that feminists have been talking about for eons, women haven't made the connection. A married secretary with three children, back at the office after a too short maternity leave, forced to do extra work because so many people in the company have been laid off, whose husband "helps" but doesn't take charge of any housework, tells a focus group she's worn to a frazzle.

"It never occurs to her," writes Henry, "that what she needs includes flextime or job-sharing . . . guaranteed family leave . . . and more consistent help from her husband, all of which are tenets of feminism."

Henry suggests that the women's movement essentially repackage itself as a movement for women, children and families, shoving most other issues into the background. "Lesbian rights, although basic in a democracy . . . will never energize the majority," she writes. She calls for new feminist leaders, nicely dressed, please ("Those who appear too 'mannish' will not gain as much support for their causes"), who will politely distance themselves from messier sorts working on abortion rights, wife-battering and other icky problems. It's unclear why she is so certain that designer suits and wholesome issues will win the day for women candidates, unless she really believes that those who lost in 1992 wore hip-waders on the campaign trail and ran on a platform of same-sex marriage rights.

But give Henry credit: she knows the difference between the media-generated monsters of "women's lib" and the real women's movement. Not so Anne Taylor Fleming, who made her name writing about feminism for numerous publications (including *Newsweek*) beginning in the '70s. Fleming describes herself in *Motherhood Deferred* (256 pages. Putnam. $23.95) as part of a "sacrificial generation," young feminists who put off pregnancy for work, waiting so long that they lost the chance. Infertility is her punishment, writes Fleming, for falling under the spell of "those angry, childless and unmarried ideologues of yore." Oddly, she had no trouble fending off the feminist rhetoric against men and marriage; she got married at 22. But then the "anti-motherhood bandwagon" rattled by and she leapt on board. Twelve years later she began trying to conceive, had no luck and finally entered the cold domain of high-tech baby-making. She had lots of company: more women "with the Scarlet 'I' writ, if not across our foreheads, certainly across our hearts . . . modern-day Hester Prynnes . . . who had . . . put work ahead of motherhood."

This is sticky stuff. It badly misrepresents the women's movement,   *10* which did a lot more agitating for day care than issuing decrees against childbearing. True, the powerful focus on work sent pregnancy to a remote file drawer labeled SOME OTHER TIME. But Fleming barely admits the possibility that her infertility might have roots someplace other than her politics. As for her politics, Fleming's own writing shows her to have been anything but a hapless zombie of the women's movement. Her first article, published in 1974, urged women not to get ahead by thinking like men but to hold on to their "specialness," their "female ethnicity." Another article was a defense of flirting, which Fleming herself admits had a touch of backlash about it.

When Fleming turns to the infertility business she knows so well, the book picks up considerably. Her account of baby-making in labs, the hope followed by the disappointment followed by a fresh round of hope, is genuinely gripping—and it captures the sadness of her plight.

After the mudslinging in these books, what a pleasure it is to find Susan Douglas and Gloria Steinem, a couple of unrepentant, unreformed feminists who liked the women's movement just fine and still do. Douglas's engagingly written "Where the Girls Are" provides a first-rate analysis of the music, movies, and TV imagery that helped shape female psyches beginning in the '50s. Dissecting TV coverage of the early years of the movement, she also sheds light on the way "feminism" turned into a dirty word. Organizers of the first major event of modern feminism, the Aug. 26, 1970, Women's Strike for Equality, issued three demands— "which you can read with a wistful sigh," writes Douglas, "since none of them has been achieved: equal opportunity for women in employment and education, twenty-four-hour child-care centers and abortion on demand." TV coverage that day and thereafter conceded the merits of equal pay, but much of the liveliest air time showed feminists as loonies. Meanwhile, a few truly radical feminists also had their moment on camera. Shulamit Firestone, for instance, told CBS News that "pregnancy is barbaric," and Ti-Grace Atkinson likened marriage to cancer. That kind of TV has legs. Today, when ordinary women like those in Henry's book hear about feminism, they automatically think man-hating. Nobody exactly rushes to bring up day care.

But a lot of ordinary women admire Gloria Steinem, radical though she seems—they like her looks and they buy her books. Her new collection of essays, *Moving Beyond Words* (296 pages. Simon & Schuster. $23), has its strengths—there's a fascinating piece about how *Ms.* Magazine tried to lure traditional women's magazine advertising (eye makeup) without running the traditional stories supporting it (new ideas for eye makeup). But more often Steinem seems to claim the role of rebel without living it. There is little new thinking here.

OK, let the record show that pregnancy is not barbaric and marriage is not cancer. But one reason it's taken so long to win the mainstream demands of 1970 may be that the radical edge of the movement has dwindled into the kind of trivial self-absorption excoriated by Sommers, and demonstrated in Steinem's last book, *Revolution from Within*. Nobody's pushing back the borders anymore, opening up space for change. The American women's movement has always had an avant-garde: Elizabeth Cady Stanton, the suffrage leader whom Sommers calls the very model of equity feminism, mortified her colleagues in the mid-19th century by demanding divorce rights and terming marriage "legalized prostitution."

In an essay on turning 60, Steinem writes: "I'm looking forward to   15 trading moderation for excess"—which is good news. And there's a precedent. In 1895 Stanton finally published a book she had been planning for many years: a roaring attack on the Bible for its misogyny. The book was a best seller, the horrified suffrage association voted to censure her, and to Stanton's pleasure, "the clergy jump round . . . like parched peas on a hot shovel." She was 80. Now *that's* a feminist.

The Responsive Reader

1. What spirit does Shapiro invoke in her introductory paragraph about the early stages of the women's movement? What key issues or concerns does she hint at? What is ironic about her title?
2. Early in her review, Shapiro reminds the reader of current buzz-words: *victim feminism, gender feminism, equity feminism.* How are they different? How important are the differences?
3. In reviewing the books by Sherrye Henry and Anne Taylor Fleming, what does Shapiro identify as the basic commitment of each author? Where does she agree with them? Where does she take issue with them? (Would you call these hostile or unsympathetic reviews?)
4. Why does Shapiro call Susan Douglas and Gloria Steinem "unrepentant, unreformed feminists"? Why or where does she agree or identify with them? (Why or how is she critical of Steinem?)
5. How does this reviewer show at the end that she sympathizes with radical feminists or the feminist avant-garde?

Talking, Listening, Writing

6. According to Shapiro, three early basic demands of feminists were equal opportunity, child care, and legal abortion. Do you subscribe to these demands? Why or why not?
7. Do you think the women's movement is anti-male?
8. Do you think the women's movement is anti-family?

Collaborative Projects

9. Working with a group, explore a question bearing on the future of the women's movement. For instance, how common is the "I-am-not-a feminist-but" attitude among women of your generation? Or, do working-class women tend to be out of touch with the feminist movement?

Thinking about Connections

Committed feminists represented in this book include Patty Fisher, Naomi Wolf, Alice Walker, Gloria Steinem, and Judi Bari. When you look back over their writing, what are common themes or commitments? What basic values or goals do they share? What are significant differences in perspective?

MY ALL-AMERICAN SON

Maria Herrera-Sobek

> *Maria Herrera-Sobek spent her childhood years in Río Hondo, Texas,
> went to high school in Gilbert, Arizona, and moved to southern California.
> She has worked in the areas of Chicana literature, women's studies, Latin
> American literature, and Hispanic folklore. The following poem is part of her
> collection* Naked Moon/Luna desnuda, *published as part of an issue of*
> The Bilingual Review *devoted to Chicana poetry. Like other parents, the
> poet is anxious about what lies ahead for the next generation. How does she
> envision the future?*

Thought Starters: If you were thinking about what the future holds for
children of your own or children of friends or relatives, what would be
your central worry or key hope?

Watching   1
My all-American son
Move in and out
Of a white world
Brown skin   5
Glistening
In a world
That loves–hates
Brown

Loves   10
Toasted
Blonde–brown
Ocean–sprayed
Sun–tanned
Oiled   15
Sleek
Shiny
Sun–soaked
Brown.

Fears   20
Earth–brown
Hawaiian

Mexican
Indian
Filipino   25
Brown.

Yet
The English
Tumbles
From his   30
American lips
Murders
The Spanish
Tongue
Slips in and out   35
Of a white world
With dignity and pride.

I know
His stand is precarious
One false move   40
And he'll be
Ejected
Rejected
Put in "his place"

American Brown   45
I ache for you.

The Responsive Reader

1. How does our world "love-hate" brown? How do you think the son would "move in and out," or slip in and out, "of a white world"?
2. Dictionaries still list a common language as a key to national identity. What role does language play in this poem?
3. Have you ever been "put in your place"? How do you think the mother expects that her son might be put in "his place"? What could be that "one false move"?
4. As you look back over the poem as a whole, what is ironic about the mother calling her son "my all-American son"?

Talking, Listening, Writing

5. Would you call this a pessimistic poem?
6. In a poem entitled "North and South," Herrera-Sobek said that North Americans are "so kind / To dogs / And cats" and "so unkind

to people." South Americans are "so cruel / To dogs / And cats / And bulls" but "oh so kind / To people." What made her say what she did? Do you think she is being unfair?

WRITING
WORKSHOP 12

The Documented Paper

When you are bringing together the best current information and best current thinking on a subject, you may be expected to provide full documentation. In a documented paper, you furnish the data a reader would need to check your sources. Where did you find the information? in what book? written by whom? published where, when, and by whom? On what page did this particular passage occur? If a quotation came from a magazine article, what was the date of the issue and the exact page number? if from a newspaper story, what edition (morning or evening, national or regional)? what section of the paper?

Authors provide full documentation when they think that someone might want to verify or challenge their evidence. When you work on a documented paper, you keep a complete record of where you found your material—so that the reader can retrace your steps. Documentation is for readers who do not just accept someone else's say-so. They want to check things out for themselves.

Where do you turn for material? Your sources for a documented paper may include articles from newspapers and periodicals, full-length books, and reference works. Input from nonprint sources may include material from interviews, radio and television programs, or lectures. You may be using material from sources first published in hard copy but also available on-line, material originally published on-line, material available on CD-ROM, or material downloaded from a wide range of Internet sources. Reference books like the *Encyclopaedia Britannica* are now available on CD-ROM, allowing you to call up an article by typing in a key word or a string of key words—or allowing you to type in a question and click for the answer. Your library is likely to be linked with other libraries nationally and internationally, so that you may be able to compensate for gaps in your library's holdings.

EVALUATING YOUR SOURCES You will need to convince your readers that you have consulted authoritative sources. What are the credentials of an author you are quoting? What is the author's credibility? When evaluating promising sources, ask questions like the following:

■ *Is the source an authority on the subject?* What is the author's track record? Does the author draw on firsthand investigation? Has the author written or lectured on the subject? Is the author associated with a prestige institution? Is the author quoted or consulted by others?

■ *Is the work a thorough study of the subject?* Does it recognize previous work in the field? Does it look in depth at case histories, relevant experiments, or key examples? Does it carefully examine statistics?

■ *Does the author turn to primary sources?* Reliable authorities often settle important questions by tracking down **primary sources**. They may consult legal documents, diaries and letters, or transcripts of speeches. They may turn to interviews with eyewitnesses, reports on experiments, or detailed statistical studies.

■ *Is the source up to date?* Does it recognize recent research or new facts? If it was first published ten or fifteen years ago, has the author updated the findings—in a later study or in a revised edition of a book?

■ *Is the source impartial or biased?* How credible is research on the health hazards of smoking if it was funded by a tobacco company? Are you going to be able to make allowance for a probusiness bias in material from the U.S. Chamber of Commerce or for a prolabor bias in material from the AFL-CIO?

SEARCHING FOR ARTICLES You will often turn for material to publications ranging from daily newspapers and weekly newsmagazines to popular science magazines and scientific and technical journals. Periodicals may appear on a weekly, monthly, or quarterly basis.

■ You may turn to leading newspapers like the *New York Times, Washington Post, Wall Street Journal, Christian Science Monitor,* or *Los Angeles Times* not only for authoritative news coverage but also for background studies, book reviews, or editorial opinion. Ranging from the archconservative to the progressive, newsmagazines and journals of commentary and opinion include *U.S. News and World Report, Time, Newsweek, Harper's, Atlantic, Commentary, New Republic, Mother Jones, Nation,* or *Ms.* magazine.

■ You may turn to experts, scholars, or scientists writing for the general public in publications like *Science, Scientific American, Psychology Today, Discover* magazine, or *National Geographic.*

■ You may draw on material in scientific, technical, or scholarly journals in areas like psychology, sociology, medicine, history, or art. For instance, for a study of trends in juvenile crime you may find relevant source material in a journal called *Crime and Delinquency.* For a paper on the implications of current brain research, your sources might include articles in journals with titles like *New Scientist, Brain, Neurology, New England Journal of Medicine,* or *British Journal of Educational Psychology.*

Computerized databases greatly facilitate your search for material in periodicals. Systems like INFOTRAC give you an instant listing of articles from hundreds of publications. (Remember to check years covered—INFOTRAC, for instance, started comprehensive indexing only in 1991.) By typing in key words or **retrieval codes**, you can call up lists of sources on subjects like child abuse, wage parity, or illegal immigration. You can call up book reviews, articles by or about a person, or information about an institution or company. When you are researching progress toward gender equity in college sports, for instance, the computer will call up articles whose titles include the words you have typed in as key words or as possible subject headings:

```
women and athletics
women and sports
sports equity
women's physical education
women and college sports
funding for college sports
gender equality in sports
```

Remember advice like the following from a fellow student:

If you don't find what you are looking for under one heading, try another. Writing about careers for women, you may find some of what you want under "Women—Employment." But if you are resourceful enough, you may find a real bonanza under headings like "Women—television industry," "Women judges," and "Women lawyers."

Other large umbrella systems can lead you to specialized databases in areas like sociology, government policy, medical research, or education. These databases will guide you to articles published by experts and professionals. For instance, for a paper on how schools are dealing with challenges to bilingual education, you may turn to a specialized education database. You will be able to tap into a statistics database providing access to relevant government statistics.

A student researcher obtained a range of leads like the following from the newspaper index that is part of INFOTRAC when looking for newspaper coverage of women's progress toward equity in sports. Look at the format:

- After the title, this database often includes a brief parenthetical note on the focus or key point of the article.
- It then tracks the exact location of the item: publication, volume number, section and page, column (with length of article in column inches).

- It then gives the author's name and possible subject headings under which the item may be catalogued.

Database: National Newspaper Index
Subject: sports for women

The girls against the boys; women have played pro ball before. But never against men. Is this exploitation, or feminism . . . or both? (Coors Silver Bullets; the first women's professional baseball team)

The Washington Post, April 24, 1994 v117 pF1 col 3 (82 col in).

Author: Laura Blumenfeld

Subjects: Baseball (Professional) - Analysis
Women athletes - Competitions

Features: illustration; photograph

AN: 15207085

Often source information includes an **abstract**—a summary of the findings or ideas developed in an article. The following printout from a sports-centered database includes an abstract that could help you decide whether the source is worth following up:

SilverPlatter 3.11   SPORT Discus 1975 - June 1994

SPORT Discus 1975 - June 1994 usage is subject to the terms and conditions of the Subscription and Licensing Agreement and the applicable Copyright and intellectual property protection as dictated by the appropriate laws of your country and/or by International Convention.

TI: Sport and the maintenance of masculine hegemony
AU: Bryson, -L
JN: Womens-studies-international-forum-(Elmsford,-N.Y.); 10(4), 1987, 349-360 Refs:37
PY: 1987
AB: Discusses two fundamental dimensions of the support that sport provides for masculine hegemony: 1) it links maleness with highly valued and visible skills, and 2) it links maleness with the positively sanctioned use of aggression/force/violence. Examines four social processes through which women are effectively

marginalized in their sport participation - definition,
direct control, ignoring, and trivialization - using
examples from the sports scene in Australia. Concludes
that <u>women</u> need to challenge the definition of sport,
take control of women's sports, persistently provide
information and reject attempts to ignore women's sport,
and attack the trivialization of <u>women</u> in sport.
AN: 213623

For articles published before the 1990s, you may have to search the multivolume print indexes in your library. The *Readers' Guide to Periodical Literature* indexes magazines for the general reader, from *Time* and *Newsweek* to *Working Woman, Science Digest,* and *Technology Review.* Other guides to periodicals for the general reader include *Applied Science and Technology Index, Biological and Agricultural Index, Business Periodicals Index, Humanities Index,* and *Social Sciences Index.*

As you track down promising sources, start a card file or computer file recording complete data for each item: author, complete title of articles, name of periodical, date, and page numbers. (Where appropriate, record the section of a newspaper or the volume number of a magazine.) Include a brief **annotation** as a reminder. A source record annotated by you might look like this:

---

periodical Guterson, David. "Moneyball! On the Relentless
room   Promotion of Pro Sports." <u>Harper's</u> magazine
            Sept. 1994: 37-46

The author is a contributing editor of <u>Harper's</u> magazine.
"I was not always so disgusted with sport; I was not
always an aging crank," Guterson pleads before launching
into a litany of the excesses of today's sports.

SEARCHING FOR BOOKS Data given on traditional index cards and on computer listings are similar, although they may be laid out differently. When you have heard of a promising book, you can look for it under the author's name or under the title. For instance, you would look under *Thurow* or under *Head to Head* for Lester Thurow's *Head to Head: The Coming Economic Battle Among Japan, Europe, and America.* However, when still looking for useful sources, you will check under subject headings. For instance, if you had not heard of Thurow's book you might be looking for books with a similar focus under subject headings like ECONOMIC FORECASTING, GLOBAL ECONOMY, INTERNATIONAL ECONOMIC RELATIONS, U.S. ECONOMIC POLICY, JAPAN—ECONOMIC POLICY, or TRADE WARS—U.S. AND JAPAN.

Computer entries may look like the following **author card**. The **call number** will direct you or a librarian to the right section and the right shelf in the library.

Call #:	LB 2343.32 F54 1991
Author:	Figler, Stephen K.
Title:	Going the distance: the college athlete's guide to excellence on the field and in the classroom / by Stephen K. Figler. Princeton, N.J.: Peterson's Guides, 1991. xi, 208 p.: illus; 23 cm.
Notes:	Includes bibliography: pp. 203-208.
Subjects:	College student orientation -- United States College athletes -- United States.
Add Author:	Figler, Howard E.

As with articles, you will want to prepare **source cards** or source entries giving complete publishing data for your record of promising sources:

HQ 1426 W565	Wolf, Naomi. <u>Fire With Fire: The New Female Power and How It Will Change the 21st Century</u>. New York: Random House, 1993.

CONSULTING REFERENCE WORKS Reference works, ranging from multivolume sets to compact manuals, provide detailed, authoritative information on specialized subjects. Many are now available on-line. You will find specialized reference works in a guide like Eugene P. Sheehy's *Guide to Reference Books,* published by the American Library Association. Here is a sampling of reference works that are often consulted:

- *The New Encyclopedia Britannica* (now an American publication), updated each year by the *Britannica Book of the Year*
- The *Encyclopedia Americana* with its annual supplement, the *American Annual*
- *Who's Who in America,* a biographical dictionary with capsule biographies of outstanding living men and women

- *Who's Who of American Women*
- *The Dictionary of American Biography (DAB)*
- *American Universities and Colleges* and *American Junior Colleges*
- *The McGraw-Hill Encyclopedia of Science and Technology,* kept up to date by the *McGraw-Hill Yearbook of Science and Technology*
- *The Encyclopedia of Computer Science and Technology*
- The *Dictionary of American History* by J. T. Adams (in six volumes)
- The *International Encyclopedia of the Social Sciences*

TAKING NOTES To record the materials for a documented research paper or library paper, you may use computer entries. You can then transfer typed quotations and the like directly to the body of your paper, without the need for retyping. (Some writers still use the traditional handwritten note cards, which they can reshuffle and organize in the order in which they will use them in their first draft.) You may also make use of newspaper clippings and photocopies of whole articles or key pages, with key passages highlighted for future use.

To ensure maximum usefulness of your notes, remember:

- *Start each note with a tag or descriptor.* Show where the material tentatively fits into your paper. Use headings like the following:

AZTECS—sacrificial rites

AZTECS—light-skinned gods

INCAS—tribal wars

- *Try to limit each entry to closely related information.* If you limit each entry to one key point, you can easily move the entry around and feed it into your project at the right spot—without having to break up an entry ranging over different points.
- *Mark all direct quotation with quotation marks.* Distinguish clearly between direct quotation (material quoted exactly word for word) and paraphrase (where you put less important material in your own words, often in condensed form.)
- *Make sure each note shows the exact source.* Include all publishing information you will need later: full names, titles and subtitles, publishers or publications, as well as dates and places. Keep track of exact page numbers: the specific page or pages for a quotation, but also the *complete* page numbers for an article.

Here are sample entries from a computer file. The student writer is investigating new perspectives on the rise in juvenile crime, recording essential input:

- statistics documenting the rise in youth crime
- comments on the failure of conventional approaches
- definition of a key concept (youth gangs redefined)

JUVENILE CRIME—STATS

In 1981, youths were charged with 53,240 violent crimes. In 1992, the figure was 104,137.
Federal Bureau of Justice

JUVENILE JUSTICE

Trying juvenile offenders as adults and locking them up for long periods of time "looks tough but is shortsighted." Institutions for adult criminals are useless when it comes to crime prevention or rehabilitation. "Juveniles in adult institutions are five times more likely to be sexually assaulted, twice as likely to be beaten by staff, and 50 percent more likely to be attacked with a weapon than youths in a juvenile facility." "Three different studies conducted over a ten-year period . . . show significantly higher recidivism rates for youths tried in adult courts compared to those tried in juvenile courts."

Michael E. Saucier, national chair of the Coalition for Juvenile Justice, speech before Congress March 1994—check issue of *Congressional Record*

REDEFINING GANGS

"Despite conventional thinking, gangs are not anarchies. They can be highly structured, with codes of honor and discipline. For many members, the gang serves as family, as the only place where they can find fellowship, respect, a place to belong. You often hear the world *love* among gang members. Sometimes the gang is the only place where they can find it." (p. 58)

"Sociopathic behavior exists within the framework of a sociopathic society. Under these circumstances, gangs are not a problem; they are a solution, particularly for communities lacking economic, social, and political options." (p. 58)

Luis J. Rodriguez, "Rekindling the Warrior," *Utne Reader* July/August 1994, pp. 58–59.

- -

The author of a successful library paper was asked what advice she would give to students working on similar research assignments. She wrote down the following "Survival Tips":

• If possible, keep all source material until you have finished the paper. Often, you will not realize until later that you want to quote a particular phrase that has been ringing in your ear or use statistics that at first you put aside. If you have thrown out the article or returned the book to the library, you have a problem.

• Make photocopies of everything that looks potentially useful. Come to the library with plenty of change and use the equipment for making photocopies or for making copies from microfilm.

• Do not channel your search too narrowly. Avoid the tunnel vision that would keep you from missing connections between your topic and related areas. For instance, I was looking for material on women's progress toward parity in sports. I at first hesitated to check a book on violence in sports, because it had no chapter on women. But the book later helped me make an essential point about violence in traditional male sports.

• Allow as much time as possible for ideas to cook. Start your project early instead of waiting until the last hectic weeks or days. The unconscious part of your mind continues to work on ideas even while you are attending to something else.

• Talk to people about your paper. Try out your ideas on different kinds of potential audiences.

ORGANIZING YOUR MATERIAL As you start to draft your paper, you will be grappling with familiar issues: What is going to be your focus? What will be the point of your paper as a whole? What will be your organizing strategy? How will you lay out your material in an order that will make sense to your readers?

Early in your project, you will start to develop a rough **working outline**—fitting the material you are collecting into a tentative overall scheme. From the beginning of your search you will be looking for questions that arise more than once or points that come up again and again. The student who investigated juvenile crime found much evidence of a trend toward treating juvenile criminals as adults, trying them in adult courts, and sending them to adult jails. As he read current newspaper articles and articles in law enforcement journals, he noted that liberal judges and liberal politicians were being accused of being soft on crime. He noted a strong trend toward harsher sentences. He found evidence of a growing impatience with and lack of sympathy for the young criminal. Many people seemed to have given up on programs for rehabilitation, on protecting the young criminal (for instance, by withholding names from the press), or on giving young people in bad trouble a second chance. He noted news reports with titles like "Teen Gets Life Term" and "Tougher Treatment for Juveniles." His first scratch outline might have looked like this:

SCRATCH OUTLINE: current get-tough mentality
                   sensationalizing juvenile crime
                   failure of "liberal" approaches
                   trying juveniles as adults

At this stage, his material pointed to a general conclusion like the following:

TRIAL THESIS: As the public gets more impatient with crime, juvenile offenders are among the prime targets of harsher treatment.

Trying not to be caught up in the pessimism reflected in many of his sources, the student writer made an effort to look at the other side. Are there advocates of more emphasis on prevention and rehabilitation? He tracked down newspaper articles about priests, teachers, or counselors trying to keep young people out of jail or out of gangs. He looked at articles with titles like "Jails or Jobs?" or "Alternatives to Hard Time." He interviewed members of the college faculty who were known for their interest in troubled adolescents. This might have been his revised and expanded working outline:

WORKING OUTLINE:
     conservative current climate
         current get-tough mentality
         sensationalizing juvenile crime
         perceived failure of liberal approaches
     getting tough on juveniles
         trying juveniles as adults
         harsh sentencing

searching for alternatives
  emphasis on prevention (education, job training)
  emphasis on rehabilitation (counseling, work camps)

The new, more positive emphasis would be reflected in an adjusted thesis:

ADJUSTED THESIS: Although juvenile offenders are among the prime targets
of a "get-tough" approach to crime, the search continues
for approaches stressing prevention and rehabilitation.

In developing a draft following such a working outline, you pull out, adapt, or combine material from your notes. An effective paper weaves material from your notes into your text to support your key points. In principle, for any point you make, imagine a reader who asks: "What made you think so?"

USING YOUR SOURCES How do you work material from written and oral sources into your paper? Experienced writers aim at the right mix of word-for-word quotation and paraphrase. In **direct quotation**, you copy material verbatim—word for word. You put the author's exact words in quotation marks. (You signal all omissions—by spaced periods; you signal your own added comments—by square brackets). In a **paraphrase**, you use *in*direct quotation. You put the author's ideas and information into your own words (no quotation marks). Often words like *that, why,* or *how* introduce indirect quotations:

DIRECT: The candidate for mayor said, "If elected, I promise to make the
homeless people on our city streets my top priority."
INDIRECT: The candidate for mayor promised *that if elected she would make
the homeless on the city's streets her top priority.*

You will often use direct quotation for a key idea, a central thesis, or an important charge or claim. Use a sentence or more of direct quotation to highlight a strong personal statement. Quote at first hand a controversial idea that might make a reader say: "Are you sure this is what the person said?"

Advocates of recovery groups claim that almost everyone is in some sense a victim—mostly, of abusive parents. "What we are hearing from the experts," John Bradshaw told an interviewer, "is that approximately 96 percent of the families in this country are dysfunctional to one degree or another."

When you paraphrase, you put what someone said or wrote into your own words. Paraphrase gives you greater flexibility than direct quotation. You can shorten a long passage, highlighting key points. You can clarify technical information by translating it into accessible language. Note that even in an extended paraphrase, you may include short quoted phrases for an authentic touch.

PARAPHRASE:
Joseph Trez, the Citadel's commandant of cadets, told a review committee that he was convinced that the women being admitted to the school were accepted by each other and by male cadets. Male cadets treated them like any other knobs. He noted that two male cadets also had nail polish remover put on their shirts and set afire.

PARAPHRASE WITH PARTIAL QUOTE:
As David Rieff says in an article on the recovery movement in *Harper's*, Americans have always felt that they can make themselves over to become something new. The great American tales are about busting loose. Their heroes find a way "of shucking off the bonds of family and tradition," striking out for new territories in order to achieve a new identity.

Study the way experienced writers *introduce* material from their sources. Who said this and where? In addition to the basic "Gloria Steinem said, '. . .'" pattern, try drawing on the full range of other **credit tags**, or introductory phrases. Here are some examples. (Note that after a tag like "he says" or "the author states," a colon may replace the more usual comma before a long or formal quotation.)

According to Susan Faludi, author of *Backlash*, the dialogue in these women's films "probes the economic and social inequities of traditional wedlock."

To quote psychologist Hilda Ignes, "Neurosis is the condition where an individual's emotional elevators go to top floor when least desired."

As Judith Guest says in *The Mythic Family*, "I have often been asked why it is that I only write about dysfunctional families. The answer that comes to mind is, what other kinds are there?"

In the words of an editor at *Ms.* magazine, "We women often dance gingerly around the kind of blokey lingo that men have built their reputations on."

David Rieff concludes: "It is a measure of the continued economic success of the United States that so many of its citizens could be so buffered from the real harshness of the world that they can spend their time anatomizing their own feelings."

Often you will want to include *credentials* of a source in your credit tag. What makes the quoted person an authority or worth listening to? What are the person's credentials?

Ann Smith, director of a Pennsylvania family service clinic, wrote *Grandchildren of Alcoholics* to "bring this group of people out of hiding and into recovery."

Lauren Teague is a clinical psychologist and vocal critic of the recovery movement. In an article called "Are We All Victims?" he says, "By concentrating on the psychological scars of affluent white Americans, we ensure that the real victims in American society will not get the attention they need to improve their lives."

How do you weave your quoted material effectively into your text? At some points in your paper, your job may be to use input from a *single source,* pulling from your notes the most important or relevant parts. Here is a sample paragraph, drawing extensively on one of several articles by a *New York Times* reporter:

Individuals who work closely with juvenile criminals often support the idea of providing guidance and discipline. Being in close contact with young offenders, they come to know their motives and their needs. For instance, Justice Michael A. Corriero is a member of the New York State Supreme Court in Manhattan who tries to balance the need for punishment or deterrence with concern for the future life of the young offender. As Jan Hoffman of the *New York Times* reports, "Judge Corriero provides juvenile offenders hope for rehabilitation." Corriero gives juveniles the chance to earn a lighter sentence by placing them in "community-based intensive supervisory programs." In the judge's view, juveniles should not receive permanent felony conviction records—criminals convicted in adult courts have permanent records—since the juvenile "can't get a job with a felony conviction." And if the juvenile cannot contribute to society, Judge Corriero asks, "Have we really protected society?" ("Punishing Youths" B1).

Just as often, you will be pulling together related material from *several sources* to prove a point. You will bring together or correlate input from a variety of source material. This way you prevent the lumpy effect that results when big chunks of undigested quotation simply follow one another. The following sample paragraph does a good job of integrating material from three different sources:

The justice system is generally moving toward trying juvenile offenders in adult courts. Marvin Owens of Virginia Beach, Virginia, was sentenced to life imprisonment by Circuit Judge Robert B. Cromwell Jr. after a jury convicted Marvin of capital murder in the "execution-style slayings of his grandmother, a half-brother, and two cousins" ("Teen Gets Life" B7). Kevin Stanford was seventeen years old when he murdered Baerbel Poor in Jefferson County, Kentucky. After he had been transferred from juvenile court to adult court, the jury convicted Stanford of murder and sentenced him to death. When his case was appealed to the Supreme Court, Justice

Scalia, in announcing the majority opinion, said that sentencing juvenile offenders to death did not violate the Eighth Amendment (*Stanford v. Kentucky* 316). A survey of 250 judges conducted by Penn and Schoen Associates and published in the *National Law Journal* found that "40 percent of the judges said the minimum age for facing murder charges should be 14 or 15, while 17 percent said it should be even lower, 12 or 13. The judges generally agreed that the criminal justice system should deal with young criminals more in the way it deals with adults" ("Tougher Treatment" A16).

Make only sparing use of **block quotations** (four lines or more indented an inch or ten spaces, *no* quote marks). Save such block quotations for special occasions—like giving an author a chance to state a key position with important ifs and buts or to record mixed feelings on a tricky subject:

> Feminists have found it difficult to find affectionate or friendly terms that do not smack of traditional male condescension, like calling someone "sweetheart" or "honey." Kate Rounds, an editor at *Ms.* magazine, talks about the difficulty of finding "a more chummy way to communicate" and a more friendly term than the formal *woman:*

> > On a recent visit to a college campus, I was terrified by a big sign reading, "Women are not 'guys'!" For some time, I'd been using "guys" instead of "women," knowing I was offending the feminist language police. So I knew I'd have to watch my mouth during this visit. (96)

DOCUMENTING YOUR SOURCES—MLA STYLE In writing a documented paper, you will be paying special attention to matters of format and style. Documentation styles vary from one area of study to another—and sometimes from one professional journal to another. Different areas of the curriculum use slightly different systems of coding information about sources.

- For papers in the humanities (English, philosophy), you will usually follow the documentation style of the Modern Language Association, outlined in the *MLA Handbook for Writers of Research Papers* (Fourth Edition, 1995).
- For papers in the social sciences (sociology, psychology, education), you will usually follow the APA style, outlined in the *Publication Manual of the American Psychological Association* (Fourth Edition, 1994).
- For papers in the sciences, you may be required to follow the style of the Council of Biology Editors (CBE), the American Institute of Physics (AIP), or the American Chemical Society (ACS).

Here are the basic features of the MLA style:

In the paper itself, you will use **parenthetical documentation**: You will give exact page references in parentheses. You may also include quick identification of sources as needed. Then, at the end of your paper, you will provide an alphabetic list of **Works Cited**. Here you give complete information about your sources. Study the way parentheses, quotation marks, underlining, colons, and other punctuation features are used in sample passages and sample entries.

Remember a few pointers: Italicize or underline the titles of books and other complete publications: *The Color Purple* or The Color Purple. (Underlining tells a printer to italicize the underlined part. Your instructor may tell you whether to use italics or underlining in your paper.) Put in quotation marks the titles of poems, articles, and other pieces that are *part* of a publication: "A Woman by Any Other Name" (the title of magazine article); "Stopping by Woods" (a poem that is part of a larger collection).

Samples of Parenthetical Documentation

Preferably, you will name author and publication in your running text. You will then usually have to give only page numbers in parentheses. But look at some of the other possibilities.

- simple page reference when you have identified the source:

```
Octavio Paz has called the meeting of the Indian and
the Spaniard the key to the Mexican national
character (138).
```

- author's name and page reference when you have *not* identified the source:

```
A prominent Latin American writer has called the
meeting of the Indian and the Spaniard the key to the
Mexican national character (Paz 138).
```

- more than one author:

```
Tests and more tests have often been a substitute for
adequate funding for our schools (Hirsenrath and
Briggers 198).
```

- abbreviated title added when you quote more than one source by same author:

```
Lin, who has called the homeless problem the result
of "social engineering in reverse" ("Homeless" 34),
examines current statistics in a scathing indictment
of official neglect (On the Street 78-81).
```

- a source you found quoted by someone else:

```
Steinbeck said he admired "strong, independent, self-
reliant women" (qtd. in Barnes 201).
```

- a reference to preface or other introductory material, with page numbers given in lowercase Roman numerals:

```
In his preface to The Great Mother, Neumann refers to
the "onesidedly patriarchal development of the male
intellectual consciousness" (xliii).
```

Note: References to the Bible typically cite chapter and verse instead of page numbers (Luke 2.1); references to a Shakespeare play usually cite act, scene, and line (*Hamlet* 3.2.73–76). After block quotations, a parenthetical page reference *follows* a final period or other terminal mark. (See sample paper for examples.)

Sample Entries for Works Cited

Preparing your final list of Works Cited tests your ability to follow a prescribed format. Look out for features that set the documentation style for your area of study apart from other styles—or from *earlier* versions of the style you are following. Indent the second line of an entry half an inch or five spaces. Leave only *one space* after periods marking off chunks of information. Abbreviate the names of months with more than four letters. Study sample entries like the following:

- *newspaper article* with date and page numbers (you may also need to specify section of paper or a special edition—"late ed." or "West Coast ed."):

```
Santos, Juan. "New Pre-Columbian Art." Fremont Times
    5 Aug. 1997: B7-8.
Bialek, Carla. "Trade and a Yin-yanging Yen." New
    York Times 22 Mar. 1994, late ed.: A4.
```

- *magazine article* identified by date with complete page numbers (the + sign shows that an article is continued later in the same issue):

```
Greenwald, John. "Toyota Road USA." Time 7 Oct. 1996:
    73-74.
Foote, Stephanie. "Our Bodies, Our Lives, Our Right
    to Decide." The Humanist July/Aug. 1992:
    2-8+.
```

- article with *volume number* (for a magazine with continuous page numbering through several issues):

```
Herzberger, David K. "Narrating the Past: History and
    the Novel of Memory in Postwar Spain." PMLA 106
    (1991): 34-45.
```

- professional journal with separate page numbering for each *issue* of the same volume (volume number is followed by number of issue):

```
Winks, Robin W. "The Sinister Oriental Thriller:
    Fiction and the Asian Scene." Journal of Popular
    Culture 19.2 (1985): 49-61.
```

- standard entry for a *book* (use shortened or abbreviated names of publishers: *Prentice* for Prentice Hall, *Princeton UP* for Princeton University Press):

```
Tan, Amy. The Kitchen God's Wife. New York: Putnam's,
    1991.
```

- book with *subtitle*:

```
Kozol, Jonathan. Amazing Grace: The Lives of Children
    and the Conscience of a Nation. New York: Crown,
    1995.
```

- *coauthored* article or book (last name first for first author only):

```
Elkholy, Sharin, and Ahmed Nassef. "Crips and Bloods
    Speak for Themselves: Voices from South
    Central." Against the Current July/Aug. 1991:
    7-10.
```

- article or book with *more than three authors*—*et al.* for "and others." However, you may decide to list all coauthors of an important work:

```
Martz, Larry, et al. "A Tide of Drug Killings."
    Newsweek 16 Jan. 1989: 44-45.
Fischer, Claude S., and Michael Hout, Martín Sánchez
    Jankowski, Samuel R. Lucas, Ann Swidler, and Kim
    Voss. Inequality by Design: Cracking the Bell
    Curve Myth. Princeton: Princeton UP, 1996.
```

- additional entry by *same author* (substitute three hyphens for name):

Steinem, Gloria. <u>Outrageous Acts and Everyday</u>
 <u>Rebellions</u>. New York: Holt, 1983.

---. <u>Revolution from Within: A Book of Self-Esteem</u>.
 Boston: Little, Brown, 1992.

- *unsigned editorial*—author not identified (alphabetize under first word other than *A, An,* or *The*):

"At the Threshold: An Action Guide for Cultural
 Survival." Editorial. <u>Cultural Survival</u>
 <u>Quarterly</u> (Spring 1992) 17-18.

- *letter to the editor*:

Wismuth, Teresa. "Saving the Forests." Letter. <u>San</u>
 <u>Jose Mercury News</u> 18 Nov. 1997: C3.

- material *edited* or collected by someone other than the author (or authors):

Shockley, Ann Allen, ed. <u>Afro-American Women Writers</u>
 <u>1746-1933: An Anthology and Critical Guide</u>.
 Boston: G.K. Hall, 1988.

Barrett, Eileen, and Mary Cullinan, eds. <u>American</u>
 <u>Women Writers: Diverse Voices in Prose Since</u>
 <u>1845</u>. New York, St. Martin's, 1992.

- material *translated* from another language:

Neruda, Pablo. <u>Selected Poems of Pablo Neruda: A</u>
 <u>Bilingual Edition</u>. Trans. Ben Belitt. New York:
 Grove, 1961.

- *later edition* of a book:

Guth, Hans P., and Gabriele L. Rico, eds. <u>Discovering</u>
 <u>Literature: Stories, Poems, Plays</u>. 2nd ed. Upper
 Saddle River, NJ: Prentice, 1997.

- special *imprint* (special line of books) of a publisher:

Acosta, Oscar Zeta. <u>The Revolt of the Cockroach</u>
 <u>People</u>. New York: Vintage-Random, 1989.

- article that is part of a *collection* or anthology:

Gutierrez, Irene. "A New Consciousness." <u>New Voices</u>
 <u>of the Southwest</u>. Ed. Laura Fuentes. Santa Fe:
 Horizon, 1992. 123-34.

- one of *several volumes*:

Woolf, Virginia. The Diary of Virginia Woolf. Ed.
      Anne Olivier Bell. New York: Harcourt, 1977.
      Vol. 1.

- *personal interview*:

Sandra Gutierrez. Personal Interview. 15 Jan. 1997.
Philip Leadbetter. Telephone Interview. 3 Dec. 1996.

- *audio* or *video source*:

The Endangered Planet. Narr. Karen Coleman. Writ. and
      prod. Loren Shell. WXRV, Seattle. 7 Nov. 1992.
Creation vs. Evolution: Battle of the Classrooms.
      Videocassette. Dir. Ryall Wilson. PBS Video,
      1982. 58 min.

- computer software:

Naruba, Mark. The Strategic Writer. Vers. 1.3.
      Computer Software. Pentrax, 1993. Mac, 128K,
      disk.

- *online* publication or CD-ROM (If there was a print publication, give first the usual publishing data and then add available data for electronic publication: database (italicized or underlined); electronic medium if applicable (such as CD-ROM); distributor or vendor; date of electronic publication. If there is no previous or parallel print publication, list the electronic publication the way you would a print publication):

Russo, Michelle Cash. "Recovering from Bibliographic
      Instruction Blahs." RQ: Reference Quarterly 32
      (1992): 178-83. Infotrac: Magazine Index Plus.
      CD-ROM. Information Access. Dec. 1993.
The CIA World Factbook. CD-ROM. Minneapolis: Quanta,
      1992.

- personal *e-mail*:

Benhurst, Teresa. "Racist Humor on the Internet."
      Personal e-mail (25 Feb. 1997).

- *Internet* sources (Eric Crump and Nick Carbone, in *English Online*, give sample citations for Internet sources like the following):

```
Slade, Robert M. "Book Review: Netiquette by Virginia
     Shea." Computer Mediated Communication
     Magazine. October 1994. World Wide Web: http://
     sunsite.unc.edu/CMC/mag/1994/oct/
     netiquette.html (30 Oct. 1994).
Pirate (Hawkins, Jim). "Welcome to My Island."
     SomeMOO. Internet. Telnet: moo.somemoo.com
     7777, @go silver's_lair, read welcome
     (3 Jan. 1993).
```

REVISING YOUR PAPER Some common revision strategies may be especially helpful when you revise a paper that has brought together a mass of information and quotation:

- *Strengthen the overall framework.* Do not allow the reader to feel lost as facts, quotations, and details pile up. Can you make sure that the four or five major stages of your paper will stand out clearly? Or that the major steps in your argument will be easy to follow?

- *Strengthen transitions.* Highlight connections between one part of the paper and the next. Check whether a *however, on the other hand,* or *finally* is needed to clarify a logical link between two points.

- *Revise for clear attribution.* Who said what? Repeat the name of the quoted author if a *he* or *she* might point to the wrong person.

- *Integrate undigested chunk quotations.* If you have too many block quotations, break them up. Work partial quotations into your own text for a smoother flow.

- *Do a final check of documentation style.* Teachers and editors of scholarly writing or research-based writing are sticklers for detail. Use capitals, indents, spacing, colons, parentheses, quotations marks, and the like exactly as the style guide for your class or for your publication says.

A SAMPLE DOCUMENTED PAPER—MLA The following student research paper observes the MLA guidelines for documentation. Study this paper as a model for the format of your own paper. No separate title page is necessary (unless your instructor requires it). Use double-spacing throughout, including block quotations and Works Cited (no quadruple-spacing after title or before and after paragraphs). Running heads (*Richards 1* and so forth) start flush right at the top of page one and continue through the Works Cited page. The extra-wide indentation for a block quotation is roughly one inch or ten typewriter spaces on the left— no extra space on the right.

Writers and readers of documented papers may lose sight of the larger purposes of a writing project as they grapple with the technicalities of research and documentation. As you study the following sample paper, pay attention to the larger questions of purpose, content, strategy, and use of evidence:

- What did the student writer set out to do?
- Who would make a good audience for this paper?
- What organizing strategy did the writer work out for the paper?
- Where did the writer turn for material?
- What use has the writer made of sources?
- How clear or helpful are the attribution and documentation of the sources?
- How balanced or persuasive are the conclusions?

Richards 1

running head
flush right

Pat Richards

Professor Guth

English 2

15 November 1994

double spacing
throughout

A Flawed Saint

"Just as the Christian Jesus said 'Forgive them, for they know
not what they do,' we pray, 'Forgive them, Great Spirit, for they
know not what they do.'" These words were spoken by Anthony Miranda,
a Costanoan Native American in the basilica of the Carmel Mission in
California on the same day that its founder, Father Junipero Serra,
was being proposed for sainthood in Rome. His words drew "shocked
gasps and stares at what many of the worshipers considered a
sacrilege." A man in the back of the basilica loudly called out,
"Why don't you take your pagan rites and get out of this church?"
The group of twenty Native Americans carrying ceremonial rattles,
feathers, and abalone shells filled with burning sage retreated to
the church cemetery. They assembled at the foot of a crude wooden
cross that marks the graves of "2,364 Christian Indians and 14
Spaniards," buried there between 1771 and 1833 (O'Neill 17).

quotes within
quote

author and page
number in
parentheses

Junipero Serra has been called "California's founding father"
and "the most overlooked man in American history" by one of the
leading religious magazines in the United States. In 1984, the
Reagan administration issued a postage stamp in his honor (Fay 71).
It has been said that "his devotion to his work was an inspiration

Richards 2

partial quotes — to those who followed in his footsteps" (Krell 310). After he died,

we are told, his parishioners "flocked to the church where his body

lay, bearing bouquets of flowers and weeping inconsolably" (Fink 48).

However, Serra has also been accused of enslaving and

torturing his converts, sending out search parties to hunt down

those who escaped from his churches, and committing genocide. His

proposed canonization (raising to official recognition as a saint)

provoked a storm of criticism from the American Indian Historical

Society. According to an article in U.S. News & World Report,

"records are replete with documentation of whippings and other

quote marks for shortened title of — harsh treatment" of the indigenous people under his jurisdiction

unsigned article ("Question" 24). Can both parties to this controversy be speaking of

the same person?

According to Augusta Fink's Monterey: The Presence of the

Past, Father Serra was born Miguel Joseph Serra in the humble town

of Petra on the island of Majorca, Spain, in 1713. In 1749, he

realized his dream of becoming a missionary when he was sent to

Mexico to help convert the Indians to Christianity. During the next

inclusive page numbers for twenty years, he founded and guided a mission among the Pame tribe

summary of information in northern Mexico and often preached in Mexico City (4-8).

According to an article in Life magazine, Serra arrived in

California in 1769 and began his work of founding the California

Missions. "Unlike the Spanish military and many of the clergy, he

immediately made friends with the local tribes." Serra died

Richards 3

"cradled in the arms of some of his 6,000 Christian converts."
According to the author of the article, "Serra has been the
unofficial state 'saint' for generations" (Fay 68-71).

credentials of
oral source

Much recent work has painted a less saintly picture of the
Spanish priest. Alma Villanueva, a professor at the University of
California at Santa Cruz, spoke to me of "mass graves" of Indians
unearthed near several of the California missions and used the term
genocide. In the book The Missions of California: A Legacy of
Genocide, the American Indian Historical Society has circulated the
same charges. The book provides numerous documented reports of the
indigenous inhabitants being subjected to "forced conversion,"
"forced labor," and "physical punishment." It includes an account
of an early settler who wrote, "For the slightest things they
receive heavy floggings, are shackled and put in stocks, and created
with so much cruelty that they are kept whole days without a drink
of water" (Costo 69).

In his book, The Ohlone Way: Indian Life in the San Francisco-
Monterey Bay Area, Malcolm Margolin quotes the explorer La Perouse,
who compared the missions in Father Serra's charge to slave colonies
he had seen in Santo Domingo:

double indent
for block quote
with bracketed
addition and
ellipsis for
omission

> We declare with pain that the resemblance [to the Santo
> Domingo slave colonies] is so exact that we saw both the
> men and the women loaded with irons, while others had a
> log of wood on their legs. . . . Corporal punishment is

Richards 4

inflicted on the Indians of both sexes who neglect their pious exercises. (162)

Margolin quotes a visitor to the mission at Santa Clara about the confinement of young unmarried women by the padres "to assure the chastity of their wards":

We were struck by the appearance of a large quadrangular building, which, having no windows on the outside, resembled a prison for state criminals. . . . The dungeons are opened two or three times a day, but only to allow the prisoners to pass to and from the church. I have occasionally seen the poor girls rushing out eagerly to breathe the fresh air and driven immediately into the church like a flock of sheep, by an old ragged Spaniard with a stick. After mass, they are in the same manner hurried back into their prisons. (161)

Fink's book reports that the last few years of Serra's life were "difficult ones." There were "few new converts and many runaways among the Indians, and a series of plagues, which were probably smallpox, had decimated the small Christianized group that remained" (48). Margolin says that "300 or more Indians out of a thousand might die during a severe epidemic year" (163).

To judge Father Serra's role in these events, we need to remember how badly the Spaniards and the Indians misunderstood each

page numbers only in parentheses

extended block quote for shocking or provocative testimony

integrating related material from different sources

Richards 5

other. They represented two vastly different cultures. In the words of another book about the California missions,

> The California Indian has often been criticized because
> he lived a life of slothfulness, not stirring himself to
> raise crops, herd flocks, or practice other disciplined
> forms of food production characteristic of more advanced
> cultures. . . . Ironically, the civilized Spaniards, who
> looked down upon the childlike Indians, suffered famines
> after they first settled in the same environment when
> their imported foodstuffs failed to arrive on time.
> (Krell 50)

author and page
number after
period ending
block quote

Serra probably never doubted the rightness of his actions. As Fink points out, the Native Americans "resisted conversion to the Christian faith, which required complete separation from the pagan community. Children presented for baptism had to live at the mission under the supervision of the padres" (43). It must be noted, however, that not even his countrymen always took his side. Governor Neve "refused to round up Indian fugitives from the missions, who, Serra felt, had broken the contract they made at baptism" (48).

The historical evidence makes one thing clear: Serra's methods were overzealous by twentieth-century standards. Some would argue that he was overzealous by anyone's and anytime's standards. When we read that Indians wept and brought flowers to his grave, we have to

Richards 6

wonder how many others were overjoyed at the news of his death. When
we are faced with documented accounts of what happened to many
indigenous inhabitants under his authority, it is hard to consider
Father Serra worthy of being made a saint. In the words of Jack
Norton, a Native American professor at Humboldt State University, a
candidate for sainthood "should epitomize virtue and kindness"

clincher quote ——— (qtd. in "Question" 24).

Richards 7

Works Cited

Costo, Rupert, and Jeanette H. Costo, eds. The Missions of

California: A Legacy of Genocide. San Francisco: Indian

Historical, 1987.

Donohue, John W. "California's Founding Father." America 11 May

1985: 306.

Fay, Martha, Linda Gomez, and Wilton Wynn. "So You Want to Be a

Saint." Life Sept. 1987: 68-71.

Fink, Augusta. Monterey: The Presence of the Past. San Francisco:

Chronicle Publishing, 1972.

Krell, Dorothy, and Paul C. Johnson, eds. The California Missions: A

Pictorial History. Menlo Park, CA: Lane, 1979.

Margolin, Malcolm. The Ohlone Way: Indian Life in the San Francisco-

Monterey Bay Area. Berkeley: Heyday, 1978.

O'Neill, Ann W. "Confrontation at the Mission." San Jose Mercury

News 26 Sept. 1987: B17-19.

"A Question of Faith in California." U.S. News & World Report 11 May

1987: 24.

Villanueva, Alma. Personal Interview. 26 June 1993.

first line of each
entry flush left,
additional lines
indented

DOCUMENTING YOUR SOURCES—APA STYLE Many publications in the social sciences follow the APA style of documentation, outlined in the *Publication Manual of the American Psychological Association* (Fourth Edition, 1994).

For brief identification of sources in the text of a paper, the APA format uses the **author-and-date** method. When using this style, include year or date of publication after the author's name: (Mineta, 1996). Do not repeat the author's name between parentheses if you have already mentioned it in your text (1996). Often, the APA style gives a source and the publication date of research without a page reference. Interested readers are expected to become familiar with the relevant research literature and consider its findings in context. However, give an exact page reference with all direct quotation.

Samples of Parenthetical Documentation

Study the following sample citations. Note distinctive features like the use of commas, the abbreviations *p.* or *pp.* for "page" or "pages," or the symbol & (the ampersand) for *and*.

- standard citation—*author and date* only:

Anorexia nervosa is a condition of extreme weight loss that results when young women compulsively starve themselves (Grayfield, 1993).

- *date only,* with author's name in your own text.

As defined by Grayfield, anorexia nervosa is a condition of extreme weight loss that results when young women compulsively starve themselves (1993).

- *page reference* for direct quotation or specific reference:

Anorexia nervosa is "not really true loss of appetite" but "a condition of emaciation resulting from self-inflicted starvation" (Huebner, 1982, p. 143).

- names of *all coauthors* for work by several authors (et al.—for "and others"—used only in second or later reference):

Much advertising promotes miracle diets promising young women beauty and success (Bennings, Vasquez, & Theroux, 1994).

The harmful effects of crash diets have been well documented (Bennings et al., 1994).

- for several publications published by the *same author in the same year*, *a, b, c,* and so on, used in order of publication:

```
Fyodor has published a series of studies challenging
the tobacco industry's claims (1995, 1996a, 1996b).
```

- *several cited sources* listed in alphabetical order, divided by semicolons:

```
Unemployment statistics obscure the continuing
increase of part-time and temporary work (Gutierrez &
Vargas, 1994; Petersen, 1995).
```

- for *unknown author,* source identified by shortened title:

```
Jury selection has become the subject of study for
self-styled "experts" ("Psyching Out Prospective
Jurors," 1996).
```

- for *institutional authorship,* acronyms or abbreviations used only in second or later citation:

```
Many promising drugs proved to have disastrous side
effects (National Institute of Mental Health [NIHM],
1994).
Research into the biochemistry of the brain has led
to genuine breakthroughs in the treatment of
emotional disorders (NIMH, 1994).
```

- letters, memos, E-mail, or telephone interviews cited as *personal communications,* with date included (do not include personal communications in your list of References):

```
Police officers tend to feel that the media tend to
give a negative slant to police work (Victor Gomez,
personal communication, March 17, 1995).
```

Sample Entries for References Directory

Use the heading "References" for your final alphabetical listing of works quoted or consulted. Note the distinctive **author–and–date** sequence, with author identification followed by the date in parentheses:

```
Stefan, L. B. (1991). Youth and the law: Getting
tough on juvenile crime. Boston: Benchmark Books.
```

In the following sample entries, study distinctive features of the APA style:

Indent *first* line of each entry one-half inch (or five typewriter spaces). Start with the last name of the author, followed by *initials* (not full first names). Then put the date in parentheses. For dates of newspapers or periodicals, do not abbreviate months (1996, September 21).

Use *lowercase* letters in titles, except for words you would normally capitalize in your text. Do not put titles of articles in quotation marks. Italicize (or underline) the name of a complete publication—newspaper, magazine, book. Use the full names of publishers, omitting tags like *Inc.* or *Co.*: Cambridge: Harvard University Press. Use *p.* or *pp.* for "page" or "pages."

- for a *newspaper article,* give date but also specify the edition of the newspaper—early or late, east or west, if appropriate: *The Wall Street Journal,* eastern ed., p. A3 (keep the article *The* in the names of newspapers like *The Wall Street Journal* or *The New York Times*):

  Lipstye, R. (1993, September 24). An immovable barrier in the fight for equity. The New York Times, p. B11.

- with a *newspaper* or *magazine article,* include complete page numbers (if a newspaper or magazine article is concluded later in the issue, use a comma between the two sets of page numbers):

  Farmelo, G. (1995, November). The discovery of x-rays. Scientific American, pp. 86-91.

  Miller, G. (1969, December). On turning psychology over to the unwashed. Psychology Today, pp. 53-54, 66-74.

- for article or book with *subtitle,* use a colon between title and subtitle:

  Claflin, T. (1993, November/December). Monumental achievement: Twenty years after Vietnam, invisible vets get their memorial. Ms., pp. 83-88.

  Kozol, J. (1995). Amazing grace: The lives of children and the conscience of a nation. New York: Crown Publishers.

- for articles or books *by several authors,* list the names of all coauthors, last names first, and put the *and*-sign (&) before the last author's name:

  Cooper, J. C., & Madigan, K. (1995, July 10). Consumers may be tight-fished, but business isn't. Business Week, pp. 29-30.

Minuchin, S., Rosman, B., & Baker, L. (1978). Psychosomatic families: Anorexia nervosa in context. Cambridge, MA: Harvard University Press.

Boyer, P. S., Clark, C. E., Hawley, S. M., Kett, J. F., Salisbury, N., Sitkoff, H., & Woloch, N. (1995). The enduring vision: A history of the American people. Lexington: D. C. Heath.

- for an *unsigned or anonymous publication,* start with the title and alphabetize by the first word of the title, not counting *The, A,* or *An.*

Losing its way: Japanese industry. (1993, September 18). Economist, pp. 78-79.

- underline (or italicize) the *volume number for a periodical,* with complete page numbers following after a comma: *6,* 152–169.

Santley, R. S. (1985). The political economy of the Aztec empire. Journal of Anthropological Research, 41, pp. 327-337.

- if needed, include both volume number and *number of the issue*—in parentheses between the volume number and the page numbers: *6*(3), 152–169 (number of issue may be needed if page numbers are not continuous for the whole volume):

Steinhausen, H., & Glenville, K. (1983). Follow-up studies of anorexia nervosa: A review of research findings. Psychological Medicine: Abstracts in English, 13(2), pp. 239-245.

- for an *editorial,* add the label *Editorial* in square brackets (if the editorial is unsigned, begin with the title):

Hernandez, C. (1994, September 27). Immigrants are not aliens. [Editorial.] Harristown News, p. 7.

What is sacred? (1995, November/December). [Editorial.] Mother Jones, pp. 3-6.

- for a *letter to the editor,* add the right label after the title:

Kosinski, L. (1996, November 12). Downsizing gets out of hand. [Letter to the Editor.] The Los Angeles Times part II: p. 7.

- start with author and title of a *book review* and include title of book reviewed in square brackets:

Sheaffer, R. (1995, November). Truth abducted [Review of the book Close encounters of the fourth kind: Alien abduction, UFOs, and the conference at MIT]. Scientific American, 273(5), pp. 102-103.

- for a *later edition of a book,* include *2nd ed.* for second edition, for instance, or *rev. ed.* for revised edition:

Zettl, H. (1997). Television production handbook (6th ed.). Belmont, CA: Wadsworth.

- for a book with an *editor's name,* put the abbreviation for "editor" (*Ed.* or *Eds.*) in parentheses:

Hartman, F. (Ed.). (1973). World in crisis: Readings in international relations (4th ed.). New York: Macmillan.

Popkewitz, T. S., & Tabachnick, B. R. (Eds.). (1981). The study of schooling: Field based methodologies in educational research and evaluation. New York: Praeger.

- put a *translator's name* (or translators' names) followed by *Trans.* after the title:

Freire, P. (1970). Pedagogy of the oppressed (M. B. Ramos, Trans.). New York: Seabury Press.

- when listing *several* works by the *same author,* repeat the author's name with each title, putting works in chronological order:

Bruch, H. (1973). Eating disorders: Obesity, anorexia nervosa, and the person within. New York: Basic Books.

Bruch, H. (1978). The golden cage: The enigma of anorexia nervosa. Cambridge, MA: Harvard University Press.

- include *volume number* for one of several volumes:

Davis, S. P. (1984). History of Nevada. Vol 2. Las Vegas: Nevada Publications.

- for a *part of a book,* use the appropriate label—preface, introduction, afterword, or the like:

Aufderheide, P. (1992). Preface. In P. Aufderheide (Ed.), Beyond PC: Toward a politics of

<u>understanding</u> (pp. 1-4). Saint Paul, MN: Graywolf
Press.

- for part of a *collection of anthology*, identify both the article or other short item and the collection of which it is a part (if you cite several articles from the same collection, give full publishing information each time):

Borges, J. L. (1972). A new refutation of time.
In S. Sears & G. W. Lord (Eds.), <u>The discontinuous</u>
<u>universe</u>: <u>Selected writings in contemporary</u>
<u>consciousness</u> (pp. 208-223). New York: Basic Books.

- for *institutional authorship*, list the organization as the author:

American Psychological Association. (1982).
<u>Ethical principles in the conduct of research with</u>
<u>human participants.</u> Washington, DC: Author.

- list an unsigned *entry in an encyclopedia* or other reference work under first word of entry (if the author of an entry is identified, include the name):

Russia. (1994). In <u>The new encyclopedia</u>
<u>Britannica</u> (15th ed.) (Vol. 10, pp. 253-255). Chicago:
Encyclopedia Britannica.

- for material obtained through a *computer service,* include the name of the system and retrieval path (for instance, name of file and item number):

Schomer, H. (1983, May-June.) South Africa:
Beyond fair employment. [On-line]. <u>Harvard Business</u>
<u>Review,</u> pp. 145, 156. DIALOG File 122, Item 119425
833160

- *for on-line publication,* an availability statement replaces the name and location of publisher provided for print publications (the information needed may be a simple document number but may also be more extensive, like in the following availability statement after the entry for an article by Bridgeman published in the on-line journal *Psycholoquy,* accessed through the File Transfer Protocol—FTP):

Available FTP: 128.112.128.1 Directory: pub/
harnad File: psych.92.3.26.consciousness.11.
bridgeman

- for previously published material from an *information service,* provide standard publishing information, followed by identification of the service and an item number (if the material had not been previously published, cite it as a complete publication published by the service):

> Kurth, R. J., & Stromberg, L. J. (1984). Using word processing in composition instruction [On-line]. ERIC, ED 251 850.

- for *CD-ROM,* include source and retrieval number or similar information:

> Croft, F. S. (1995). Cruising in cyberspace. [CD-ROM]. VocEd File: Item 875623.

- for *nonprint media,* include a label for the medium used (in square brackets).

> Maas, J. B. (Producer), & Gluck, D. H. (Director). (1979). Deeper into hypnosis [Film]. Englewood Cliffs, NJ: Prentice-Hall.
>
> Clark, K. B. (Speaker). (1976). Problems of freedom and behavior modification [Cassette Recording]. Washington, DC: American Psychological Association.
>
> DiSanto, F. Alienation [Artwork]. San Jose, CA: Institute of Mexican American Art.
>
> Vitale, K. (Interviewer). (1996, May 6). Interview with C. Lobos. Behind the news [Radio program]. Washington, DC: Public Broadcasting Service.

SAMPLE RESEARCH PAPER PAGES—APA The following pages are the opening pages of a research paper formatted in the APA style. The sample pages are followed by the complete list of References. Note the use of **running heads** using a shortened title—not the student writer's name. Note the use of the **author–date style** both in the brief parenthetic references in the text and in the detailed list of References at the end. Note the use of specific page references for direct quotations.

Child Criminals 1

running head
using shortened
title

James Perry

Professor Guth

English 176

21 November 1995

Child Criminals in Adult Courts--A Crime in Itself?

In August 1993, at a day camp in Savona, New York, Eric Smith,
a 13-year-old, brutally murdered a 4-year-old. Eric grabbed the
younger boy in a headlock, smashed his head three times with a rock,
stuffed a napkin and a plastic bag in his mouth, pummeled his body
with a rock, and poured a drink over his body. His trial began on
August 1 in Bath, New York. Despite his young age, Eric was tried
as an adult, because of the severity of his crime and also because
of a law allowing children as young as thirteen to be tried as
adults when accused of murder (Nordheimer, 1994, p. B5). His act
was indicative of some frightening trends in America--an increase
in the severity of juvenile crime, and a decrease in the age at
which children commit crimes. His trial also shows a current trend
in American juvenile justice--children are being tried in adult
courts in more cases and at younger ages. Experts, elected
representatives, and the general public have been grappling with
the issue of how to deal with juvenile crime, and treating youths as
adults is currently a popular solution. Many issues are relevant in
the debate over whether to try children as adults--how major a
problem is juvenile crime; is being harsh with juvenile criminals in

author and date
with page
number

Child Criminals 2

the best interest of the defendants and in society's best interest, in terms of rehabilitating criminals, deterring and reducing crime, and justice; is treating child criminals as adults the most effective and most cost-efficient way of dealing with them; and so on. The alternative to treating juveniles as adults I intend to treat in this paper is a more rehabilitative approach--some experts advocate more preventative efforts, as opposed to more punishment-oriented programs such as trying youths in adult courtrooms. In this paper, I intend to show the causes for the current sentiment toward trying youths as adults. Then I intend to argue that while juvenile crime is a problem, it may not be the epidemic that it has been made out to be, and that although it is necessary to be firm in dealing with juvenile criminals, the best way to deal with them may not necessarily be through adult courts and strictly "getting tough."

preview of the argument

In a way, the American justice system seems to be coming full circle. The nation's first juvenile court was established in 1899 in Cook County, Illinois, as a way to deal with young offenders in a more rehabilitative style, as opposed to the harsher justice found in adult courts (Andrews, 1994). However, by the 1960's, the public became more concerned about juvenile crime, as the youth population was growing and becoming more violent. Americans have begun to question the principles and effectiveness of the current juvenile justice systems, and have argued in favor of harsher, firmer alternatives. The 1966 U.S. Supreme Court case Kent vs. United

author and date in parentheses

Child Criminals 3

States established guidelines for the transfer of young offenders to adult courts. The youths' threat to the safety of the public and amenability to treatments within the juvenile justice system were to be considered (Houghtalin & Mays, 1991). Since this time, more and more laws have been proposed and implemented to make it easier, and in some cases mandatory, for youths to be sent to adult courts for certain crimes, both violent and non-violent. The public seems to want young criminals to be held responsible for their crimes and to be punished, and they believe that this can best be done in adult courts, where child criminals presumably will face harsher sentencing, often including time in adult prisons.

Measures to treat juvenile offenders as adults have been proposed and supported for several reasons in recent years. While some experts advocate and have implemented more preventive measures, these are difficult to implement and would have more of a long-term effect, leaving Americans wondering "what we are supposed to do in the meantime" (Methvin, 1994, p. 95). Bob Herbert argues that attempts to rehabilitate young offenders and treat them lightly are "well-intentioned" but "out of touch with the increasingly violent reality of juvenile crime" (1994, p. E15). Other measures have failed to reduce juvenile crime; for instance, gun control laws are not believed to have a significant effect on violent crime by youths, since they tend to obtain the guns through illegal means anyway (Witkin, 1991, p. 28). Although experts

quoted phrases

disagree as to the extent and seriousness of current juvenile crime, the fact is that the public feels that juvenile crime is a major problem, and they support measures to deal with it. Assistant Maryland public defender feels that the public's focus on juvenile crime created the "political climate" that exists supporting anti-juvenile crime measures (Stepp, 1994, p. A12).

Many officials within the justice system feel that some young criminals should be treated as adults and tried in adult courts. A study published in August 1994 showed that many judges in the juvenile justice system feel that "the criminal justice system should deal with young criminals more in the way it deals with adults." For instance, two out of five judges surveyed feel child offenders should be eligible to receive the death penalty in some situations, and a majority felt that the minimum age for facing murder charges should be lowered ("Tougher Treatment," 1994, p. A16). Former administrator of the Office of Juvenile Justice and Delinquency Prevention Ira Schwartz feels that "juvenile court judges and youth probation workers are among the staunchest supporters of jailing for juveniles" (1989, p. 18).

short title for
unsigned article

Many legislators, and a large portion of the general public, share the sentiments of these justice authorities. Maryland Delegate Joseph F. Vallario Jr. feels that "if [youths] want to do adult-type crimes, we're going to treat them like adults" (Stepp, 1994, p. A12). Another Maryland Delegate, Ulysses Curie, writes

bracketed
addition

Child Criminals 5

that due to the increasing violence and youth of juvenile offenders, "the juvenile system must be changed to respond to this reality" by treating youths more like adults (1994, p. C8). Both Democrats and Republicans support measures to treat young criminals more like adults; both of the Maryland delegates quoted above are Democrats, and a major part of the Republicans' "Contract With America" was the "Taking Back Our Streets Act," which supported harsher punishment of crime ("Youth and Crime," p. 18). In recent years, many states have added legislation that lowered the ages at which youths can be tried as adults for certain crimes, added new crimes to those for which a juvenile may or must be tried as an adult, implemented mandatory sentencing for children convicted of certain crimes, and so on. For instance, in 1993, Louisiana added attempted murder and aggravated battery to the list of offenses for which a juvenile may be tried as an adult.

A rare dissenting opinion was registered by Supreme Court Justice Brennan in Stanford v. Kentucky (1992). Citing an earlier court opinion, he said:

> The reason why juveniles are not trusted with the privileges and responsibilities of an adult also explains why their irresponsible conduct is not as morally reprehensible as that of an adult. Adolescents are more

normal indent for block quotation

end of sample pages—references pages follow

date in parentheses

indent first lines

Child Criminals 12

References

Andrews, J. H. (1994, March 7). Criminals, but still children. Christian Science Monitor, p. 17.

lower case in titles

Armstrong, S. (1994, March 7). Colorado tries more carrot and less stick in punishing juvenile crimes. Christian Science Monitor, pp. 1, 4.

Bayh, B. (1989). Foreword. In I. M. Schwartz, (In)justice for juveniles: Rethinking the best interests of the child (pp. xi-xiii). Lexington: Heath-Lexington.

Curie, U. (1994, February 6). Reality requires tougher responses to juvenile crime. The Washington Post, p. C8.

Fiagone, C. (1995, February 13). Jacksonville's tough answer to problem of youth crimes. Christian Science Monitor, pp. 1, 14.

Herbert, B. (1994, July 24). Little criminals, big crimes. The New York Times, late ed., p. E15.

Houghtalin, M., & Mays, G. L. (1991). Criminal dispositions of New Mexico juveniles transferred to adult court. Crime and Delinquency, 37, pp. 393-407.

Kotlowitz, A. (1994, February 13). Their crimes don't make them adults. The New York Times Magazine, pp. 40-41.

McLean, G. (1986, December 12). Adult prison is no place for a kid. Christianity Today, p. 13.

Methvin, E. H. (1994, April). Behind Florida's tourist murders. Reader's Digest, pp. 92-96.

Child Criminals 13

Nordheimer, J. (1994, August 2). Murder trial begins for teen-ager. The New York Times, late ed., p. B5.

Schwartz, I. M. (1989). (In)justice for juveniles: Rethinking the best interests of the child. Lexington: Heath-Lexington.

Stanford v. Kentucky, 106 U.S. 339 (1992).

Stefan, L. B. (1991). Youth and the law: Getting tough on juvenile crime. Boston: Benchmark Books.

Stepp, L. S. (1994, October 15). The crackdown on juvenile crime--Do stricter laws deter youths? The Washington Post, pp. A1, A12.

Tougher treatment urged for juveniles. (1994, August 2). The New York Times, late ed., p. A16.

Witkin, G. (1991, April 8). Kids who kill. U.S. News & World Report, pp. 26-32.

Youth and cirme. (1995, January 10). [Editorial.] Christian Science Monitor, p. 18.

A GLOSSARY OF TERMS

abstraction A general idea (often *very* general) that "draws us away" from the level of specific data or observations; large abstractions are concepts like justice, dignity, and freedom

ad hominem Getting personal in an argument; distracting from the merit of ideas by attacking the person, character, or private life of an opponent (Latin for "directed at the person")

allusion A brief mention that brings a whole story or set of associations to the reader's mind

analogy A close comparison traced into several related details, often used to explain the new in terms of the familiar

analysis Explaining a complex phenomenon by identifying its major parts, stages, or causes

bandwagon Trying to sway people by claiming that the great majority is on the speaker's or writer's side (and that he or she must therefore be right)

brainstorming Freely calling up memories, data, or associations relevant to a topic, without at first editing or sorting them out

cause and effect The logical connection between actions and their consequences, making us focus on reasons and results

claim What we assert in an argument and then need to support with evidence or examples

classification The setting up of categories that help us sort out a mass of data

cliché A tired, overused expression that may have been clever or colorful at one time but has long since lost its edge

cluster A network or web of ideas centered in a key term or stimulus word, from which various strands of ideas and associations branch out

comparison Tracing connections to demonstrate similarities and contrast differences

connotation The attitudes, emotions, or associations a word carries beyond its basic factual meaning (or denotation)

context What comes before and after a word or a statement and helps give it its full meaning; the setting or situation that helps explain what something means

data Facts, observations, or statistics that provide the input for reasoning or interpretation

deduction The kind of reasoning that applies general principles to specific situations

definition Staking out the exact meaning of a possibly vague, ambiguous, or abused term

dialectic The kind of reasoning that makes ideas emerge from the play of pro and con; ideally, dialectic proceeds from thesis (statement) to antithesis (counterstatement) and from there to synthesis (a balanced conclusion)

discovery frames Sets of questions that help a writer explore a topic

doublespeak A verbal smokescreen designed to cover up unpleasant facts (such as calling an airplane crash "unscheduled contact with the ground")

draft A possibly unfinished or tentative version of a piece of writing, subject to revision

fallacy A common pattern of faulty logic, leading to wrong conclusions

figurative language Language using imaginative comparisons, such as calling someone a gadfly (metaphor) or punctual as a clock (simile)

hasty generalization Generalizing from a limited sample, such as labeling a brand of cars defective because two that you know about were

image Something we can vividly visualize; something that appeals vividly to our senses

induction The generalizing kind of reasoning that finds the connecting thread or common pattern in a set of data

inference The logical jump from facts or observations to what we interpret them to mean

innuendo Damaging hints stopping short of outright charges that could be challenged and refuted

jargon Pretentious, overblown pseudoscientific or unnecessarily technical language

metaphor An imaginative comparison that treats one thing as if it were another, without using a signal such as *like* or *as* ("he *surfed* to the speaker's table on a *wave* of applause")

narrator In fiction, the person—real or imaginary—telling the story

paraphrase Putting a statement or passage into one's own words

peer review Feedback given to a writer by classmates or fellow writers

persona The identity assumed or the public role played by a writer in a piece of writing (the persona may be different from the writer's private personality)

post hoc fallacy Short for *post hoc ergo propter hoc,* Latin for "it happened after this; therefore it's because of this"; blaming something on a highly visible recent event rather than on true long-range causes (there was an earthquake after a nuclear test; therefore the test triggered the earthquake)

premise A basic shared assumption on which an argument is built

rationalization A creditable, reasonable-sounding explanation that clears us of blame

redundancy Unintentional duplication that makes for dense, lumpy prose: "The problem will *eventually* resolve itself *in due time*"

rhetoric The practice or the study of effective strategies for speech and writing (sometimes used negatively to mean empty or deceptive use of language)

simile An imaginative comparison signaled by such words as *like* or *as* ("the library had bare solid walls *like a prison*")

slanting Presenting only evidence or testimony that favors your own side

syllogism A formal deductive argument that moves from the major premise ("mammals need air to breathe") through the minor premise ("whales are mammals") to a logical conclusion ("whales need air to breathe")

thesis The central idea or unifying assertion that a paper as a whole supports; the claim a paper stakes out and defends

transition A link showing the logical connection between one sentence or paragraph and the next

valid Logically correct (but logically correct reasoning may lead to untrue conclusions if based on faulty premises)

CREDITS

Pamela Alexander, "Flight" (For Amelia Earhart) from *Navigable Waterways,* Yale University Press, 1985. Copyright © 1985 by Pamela Alexander. Reprinted by permission of the author.

Anonymous, "Homeless Woman Reveals Misery of Living in Car" from *San Jose Mercury News,* December 8, 1991.

Amoja Three Rivers, "Cultural Etiquette: A Guide" in *Ms.* Magazine, September/October 1991. Reprinted by permission of Amoja Three Rivers.

Roger Angell, "Return of the Cliché Expert" from *The New Yorker,* Dec/Jan 1996/97. Reprinted by permission. Copyright © 1996 by Roger Angell. Originally in *The New Yorker.* All rights reserved.

Maya Angelou, "Step Forward in the Car, Please" from *I Know Why the Caged Bird Sings.* Copyright © 1969 and renewed 1997 by Maya Angelou. Reprinted by permission of Random House, Inc.

Arthur Ashe, "A Black Athlete Looks at Education" from the *New York Times,* February 6, 1977. Copyright © 1977 by The New York Times Co. Reprinted by permission.

Nanette Asimov with Toni Cook, "Ebonics: Opening Pandora's Box" from *The Sunday Examiner and Chronicle,* January 19, 1997. Copyright © 1997 San Francisco Chronicle. Reprinted by permission.

Margaret Atwood, "Dreams of the Animals" from *Procedures for Underground, Selected Poems 1965–1975.* Copyright © 1976 by Margaret Atwood. Reprinted by permission of Houghton Mifflin Co. All rights reserved.

Jenny Lyn Bader, "Larger Than Life" from *Next: Young American Writers on the New Generation* by Eric Liu, editor. Copyright © 1994 by Jenny Lyn Bader. Reprinted by permission of the author and W. W. Norton & Company, Inc.

Toni Cade Bambara, "The Lesson" from *Gorilla, My Love.* Copyright © 1960, 1970, 1971, 1972 by Toni Cade Bambara. Reprinted by permission of Random House, Inc.

Judi Bari, "The Feminization of Earth First!" from *Ms.* Magazine, May/June 1992. Copyright © 1992. Reprinted by permission.

William J. Bennett, "Love, Marriage, and the Law." Copyright © 1996, Washington Post Writers Group. Reprinted with permission.

Carl Bernstein, "The Idiot Culture" abridged from *The New Republic,* June 8, 1992. Copyright © 1992 by The New Republic. Reprinted by permission of the publisher.

David Bernstein, "Mixed Like Me" from *Next: Young American Writers on the New Generation* by Eric Liu, editor. Copyright © 1994 by David Bernstein. Reprinted by permission of the author and W. W. Norton & Company, Inc.

Mary Kay Blakely, "Memories of Frank" from *Wake Me When It's Over.* Copyright © 1989 by Mary Kay Blakely, published by Times Books. No part of this material may be reproduced in whole or part without the express written permission of the author or her agent, Phyllis Wender of Rosenstone/Wender, 3 E 48th St., 4th Fl., New York, NY 10017.

Deborah Blum, "The Monkey Wars" from *The Sacramento Bee,* 1992. Reprinted with permission of Deborah Blum.

Robert Bly, "The Community of Men" from *Iron John: A Book About Men.* Copyright © 1990 by Robert Bly. Reprinted by permission of Addison-Wesley Longman.

Daniel J. Boorstin, "Why I Am Optimistic About America" from *Parade* Magazine,

July 10, 1994. Copyright © 1994 by Daniel J. Boorstin. Reprinted by permission of the author and *Parade* Magazine.

Sterling A. Brown, "Sister Lou" from *The Collected Poems of Sterling A. Brown,* edited by Michael S. Harper. Copyright © 1980 by Sterling A. Brown. Reprinted by permission of HarperCollins Publishers, Inc.

Fox Butterfield, "Why They Excel" from *Parade* Magazine, January 21, 1990. Copyright © 1990 by Fox Butterfield. Reprinted with permission from the author and *Parade* Magazine.

Gregorio Cerio, "Were the Spaniards Cruel?" from *Newsweek,* Fall/Winter 1991. Copyright © 1991 by Newsweek, Inc. All rights reserved. Reprinted by permission.

Lorna Dee Cervantes, "Refugee Ship" is reprinted with permission from the publisher of *A Decade of Hispanic Literature* (Houston: Arte Publico Press — University of Houston, 1982).

Frank Chin, excerpt originally appeared in the novel *Donald Duk* by Frank Chin, Coffee House Press, 1991. Copyright © 1991 by Frank Chin. Reprinted by permission of the publisher.

Sandra Cisneros, "Mericans" from *Woman Hollering Creek and Other Stories.* Copyright © 1991 by Sandra Cisneros. Published by Vintage Books, a division of Random House Inc., and originally in hardcover by Random House Inc. Reprinted by permission of Susan Bergholz Literary Services, New York. All rights reserved.

"Citing Abuse, 2 Women Leave Citadel" from the *New York Times,* January 13, 1997. Copyright © 1997 by The New York Times Co. Reprinted by permission.

Gregory Clay, "A Black Journalist Urges O. J. to Admit the Truth" from the *San Francisco Chronicle,* 2/9/97. Copyright © 1997 the San Francisco Chronicle. Reprinted by permission.

Richard Cohen, "Children Are Our Future—Unfortunately They're Bigots" from the Richard Cohen column. Copyright © 1993 Washington Post Writers Group. Reprinted with permission.

Mary Crow Dog with Richard Erdoes from *Lakota Woman.* Copyright © 1990 by Mary Crow Dog and Richard Erdoes. Used by permission of Grove/Atlantic, Inc.

Marie de Santis, "Last of the Wild Salmon" from *This World,* San Francisco Chronicle, July 21, 1985. Reprinted by permission of the author.

John Fire Lame Deer, "Listening to the Air" from *Lame Deer: Seeker of Visions.* Copyright © 1972 by John Fire/Lame Deer and Richard Erdoes. Reprinted with the permission of Simon & Schuster.

Barbara Ehrenreich, "Their Dilemma and Mine" from *The Worst Years of Our Lives,* pp. 430-432. Copyright © 1990 by Barbara Ehrenreich. Reprinted by permission of Pantheon Books, a division of Random House, Inc.

Ira Eisenberg, "The Press and the Ebonics Story" by Ira Eisenberg in *The San Francisco Chronicle,* 1/3/97. Reprinted by permission of Ira Eisenberg, who is a San Francisco Bay Area journalist.

Lolis Eric Elie, "Naysayers Miss Point" from *Times-Picayune,* 1/17/97. Reprinted courtesy of The Times-Picayune Publishing Corporation.

Black Elk, "The Earth Is All That Lasts" from *Black Elk Speaks* by John O. Neihardt by permission of the University of Nebraska Press. Copyright 1932, 1959, 1972 by John G. Neihardt. Copyright © 1961 by the John G. Neihardt Trust.

Ralph Ellison, "Mister Toussant" from *Flying Home and Other Stories* by Ralph Ellison. Copyright © 1996 by Fanny Ellison. Reprinted by permission of Random House, Inc.

Philip Elmer-Dewitt, "Bards of the Internet" from *Time* Magazine, 7/4/94. Copyright © 1994 by Time, Inc. Reprinted by permission.

Louise Erdrich, "Indian Boarding School: The Runaways" from *Jacklight: Poems by*

Jerome P. Kassirer, "Federal Foolishness and Marijuana" from the *Associated Press.* Copyright © 1997 by the Associated Press.

Matthew Kauffman, "The Day the Slaves Got Their Way" from *The Hartford Courant,* July 16, 1989. Reprinted by permission of the publisher.

Stanley Kauffman, "The Merchant of Venus" from *The New Republic,* January 20, 1997. Copyright © 1997 *The New Republic.* Reprinted by permission.

Garrison Keillor, "Protestant" from *Lake Wobegon Days.* Copyright © 1985 by Garrison Keillor. Used by permission of Viking Penguin, a division of Penguin Books USA Inc.

Martin Luther King, Jr., "I Have a Dream." Reprinted by arrangement with The Heirs to the Estate of Martin Luther King, Jr., c/o Writers House, Inc. as agent for the proprietor. Copyright © 1963 by Martin Luther King, Jr. Copyright renewed 1991 by Coretta Scott King.

Ynestra King, "The Other Body: Disability and Identity Politics" from *Ms.* Magazine, March/April 1993. Reprinted by permission of the author. Ynestra King is currently a Visiting Scholar at Columbia University in New York City where she lives with her son Micah.

Charles Krauthammer, "Saving Nature, But Only for Man" from *Time* Magazine, 6/17/91. Copyright © 1991 by Time Inc. Reprinted by permission.

Ursula K. Le Guin, "Along the Platte" from *Dancing at the Edge of the World.* Copyright © 1983 by Ursula K. Le Guin. Used by permission of Grove/Atlantic, Inc.

Li-Young Lee, "Persimmons" copyright © 1986 by Li-Young Lee. Reprinted from *Rose* by Li-Young Lee, with permission of BOA Editions, Ltd., Rochester, NY.

Nguyen Louie, "A Daughter's Story" from *Conversations Begin, Mothers and Daughters Talk.* Copyright © 1996 by Christina Looper Baker and Christina Baker Klein. Used by permission of Bantam Books, a division of Bantam Doubleday Dell Publishing Group, Inc.

Andrea Freud Loewenstein, "Sister from Another Planet Probes the Soaps" from *Ms.* Magazine, November/December 1993. Copyright © 1993. Reprinted by permission.

Arturo Madrid, "Diversity and Its Discontents" in *Black Issues in Higher Education,* Vol. 5, No. 4, May 1988. Reprinted by permission of the Tomás Rivera Center.

Randall E. Majors, "America's Emerging Gay Culture" from *Intercultural Communications: A Reader,* Sixth Edition by Larry A. Samovar and Richard E. Porter, Wadsworth 1991. Copyright © 1991 by Randall E. Majors. Reprinted by permission of the author.

Jorge R. Mancillas, "Assimilation Is More Than ABCs" from *The Los Angeles Times,* Wednesday, November 17, 1993. Copyright © 1993 by Jorge R. Mancillas. Reprinted by permission of the author.

Nathan McCall, "Time" from *Makes Me Wanna Holler,* pp. 271-279. Copyright © 1994 by Nathan McCall. Reprinted by permission of Random House, Inc.

Harvey Milk, "A City of Neighborhoods" from *The American Reader,* HarperCollins, 1991. Copyright © 1978 by the Estate of Harvey Milk. Reprinted by permission of Scott Smith.

Susan J. Miller, "My Father's Other Life" in *Harper's Magazine* 1994, abridged from *Granta* #47, Summer 1994. Copyright © 1994 by Susan J. Miller. Reprinted by permisison of the author.

Janice Mirikitani, "For My Father" from *Awake in the River, Poetry and Prose* by Janice Mirikitani, Isthmus Press, San Francisco, CA 1978. Copyright © 1978 by Janice Mirikitani. Reprinted by permission of the author.

Farley Mowat, "The Snow Walker" from *The Snow Walker.* Copyright © 1975 by McClelland & Stewart. Reprinted by permission of Little, Brown & Company.

Steven Musil, "Emotions Clouding Rational Decisions" from *The Spartan Daily,* December 12, 1989. Reprinted by permission of the publisher.

INDEX OF AUTHORS AND TITLES